The Practice of Public Relations

Second Edition

Fraser P. Seitel

Vice President, Director of
Public Affairs, The Chase
Manhattan Bank

Lecturer, University College,
Pace University

Charles E. Merrill Publishing Company
A Bell & Howell Company
Columbus Toronto London Sydney

Published by
Charles E. Merrill Publishing Company
A Bell & Howell Company
Columbus, Ohio 43216

This book was set in Souvenir.
Production Editor: Tracey E. Dils
Text Designer: Cynthia Brunk
Cover Design: Tony Faiola
Cover Painting: Marko Spalatin

Library of Congress Catalog Card Number: 83-62025
International Standard Book Number: 0-675-20104-7
Printed in the United States of America
1 2 3 4 5 6 7 8 9 10—88 87 86 85 84

To Rosemary, Raina, and the Geeter.

Public relations—what it is and what it isn't—is understandably a subject of interest and concern to those who work, teach, or study in the field.

Some approach this definitional conundrum from the standpoint of concept, principle, and theory—the "what ought to be and why" approach. Others take the "what you see is what you get" approach, defining public relations in terms of what activities are carried out in the name of public relations.

But neither approach is wholly satisfactory. The theoretical approach leaves out some very practical considerations of what *will* work; the focus is sometimes too narrowly on the *ideal*, rather than the *real*. And saying that the on-the-job tasks of someone in public relations define public relations leaves open the question of what to do with the switchboard receptionist whose job description requires "significant public relations contact with customers and clients."

The second edition of *The Practice of Public Relations* charts a course midway between these too-confining schools of thought and represents a most happy medium for the student of public relations, whether that student is a neophyte preparing for a first career or a seasoned veteran looking for new insights and a fresh approach.

It presents an adroit juxtaposition of the basic principles that ought to (and do in many cases) guide public relations activity with examples from public relations as it is actually practiced by "real world" corporations, associations, and institutions.

A central theme that runs throughout this second edition is that public relations is a management process, an integral part of the policy and decision-making apparatus of any organization. The idea that public relations professionals are more than low-grade skilled communication technicians is not new, but is presented here in a refreshingly original way. Through interviews with public relations executives from business and industry, government, counseling firms, and public relations agencies, and through a generous sprinkling of up-to-date case studies, mini-

FOREWORD

cases, and features, Fraser Seitel illustrates the important management dimensions of the practice of public relations.

From the Love Canal Case to Procter & Gamble's handling of satanic rumors about its moon and stars trademark to Johnson & Johnson's crisis with Tylenol to the Sony "Walkman" to movie idol E.T.'s favorite candy, the reader experiences how public relations *works* or doesn't work.

Despite this emphasis on public relations as management, the basics aren't ignored, making this book especially useful as an introductory overview of the range and breadth of public relations. Public relations skills—writing, editing, researching—are dealt with quite thoroughly in several excellent chapters on these nitty-gritty tools of the public relations trade.

Significant attention is paid in this second edition to change, both within the profession and in the external environment of public relations. Changing technologies, notably cable and satellite broadcasting and computers, as well as changing lifestyles of public relations audiences and changing concerns and issues that confront organizations in today's society, are explored along with the tools public relations professionals will need to deal with these changes.

Students—both the neophytes and the seasoned veterans—will find Mr. Seitel's book a useful public relations tool in itself. It can provide an important focus for learning more about public relations—about what it is and perhaps, more important, what it ought to be.

Judy VanSlyke Turk
Assistant Professor
Louisiana State University

PREFACE

This second edition of *The Practice of Public Relations* is a lot better than the first.

The book has retained its practical emphasis. Public relations is, at base, a practical field, and the knowledge provided here is designed to be used. As a professional communicator, the public relations practitioner must know how to write, how to speak, and how to counsel others in their communications. This book is structured to help readers do just that.

The sixty hypothetical and real-life case studies of the first book have been expanded to include several of the most complex conundrums to confront the public relations profession in recent years, from Watergate to Three Mile Island to Love Canal to the Tylenol murders.

While the first edition deemphasized theory, this book examines more closely the philosophical underpinnings that make public relations so relevant in today's society. This theoretical insight provides the backdrop against which the practical knowledge can be made more useful.

This edition has one other unique wrinkle: interviews with twenty-three of the most well-known professionals in the public relations field, each addressing the aspect of public relations he or she knows best. Their insights alone are well worth the reader's attention.

So "net/net," as the bankers say, I am pleased with this effort. It's relatively easy to read, brutally practical, not too theoretically ponderous, yet weighty enough to provide a fair, accurate, and hopefully enticing introduction to the increasingly influential practice of public relations.

ACKNOWLEDGMENTS

Anybody who says that updating a textbook is easy hasn't tried it. The second edition of this one was a lot more work than the first.

Thank goodness there were so many

good-hearted and knowledgeable people around to help this effort through to publication.

I am most grateful indeed to the twenty-three public relations experts who agreed to share their considerable knowledge and experience in the interviews that accompany each chapter. Their contributions alone make this a unique textbook.

Elaine Hannon, a research assistant of amazing skill and persistence, also provided a major contribution. She was invaluable in tracking down bits and pieces of information along the way. So too was Yolanda Rhymer, a veteran of the manuscript wars, who made sure that the finished product emerged in an organized and presentable fashion.

Beyond these principal contributors, I am grateful as well for: the artistic contributions of Dennis Portelli and Lou Braun; the photographic expertise of Bill Devine, Ray Juschkus, and Art Lavine; and the processing proficiency of Laura Doran, Ivy Blunt, and the erstwhile Phyllis Lowenthal.

I am also very much indebted to colleagues at leading universities whose constructive critiques of the first edition helped make this second edition an all-around better book: Professors Paul Brennan (Nassau Community College), Carol L. Hills (Boston University), George Laposky (Miami-Dade Community College), Mack Palmer (University of Oklahoma), and Roger B. Wadsworth (Miami-Dade Community College). Professor Palmer, in particular, was a great help in lightening the tone of this book. He and Professor Brennan also assisted by critiquing this edition's first draft.

In addition to these academic leaders,

I also am grateful to the public relations teachers whose insightful suggestions aided my earlier edition: Professors James E. Grunig (University of Maryland), Robert T. Reilly (University of Nebraska at Omaha), Kenneth Rowe (Arizona State University), Dennis L. Wilcox (San Jose State University), and Albert Walker (Northern Illinois University).

I am also most grateful to Professor Judy VanSlyke Turk, Assistant Professor, Louisiana State University.

In addition to all these people, several other special souls deserve recognition.

Sam Justice, a respected journalist/public relations counselor/communications professor, was an integral element in the launch of the first edition. Dan Pliskin, a professor without peer in the classroom or on the golf course, encouraged the original effort. Joe Snyder, communications counselor extraordinaire, not only provided strategic guidance but also lent the editorial talents of Vanessa Reed, whose contribution was very much appreciated. So too was the sage counsel of John Ducas.

Finally, A. Wright Elliott, corporate communications director of the Chase Manhattan Bank, was, as always, totally supportive through the duration of the project.

Last but never least, the three most important people in the world, Rosemary, Raina, and David Seitel provided essential moral support to make sure that Dad finished the job. For that, they get my gratitude, and hopefully, a goodly amount of royalties as well.

Fraser P. Seitel
February 1, 1983

CONTENTS

Public relations takes on weightier assignments

By Guy Halverson
Business and financial correspondent of
The Christian Science Monitor
Washington

United States corporations—increasingly assailed by strident citizen action groups and government agencies demanding increased financial disclosure—are finding their public relations departments more valued than ever.

Once considered a "back room" or "sideline" post in many corporations, the "PR"—or public relations—officer now is often ranked among the highest paid personnel in a firm.

Moreover, many "PR officers" now are technical specialists such as attorneys, engineers, or accountants.

While precise national statistics are somewhat difficult to come by, "PR" officials throughout the US certainly number in the thousands. According to Jack O'Dwyer, who publishes a journal for public relations officials, there are between 10,000 and 20,000 business-oriented public relations personnel in the US.

If PR officials working for public or nonprofit organizations, such as schools, government units, or citizen action groups are added, the total PR community may total as high as 100,000 people, Mr. O'Dwyer believes.

Public relations officials say that the nature of their trade—at least at the corporate level—has changed considerably over the past several years.

• Scores of major firms are increasing the size of their public relations staffs, boosting budgets, registering formal lobbyists with both the local and federal government, and in some cases, also hiring outside PR agencies.

• Top PR officials—usually having titles such as "vice-president of corporate affairs," "public affairs," or "consumer affairs"—are being recruited directly out of technical backgrounds. Salaries are rising higher and higher.

• Most importantly, firms are aggressively taking to the "hustings"—attempting to reach out directly to the public through television and print media—to present the "corporate story" in the best possible light.

These days, many companies hope their PR people can head off prospective difficulties, particularly from political activists. For example, the San Francisco-based Wells Fargo Bank recently set up a "social policy" review committee of bank officers to assess the social impact of overseas loans to nations considered politically repressive.

Public relations work, says Lona Jupiter, vice-president and assistant manager (for public relations) at Wells Fargo, is "much more demanding" than ever before. "We now have to know much more about the details of our business."

Mrs. Jupiter recalls that several years ago Wells Fargo had to move the month of its annual meeting from March to April so that there would be more time to gather the huge amount of technical mathematical "breakouts" on bank statistics now required under disclosure laws. Before then, she recalls, one used to be able to just list earnings figures, deposit totals, and relatively little else. Now, a corporation must list "many types of calculations" and analytical projections.

According to Mr. O'Dwyer, PR officials today are spending perhaps the main part of their time dealing with "social issues."

"Clearly," says Robert Hayes, a corporate public affairs official with the giant Boise-Cascade Company, "corporations face a distrusting or mistrustful public today."

But, he adds, "You can't give up trying to educate the public about what [businesses] do."

For Boise Cascade, says Mr. Hayes, that means working through trade groups like the Business Roundtable or the American Forest Products Association as well as seeking to take the corporate message directly to the public through advertising.

Seeking to influence the drafting of federal legislation has also become a main objective of many PR offices. By one informal count, there now are between 1,600 and 2,000 trade groups in Washington—each in effect, a "PR" agency. In addition, more than 500 corporations have set up PR offices here, in addition to those at their headquarter offices.

THE
BASICS

PART
ONE

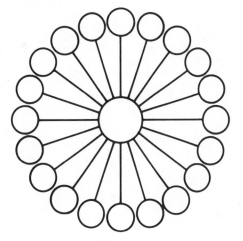

COMING OF AGE

I n the 1980s, the practice of public relations stands at a crossroads.

On the one hand, public relations
has finally arrived. In an age, as columnist
George Will puts it, "of skimmed surfaces, of
facile confidence that reality is whatever can
be seen and taped and reported,"[1] the practice of public relations has acquired new-
found respect. Indeed, in an era of unrelent-
ing questioning by the media and the public,
an organization must not only be sensitive to
but highly considerate of its many publics.

A primary vehicle through which an
organization shows its public sensitivity and
consideration is its public relations professionals. Accordingly, the practice of public
relations has shed its old misconceptions,
acquired new responsibilities, and inherited
an increasing amount of power, prestige, and
pay in the 1980s.[2]

The striking metamorphosis of public
relations from a misunderstood trade to a
respected profession will likely continue
through the 1980s.

On the other hand, along with its new
stature, the practice of public relations is
now faced with unprecedented pressure.

○ The very name *public relations* is being
challenged by such euphemisms as public affairs, corporate communications,
public information, and a variety of
others.

○ As public relations positions take on
greater credibility, the competition to fill
them becomes more intense. Today, the
profession finds itself vulnerable to encroachment by people without public
relations backgrounds, such as lawyers,
marketers, and general managers of
every stripe.

1
What is public relations?

○ Educational institutions, who themselves have recognized the need to practice public relations intensively, have nonetheless been slow to recognize the need to teach it.

○ While organizations throughout society desperately need professionals of universal interests and broad-reaching ideas in sensitive public relations jobs, there is a continuing trend toward specialization in the field.

○ The field is still plagued by misrepresentations of what it's all about. More often than not, the public's perception is that public relations is *aimed at* not *for* them; that they are the *object* of public relations, not the *beneficiaries*.[3]

The public relations profession is buffeted by countervailing pressures. It has earned the respect of management, yet must still fight for its identity among the general public. It has earned acceptance in most organizations, yet must fight for its rightful role in society. It is blessed with unlimited opportunities in the years ahead, yet its very survival is threatened by encroachment from outsiders.

Few other professions are subject to as continuous a current of controversy as the practice of public relations. In any event, it is irrefutable that public relations today, in a comparatively short time and despite a number of handicaps, has evolved from a fringe function to a basic element of society. It is indeed a force to be reckoned with.

OVERVIEW OF PUBLIC RELATIONS

Public relations affects almost everyone who has contact with other human beings. All of us, in one way or another, practice public relations daily.

To be sure, public relations is not yet a profession like law, accounting, and medicine, in which practitioners are trained, licensed, and supervised. There is nothing to prevent someone with little or no formal training from "hanging out a shingle" as a public relations specialist. Such frauds embarrass professionals in the field. Thankfully, these phonies are becoming harder and harder to find.

Over the last decade, public relations has steadily built its reputation, increased its prominence, and earned respect across a wide span of society. As today's institutions strive to understand more clearly the forces of change, to adapt their activities to new pressures and aspirations, and to listen and communicate more effectively, public relations has become more important. Institutions rely on their practitioners to help win public support and trust. Without such public support, they know they will be rendered powerless.

As the field increases in prominence, it grows in professional stature. The Public Relations Society of America, with a national membership of over 11,000, has accredited about one-third of its members through a standardized examination. The Society has also investigated legal licensing—similar to the accounting and legal professions—of public relations practitioners.

The Society's main objective is to increase the field's professionalism. It has a code of standards (see Appendix A), which dwells heavily on a practitioner's ethical responsibilities. The Society also provides additional opportunities in specialized areas of practice: association, corporate, counseling, educational institutions, educators, financial institutions, government, health, investor relations, and utilities. These sections have their own publications, seminars, and programs.

Today, less than 10 percent of the more than 100,000 practitioners in the United States are members of the Society. Thousands of practitioners are former newspaper reporters and magazine writers, journalism school graduates, advertising agency alumni, and lawyers. Increasingly, one also can find individuals formally educated in public relations practice.

In an attempt to begin to understand what public relations is and what it can and cannot accomplish, here are a few approaches toward defining public relations.

APPROACHES TO A DEFINITION

First, public relations is not:

○ the $5 million quarterback glad-handing the local businessmen at the cigar company's annual luncheon

○ the sultry screen actress seductively caressing the after-shave lotion to the clicks of photographers' shutters

○ the fast-talking hustler eagerly touting his "contacts" to a prospective client

○ a U.S. President's brother (Billy Carter), the former heavyweight champions of the world (Joe Louis/Muhammed Ali), or the palimony roommate of a famous actor (Michelle Triola Marvin).

Yet all of these and worse have, from time to time, been mistaken as part of the practice of public relations. As one of the industry's leading publications, *PR Reporter*, put it (only slightly tongue-in-cheek): "Ex-convicts, child molesters, political fixers, call girls and their procurers, gambling casino bouncers and a variety of glad-handing front men have been described as 'public relations counselors.' "[4]

A similar thought was expressed by John Sattler, former director of public relations at Ford: "Public relations is an easy and all-encompassing label to hang on people and events. Like cosmetics, it can be thought to cover all types of imperfections and blemishes. It was bound to attract varying levels of capability and competence and motives . . . and has its share of 'schlock' operators."[5]

While all organizations have, by their existence, some kind of public relations, not all enjoy *good* public relations. And that's what this book is all about—good public relations, the kind you must work at.

Whereas *marketing* and *sales* have as their primary objective to sell an organization's products, public relations attempts to "sell" the organization itself. Central to its concern is the public interest.

Advertising also generally aims to sell products through paid means. Good public relations, on the other hand, cannot be bought; it must be earned. And the credibility derived from sound public relations work may far exceed that gained through paid advertising.

Product publicity, although an aspect of public relations, is more closely aligned with advertising. In general, the elements of the marketing mix—advertising, product promotion, sales, publicity, and the like—may be but a small part of public relations. As Louis B. Lundborg, retired chairman of Bank America, has pointed out, "If the person who advises top management on the public implications of company policies and decisions . . . can be influenced by pressures from advertising or marketing forces, he is worthless to management as a PR counselor."[6]

The earliest college teachers of public relations exhorted students to:

learn new ways of using knowledge you already have—a different viewpoint, as if you moved to one side and looked at everything from unfamiliar angles. Project yourself into the minds of people you are trying to reach, and see things the way they do. Use everything you've learned elsewhere—English, economics, sociology, science, history—you name it.[7]

INTERVIEW
Walt Seifert

Walt Seifert is professor of public relations in the School of Journalism at Ohio State University. He has taught at Ohio State since 1958. In 1967, he founded the Public Relations Student Society of America (PRSSA) and in 1976, he founded the Educator's Section of PRSA. A former newspaper reporter, Mr. Seifert was a public information officer in the U.S. Navy during World War II, an account executive

for N. W. Ayer & Son, and spent ten years in public relations with Byer & Bowman in Columbus, Ohio. More than 500 graduates of Professor Seifert's classes are now practicing public relations.

What are the most striking changes in the public relations profession since you began in the practice?

Since I started as a manager of the Bermuda News Bureau in 1938, I have watched this emerging profession develop fast in both qualitative and quantitative senses. In today's highly competitive society, it is widely understood that any individual, organization, or institution that seeks public support must hire professional communicators to advocate in the Court of Public Opinion as it hires lawyers to advocate in the courts of law.

What changes have you noticed among public relations students?

Today's public relations students, like all other students, are concentrating on their goals and their glands—and are much more job-oriented than the angry students in the 70s.

How do you define public relations?

Several decades later, it is still widely felt that a broad background is essential to effectively manage public issues. While specific definitions of public relations may differ, most who practice it agree that good public relations requires a firm base of theoretical knowledge, a strong sense of judgment, solid communication skills, and, most of all, an uncompromising attitude of professionalism.

Public relations is "doing good and making sure you get caught." Another way of saying this is "good deeds made known."

What distinguishes a good public relations practitioner?

A good public relations practitioner touches all four bases in the professional PR process: *R*(esearch), *A*(ction), *C*(ommunicating), and *E*(valuating). This requires planning, doing, telling, and proving. A mediocre practitioner only communicates.

What advice do you give your students who want to become professional public relations practitioners?

Study under a seasoned public relations professional, whether he has fancy academic degrees or not. Join the student society and make contacts at PRSSA meetings and conventions. Work on PRSA accounts, summer PR jobs, and academic internships that will give you experience and a strong portfolio. Get lots of bylined clips from your school newspaper.

Why should a student be interested in a career in public relations?

In the last 22 years at least 500 graduates of our classes have entered fulltime PR work. More than 92 percent say they like it, and almost all are still in it.

How easy is it to get a job in the field?

It is still relatively easy for graduates to get PR jobs if they have a decent academic record supplemented with strong collegiate PR experiences.

What are the most significant challenges confronting public relations today?

Public relations, like many other professions, is highly differentiated. At the top are the seasoned counselors who sit with management at the policy-making table. At the bottom are youngsters at the news bureau or house organ level. No two practices are alike, but success comes fast to those who have lots of natural intelligence, talent, and desire. The need for clear, effective communication keeps growing.

Twenty years from now, what will be the stature of public relations?

Public relations, as a profession, will keep growing bigger and better as rival organizations compete for approval and seek to offset the negativism of our national mass media.

If you had your career to start over again, what would you do?

I would do exactly what I have done for almost 50 years: pay my dues by proving myself in many phases of real-life PR practice, and then settle back to the easy, inspiring world of academe.

Is there anything else you'd like readers of this book to know?

The only thing between you and the top of the ladder is the ladder!

SEARCHING FOR A SINGLE DEFINITION

What, then, is public relations?

While a lot of people seem to have a pretty good idea, few seem to agree. American historian Robert Heilbroner describes the field as "a brotherhood of some 100,000, whose common bond is its profession and whose common woe is that no two of them can ever quite agree on what that profession is."[8]

Basically, Heilbroner is right, although he can't say there haven't been a great many efforts over the years to come up with a suitable public relations definition. Perhaps the first recorded definition of public relations was found in the Bible: "To do good, and communicate, forget not."[9]

In 1923, Edward Bernays described the function of his fledgling public relations counseling business as one of providing "information given to the public, persuasion directed at the public to modify attitudes and actions, and efforts to integrate attitudes and actions of an institution with its publics and of publics with those of that institution."[10]

In 1939, *Fortune* magazine, in an article entitled, "The Public Be Not Damned," said "public relations is the label used to describe, at one and the same time, techniques and objectives" and "the conduct of individual businesses, as organizations of people banded together in an effort to make a living for themselves and a profit for investors."[11]

In 1944, the Dictionary of Sociology defined the field as "the body of theory and technique utilized in adjusting the relationships of a subject with its publics. These theories and techniques represent applications of sociology, social psychology, economics and political science, as well as of the special skills of journalists, artists, organizational experts, advertising men, etc. to the specific problems involved in this field of activity."[12]

However, as late as 1960, *Webster's Dictionary* showed little understanding when it defined public relations as "relations with the general public through publicity; those functions of a corporation, organization, branch of military service, etc. concerned with informing the public of its activities, policies, etc. and attempting to create favorable public opinion."

Today, while a generally accepted definition of public relations still eludes practitioners, substantial headway toward a clearer understanding of the field is being made. One of the most ambitious searches for a universal definition was that commissioned in 1975 by the Foundation for Public Relations Research and Education. Sixty-five public relations leaders participated in the study, which analyzed 472 different definitions and offered the following sentence:

> Public relations is a distinctive management function which helps establish and maintain mutual lines of communications, understanding, acceptance, and cooperation between an organization and its publics; involves the management of problems or issues; helps management to keep informed on and responsive to public opinion; defines and emphasizes the responsibility of management to serve the public interest; helps management keep abreast of and effectively utilize change, serving as an early warning system to help anticipate trends; and uses research and sound and ethical communication techniques as its principal tools.[13]

FEATURE

Rocky Mountain News

March 3, 1981

Trying 36-24-36 PR

The former Rebecca Ann King was once a queen, or about as close to being a queen as you get in this country. She was Miss America, vintage 1974, and there's nothing wrong with that.

But the 30-year-old looker, whose name is now Dreman, has been named public affairs director for the Regional Transportation District at $42,000 a year, and there very well may be something wrong with that.

We're not saying she's just another pretty face. She did, after all, win a law degree at the University of Denver, she has been on speaking tours to raise money for cancer and asthma research and she has been a consultant for a number of large firms.

But just how qualified is she for this job? There are people out there—a lot of them—who have mastered the difficult field of public relations through years of hard work. Dreman may be bright, and with measurements that read 36-24-36, a real attention getter, but there's nothing to indicate she's an expert at explaining complicated issues to the public.

And what about the salary of 42 grand a year? It's true, RTD has had a hard time getting its message across—namely, ride the bus and leave the driving to us—but does it take that kind of money to persuade a skilled PR hand to climb aboard?

Dreman is no stranger to controversy. After winning the Miss America Pageant in Atlantic City, critics said she wasn't the prettiest or the most talented contestant, and she said, ''If they don't like me, that's fine.'' Then, in her first official appearance as Miss America, she said she favored legalizing marijuana and abortion. That caused something of a stir.

If she thinks the going was tough then, however, wait until she has to explain why buses don't arrive on time or why routes are always being changed or why costs of the Denver mall keep going up and up or why the RTD board should be permitted junkets at taxpayer expense.

Some people have accused the RTD of being inept. Interesting, isn't it, that the agency was inept in hiring someone whose job it will be to justify that ineptness.

While decisions to fill public relations positions may still be clouded by irrelevant factors from time-to-time, as this editorial implies there is increasing recognition in society of the complexities involved in professional public relations work.

Another definition emerged from an assembly of public relations associations in 1978:

> Public relations practice is the art and social science of analyzing trends, predicting their consequences, counseling organization leaders and implementing planned programs of action which will serve both the organization's and the public's interest.[14]

In 1980, the Task Force on the Stature and Role of Public Relations, chartered by the Public Relations Society of America, offered two definitions that project a perspective of the field at the highest policy-making level and encompass all its functions and specialities:

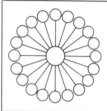

MINICASE

The railroaded railroad

The Grand Northern Railroad couldn't get a break.

In the summer came the floods. In the winter came the snow. In between came the cows mistaking the GN tracks for grazing land. For the 50,000 commuters who depended on the Grand Northern to get them to and from work each day, it meant perpetual and massive delays.

The GN—or as it was derisively labeled by its riders, the Grand Nuisance—was a laughing stock.

One afternoon, Grand Northern's president decided to take action. He called a press conference.

"From now on," he told the skeptical journalists, "this railroad will run on time every time. We will make a concerted effort to improve all phases of our customer service. You're going to see a real change in this railroad." He went on to announce a special program that would award bonuses to staff members demonstrating superior service to customers.

The next morning, sixteen miles from its destination, in the middle of an expansive open field miles from civilization, the GN Mainliner—pride of the GN fleet—sputtered miserably, coughed one last puff of steam, and collapsed with a groan; leaving hundreds of irate commuters to ponder their morning headline, "Grand Northern Promises 'Real Change' for Passengers."

QUESTIONS

1 What's wrong with Grand Northern's public relations strategy?
2 Was the timing of the press conference appropriate?
3 Was the content of the conference appropriate?
4 How might Grand Northern be treated in the next day's paper?
5 If you had been the firm's public relations counsel, what would you have advised GN's president about his press conference idea?

○ Public relations helps an organization and its publics adapt mutually to each other.

○ Public relations is an organization's efforts to win the cooperation of groups of people.[15]

Communications counselor L. L. L. Golden has suggested that more people would understand the field if the term *relations with the public* were substituted to describe it.[16] While it is unlikely that a generally accepted definition of public relations will soon—or perhaps ever—be agreed upon, the attempts mentioned here provide some idea of the scope of the practice.

R-A-C-E FORMULA

Communications professor John Marston suggested that public relations be defined in terms of four specific functions: a) research, b) action, c) communication, and d) evaluation.[17]

Applying the R-A-C-E approach, one researches attitudes on a particular issue, identifies action programs of the organization that speak to that issue, communicates these programs to gain understanding and acceptance, and evaluates the effect of the communication efforts on the public.

This formula is similar to one of the most repeated definitions of public relations, developed by Public Relations News, a leading newsletter for practitioners: Public relations is the management function which evaluates public attitudes, identifies the policies and procedures of an individual or an organization with the public interest, and plans and executes a program of action to earn public understanding and acceptance.[18]

The key word in this definition is *management.* Although most practitioners believe the field is close to the top of the policy-making pyramid, some think the word management is not part of a definition. For example, the Public Relations Society of America did not include it for "simplicity" reasons. Its definition called public relations "the function that maintains an organization's relationships with society in a way that most effectively achieves the organization's goals."[19]

Underlying these definitions is an unstated word: *performance.* Without proper performance, good public relations is impossible. Stated another way, performance must precede publicity. Or yet another way, in the less grandiose terminology of public relations professor Mack Palmer, "First lay the egg, then cackle."

SHORTHAND DEFINITIONS

Other attempts to define the field have been simpler than the previously discussed approaches, although no less germane.

At the British Institute of Public Relations: "Public relations is a deliberate, planned, and sustained effort to establish and maintain mutual understanding between an organization and its publics."

At *Fortune* magazine: "Public relations is good performance today publicly appreciated because it is adequately communicated."

To one counselor: "Public relations is communicating truth—good works well told."

To others, it's:

"Persuasive communication designed to influence specific publics."

"The winning of public acceptance by acceptable performance."

"Doing good and getting credit for it."

"*Performance* plus *Recognition*."

This book will define *public relations* as the management of communications between an organization and its publics. But whichever definition you prefer, it is clear that the more we try to define it, the more we understand about the scope of the practice. That no one can agree about a definition shows that public relations is an evolving profession.[20]

INTERPRETING MANAGEMENT TO THE PUBLIC

At base, practitioners are interpreters. On the one hand, they must interpret the philosophies, policies, programs, and practices of their management to the public; and on the other hand, they must translate the attitudes of the public to their management.

To accomplish these tasks accurately and truthfully, they must gain attention, understanding, acceptance, and ultimately, action from target publics. To do this, they first have to know what management is thinking. Lewis A. Lapham, former vice-chairperson of Banker's Trust Company, admitted that he'd learned "in tears and sweat, if not in blood, that public relations philosophy, inspiration, and action must flow from the top."[21]

So good public relations can't be practiced in a vacuum. No matter what the size of the organization, a public relations department is only as good as its access to management. For example, it's useless for a political press secretary to explain the reasoning of an important decision if the secretary hasn't first found out what the senator had in mind. So too, an organization's public relations staff is impotent without the first-hand knowledge of the reasons for management's decisions and the rationale for organizational policy. As Lapham put it, "No matter how skillful the public relations techniques and technicians, they simply cannot succeed if top management is unaware of or sidesteps its responsibilities in describing its place in the community and in defining its objectives."[22]

The public relations policy of Standard Oil of Indiana is an example of sound objectives:

> We are in business to find oil, make good products, and sell them at fair prices and profits. We try to operate in the best interest of shareholders, employees, customers, and the public. We believe our company and all business and industry can do this best under American free enterprise and competitive private management. Our public relations policy is to treat people right, heed their opinions and keep them informed.[23]

The public relations department can counsel management. It can advise management. It can even exhort management to action. But management must call the tune on organizational policy. Practitioners must fully understand the why's and wherefore's of policy and communicate the ideas accurately and candidly to the public. Anything less can lead to major problems.

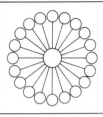

MINICASE

The uninformed PR veep

Osterman, Bimbo Manufacturing's public relations vice-president, sensed trouble when he walked in at 8:30 and found his boss waiting for him, shaking his head disgustedly.

"It's trouble, Herb," the boss fumed. "We're sending out hundreds of pink slips in the morning mail. The press is gonna be all over us if word leaks out."

"You mean we're not going to announce the layoffs? Osterman asked incredulously. "We're intending to 'stonewall' it?"

"What's there to announce?" his boss rumbled. "Any way you slice it, it's bad news, and we can't win by saying anything."

"I suppose you're right," Osterman reasoned. "In that case, don't give me any of the details. That way, if I do get called, I won't be lying when I tell 'em I know nothing more about it than we've effected some layoffs. Agree?"

"Absolutely."

QUESTIONS

1 Do you, too, agree with Osterman's approach?
2 What might a reporter think of Osterman and Bimbo Manufacturing upon getting wind of the story?
3 Do you think a reporter would write a story about the layoffs even without Osterman's help?
4 If so, how might Bimbo Manufacturing be treated in the article?
5 What would you have done in Osterman's place?

INTERPRETING THE PUBLIC TO MANAGEMENT

The flip side of the coin is interpreting the public to management. Simply stated, this task means finding out what the public really thinks about the firm and letting management know. Regretfully, recent corporate history is filled with examples of public relations departments failing to anticipate clearly the true sentiments of the public.

For example, in 1962, U.S. Steel produced a credible argument that a rise in steel prices was in the public's best long-term interest. The decision, however, was ill-timed and denounced by three government agencies and many national leaders. President Kennedy condemned the company's move as a blatant act of "contempt for 185 million Americans." Then both the company and the industry were subject to scornful broadsides from all quarters.

In another incident several years later, General Motors did not pay much attention to a little-known consumer activist named Ralph Nader, who spread the message that GM's Corvair was "unsafe at any speed." When Nader's assault began to be believed, the automaker assigned private detectives to trail him. In short order, General Motors was forced to acknowledge its act of paranoia, and the Corvair was eventually sacked at great loss to the company.

As a further illustration, in the mid-1970s, as the price of gasoline and oil company profits rose rapidly, Mobil infuriated a suspicious public by purchasing Marcor, parent of the Montgomery Ward department store chain, instead of spending its earnings on new oil exploration and development.

Government leaders, too, sometimes incorrectly interpret the public's sentiments. Late in his Presidency, Jimmy Carter tried to enlist public support for his flagging economic program with a nationally televised address that discussed "America's malaise" and the need to get the nation moving again. Carter's speech, it was generally agreed, backfired because many Americans resented the notion that they and their country were languishing. The Carter "malaise speech" was later used to great advantage by Ronald Reagan in his successful bid for the Presidency in 1979.

These examples indicate that organizations are often insensitive to the public's concerns. As Joseph T. Nolan, public affairs director of Monsanto Company, has put it,

> Nobody has a larger stake in our economic system—or a larger say in our society—than U.S. business. Whether that system and that society continue to work to the satisfaction of business will depend, ultimately, on how successfully individual businesses demonstrate that they can work for the good of everybody.[24]

THE PUBLICS OF PUBLIC RELATIONS

The term *public relations* is really a misnomer. "Publics relations" or "relations with the publics" would be more to the point. Practitioners must communicate with many different publics—beyond the "general" public—each having its own special needs and requiring different types of communications. Often, the lines that divide these publics are thin and the potential overlap is significant. Therefore priorities, according to organizational needs, must always be reconciled. (See Figure 1-1.)

Technological change, in particular, has brought greater interdependence among people and organizations. There is growing concern in organizations today about managing extensive webs of interrelationships. Indeed, managers have become interrelationship conscious.

Internally, managers must deal directly with various levels of subordinates as well as with cross relationships that arise from subordinates interacting with one another. Externally, they must deal with a system that includes government regulatory agencies, labor unions, subcontractors, consumer groups, and many other independent—but often related—organizations.

The public relations challenge in all this is to effectively manage the communications between managers and the various publics with whom they interrelate.

Definitions differ on what precisely constitutes a *public*. One definition suggests that a public arises when a group of people a) face a similar indeterminant situation, b) recognize what is indeterminant and problematic in that situation, and c) organize to do something about the problem.[25]

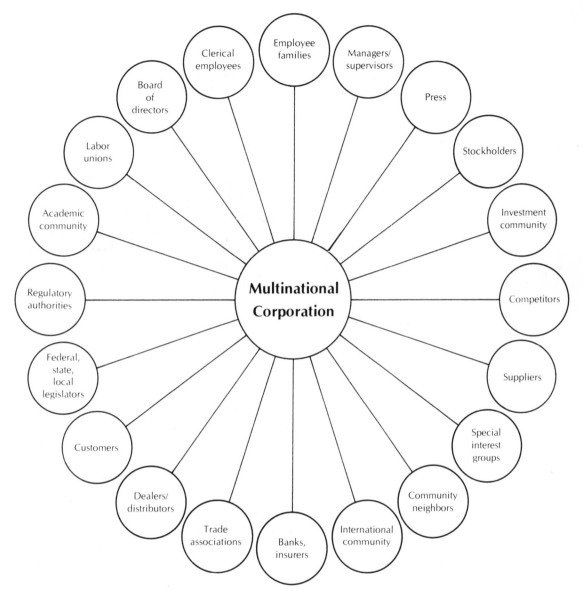

FIGURE 1-1. Twenty key publics of a typical multinational corporation.

SOURCE: Artist Lou Braun.

This framework can be used to define three stages in the evolution of a public:

1 **Latent publics,** when a group is in an indeterminate situation but does not recognize the situation as a problem. For example, in the early 1980s, the vast majority of airline employees for such companies as Braniff, Laker, Continental, and World probably had little idea that the combination of airline deregulation and rising energy prices might have negative consequences for them. They quickly got the message when all three companies began to totter and fall toward the brink of bankruptcy.

2 **Aware publics,** when the group recognizes the problem.

3 **Active publics,** when the group organizes to do something about the problem.[26]

This three-stage approach to defining publics may help practitioners design communications strategies to respond to each level of the evolutionary process.

Publics may also be classified into several overlapping categories:

1 **Internal and External** Internal publics are inside the organization: supervisors, clerks, managers, stockholders, and the board of directors. External publics are those not directly connected with the organization: the press, government, educators, customers, community, and suppliers.

2 **Primary, Secondary, and Marginal** Primary publics can most help—or hinder—the organization's efforts. Secondary publics are less important, and marginal publics are least important of all. For example, members of the Federal Reserve Board of Governors, who regulate banks, would be the primary public for a bank awaiting a regulatory ruling, while legislators and the general public would be "secondary."

3 **Traditional and Future** Employees and current customers are traditional publics, while students and potential customers are future ones. No organization can afford to become complacent in dealing with its changing publics. Today a firm's publics range from women to minorities to senior citizens to homosexuals. Each could be important to the future success of an organization.

4 **Proponents, Opponents, and Uncommitted** An institution must deal differently with those who support it and those who oppose it. For supporters, communications that reinforce beliefs may be in order. But to change the opinions of skeptics calls for strong, persuasive communications. Often, particularly in politics, the "uncommitted" public is crucial. Many a campaign has been decided because the "swing vote" was won over by one of the candidates.

The typical organization is faced with a myriad of critical publics with whom it must communicate daily. It must be sensitive to their needs and concerns, communicating with each in a timely and effective manner. While management must always speak with one voice, its inflection, its delivery, and its emphasis should be sensitive to each public.

THE ESSENCE OF PUBLIC RELATIONS PRACTICE

Ethics, truth, credibility—that's what good public relations is all about. Cover-up, distortion, and subterfuge is the antithesis of good public relations.

Much more than *customers* for their products, managers today desperately need *constituents* for their ideas. In the 1980s, the role of public relations will be much more to guide management in framing its ideas and in making its commit-ments. The counsel that management will need must come from advisors who understand public attitudes, public moods, public needs and public aspirations.[27]

That public relations professionals will provide that needed counsel is indis-putable for many reasons:

○ The growth of people's influence all over the world makes essential the role of public relations as a detector, interpreter, and communicator.

○ The growing diversity of people and their interests demands greater sophistica-tion and skill to deal with them.

○ Growing specialization in all fields is increasing the need for broader under-standing and professional communications skills.

○ The decline in writing skills in society increases the need for those who have such skills.

○ There is a growing number of media and voices using the channels of commu-nication.

○ Technology and the spread of knowledge increasingly have made the world the province of public relations.

○ Finally, the tendency for leaders of organizations to look inward creates a pressing need for those able to provide outside viewpoints and reach outside groups to earn "goodwill" for their organizations.[28]

Winning this elusive commodity of goodwill takes time and effort. Credibility can't be won overnight, nor can it be bought. If management policies aren't in the public's best interest, no amount of "public relations" can obscure that reality. Public relations is not effective as a temporary, defensive measure to compensate for management misjudgment. If management errs seriously, the best—and only—public relations advice must be to get the story out immediately.

So, if public relations has come of age as a serious and substantive profession, does that mean the end of the slick-talking "image merchant"? Hardly. People will always be interested in "finding the angle" or "sneaking one by" in the flim-flammiest traditions of P. T. Barnum. But clearly the profession is growing more sophisticated, with many practitioners thinking of their work in the same vein as counselor Emanuel Goldberg:

> Public relations today is not product publicity, lavish trips or gifts to the media at Christmas, or a smile at the teller's window. It's a very deep kind of private and public service. It conceives themes and programs, advises management on thorny issues, deals constructively with a wide variety of oft-conflicting publics . . . writes capably and imaginatively, surveys attitudes, promotes good community, race and employee rela-tions, plans for emergencies, creates radio and television programs, gets into publishing and films and slides and exhibits, adapts to similar tasks overseas, meets with analysts, brokers, and money managers, collaborates in marketing and advertising campaigns, and on and on and on.[29]

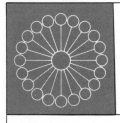

CASE STUDY
Watergate

I felt sure that it was just a public relations problem that only needed a public relations solution.

Richard M. Nixon,
RN: The Memoirs of Richard Nixon
(New York: Grosset & Dunlap, 1978), p. 773.

In 1972, Richard Nixon was elected President of the United States in a landslide. His opponent, Senator George McGovern, won only Massachusetts and the District of Columbia.

Two years later, on August 9, 1974, Nixon resigned in disgrace and humiliation. His administration had been tarnished with illegal wiretapping, illegal surveilance, burglary, and unlawful use of the law. The President and his men were toppled by the most profound political scandal in the nation's history, which grew out of a series of break-ins at Washington Democratic National Headquarters in a building named *Watergate*.

One notion raised in the aftermath of Watergate was that the President and his advisors were too concerned about "public relations," about "covering up" the facts, and that this concern led to their downfall. This castigation of public relations for its supposed role in Watergate is ironic. For had Nixon or his aides been able to comprehend the broad ramifications and deal with them straightforwardly, they may have been judged with more compassion and spared their severe and precipitous fall. (While the field of public relations took the heat for the Watergate scandal, most of Nixon's key public relations advisors came from the field of advertising.)

As excerpts from transcripts indicate, neither the President nor his advisors knew much about good public relations. By ignoring virtually every elementary public relations principle, they blundered away any chance of many Americans understanding and forgiving them their misjudgments.

Here are six of the more onerous miscalculations from the Watergate saga:

1   In late 1972, while rumors abounded that the administration was corrupt, the White House remained silent. As the President concluded in a conversation with top aides, H.R. Haldeman and John Dean, "We take a few shots and it will be over. Don't worry."

 Evidently, Nixon felt the public would grow tired of the perpetual pounding on Watergate. Therefore his strategy: "Hang tough and ignore it."

2   The spotlight on Watergate intensified and the media refused to let up. Nixon ordered Dean to prepare an "enemies list" of journalists and others who opposed the administration, saying, "I want the most comprehensive notes on all those who tried to do us in."

Evidently, he felt that going directly after particular individuals would stifle their efforts. This step, according to Dean, was to use "available federal machinery to screw our political enemies."

3 In early 1973, the Senate's investigation dominated national news. The President and his aides were invited to appear, but they declined on the grounds of "*executive privilege.*"

4 Like *executive privilege*, the term *national security* also received an extensive workout during the Watergate period. In March 1973, the President discussed with Haldeman and Dean the break-in at the office of the psychiatrist Daniel Ellsberg, an administration "enemy" who had leaked secret Pentagon papers to *The New York Times*. Dean suggested that the break-in be defended as "national security." The President agreed, saying, "We had to get information for national security grounds. We had to do it on a confidential basis. Neither [the FBI nor the CIA] could be trusted."

Several years later, both Dean and Haldeman were imprisoned, primarily due to their roles in this break-in.

5 In October 1973, Nixon had had enough of Archibald Cox, the special prosecutor he appointed to get to the bottom of the Watergate case. When Cox persisted in trying to secure the release of the President's confidential tapes, Nixon ordered Attorney General Elliot Richardson to fire him. Richardson refused and resigned. Deputy Attorney General William Ruckelshaus, the next in line, also refused and was fired. Finally, Solicitor General Robert Bork, the third person in line, fired Cox.

In one fell swoop, Nixon's "Saturday Night Massacre" became a new cause celebre, and the Watergate fires were reignited.

6 The President's relations with the media steadily deteriorated. About a major report by Dean on Watergate, Nixon told an aide, "We've got to keep our eye on the Dean thing—just give them some of it, not all of it . . . just take the heat."

Facing an audience of several hundred newspaper editors in November 1973, the President rambled, "In all of my years of public life, I have never obstructed justice. And I think too that I could say that in my years of public life, that I welcome this kind of examination, because people have got to know whether or not their President is a crook. Well, I am not a crook."

Later on, the President instructed Press Secretary Ronald Ziegler that in responding to substantive press queries, "Just get out there and act like your usual cocky, confident self."[30]

QUESTIONS

1 How sound was the early White House public relations strategy to "hang tough" in the midst of media flak?

2 Why didn't Watergate go away?

3 Why was the compilation of an "enemies list" a mistake?

4 Did the list serve any purpose for Nixon?

5 Was "executive privilege" justified in the administration's refusal to appear before the Senate Watergate Committee?

6 What were the public relations consequences of invoking executive privilege?

7 How would you have interpreted the "Saturday Night Massacre" if you were a disinterested observer?

8 What public relations/credibility problems might have been caused by the break-in of Ellsberg's psychiatrist's office and the subsequent "national security" explanation defending it?

9 How would you assess Nixon's media relations philosophy?

10 If you had been Nixon's public relations counselor, what would you have recommended upon learning the full story about Watergate?

Hint in answering questions:

British statesman Edmund Burke once said, "It is not what a lawyer tells me I may do, but what humanity, reason and justice tell me I ought to do."

NOTES

1 George F. Will, "Well, I Don't Love You E.T.," *Newsweek*, 19 July 1982, p. 76.

2 Robert K. Gray, "Public Relations," *Washington Journalism Review*, January/February 1980, p. 43.

3 Philip Lesley, "Report and Recommendation: Task Force on Stature and Role of Public Relations," *Public Relations Journal*, March 1981, p. 32.

4 *PR Reporter*, 15, no. 16 (17 April 1972):1.

5 John E. Sattler, remarks at a seminar of the Public Relations Society of America, Dearborn, Mich., April 1, 1976.

6 Louis B. Lundborg, "Executive Survival Kit," *Industry Week*, 14 April 1980, p. 12.

7 Berton J. Ballard, lecture at San Jose State University, San Jose, Calif., 1948. Cited in Pearce Davies, "Twenty-Five Years Old and Still Growing," *Public Relations Journal*, October 1977.

8 Cited in Scott M. Cutlip and Allan H. Center, *Effective* Public Relations, 5th ed. (Englewood Cliffs, N.J.: Prentice-Hall, 1978), p. 5.

9 Heb. 13:16.

10 Edward L. Bernays, *"Crystallizing Public Opinion"* (New York, Liveright Publishing Corp., 1961), p. LV.

11 "The Public Be Not Damned," *Fortune*, March 1, 1939, p. 83.

12 Pratt Henry Fairchild (ed.), *Dictionary of Sociology*. (New York, N.Y.: Philosophical Library, 1944.)

13 Rex F. Harlow, "Building a Public Relations Definition," *Public Relations Review*, 2, no. 4 (Winter 1976):36.

14 First World Assembly of Public Relations Associations, Mexico City, Mexico, 1978.

15 Philip Lesley, op cit., p. 30.

16 L. L. L. Golden, *Only by Public Consent* (New York: Hawthorn Books, 1968).

17 John E. Marston, *The Nature of Public Relations* (New York: McGraw-Hill, 1963).

18 Denny Griswold, *Public Relations News*, the International Public Relations Weekly for Executives, 127 East 80th Street, New York, N.Y. 10021.

19 C. Thomas Wilck, "Toward a Definition of Public Relations," *Public Relations Journal*, December 1977, p. 26.

20 Counselor John Cook provides an irreverant and insightful analysis of the various definitions, myths, and premises of public relations in "PR Without the BS," *Public Relations* Quarterly, Spring 1974.

21 Cited in John F. Budd, Jr. *An Executive's Primer on* Public Relations (Philadelphia: Chilton, 1969), p. xii.

22 Ibid.

23 Standard Oil Company (Indiana), 200 E. Randolph Dr., Chicago, Illinois 60601.

24 Joseph T. Nolan, "Protect Your Public Image with Performance," *Harvard Business Review*, March-April 1975, p. 142.

25 John Dewey, *The Public and Its Problems* (Chicago: Swallow Press, 1927).

26 James E. Grunig, "Defining Publics in Public Relations: The Case of a Suburban Hospital," *Journalism Quarterly*, Spring 1978.

27 Robert Cushman, Chairman, Norton Company, Remarks at the New England Chapter of the Public Relations Society of America, Worcester, Mass., 27 February 1980.

28 Philip Lesley, op cit., p. 17.

29 Emanuel Goldberg, "Public Relations: Before and After Watergate," *Congressional Record*, 120, no. 177 (17 December 1974):40591.

30 This case is adapted from one of the more significant analyses of Watergate as a study in public relations: Joseph T. Nolan, "Watergate: A Case Study in How Not to Handle Public Relations," *Public Relations Quarterly*, Summer 1975. Used with permission. Also see Gladys Engel Lang and Kurt Lang, "Polling on Watergate: The Battle for Public Opinion," *Public Opinion Quarterly*, Vol. 44:530–547.

SUGGESTED READING

Armstrong, Richard A. "Public Affairs vs. Public Relations," *Public Relations Quarterly*, Fall 1981, p. 26.

Bernays, Edward L. *Crystallizing Public Opinion*, New York: Liveright Publishing Corporation, 1961, pp. 1v–1vi.

Canfield, Bertrand R., and **Moore, H. Frazier.** *Public Relations: Principles, Cases and Problems.* 6th ed. Homewood, Ill.: Richard D. Irwin, 1973.

Center, Allen H. and **Walsh, Frank E.** *Public Relations Practices: Case Studies*, 2nd ed., Englewood Cliffs, New Jersey: Prentice-Hall, 1981.

Chaffee, Steven H., and **Petrick Michael J.** *Using the Mass Media: Communications Problems in American Society.* New York: McGraw-Hill, 1975.

Chase, W. Howard, "New Standards for Measuring Public Relations." *Public Relations Journal* 31, no. 2 (February 1975): 18–21.

Cole, Robert S. *The Practical Handbook of Public Relations*, Englewood Cliffs, New Jersey: Prentice-Hall, Inc., 1981.

Cook, John. "PR without the BS," *Public Relations Quarterly*, Spring 1975, pp. 6–25.

Cutlip, Scott M., and **Center, Allen H.** *Effective Public Relations*, 5th ed. Englewood Cliffs, N.J.: Prentice-Hall, 1978.

Haimann, Theo, Scott, William G., and **Connor, Patrick E.** *Managing the Modern Organization*, Boston: Houghton Mifflin, 1978, p. 41, Chapter 8.

Hall, Babette. *Public Relations, Publicity and Promotion*, New York: David McKay, 1970.

Harlow, Rex F. "Building a Public Relations Definition." Public Relations Review, 2, no. 4 (Winter 1976): 34–41.

Hill, John W. *The Making of a Public Relations Man*, New York: David McKay Company, Inc., 1963, pp. 131–143.

Hill and Knowlton Executives, *Critical Issues in Public Relations*. Englewood Cliffs, N.J.: Prentice-Hall, 1975. Essays and speeches dealing with the role of public relations.

Kadon, Ann and **John.** *Successful Public Relations Techniques*, Scottsdale, Arizona: Modern Schools, 1976.

Lesley, Philip. "Report and Recommendations: Task Force on Stature and Role of Public Relations," *Public Relations Journal*, March 1980, pp. 21–44. Overview analysis of the entire public relations profession and indications of the likely course it might take in the years ahead.

Lesley, Philip. "The Stature and Role of Public Relations," *Public Relations Journal*, January 1981, pp. 14–17. A blue-ribbon task force analysis of the future of the profession.

Lesley, Philip, ed. *Public Relations Handbook*. 2nd ed. Englewood Cliffs, N.J.: Prentice-Hall, 1978. Chapters on problems that plague nonprofit organizations, trade associations, schools and universities, newspapers, and other groups. This manual also offers valuable information on numerous communication techniques.

Lewis, H. Gordon. *How to Handle Your Own Public Relations*, Chicago: Nelson-Hall, 1976.

Lloyd, Herbert. *Public Relations*. New York: International Publishing Service, 1974.

Margulies, Walter P. "Back to Fundamentals," *Public Relations Journal*, April 1982, pp. 50–51.

Marston, John E. *Modern Public Relations*, New York: McGraw-Hill, Inc., 1979.
"The New Public Relations," *Public Relations Journal*, January 1981, pp. 29–33.

Newson, Doug, and **Scott, Alan.** *This is PR: The Realities of Public Relations*. Belmont, Calif.: Wadsworth, 1976.

Nolte, Lawrence W. Fundamentals of Public Relations. 2nd Ed. New York: Pergamon Press, 1979.

Read Jr., Nat B. "Laws of Public Relations," *Public Relations Journal*, May 1982, p. 20.

Reilly, Robert T. *Public Relations in Action*, Englewood Cliffs, New Jersey: Prentice-Hall, Inc., 1981.

Siefert, Walter W. "The Sin of Silence." *Public Relations Journal* 31, no. 1 (January 1975): 11–12.

Simon, Raymond. *Public Relations: Concepts and Practice*. Columbus, Ohio: Grid, 1976.

Simon, Raymond. *Public Relations Management: Cases and Simulations*, Columbus, Ohio: Grid Inc., 1977.

Simon, Raymond. *Publicity and Public Relations Worktext*, 4th ed., Columbus, Ohio: Grid Inc., 1978.

Stanton, William J. *Fundamentals of Marketing*, New York: McGraw-Hill, 1978, pp. 410–411, 458–461.

Stephenson, Howard. *Handbook of Public Relations*. 2nd ed. New York: McGraw-Hill, 1971.

Voros, Gerald J. and **Alvarez, Paul.** *What Happens in Public Relations*, New York: American Management Associations, 1981.

Weston, William. "Public Relations: Trustee of a Free Society." *Public Relations Review* 1, no. 2 (Fall 1975):5–14.

RESPONDING TO A COMPLEX SOCIETY

The practice of public relations has been shaped by several underlying and pervasive trends in our complex, industrialized society.

Three fundamental trends, in particular, are directly related to the evolution of public relations:

1 the growth of "big institutions";

2 the increasing incidence of conflict and confrontation in society;

3 the heightened awareness of people everywhere because of more sophisticated communications technology.

The "bigness" of today's society has played a significant role in the development of public relations. The days of the mom and pop grocery store, the tiny community college, and the small local bank rapidly are disappearing. In their place have emerged supermarket chains and 24-hour-a-day 7-Elevens, statewide community college systems, with populous branches in several cities and, multi-bank, multi-state banking networks, such as First Interstate Bancorporation, a federation of medium- and larger-sized banks with offices throughout the western United States.

As institutions have grown larger, as the U.S. population has burgeoned to over 220 million, as people have had to deal increasingly with bureaucracy, so too have institutions themselves refined their methods of communicating with their publics. Specifically, the public relations profession has evolved to interpret these large institutions to the publics they serve.

○ The increasing incidence of conflict and confrontation in society is yet another reason for the evolution of public relations.

2
The Evolution of Public Relations

○ Women's rights and affirmative action, consumerism and environmental aware-ness, labor-management disputes, and the unhappiness of the public in gen-eral with large institutions all have contributed materially to the need for more and better communications and the existence of more and better communi-cators.

○ A final factor in the development of public relations is the heightened awareness of people everywhere. First came the invention of the printing press. Later it was the pervasiveness of mass communications: print media, radio, and television. Then it was the development of cable, satellite, video tape, video discs, video typewriters, portable cameras, word processors, and all the other communica-tions technologies that have delivered Marshall McLuhan's "global village." All have contributed to the necessity in today's society to better understand and manage the communications process.

ANCIENT BEGINNINGS

Although we think of public relations as a twentieth century phenomenon, its roots are ancient. Leaders in virtually every great society throughout history understood the importance of influencing public opinion through persuasion.

For example, the Iraqis of 1800 B.C. hammered out their messages on stone tablets so that farmers could learn the latest techniques of harvesting, sowing, and irrigation.[1] The more food the farmers grew, the better the citizenry ate and the wealthier the country became: a good example of planned persuasion to reach a specific public for a particular purpose. Or, in other words, public relations.

Later on, the Greeks put a high premium on communication skills. The best speakers, in fact, were generally elected to leadership positions. Occasionally, aspiring Greek politicians enlisted the aid of Sophists (individuals renowned for both their reasoning and rhetoric) to help fight verbal battles. Sophists would gather in the amphitheaters of the day and extoll the virtues of particular political candidates. Often, their arguments convinced the voters and elected their employer. Thus, the Sophists set the stage for today's lobbyists, who attempt to influence legislation through effective communication techniques.

The Romans (particularly Julius Caesar) were also masters of persuasive techniques. Faced with an upcoming battle, Caesar would rally public support through assorted publications and staged events. Similarly, in the United States in World War I, a special public information committee, the Creel Committee, was formed to channel the patriotic sentiments of Americans in support of the U.S. role in the war. Stealing a page from Caesar, the committee's massive verbal and written communications effort was successful in marshalling national pride behind the war effort.

Even the Catholic Church had a hand in the early beginnings of public relations. In the 1600s, under the leadership of Pope Gregory XV, the Church established a College of Propaganda to "help propagate the faith." In those days, the term *propaganda* did not have a negative connotation; the Church simply wanted to inform the public more clearly about the advantages of Catholicism.

EARLY AMERICAN EXPERIENCE

Three individuals, in particular, helped influence the American public relations field prior to the 1900s: a revolutionary, a writer, and a ringmaster.

ADAMS

Sam Adams led the communications phase of the American Revolutionary War with the same zeal and competence with which George Washington led the military phase. As an arouser of public awareness, Adams was a master. He was a hard-core revolutionary, who bitterly opposed the pro-British sentiments of many of his fellow colonists. Systematically, through a series of planned communications, Adams and his colleagues set out to break down British loyalties and build up revolutionary fervor. He organized the Committees of Correspondence as a kind of "revolutionary Associated Press" to speedily disseminate anti-British information throughout the colonies.

Adams staged events—the Boston Tea Party is one memorable example—to dramatize the mission of the revolutionaries. Adams exploited British transgressions with screaming publicity, labeling the enemy's shooting of several Boston dockhands as "the Boston Massacre" and successfully sending shockwaves through the countryside.

While his methods occasionally may have been devious, Adams was nonetheless extremely persuasive.

KENDALL

So was Amos Kendall. As a writer and editor in Kentucky, Kendall was selected by President Andrew Jackson to serve in his administration in 1829. Within weeks, Kendall became a member of Old Hickory's "Kitchen Cabinet," and he eventually turned out to be one of Jackson's most influential assistants.

Kendall performed just about every White House public relations task. He wrote speeches, state papers, and messages, and turned out press releases. He even conducted basic opinion polls. Although Kendall is generally credited with being the first authentic presidential press secretary, his functions and role went far beyond that.

Among Kendall's most successful ventures in Jackson's behalf was the development of the administration's own newspaper, *The Globe*. Although it was not uncommon for the governing administration to publish its own "national house organ," Kendall's deft editorial touch refined the process to increase its effectiveness. It was not uncommon for Kendall to pen a Jackson news release, distribute it for publication to a local newspaper, and then reprint the press clipping in *The Globe* to underscore Jackson's nationwide popularity. Indeed, that popularity continued unabated throughout Jackson's years in office, with much of the credit going to the President's public relations advisor.*

---

* Kendall was most decidedly not cut from the same swath as today's neat, trim, buttoned-down press secretaries. On the contrary, Jackson's man was described as "a puny, sickly looking man with a weak voice, a wheezing cough, narrow and stooping shoulders, a sallow complexion, silvery hair in his prime, slovenly dress, and a seedy appearance" (Fred F. Endres, "Public Relations in the Jackson White House," *Public Relations Review*, 2, no. 3 [Fall 1976]:5–12).

When you taught the first public relations class, did you ever envision the profession growing to its present stature?

I gave the first course in public relations after *Crystallizing Public Opinion* was published in 1923. I decided that one way to give the term *counsel on public relations* status was to lecture at a university on the principles, practices, and ethics of the new profession. New York University was willing to accept my offer to do so. But I never envisioned at that time that the profession would spread throughout the United States and then throughout the free world.

What were the objectives of that first public relations course?

The objectives were to give status to the new profession. Many people still believed the term *counsel on public relations* was a euphemism for publicity man, press agent, flack. Even H. L. Mencken in his book on the American language ranked it such. But in his *Supplement to the American Language* published years later, he revised his viewpoint and used my definition of the term.

E dward L. Bernays is a public relations patriarch. In 1923, he wrote the seminal book on the subject, *Crystallizing Public Relations,* which laid down the principles, practices, and ethics of the profession. In that same year, he taught the first college course in public relations at New York University. A nephew of Sigmund Freud, Mr. Bernays pioneered the application of the social sciences to public relations. In partnership with his wife, he has advised presidents of the United States, industrial leaders, and legendary figures from Enrico Caruso to Eleanor Roosevelt. Indeed, Mr. Bernays, himself, is a legend in the field of public relations.

What are the most significant factors that have led to the rise in public relations practice?

The most significant factor is the rise in people power. Theodore Roosevelt helped bring this about with his "Square Deal." Woodrow Wilson helped with his "New Freedom," and so did Franklin Delano Roosevelt with his "New Deal." And this tradition was continued as time went on.

Do you have any gripes with the way public relations is practiced today?

I certainly do. The meanings of words in the United States have the stability of soap bubbles. Unless words are defined as to their meaning by law, as in the case of other professions—for instance law, medicine, architecture—they are in the public domain. Anyone can use them. Recently, I received a letter from a model agency offering to supply me with a "public relations representative" for the next trade fair at which we might exhibit our client's products. Today, any plumber or car salesman or unethical character can call himself or herself a public relations practitioner. Many who call themselves public relations practitioners have no education, training, or knowledge of what the field is. And the public equally has little understanding of the meaning of the two words. Until licensing and registration is introduced, this will continue to be the situation.

What pleases you most about current public relations practice?

What pleases me most is that there are, indeed, practitioners who regard their activity as a profession, an art applied to a science, in which the public interest and not pecuniary motivation is the primary consideration; and also that outstanding leaders in society are grasping the meaning and significance of the profession.

What's the most significant problem that confronts the profession?

The most significant problem confronting the profession is this matter of definition by the state of what the profession is—defining it,

registering and licensing practitioners through a board of examiners chosen from the profession, and developing economic sanctions for those who break the code of ethics. This is what other professions have done to protect the public interest and their own interests.

How would you compare the caliber of today's public relations practitioner with the practitioner of the past?

The practitioner today has more education in his subject. But unfortunately, education for public relations varies with the institution where it is being conducted. This is due to the lack of a standard definition. Many institutions of higher learning think public relations activity consists of skillful writing of press releases and teach their students accordingly. This is of course not true. Public relations activity is applied social science.

Where do you think public relations will be twenty years from now?

It is difficult to appraise where public relations will be twenty years from now. I don't like the tendency of advertising agencies gobbling up some large public relations organizations. That is like surgical instrument manufacturers gobbling up surgical medical colleges or law book publishers gobbling up law colleges. However, if licensing and registration take place, as they well may, then the profession is assured a long lifetime.

Is there anything else you'd like readers of this book to know?

There is of course much else I would like readers of this book to know. I would suggest that they read and read and read the books and periodicals that appeal to them, and that are reported on in the bibliographies they read.

BARNUM

Most public relations professionals would rather not talk about Phineas T. Barnum as an industry pioneer. Barnum was a press agent—pure and simple. His end was to make money, and his means was to use publicity. He remained undaunted when the facts sometimes got in the way of his promotional ideas. "The public be fooled" might have been his motto.

Like him or not, Barnum was a master publicist. In the 1800s, as owner of a major circus, Barnum generated article after article for his traveling show. He purposely gave his star performers short names—for instance, Tom Thumb, the midget, and Jenny Lind, the singer—so that they could easily fit as headlines into narrow newspaper columns. He staged bizarre events, like the legal marriage of the "fat lady" to the "thin man" to drum up free newspaper exposure. While today's practitioners scoff at Barnum's methods, some press agents still practice his techniques.

Nevertheless, when today's public relations professionals bemoan the specter of "shysters" and "hucksters" that still overhangs their field, they inevitably place the blame squarely on the fertile mind and silver tongue of Phineas T. Barnum.

EMERGENCE OF THE *ROBBER BARONS*

The American Industrial Revolution ushered in many things at the turn of the century, not the least of which was the field of public relations.

The twentieth century began with the small mills and shops, which served as the hub of the frontier economy, giving way to massive factories. Country hamlets, which had been the centers of commerce and trade, were replaced by sprawling cities. Limited transportation and communications facilities became nationwide railroad lines and communications wires. Big business had taken over, and the businessman was king.

The men who ran America's industries—and without exception, they were all male—seemed more concerned with making a profit than improving the lot of their fellow citizens: railroad owners like William Vanderbilt, bankers like J. P. Morgan, oil magnates like John D. Rockefeller, steel impresarios like Henry Clay Frick. Each "ruled" the fortunes of thousands of others.

Typical of the reputation acquired by this group of industrialists was the famous—or perhaps apocryphal—response of Vanderbilt when questioned about the public's reaction to his closing down the New York Central: "The public be damned!"

Little wonder that Vanderbilt and his ilk were cursed by Americans as robber barons who cared little for the rest of society. While most who depended on these industrialists for their livelihood felt powerless to rebel, the seeds of discontent were sprinkled liberally throughout the culture. It was but a matter of time before the robber barons got their comeuppance.

ENTER THE MUCKRAKERS

When the ax fell on the robber barons, it came in the form of criticism from a feisty group of journalists dubbed *muckrakers*.

The "muck" that these reporters and editors "raked" was based on the scandalous operations of America's business enterprises. Upton Sinclair's novel *The*

FEATURE
P. T. Barnum revisited: the days of super hype

Although most public relations professionals disagree with the publicity-seeking antics attributed to P. T. Barnum, "publicity for publicity's sake" is still very much in vogue, especially in the numerous national photo magazines.

In a return to the kind of media "hype" that Barnum made famous over 100 years ago, today's magazine journalists occasionally sacrifice everything—including objectivity and news judgment—to land a story about a "hot personality" or a "hot project."

This is especially true in the case of the movie industry where personality journalism—also labeled *disposable journalism*—reigns supreme.

For example, in the summer of 1982, with America mired in a nagging recession, Hollywood launched a gaggle of escapist movies, built around exotic personalities, to take the country's mind off its economic problems. Hollywood publicists had a field day as personality-oriented magazines such as *People* and *Us,* and news magazines such as *Time* and *Newsweek* made a mad dash to pick up on the summer movie mania.

In the first month of their runs, largely because of the lavish magazine publicity they received, many of the summer films did spectacularly. *Conan The Barbarian* grossed $33 million. *Star Trek II* grossed $51 million. *Rocky III* grossed $56 million. And *E.T.,* the blockbuster of all time, grossed $87 million in its first month in movie theaters.

The success of these movies was quickly followed by dolls, video games, magazines, coloring books, lunch pails, and assorted other merchandising spin-offs. Not since *Gone With The Wind* bibles and Scarlett O'Hara panties had the country seen such a barrage of publicity/marketing hoopla to promote motion pictures.[2]

As *Newsweek* cultural affairs editor Charles Michener summarized the craze, "There's a great deal of public apathy toward news. The line is growing very blurred between news and entertainment. It's big business, and agents and PR people are now in the position of playing magazines off against each other in ways that they never could before. It obviously has to do with people seeking escape."[3]

Jungle attacked the deplorable conditions of the meat-packing industry. Ida Tarbell's *History of Standard Oil* stripped bare the public facade of the nation's leading petroleum firm. Magazines like *McClure's* struck out systematically at one industry after another.

The captains of industry, so used to getting their own way and having to answer to no one, were wrenched from their environment of peaceful passivity and rolled out on the public carpet to answer for their sins. Journalistic shock stories soon led to a wave of sentiment for legislative reform.

"Trust busting" was the order of the day. Conflicts between employers and employees began to break out, and newly-organized labor unions rose to the fore. The Socialist and Communist movements began to take off. In short, it was "a period when free enterprise reached a peak in American history, and yet at that very climax, the tide of public opinion was swelling up against business freedom, primarily because of the breakdown in communications between the businessman and the public.[4]

For a time, these men of inordinate wealth and power found themselves limited to defend themselves and their activities against the tidal wave of public condemnation. They simply did not know how to get through effectively to the public.

To tell their side of the story, the business barons first tried using the lure of advertising to silence journalistic critics. They tried to buy off critics by paying for ads in their papers. It didn't work. Next, they paid publicity people, or press agents, to present the company's side. Often, these hired guns painted over the real problems involved and presented the client's view in the best possible light. The public saw through this approach.

Clearly, another tack had to be discovered to get the public to at least consider the point-of-view of business. Business leaders began to realize that while a corporation could have capital, labor, and natural resources, if it lacked intelligent management, particularly in the area of influencing public opinion, then it was doomed to fail. The best way to "influence" public opinion, as it turned out, was through the vehicles of honesty and candor. This simple truth was the key to the eventual success of American history's first public relations counselor, Ivy Lee.

IVY LEE: THE FATHER OF MODERN PUBLIC RELATIONS

Ivy Ledbetter Lee was a former Wall Street newspaper reporter who plunged into publicity work in 1903. Lee neither believed in Barnum's "the public be fooled" approach nor in Vanderbilt's "the public be damned" philosophy. To Lee, the key to business acceptance and understanding was "the public be informed."

Lee firmly believed that the only way business could answer its critics convincingly was to present its side honestly, accurately, and forcefully. Instead of merely appeasing the public, Lee felt a company should strive to earn public confidence and good will. Sometimes, this task meant looking further for mutual solutions. Other times, it even meant admitting the company was wrong.* Hired by the anthracite coal industry in 1906, Lee set forth his beliefs in a "Declaration of Principles" to newspaper editors:

> This is not a secret press bureau. All our work is done in the open. We aim to supply news. This is not an advertising agency; if you think any of our matter ought properly to go to your business office, do not use it. Our matter is accurate. Further details on any subject treated will be supplied promptly, and any editor will be assisted most cheerfully in verifying any statement of fact . . . In brief, our plan is frankly and openly, on behalf of

---

* That Lee dramatically influenced the standards of the emerging profession is obvious from an observation made in 1963 by Earl Newsom, prominent public relations counsel, who told a colleague, "The whole activity of which you and I are a part can probably be said to have had its beginning when Ivy Lee persuaded the directors of the Pennsylvania Railroad that the press should be given the facts on all railway accidents—even though the facts might place the blame on the railroad itself.[5]

business concerns and public institutions, to supply to the press and public of the United States prompt and accurate information concerning subjects which it is of value and interest to the public to know about.[6]

In 1914, Lee was hired by John D. Rockefeller, Jr., who headed one of the most maligned and misunderstood of America's wealthy families. As Lee biographer Ray Eldon Hiebert pointed out, Lee did less to change the Rockefellers' policies than to give them a public hearing.[7]

For example, when the family was censured scathingly for its role in breaking up a strike at the Rockefeller-owned Colorado Fuel and Iron Company, they hired (at Lee's recommendation) a labor relations expert to determine the causes of an incident that had led to several deaths. The end result of this effort was the formation of a joint labor-management board to mediate all workers' grievances on wages, hours, and working conditions. When the chairman of the Colorado company balked at the plan, John Jr. (again on Lee's advice) personally toured the mines, listened to the miners' complaints, and even danced with the miners' wives at a social function. By the end of his visit, Rockefeller was not only a hero to the miners but a new man to the public. Years later, John Jr. admitted that the public relations outcome of the Colorado strike "was one of the most important things that ever happened to the Rockefeller family.[8]

In working for the Rockefellers, Lee tried to "humanize" them, to feature them in real-life situations, such as playing golf, attending church, and celebrating birthdays. Simply, Lee's goal was to translate the Rockefellers into terms that every individual could understand and appreciate. Years later, despite their critics, the family came to be known as one of the nation's outstanding sources of philanthropic support.

Lee's contributions to the development of public relations went beyond his work with the Rockefellers. He urged the American Tobacco Company, for example, to initiate a profit-sharing plan. He advised the Pennsylvania Railroad to beautify its stations. He educated the American public about ocean travel to overcome the impressions of the *Titanic* and *Lusitania* disasters. In addition, he was instrumental in working with Admiral Richard Byrd and aviator Charles Lindbergh to combat the public's fear of flying.

Ironically, even Ivy Lee could not escape the glare of public criticism. In the late 1920s, Lee was asked to serve as advisor to the parent company of the German Dye Trust, which, as it turned out, was an agent for the policies of Adolf Hitler. When Lee realized the nature of Hitler's intentions, he advised the Dye Trust cartel to work to alter Hitler's ill-conceived policies of restricting religious and press freedom. For his involvement with the Dye Trust, Lee was branded a traitor and dubbed "Poison Ivy" by members of Congress investigating un-American activities. The smears against him in the press rivaled the most vicious against the robber barons.

Despite his unfortunate involvement with the Dye Trust, Ivy Lee is recognized as the individual who brought honesty and candor to public relations. Lee, more than anyone before him, lifted the field from a questionable pursuit—seeking positive publicity at any cost—to a professional discipline designed to win public confidence and trust through communications based on candor and truth.

Little wonder that Lee is generally recognized as "the father of modern public relations."

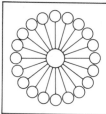

MINICASE
The "double reverse" discrimination

Public relations counselor Sylvia Emmons knew that Seton Filmways had a problem. Emmons believed that management sincerely felt it had not systematically discriminated against hiring minority workers. Nevertheless, in a town like Lyle, where minority residents outnumbered whites 2 to 1, Seton's 20,000-member staff included only 2,000 minority members. Clearly, thought Emmons, something was wrong.

In the best tradition of Ivy Lee, Emmons counseled Seton management that it could not remain silent in the face of mounting community criticism. She suggested that management appoint a representative to meet with community leaders to explore options that would increase minority employment in the company.

Management was sensitive to increased press coverage of Seton's minority hiring practices and agreed to allow Emmons to negotiate in the company's behalf with the community leaders. After several months of discussion, the public relations consultant reached agreement on a formula and long-term goals for Seton's hiring of minority workers. The formula and goals were hailed in the Lyle press as a "great step forward." Seton was held up as a model of progress.

THE GROWTH OF MODERN PUBLIC RELATIONS

Ivy Lee, in effect, opened the gate. Once he helped establish that firms had a responsibility to inform their publics, the practice began to grow in every sector of American society.

GOVERNMENT

During World War I, President Woodrow Wilson established the Committee on Public Information under journalist George Creel. The Creel Committee, as previously mentioned, proved an effective force, mobilizing public opinion in support of the war effort and stimulating the sale of war bonds through "Liberty Loan" publicity drives. Not only did the war effort get a boost, but so did the field of public relations.

The public relations field received an even bigger boost during World War II. With the Creel Committee as its precursor, the Office of War Information (OWI) was established to convey the message and the purpose of the United States at home and abroad. Under the directorship of Elmer Davis, a veteran journalist, the OWI laid the foundations for the United States Information Agency as the "voice of America" around the world.

But Seton management was having second thoughts. Several members of the firm's Executive Committee thought the goals "too ambitious." After a lengthy meeting, management convinced the chairperson to send Emmons back to the table to "renegotiate" Seton's position.

The community leaders were furious about Seton's repudiation of the agreement negotiated in good faith with management's representative. They called a press conference and threatened Seton with a national boycott. The story was picked up on the United Press wire. It made network television news. From Washington came word that two national civil rights leaders were flying to Lyle to pick up the gauntlet against Seton.

The next day, deeply embarrassed by the national publicity, Seton's chairperson ignominiously announced the company was reversing itself once again and would immediately institute the original minority hiring agreement.

QUESTIONS

1 Did management do the right thing in sending Emmons out to "do battle" with the community groups?

2 Was management sensitive to the public relations consequences of this issue?

3 What factors should management have considered during the meeting on the Emmons agreement?

4 How might this entire incident affect Seton's image with its minority customers? With the community? Current employees? Potential employees? The investing public?

5 How might Seton have avoided its public relations problems?

World War II also saw a flurry of activity to sell war bonds, to boost the morale of those at home, to spur production in the nation's factories and offices, and, in general, to support as furiously as possible, America's war effort. By virtually every measure, this full-court public relations offensive was an unquestioned success.

The proliferation of public relations officers in World War II led to a growth in the number of practitioners during the peace-time era that followed. And this was probably a good thing, especially in light of the feisty, combative attitude of President Harry Truman toward many of the country's largest institutions. For example, in a memorable address over radio and television, President Truman, on April 8, 1952, announced that as a result of a union wage dispute, "the government would take over the steel plants." The seizure of the steel mills touched off a series of historical events that reached into Congress and the Supreme Court and stimulated a massive public relations campaign, the likes of which had rarely been seen outside the government.[9]

COUNSELING

The steel industry's public relations signals were called by the counseling firm of Hill and Knowlton. This national communications conflict between the president and big business was the first of many such battles that have marked the government-business relationship in the ensuing years.

John W. Hill entered public relations in 1927 after a dozen years as a journalist. Together with William Knowlton, Hill founded Hill and Knowlton, Inc. in Cleveland. Hill soon came east and Knowlton dropped out of the firm. The agency quickly became the largest public relations operation in the world, with 600 employees in twenty countries and forty U.S. cities. Hill stayed active in the firm for half a century. Close to his fiftieth anniversary in public relations, he mused about the field's beginnings:

> In 1927, public relations was just in its infancy. Think of the contrast of the present with fifty years ago. Less than a handful of counseling firms anywhere in the world and barely a handful of practitioners tucked away and lost in the offices of a very few large corporations—far removed from the executive suite.[10]

In addition to Hill, Creel Committee associate chairman Carl Byoir launched his own public relations counseling firm in 1930. Like Hill and Knowlton, Carl Byoir and Associates, Inc. remains today as one of the world's principal public relations agencies.

Besides Byoir and Hill, Earl Newsom and Pendleton Dudley founded early firms, which still enjoy prominence today. Newsom, who began Newsom & Co. in 1935, generally limited his public relations practice to counseling companies like Ford, General Motors, and Jersey Standard. Author Irwin Ross paid tribute to Newsom's success in his otherwise critical treatment of public relations, *The Image Merchants:*

> The goal of a good many public relations men is someday to attain the lonely eminence of Earl Newsom. His fees are high; his clients include some of the most august names in the corporate roster; and his work involved pure 'consultation.'[11]

Dudley, like Newsom, got started early and remained in public relations until his death at age 90 in 1966. Dudley's firm is today Dudley-Anderson-Yutzy, one of the most admired agencies for introducing innovative techniques to win public approval.

Another early counselor, Harold Burson, emphasized marketing-oriented public relations to build his agency, Burson-Marsteller, to its current position of ranking neck-and-neck in worldwide billings with Hill and Knowlton. Burson also has been particularly active in promoting public relations education.

CORPORATIONS

Corporate public relations was not without its important pioneers in the 1920s and 30s. Arthur W. Page became American Telephone and Telegraph's (AT&T) first public relations vice-president in 1927. Page was a pacesetter, helping to manage AT&T's reputation as a prudent and proper corporate citizen. Indeed, Page's "five principles of successful corporate public relations" are as relevant now as they were in the 1930s:

1 To make sure management thoughtfully analyzes its overall relation to the public.
2 To create a system for informing all employees about the firm's general policies and practices.
3 To create a system giving contact employees the knowledge needed to be reasonable and polite to the public. (Contact employees are those having direct dealings with the public.)

FEATURE
The growth of public relations education

Public relations education has soared since Bernays's first course at New York University in 1923.

In the 1950s, education in public relations experienced a sudden growth spurt. In 1951, there were 12 schools with new major programs in public relations. By 1955, there were 28, and 66 schools offered some instruction in the subject.

Growth continued in the 1960s. By 1964, over 40 colleges and universities gave major programs or sequences in public relations, and 280 institutions provided some classroom work in the field.

By 1970, there were about 100 schools offering concentrated work in public relations, with nearly 300 schools offering at least one course dealing with the profession.

By 1980, there were 18,000 students enrolled in public relations degree programs. Public relations graduate enrollment in 1980 stood at around 4,000 students—nearly double the entire student enrollment in public relations degree programs ten years earlier.

While discussion continued in the mid-1980s about where public relations education should appropriately be housed—in journalism, business, or liberal arts—the profession's role as an academic pursuit seemed to be gaining further strength. Indeed, the largest jump in the history of public relations enrollments took place between 1975 and 1980 when the number of undergraduates in public relations courses doubled and the number of graduate students in public relations rose by two-thirds.[12]

4 To create a system drawing employee and public questions and criticism back up through the organization to management.

5 To ensure frankness in telling the public about the company's actions.[13]

Paul Garrett was another who felt the need to be responsive to the public's wishes. A former news reporter, he became General Motors' first director of public relations in 1931. Garrett once reportedly explained that the essence of his job was to convince the public that the powerful auto company deserved trust, or in other words, "to make a billion-dollar company seem small."

EDUCATION

One public relations pioneer who began as a publicist in 1913 was Edward L. Bernays, nephew of Sigmund Freud and author of the landmark book, *Crystallizing Public Opinion* (See page 26.) Bernays was a true public relations scholar, teaching the first course in public relations at New York University in 1923. Bernays's seminal writings in the field were among the first to disassociate public relations from press agentry or publicity work. As Bernays wrote later,

> At first we called our activity 'publicity direction.' We intended to give advice to clients on how to direct their actions to get public visibility for them. But within a year we changed the service and its name to 'counsel on public relations.' We recognized that all actions of a client that impinged on the public needed counsel. Public visibility of a client for one action might be vitiated by another action not in the public interest.[14]

Historian Eric Goldman credited Bernays with "[moving] along with the most advanced trends in the public relations field, thinking with, around and ahead of them."[15]

Other leading public relations educators included Milton Fairman, a Chicago news reporter and corporate public relations practitioner who later served as president of the Foundation for Public Relations Research and Education; Rex F. Harlow, who formed the American Council on Public Relations in 1939 and later presided over its merger with the Public Relations Society of America (PRSA) in 1947; and W. Howard Chase, a founding member of the PRSA, who advocated that public relations professionals should concern themselves with "public issues management" rather than with more narrow communications problems.

PUBLIC RELATIONS COMES OF AGE

As noted at the beginning of this chapter, public relations really came of age as a result of the confluence of three general factors in our society: the growth of large institutions and their sense of responsibility to the public, the increased conflicts and confrontations between interest groups in society, and the heightened awareness of people everywhere brought about by increasingly sophisticated communications technology.

GROWTH OF LARGE INSTITUTIONS

Ironically, the public relations profession received perhaps its most major forward thrust when business confidence suffered its most severe setback. The economic and social upheaval caused by the Great Depression of the 1930s provided the impetus for corporations to seek public support by telling their stories. Public relations departments sprang up at scores of major companies, among them Bendix, Borden, Eastman Kodak, Eli Lilly, Ford, General Motors, Standard Oil, Pan American, and U.S. Steel. The role that public relations played in helping regain post-Depression public trust in big business helped project the field into the relatively strong position it enjoyed during World War II.

As noted, the Truman years marked a challenging period for public relations practitioners. The Truman era was characterized by controls on information in the name of national security, Communist scares, and a general antagonism between government and big business. While big business became more and more cognizant of the vulnerable, public role it played in American society, so too did corporate managers become increasingly aware of the important role that could be played by skillful public relations practitioners.

CONFLICT AND CONFRONTATION

Disenchantment with big institutions reached a head in the 1960s. The conflicts during the early part of the decade between private economic institutions—especially large corporations—and various disenfranchised elements of society arose from long-standing grievances. As one commentator put it, "Their rebellion was born out of the desperation of those who had nothing to lose. Issues were seen as black or white, groups as villainous and virtuous, causes as holy or satanic, and leaders as saints or charlatans."[16]

The social and political consternation of the 1960s manifested itself in many forms. Ralph Nader began to look pointedly at the inadequacies of the automobile industry. Women, long denied equal rights with men in the workplace and elsewhere, began to mobilize into activist groups, such as the National Organization of Women (NOW). Environmentalists, worried about threats to the land and water by business expansion, began to support groups such as the Sierra Club. Minorities—particularly Blacks and Hispanics—began to petition and protest for their rights, through such groups as the Congress on Racial Equality, National Association for the Advancement of Colored People (NAACP), and the Student Nonviolent Coordinating Committee. Homosexuals, senior citizens, birth control advocates, and social activists of every kind began to challenge the legitimacy of large institutions.

Not since the days of the robber barons did large institutions so desperately need professional communications help.

HEIGHTENED PUBLIC AWARENESS

The 1970s brought a partial resolution of the problems that afflicted society in the 1960s. Many of these solutions came through government in the form of affirmative action guidelines, senior citizen supports, consumer and environmental protection acts and agencies, aids to education, and a myriad of other laws and statutes.

As for society's large institutions—particularly big business—they began to clearly recognize their responsibilities as "social creatures." Business began to contribute to charities. Managers began to consider community relations as a first-line responsibility. The general policy of corporations confronting their adversaries was abandoned. In its place, most large companies adopted a policy of conciliation and compromise.

In truth, institutions in the 1980s had little choice but to get along with their publics. Largely because of the increasingly more sophisticated communications technology, the public-at-large was more aware and better informed than in any previous period.

For example, in the early 80s, 77 million American homes had televisions, with 45 percent expected to be wired for cable by 1985. The potential of two-way communications systems through cable, satellite, computer, and video disc technologies promises to further revolutionize the information transmission and receiving process. As a result, publics have become much more segmented, specialized, and sophisticated. And public relations professionals have had to discard many of the traditional methods used to reach and influence these publics. With companies facing the new reality of instant communication through desk top video display terminals, instant file and retrieval through centralized data banks, and comprehensive management information systems, the public relations challenge for the 1980s has become significant indeed.

FEATURE
War in the satellite era

Nowhere has the new communications technology been more striking than in its use as a persuasive tool in the politics of war in the 1980s.

Using the 1979 capture of American embassy employees as the linchpin, Iranian militants in Tehran launched a massive, long distance, nonstop media campaign to convince the world of their nation's mistreatment at the hands of the Shah. Angry mobs of Iranian militants were beamed live and in blazing color to millions of Western homes on a nightly basis—only serving to infuriate viewers and further strain anti-Iranian feelings.

In the summer of 1982, hopelessly surrounded in the suburbs of West Beirut, Lebanon, by the Israeli army, Palestinian Liberation Organization Chief Yasir Arafat also tried to use the world media to slip out of his predicament.

When he was visited by a U.S. congressional delegation with an accompanying television camera crew, Arafat signed a document in his bunker—in full view of the television cameras—obstensibly recognizing Israel's right to exist.

Within an hour of Arafat's televised encounter with the congressmen, authoritative Palestinians in the West rushed to clarify that what their leader *really* meant in signing the document was that "Israel would be recognized when we get an independent Palestinian state."

While the embarrassed congressmen blamed Arafat for the misunderstanding, and he blamed them, at least one aspect of this particular Mideast debate was crystal clear: television, video tape, and satellite technology in the 1980s had become prominent factors in the politics of war.

PUBLIC RELATIONS TODAY

Today, public relations is big business:

More than 100,000 practitioners work in public relations in the United States alone.

The Public Relations Society of America, organized in 1947, boasts a growing membership of over 10,000 in about eighty chapters nationwide.

The Public Relations Student Society of America, formed in 1968 to facilitate communications between students interested in the field and public relations professionals, has 3,000 student members at more than eighty colleges and universities.

More than 2,000 U.S. companies have public relations departments.

More than 700 public relations agencies, some billing millions of dollars per year, exist in the United States.

More than 200 trade associations have public relations departments.

Top communications executives at major companies and agencies draw salaries into six figures.

Boston University's Graduate School of Public Communication is devoted primarily to instruction in public relations activities.

The scope of modern public relations practice is vast. Press relations, employee communications, public relations counseling and research, local community relations, audiovisual communications, contributions, and numerous other diverse activities fall under the public relations umbrella.

While those engaged in public relations work occasionally seem preoccupied excessively about the proper title of their calling—public relations, external affairs, corporate communications, public affairs, corporate relations, ad infinitum—whatever its name, the field has solidly entrenched itself as an important, influential, and professional component of our society.

CASE STUDY
The public relations of Henry Ford

Your life, your character, and your achievements should be an inspiration to every laboring man; to every good American citizen; and to every rich man and capitalist in the country—plain, simple, good-hearted, just, generous Henry Ford!

Editorial, *Denver Post*,
22 September 1920

Whatever his ignorance of history, Ford, as a spotlight artist and consummate master of the increasingly difficult work of prying the newspapers loose from vast gobs of free publicity, stands without peer in the industrial life of America.

Editorial, *Arkansas Democrat*,
September 1920

Henry Ford, one of the world's leading industrialists, was an enigma. He was ignorant, cynical, and narrow-minded, while at the same time flexible, insightful, and compassionate. Some loved him. Others despised him. But most agreed that in addition to being a master businessman, Ford was also an innovator when it came to promoting his company's public image.[17]

Certainly, Ford's heavy-handed tactics landed him occasional public black eyes. But he also orchestrated many public relations breakthroughs.

In 1913, the Ford Motor Company distributed more than $11 million in dividends to its stockholders and hundreds of thousands of dollars to a select group of executives. It also managed to lower the price of its cars to the public.

Things were moving along so well in 1913, in fact, that only one question perplexed Henry Ford: What can be done for the workers?

Ford's answer was, said the *London Economist*, "the most dramatic event in the history of wages." Simply stated, Ford decided to let the company's workers share in the firm's profits. Instead of waiting until the end of the year to distribute each employee's share of the profits, Ford proposed to make the awards in advance as part of the periodic pay process and based on earnings projections for the year.

Ford's "Five-Dollar Pay Plan,"—the smallest amount to be paid any worker was $5 per day—drew immediate world-wide raves. The *New York Herald* called it "an epoch in the world's industrial history." The *New York Evening Post* hailed it as "a magnificent act of generosity." And the *Toledo Blade* regarded it as a "lordly gift."

While other industrial leaders were dismayed by the Ford announcement and warned that it would lead to financial and factory disorganization, the value of publicity to Ford Motor Company probably greatly exceeded the eventual $6 million the company shelled out in the profit-sharing money to its workers.

In 1915, Henry Ford announced he was a confirmed pacifist. "I would give everything I possess if I could stop the war," he reportedly told a number of journalists.

So Ford set out to singlehandedly do just that by launching a special "peace ship," boarded by "the most influential peace advocates in the country." While some newspapers scoffed that "Henry has P. T. Barnum skinned a mile," the automaker set sail from Hoboken, New Jersey on December 5, 1915 along with 100 "American peace delegates who would help form a commission for continuous mediation" with the enemy. The ship also carried 54 reporters from around the world.

On December 22, after landing in Norway, Ford called a press conference to talk about—not mediation—but rather the new tractor his company had perfected. The tractor, he argued, could realize a greater profit than could the manufacture of guns. Therefore, Ford said he would seek to convince arms manufacturers to switch to making tractors.

Ford continued to hold press conferences and to promote peace in Europe until he gave up and returned to America in 1917. He was generally greeted as a returning hero, a man who, as the *New York American* put it, "deserves respect, not ridicule." Despite criticism from several American newspapers, Ford's voyage had won him the admiration of people around the world.

Ford also introduced the concept of giving customers rebates for purchasing a Model T. In 1914, Ford announced plans to rebate $40 to $60 to each Model T purchaser should sales exceed 300,000 units during the following year.

While the company's unprecedented customer profit-sharing announcement was overshadowed in the press by the outbreak of World War hostilities, Ford was universally hailed for his sales promotion genius.

A year after the announcement, the company claimed to have sold more than 300,000 Model T's during the previous year and refunded $50 to each buyer, about 9 percent of the average purchase price.

Henry Ford also established his company as the first American business firm to organize a motion picture department.

Ford spared no expense in staffing and equipping his department. He even called in Thomas Edison to consult. By 1916, the department was producing a ten to fifteen minute newsreel offered without charge to theaters across the country. While the newsreels dealt with a variety of subjects and included no commercials, a Model T occasionally flitted through the scenes.

Ford soon realized that the individual newsreels quickly became obsolete and could only provide a limited return for his investment. So he decided to move into historical and educational films. "The Ford Educational Weekly" soon became the nation's first series of historical, geographical, travel, and educational films. They received extensive exposure in theaters throughout America. They were distributed free and, like the newsreels, carried no commercials, except for the line on the title frame, "Distributed by the Ford Motor Company."

Later on, Ford moved into the sales-promotional film area. These films, which concerned everything from the Ford Motor Company as a whole to Model T's and tractors, were designed for smaller audiences rather than large theaters. Fraternal lodges, church groups, luncheon clubs, county fairs, and schools were all potential borrowers for these Ford films. Generally, Ford sales representatives accompanied the films to a community. This method proved to be one of the most effective schemes to communicate "the gospel according to Henry Ford."

QUESTIONS

1   Timing is often critical in public relations. What do you think about Ford's announcement, in the midst of worldwide depression, to allow employees to share in the company's profits?

2   If you were Ford's public relations advisor, how would you have handled the criticism from other business leaders of the employee profit-sharing plan?

3   Ford's profit-sharing plan eventually cost about $6 million. How could he have measured the "publicity return" on the announcement?

4   How would you assess the end result of the "peace ship" expedition in terms of the public image of Ford and his company?

5   Might there have been some ulterior motive to Ford's overseas visibility? (Hint: Prior to the trip, Ford Motor's overseas sales were negligible.)

6   What is your assessment of the customer rebate idea as a public relations opportunity? How might Ford have improved the timing of the rebate announcement?

7   Was it a good idea for Ford to start a motion picture department?

8   Why would Ford have chosen not to advertise Ford Motor's products in the films?

9   How might Ford have "measured" the bottom line benefit of showing free films to the public?

NOTES

1   Scott M. Cutlip and Allen H. Center, *Effective Public Relations*, 5th ed. (Englewood Cliffs, N.J.: Prentice-Hall, 1978).

2   "Hollywood's Hottest Summer," *Time*, 19 July 1982, p. 63.

3   Peter S. Greenberg, "Star Wars," *New Times*, 6 February 1978, p. 39.

4   Ray Eldon Hiebert, *Courtier to the Crowd: The Story of Ivy L. Lee and the Development of Public Relations* (Ames, Iowa: Iowa State University Press, 1966).

5 Rex Harlow, "A Public Relations Historian Recalls the First Days," *Public Relations Review,* Summer 1981, p. 39–40.

6 Cited in Sherman Morse, "An Awakening in Wall Street," *American Magazine,* 62 (September 1906):460.

7 Ray Eldon Hiebert, op. cit.

8 Cited in Alvin Moscow, *The Rockefeller Inheritance* (Garden City, N.Y.: Doubleday, 1977), p. 23.

9 John W. Hill, *The Making of a Public Relations Man* (New York, N.Y.: David McKay Company, Inc., 1963), p. 69.

10 John W. Hill, "The Future of Public Relations," speech delivered at the Seventh Public Relations World Congress, Boston, Mass., Aug. 14, 1976.

11 Irwin Ross, *The Image Merchants* (Garden City, N.Y.: Doubleday, 1959), p. 85.

12 Albert Walker, "End of Decade Survey Shows Academic Growth in Public Relations," *Public Relations Review,* Summer 1982, pp. 46–60.

13 Cited in Noel L. Griese, "The Employee Communications Philosophy of Arthur W. Page," *Public Relations Quarterly* (Winter, 1977).

14 Edward L. Bernays, "Bernays' 62 Years in Public Relations," *Public Relations Quarterly,* Fall 1981, p. 8.

15 David L. Lewis, "The Outstanding PR Professionals," *Public Relations Journal* (October 1970), p. 84.

16 S. Prakash Sethi, "Business and Social Challenge," *Public Relations Journal,* September 1981, p. 30.

17 Clearly the most comprehensive treatment of Henry Ford's public relations is David L. Lewis, *The Public Image of Henry Ford* (Detroit, Mich.: Wayne State University Press, 1976).

SUGGESTED READING

Barber, Richard J. *The American Corporation: Its Power, Its Money, Its Politics.* New York: E. P. Dulton, 1970.

Bernays, Edward L. "Bernays' 62 Years in Public Relations," *Public Relations Quarterly,* Fall 1981, p. 8.

Bernays, Edward L. *Crystallizing Public Opinion,* New York: Liveright Publishing Corporation, 1961, pp. xlviii–lvi.

Cornwell, Elmer E., Jr. *Presidential Leadership of Public Opinion.* Bloomington, Ind.: Indiana University Press, 1963.

Dennis, Lloyd B. "The 'Promises, Promises' Era Is Turning," *Public Relations Quarterly,* Winter 1981-82, pp. 13–17. A listing of important trends concerning social responsibility during the rest of this decade.

Friedman, William H. "Public Relations and The Sense of History," *Public Relations Quarterly,* Summer 1981, pp. 26–27.

Gunther, John. *Taken at the Flood—The Story of Albert Lasker.* New York: Harper and Row, 1960. Although advertising was his profession, Lasker made many contributions to public relations.

Harlow, Rex. "A Public Relations Historian Recalls The First Days," *Public Relations Review,* Summer 1981, pp. 33–42. Harlow's years of experience in the field and his detailed recollection of personalities and events have enabled him to recreate here the excitement of the first days of public relations.

Hill, John W. *The Making of the Public Relations Man.* New York: David McKay, 1963.

Irwin, James W. "Four Decades of Public Relations." *Public Relations Quarterly* 12 (Spring, 1967):21–28.

Lyon, Peter. *Success Story: The Life and Times of S.S. Mc Clure,* (New York: Charles Scribner's Sons, 1963.

Sethi, S. Prakash. "Business and Social Challenge," *Public Relations Journal,* September 1981, pp. 30–31, 34. An overview of the evolving relationship between business and society during the last two decades.

Simon, Raymond. *Public Relations: Concepts and Practices,* Columbus, Ohio: Grid, Inc., 1976, Chapter 2.

Stephenson, Howard. *Handbook of Public Relations,* 2nd ed., New York: McGraw-Hill Book Company, p. 190.

Walker, Albert. "End of Decade Survey Shows Academic Growth In Public Relations," *PR Review,* Summer 1982, pp. 46–60.

PUBLIC RELATIONS AS
MANAGEMENT PROCESS

More and more today, public relations is being regarded as a management process in itself.

Like other management processes, professional public relations work emanates from clear strategies and bottom-line objectives, which flow into specific tactics, each with its own discrete budget, timetable, and allocation of resources. Stated another way, public relations today is much more a planned, persuasive social/managerial science than it is a knee-jerk, damage control reaction to sudden flare-ups.

On the organizational level, as public relations has enhanced its overall stature, it increasingly has been brought into the general management structure of institutions. Indeed, as will be discussed, the public relations function works most effectively when it reports directly to top management.

On the individual level, public relations practitioners increasingly are expected to have mastered a wide variety of technical communications skills, such as writing, editing, placement, production, programming, and so on. At the same time, by virtue of their relatively recent role as integral parts in the general management process, public relations professionals are expected to be fluent in management theory and technique. In other words, public relations practitioners themselves must be, in every sense of the word, managers.

3
Organizing for Public Relations

JUST WHAT IS IT YOU DO EXACTLY?

Sometimes it's tough to say just what the job of public relations is. It's not that practitioners don't know what they do, but rather, they have trouble categorizing it.

For example, chances are good that public relations people were involved somewhere along the line in these ventures:

- a press conference
- an annual report
- a newspaper interview
- a speech by a politician or community leader
- a school official leading a community service drive
- a security analyst presentation by top executives
- an educational television program, funded by a business firm
- an institution's facilities brochure
- a groundbreaking, topping-out, or grand opening ceremony
- a corporate contribution to a minority enterprise
- a college blood drive to benefit a local hospital
- a charity dinner
- a company-wide graphics program that changes the look of packaging, stationery, signs, publications—and the firm's image

This list covers just the obvious. Far more subtle is the constant counseling of management by public relations people on issues of policy that affect an organization's publics.

In sum, whenever communications, key publics, and questions of public policy come together, a good public relations staff or agency will be involved in devising and implementing appropriate strategies.

REPORTING TO TOP MANAGEMENT

In some companies, practitioners play a minor role—perhaps reporting to the marketing director—and deal with only the most rudimentary communications for employees or the public. In such organizations, they rarely participate in the management decision-making process. Frequently in such an environment, they and their staff are viewed as "second-class citizens."

However, in other organizations—both profit and nonprofit—public relations is given a more prominent role in management decision-making. Frequently, the public relations director reports directly to top management—generally to the chief executive officer. The reason for this is simple. If public relations is to be the *interpreter* of management, then it must know what management is thinking on virtually every public issue at any moment. If public relations is made subordinate to any other discipline—marketing, advertising, legal, and so on—then its independence, its credibility, and ultimately, its value as an objective management counselor, will be sacrificed.

Public relations, after all, is a staff advisory rather than a line, profit-making function. While the marketing and advertising groups must, by definition, be advocates for their specific products, the public relations department has no such mandated allegiance. Public relations, rightfully, should be the "corporate conscience." An organization's public relations professionals should enjoy enough autonomy to tell management, as sportscaster Howard Cosell might put it, "like it is." Specifically, if an idea doesn't make sense, if a product is flawed, if the general institutional wisdom is wrong, it is the duty of the public relations professional to challenge the consensus.

This is not to say that advertising, marketing, and all the other disciplines shouldn't enjoy a close partnership with public relations. Clearly, they must. Each discipline has to maintain its own independence and identity while working to build a long-term, mutually beneficial relationship for the good of the organization. On the other hand, public relations should never shirk its overriding responsibility to enhance the organization's credibility through ensuring that corporate actions are in the public interest.

SCOPE OF THE PRACTICE

The duties and responsibilities of public relations practitioners are as diverse as the publics with whom different institutions deal.

For example, here is a partial list of potential public relations duties:

1 **Reaching the employees** through a variety of internal means, including newsletters, television, and meetings. Traditionally, this role has emphasized "news-oriented" communications rather than "benefits-oriented" ones, which are usually the province of personnel departments.

2 **Coordinating relationships with the print and electronic media.** This responsibility includes arranging and monitoring press interviews, writing news releases and related press materials, organizing press conferences, and answering media inquiries and requests. A good deal of media relations work is spent attempting to gain favorable news coverage for the firm.

3 **Coordinating activities with legislators** on the local, state, and federal levels; includes legislative research activities and public policy formation.

4 **Orchestrating interaction with the community.** Activities might consist of open houses, tours, and employee volunteerism designed to reflect the supportive nature of the organization to the community.

5 **Managing relations with the investment community,** including the firm's present and interested potential stockholders. This task emphasizes personal contact with securities analysts, institutional investors, and private investors.

6 **Supporting activities** with customers and potential customers; activities range from "hard-sell" product promotion activities to "soft" consumer advisory services.

7 **Coordinating the institution's "printed voice" to its publics** through reprints of speeches, annual reports, quarterly statements, and product and company brochures.

8 **Coordinating relationships with outside specialty groups** such as suppliers, educators, students, nonprofit organizations, and competitors.

9 **Managing the "institutional"—or nonproduct—advertising image.** Increasingly, public relations practitioners are being called upon to assist in the management of the more traditional product advertising.

Edward M. Block is vice president/ public relations and employee information at AT&T Co. Mr. Block joined the Bell System in 1952 and served in a variety of increasingly important public relations positions before assuming the top AT&T communications post in 1975. A former sports writer, reporter, and photographer, Mr. Block is a director of numerous organizations and the recipient of many awards in the communications field.

Do you think that the communications department should always report directly to the chief executive officer (CEO)?

It's unwise to be dogmatic. I've had it both ways, and I know it can work both ways. The reason that direct reporting is preferable, at least conceptually, is that the large institution in society—and certainly the corporation—functions most effectively when it is *governed*. The CEO who does not control constituency communications will not for long control policy. The CEO who possesses no direct mechanism for assuring timely, accurate feedback, and counsel is handicapped in the formulating and establishing of sound policy. The effective CEOs increasingly understand this. That's why they want to hold a single, competent executive responsible for communications. It therefore follows that direct reporting will, in most circumstances, best serve the needs of the CEO.

What's the ideal organization for a public relations department?

Public relations is not so much a department as it is an array of management functions, which must be explicitly linked, coordinated, and delegated in harmony with the overall organization scheme and business purposes of the enterprise. Hence there can be no ideal, because no two corporations are exactly alike. But having said that, I tend to hold with the conventional wisdom that shapes most public relations departments: you must have a single executive with overall responsibility. You must explicitly delegate the authority necessary to carry out the responsibility. You must provide sufficient resources for media relations, employee information, financial information, community relations, public opinion sampling, issues assessment, public relations planning, graphics and corporate identification, institutional advertising, and all the rest.

Why hire a public relations agency?

You might want to employ an agency for short-term projects, peaks in work load, and for matters in which you and/or your staff lack experience or expertise. In short, you would use an agency to augment your own staff and avoid continuing expense for resources you don't need on a continuing basis. Some public relations executives employ counsel as a convenient means of "having someone to be dumb in front of" (a wise outside counselor to assist you with your inside counseling and to have a fresh head to help in assessing new or difficult issues). However, no outsider can know your business as well as you know it. No outsider can really ensure continuity of experience and expertise with respect to your business. No outsider can truly be held accountable by a CEO.

What are the primary attributes you look for in a subordinate?

Brains. Guts. Writing skills. Knowledge of the business. Ability to anticipate how stakeholders will react.

How important is the planning function in public relations?

The management art we have come to call public relations embraces only three functions: 1) communicating with constituencies on behalf of the institution, 2) communicating to senior management on behalf of the constituencies, 3) counseling and mediating as policies are developed, established, and implemented. None of these functions can be carried out coherently and effectively without careful planning on a continuing basis, and AT&T maintains a discrete organization within the public relations department for this purpose.

What are the most important qualities of a successful public relations professional?

Again, we place great emphasis on clear, effective writing. Clear writing is a manifestation of clear thinking—they go together. There also appears to be some correlation between good writing and those precious but undefinable characteristics: innovativeness, creativity, insightfulness. Guts is an inelegant word but it conveys a sense of what is so important and so often lacking in the corporate setting: initiative. Risk taking. Willingness to take decisive action—and to take consequences. Willingness to assist another individual or another department and let them get the credit if the desired outcome is achieved. Willingness to step up to an issue or a decision; to articulate a reasoned position. Finally, a commitment to excellence in small ways as well as large. It is also possible to describe some characteristics which identify people who will never be successful. Nine to fivers. Whiners and complainers. Blame avoiders. Decision avoiders. Hip shooters. Politicians and posturers.

How important is the public relations function at AT&T?

The nature of AT&T's business as well as its size guarantees the importance of the public relations function. A vice president has been in charge of the function since 1926. A theology of public relations was articulated and institutionalized by the founder of the Bell System long before a public relations department even existed. But "respect" is earned not conferred. The hierarchial status of the officer in charge, the size of the budget, a corporate culture which embraces public relations as a given are all helpful. But it is effective performance day in and day out, year in and year out, which gives authority to a public relations organization. When performance slips, so too does respect.

Is there anything else you'd like readers of this book to know?

Yes. Arthur Wilson Page, the man who was elected AT&T vice president in charge of public relations in 1926, said it all: "Public relations is 90 percent doing and 10 percent talking about it." By that he meant that what the corporation does is more important than what it says if the objective is to achieve satisfactory public relations. His advice may be humbling but at least it tells us where we had better devote our best efforts, because there is as yet no evidence that Mr. Page was wrong.

10 **Coordinating the graphics and photographic services** of the organization. To do this task well, one needs knowledge of typography, layout, and art.

11 **Opinion research,** which involves assisting in the public policy formation process through the coordination and interpretation of attitudinal studies of key publics.

12 **Managing the gift-giving apparatus.** This activity, performed in both corporations and foundations, ordinarily consists of screening and evaluating philanthropic proposals and allocating the organization's available resources.

13 **Coordinating special events,** including travel for the company management, corporate celebrations and exhibits, dinners, ground-breakings, grand openings.

14 **Management counseling,** which involves advising administrators on alternative options and recommended choices in light of public responsibilities.

PLANNING FOR PUBLIC RELATIONS

Before organizing for public relations work, objectives and strategies must be established.* Simply, the broad environment in which the company operates must dictate overall business objectives, which in turn dictate specific public relations objectives and strategies. Once these objectives have been defined, the task of structuring a public relations department should flow naturally

For example, a firm that wishes to broaden its stockholder base would probably consider an investor relations unit a necessity. Another firm with the objective of selling 30 percent more of a particular product might organize a broad-based product publicity capability. Conversely, a nonprofit agency, concerned with waning employee morale, might gear up for a heavy internal communications organization. In each case, the specific objectives determine the structure.

Setting objectives, formulating strategies, and planning all are absolutely essential if the public relations function is to be considered of equal stature with other components in an organization.

Planning requires time, especially time to think. Unfortunately, public relations people have precious little time. By the very nature of the job, they are on call to management, frequently drafted to serve as "fire fighters." For example:

A wildcat strike breaks out in a steel plant, and public relations is asked by the press for details.

A stockholder launches a sudden proxy fight, and public relations is asked for management's reaction.

A branch office is held up by armed robbers, and public relations is called to report on how much they got.

---

* In a study of 185 firms in Fortune's top 1,000 U.S. corporations, slightly more than half the responding executives reported that their corporation had established public relations objectives (W. Harvey Hegarty, John C. Aplin, and Richard A. Cosier, "Achieving Corporate Success in External Affairs: A Management Challenge" [Research study by faculty members in the Graduate School of Business Administration at Indiana University, Bloomington, July 29, 1977]).

Such activities may be exciting, but they don't do much for long-range planning. Indeed, if a conscious effort isn't made, planning and objective-setting time can easily get lost. Priorities for the perpetual fire fighter become very short-term oriented, with most days spent squelching brush fires and doing little else.

But fire fighting, while it may solve immediate dilemmas, won't do much to advance the institution or its public relations function. Thoughtful planning is critical, and good public relations professionals clearly understand this fact.

The fire-fighting aspects of many public relations jobs have caused practitioners to master the art of _contingency planning_. The contingency approach borrows from systems theory and enables public relations managers first, to anticipate the major internal and external factors with which they must deal and second, to plan, in a contingency sense, how to cope with these environmental demands. The point is that public relations professionals must have the flexibility to respond quickly to changes in the environment. While the practitioners can't predict to the moment when the strike or the proxy fight or the robbery will occur, they can—and should—be prepared for just such a contingency.

MEASURING PUBLIC RELATIONS OBJECTIVES

The only good goals are ones that can be measured. Public relations objectives, just like those in other business areas, must be results-oriented. As Boston Red Sox pitcher Johnny Sain used to say, "Nobody wants to hear about the labor pains, but everyone wants to see the baby."

Good objectives stand up to the following questions:

○ Do they clearly describe the end result expected?
○ Are they understandable to everyone in the organization?
○ Do they list a firm completion date?
○ Are they realistic, attainable, and measurable?
○ Are they consistent with management's objectives?[1]

While the methods of measuring program effectiveness are still rather rough, four common types of research prevail:

1 **Environmental monitoring,** in which research is used to identify changes in public opinion affecting an organization.
2 **Public relations audit,** in which research is used to identify audiences, to determine a corporate image among an audience, or to evaluate the effect of a specific public relations program.
3 **Communications audit,** which typically consists of a content analysis of messages, a readability study, or a readership survey. A spinoff of this, the _social audit_, is research conducted to measure the extent to which an organization is meeting its social responsibilities.[2]
4 **Management by objectives** (MBO) is a highly popular managerial appraisal technique, which requires that public relations managers and subordinates think in terms of measurable objectives and goal priorities. While this is difficult in many instances—particularly in light of the content of many public relations

projects—nonetheless, the existence of tangible, measurable objectives can give public relations workers a powerful source of feedback on performance. While procedures for implementing MBO programs differ, there are four points that all programs have in common:

a) specification of the organization's goals with objective measures of the organization's performance; b) conferences between a superior and a subordinate about the subordinate's goals; c) agreement between the superior and subordinate on the subordinate's goals that are consistent with the organization's goals; d) review of progress by the superior and the subordinate toward achievement of jointly-determined goals.

Again, in public relations work, the tying of public relations goals to the goals of the organization not only helps make the function more measurable but also more meaningful in the eyes of senior management.

Despite the relatively rough state of most measurement techniques in public relations, an organization with clear-cut objectives will be able to more accurately evaluate the level of its performance.

PROGRAMMING/BUDGETING FOR PUBLIC RELATIONS

Like any other business activity, public relations programs must be bolstered with sound budgets and principles of cost control.

Specifically, after identifying strategies and objectives, the public relations practitioner must detail the particular tactics that will help deliver those objectives. At this point, the practitioner also should begin to estimate costs. The key to budgeting may lie in performing the following two steps: First, estimate the extent of the resources—both manpower and purchases—needed to accomplish each activity. Then, estimate the cost and availability of those resources.[3]

With this information in hand, the development of a budget and monthly cash flow for a public relations program becomes easier. Such data also provide the milestones necessary to audit program costs on a routine basis and to make adjustments well in advance of budget crises.

Most public relations programs operate on limited budgets. Therefore, whenever possible, adaptable programs—ones that readily can be recycled and redesigned to meet changing needs—always should be considered. For example, television, magazine, and newspaper advertising generally is too expensive for most public relations budgets. On the other hand, special events, personalized literature, direct mail, personal contacts, or promotional displays are the kinds of inexpensive communications vehicles that can be easily duplicated.[4]

Regrettably, because of the general—even predictable—nature of many public relations programs, the field still is afflicted with too much "seat-of-the-pants programming." Lacking specific budgets and cost controls, such programs are susceptible to failure either because they run out of money or become too expensive for their benefits to justify their costs. This is particularly true in larger corporations.

Alternatively, in public relations agencies, where clients pay for public relations work, the cost of staff time and expenses/purchases involved in each activity is closely calculated. Before staff time can be estimated, an hourly rate must be

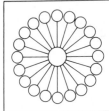

MINICASE
Harried Harry

Harry Detweiler runs the public information unit of the State Commerce Department.

Harry purposely left last Thursday wide open to plot the department's objectives and strategies for next year.

At 9:10, his secretary buzzed for his reaction to last night's basketball championship. He chatted about it for a few minutes, hung up and went back to "planning." At 9:30, the commissioner called and asked if he'd mind getting back to an outside consultant who had just called. Harry got right on it. He promised to send the consultant the materials he requested, hung up, and then searched for and found the information. He buzzed his secretary to make sure it got delivered to the consultant.

At 10:15, *Business Week* called to find out how the department viewed the regional economy. Harry thought of farming out the request to one of his subordinates but decided instead to personally call a department economist with the query. While he was on with the economist, both *The Wall Street Journal* and an environmentalist left messages for call backs.

The *Journal* wanted an item for its "Business Bulletin" column on the state's health insurance plan. It took Harry a while to track down the right person to answer the question. The environmentalist's call was a bit tricky, dealing with the department's reduction in air purification requirements for new plants. Harry tried to answer the question as best he could and advised the caller to seek further clarification from the state environmental commissioner.

By 11:30, Harry was off the phone and ready to order lunch at his desk when Vince Ripkoon invited him out to eat. Harry accepted. By 2:15, Harry was back in the office to discover five call-back slips and the news that his secretary had scheduled an afternoon meeting with several transportation department staff members interested in starting an inter-agency house organ.

"Planning," Harry sighed dejectedly as he packed up his materials, "is impossible in a madhouse like this."

QUESTIONS

1 Is Harry right?
2 What's wrong with his approach to planning?
3 What might he have done with the various phone calls he received?
4 Should he have interrupted the planning process to talk to the press, the environmentalist, and the transportation department staff people?
5 If you were Harry's boss, upon what criteria might you base your review of his accomplishments?

established through analysis of hourly salaries multiplied by an overhead factor—three or four times, for example. Such overhead can vary greatly depending on what is included, such as employee benefits, rents, utilities, equipment and furniture, office supplies, and the like. Importantly, public relations counseling overhead also includes a factor for profit.

Most public relations agencies treat client costs in a similar manner to legal, accounting, and management consulting firms. The client pays only for services rendered, often against an established monthly minimum for staff time. Time records are kept by every employee—from chairperson to mail clerk—on a daily basis. This mechanism helps assure public relations agency clients of efficient budgetary and cost control. Put another way, clients can be much more certain of exactly what they are paying for.

ORGANIZING THE PUBLIC RELATIONS DEPARTMENT

Once a company has analyzed its environment, established its objectives, set up measurement standards, and thought about appropriate programs and budgets, it is ready to organize a public relations department.

Departments range from one-person operations to firms like General Motors, with a staff of more than 200 persons—half professionals and half support staff—

FEATURE

National Consumer Finance Company public relations objectives

Objective 1:
To demonstrate that the company—despite its bigness—is an integral, concerned, and socially responsible member of its communities.

Targets:

1 Distribute to the local press one by-lined article per month from local branch managers in each target market.

2 Appoint one local Consumer Advisory Board, composed of local residents, to assist management in each target market.

3 Place at least two company officers on United Fund, Red Cross, Boy Scouts, and major hospital boards in each target market.

4 Sponsor at least one Little League team in each small target market and at least two in each large target market.

5 Orchestrate at least three local speaking engagements per quarter for general managers in each target market.

6 Make branch office community rooms and parking lots available to local groups, aiming for major sponsorship per quarter in each target market.

7 Place at least three stories per quarter in local newspapers that include references to and quotations of local company management in each target market.

responsible for relations with the press, investors, civic groups, employees, and governments around the world. Oil companies such as Mobil and Exxon and banks such as Chase and Citibank have departments well in excess of 100 staff members.

Typically, most departments begin as small operations and grow as the business environment changes. For example, the increasing importance of public relations with investors, employees, and minority groups has created new areas for department expansion. As an exhaustive study by The Conference Board pointed out, there is no one best way to organize for public or external relations.[5] Some firms use decentralized organizational structures, with public relations reporting to a communications professional, public affairs reporting to a legal professional, and investor relations reporting to the head accountant. In other companies, the public relations or communications function is organized centrally, under one executive who is responsible for dealing with many of the firm's key publics.

As to the names of the departments in which public relations is housed, organizations use a wide variety of names for the function. Ironically, the trend in the 1980s seems to be away from use of the traditional term *Public Relations* and towards *Corporate Communications*. In one comprehensive analysis, about 30 percent of the organizations surveyed still used Public Relations, while Corporate Communications or just plain *Communications* was used by nearly 20 percent. About 8 percent used *Public Affairs* and another 8 percent used *Advertising/Public Relations*. Among the other titles found to be in use were *Corporate Relations* and *Public Information*.[6]

ORGANIZING FOR COMMUNICATIONS AT THE CHASE MANHATTAN BANK

A typical organization for communications activity can be found at New York's Chase Manhattan Bank (see Figure 3-1). Chase is a multinational financial services company with more than 35,000 employees in over 2,000 locations worldwide. The bank's communications activities are managed by the Corporate Communications Group, with a staff of more than 100 professionals. The staff is headed by an executive vice-president/director, who reports directly to the chairman of the board and chief executive officer and on a "dotted line" to the bank's president and chief operating officer. Thus, by the very nature of these reporting relationships, the communications director is "plugged in" to most major corporate decisions.

Chase's Corporate Communications group is divided into several individual components, responsible for distinct communications activities:

1   **Public affairs** is responsible for communications with the bank's publics through the media, management speeches, and shareholder publications such as the annual and quarterly reports. The division also is responsible for supervising the bank's community relations, consumer affairs, and its philanthropic giving program, in which 2 percent of Chase's after-tax profits is contributed annually to hundreds of charities of every kind. Finally, the division maintains Chase's archives, where important historical records are housed.

2   **Investor relations** is responsible for contact with securities analysts and investors. The division is headed by an investment professional comfortable with the jargon and workings of Wall Street.

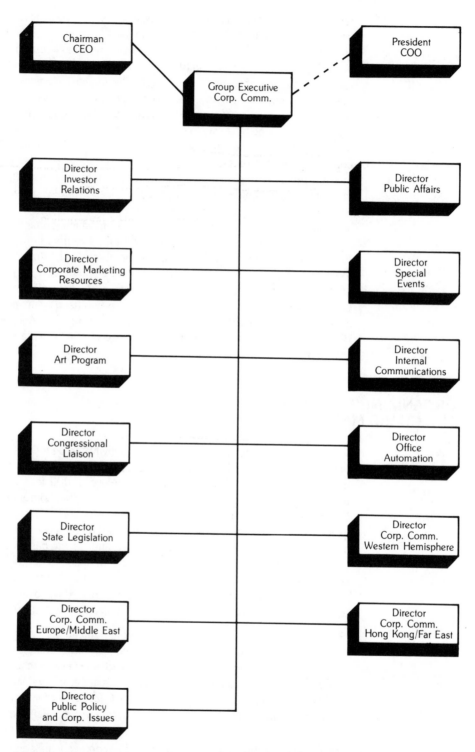

Chase Manhattan Bank
Corporate Communications Group

FIGURE 3.1 Chase Manhattan Bank's communications operation is headquartered in the Corporate Communications group, composed of more than 100 professionals who perform a variety of discrete functions.
SOURCE: Artist Cal Austin

3 **Internal communications** coordinates the bank's communications to its staff through a variety of upward and lateral communications methods, including television, brochures and newsletters, bulletin boards, and face-to-face meetings. The unit is staffed by specialists in the field.

4 **Corporate marketing resources** coordinates the bank's advertising in its many markets. Often, the division serves as a consultant to line marketing departments, who control their own advertising budgets. In addition to responsibilities for market research and planning, the unit manages the bank's relationships with its advertising agencies.

5 **Congressional liaison** is the bank's lobbying and policy formulating arm. The unit includes the bank's three registered Washington lobbyists as well as a research staff to assist in policy development.

6 **Special events** coordinates the bank's presentation at conferences, conventions, and seminars. External events personnel are experts in scheduling, planning, and design and are responsible for ensuring that Chase's presentation "on the road" is tastefully executed.

7 **The state legislation** unit is responsible for the bank's role in Albany, New York's state capital, as well as in other states around the country. This function becomes particularly important in the 1980s as banks like Chase are granted the privilege of expanding their activities across state lines.

8 **Office automation** enables the Corporate Communications group to stay on the cutting edge of new communications technology, such as word processing and electronic mail. At Chase, fittingly, the Communications group serves as the bank's guinea pig in experimenting with the latest technology to deliver information.

9 **The bank's art program** consists of over $3 million of art purchased to enhance Chase's premises around the world. It is staffed by a group of experienced fine arts professionals, who perform a unique and important role for a financial institution.

10 **Public policy and corporate issues** has primary responsibility to keep the bank abreast of emerging public issues. Through a pervasive "issues contact network" within the bank, this unit counsels senior management on breaking legislative developments.

In addition to its New York staff and Washington and Albany representatives, Chase employs representatives in major markets overseas. These officers report directly to New York communications personnel so that the bank can present a unified and cohesive appearance around the world.

ORGANIZING THE PUBLIC RELATIONS AGENCY

The biggest difference between an external agency and an internal department is perspective. The former is outside looking in; the latter is inside looking out (often, quite literally, for itself).

Sometimes the use of an agency is necessary to escape the tunnel vision syndrome that afflicts some firms, where a detached viewpoint is desperately

FEATURE
Who says counselors aren't busy?

Despite keeping meticulous records of their time, public relations counselors still are treated as something of an enigma by many people. Occasionally, the question is asked, "What exactly do they do?" In answer, the Henry J. Kaufmann & Associates, Inc. firm in Washington, D.C. reported that it did the following in 1981:

○ Received over 200,000 phone calls,
○ Made 220,000 phone calls,
○ Received 264,000 pieces of mail,
○ Wrote 5,000 checks—over $8 million— to outside suppliers

○ Received about 6,500 visitors,
○ Traveled 284,900 miles on business trips,
○ Made at least 200 trips to New York,
○ Used 36 miles of typewriter ribbon,
○ Produced 433,602 copies on the copying machine,
○ Used 23,000 pages of legal pads,
○ Consumed 20,400 cups of coffee, and
○ Contributed 160 jobs to the economy, assuming that one job is created for every $50,000 paid to suppliers.[7]

needed. An agency unfettered by internal corporate politics might be better trusted to present management with an objective reading of the concerns of its publics.

An agency has the added advantage of not being taken for granted by a firm's management. Unfortunately, managements sometimes have a greater regard for an outside specialist than an inside one. This attitude frequently defies logic, but nonetheless, it's often true. Generally, if management is paying (sometimes quite handsomely) for outside counsel, it tends to listen carefully to the advice.

Agencies also may fit certain unique needs of an organization. A company may need a technically complex speech, a specially targeted consumer program, or a particularly pointed financial relations project. Such needs may be filled quickly and professionally by outside counsel.

Public relations counsel is, by definition, a highly personalized service. A counselor's prescription for a client depends primarily on what the counselor thinks a client needs and how that assessment fits the client's own perception of those needs. Often, an outsider's fresh point-of-view is helpful in focusing a client on particular problems and opportunities and how best to conquer or capitalize on them.

On the other hand, since outside agencies are just that—outside—they are often unfamiliar with details affecting the situation of particular companies and the idiosyncracies of company management. The good external counselor must constantly work to overcome this barrier. The best client-agency relationships are those with free-flowing communications between internal and external public relations groups so that both resources are kept informed about corporate policy, strategies, and tactics.

A well-oiled, complementary department/agency relationship can only result in a more positive communications approach for an organization.

ORGANIZING FOR PUBLIC RELATIONS AT HILL AND KNOWLTON

Hill and Knowlton (H and K) is not a typical agency. While the majority of agencies are smaller shops with several counselors, Hill and Knowlton, by contrast, is by most measures the world's largest agency.

Headquartered in New York City, H and K has grown from a two-man operation with one client to a 1,000-staff member operation of $46 million income with offices in more than thirty countries.

H and K however, is typical of the growing trend of public relations agencies to merge with advertising agencies. In H and K's case, it was acquired in the early 1980s by J. Walter Thompson, a huge New York advertising agency. Prior to the H and K/ Thompson merger, Hill and Knowlton's counseling colleague, Carl Byoir & Associates, merged with Chicago's Foote, Cone & Belding Communications, the ninth largest advertising agency.

Although such mergers have caused consternation and speculation within the public relations community, thus far agencies such as H and K have been able to maintain their autonomy, identity, objectivity, and independence to function effectively as counselors. Indeed, the partnership between advertising and public relations agencies makes sense from a number of standpoints:

1 More resources available,

2 Increased exposure and influence,

3 More disciplined management between the public relations and advertising functions, and

4 greater use of advertising as a public relations tool.

H and K for example, remains a full-service agency whose client list reads like a Who's Who of American industry. American Airlines, Campbell Soup, Procter & Gamble, Sperry Rand, the Iron and Steel Institute, and more than 100 others are all H and K customers. The guiding philosophy at Hill and Knowlton is teamwork, with individual service specialists working in concert with account executives to manage client relationships.

The agency is organized into a variety of specialty areas—some, of the most specialized variety—on which account executives may call for particular expertise. For example, here are 22 of the more exotic Hill and Knowlton resource units:

1 **Financial Relations** Counsels clients on financial problems, Securities and Exchange Commission disclosure, and financial reporting requirements.

2 **Proxy Solicitation and Shareholder List Analysis** Specializes in working for public companies to raise annual meeting vote totals. In addition to proxy solicitation, the group acts as information agent in tender offers, works for passage of a wide variety of management proposals, and aids companies during hostile takeover situations.

3 **Financial Media Relations** Keeps in constant touch with financial editors and reporters to initiate stories about H and K clients and offer quotable corporate spokespersons.

4 **Publicity and Marketing** Presents clients' products, services, and concepts to target audiences through the mass media, merchandising, and product promotions.

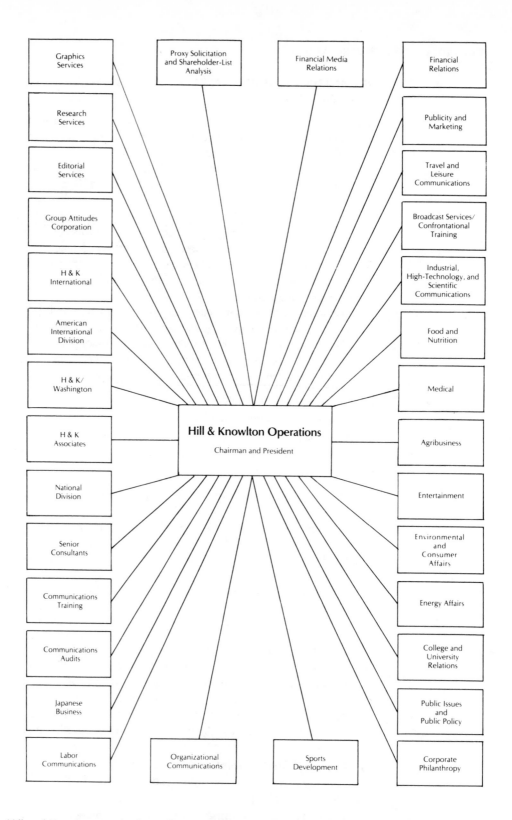

FIGURE 3-2. Hill and Knowlton, a subsidiary of the JWT Group and the largest public relations agency in the world, is compartmentalized into a diverse cross-section of speciality areas.

Source: Artist Candida Alvarez

5 Sports Development   Assists clients in becoming aligned promotionally with the sports, recreation, and leisure-time markets as well as offering professional and amateur sports teams a full range of counseling services.

6 Travel and Leisure Communications   Establishes relationships with the travel media and representatives of carriers, tourist boards, tour operations, hotel groups, and other industry leaders to promote public relations programs for major destinations, hotel groups, resort properties, airlines, cruise companies, and world's fairs.

7 Broadcast Services/Confrontation Training   Produces documentary programs on both videotape and film, news clips, and multimedia presentations; feeds audio programs to key market stations; creates or acquires public television programs and builds audiences for them; and plans radio and television media tours. It also counsels clients on the use of the media in responding to questions about policies or products that are under attack.

8 Industrial, High-technology, and Scientific Communications   Provides specialized news and information for industry groups, the general public, and the business community in the areas of electrical, mechanical, and chemical engineering, electronics, computer sciences, chemistry, architecture, medicine, pharmacy, technical and business journalism, and marketing.

9 Food and Nutrition   Reaches consumers of all ages with educational and publicity programs highlighting food, beverage, and spirits products and services.

10 Medical   Provides information on medical and health-related issues for hospitals, medical associations, pharmaceutical companies, health-maintenance organizations, and insurance companies.

11 Agribusiness   Provides consistent, continuing communications to generate increased government and public understanding for companies involved in agriculture.

12 Entertainment   Provides a full range of communications services for movie studios, television production companies, cable television operators and programming services, and the recording industry.

13 Environmental and Consumer Affairs   Helps clients deal with environmental and occupational health issues, consumer issues, and problems involving the medical and scientific aspects of products.

14 Energy Affairs   Counsels a variety of clients, including major utilities companies, on emerging legislative and regulatory trends and how best to make positions known to legislators and regulators.

15 Public Issues and Public Policy   Counsels clients in corporate social responsibility policies and practices, emerging issues, response management, issues analysis, and the creation of issues management response systems to improve a company's ability to identify, analyze, and evaluate the impact of social and public policy issues, both present and emerging.

16 Corporate Philanthropy   Helps develop contribution strategies, programs, and corporate giving policies that achieve both corporate and social goals.

17 Labor Communications   Provides specialized communications counseling in areas dealing with the tensions and crises that grow out of plant relocations, layoffs, strikes, divestitures, labor contract negotiations, unit organizing drives, and plant closings.

18 Japanese Business Services the unique communications needs of U.S.-based Japanese firms who may need assistance in dealing with the different cultural patterns between Japanese and American approaches to problem-solving such as marketing forecasting, political analysis, and dealing with U.S. employees and the media.

19 Organizational Communications Provides counseling on equal employment opportunity problems, productivity questions, turnover problems, plant start-ups or closures, and other situations involving employees.

20 Communications Audits Specializes in studies and analyses that help organizations measure the effectiveness of their communications and reposition themselves, if necessary, to meet changing conditions.

21 Communications Training Provides training courses, tailored specifically to client needs, to update and improve general communication skills.

22 Senior Consultants Offers a group of carefully selected senior practitioners to serve as added support for account supervisors and their teams in dealing with complex social and public issues.

In addition to all these specialized services, Hill and Knowlton has a national group with thirty-seven offices in the United States, more than seventy affiliate and associate offices around the world, a Washington group, special graphics, research and editorial services units, and the Group Attitudes Corporation, a subsidiary that conducts original survey research.

As organizational needs change, so too does the makeup of Hill and Knowlton's specialty service areas. Like other smart counseling firms, Hill and Knowlton seems well aware that in order to prosper, it must be flexible enough to meet the ever-changing needs of its clients.

WHAT'S IT PAY?

Without question, the communications function has increased in importance and clout. And, while salaries may not have increased in proportion to decision-making power, they nevertheless are headed upward. Indeed, the top communications professionals in many large corporations today draw salaries in excess of $100,000—not including perquisites and bonuses.

Entry-level jobs for writers and researchers generally fall into the $10,000 to $20,000 range. Managers of individual units—press relations, editorial services, and financial communications, for example—may earn anywhere from $20,000 to $50,000. Public relations directors may range in salary from the $30s to the high $70s and $80s. Salaries for communications directors are even higher. Every industry and most companies within an industry have different criteria for certain jobs and therefore do not pay the same.

FEATURE

The image doctors: personal packaging consultants

Among the most unusual "boutique" services offered by communications agencies are those concerned with "personal packaging."

Dubbed *the image doctors*, these consultants will, for a fee, polish rough executive edges. Among other things, they will "lower the pitch of your voice, remove your accent, correct your body language, modify your unacceptable behavior, eliminate your negative self-perceptions, select your wardrobe, restyle your hair and teach you how to speak off the cuff or read a speech without putting your audience to sleep."[8]

Prices vary depending on the service offered, but private rates of $2,000 or more are not unusual. Here's a breakdown of the services:

Speech and Public Appearance Consultants A growing breed, interested in improving the public speaking performance of the corporate executive. Generally, they rely on heavy use of videotape playback so that speakers can experience themselves for better or usually worse. The objective of such instruction is to get the executive to relax at the podium, before the microphones, or in front of the camera.

Dress Consultants In business, so they say, "clothes make the man." Sometimes, companies will hire dress consultants to convert key executives from "shlep status" to fashion plate. Often, a computer is used to match a client's personality and position with a "certain look." After a wardrobe is shaped up, clients may be counseled on such extras as movement and voice projection.

Personal Public Relations Consultants The pinnacle of image counseling is occupied by a few specialists who deal in "personal public relations." This select group counsels clients on the fine points of "professional grooming," from career management guidance to speech training, from behavior modification to attracting the right media exposure. Such specialists are well paid and boast a roster of satisfied clients.

While such firms are not your typical counselors, they do represent a growing and lucrative portion of the communications agency market.

On the agency side, since account executives are "on the line" earning income for the firm, salaries may be higher than corporate staff salaries. Job security in an agency, however, is usually less than that offered by a corporation.

As noted, agencies generally work on monthly retainer fees, based on hourly rates. Counseling charges vary by region. For example, the average hourly rate in the Northeast is $84; in the Pacific, $74; in the Mountain States, $70; in the Midwest, $69; in the South, $69; and in New York City $97.[9]

In terms of client costs, it is not unusual for American companies and trade associations today to pay agencies well in excess of $100,000 a year for public relations support.

TABLE 3-1 Fifty largest U.S. public relations operations, independent and ad agency affiliated for year ended Dec. 31, 1982. *Denotes advertising agency subsidiary

	1982 Net Fee Income	Employees as of Oct. 15, 1982	% Change from 1981 Income
1 Hill and Knowlton*	$54,000,000	1,050	+14.8
2 Burson-Marsteller*	50,550,000	1,060	+23.0
3 Carl Byoir & Associates¹	21,887,000	480	+ 4.9
4 Ruder Finn & Rotman	16,300,000	400	+ 7.2
5 Daniel J. Edelman	8,500,000	176	+ 4.8
6 Doremus & Company*²	8,315,014	159	+24.2
7 Manning, Selvage & Lee*	8,304,000	142	+15.5
8 Ketchum PR*	7,802,484	118	+31.2
9 The Rowland Company	7,480,629	123	+ 3.4
10 Ogilvy & Mather PR*³	7,432,000	133	+ 8.3
11 Fleishman-Hillard	6,191,000	104	+45.6
12 Rogers & Cowan	6,054,000	121	+13.1
13 Gray and Company	—	107	—
14 Robert Marston and Associates	5,251,000	70	+21.6
15 Booke Communications Incorporated Group	5,239,000	78	+ 8.9
16 Creamer Dickson Basford*	4,810,000	100	+ 3.2
17 Bozell & Jacobs PR*	4,460,000	89	− 4.3
18 Baron/Canning and Company	3,782,000	49	+16.6
19 Dudley-Anderson-Yutzy PR	3,449,000	65	+ 9.2
20 Ayer Public Relations Services*	3,446,500	45	+ 5.6
21 Golin/Harris Communications	3,368,725	64	+17.4
22 Regis McKenna	3,010,269	50	+34.9
23 Kanan, Corbin, Schupak & Aronow	2,617,652	36	+18.5
24 Aaron D. Cushman and Associates	2,601,350	52	+ 2.3
25 Financial Relations Board	2,585,868	59	+ 6.8
26 The Strayton Corporation	2,410,000	36	+28.5
27 Porter, Novelli and Associates*	2,235,000	43	+31.3
28 Hank Meyer Associates	2,159,074	22	− 7.6
29 The Rockey Company	2,145,000	43	+16.6
30 The Hannaford Company	2,103,337	35	+17.6
31 Dorf/MJH	2,032,817	51	+72.2
32 Anthony M. Franco	2,000,000	42	+24.6
33 Richard Weiner	1,950,000	43	+37.9
34 Gibbs & Soell	1,877,660	38	− 4.9
35 Padilla and Speer	1,862,071	29	+19.4
36 Geltzer & Company	1,800,300	30	+ 2.2
37 Lobsenz-Stevens	1,735,000	33	+ 8.5
38 Public Relations Board	1,628,556	48	+ 2.3
39 ICPR	1,511,000	32	−11.3
40 John Adams Associates, Inc.	1,476,736	27	+97.3
41 Charles Ryan Associates	1,378,444	23	+14.4
42 Porter, LeVay & Rose	1,339,425	24	+50.4
43 Cohn & Wolfe	1,317,000	40	+81.5
44 Simon/Public Relations Inc.	1,290,000	23	+45.7
45 Gross and Associates/PR	1,247,308	26	−18.1
46 Woody Kepner Associates	1,221,000	18	+21.6
47 Edward Howard & Co.	1,214,363	21	−17.3
48 Mallory Factor Associates	1,214,000	20	+29.7
49 Smith & Harroff	1,190,000	13	+ 1.8
50 Public Communications, Inc.	1,180,000	24	−17.0

¹Acquired Newsome & Company, Inc. Nov. 1, 1982. ²Includes all wholly owned BBDO International PR Units. ³Includes AAB Assessoria Administrativa Ltda. acquired Feb. 1, 1982. SOURCE: © 1983 The J. R. O'Dwyer Company Inc. May not be reproduced or photocopied in any form without permission.

FEATURE
The typical public relations practitioner

What does the "typical" public relations professional look like? Here's what a 1981 survey conducted by PR Reporter revealed:[10]

He—only 30 percent of respondents were female—was 48 years old, had been in public relations between ten to fourteen years, had worked for his present employer between four to five years, and had been in his current position between two to three years.

Despite this survey, the Public Relations Society of America reported in 1982 that women composed 36 percent of its member-ship and that in the Public Relations Student Society of America, women composed 76 percent of the membership. Moreover, according to the Bureau of Labor Statistics in 1982, of the 123,000 public relations practitioners in the United States more than 45 percent reportedly were women.

One of the most atypical was the woman named in 1982 to head the General Electric public relations group. She became the second woman vice president at General Electric and reportedly earned $200,000 annual salary, exclusive of bonuses and other benefits.

TABLE 3–2 Comparison of 1981 and 1980 median salaries of top level public relations/ public affairs practitioners in U.S. and Canada, and by Type of Organization

Type Organization	Median Salary 1981	Median Salary 1980	1981 Salary Range	Median Change*
All U.S. organizations	$38,000	$35,000	$16,000-125,000	
All Canadian organizations	38,600	33,000	19,000-200,000	
PR firms	50,000	45,000	16,000-200,000	$5,625
Advertising agencies	38,000	36,500	16,000- 80,000	4,500
Other consulting	—	38,000	21,000-100,000	—
Banks	35,000	34,000	18,000- 85,000	3,850
Insurance companies	35,000	29,500	11,000-120,000	3,200
Consumer product companies	44,700	37,500	26,000-117,000	4,500
Industrials	45,200	36,000	17,000-127,000	4,750
Conglomerates	43,200	42,000	17,000-148,000	4,600
Transportation	—	33,800	8,000- 78,000	—
Utilities	41,000	36,500	19,000- 75,000	5,950
Hospitals	30,000	23,650	15,000- 65,000	3,250
Educational	32,800	27,700	14,000- 67,500	2,900
Trade/professional associations	38,700	36,000	16,000- 75,000	3,600
Other nonprofits	33,000	30,000	11,000- 72,000	3,000
Government	31,000	29,000	15,000- 50,000	2,975

*Calculated on the difference between 1981 and 1980 salaries as reported by *each* respondent.

Note: Median salary and median change are not shown when sample is too small.

SOURCE: Based on responses of 720 subscribers to PR Reporter in "Seventeenth Annual Survey of the Profession," *PR Reporter* Vol. 24, No. 39, Oct. 12, 1981.

FEATURE
The perfect public relations manager

In a speech on Feb. 27, 1980, Robert Cushman, chairman and chief executive officer of Norton Company of Worcester, Mass., laid out nine requisites for perfect public relations managers:

1 They should be students of public attitudes and perceptions, who understand that communications is not just what you *say* but what others hear.

2 They must understand a variety of different publics and what makes them tick—from security analysts to hard hats, from state senators to Mexican Americans.

3 They must have ideologies, yes—but with enough flexibility and empathy to understand conflicting views and the role of trade-offs.

4 They must be honest, open, and accessible.

5 They must hold a deep interest in what's going on in the world; they should be concerned about Iran, Afghanistan, the election, energy, inflation, education, tax reform, the capital problems of business, new economic philosophies, and new trends in art, music, and public tastes. In short, they should be renaissance people.

6 They must have ideas and be responsive to the ideas of others.

7 They must be good writers.

8 They must be in touch with the real world and protect senior managers from insulating themselves from what is happening out there.

9 Most of all, they must talk straight to me and other members of management. We don't want to be patronized. We don't want sycophants. We want advisors who will advocate, debate, and defend their thinking and proposals.[11]

WHAT MANNER OF MAN/WOMAN?

What kind of individual does it take to become a competent public relations professional?

New York counselor Art Stevens speculated that in most peoples' minds, a "PR man"—and presumably "PR woman"—would appear something like this:

A man steps into a phone booth and says the magic words *corporate image*. Suddenly there is a flash of typewriter ribbon, and he becomes "PR Man"—a wide smile fixed on his face. His fingers flex in anticipation of countless handshakes; his mind forms strings of pleasant, glib words; his amino acids brace themselves for the four martinis that he must down during the traditional three-hour lunch.

His looks take on the appearance of Tony Curtis in *Sweet Smell of Success*. There's also a touch of Jack Lemmon in *Days of Wine and Roses*. Beads of perspiration form on his brow as he anticipates the excitement and satisfaction of conning the world. No one knows precisely what he does and how he does it, but he conveys glamor and intrigue.[12]

If only that "glamor and intrigue" were true. Regrettably, most practitioners would moan, "It simply ain't so!" More precisely, in order to make it, a public relations practitioner ought to possess a set of specific, technical skills as well as an appreciation of the proper attitudinal approach to the job.

On the technical side, these five skills are important:

1 **Knowledge of the Field** An understanding of the underpinnings of public relations, of culture and history, and of philosophy and social psychology.

2 **Communications Knowledge** An understanding of the media and how they work, of communications research, and, most importantly, of how to write.

3 **Business Knowledge** An understanding of how business works, a bottom-line orientation, and a knowledge of one's company and industry.

4 **Knowledge of Bureaucracy** An understanding of how to get things done in a bureaucratic organization, how to use and gain power for best advantage, and how to maneuver in a politically-charged environment.

5 **Management Knowledge** An understanding of how public policy is shaped and an appreciation of the various pressures on and responsibilities of senior managers.

In terms of attitude, public relations professionals ought to possess the following four characteristics:

1 **Communications Orientation** A bias toward disclosing rather than withholding information. Public relations professionals should *want to* communicate to the public. They should practice the belief that "the public has a right to know."

2 **Advocacy** A desire to be advocates for their employers. Public relations people must believe in what their employers stand for. While they should never distort, lie, or hide facts, occasionally it may be in an organization's best interest to avoid comment on certain issues. If practitioners don't believe in the integrity and credibility of their employer, their most honorable course is to quit.

3 **Counseling Orientation** A compelling desire to advise senior managers. Top executives are used to dealing in "tangibles," such as balance sheets, costs per thousand, and cash flows. Public relations practitioners understand the "intangibles," such as public opinion, media influence, and communications messages. Practitioners must be willing to support their beliefs—often in opposition to lawyers or personnel executives. They even must be willing to disagree at times with management. Far from being "yes men," the public relations practitioner often must have the gumption to counsel, "no."

4 **Personal Confidence** A strong sense of honesty and ethics, a willingness to take risks, and, not unimportantly, a sense of humor. In sum, public relations professionals must have the courage of their convictions and the personal confidence to represent proudly a curious—yet critical—role in any organization.

It all boils down to a single most important quality: professionalism. Public relations neither takes a false smile nor a glad hand. But it does take solid communications, human relations, and judgmental and learning skills. Most of all, it takes work.

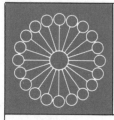

CASE STUDY
The loquacious bank economist

New York's Gonzo National Bank was the largest bank in the world in terms of total assets and deposits. Many of these deposits emanated from foreign customers, including foreign multinational companies and foreign banks. Indeed, the Japanese were among the most important and most prosperous of all Gonzo customers.

In August, the United States began putting strong pressure on the Japanese to revalue the yen, so that as a result, Japanese goods would cost more to purchase than those of American competitors. In America, more dollars would have to be paid out to purchase Japanese imports. Therefore, a revaluation upward of the Japanese yen would be deleterious to the Japanese economy while stimulating the American economy.

On the evening of September 15, after several weeks of intense American pressure, the Japanese reluctantly announced that they would revalue the yen.

At Gonzo National, management internally welcomed the Japanese announcement, interpreting it as a boon to the sagging U.S. economy. They agreed, however, that no public statement would be made for fear the bank's good Japanese clients would consider such a statement as rubbing salt in the wound. They further agreed that the bank's public relations department would respond to the Japanese announcement with a simple "no comment."

At 8 A.M. after the Japanese announcement—September 16—vacationing Gonzo National economist H. John Hollingsworth was at home eating breakfast when the telephone rang. He answered it, and on the line was his next door neighbor Lawrence Shields, international business editor of the Associated Press wire service. Shields was interested to know what Hollingsworth thought of last night's Japanese announcement.

"What do I think of it?" Hollingsworth replied. "Why I think it's great. A change in the yen rate was a key part needed to make the U.S. plan work. It's a victory for America."

Shields thanked his neighbor for the information and hung up. Hollingsworth went back to his morning coffee.

Fifteen minutes later, a bulletin went out over the 4,000 Associated Press news wires in newspapers and brokerage houses throughout the world. It read:

> AP, NEW YORK, 8:15 A.M.—Gonzo National Bank calls Japanese revaluation announcement a great victory for America. Economist H. John Hollingsworth of New York's 80-billion dollar Gonzo National Bank today said yesterday's decision by the Japanese government to revalue the yen was "a key part needed to make the United States plan work. It's a victory for America."

Within six minutes John T. Knoll, public relations director for Gonzo National, received a call from the bank's president. The president told him that the Dow Jones ticker machine in his office had just carried an item reporting that Gonzo National had called the Japanese revaluation "a great victory for the U.S." The president asked Knoll to come up to his office immediately.

At 8:24 A.M. Knoll and the president began to weigh the consequences of the inadvertent announcement. The president pointed out that the Japanese had "hundreds of millions of dollars of deposits in our bank." He said he personally was friendly with the American representatives of Mitsubishi Bank, Bank of Tokyo, and several other large Japanese banks with offices in New York City. "When these fellows see that statement," he said, "they'll be livid." The president suggested to Knoll that the Japanese were "proud people" and that the revaluation was something they felt forced into.

"Revaluation was understandably unpopular among Japanese business leaders," the president said, "and now it look like the Gonzo National is rubbing it in. We've got real trouble," he concluded.

As the president chronicled customer relations and real business problems that the announcement had evoked, Knoll began contemplating the media ramifications. The newspapers, he thought, would see the announcement on the wire and tomorrow morning's headlines could be frightening. Indeed, even if Gonzo's Japanese customers didn't see the story on the news wires in their offices, they would still probably read about the announcement in tomorrow's newspapers.

Obviously, thoughtful action had to be taken quickly.

"John," the president said solemnly, "it's 8:30. At 8:45, I'd like to see you back here with a plan for our reaction to this mess. As I see it, we've got public relations considerations with respect to media reaction on one hand and Japanese customer reaction on the other. Failure to handle either effectively will cost us an enormous amount of business. Go back to your office and think about it. I'll see you in fifteen minutes."

QUESTIONS

1 What recommendation would you make to the president about Gonzo National's public response to the initial statement?

   Would you issue another statement? Why or why not? If you issued another statement, what would it say? Who would it come from? When would it be issued? To whom would it be issued?

2 What recommendation would you make to the president about Gonzo National's contacting Japanese clients? Would you attempt to contact them? Why or why not? If you would contact them, how should it be done? When should it be done? What should be said? Who should say it?

NOTES

1 Richard H. Truitt, "Wanted: Hard-Headed Objectives," *Public Relations Journal,* August 1969, pp. 12, 13.

2 "Measurement in Public Relations—An Overview," *Public Relations Review,* 3, no. 4 (Winter 1977):6, 7.

3 Jack Tucker, "Budgeting and Cost Control: Are You a Businessman Or a Riverboat Gambler?" *Public Relations Journal,* March 1981, p. 15.

4   Donald T. Mogavero, "When the Funds Come Tumbling Down," *Public Relations Journal,* October 1981, p. 13.

5   "Managing Corporate External Relations: Changing Perspectives and Responses," The Conference Board, Report 679, New York, N.Y., 1976.

6   Jack O. Dwyer, *O'Dwyer's Directory of Corporate Communications,* (New York, N.Y.: J. R. O'Dwyer Co., Inc., 1982).

7   Leo J. Northart, "Editor's Notebook," *Public Relations Journal,* May 1982, p. 6.

8   Jacqueline A. Thompson, "The Image Doctors: A Guide to the Personal Packaging Consultants," *MBA Magazine,* September 1977, pp. 23-30.

9   "Counselors Charge Average of $78/HR Nationwide Survey Finds," *PR Reporter,* 12 October 1982.

10 "Profile of a Typical Practitioner," *PR Reporter,* Vol. 24, No. 39, 12 October 1981.

11 Robert Cushman, Speech before the New England Chapter of the Public Relations Society of America, 27 February 1980.

12 Art Stevens, "Public Relations: The Image of the Imagemaker," *AMA Management Review,* November 1971.

SUGGESTED READING

Burger, Chester. "How to Manage 'Demon Time'." *Public Relations Journal* 31, no. 6 (June, 1975):16–18. Time is all-important and practitioners must know how to manage it.

Burger, Chester. "So You Want To Start Your Own Business," *Public Relations Journal,* August 1981, pp. 20–22.

Chase, Howard. "The Corporate Imperative Management of Profit and Policy," *Public Relations Quarterly,* Spring 1982, pp. 25–29. The new organizational design described here is intended to bring order, logic, control, effectiveness, and economy to the twin responsibilities of corporate management: profit and public policy.

Curry Jr., Talmer E. and **Haerer, Deanne N.** "Flexi-Time: Is It For You?" *Public Relations Journal,* March 1981, pp. 54–57.

Fairman, Milton. "The Practice of Public Relations." Address to the fifteenth annual meeting of the Institute of Public Relations Society of America, 13 June 1973, at University of Texax, Austin, Texas. Available from Foundation for Public Relations Research, New York, N.Y.

Forrestal, Dan J. "Low Profile: The Two Most Harmful Words in PR Strategy." *Public Relations Journal* 31, no. 6 (June, 1975):22–24.

Geltzer, Howard, and **Ries, Al.** "The Importance of Positioning in Public Relations." *Public Relations Journal* 31, no. 11 (November, 1975):22–24.

"Guidelines for Public Relations Professionals," *Public Relations Journal,* January 1981, p. 33.

Haimann, Theo, Scott, William G., and **Connor, Patrick E.** *Managing the Modern Organization,* Boston: Houghton Mifflin Company, 1978, Chapter 1, 8-14, 17.

Hill, Don. "In Search of Excellence," *Public Relations Journal,* May 1982, pp. 36–37. Setting behavioral goals and measuring the results breed excellence in public relations programming, but too often these key elements are missing.

Mogavero, Donald T. "When the Funds Come Tumbling Down," *Public Relations Journal,* October 1981, p. 12.

Naver, Michael. "How to Think Like a Manager in Not-For-Profit Public Relations," *Public Relations Journal,* October 1981, pp. 23–24.

Safire, Bill. *The Relations Explosion,* New York: Macmillian, 1963.

"Seventeenth Annual Survey of the Profession," *PR Reporter,* Oct. 12, 1981. Median salary rise again lags behind inflation rate; analysis of how individual salaries are affected by years in public relations, organizational level, education, and other factors.

Stephenson, Howard. Handbook of Public Relations. 2d ed. New York: McGraw-Hill, 1971.

Strenski, James B. "Pert Charting Public Relations," *Public Relations Journal* 31, no. 2 (February, 1975):22–23.

Tucker, Jack. "Budgeting and Cost Control: Are You a Businessman or a Riverboat Gambler?" *Public Relations Journal,* March 1981, pp. 14–17. Effective public relations programs cannot be developed without a budget or implemented without controls.

Wright, Donald K. "Accreditation's Effects on Professionalism," *Public Relations Review,* Spring 1981, pp. 48–61. The author attempts to chart the "professionalism" of public relations by comparing practitioners' rankings of occupational values with criteria associated with the concept of professionalism.

A PERISHABLE COMMODITY

Public opinion is an elusive and fragile commodity. It is difficult to move most people toward a strong opinion on anything. It is even harder to move them away from an opinion once they reach it.

For public relations professionals, the concept of public opinion—and its power—must be understood and confronted. Indeed, meaningful public relations practice can be undertaken only upon understanding the bases for and nuances of public opinion.

At the root of public relations work lies the objective of attempting to influence public opinion, the attitudes that support it, and the actions taken in its behalf.

For an organization, the ultimate reflection of public opinion lies in its so-called "corporate image," the overall impression that it conveys to its publics. Obviously, every individual views every organization differently. One overriding goal of public relations professionals is to convince the vast majority to view their organization in a favorable light. Clearly, this revolves most centrally around the proper—and profitable—performance of the organization. But it also has much to do with an organization's understanding of and influence on public opinion.

4

The Court of Public Opinion

DEFINING PUBLIC OPINION

Public relations educator Walt Seifert insists that "the United States Supreme Court is not the highest in our land. Our highest court is the Court of Public Opinion, which meets every hour."[1]

He has a point.

Public opinion is highly influential in our society. Favorable public opinion can help elect a political candidate, sell a consumer product, or raise the price of a corporate stock. Unfavorable public opinion, on the other hand, can be the kiss of death for an individual, a product, or an institution.

Public opinion, like *public relations,* is not easily defined.

Newspaper columnist Joseph Kraft called public opinion "the unknown god to which moderns burn incense." Edward Bernays called it, "a term describing an ill-defined, mercurial, and changeable group of individual judgments."[2] And Princeton professor Harwood Childs, after coming up with no less than forty different—but nonetheless viable—definitions, concluded with a definition by Herman C. Boyle: *"Public opinion* is not the name of something but the classification of a number of somethings."[3]

Splitting public opinion into its two components, *public* and *opinion,* is perhaps the best way to understand the concept. Simply defined, *public* signifies a group of people who share a common interest in a specific subject—stockholders, for example, or employees, or community residents. Each group is concerned with a common issue—the price of the stock, the wages of the company, or the building of a new plant.

An *opinion* is the expression of an attitude on a particular topic. When attitudes become strong enough, they surface in the form of opinions. When opinions become strong enough, they lead to verbal or behavioral actions.

A corporate executive and an environmentalist from the Sierra Club might differ dramatically in their attitudes about the relative importance of pollution control versus continued industrial production. Their respective opinions on a piece of environmental legislation might also differ radically. How their organizations respond to that legislation—by picketing, petitioning, or lobbying—might also differ.

DEFINING ATTITUDES

If an opinion is an expression of an attitude on a particular topic, what then is an attitude?

Simply, it's a predisposition to think a certain way about a certain topic. Many similar attitudes in a society form the building blocks of public opinion.

Attitudes are based on a number of characteristics:

1 **Personal** The physical and emotional ingredients of an individual, including size, age, and social status.

2 **Cultural** The environment and lifestyle of a particular geographic area, such as Japan versus the United States or rural America versus urban America. National political candidates will often tailor messages to appeal to the particular cultural complexion of specific regions of the country.

3 **Educational** The level and quality of a person's education. To appeal to the increased number of college graduates in the United States today, public communication has become more sophisticated.

4 **Familial** People cannot escape their roots. Children acquire their parents' tastes, biases, political partisanships, and a host of other characteristics. While some obstetricians insist that children pick up most of their knowledge in the earliest years, few would deny the family's strong role in helping mold attitudes.

5 **Religious** Religion is making a comeback. In the 1960s, many young people turned away from formal religion. In the 1980s, religious fervor appears to be reemerging. From followers of traditional Christianity and Judaism to disciples of Hare Krishna and the Reverend Sun Yung Moon to the believers in the various fundamentalist sects of the Bible Belt—religion and its influence on attitudes is back.

6 **Social class** As people's social status changes, so too do their attitudes. For example, a college student unconcerned with making a living may dramatically change his attitude about such concepts as big government, big business, wealth, and prosperity after entering the job market.

7 **Race** Ethnic origin increasingly today helps shape people's attitudes. The history of Blacks and Whites in America has been a stormy one, with peaceful coexistence often frustrated. Nonetheless, minorities in our society, as a group, continue to improve their standard of living. In so doing, in the case of blacks, Chicanos, Puerto Ricans, and others, they have retained distinct racial pride in and allegiance to their cultural heritage.

These are but a few of the dominant influences in the formation of attitudes. Such other factors as experience, economic class, political and organizational memberships, among many others lead to the formation of opinions. Once others with similar attitudes reach similar opinions, a *consensus,* or *public opinion,* is born.

TYPES OF ATTITUDES

Strictly speaking, attitudes are either positive, negative, or nonexistent. A person is either for it, agin'it, or couldn't care less.

Studies show most people don't care much one way or the other. For any one issue, a small percentage of people will express strong support and another small percentage will express strong opposition. The vast number will be right smack in the middle—passive, neutral, indifferent. Former Vice-President Spiro T. Agnew called them "the silent majority." In many instances—political campaigns being a prime example—this "silent majority" hold the key to success because they are most readily influenced by a communicator's message.

It's hard to change the mind of a person who is staunchly opposed to a particular issue or individual. Likewise, it's easy to reinforce the support of a person

Herb Schmertz is vice president for public affairs at Mobil Oil Corporation. He is a director of Mobil Corporation and a director of Mobil Oil Corporation. He is responsible for corporate public relations, domestic and international government relations, and investor relations. By all accounts, Mr. Schmertz is just about the most well-known public relations man in the United States. Through his leadership, Mobil has developed a reputation as perhaps the nation's most outspoken corporation. A frequent critic of the media, Mr. Schmertz regularly appears as a guest columnist in print and a guest commentator on television. He also is co-author of the novel, *Takeover.*

Why is Mobil so outspoken in its views?

The answer is twofold. First, Mobil is committed to dialogue. A pluralistic society demands vigorous competition in the marketplace of ideas. We believe that nobody speaks for any business better than the business itself.

Second, we believe that companies, like individuals, have distinct personalities. Our personality includes a sensitivity to the environment in which we operate. The ultimate survival of any single institution in our society is closely linked to the strength and vitality of all our free institutions—our universities, our free press, our churches, and our cultural groups. Mobil's top management obviously supports participation in the marketplace of ideas and our concern for the world around us. Without management's support, none of our programs would work.

What are the advantages of such an approach? The disadvantages?

We know that 100 percent support for our views and philosophies cannot be achieved. We risk rebuttal and perhaps attack by those who have a vested political interest in opposing us. However, by participating in the debate over political and economic issues, we have broadened the spectrum of facts, views, opinions, and philosophy available for our publics to consider in making decisions.

Does it bother you that others criticize this out-front approach?

No, we are committed to our program. We want to speak our piece in the marketplace of ideas, without trying to dominate that market. We know that if our ideas don't make sense and if we are not credible over a long period of time, then our ideas will get shot down and will deserve to. We have created a constituency that didn't exist and would not have existed without this program.

What's your opinion of the media?

The nature of television operating under the tyranny of the 25-second bite makes it inherently less fair and less accurate than print media. Newspapers have the space to develop complicated ideas, accept letters to the editor, print corrections, and even accept advocacy advertising. Yet, I believe the media in general tend toward sensationalism, to reporting gossip and recriminations, without thoroughly exposing the political motivations that give rise to them.

What gains has Mobil made with the media since the inception of its program?

I think the campaign is having an impact on the media. They are more careful about what they say about us and about energy in general.

What should be the proper relationship between the media and business?

The current adversary relationship between business and the media serves no purpose. If a relationship of mutual trust were to develop, the press would undoubtedly have better access to businessmen and the result would be a better informed American public.

The basic purpose of journalism should be to inform, and information can best be solicited from the business community in an atmosphere free of cat-and-mouse games. Journalists have to rediscover the objectivity that used to be their stock in trade and free themselves of the "I make the news I report" syndrome.

The purpose of an interview should not be to put the businessman on the spot or to make him look stupid. All terms should be understood in advance—what questions will be asked, who will participate in the interview, and where the reporter wants the interview to go. If the businessman is fully informed and prepared, a factual and mean-

ingful exchange will ensue. The viewer will have the opportunity to learn something.

What do you advise your top management in dealing with the media?

Our top management has made a basic decision: that senior people in the company should make themselves available for everything from print and electronic interviews to talk shows and should try to impart information and understanding without fretting over the possibility that they might make a bobble now and then.

Have you measured quantitatively the impact of Mobil's ad program?

We do not measure the results of our ads scientifically, but I don't believe that the true effectiveness of issues advertising can be measured anyway. However, there has been some effect on our company's stockholders. Polls of our new stockholders show that one of the reasons they purchase our stock is our issues advertising. I would not interpret this to mean they just like our ads, but that they believe this is a company that believes in protecting shareholder interests.

Do you think Mobil's op-ed ads have outlived their usefulness?

No. Our op-ed ads deal with current political and economic issues that are of fundamental importance to Mobil and to its industry. We want to bring our dialogue to the attention of those opinion leaders who read the op-ed page regularly—those readers we feel are best able to grasp complex issues and sophisticated concepts. We believe it is important to continue to infuse our views, facts, and philosophy into the mix for the consideration of these opinion leaders.

How important is it for managers to be available to the media?

I think it is very important for information and management personnel to be available in the hope that a better informed press corps will lead to better balanced and more complete reporting.

who is wholeheartedly in favor of an issue or an individual. Social scientist Leon Festinger discussed this concept when he talked about *cognitive dissonance,* saying that individuals tend to *avoid* information that is dissonant or opposed to their own points of view, and they tend to *seek out* information that is consonant, or in support of their own attitudes.[4]

In other words, if one regularly reads the liberal *Village Voice,* one probably wouldn't read the conservative *National Review,* and vice versa. In effect, this case would be cognitive dissonance in action.

As Festinger's theory intimates, the people whose attitudes can be influenced most readily are those who have not yet made up their minds. In politics, as noted in Chapter 1, this group is often referred to as the *swing vote.* Many an election has been won or lost on last-minute appeals to these politically undecided voters. It is also possible to introduce information that may cause "dissonance" in the mind of a receiver.

Understanding this theory and its potential for influencing the silent majority is extremely important for the practitioner, whose objective is to win support through clear, thoughtful, and persuasive communication.

Moving a person from a latent state of attitude formation to a more aware state and finally to an active one becomes a matter of motivation.

SOURCES OF MOTIVATION

People are motivated by different factors. And no two people will likely respond the same way to the same set of circumstances. Each of us is motivated by different drives and needs.

The most famous delineator of what motivates people was Dr. Abraham Maslow, whose "hierarchy of needs" helps define the origins of motivation which, in turn, help explain attitudes and public opinion.

Maslow postulated a five-level hierarchy of needs.

1   The lowest order of needs, according to Maslow, was the *physiological needs,* encompassing a person's biological demands—food and thirst, sleep, health, bodily needs, exercise and rest, and sex.
2   A second level was that of *safety needs,* including security, protection, comfort and peace, and orderly surroundings.
3   A third level was that of *love needs,* such as acceptance, belonging, love and affection, and membership in a group.
4   A fourth level was that of *esteem,* the need for recognition and prestige, confidence and leadership, competence and strength, intelligence and success.
5   The highest order of needs were ones of *self-actualization,* or simply "becoming what one is capable of becoming." Self-actualization involves self-fulfillment and achieving a goal for the purpose of challenge and accomplishment.

By Maslow's definition at least, the needs at each level compose the fundamental motivating factors for any individual or public.

TYPES OF PUBLICS

As noted, the *publics* of pubic relations are diverse and vary from firm to firm. Virtually every discrete subpublic of an organization—from line managers to staff managers to union workers to nonunion workers to per-diem employees and on and on—require separate communications to deal with separate opinions.

However, in a general sense, public opinion might be segregated into four overall types of publics:

1   **The general public** has little interest in either the facts surrounding public issues or the issues themselves and could better be categorized the *nonpublic*.
2   **The attentive** public at least knows that certain issues are prominent in the public arena.
3   **The informed public** not only knows the issues but participates in the dialogue concerning them.
4   **The elite public** initiates and defines the issues and manages the public discussion about them.[5]

The elite public frequently becomes a catalyst in the formation of public opinion. When Spiro Agnew was vice-president, he delighted in classifying the "effete snobs" who ran the liberal eastern media as the true elite public manipulating U.S. public opinion.

Agnew's categorization, however, was too flip. Opinion elites—or opinion leaders—are broad-based and changeable. Generally acknowledged opinion leaders occupy decision-making positions in corporations, the media, the academic community, or the government. But just as often, depending on the issue, opinion-influencers may not fit the stereotype of the community leader. As AT&T vice-president Ed Block has pointed out, "The Bell System companies did quite a bit of research among leaders and discovered, to the surprise of some of us, that people in positions of community leadership are vastly different [from the generally acknowledged group of opinion leaders]."

In attempting to influence public opinion, it is important to keep firmly in mind the specific public to whom a communication is aimed. Choosing one elite public over another involves trade-offs that must be carefully weighed in advance of the communication.

INFLUENCING PUBLIC OPINION

Conducted wisely, public relations has the power to influence public opinion. A thoughtful campaign can crystallize attitudes, reinforce beliefs, or occasionally change the public's mind.

But the process can't be approached haphazardly. First, the opinions to be changed or modified must be identified and understood. Second, the target publics must be clear. Finally, the practitioner must have a sharp focus of the objectives that influence particular publics and opinions.

FEATURE
When fantasy collides with reality . . .

The operative word at California's Disneyland is "fantasy."

At least that's the feeling that Disneyland officials would like to leave with visitors. In terms of influencing public opinion about "The Magic Kingdom," Disneyland management works hard to maintain a dreamy impression.

According to *The Wall Street Journal,* perhaps Disneyland officials have worked too hard at preserving the impression of "fantasy."

In mid-1981, the Journal revealed that a spate of incidents at Disneyland had raised questions about whether the park "values its magical atmosphere so highly that it won't call for paramedics when a visitor falls ill or is seriously injured."[6]

Specifically, the Journal cited three incidents in which Disneyland medical personnel, arriving in unmarked first-aid vans, refused to call local health officials or paramedics for fear of tarnishing the fantasy image. In one reported incident, a teenager was stabbed in the chest in the park's Tomorrowland section, was treated by a Disneyland nurse, and died a few minutes after reaching the hospital. Local health officials claimed the boy could have been saved had paramedics been called.

As one health official put it, "It's just the whole image thing. I've seen minor injuries taken care of, and the patients are basically just swooped away and it's back to the serene esthetics."

At other similar theme parks, policies regarding the use of local paramedics evidently are more relaxed. At Walt Disney World in Florida, for example, a spokesman says the park does use paramedics, although, "they don't come right into the park."

Clearly, the scream of ambulance sirens, at least to some theme park officials, definitely disrupts the public aura of a wonderland.

Dr. G. Edward Pendray, a former editor of *Public Relations Journal,* offered the following nine maxims in dealing with public opinion:

1 **The better they know you, the more they'll like you—providing you deserve it.** Organizations often feel that their poor image stems from a general lack of knowledge of their activities. Becoming better known means that liabilities as well as assets will be highlighted. So a firm that seeks the limelight must also accept the attendant responsibility.

2 **Change yourself. It's easier than changing the public.** The public will never change its thinking about you unless you, on your own, reform any questionable policies and practices.

3 **Speak the language of action.** If you want to be listened to, support your words with actions. Words, in themselves, are hollow.

4 **Weary not in well-doing.** Public opinion takes time to develop. Don't give up good programs if they don't meet with immediate public recognition. Give it time to build.

5 **Truth rides the storm; half-truth and falsehood blow away.** Always base public relations programs on truth. There simply is no substitute.

6 **Put your heart where your money is.** Money alone can't buy favorable public opinion. Back up your money with personal participation. The public will get the message.

7 **You may like cake, but you can fish better with worms.** You must tell your story in terms of the public's needs, and not your own. If you have an abstract idea to put across, bait the hook with human interest, not self-interest.

8 **People interest people most.** People want to hear about other people. They're less interested in a firm. Express things in terms of human interest.

9 **Watch that log—it may be a crocodile.** Clever or easy solutions rarely work. Before taking any public stand, an organization must thoroughly examine all the ramifications.[7]

Thoughtfully applying these rules before embarking on a campaign to influence public opinion can pay off in long-lasting benefits. Alternatively, ignoring them can cause decisive setbacks in the court of public opinion.

POLISHING THE CORPORATE IMAGE

Most organizations today and the people who manage them are extremely sensitive about the way they are perceived by their critical publics. In one nationwide survey of 100 top executives, more than half considered it "very important to maintain a good public image."[8]

That is not to say that some corporate managements today are reluctant to stick their collective neck out. As former General Motors executive John DeLorean described the executive thinking at his alma mater, "General Motors management feels that the corporation simply draws the lion's share of criticism. The best way to reduce this inevitable criticism, as top management sees it, is to keep a low, faceless profile."[9]

Ironically, in General Motors' case, the company was one of the first U.S. corporations to maintain a high-profile, "industrial statesman" approach to public affairs.* Indeed, few firms today can afford to keep a low profile.

Consider the following:

○ Procter & Gamble voluntarily recalled and permanently removed from the market its successful Rely tampons product, when it was suspected that Rely contained carcinogenic agents.

○ McDonald's reluctantly went public to defuse a quickly-spreading rumor that among the tasty ingredients in its patented hamburger were ground worms.

○ J. P. Stevens, the nation's second largest textile manufacturer, reluctantly agreed to reconsider its labor practices when a group of activists successfully focused national media attention on the firm's treatment of its employees.

○ New York City judges, smarting from attacks on their efficiency, integrity, and judgment, hired a public relations firm to improve their sagging image.

---

* Also, ironically, John Delorean was arrested in a 1983 blaze of publicity, for attempted cocaine smuggling.

○ Several of the nation's largest banks went public in opposition to the apartheid policies of the South African government after considering the merits of arguments raised by church groups about lending money to South Africa.

Most organizations today understand clearly that while it takes a great deal of time to build a favorable image for a corporation, it takes only one slip to create a negative public impression. In other words, the corporate image is a fragile commodity. Most firms also believe that a positive corporate image is essential for continued long-term success.

As Communications Director Ray D'Argenio of United Technologies has put it, "Corporate communications can't create a corporate character. A company already has a character, which communications can reinforce."[10] In the case of D'Argenio's own company, United Technologies distinguished itself largely through an aggressive and unique advertising campaign that dared to be different. "We didn't seek to dissolve into the mainstream of companies," says D'Argenio. "Rather, we wanted to be distinct." So successful was the United Technologies advertising campaign that few readers needed the corporate logo to remind them that the company was the sponsor of a simple yet novel series on subjects from creativity to proper language to the importance of the individual in society.

While every employee in an organization plays a part in shaping a firm's public image, the public relations department is technically responsible. A practitioner must realize that image—a function of a company's mission, objective, people, and performance—must be based on fact.

FIGURE 4-1. While many companies attempted to construct a differentiable corporate image through advertising, few succeeded as well as United Technologies, which kept its messages succinct, savvy, and sparkling.

SOURCE: A message as published by *The Wall Street Journal* by United Technologies Corporation, Hartford, Connecticut

**It's What You Do–
Not When You Do It**

Ted Williams, at age 42,
slammed a home run
in his last official
time at bat.
Mickey Mantle, age 20,
hit 23 home runs
his first full year
in the major leagues.
Golda Meir was 71 when
she became Prime Minister
of Israel.
William Pitt II was 24
when he became
Prime Minister of
Great Britain.
George Bernard Shaw was 94
when one of his plays
was first produced.
Mozart was just seven
when his first composition
was published.
Now, how about this?
Benjamin Franklin
was a newspaper columnist
at 16,
and a framer of The United
States Constitution
when he was 81.
You're never too young
or too old
if you've got talent.
Let's recognize
that age has little to do
with ability.

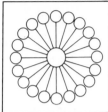

MINICASE
The loaned-out executives

One week before the nation's largest manufacturer of ball bearings, Laskow Industries, was to announce its revolutionary "Executive-On-Loan" program, the firm's public relations director called his staff together to discuss strategy.

The Laskow public relations problem was unique.

To begin with, the Executive-On-Loan program was the *first* in the country to "donate" a group of twenty-five corporate executives to full-time projects working with community agencies. Each executive would be given a management position in an agency in the city's ghetto areas. Laskow's top management had decided to devote $100,000 per year in support of this Executive-On-Loan approach.

The job of public relations was to structure the announcement of the program so that the firm reaped maximum public opinion benefits. The critical issue for the public relations staff was to determine how the program should be announced to reach key publics. The director felt that Laskow had three options:

1   To hold a press conference inviting the national media.
2   To give the story exclusively to the minority press.
3   To give the story exclusively to one specific news organization with an elite readership, such as *The New York Times.*

After thrashing the decision about, the director and her staff decided to choose option 3. Two days later, both Laskow's president and its public relations director hosted a private luncheon for the business editor of *The New York Times.* They explained the details of the program and invited the editor to write an exclusive story.

The next day, *The New York Times* carried a front page, three-column story about the Laskow program, including the president's photograph.

QUESTIONS
1   Would you consider the outcome a public relations success?
2   Why did Laskow choose option 3 to publicize its program?
3   What specific publics was Laskow hoping to influence by placing the story in *The New York Times?*
4   What might have resulted had Laskow chosen option 1?
    Option 2?
5   Do you think Laskow's public relations decision helped influence opinion about the company?

DISCOVERING THE CORPORATE IMAGE

Helping an organization discover its own special and distinct corporate image is an important function of the public relations practitioner. In getting to the roots of a particular corporate image, the practitioner must ask the following basic questions:

What is the firm's present corporate image? How does the public perceive the company? Does this perception differ with that of management? Often, research turns up significant discrepancies.

For example, one computer company, which prided itself on its frequent communication with Wall Street analysts, was surprised to learn that it was perceived by analysts as "pushy."

In another example, a food chain that considered its new menu to be up-to-date discovered that anyone under forty still thought of the firm as "old and stodgy."

One public utility, active in community affairs, was amazed to discover that few in the community appreciated the full extent of the firm's public service activities.

FIGURE 4-2. *Corporate logos: Instant identification.* These corporate logos are so identifiable that one glance tells what companies they are: the Chase Manhattan Bank octagon, the Prudential rock, the Hartford deer, and the Blue Shield snake. As previously mentioned, U.S. Steel spent millions to develop its modern trademark, USS. Xerox's problem is that its name and logo are so widely used that it must fight a continual battle to have the name treated as a proper adjective with a capital X rather than a verb with a lower-case x.

What corporate image does the firm want?   An organization can't be all things to all people. One department store might decide, for instance, that its market is the upper-middle class. Another store might shoot for an even more elite market. Still another might wish to project the image of a discount merchant, servicing the less well-to-do. Before an organization can take action in achieving a new corporate image, it must first decide the specific kind of image it wishes to attain.

How do the company's various entities—products and/or services—affect the image of the company? Does this vary by audience?   Many times, a company's divisions, subsidiaries, or products will have a completely different image than the rest of the firm. Often this is a good idea, but sometimes it isn't. Specifically, if a firm wishes to be looked upon as a consistently high class/high quality operation, a profitable yet low-class/low quality area within that corporation might be detrimental to the overall corporate image. This is the kind of tough issue with which an organization must grapple if it wishes to convey a cohesive corporate image among all of its parts. Then too, different audiences associated with different elements of an organization may perceive the firm's image to be something completely different from other audiences who deal with other organizational elements. Often, this is exactly what the organization wants.

What must a firm do to win a new corporate image?   Often, the process starts with changing the internal "culture." The company's procedures might need revision. Product lines might require reexamination. If the firm truly wishes to change, corporate philosophies might have to be shaken. Sometimes the very name of the company needs to be changed to shed an old image and don a new one.

Clearly, the most important aspect in image-building is that all members of the organization work together to establish sound policies and promote solid performance. If the various voices of the organization are unified, if the messages of the organization's different parts are the same, and if the operations of the firm are positive, then the goal of achieving a new corporate image can be attained.

THE CORPORATE IMAGE AT MOBIL OIL

The serious energy shortages of the mid-1970s and the subsequent skyrocketing oil prices created a groundswell of negative public opinion directed toward the nation's largest oil companies. A traditionally closed-mouthed group, the oil companies were momentarily caught off guard by the barrage of media accusations.

Each of the so-called "seven sisters" chose a different manner of responding to the criticism. Some opened up to the public their side of the story. Others began massive defensive advertising. Still others began sponsoring public affairs programs on television.

Mobil Oil did all these things and much, much more; it came out swinging in every direction (Figure 4-3). First, it sponsored a series of feisty ads on the opposite-editorial ("op-ed") pages of major newspapers, offering its own opinion about energy, the need to accumulate capital in society, and the role of business generally.

FIGURE 4-3. *Mobil materials.* Among the arrows in Mobil Oil's public relations quiver were these op-ed advertisements, which weekly noted the company's viewpoint on matters from national energy policy to the importance of profits in society; "Observations" columns, which editorialized on economic and energy-related issues; cartoons, which mainly poked fun at bureaucrats; and sponsorship of public affairs television programs, a more "soft-sell" approach.
SOURCE: © 1975 Mobil Oil Corporation. Used with permission.

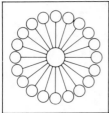

MINICASE
The peripatetic profile

In the early days, the public image of Bupkis Iron and Steel couldn't have been better.

Everything that President "Happy" Helen Sylvia touched turned to gold. Major acquisitions were consummated. Sales and earnings mushroomed. Orders piled in. Most of the credit, deservedly, was heaped on "Happy" Helen Sylvia.

For her part, "Happy" Helen basked in the limelight. She talked to anyone and everyone willing to listen and take notes. Her face graced all the trade journals. The *Wall Street Journal* devoted a front-page story to her. Everything was rosy for "Happy" Helen and Bupkis Iron and Steel.

At which point the economy fell out of bed. The auto companies cut back on their orders. Iron and steel products were less in demand. Foreign competition started flooding the American marketplace. For two years, Bupkis' sales and earnings took a nose dive.

Through it all, Helen hid. She avoided the press, refused interviews, and did not want to talk about the company's problems. *Low profile* were the watchwords at Bupkis during this period; Helen absolutely forbid any of her colleagues to discuss publicly what was going on.

When the economy bottomed out and began its trek upward, "Happy" Helen emerged from her cocoon. Bupkis rebounded. Sales started up again. Earnings looked good. The time had come, Helen reasoned, to hold a major press conference to signal the turnaround.

Arrangements were made, reporters invited, and company executives briefed for the full disclosure that was Helen's objective. But *The New York Times* didn't make it. Neither did the *Wall Street Journal. Forbes* and *Business Week* said they couldn't attend. Even *Iron Age,* which generally made most industry functions, couldn't spare a body.

"Why?" pondered a saddened "Happy" Helen, as she surveyed the empty room. "Why?"

QUESTION
Why?

It then sent key executives to cities around the country to appear on over 100 talk shows, news broadcasts, and radio call-in programs to explain its side of the energy crisis.

It sponsored a series of energy-related cartoons for newspapers. It created and placed a series of editorial columns, called *Observations,* again discussing the

FEATURE

The name game: a "new look" for the corporate image

Walter P. Margulies, president of Lippincott and Margulies, probably said it best: "The nostalgic and the quaint have no place in the world of corporate identity."[11]

Margulies should know. Together with a handful of other design consultants, he has helped a growing number of U.S. corporations change their names, their trademarks, and their "communications looks" in order to keep up with a changing society. As previously mentioned, corporate identity consultants have become lucrative factors in the communications agency marketplace. In 1981 alone, 572 organizations changed names, including 257 banks.

Sometimes such corporate identity consultants point out obvious incongruities between a firm's traditional logo and its more recent

activities. For example, RCA was advised to get rid of its fox terrier mascot, Nipper, in light of its involvement with advanced missile technology and the space program. Curiously, the company first adopted and then

The new Nipper

implications of the energy situation. It channeled millions of dollars into the sponsorship of public affairs programs such as "Masterpiece Theatre" on the public broadcasting network. And whenever it found itself misenterpreted by a story in the media, it lashed back.

Mobil's corporate image offensive was unprecedented. As *Fortune* magazine somewhat dourly admitted, "Few organizations of any kind can rival Mobil in the artfulness and sophistication with which it presses its opinions, whether it is advocating a national energy policy, resisting congressional proposals to end vertical integration in the oil industry, or championing the cause of mass transit."[12]

The cornerstone of Mobil's public relations thrust was its op-ed advertising campaign. Ironically, the ads rarely mentioned the company's service stations or its products. Rather, they emphasized corporate issues: the free enterprise system, energy conservation, and the importance of profits. Mobil's clear intent in sponsoring this kind of bold, aggressive, full-scale campaign was to speak out in defense of its interests, the interests of the oil industry, and what it perceived to be the national interest.

Mobil's decision to disavow the low profile and to speak up for its beliefs was criticized by some as throwing money away in a counterproductive effort that only served to antagonize critics. Indeed, research on the Mobil program was inconclusive

rejected the advice, choosing to restore in 1978 its famous trademark. More often, as in the case of U.S. Steel Corporation, the consultants suggest a new graphics approach adopted after thee years of planning, testing, market research, and self-analysis. (Figure 4-2 shows various company logos, including U.S. Steel.) Frequently, the consultants suggest name changes for specific reasons.

Here are some examples.

International Utilities, a billion-dollar conglomerate based in Philadelphia, realized that investors thought of it primarily as a utility—even though it had grown to a business that ranged from trucking to shipping to the production of macadamia nuts. After a thorough study of possible names, the company became *I.U. International.*

United Aircraft, a traditional supplier of flight products, had expanded into other industrial and commercial spheres such as electric power generation and transmission, laser technology, and marine propulsion.

Consequently, it decided to become *United Technologies Corporation* to more accurately reflect its new identity.

Perhaps the granddaddy of all corporate identity programs was the $110 million name change undertaken by the Standard Oil Company of New Jersey to become *Exxon* on all its signs, stationery, and pumps.

Why do firms go to the trouble of changing their names? There is no one answer. Some do it because of a change in their product mix. Others do it because they want their name and logo to more accurately convey their idea of the firm's image. (Occasionally, however, it is difficult to understand why a company would adopt a name reminiscent of alphabet soup—for example, the MBPXL Corporation!) Others adopt new names to keep up with the times. Still others do it because it just seems to make sense; as one executive of New York's First National City Bank put it when his company changed its name, "Everybody calls us Citibank anyway, so we thought we might as well make it official."

in terms of its success in changing public opinion about big oil companies. Nonetheless, Mobil's outspokenness helped convey a corporate image of a profitable company, committed to the free enterprise system, and confident enough to represent and defend that system in the public arena.

BEWARE: THE TRAPS OF PUBLIC OPINION

Analyzing public opinion is not as easy as it looks.

Once a company wins favorable public opinion for a product or an idea, the trick is to maintain it. The worst thing to do is sit back and bask in the glory of a positive public image—that's a quick route to image deterioration.

Public opinion is changeable, and in assessing it, communicators are susceptible to a number of subtle yet lethal traps:

Cast in stone. This fallacy assumes that just because public opinion is well established on a certain issue, it isn't likely to change. Not true. Consider an issue like women's liberation. In the early 1960s, people laughed at the handful of women raising a ruckus about equal rights, equal pay, and equal treatment. By the early

1970s, women's liberation pervaded every sector of our culture, and nobody laughed. In the space of a decade, public opinion about the importance of this issue had shifted substantially.

Gut reaction.   This fallacy assumes that if management feels in its corporate "gut" that the public will feel strongly in a certain direction, then that must be the way to go. *Be careful;* some managements are so cut off from the real world that their "knee jerk" reactions to issues often turn out to be more "jerk" than anything else. One former auto company executive, perhaps overstating the case, described the problem this way: "There's no forward response to what the public wants today. It's gotten to be a total insulation from the realities of the world." In any event, management's instincts in dealing with the public may be questionable at times. Generally, gut-reaction judgments should be avoided in assessing public opinion.

General public.   As noted, there's no such thing as the general public. Even the smallest public can be subdivided. No two people are alike, and messages to influence public opinion should be as pointed as possible rather than scatter shot. Sometimes individuals might qualify as members of publics on both sides of an issue. In weighing the pros and cons of lower speed limits, for example, many people are both drivers and pedestrians. So categorizing them into one general group can be a mistake.

Words move mountains.   Perhaps they do, sometimes; but public opinion is usually influenced more by events than words. For example, in 1979, nuclear power foes lacked a solid political base until an accident at Pennsylvania's Three Mile Island plant rallied public sentiment against the proponents of nuclear power.

Brother's keeper.   It's true that most people will rise up indignantly if their fellow person has been wronged. But they'll get a lot more indignant if they feel they themselves have been wronged. In other words, *self-interest* often sparks public opinion. An organization wishing to influence public opinion might be well advised to initially ask: "What's in this for the people whose opinion we're trying to influence?"

Figuring out the flows and ebbs of opinion is always tricky, but attempting to harness it is often worth the risk. Its power remains one of the most awesome elements in our democracy.

THE PUBLIC'S PERCEPTION OF PUBLIC RELATIONS

Most practitioners would probably say that few of their fellow citizens know very much about the field. An even greater number would probably argue that generally, public relations has a pretty rotten name among nonpractitioners.

However, according to certain survey data, they'd be wrong on both counts.[13] As these data reveal, more than half the population has at least a general idea of what the field is all about. Compared to similar professionals, such as those in advertising, practitioners are judged more ethical, more concerned with the public welfare, and are thought to be more useful to society.

An earlier 1974 study revealed that most people have a high opinion of the *purposes* of public relations. Only 18 percent believe practitioners are hired mainly "to make organizations look better than they are." By and large, at least according to this research, the public seems to think practitioners spread useful information in the public interest.

Here are the 1981 questionnaire results (in percentages of the total polled):

1   Many people today work in what can be called the *communications industry.* Here is a list of some of the major fields of work within that industry. We'd like to know how clear an idea you feel you have of the kind of work people in those fields do. Do you feel you have a pretty clear idea, just a general idea, or know very little about the kind of work they do?

	Clear Idea	General Idea	Little Idea	Don't Know
People in the press (TV and newspapers)	21%	45%	29%	5%
People in advertising	20%	39%	34%	6%
People in public relations	15%	36%	41%	8%
People in magazine publishing	12%	34%	46%	8%
People in book publishing	11%	31%	50%	9%

2   Now we'd like your impressions of the kind of people who work in just a few of the fields. Here's a list of words and phrases. Would you call off all those that fit your impression of people in advertising? In public relations? In the press?

	Advertising	Public Relations	Press
Intelligent	43%	41%	50%
Concerned with the public welfare	8%	28%	31%
Dishonest	17%	6%	8%
Ethical	6%	11%	16%
Slick	34%	14%	10%
In it more for the money than anything else	42%	16%	13%
Ambitious	43%	33%	39%
Hard working	30%	32%	45%
Perform a useful function in society	22%	32%	49%
None of them (vol.)	1%	1%	1%
Don't know	11%	19%	11%

3 Thinking now just about public relations people, here is a list of reasons why organizations have been said to hire public relations people. Which two or three of those reasons do you think are the *main* reasons that most organizations hire public relations people?

a. To provide the press and the public with information about their organizations.	57%
b. To keep the management of the organizations they work for informed about the public's interests and concerns.	46%
c. To represent the public's interests within their organizations to insure that the public doesn't get overlooked.	27%
d. To keep their organizations out of trouble with the government, the public, and other groups, by identifying potential problems before they become serious.	27%
e. To whitewash things that are bad about the organizations they work for and try to make them look good.	18%
f. To think up stunts and gimmicks and hire pretty girls to get publicity for their organizations and what they do or sell.	11%
g. To make deals and payoffs to get out of trouble with the law, or to prevent legislation that will adversely affect their organizations.	6%
None.	1%
Don't know.	14%

ONE STEP AHEAD OF PUBLIC OPINION

Influencing public opinion remains at the heart of professional public relations work. Perhaps the key to realizing this objective is anticipating or keeping ahead of trends in our society.

Anticipating trends, of course, is no easy task. In the 1980s, major forces seem to be at work that potentially could have a dramatic impact on public opinion. Among them:

○ Accelerated technology.
○ Satellite television advancements.
○ A climate of mediocrity.
○ The sexual revolution.
○ A universal sense of entitlement.
○ A growing concern for big government.
○ Decline in U.S. supremacy.

Many such trends will be in conflict with one another. Some will be ephemeral, others longer-lasting. Most will have to be scrutinized, analyzed, and evaluated by organizations in order to deal more effectively with the future.

As public relations counselor Philip Lesley has pointed out, "The real problems faced by business today are in the outside world of intangibles and public attitudes.[14] To keep ahead of these intangibles, these public attitudes, and these kernels of future public opinion, managements will turn increasingly to professional public relations practitioners for guidance.

CASE STUDY
The tragedy of Love Canal

A heartless corporation dumped toxic chemicals in Love Canal, then walked away from the problem, leaving behind a neighborhood full of victims.

Advertisement for *Reason* magazine in *The Washington Monthly,* June 1982.

Love Canal was a tragedy, pure and simple. The story began as a community relations dilemma and gradually mushroomed into a national public relations nightmare, which dramatically influenced public opinion about chemical wastes and waste sites.

Here, in some detail, is the chronology of events of Love Canal.

1910	Visionary John Love digs Love Canal to create electricity, but project is abandoned in light of a better, competitive project, Niagara Falls.
Early 1940s	Hooker Chemical, a wholesale chemical company with no consumer franchise, buys Love Canal as a potential site to dispose of wastes at its Niagara Falls plant.
1942	Hooker completes the legal transactions to commence dumping of what ultimately amounts to approximately 21,800 tons of company waste into Love Canal.
1942–1951	Following standard operating procedures, Hooker dumps its chemical wastes into the Canal, covering the waste with layers of clay. Other wastes besides those from Hooker also are dumped into the Canal. In light of the soil characteristics of the area as well as the sparse population surrounding the Canal, it constituted an excellent dumping ground for the chemicals.
1952	Niagara Falls Board of Education insists that Hooker sell the land adjacent to the Canal to construct a school.
1953	Hooker, under pressure, sells the property to the Board for $1. The School Board agrees to assume "all risk and liability." Hooker engineers advise the Board that the clay cap encasing the dump site must not be disturbed. However, the Board allows a highway to be built over the southern tip of the site, leases some of the land for development, and allows the soil to

be removed for landfill. Finally, the School Board votes to construct a school next to the Canal. As part of this project, foundations are dug for homes, risking penetration of the Canal's clay cover.

1954 In removing 3,000 cubic yards of fill from Love Canal, an architect reports hitting "a soft spot in the ground, which turned out to be a drain-filled ditch trench, which gave off a strong chemical odor." Upon further investigation, the excavator makes contact with a pit filled with chemicals. He immediately stops work.

1955-1957 The new school building adjacent to the Love Canal opens its doors to 500 students. Meanwhile, thousands of cubic yards of soil are moved from the top of the Canal in order to grade the surrounding area. Among the only modifications is the movement of the location of the kindergarten playground so as not to interfere with chemical deposits.

1957 Hooker publicly—and strongly—warns the community, through local newspaper ads, about the potential dangers of Love Canal. Nonetheless sewers are dug at the Canal, penetrating the clay cover for the first time. The Hooker warnings quickly are forgotten.

1958 Children, playing on the landfill area of Love Canal, contract chemical burns from exposed residues on the surface of the Canal. Hooker, wishing to avoid legal repercussions, privately warns the School Board again.

1968 The New York State Department of Transportation rips into the Canal at the southwestern end during construction of a new expressway.

1976 Niagara Falls experiences record rains that pour into the by-now *opened* Love Canal, forcing large quantities of chemicals up and out into the community. Such lethal chemicals as tolurene, leachate, and 3-4-5-T or "Agent Orange" are liberally dumped into neighborhood basements. People begin to become increasingly concerned about the dangers of Love Canal.

Hooker proposes to pay one-third of an estimated $850,000 cleanup bill, but the city fails to come up with the balance, and the plan is aborted. Also in 1976, the U.S. Congress passes the Resources Conservation and Recovery Act, the first cradle-to-grave tracking system for hazardous waste.

1978 Reporter Michael Brown begins reporting on problems at Love Canal in the *Niagara Gazette*. The Love Canal Home Owners Association is formed to bring attention to the chemical waste problems. The Home Owners Association alleges that area children have contracted birth defects because of the chemical wastes of Love Canal. Governor Hugh Carey, running for reelection, seizes the issue and vows that the state of New York will buy the 85–90 homes in the Love Canal area and evacuate all residents to hotels until the Love Canal problem can be resolved.

1979   In rapid succession, Hooker plants around the nation become lightning rods for controversy:

In White Springs, Florida, the Hooker plant is found to be sending phosphate piles into the land, killing fish and fowl.
In Lathrop, California, Hooker reportedly dumps waste into an open pit, which contaminates ground water and allegedly leads to the death of a dog.
Hooker's Montague, Michigan plant reportedly allows chemical waste to seep into the White River leading directly to Lake Michigan.
And in Niagara Falls itself, another Hooker plant allegedly dumps wastes into Bloody Run Creek, causing illnesses to local residents similar to those reported around Love Canal.

1979   Hooker, after observing a general policy of silence on the advice of legal counsel, decides to become more public. Up until now, Hooker has shunned the limelight, perhaps believing that it has no legal liability for Love Canal-related problems and therefore has no responsibility to "go public." However, with the name Love Canal now synonomous with images of poisoned water, deformed babies, and negative public opinion toward chemical dumping, the company decides to change its tune.

It hires a respected public relations agency, Daniel J. Edelman, to help launch an extensive public relations offensive. It creates an internal Issues Group, to deal with Love Canal-related concerns. It authors "white papers" and "Fact Line" pamphlets to clarify the facts about Love Canal. It also appoints a senior Environmental Ombudsman to help organize the company's response to environmental problems. And it keeps its employees much more aware of company positions and actions. Indeed, bumper stickers begin appearing in Upstate New York bearing a picture of a Hooker hardhat with the legend "I work for Hooker and am proud of it." Obviously encouraged by the settlement of a suit with the Michigan Attorney General over its Montague, Michigan plant, Hooker decides to allow its president to be interviewed by reporter Mike Wallace on the CBS network show, "60 Minutes." This proves to be a serious mistake. Although the interview lasts two hours, in the eight-and-a half minutes that make the air, the president is barbecued. When Wallace produces a personal letter to the president intimating that the "Lathrop Plant is a time bomb," the shocked executive replies (before 40 million Americans) "I've never seen that before." After the show, Hooker cries foul and prepares its own 15-minute rebuttal tape.

1980   In April, the State of New York files a $365 million lawsuit against Occidental Petroleum, Hooker Chemical Company, and Hooker Chemicals & Plastics Corp. accusing them of responsibility for the Love Canal problems.

On May 17, the Environmental Protection Agency (EPA) holds a press conference to release the results of a preliminary genetic study showing chromosome damage in 11 of 36 Love Canal residents tested. The private laboratory that performed the tests for the EPA acknowledges that the preliminary findings are not definitive. Hooker reconfirms its concern for the health and well-being of all residents of the Love Canal community and calls for an immediate follow-up of the EPA report by a scientifically-sound study.

On May 21, President Carter declares a state of emergency in the Love Canal area, paving the way for the evacuation of up to 710 families. Eight days later, a New York State Assembly task force issues a report that claims the U.S. Military had dumped dangerous wastes in the Love Canal and that the government's dumping began before Hooker first used the property. The federal government denies the charges. Finally in 1980, the U.S. Congress establishes a "Superfund," under which petrochemical producers are taxed with a special assessment to clean up abandoned hazardous waste disposal sites nationwide.

1982   The EPA issues a definitive report on Love Canal, concluding that Hooker effectively had contained the central dump site and that in terms of toxic chemicals, the zone around Love Canal was as habitable as the rest of the Niagara Falls area.

In an editorial, *The New York Times,* opining on the EPA's 1982 finding, summarized that after four years of "incomplete, misleading or erroneous scientific information," the residents of Love Canal—and indeed the public-at-large— "have paid a heavy price for the confusion."

The editorial concluded, "The first lesson of Love Canal turns out to be very much like that of Three Mile Island: such complex situations must be handled, above all, with credibility."

Rightly or wrongly, the term "Love Canal" had passed into common usage as a symbol of corporate indifference to the hazards of chemical wastes, much as "Watergate" became a generic term for government corruption. With most of the public now acutely aware of the dangers—real or perceived—in disposing of hazardous wastes, the tragedy of Love Canal had clearly taken its toll on public opinion.

QUESTIONS

1   How would you rate Hooker's handling of Love Canal? Did the reality jibe with the perception?

2   What do you think Love Canal did for the reputation of Hooker Chemical?

3   Would the company have been wise to expand on its 1976 proposal to pay one-third of the cleanup bill for Love Canal?

4 If you had been Hooker's management in the late 1970s, would you have heeded legal advice to maintain a low profile in the face of criticism about Love Canal?

5 Would you have recommended that Hooker come out of its low profile closet by agreeing to the "60 Minutes" interview?

6 Did the fact that Hooker was a wholesale rather than a retail company with no "trade name to trade on" help or hinder it in dealing publicly with Love Canal?

7 Does it surprise you that in the spring of 1982, Hooker's parent decided to change the company's name from the Hooker Chemical Company to the Occidental Chemical Company? Why not?

For further information on the Love Canal case, consult Eric Zuesse, "Love Canal: The Truth Seeps Out," *Reason*, February 1981; "Notoriety Makes Love Canal a Symbol Which Hooker Treats as a Local Issue; Classic Case of Legal Facts vs. Public Feeling," *PR Reporter*, Vol. 23, No. 35, Sept. 8, 1980; "The War of Words at Love Canal," *The New York Times*, July 17, 1982, p. 18; and A. J. Carter, "Niagara Families Battle Illness," *Newsday*, April 30, 1979.

NOTES

1 Walt Seifert, "Our Highest Court: Public Opinion," *Public Relations Journal*, December 1977, p. 24.

2 Cited in Edward L. Bernays, *Crystallizing Public Opinion* (New York: Boni & Liveright, 1961), p. 61.

3 Boyle as cited in Harwood L. Childs, *Public Opinion: Nature, Formation, and Role* (Princeton, N.J.: Van Nostrand, 1965), p. 15.

4 Leon A. Festinger, *A Theory of Cognitive Dissonance* (New York: Harper & Row, 1957), p. 163.

5 Edward M. Block, "How Public Opinion Is Formed," *Public Relations Review*, III, no. 3 (Fall 1977).

6 John Andrew, "Disneyland's Way of Dealing With Injuries Is Questioned," *The Wall Street Journal*, 25 March 1982, pp. 1, 42.

7 G. Edward Pendray, "PR Folklore," *Public Relations Journal*, October 1970, p. 20.

8 "Image Is a Priority to 53% of Executives Surveyed," *The Wall Street Journal*, 23 July 1981.

9 J. Patrick Wright, *On A Clear Day You Can See General Motors* (New York, N.Y.: Avon Books, 1980), p. 279.

10 Ray D'Argenio, Speech at Communications Executive of the Year Luncheon, sponsored by Corpcom Services, Inc., 10 December 1981.

11 Cited in Stewart Alter, "Margulies Advises Companies to Start Modern," *ANNY*, 13 August 1976, p. 15.

12 Irwin Ross, "Public Relations Isn't Kid-Glove Stuff at Mobil," *Fortune*, September 1976, p. 106.

13 Research based on a random interview sample of 1,999 *Roper Reports*, no. 18-5 (New York: The Roper Organization Inc., May 1981). Used by permission.

14 Philip Lesly, "How the Future Will Shape Public Relations And Vice Versa," *Public Relations Quarterly*, Winter 1981-82, p. 7.

SUGGESTED READING

Anshen, Melvin. *Managing the Socially Responsible Corporation.* New York: Macmillan, 1974.

Bernays, Edward L. "Public Dissatisfaction With Institutions," *Public Relations Quarterly,* Summer 1981, p. 15.

Bowman, Lewis, and Boynton, G.R. *Political Behavior and Public Opinion.* Englewood Cliffs, N.J.: Prentice-Hall, 1974.

Cantril, Hadley. *Gauging Public Opinion.* 1947. Reprint. Port Washington, N.Y.: Kennikat Press, 1971.

"Corporate Image Check List," *Public Relations Journal,* April 1982, p. 50. A listing of key questions that the professional communicator, creating an ongoing communications strategy for an organization, must answer.

Domhoff, G. William. *Who Rules America?* Englewood Cliffs, N.J.: Prentice-Hall, 1968.

Erikson, Robert J., and **Luttberg, Norman.** *American Public Opinion: Its Origin, Contents and Impact.* New York: John Wiley and Sons, 1973.

Free, Lloyd A., and **Cantril, Hadley.** *The Political Beliefs of Americans: A Study of Public Opinion.* New Brunswick, N.J.: Rutgers University Press, 1967.

Gallup, George. *The Sophisticated Poll Watcher's Guide.* Princeton, N.J.: Princeton Opinion Press, 1973.

Hanson, James, and **Abelson, Herbert I.** *Persuasion: How Opinions and Attitudes Are Changed.* 3rd ed. New York: Springer Publishing, 1976.

Johnston, David C-H. "Communicating Your Social Role," *Public Relations Journal,"* December 1981, pp. 18–19. A comparison between a company's social role and its economic mission.

Lane, Robert E., and **Sears, David O.** *Public Opinion.* Englewood Cliffs, N.J.: Prentice-Hall, 1964.

Lerbinger, Otto. *Designs for Persuasive Communications.* Englewood Cliffs, N.J.: Prentice-Hall, 1972.

Lesley, Philip. "How the Future Will Shape Public Relations—and Vice Versa," *Public Relations Quarterly,* Winter 1981–82, pp. 4–8.

Lippmann, Walter. *Public Opinion.* New York: Harcourt Brace and Co., 1922. Reprint. New York: Macmillan, 1965. Still a classic.

Margulies, Walter P. "Back to Fundamentals," *Public Relations Journal,* April 1982, pp. 50–51. The public relations professional has the primary responsibility for vigilance over the corporation's image.

Mitchell, Malcolm G. *Propaganda, Polls,* and Public Opinion: Are the People Manipulated? Englewood Cliffs, N.J.: Prentice-Hall, 1977.

Monroe, Alan D. *Public Opinion in America.* New York: Dodd Mead, 1975.

Nie, Norman; Verba, Sidney; and **Petrocik, John R.** *The Changing American Voter.* Cambridge, Mass.: Harvard University Press, 1976.

Nolan, Joseph T. "Protect Your Public Image with Performance." *Harvard Business Review,* March/April 1975, pp. 135–42.

Nowling, J.R. "The Professional's Way," *Public Relations Quarterly,* Winter 1981–82, pp. 21-22.

Ronson, Ralph L., and **Fine, Gary Alan.** *Rumor and Gossip: The Social Psychology of Hearsay.* New York: Elsevier North-Holland, 1976.

Simon, Raymond. *Public Relations Concepts & Practices,* Grid Publishing, Chapter 5.

Simon, Rita, ed. *Public Opinion.* Chicago, Ill.: Rand McNally, 1974.

Simons, Herbert W. *Persuasion: Understanding, Practice, and Analysis.* Reading, Mass.: Addison-Wesley, 1976.

Steinberg, Charles S. *The Creation of Consent.* New York: Hastings House, 1975.

Welch, Susan, ed. *Public Opinion: Its Formation, Measurement, and Impact.* Palo Alto, Calif.: Mayfield, 1975.

A PROFESSIONAL
COMMUNICATOR

The public relations practitioner is, at base, a *professional communicator.* The practitioner, above all others in the organization, must know how to communicate. This knowledge sets the public relations professional apart from others.

Fundamentally, communication is a process of exchanging information, of imparting ideas, and of making oneself understood by others. It also, importantly, means *understanding* others in return. Indeed, understanding is critical to the communications process.

If one person sends a message to another who disregards or misunderstands it, then communication hasn't taken place. But if the idea received is the one intended, then communication has been accomplished.

Stated another way, a boss who sends subordinates mountains of memos isn't necessarily communicating with them. Different people may interpret the same messages differently. If the idea received is not the one intended, then the sender, rather than communicating, has done little more than convert personal thoughts to words. And there they lie.

5
Communi-
cations:
The Backbone
of Public
Relations

While all of us are endowed with some capacity for communicating, the public relations practitioner must be better than most. The effectiveness of public relations professionals is determined, in large measure, both by their own ability to communicate and by their ability to counsel others on how to communicate.

Before a public relations practitioner can earn the respect of management and become a trusted advisor, he must demonstrate a mastery of many communications skills—writing, speaking, listening, promoting, and counseling. Just as the controller is expected to be an adept accountant and the legal counsel expected to be an accomplished lawyer, so too is the public relations professional expected to be an expert communicator.

This ability is the key to success, although expertise in management and marketing also contributes. Thus it's essential that practitioners understand the theory behind interpersonal communications; in other words, *how* people communicate.

THE S-E-M-D-R APPROACH

Among the most traditional models of communication is the S-M-R approach. This model suggests that every communication begins with a sender or source, who issues a message to a certain receiver, who then decides what action to take, if any, on the communication. To this model must be added the element of feedback, because good communication involves dialogue between parties.

The model has been modified to include additional elements: an encoding stage, in which the source's original message is translated and conveyed to the receiver; and a decoding stage, in which the receiver interprets the encoded message and takes action. This evolution from the traditional model has resulted in the S-E-M-D-R method, which illustrates graphically the role of the public relations function in modern communications—for both the encoding and the decoding stages are of critical importance in communicating any public relations message.

THE SOURCE

The source of a message is the central person or organization doing the communicating. The source could be a politician giving a campaign speech, or a school announcing curriculum changes, or even, as one superior court judge in Seattle ruled, a topless go-go dancer in the midst of gyrating.*

While the source usually knows how she wants the message to be received, there is no guarantee she'll be understood that way, by the receiver. In many cases— a public speech, for example—the speaker is relatively limited in how much he can influence the interpretation of the message. While he can use gestures or voice tone or volume to convey special importance to certain remarks, whether or not the audience understands what he wants them to may ultimately depend on other factors, particularly the encoder.

---

* According to the judge, topless go-go dancing is protected by the First Amendment because it is a way of communicating. "I don't have to like the message to say that she has a right to convey the message," the judge ruled in dismissing charges against a topless dancer ("Dancing to the First Amendment," *Forbes,* 15 September 1972, p. 23).

THE ENCODER

What the source wants to relate must be translated from an idea in her mind's eye to a communication. In the case of a campaign speech, for example, a politician's original message may be subject to reinterpretation by at least three independent encoders:

1 The politician may consult a *speech writer* to help put ideas into words on paper. Speech writers become encoders in that they must first clearly understand the politician's message and then effectively translate that message into language that the audience will at least understand and, hopefully, accept.

2 Once the speech is written, it may be further encoded into a *news release*. Here, the encoder—perhaps a different individual than the speech writer—selects what he believes to be the most salient points of the speech and provides them to media editors in the form of a news release.

3 An editor may take the news release and retranslate it when reporting to the voters, the ultimate audience of the politician's message.

Thus, the original message in the mind of the politician has been "massaged" three separate times before it ever reaches the intended receivers. Each time, in all likelihood, the particular encoder has added new subjective shadings to the politician's original message. Indeed, the very act of encoding depends largely on the encoder's own personal experience.

Words. Words are among our most personal and potent weapons. Words can soothe us, bother us, or infuriate us. They can bring us together or drive us apart. They can even cause us to kill or be killed.

Words mean different things to different people, depending on their backgrounds, occupations, education, and geographic location. What one word means to you might be dramatically different from what the same word means to your neighbor.

Take the word *cool.* In American vernacular, if a person is cool, then he's good. If a person is not so hot, than he's bad. So *cool* is the opposite of *not so hot.* But wait a minute; *not so hot* must also be the opposite of *hot.* Therefore, in a strange and convoluted way, cool equals hot!

$$cool \neq not\ so\ hot$$
$$hot \neq not\ so\ hot$$
$$cool = hot$$

The point is that the words used in the encoding stage have a significant influence on the message conveyed to the ultimate receiver. Thus the source must depend greatly on the ability of the encoder to accurately understand and effectively translate the message to the receiver.

THE MESSAGE

Once an encoder has taken in the source's ideas and translated them into terms she can understand, the ideas are then transmitted in the form of a message. The message may be carried by a variety of communications media: speeches, newspapers, news releases, press conferences, broadcast reports, and face-to-face

Ron Nessen is executive vice president and managing director of Marston and Rothenberg Public Affairs, Inc., the Washington office of Robert Marston and Associates. He spent five years as an editor with United Press International before joining NBC-TV in 1962. During 12 years as a network correspondent, Mr. Nessen covered news from Washington, New York, London, Mexico City, and the Far East. Mr. Nessen joined the Marston organization in 1980, after serving as President Gerald Ford's Press Secretary. He is the author of *It Sure Looks Different From The Inside,* a book about his experiences in the White House, and a novel, *The Hour,* about a TV news magazine show.

What did you think of public relations practitioners as communicators when you were a network news correspondent?

Due to the nature of my NBC assignments, I dealt mainly with public relations practitioners for political candidates, government agencies, and the military. I found them generally helpful in providing basic information, arranging interviews, assisting with logistics details, etc., although my attitude was the standard journalist's skepticism.

Did your attitude change once you became press secretary?

Yes. Going from being a news recipient to a news dispenser, I discovered that public relations practitioners have far more useful information to pass on to reporters than the reporters realize. Journalistic skepticism, in fact, sometimes hinders the amount of news transmitted.

meetings. Communications theorists differ on what exactly constitutes the message. Here are three of the more popular explanations:

1 The **content** is the message. According to this theory, far and away the most popular, the content of a communication—what it says—constitutes its message. According to this view, the real importance of a communication—the message— lies in the meaning of an article, or in the intent of a speech. Neither the medium

What was your biggest problem in dealing with the press as President Ford's Press Secretary?

In a general sense, my most significant challenge was trying to reverse the hostile and suspicious attitude that had grown up between the White House and the press corps as a result of the Vietnam and Watergate periods. More specifically, my most frustrating problem was trying to devise a communications plan that would reverse President Ford's public image as a bumbler.

How did your attitude about the press change as a member of the Ford White House?

I reluctantly concluded that the press needed to report in greater depth, particularly when focusing on complex economic, energy, and foreign policy issues. Viewed from inside the White House, some of the news coverage appeared to me to be shallow.

What is your assessment of the state of business coverage by television journalists?

Again, my major complaint has to do with lack of depth. While most major newspapers and magazines have a staff of economic and business experts among their reporters, television correspondents tend to be generalists. The resut is business coverage on television that too often dwells on the trivial, the obvious, or the unsavory. Given its impact on American life, business is probably the most *under*covered institution by television.

What advice do you give subordinates in dealing with the media?

I tell subordinates that the three most important words I know in dealing with the media are: "plan . . . plan . . . plan." Dealings with the press must be prepared for as carefully as meetings with stockholders, creditors, regulatory agencies, legislative bodies, or boards of directors. I urge subordinates to be open and truthful with reporters, to tell *their* story *their* way, and—most of all—not to think of the media as the enemy.

What, in your view, is the general perception of public relations professionals among journalists?

Privately, many journalists perceive public relations professionals as helpful resources for information and guidance. Unfortunately, the public attitude of some journalists is indicated by their use of the derogatory expression "flacks."

Was yours a difficult transition from journalism to public relations?

It was an easy transition, for two reasons. First, President Ford had an enlightened, open, and relaxed attitude toward reporters. He liked them, and they liked him. He was determined to repair the strains between the White House and the press which had developed during the administrations of his two predecessors. Second, I considered the goal of my job as White House communicator namely, to fully inform the American public about the complex issues facing our nation.

through which the message is being communicated nor the individual doing the communicating are as important as the content.

2   The **medium** is the message. Other communications theorists—the late Canadian professor Marshall McLuhan being the best known—argue that the content of a communication is not the message at all. According to McLuhan, the content is less important than the vehicle of communication.

McLuhan's argument stems largely from the fact that many people today watch television. He said that television is a "cool" medium; that is, someone can derive meaning from a TV message without working too hard. On the other hand, reading involves hard work to fully grasp the idea; as such, newspapers, magazines, and books are "hot" media. Furthermore, McLuhan argued, a television viewer can easily become part of that which he is viewing. In other words, the television program becomes the message, and the viewer himself becomes part of the "content" of that message. Indeed, the steady barrage of TV film on fighting in Vietnam in the 1960s and Lebanon in the 1980s probably greatly influenced public opinion about the wars. These nightly broadcasts became, for many viewers, antiwar messages.

One direct outgrowth of this "medium is the message" theory was development in the mid-1970s of the "friendly team" style of local television news reporting. Often called the "Eyewitness" approach, this format encouraged interaction among TV newscasters in order to involve viewers as part of the news team "family." McLuhan felt that the spread of this format throughout the country was an example of local media serving "as service environments that envelop the entire life of man and society in totally new conditions."[1] While many have scoffed at McLuhan's somewhat mystical approach to communications, many politicians have taken the professor's words to heart.

3 The **man** or **woman** is the message. Still other theorists argue that it is neither the content nor the medium that is the message, but rather the speaker.

For example, Hitler was a master of persuasion. His Minister of Propaganda, Josef Goebbels, used to say, "Any man who thinks he can persuade, can persuade." Hitler practiced this self-fulfilling communications prophesy to the hilt. Feeding on the perceived desires of the German people, Hitler was much less concerned with the content of his remarks than with their delivery. His maniacal rantings and frantic gestures seized public sentiment and sent friendly crowds into a frenzy. In every way, Hitler himself was the primary message of his communications.

Today, in a similar vein, we often refer to a leader's *charisma*. Frequently, the charismatic appeal of a political leader may be more important than what that individual says. President John F. Kennedy, for example, could move an audience by the very inflection of his words. Hubert Humphrey could bring a group to its feet, merely by shaking a fist or raising the pitch of his voice. And Ronald Reagan was second to none in communications skill. In such cases, the source of the communication has been every bit as important as the message itself. Simply, "the man" has contributed in a major way to "the message."

THE DECODER

After a message has been transmitted by an encoder from a source and before action can be taken, it must be decoded by a receiver.

This stage is like the encoding stage in that the receiver takes in the message, translates it into his own common terms, determines its usefulness, and then takes action. Obviously language again plays a critical role. The decoder must fully understand the message before acting on it; if the message is unclear or the decoder is unsure of its intent, there's probably little chance the action taken by the receiver will be the one desired by the source. Messages must be in common terms.

FEATURE
The language of the 1980s

In the 1980s, words took on new and curious meanings.

Depending on one's line of work, field of study, or geographic base, some American vocabulary became almost indecipherable to the unschooled ear. To wit, these examples of current terminology from a statesman, a computer analyst, and a resident of Los Angeles' San Fernando Valley:

The Statesman[2]

"to caveat"—to qualify one's statement

"to context it"—to put one's remarks in context

"post-hostage-return-attitude"—the attitude prevalent in the United States after the return of the Iranian hostages

"epistemologicallywise"—relating to epistemology

The Computer Analyst[3]

"bit"—the smallest piece of a binary number

"bomb"—a piece of computer equipment that ceases to function

"chip"—tiny wafer of silicon or equally tiny complete circuit

"down"—inoperative

"glitch"—a source of malfunction

"handshaking"—sending one line of data and asking the receiving machine if the line was received intact before sending another line

"real time"—operating in response to "real world" events occurring at the same time the information is being processed

"wetwear"—organic hardware that conceives of and writes the abstract software that drives the mineral hardware (e.g., the human brain)

The Valley Girl[4]

"grody old grownups"—out-of-touch older people

"airhead"—a total dummy

"to the max"—the ultimate

"total bummer"—a very bad thing

"freaking out"—going crazy

"space cadet"—a weird person

"tubular"—awesome, almost too great to be described

"yucky"—yucky

Little wonder, with vocabulary like the above, many people in the 1980s—particularly the nonbureaucrats, non-computer-sensitized, and "grody old grownups" among us—have a tough time understanding exactly what's going on.

A good example of this problem, although apocryphal, is the following exchange between the Bureau of Standards of the U.S. Department of Commerce and a New York plumber. The plumber had written the Bureau that she had found hydrochloric acid fine for cleaning drains and asked the Bureau if the acid were harmless for this purpose.

Washington replied, "The efficacy of hydrochloric acid is indisputable, but the chlorine residue is incompatible with metallic permanence."

The plumber, unfamiliar with scientific terminology, replied that she was mighty glad that the Bureau agreed with her.

The Bureau answered with a note of alarm: "We cannot assume responsibility for the production of toxic and noxious residues with hydrochloric acid and suggest that you use an alternate procedure."

The plumber replied that she was happy that the Bureau still agreed with her.

The Bureau finally exploded, "Don't use hydrochloric acid, you jackass. It eats the hell out of your pipes."[5]

PERCEPTION

How a receiver decodes a message depends greatly on that person's own perception. How an individual looks at and comprehends a message is a key to effective communications.

Remember that everyone is biased; no two people perceive a message identically. Personal biases are nurtured by many factors, including stereotypes, symbols, semantics, peer group pressures, and especially in today's culture, the media.

1 *Stereotypes* are rampant in our culture. Everyone lives in a world of his or her own stereotypical figures. Ivy Leaguers, Midwesterners, feminists, bankers, politicians, PR types, and thousands of other characterizations cause people to think of certain specific images.

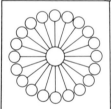

MINICASE
The erring encoder

To swing the election, Representative Rankle desperately needed the votes of the Booneville Urban League Chapter.

"It's up to you, Herby," Rankel confided to his chief speech writer, Herbert Mertz, "to make sure we get the key points across in my speech tonight to let 'em know I'm up-to-speed on the issues—particularly campaign contributors and busing."

On the former issue, Rankle was well aware of rumors that his campaign was subsidized by several underworld figures. On the latter issue, Rankle knew that the recent burning of a school bus had created an enormous amount of tension among Urban League members.

"Make it clear, Herby, that I am against revealing the names of campaign contributors because I believe in protecting an individual's right to privacy, and I don't intend to focus the spotlight of public attention on those who have contributed to my campaign. I wouldn't like it if I were they, and I know they wouldn't either. As far as busing, let 'em know that I know the debate is a hot one, but that I simply will not accept the old, pat answers. I intend to seek revolutionary solutions on this issue of heated debate."

Public figures, for example, are type cast regularly. The "dumb blonde," the "bigoted blue collar worker," and the "shifty used car salesman" are the kinds of stereotypes our society—and particularly television—perpetuates.

And consider the plight of the poor businessman. As syndicated cartoonist Charles Saxon wrote, "The big problem for cartoonists is that most businessmen don't fall into comfortable stereotypes."[6] Nonetheless, cartoonists are obligated to come up with stereotypes. Therefore, the ubiquitous businessman caricature is middle-aged, looks like he might be posing for a portrait in *Fortune*, rarely relaxes his facial features, and, in general, looks overblown and pompous.

Like it or not, most of us are victims of such stereotypes. For example, research indicates that a lecture delivered by a person wearing glasses will be perceived as "significantly more believable" than the same lecture delivered before the same audience by the same lecturer without glasses. The stereotyped impression of people with glasses is that they are more trustworthy and more believable.

2 *Symbols* too are determinants of perception. The clenched fist salute, the swastika, and the "thumbs up" sign all leave distinct impressions with most people.

Marshalled properly, symbols can be used as effective persuasive elements. The Statue of Liberty, the Red Cross, the Star of David, and many others have been used traditionally for positive persuasion. Indeed, in the Falkland Islands

---

"I understand perfectly, Congressman," Mertz smiled. "Just leave the writing to me."

Regrettably for Rankle, that's exactly what he did. It took only a few sentences to convince the audience that Rankle was either crooked, stupid, incredibly insensitive, or a combination of all three. Here's how his speech began:

I intend tonight, ladies and gentlemen, to address two subjects that I know are on your minds—campaign contributors and busing.

On the former, I believe quite strongly that a candidate should never disclose the names of his campaign contributors. I know my contributors well, and I know that such disclosure would frankly embarrass them. Were I in their position, I have no doubt that I, too, would be embarrassed!

Let me be equally frank on school busing—indeed, another *burning* issue in our community. Neither I nor my running mates will sit by when others call for the old and pat solutions. We will fight their every move. In a word, my colleagues and I are *revolting!* Tonight, I intend to prove it.

QUESTIONS

1 Where did Mertz go wrong in encoding the message?

2 Might Mertz have felt his encoding was correct?

3 How many faux pas did Rankle commit in his remarks?
   Might they be enough to cost him the election?

4 Had you been Mertz, what would you have done differently in encoding the speech?

FEATURE

The medium is the message—especially if you want to be president

At least since the days of the famous Nixon-Kennedy debates, and maybe earlier, television has played a major role in presidential politics.

While presidents Kennedy, Johnson, and Nixon are all generally credited with using television to help sell their ideas, more recent presidents have refined the use of the medium to an even greater degree.

President Gerald Ford, although not particularly known for his public speaking presence, did quite well on television. He should have, for he rehearsed assiduously for TV appearances. He took great pains to practice his lines, his gestures, and even his movements in front of the cameras. The result, according to one veteran *New York Times* reporter, was "a cool performer." While he did not have the grinning assurance of President Kennedy, he did not strain and perspire like President Nixon."[7] All-in-all, Ford was a very effective user of the television medium.

The first true television president was Jimmy Carter, who after taking his oath of office, strolled down Pennsylvania Avenue all the way to the White House, every step captured by the TV cameras. In addressing the nation, Carter sometimes took the unprecedented step of dressing casually—in cardigan sweaters rather than dark suits—to subtly convey a TV message of confidence, informality, and the very antithesis of the "imperial presidency."

Many in the press were clearly confused by Carter's use of symbols and images to enhance his popular appeal. As one veteran journalist put it, "All of us of the pre-TV era who were brought up on the English language look for words and think in terms of language. That creates problems and misunderstandings for us; to us it [symbols] looks like a stunt and may not come off too well. But not to other people."[8]

If President Carter was good at using television, President Ronald Reagan was great. Clearly, he had the most experience in the medium, having begun as a movie actor and later as a media spokesman for General Electric. Just how good Reagan was on television was underscored in the first Carter-Reagan televised presidential campaign debate in 1980. While Carter the incumbent was austere and formal, Reagan the challenger was loose and relaxed. So much so that after the debate, Reagan strolled across the stage to warmly extend his hand to his opponent—in full view of millions of TV watchers.

After his election, President Reagan used television to maximum effectiveness. In his first year, he appealed to the nation to "write your Congressman" in support of his initial budget-cutting measures. The "nation" responded, and Congressional offices were deluged. Later, when forced to reverse economic direction and institute a tax increase, Reagan again turned to television to seek the support of his fellow taxpayers. Again, he got it.

The intelligent use of television by Ford and Carter and the overwhelmingly effective use of the medium by Reagan indicate that future presidential aspirants and office-holders will likely continue to regard the TV medium as a primary delivery vehicle for communicating their messages.

invasion by Argentina in 1982, England used the symbol of its Queen—and the honor of the Crown—to promulgate public sentiment behind the war effort to win the islands back. And later that same year, a disgruntled antinuclear activist tried to hold the Washington Monument "hostage" as a symbol of a threatened nation.

3   *Semantics,* or the science of what words really mean, also influences perception. Public relations professionals largely make their living by knowing how to use words to effectively communicate desired meanings. Occasionally, this is tricky, since the same words may hold contrasting meanings to different people. Especially vulnerable are popular and politically-sensitive phrases such as "capital punishment," "law and order," "liberal politician," "right winger," and on and on until . . . You reach the point where the Oakridge Mall in San Jose, California demanded that the gourmet hamburger restaurant on its premises, whose logo depicted a smiling hamburger with a monacle and top hat, either change its "suggestive name" or leave the mall. The restaurant's name? "Elegant Buns."

The point is that semantics must be handled with extreme care, because language and the meanings of words change constantly. Good communicators always will consider the consequences of the words they plan to use *before* using them.

4   *Peer groups,* too, have a great bearing on perception. For example, in Solomon Asch's famous study, students were asked to point out in progression the shortest of three lines:

A   _____

B   _____

C   _____

Although line B is obviously shortest, each student in the class except one was told in advance to answer that line C was shortest. The object of the test was to see how many times the one student not "set up" would agree with his peers. Results generally indicated that, to a statistically significant degree, all students, including the unknowing one, chose answer C. Peer pressure prevails.

5   The *power of the media* to influence perception—particularly as an agenda setter or reinforcement mechanism—is also substantial. A common complaint among lawyers is that their clients cannot receive fair trials because of pretrial publicity leading to preconceived verdicts among potential jurors who read newspapers and watch television.

In one famous case in Georgia, an army officer was put on trial in 1970 for the savage killing of his wife and two children. The officer claimed that he was innocent and that a "band of hippies" had stabbed him and killed his family. Georgia newspapers publicized the case extensively, running photographs of the soldier and commentary about the circumstances of the murders. Neither the soldier nor his lawyer would talk to the press.

A random telephone survey of Georgians, taken a week before the trial, indicated that most people thought the soldier was guilty. Several weeks later however, the Army dropped murder charges against him when it couldn't make a

Words can get you in a lot of trouble. Public relations professionals, who deal on a daily basis with the arcane province of semantics, must be aware of and sensitive to the potential explosiveness of words and phrases. The following random list of culturally-biased phrases is a case-in-point. How many of these can you adequately define? Are you sure?

○ over-the-hill
○ cool your jets
○ Catch-22
○ out-of-the-blue
○ go for it
○ stonewall it

○ a "10"
○ we blew it
○ a boo-boo
○ get it together
○ jive turkey
○ shot full of holes
○ flipped out
○ circular file
○ deep six it
○ put it on the back burner
○ the bottom fell out
○ wasted
○ workhorse
○ taking care of business (TCB'ing)

case. (Ironically, nine years later the man was convicted of murder for the three killings, subsequently released, and then, in 1982, found guilty on appeal.)

The point remains that people often base perceptions on what they read or hear without bothering to dig further to elicit the facts of a situation. While appearances are sometimes revealing, they are often most deceiving.

THE RECEIVER

You really aren't communicating unless someone's at the other end to hear and understand what you are saying.

This problem is analogous to the old conundrum of the falling tree in the forest: Does it make a noise when it hits the ground if there's no one there to hear it? Regardless of the answer, communication doesn't take place if a message doesn't reach the intended audience of receivers and exert the desired effect on those receivers.[9]

Sometimes, while the message might reach the correct receivers, their perceptions of that message might not be what was intended. Here are two examples:

When [the former addict] . . . was put in charge of an antidrug addiction program, [he] . . . commented that 'the first thing that impressed me . . . was that people were talking about things I didn't understand. *Values*—that's what you get when you go to Macy's; *Principles*—those are the guys in schools; *Conviction*—that's what you get when you go in front of a judge.'

When it was first offered, only four girls enrolled in a special female weight lifting course at the University of California. The following semester, the instructor changed the course name from "Weight Lifting" to "Weight Training for Figure Control." A short time later, 200 women had enrolled in the course.[10]

Even if a communication is understood clearly, there is still no guarantee that the action triggered will be the desired one. In fact, a message may trigger several different effects. For instance:

1 **It may change attitudes.**   This goal, however, is a very tough task and rarely happens.

2 **It may crystallize attitudes.**   This outcome is much more common. Often a message will influence receivers to take actions they might have already been thinking about taking but needed an extra push to accomplish. For example, a receiver might want to contribute to a certain charity, but seeing a child's photo on a contribution canister might crystallize the attitude sufficiently to trigger action.

3 **It might create a wedge of doubt.**   Communications can sometimes force receivers to modify their points of view. A persuasive message can cause receivers to question their original thinking on an issue.

4 **It may do nothing.**   Often, communications result in no action at all. When the American Cancer Society waged an all-out effort to cut into cigarette sales, the net impact of the communications campaign was hardly significant. Receivers may have been exposed to the anticigarette messages and understood them, but they did not feel compelled to act.

FEATURE

Are you sure you saw what you thought you saw?

First, read the sentence below:

FINISHED FILES ARE THE RE-
SULT OF YEARS OF SCIENTIF-
IC STUDY COMBINED WITH THE
EXPERIENCE OF MANY YEARS.

Now, count the F's in the sentence. Count them only once and do not go back and count them again.

Question
How many F's are there?

Answer
There are six F's. However, because the capital F in OF sounds like a capital V, it seems to disappear. Most people perceive only three F's in the sentence. Our conditioned, habitual patterns ("mental blocks") restrict us from being as alert as we should be. Frequently, we fail to perceive things as they really are.

FEEDBACK

Feedback is critical to the process. A communicator must get feedback from a receiver to know what messages are or are not getting through and how to structure future communications. Occasionally feedback is ignored by professional communicators, but this is always a mistake.

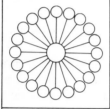

MINICASE

The awkward acquisition

Negotiations for Centurion's new acquisition had been lengthy and complex. But finally, they were near completion. The company, on the advice of legal counsel, decided to announce the negotiations to the public. Since the idea to announce was counsel's, Centurion decided to let the lawyers write the news release.

However, the release was incomprehensible. In five pages, it listed all technicalities, conditions, and disclaimers associated with the acquisition.

"This release," smiled an obviously pleased chief counsel, "will satisfy everyone at the SEC."

Maybe, but the media became very confused. Even though the story was a major one, many editors passed it up because they couldn't understand the release's awkward sentence structure and terminology. Even worse, three reporters tried to rewrite the story and in doing so, made major errors—in one case confusing Centurion with the firm to be acquired.

Customers and shareholders flooded the Centurion switchboard. A good many brokers, confused by the original release, called for clarification. Other brokers, not given the benefit of the original release, moved to sell their stock after perusing the trade press reports.

What should have been a positive Centurion announcement had become a public relations nightmare.

QUESTIONS
1 What was Centurion management's big mistake?
2 Why should the attorneys not have written the release?
3 Do you think the lawyers were right that the press release would have "satisfied" the SEC? The shareholders? The press? The public?
4 In light of the extraordinarily technical nature of the intended acquisition and the concern about SEC interpretation of the release, what procedure should have been followed in writing it?

Whether the objectives of a communication have been met can often be assessed in such ways as amount of sales, number of letters, or number of votes obtained.

If individuals take no action after receiving a communication, feedback must still be sought. In certain cases, although receivers have taken no discernible action, they may have understood and even passed on the message to other individuals. This person-to-person relay of received messages creates a two-step flow of communications—first vertically from a particular source and then horizontally from interpersonal contact.

The targeting of opinion leaders as primary receivers is based on the hope that they will distribute received messages horizontally within their own communities. In any event, it's always a sound investment to research how many people saw a message, how many agreed with it, how many acted on it, and what action they took. Without measurement, an organization is communicating blindly.

BARRIERS TO COMMUNICATIONS

When the communications network breaks down, misunderstandings, friction, and inconveniences arise. Breakdowns often are caused by numerous communications barriers.

Frequently, complex ideas are difficult to communicate and even more difficult to understand. Messages also occasionally are distorted if they are transmitted through many layers of an organization. Moreoever, communications in the public media are limited by time and space constraints as well as elements of timing, selectivity, and even censorship. A case in point was the war in the Middle East in 1982 between Israel and the Palestinian Liberation Organization in which Israeli officials scrutinized each piece of American film footage, broadcast, and print copy before it was beamed back to the United States.

Many other barriers to communication arise in specific situations; emotional reactions, superstitions, physical conditions, prejudices, indifferences to the message, and so on can all cause serious problems in delivering messages. Unless the senders of messages or their public relations advisors are aware of the existence of such barriers, the ability to communicate effectively may be impaired.

THE TRICK TO COMMUNICATING EFFECTIVELY

There really is no trick to effective communication. Other than some facility with techniques, hard work and common sense are the basic guiding principles.

Naturally in every case, communication is less important than performance. Organizations must back up what they say with action. Slick brochures, thoughtful speeches, intelligent articles, and a good press may capture the public's attention; but in the final analysis, the only way to obtain continued public support is through proper performance.

FEATURE
A good communicator's dozen

1   Plan communications carefully, keeping the audience clearly in mind.

2   Know the purpose of the communication in advance of communicating.

3   Be flexible in adapting to the audience, content, purpose, and medium.

4   Don't expect complete understanding the first time around; always follow-up.

5   Keep aware of nonverbal overtones, such as the mood of the audience, the flow of the presentation, the graphics, and the delivery of the message.

6   Be a good listener.

7   Remember that actions speak louder than words.

8   Neither overestimate nor underestimate the receiver's knowledge of the topic.

9   Avoid words that antagonize the audience.

10 Give reasons that are meaningful to the receiver, not the source.

11 Get feedback.

12 Work on building a long-term relationship with receivers.

CASE STUDY
Chantilly laced

The Chantilly National Bank and Trust Company not only was the most well-known bank in Chantilly, Ohio, it also was the most prominent financial institution in the entire midwest.

For many years, Chantilly's earnings steadily improved, until the Ohio bank had become fully competitive with its money center rivals on the East and West Coasts. The reputation of Chantilly's management was impeccable. Its people were coveted by other institutions. Its systems, controls, policies, and programs were the envy of the banking industry.

Its communications approach was equally laudable. Chantilly's philosophy was one of "proactive" communications. It regularly held briefings with the media and securities analysts. Its management gave frequent speeches and held leadership positions in industry associations. Management also took strong public positions on industry issues. Chantilly was active politically and known for its outspokenness in standing up for what it believed in.

That's why in the summer of 1983, it came as a shock to most industry analysts when Chantilly National Bank began experiencing problems.

○ First, a front-page article in *The Wall Street Journal* suggested that Chantilly's loan portfolio was in rocky shape. The article pointed out that a number of prominent credits in the Chantilly portfolio were experiencing rough times.

○ The *Journal* article was followed by a number of major corporate bankruptcies, each of which seemed to announce Chantilly Bank as a primary lender.

○ The coup de grace occurred in the fall of 1983. A small, Texas bank, known widely for its hip-shooting policies on energy-related loans, declared bankruptcy. It was immediately revealed that a number of much larger banks had participated with the bankrupt Texas institution in lending to questionable energy companies. The most prominent bank among these larger lenders was Chantilly National Bank and Trust Company.

This particular revelation—about Chantilly's role with the bankrupt Texas bank—was the last straw. Immediately thereafter, Chantilly got "laced" by most of its key constituents.

The media, the analysts, the shareholders, the employees, and the public all clamored for clarification from Chantilly management. In the face of this firestorm of negative publicity, Chantilly was strangely silent.

Weeks passed, Chantilly's stock plummeted, but still the bank shunned making a comprehensive public explanation. Instead, it chose to issue cryptic press statements on the earnings impact of its problems. Finally, four weeks after the crisis reached its apex, Chantilly did a communications about-face.

○ First, senior Chantilly officials flew to New York City to meet with securities analysts in an effort to restore confidence in the bank. At the meeting, which was "off limits" to the media, the bank discussed specific problem loans in-depth. This disclosure was unprecedented in the banking industry. Most financial institutions firmly refuse to discuss particular details of proprietary customer relationships. And in this instance, Chantilly sought and received customer approval before doing so.

○ The next day, back in Ohio, the bank's chairman conducted a wide open press conference, reiterating in detail what the analysts had been told the day before about the bank's problem loans.

The immediate impact of the public relations turnabout was positive. The bank's stock, for the first time in a month, experienced a slight uptick. One journalist reported the bank had taken "the extraordinary step of inviting in a handful of reporters and revealing the skeletons of decimated corporations in its closets in an unusual exhibition of candor aimed at restoring its stature in the financial community."

Other reviews, however, were not as sanguine. Several analysts pooh-poohed the disclosures. "Certainly they haven't served to clarify things in my mind," said one. Said another, "I still think they're not telling the whole story."

Indeed, despite the excruciating lengths to which Chantilly went in detailing specific problem loans, in the days following the press conference, new corporate bankruptcy petitions were filed in which Chantilly was named as a creditor.

Nonetheless, Chantilly's communications mea culpa with the analysts and journalists did serve to take some of the public heat off the bank. When asked why the bank had not revealed its problems earlier, Chantilly's chairman cited an Ohio privacy law that legal counsel had advised "prevented the bank from making such disclosures."

As a macabre postscript (as if things weren't bad enough) in the midst of Chantilly's loan problems, the windows on the bank's new San Francisco office tower blew out in a freak storm, injuring pedestrians and causing a furor on the coast.

Concluded a harried Chantilly public relations officer, "Who would ever believe this?"

QUESTIONS

1 How would you rate the way Chantilly handled its communications in the face of its problems?

2 Had you been Chantilly's public relations director, what communications course would you have recommended that management take?

3 Do you agree with the timing of the analyst meeting and press conference to disclose Chantilly's problem loans?

4 What about the specific loan problems disclosed at the meetings? From what you know, do you think this was enough disclosure? Too much?

5 Again, if you were Chantilly's public relations director, how would you have responded to the suggestion by the bank's legal counsel that Ohio privacy law prevented you from comprehensively discussing your problems?

6 Now that the public relations damage has been done, what communications posture do you think the bank should adopt going forward?

NOTES

1 Marshall McLuhan, "Sharing the News, Friendly Teamness; Teeming Friendliness," brochure, McLuhan Associates and American Broadcasting Companies, 1971.

2 Former Secretary of State Alexander M. Haig, Jr. was quoted often for this kind of unique word choice, affectionately labeled "Haigspeak" or "Haigledygook". See "Why Haig Quit: Contexting It," *Newsweek*, 5 July 1982, p. 24.

3 The world of computers developed this kind of language all its own. See Don Ethan Miller, *The Book of Jargon*, (New York, N.Y.: Macmillan Publishing Co., Inc., 1981).

4 In 1982, an album by rock and roll singer Frank Zappa and his daughter, Moon, swept the nation. Called "Valley Girl," the record spoofed the language of the trend-obsessed teenagers of the San Fernando Valley suburbs of Los Angeles. See *"It's Like Tubular!" Newsweek*, 2 August 1982, p. 61.

5 Bertram R. Canfield and H. Frazier Moore, *Public Relations Principles: Cases and Problems* (Homewood, Ill.: Richard D. Irwin, 1973), pp. 67, 68.

6 Dom Bonafede, "Uncle Sam: The Flimflam Man?" *Washington Journalism Review*, April-May 1978, p. 67.

7 Clifton Daniel, "The New Ford Show: Smooth and Cool," *The New York Times*, 14 January 1975, p. 20.

8 Charles Saxon, "How to Draw a Businessman," *The New York Times*, 28 March 1982.

9 H. Zane Robins, vice-president and general manager of Burson-Marsteller Associates, remarks at a meeting of the American Management Association, Chicago, Ill., January 20, 1969.

10 John E. Cook, "Communication Criteria: Necessary and Effective," *Public Relations Journal*, January 1974, p. 31.

SUGGESTED READING

Asimov, Isaac. "The Electronic Revolution," *Public Relations Quarterly*, Spring 1982, pp. 4–5.

Berlo, David K. *The Process of Communication, An Introduction to Theory and Practice.* New York: Holt, Rinehart & Winston, 1960. Beginners in the study of communications will benefit from reading this book.

Bettinghaus, Erwin P. *Persuasive Communication.* New York: Holt, Rinehart & Winston, 1973.

Bleecker, Samuel E. and **Lento Ph.D., Thomas V.** "Public Relations In a Wired Society," *Public Relations Quarterly*, Spring 1982, pp. 6–12.

Brown, David S. "Barrier to Successful Communication: Part 1, Microbarriers," *Management Review* 64, no. 12 (December 1975): 24–29. Discusses how to overcome communication barriers.

Brush, Douglas P. "The New Technology," *Public Relations Journal*, February 1981, pp. 10–13.

Budd Jr., John F. "Credibility vs. 'Con' " *Public Relations Quarterly*, Spring 1982, pp. 13–14.

Burger, Chester. "The Edge of The Communications Revolution," *Public Relations Review*, Summer 1981, pp. 3–12. Predictions of how "the new communications technology" will change corporate America.

Coyle, Lee. "RSVP: The Ohio Bell Approach," *Public Relations Journal*, February 1981, p. 24.

Cramer, D. D., and **Wandling, W. A.** "New Approach to Effective Communications." *Cross-Reference*, November 5, 1975, pp. 8–10.

Forney, T. Michael. "The New Communication Technology," *Public Relations Journal*, March 1982, pp. 20–23.

Fraser, Edith A. "Association Public Relations: The State of The Art," *Public Relations Journal*, October 1981, pp. 18–21, 30. A description of several important trends occurring in the use of communications in the 1980s and their effect on public relations.

Goodman, Ronald and **Ruch, Richard S.** "In the Image of the CEO," *Public Relations Journal*, February 1981, pp. 14–19.

Haimann, Theo, Scott, William G., and **Connor, Patrick E.** *Managing the Modern Organization*, Boston: Houghton Mifflin, 1978, p. 41, Chapter 30.

Hakensen, David. "Creativity In A 'High-Tech' Mode," *Public Relations Journal*, March 1982, p. 29.

Hecht, Andrea Platt. "How to Bring Middle Management Into the Communication Process," *Public Relations Journal*, October 1981, p. 16.

Johnston, David C-H. "Communicating Your Social Role," *Public Relations Journal*, December 1981, p. 18.

Kahn, Charles. "Psycho-linguistics and Business Communications," *Journal of Systems Management* 26, no. 6 (June 1975): 22–25.

Keltner, John W. *Elements of Interpersonal Communication.* Belmont, Calif.: Wadsworth, 1970.

King, Stephen W. *Communications and Social Influence.* Reading, Mass.: Addison-Wesley, 1975.

Kopee, Joseph A. "The Communication Audit," *Public Relations Journal*, May 1982, pp. 24–27. A description of a communication audit: what it does, how to it, what it costs, and why it should be an essential part of internal and external communication plans and programs.

Lindaver, J. S. *Communicating in Business.* Riverside, N.J.: Macmillan, 1974.

Lloyd, L. *Communications and Intervention Strategies.* Baltimore, Md.: University Park, 1975.

Lund, Philip R. *Compelling Selling: A Framework of Persuasion.* New York: American Management Association, 1974.

McCallister, Linda. "The Interpersonal Side of Internal Communications," *Public Relations Journal*, February 1981, pp. 20–23. Most organizations monitor their formal communications, but little attention is given to person-to-person relationships. Here, the communications professional is given tips on how to improve internal communication.

Marston, John E. "A Strategy for PR Communications," *Public Relations Journal* 31, no. 9 (September 1975): 10.

Okun, Sherman K. "How to be a Listener." *Nation's Business* 63, no. 8 (August 8, 1975): 59–62.

Prestanski, Harry. "Human Information Processing In The Development And Implementation Of Public Relations Programs," *Public Relations Quarterly*, Summer 1981, pp. 16–20.

Rivers, William L., and **Schramm, Wilbur.** *Responsibility in Mass Communications.* New York: Harper and Row, 1969.

Robinson, Edward J., *Communication and Public Relations,* Columbus, Ohio: Charles E. Merrill, 1966.

"The New Public Relations," *Public Relations Journal*, January 1981, pp. 29–33.

Turnbull, Arthur T., and **Baird, Russell N.** *The Graphics of Communication.* New York: Holt, Rinehart & Winston, 1975. Describes the main elements of graphics communication and several new technological advances.

Williams Ph.D., Patrick R. "The New Technology and Its Implications for Organizational Communicators," *Public Relations Quarterly*, Spring 1982, pp. 15–16.

Wilson, John and **Arnold, Carroll.** *Dimensions of Public Communications.* Rockleigh, N.J.: Allyn and Bacon, 1976.

Yorks, L. "I Speak Your Language: Developing and Maintaining Effective Communication." *Data Management* 13 (September 1975): 34–35.

BEGINNING TO LISTEN

In the early 1980s, the Sperry Rand Corporation advertised a basic strength in a most unique and effective manner. "We Listen" was the company's simple yet profound theme.

Public relations professionals too have begun to "listen"—both inside and outside their organizations. Indeed, the element of "listening" has become an increasingly important part of the public relations practitioner's job.

Another name for "listening" in public relations work is *research,* particularly the kind that involves public opinions, attitudes, and reactions to the policies and practices of an organization. Not too long ago, the broad majority of practitioners contended that public relations work could not be measured because it was too creative and intangible. Today, however, the idea of measuring public relations work has steadily gained acceptance.[1]

It is understandable that research in the 1980s should begin to emerge as an important function of public relations. In an era of scarce resources, management wants facts and statistics from public relations professionals to show that their efforts contribute not only to overall organizational effectiveness but also to the bottom line. Consequently, each time a public relations program is proposed, it should be accompanied by a research scheme, preferably in the planning and development stages of the program. And while research will not necessarily provide unequivocable proof of a program's effectiveness, it will allow a means by which public relations professionals can add credibility to their own intuition.

6
Research

Paul H. Alvarez is chairman and chief executive officer of Ketchum Public Relations based in New York City. Mr. Alvarez joined Ketchum Public Relations in 1971 as an account supervisor in its Pittsburgh office. In 1973, he was named a vice president and subsequently became director of public relations for the Los Angeles office of Botsford Ketchum, a wholly-owned subsidiary of Ketchum MacLeod & Grove, Inc. In 1976, he was named a senior vice president-associate director of public relations. Two years later, he was named executive vice president. A year later, Mr. Alvarez became Ketchum chairman. Prior to joining Ketchum,

Mr. Alvarez had extensive experience in agency and corporate public relations work. A frequent university lecturer in public relations, he also serves on the public relations advisory board of the School of Journalism at the University of Florida.

How important is the function of research in public relations practice today?

Corporate management has been increasing its pressure and demands on public relations staffs and agencies to prove they do work. Communication research is a highly effective tool for convincing management that the public relations discipline has an important role to play in achieving corporate objectives. Research can demonstrate that public relations improves the company's effectiveness and contributes to the critical bottom line of profit. Research is now an important ingredient in planning, carrying out, and evaluating successful marketing communications programs.

Can you really measure public relations success?

For years, public relations has lagged behind advertising in its techniques to measure communication success or failure. Clippings and broadcast time are no longer true measures for the evaluation of public relations programs. As the time and money that is spent on public relations programs increases, practitioners are forced to provide quantitative facts and figures on their work. Several evaluation systems have been developed that address this crucial issue. James S. Tirone, public relation director-measurement for AT&T, has developed a system for evaluating and measuring the results of public relations programs. The AT&T system measures publicity placements as being positive, negative, or neutral in terms of the goals of the overall program. Here at Ketchum Public Relations, we have devised and are now implementing for our clients a computer-based measurement system called "The Ketchum Publicity Tracking Model," which evaluates public relations results on *both* a quantitative and qualitative basis. Public relations practitioners have made great strides to improve the measurement of the discipline and must continue to do so in the future.

What are the most popular research methods in the public relations field today?

There are primarily three methods of research that can be labeled most popular in use today: the survey, the focus group, and communication audits. The survey consists of the sample, the questionnaire, the interviews, and the analysis of results. Focus groups usually consist of eight to twelve people with a moderator encouraging in-depth discussion of a designated topic. The communication audit is one of the most important and widely-used types of research. Determining the target audience, addressing their concerns, and designing your message accordingly are necessary factors to successful public relations programming. An audit is designed to determine the status of a corporate relationship with its target audience, the concerns of that group, and what the corporation must do to improve that relationship.

What can a practitioner expect to derive from research?

Successful public relations programs begin with solid research. Research is crucial to the development and implementation of innovative programs. It helps the practitioner create the "big idea" that works. Research may serve to make public relations less amorphous and more clear to those with a lesser understanding of the discipline.

What do you say to a practitioner who challenges the necessity of research in public relations work?

Without research as your basis, you might as well not devote funds to a public relations program. The public relations discipline has moved out of the "bargain basement" in communications methods, and research is now a required aspect of any communications program. Without it, communicating client messages to the consumer is very difficult. Successful product publicity, without the knowledge of the target audience and its interests, is nearly impossible. Certainly it does not justify the funds allocated to the program.

What is the future of public relations research?

In the past, corporate public relations programs concentrated their time and money on reaching certain predictable audiences thought to be of the greatest importance to the corporation. Today, public relations research studies cannot make sweeping assumptions "thought to be" true about target audiences. Assumptions about consumer attitudes cannot be made solely on the basis of demographic characteristics. Lifestyle and psychographic variables are now accounted for in the development of the target audience portfolio. It is this change in research that has propelled public relations to the forefront of the total communications mix.

AN UNGLAMOROUS/DEMYSTIFIED PRACTICE

Research isn't a glamorous part of public relations, yet it is essential for effective communications. Traditionally it has not been practiced vigorously. One problem has been the number of exogenous factors that can influence a person's attitude toward an organization or idea. The dearth of research in public relations has been a source of concern to academic and practical research specialists in the field. Fortunately, in recent years research has begun to awaken from its serene state.[2]

Most people associate public relations with *conveying* information. While that idea is true, research must be the obligatory first step in any project. A firm must acquire accurate data about the publics, products, and programs with which it is concerned.

It's a difficult task to delve into the minds of others, whose backgrounds and points of view may be quite different from one's own, with the purpose of understanding why they think as they do. Research skills are partly intuitive, partly an outgrowth of individual temperament, and partly based on acquired knowledge. There is nothing mystifying about them.

Fundamentally, research involves recognizing and acting on the perceived needs of others. At its most complex stage, it may require charting past, present, and potential behavior patterns. Although we tend to think of research in terms of impersonal test scores, interviews, or questionnaires, they are only a small part. The real wisdom is in *using* research—knowing when to do what, with whom, and for what purpose.[3]

RESEARCH APPLICATIONS

Traditionally, public relations practice was based more on intuition and feeling than on analytical research. Properly applied research, however, can bolster public relations judgments by basing them on a more empirical foundation.

Most frequently, research may confirm assumptions about public opinion on a given issue, product, or company. Often, intuition may be accurate, with research serving to corroborate the validity of a company's communications thrust.

When limited information is available, research can help clarify issues. Attitudes are often fuzzy; people may say they *like* something without being specific about the particular characteristics they admire. Research probes deeper to determine what specifically about an issue or a product appeals to someone.

Research also can help position public relations efforts within a business framework. By tying such research to business goals, communications programs can be more specifically structured to complement a firm's line objectives.

For example, an organization whose news releases are used frequently by the local newspaper can't be certain without research whether the image conveyed by the releases is that which the organization seeks. By analyzing the news coverage, however, the firm can get a much clearer picture of the effectiveness of its communication. Such "content analysis" might be organized along specific criteria, such as the following:

○ **Frequency of Coverage**   How many releases were used?
○ **Placement within the Paper**   Did releases appear most frequently on page one or seventy-one?
○ **Messages Conveyed**   Did the releases used express the goals of the organization or were they simply informational in content?
○ **Editing of Releases**   How much did the newspaper edit the copy submitted? Did it materially change desired meanings?

Obviously, there is nothing mysterious about such content analysis. While this kind of research might seem simple, it can often reveal those facets of a public relations program that need to be modified to enhance the persuasiveness of an organization's communication.

COMMON OBJECTIVES OF RESEARCH

To make research meaningful, specific objectives must be set. Some common objectives in public relations research include:

Determining the public's basic attitudes.   To influence a group's opinion, an organization must understand the background and make-up of its audience. For example, the management of a large department store about to enter a rural community might be wise to first assess how residents feel about large stores in general. After knowing their feelings, it can attempt to win public support.

Finding the majority opinion.   Often, the loudest opinions are those of a vocal minority rather than the quieter *majority*. Listening to those who speak the loudest therefore may not accomplish a firm's objectives. In fact, it may even be counterproductive. Research helps unearth the public's true feelings.

Test marketing themes and media.   Public image or issue advertising campaigns are costly. It's good sense to test public response before spending money for a campaign. A series of "sounding-board sessions" might be held with knowledgeable leaders in a particular field or community. In-depth interviews with carefully selected subjects might be another alternative. Effectiveness can also be gauged by exposing the proposed promotional messages and media to representative public samples.

Determining the opposition's strength.   There are at least two sides to every issue. It is natural to want to strike back when attacked. But often, this strategy is counterproductive. For example, before a political candidate spends time or money on squelching the opposition's view, research should be applied to determine just how potent the issue is in the minds of the electorate.

Revealing potential trouble spots.   Research should be an ongoing process, whether or not problems exist. Continually updating research can reveal potential trouble spots, such as lingering labor unrest, concern over safety conditions, unhappiness with current communications channels, and dissatisfaction with certain products.

TYPES OF RESEARCH

Public relations research can be informal and formal. Professionals research informally every day, in preparing speeches, background memos, and news releases. Formal research is done on a less regular, more strategic basis. Typical activities include defining present levels of awareness and understanding of a product, identifying areas of insufficient information among audience segments, predicting the probable effects of a proposed course of action, and analyzing the effect of a planned expansion or diversification program.

Most research involves at least one of the following techniques: fact finding, opinion surveys, or motivational studies.

Fact finding consists primarily of reading and filing material that in any way relates to the industry or organization. The public relations department is the organization's nerve center and stores original surveys or research conducted by other sources, such as government or trade groups, newspapers, and industry. An increasingly popular type of fact-finding research is the *communications audit,* discussed later, which periodically monitors public relations program results against specific objectives.

Opinion surveys go beyond mere fact-gathering and attempt to identify what people think about a firm, its employees, or its products. Surveys attempt to expose real perceptions of a representative sample of publics.

A motivational study, or attitudinal research, explores in-depth why people feel the way they do. It attempts to reveal the bases of deep-seated attitudes. Interviewees are encouraged to talk freely and explain their viewpoints. Although fact-finding and opinion surveying are used more widely, motivational analysis presents a more scientific vehicle for probing public attitudes toward an organization.[4]

FACT-FINDING

Facts are the bricks and mortar of public relations work; no action can be taken unless the facts are known, and the fact-finding process must be continuous.

Most companies track references to them in the media. Some use elaborate *trend watching* units to monitor information that may be remotely related to the business of the organization. Such phenomena as population shifts, crop and weather projections, and cultural habits are followed to keep updated on changing public preferences.

This type of research begins with a "fact file," consisting essentially of the following data:

1 **Organization statistics,** such as the assets of the company, locations of the firm, number of people employed, and products produced.

2 **Charters and bylaws of the organization.**

3 **Publications of the organization,** such as news releases, annual reports, financial reports, speeches, advertisements, and brochures.

4 **Photographs,** especially of key executives and facilities.

5 **Biographies** of key current and former executives.

FEATURE

Consumerism at the crossroads: a public opinion research program for Sentry Insurance[5]

PROBLEM:

Coping with consumerism. American business has spent much time and money responding to consumerist demands. The American public has footed a large part of the "consumerism bill." Yet despite all the legislation and business activity, scarcely any information on the consumer movement has been available.

OBJECTIVE:

To provide the public and business community, as well as activists, legislators, and regulators with a definitive body of information on the consumer movement to learn what they believe it has accomplished, where they believe it has been a positive as well as counterproductive force, whether the views of activists reflect those of the public, and what direction the movement should take.

APPROACH:

Commission a sweeping national opinion research survey on the consumer movement, to provide the information and perspective needed for a more effective and reasonable approach to meeting consumer needs and consumerist demands. Develop a communications program to reveal the findings.

RESULTS:

1 *Washington Briefing*—A two-hour luncheon-briefing was attended by 175 senators, representatives, regulators, activists, etc. Copies of the survey were hand-delivered to each member of Congress.

2 *White House Briefing and Press Conference*—A White House press conference was attended by representatives from virtually all major news organizations.

In attendance were Sentry's chief executive and the consumer affairs advisor to the President.

3 *New York Press Conference*—Some 75 members of the national press and about 100 consumer affairs representatives attended. More than 1,300 newspaper and magazine articles appeared.

4 A corresponding *employee survey* produced almost a 100 percent response.

5 The *survey report* was mailed to 3,500 members of the business community the same day as the New York press conference. Sentry received over 50,000 requests for the survey report.

6 Major associations, such as the National Retail Merchants Association, devoted special segments of their annual conventions to a discussion of *Consumerism at the Crossroads* led by a senior Sentry executive.

7 Because of the importance of the survey, Sentry's chief executive was named *"Consumer Man of the Year"* by the Society of Consumer Affairs Professionals in Business.

8 An *attitude and awareness study* to measure the survey's impact found that 5 percent of the public, a very substantial number, had heard of *Consumerism at the Crossroads*.

As a postscript, the White House requested that the monograph on *Consumerism at the Crossroads* serve as a framework for an Executive Branch position paper on how further consumer legislation could better serve the public while making less onerous demands on business.

6 **Press clippings** from newspapers, magazines, and trade publications, as well as radio and television transcriptions that mention the firm.

7 **Associated literature** from trade unions, trade associations, and industry sources.

8 **Media lists** of key editors and journalists with whom the firm deals.

9 **Competitive literature,** including press coverage of competitors, as well as their reports, speeches, and brochures.

10 **Public opinion studies,** especially those pertaining to the organization and the industry.

11 **Pending legislation,** including pending bills and references to upcoming government hearings.

12 **Reference literature** about the company and the industry in particular, but also including national information and research services.

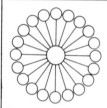

MINICASE
The leadership image

Joanne "Jo Jo" Klein didn't get to be head of the world's largest manufacturing company without a great deal of sharp, intuitive judgment. Klein's Robby Industries now ranks as the nation's top consumer products company.

Although most of Robby's success has been in toiletries, the company is ready to expand into health care products and detergents, among others.

Klein is adamant about keeping the Robby brand name tied "to each and every new product we introduce, regardless of the market." She reasons that because Robby occupies a "leadership image" in most of its current markets, consumers "will be more than willing to trust the Robby name whether it's on detergents or cologne."

Research, she believes would be of "minimal value," since Robby's image is so good and so well known "we are almost guaranteed of picking up a major share of the market regardless of what consumer market we're speaking of."

QUESTIONS

1 Why is Klein's view simplistic?
2 Is it necessarily true that Robby's "leadership image" will prevail in marketing foot powder as it does in marketing soap? Why not?
3 What could research in this case reveal that Klein may be overlooking?

FEATURE

Of computers, word processors, and databases: the brave new world of public relations research

Public relations, like most other fields, rapidly is approaching the day when a practitioner will research an article, speech, or news release in the comfort of her home or office, with instant access to worldwide databases, including those of universities, research organizations, governments, and her own organization's computerized files.

Up-to-date information will be available on almost any subject. And where once it took weeks to complete a research project, soon the same project will be completed in minutes, through the docile assistance of a computer terminal.

The day is rapidly approaching when the vast majority of public relations researchers will gather their material, write their articles, correct their syntax and grammar, switch paragraphs, add or delete sentences, and finally, produce perfect, finished, original copy without typewriters, typewriter paper, ribbons, carbon paper, correction fluid, or dirty hands.

The day of the computer, word processor, and database is upon us. And public relations research will reap the benefits.

Already, most large offices are moving toward word processing automation to handle information. Word processing equipment already has reduced many legal, business, and medical costs, for example, by automatically producing frequently-used forms and standard letters from memory units. In public relations work, manuscripts and releases can be produced on the keyboard-cathode ray tube (CRT) unit, easily edited, and printed out as many times as desired through the equipment's memory.

Instead of reproducing manuscripts only on paper, word processing equipment also permits their reproduction on magnetic tapes or discs, known variously as *floppy discs* or *data discs,* which already are accepted by many wire services.

Particularly important for public relations research are electronic data bases, which store vast quantities of information on current or historical subjects. Several data base vendors, in fact, access other specialized bases, not available to the public directly.

One such base is Lockheed's DIALOG, begun in 1972, which accesses nearly 150 data pools throughout the nation, dealing with social sciences, arts, humanities, business and finance, current affairs, mass media, and statistics of all kinds.

DIALOG accesses citations to articles and stories in more than 40,000 journals and

(Feature continues on pages 130 and 131)

THE COMMUNICATIONS AUDIT

An increasingly popular use of fact-finding research in public relations work is the communications audit. In essence, the communications audit analyzes an organization's communications, internal and/or external; it "takes a snapshot" of communication needs, policies, practices, and capabilities, assessing the current state of communications in the organization and suggesting improvements for the future.

magazines in as many as forty languages. Abstracts of many of these are available for immediate printout. Indeed, in many cases, this condensed information is all that the public relations researcher needs—although, upon request, complete articles usually are available to the user by mail.

Another similar system is Mead Data Central's NEXIS Information Retrieval System, which uses key words or phrases to find relevant articles in leading international journals. At a touch of a button, NEXIS delivers full texts of all articles.

Basically, there are two separate costs in using such computer research. First, each database has a fixed on-line fee for computer use. Second, a user must pay for the telephone service that delivers the information to him. In the case of NEXIS, for example, a $50 per month subscription fee is charged plus an average of $1.25 to $1.50 per minute for searches that average a few minutes in duration.

While there are literally hundreds of computer-based and other research services available to public relations practitioners, here is an additional short list of a few of the better known:

ERIC
% Dr. Albert Walker
Department of Journalism, Northern Illinois University
DeKalb, ILL. 60115
(815) 753-1925

This data bank, an agency of the U.S. Department of Education, may be accessed through data bank vendors as well as public and university libraries. Documents that qualify for input include policy manuals, speeches, research studies, student papers, and proceedings of professional meetings. An associated data bank for speech research is in Falls Church, Virginia.

FACTS ON FILE
460 Park Avenue South
New York, N.Y. 10016
(212) 683-2244

Annual subscription is $355 for this weekly digest and index of news. Information is summarized daily from leading U.S. and foreign periodicals, the publications of Commerce Clearing House, Congressional Quarterly, Congressional Record, State Department Bulletin, Presidential documents, and official press releases. Subject areas are as diverse as the news of the day.

FIND/SVP
The Information Clearing House
500 Fifth Avenue
New York City, N.Y.
(212) 354-2424

Works on a monthly subscription basis, $250 fee for one-time special projects; fee based on time involved and number of sources

Stated another way, communications audits are "benchmarks" against which future communications programs may be applied.

The scope of an audit depends entirely on the size and complexity of an organization's demands. Such audits make undeniable sense and probably should be conducted every several years to provide an organization with a fresh look at its communications program.

consuted. FIND has information in such categories as financial (interim and annual reports), general information, marketing, health care, and medical, chemical, transportation, and consumer packaged goods.

Information for Business
35 West 39th Street
New York City, N.Y.
(22) 840–1220

Minimum fee is negotiable; fees for special projects depend on the nature of the project. I is generally a custom-research organization.

Packaged Facts
274 Madison Avenue
New York City, N.Y.
(212) 532–5533

No set fees. Firm gives estimates in advance for special projects; has specialized services. Researches information on colorful and historical events for publicity use, does market research using published information, has back-dated clipping services.

The New York Times Information Service, Inc.
3 Park Avenue - 41st Floor
New York City, N.Y.
(212) 683–2208

Fees are charged on the time unit used (hours, minutes, seconds), and there is no set hourly fee. Must have a time-sharing computer terminal with telephone hook-up. The data bank contains information from *The New York Times* plus seventy other major publications, both national and international.

The Dow Jones News Retrieval Service
P. O. Box 300
Princeton, NJ
(201) 452–2000

Monthly fee is $50 with a one-year minimum subscription, plus hourly usage fee of $40. One must also have a time-sharing terminal that can be leased from Dow Jones or any equipment lessor. Contains information on about 6,000 publicly owned corporations, industry information on fifty categories and on twenty government regulatory agencies; information taken from the Dow Jones ticker, *Wall Street Journal*, and *The New York Times*. Information is stored for ninety days in most categories.

Among the better recent writings on the role of the new technology in public relations research are: A. E. Jeffcoat, "A Touch of Amazement," *Public Relations Journal*, May 1981, and George L. Beiswinger, "Database Update," *Public Relations Journal*, March 1982.

Basically, the communications audit methodology follows a standard research course in terms of the preparation of a questionnaire, its administration, the summary of responses received, and an evaluation of results. Subjects covered can range from the communications philosophy and goals of an organization to its existing vehicles and their usage. The beauty of such an audit is that it almost always makes sense, no matter how confident an organization is that its message is getting through.

SURVEYS

Surveys are now an essential tool in virtually every aspect of public relations work—from investors, to employees, to the community. Before initiating a survey, one must:

1 Determine what specifically is needed from the research
2 Preliminarily investigate past findings in similar research analyses
3 Consider and define the study's concepts and terms
4 Develop a hypothesis
5 Determine an appropriate study design
6 Gather the data
7 Analyze the data for conclusions and recommendations.

Outside help may be required. Firms that design and conduct surveys include the Lou Harris Organization, the Gallup Organization, Yankelovich, Skelly and White, Opinion Research Corporation, and the Roper Organization. Practitioners may purchase proprietary studies or "piggyback" onto existing surveys for less cost. Typical opinion surveys, including those conducted in-house with internal resources, must incorporate four essential elements:

1 **The sample,** or target group selected, must be representative of the total public whose views are sought.
2 **The questionnaire** should derive appropriate information without biasing responses.
3 **The interview** should be structured so that unbiased answers are reported.
4 **The analysis** must provide a reliable basis for recommending action.

The sample.   Once a survey population has been determined, a researcher must select the appropriate sample, or group of respondents, to answer survey questions. Sampling is tricky. A researcher must be aware of the hidden pitfalls in choosing a representative sample, not the least of which is the perishable nature of most data. Survey findings are rapidly outdated because of population mobility and changes in the political and socioeconomic environment. Consequently, research has to be completed quickly.

Quota sampling.   Quota sampling is one sample type. It allots interviews to a certain number of women, men, blacks, whites, rich, poor, and so on. Quotas are imposed in proportion to each group's percentage of the population. The advantage of quota sampling is that it increases homogeneity of a sample population, thus enhancing the validity of a study. However, it's hard to classify interviewees by one or two discrete demographic characteristics. For example, a particular interviewee may be black, Catholic, female, under 25, and a member of a labor union all at the same time. The lines of demographic demarcation can be blurred.

Delphi panels.   The Delphi method of surveying, which segregates a specially-selected sample, recently has gained favor in public relations research. The Delphi process is a means of forecasting public opinion trends by gathering data from an identified group of experts in a uniquely open manner. First developed by the Rand research group in the early 1950s, the Delphi process invites a group of experts to independently and anonymously submit answers to the same questionnaires. The answers are then passed around for written criticism by other participants until a consensus for natural development of a trend is established.[6]

Random sampling. Random probability sampling differs from quota sampling in that each member of a population has an equal chance of being selected. For example, in an *area sample,* geographical units are selected at random and then surveyed. Election polling uses a random approach; while millions of Americans vote, only a few thousand are ever polled for election preferences. In another instance, the Nielson national television sample consists of 1,250 homes out of over 83 million TV households. And the Census Bureau uses a sample of 60–75,000 out of some 88 million households to obtain estimates of employment and other population characteristics.

How large should a random sample be? The answer depends on a number of factors, one of which is the size of the population. The more alike the population elements are in regard to the characteristics being studied, the smaller the sample required. Indeed, in most random samples, the following population-to-sample ratios would apply, within a 5 percent margin of error:[7]

Population	Sample
Infinity	384
500,000	383
100,000	383
50,000	381
10,000	370
5,000	375
3,000	341
2,000	322
1,000	278

Random sampling owes its accuracy to the laws of probability, which are best explained by the example of a barrel filled with 10,000 marbles—5,000 green ones and 5,000 red ones. If a blindfolded person selects a certain number of marbles from the barrel—say 400—the laws of probability suggest that the most frequently drawn combination will be 200 red and 200 green. These laws further conjecture that within certain margins of error:

1 A very few marbles can represent the whole barrel.
2 The "barrel" could be any size—city, state, or nation.

The appropriate margin of error should always be noted. This margin explains how far off the prediction may be. In other words, while a random sample may fairly represent a larger universe, it is possible, within a certain margin of error, that the results of the research may not be *statistically significant*. In other words, they may not accurately or conclusively represent the real view of the universe.

This is particularly critical in political polling, where pollsters are quick to acknowledge that their results may accurately represent the larger universe—but normally within a 2 or 3 percent margin of error. This means that the results could be as much as 3 percent more or less for a certain candidate. Therefore, if a pollster says a candidate will win with 51 percent of the vote, what he really means is that the candidate could receive as much as 54 percent or as little as 48 percent of the vote—enough to *lose* the election.

Political polls are fraught with problems. They cannot scientifically predict outcomes. Rather, they freeze attitudes at a certain point in time. People's attitudes obviously change with the tide of events. For instance, in 1980, right after the Republicans met in Detroit, Ronald Reagan stood 25 to 30 points ahead in all Presidential polls. Later, when the Democrats convened in New York, Jimmy Carter almost caught up with Reagan in the polls. Up until election day, in fact, most polls had the two candidates running neck-in-neck. Nonetheless, Reagan won the election by a convincing 11 percentage points.

Perhaps the most notorious political poll was that of the *Literary Digest* in 1936, which used a telephone polling technique to predict that Alf Landon would be the nation's next President. Landon, of course, suffered one of the worst drubbings in American electoral history at the hands of Franklin Roosevelt. It probably was little solace to the *Literary Digest* that most of its telephone respondents, many of whom were Republicans wealthy enough to afford phones, did, indeed, vote for Landon.

While political polls clearly are not infallible, they can offer a valuable insight into public opinion.[8]

Questionnaires.   Before creating a questionnaire, it's wise to talk informally with the type of people the study is designed to reach. These talks should yield insights into how target publics think. In formulating the questionnaire, keep questions unbiased, unambiguous, and simple, seeking only *yes, no,* or alternative choice answers. Figure 6–1 illustrates an internal survey using a simple "rating" format.

A researcher should ask the following questions after preliminarily writing questions:

1   What am I trying to find out by asking this question?
2   Have I given the respondent an appropriate range of choices?
3   Have I phrased things in such a way that the average, unsophisticated respondent will know what I am talking about and be able to respond meaningfully?
4   Have I phrased things in such a way that the words will influence the respondent's answers?
5   Are the questions in a logical sequence as now placed, or will the present order tend to distort the answers?

In general, questionnaires should be designed to seek only one answer per question and to avoid emotionally-charged words that could influence the interviewee. A survey that does not conform to these requirements risks yielding meaningless or even misleading results.

The Chase Manhattan Bank, N.A.
1 Chase Manhattan Plaza
New York New York 10015

May 11, 1977

TO ALL STAFF MEMBERS

We are currently in the midst of revitalizing our corporate internal communications programs and practices. At this point, however, to move forward and to do the job right, we need some information from you.

To begin with, we need to know what you think about the various corporate internal communications programs already in place. We also need to know what kinds of information you need to keep in tune with Chase and its overall directions. And, finally, we need to know what information you feel is necessary in fulfilling your particular responsibilities.

The ideal way to get this information would be to talk with each of you directly, but this is obviously unrealistic. But we can speak with many of you indirectly through the survey that we are conducting.

We are extremely interested in having your opinion on this critical matter, and therefore urge you to take the time to give us serious, thoughtful answers to the questions that are attached.

We are firmly committed to establishing a vital internal communications program which is responsive to your information needs. You can be sure that we'll be listening to what you have to say.

Sincerely,

---

1 In general, would you say that the information Chase gives its employees keeps you:

1) Very well informed
2) Reasonably well informed
3) Somewhat informed
4) Not too well informed
5) Not informed at all

2 Generally, when Chase gives information to employees, how do you feel about it?

1) Always believe it
2) Usually believe it
3) Believe it about half the time
4) Seldom believe it
5) Never believe it

3 Overall, how would you rate the timeliness of the information you receive about the bank and your job?

1) Very good
2) Good
3) So-So
4) Poor
5) Very poor

Please rate the *importance* of each of the following as a *source of information.*

	VERY IMPOR-TANT	IMPOR-TANT	SOME-WHAT IMPOR-TANT	NOT TOO IMPOR-TANT	NOT AT ALL IMPOR-TANT	NEVER RECEIVED INFORMATION FROM THIS SOURCE
4. Your Supervisor	1	2	3	4	5	9
5. Chase Manhattan News	1	2	3	4	5	9
6. Staff Bulletin	1	2	3	4	5	9
7. Benefits News	1	2	3	4	5	9
8. Recorded Message Service	1	2	3	4	5	9
9. Annual Report	1	2	3	4	5	9
10. Chase Quarterly	1	2	3	4	5	9
11. Bulletin Boards	1	2	3	4	5	9
12. Consumer Sense	1	2	3	4	5	9
13. Benefits Booklets	1	2	3	4	5	9
14. Orientation	1	2	3	4	5	9
15. Other Chase Employees (The grapevine)	1	2	3	4	5	9

Have you any comments on your answers to questions 4-15? Include suggestions for improvement in any of the above sources of information. PLEASE WRITE IN SPACE PROVIDED BELOW.

FIGURE 6-1. *Chase employee questionnaire.* In the area of internal communications and morale, companies constantly devise questionnaires to seek employee opinions about current communications channels. This figure (above) shows the introduction to and first portion of a survey distributed to a random sampling of Chase Manhattan Bank employees.

SOURCE: Courtesy of The Chase Manhattan Bank

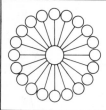

MINICASE
The Cuyhoda County questionnaire

Maxine Fine is director of public information for Cuyhoda County. In anticipation of the county's attempt to attract industry from other parts of the region, Fine plans an attitude survey of Cuyhoda County residents to reveal the benefits they see in living in the county.

She hopes to reveal the qualities that make Cuyhoda County attractive to most people, as well as any unattractive qualities that may annoy residents. Here's her survey:

1 Do you enjoy living in Cuyhoda County?
(Very much, considerably, not at all)

2 What is the most attractive quality about the county?
(Schools, transportation access, recreation)

3 What is the most unattractive quality of the county?
(Crime, climate, racial mix)

4 On the whole, how would you rate Cuyhoda County as a place to work?
(Excellent, good, poor)

5 How important to you is continued industrial development in the county?
(Very important, not very important, no opinion)

6 On a scale of 1 to 5, how would you rate your enthusiasm toward Cuyhoda County?
(1, 2, 3, 4, 5)

7 Finally, if you were asked to list the major benefit that a new resident could expect by moving to Cuyhoda County, what would it be?

Thank you.

QUESTIONS

1 Do you think Fine will be able to derive meaningful results from the data she collects?

2 How would you rate her questions in terms of "specificity"?

3 Will each question evoke only one answer?

4 What problems are raised by the format of the questionnaire?
By the wording of the questions? By the choice of language?

The interview.   Research interviews can provide a more personal, firsthand "feel" for public opinion. Interviews may be conducted in a number of ways, including face-to-face, telephone, mail questionnaires, and drop-off interviews.

Personal interviewing, because it permits in-depth polling, is considered most reliable. Such interviews can be conducted one-on-one or through survey panels, often called *idea juries.* These panels can be used, for example, to measure the buying habits or the impact of public relations programs on a community or organizational group, or to generally assess attitudes toward certain subjects.

In contrast, **telephone interviews** suffer from a high refusal rate. Many people just don't want to be bothered. Such interviews also may present an upper-income bias because lower-income earners often lack telephones. On the other hand, the increasing use of unlisted numbers by those of upper-income status may serve to mitigate this bias.

Mail interviews, although economical, often suffer from low response rates. Frequently, those who do return mail questionnaires are people with strong biases either in favor of or in opposition to—usually the latter—the subject at hand. One way to generate a higher response from mail interviews is through the use of self-addressed, stamped envelopes, or enclosed incentives, such as dollar bills or free gifts.

Drop-off interviews combine face-to-face and mail interview techniques. An interviewer personally drops off a questionnaire at a household, usually after conducting a face-to-face interview. Because the interviewer has already established some rapport with the interviewee, the rate of return for this technique is considerably higher than for straight mail interviews.

Rapport with an interview subject may be established in several ways. For instance, it may make sense to begin an interview with nonthreatening questions, saving the tougher, more controversial ones—on income level or race, for example—until last. Another approach is to depersonalize the research, i.e. explain that others have devised the survey and that the interviewer's job is simply to carry it out.

In any event, it is always wise to check with a research expert before embarking on any type of research interview. Often, another viewpoint is helpful in organizing and conducting interviews, developing questionnaires, and phrasing questions. Of course the interviewer should avoid introducing personal biases in the questioning. To avoid unconsciously presenting such biases, try out sample questions in advance on a number of indifferent parties.

THE ANALYSIS

After conducting survey interviews and compiling results, the researcher must then analyze the findings. Often a great deal of analysis is required to produce meaningful recommendations.

In reaching conclusions, margins of error must be noted and allowed for. To guard against reaching wrong or misleading conclusions, statistical levels of significance should be consulted for each research study to characterize the validity of the data. If results are "statistically significant," they are considered valid—too large to be reasonably attributed to chance.

MEASURING RESULTS

As noted, public relations research has made substantial gains in recent years in quantifying the results of public relations activity. Yet, in fairness, public relations research still is in its infancy.

Beyond the escalating use of the computer, companies have stepped up efforts in opinion sampling. Counseling firms such as Hill and Knowlton enlist separate departments to conduct attitude and opinion surveys for clients. A typical Hill and Knowlton opinion survey for security analysts might include the following types of questions:

○ What is your opinion of our client's current position in the market?
○ Why are investors skeptical about this company?
○ How can our client change its image in the marketplace?
○ How can our client improve its financial communications?
○ How do you assess our client's management capability?
○ What do you believe our client's earnings growth potential will be over the next few years?

Public relations research will increase in importance as managements continue to stress quantifiable results. Management wants proof that its departments are either making money or justifying their expenses. Public relations is no exception; managements continue to stress quantifiable results, especially to confirm support for the organization's position. The public relations area must keep management informed of results of its research and involve management in research objectives and methods of accomplishing them.

The intelligent use of research represents a technology for both defining problems and evaluating solutions. The day of the seat-of-the-pants practitioner is over. While intuitive judgment remains a coveted and important skill, management must see measurable results. As the editor of *Public Relations Journal* put it,

> The pressure is on. Public relations results and effectiveness will either measure up under searching examination by vigilant and cost-conscious managements, or the profession will languish in a melange of press agentry, publicity, and promotion.[9]

On the other hand, informed managements recognize that public relations may never reach a point where its results can be fully quantified. Management confidence is still a prerequisite for active and unencumbered programs. Such confidence can only be enhanced as practitioners become more adept in using research.

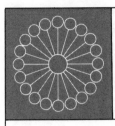

CASE STUDY
The Atwater attitude survey

The Atwater Insurance Company published the *Atwater Advocate,* its employee newspaper, since the year the company was founded. In those thirty-five years, Atwater has never surveyed what employees think about the paper. Largely for this reason, Atwater's public relations director, Katherine Weber, decided to launch a staff survey to see how employees assess the *Advocate.*

Having taken a research course in college, Weber decided to construct the survey herself. Here is her methodology:

1   The sample will be composed of representatives of each of Atwater's fifty departments. In each case, the department head will select three employees to submit to interviews about the *Advocate.* Weber reasons that this sample of 150, representing 10 percent of the 1,500-employee staff, is a fair reflection of all employee attitudes.

2   The questions asked of the employees will be free-form; that is, employees will be asked generally to talk about their views of the *Advocate,* rather than responding to detailed, specific questions regarding aspects of the paper.

3   Interviews will be conducted through combined departmental groups. In each interview, fifteen interviewees, representing five separate departments, will be polled. Each member of the group of fifteen will be asked for his or her views on the *Advocate,* with discussions centering on particular topics of concern to the individual groups.

4   Results of the interview sessions will be translated by the interviewer into a three-page discussion summary. At the end of the project, the fifteen summaries will be analyzed and specific recommendations drawn to modify the *Advocate* if necessary.

QUESTIONS

1   How would you assess Weber's research methodology?
2   Is the proposed sample a fair one?
3   Is it wise to conduct free-form discussions rather than ask specific questions?
4   What problems could result from structuring interviews in groups of fifteen, representing five separate departments?
    How could this interview format be improved?
5   Do you think this research project will yield meaningful results?

NOTES

1 Ray Chapman, "Measurement: It is Alive And Well in Chicago," *Public Relations Journal,* May 1982, p. 28.

2 Walter K. Lindenmann, "The Missing Link in Public Relations Research," *Public Relations Review,* Vol. V, no. 1 (Spring 1979), p. 30.

3 Robert Van Riper, "The Uses of Research in Public Relations," *Public Relations Journal,* February 1976, p. 18.

4 Walter K. Lindenmann, "Opinion Research: How It Works; How to Use It," *Public Relations Journal,* January 1977, p. 13.

5 This research program, orchestrated by Peter Small and Associates, Inc., won a 1977 Silver Anvil Award from the Public Relations Society of America. "The Sentry Consumerism Study," *Corporate Public Issues,* Vol. III, no. 19, 15 October 1978.

6 Richard J. Coyle and Lowndes F. Stephens, "Why Practitioners Should Master Sampling and Survey Research," *Public Relations Journal,* February 1979, p. 15.

7 David Gergen, "Collector's Items," *Public Opinion,* November/December 1978, p. 60.

8 In 1980, the Foundation for Public Relations Research and Education organized a delphi survey of 30 public relations scholars and practitioners to come up with the most important research questions for public relations in the 1980s. For the results, see Mark McElreath, "Priority Research Questions in Public Relations for the 1980s," Foundation for Public Relations Research and Education, 1980.

9 Leo J. Northart, "Editor's Notebook," *Public Relations Journal,* July 1979, p. 8.

SUGGESTED READING

Adler, Irving. *Probability and Statistics for Everyman.* New York: New American Library, 1963.

Backstrom, Charles H., and **Hursh, Gerald D.** *Survey Research.* Evanston, Ill.: Northwestern University Press, 1963.

Barzun, Jacques, and **Graff, Henry F.** *The Modern Researcher.* New York: Harcourt Brace Jovanovich, 1957. A "must-have" for anyone in the business of collecting facts.

Beiswinger, George L. "Database Update," *Public Relations Journal,* March 1982, pp. 37–39.

Chapman, Ray. "Measurement: It Is Alive and Well In Chicago," *Public Relations Journal,* May 1982, pp. 28–29. A survey of PRSA chapter members reveals broad support for measuring effectiveness of public relations programs and the use of a variety of tools.

Finn, Peter. "Demystifying Public Relations," *Public Relations Journal,* May 1982, pp. 12–17.

Hanson, James, and **Abelson, Herbert I.** *Persuasion: How Opinions and Attitudes Are Changed.* 3rd ed. New York: Basic Books, 1976. Correlates all research data to the standard theories of persuasion.

Hill, Don. "In Search Of Excellence," *Public Relations Journal,* May 1982, pp. 36–37.

Jeffcoat, A.E. "A Touch of Amazement," *Public Relations Journal,* May 1981, pp. 34–36.

Katz, Elaine Falk. "Measuring the Measurers," *Public Relations Journal,* May 1982, pp. 30–31, 33.

Kopec, Joseph A. "The Communication Audit," *Public Relations Journal,* May 1982, pp. 24–27.

Leffingwell, Roy J. "Flying By The Seat Of Our Pants," *Public Relations Quarterly,* Summer 1981, p. 25.

Leffingwell, Roy J. "Recognizing There is a Problem," *Public Relations Quarterly,* Spring 1981, p. 29.

Leffingwell, Roy J. "Social Science Research Findings Could Save Us A Great Deal Of Money," *Public Relations Quarterly,* Winter 1981–82, p. 30.

Lindenmann, Walter K. "Polls: Are We Taking Them Too Literally?" *Public Relations Journal,* May 1981, pp. 21–23. Practitioners rely heavily on polls, and that could lead to some wrong answers and, even worse, to some fatal conclusions.

Mendenhall, William, and **Reinmuth, James E.** *Statistics for Management and Economics.* North Scituat, Mass.: Duxbury Press, 1971. Comprehensive but simple treatment of the subject.

Meyer, Philip. *Precision Journalism: A Reporter's Introduction to Social Science Methods.* Bloomington, Ind.: Indiana University Press, 1973. Provides the basic steps for interpreting statistics, polls, and surveys.

"Modest Proposals for Measurement," *Public Relations Journal,* May 1981, pp. 32, 44. Proposals on how to measure the true worth of public relations.

Nafziger, Ralph O., and **White, David M.** *Introduction to Mass Communications Research.* Baton Rouge, La: Louisiana State University Press, 1963.

Nagel, Gerald D. "Finding A Better Way To Spend Your Time," *Public Relations Journal,* May 1982, pp. 18–20. Content analysis is an easy, do-it-yourself way to increase effectiveness and the quality of work.

Nagel, Gerald S. "How to Conduct Basic Research," *Public Relations Journal,* May 1981, pp. 26–29. A step-by-step procedure on conducting a do-it-yourself survey.

Namenwirth, Miller & **Weber,** "Organizations Have Opinions: A Redefinition of Publics, *Public Opinion Quarterly,* 45, Winter 1981, pp. 463–476.

National Association of Broadcasters. *A Broadcast Research Primer.* Washington, D.C.: National Association of Broadcasters, 1971. Excellent reference.

Norton, Alice. *Public Relations: Guide to Information Sources.* Detroit, Mich.: Gale Research, 1970.

Reardon, Kathleen Kelly. "The ABC's of Research," *Public Relations Journal,* May 1981, pp. 21–23.

Rivers, William L. *Finding Facts: Interviewing, Observing, Using Reference Sources.* Englewood Cliffs, N.J.: Prentice-Hall, 1975.

Selitz, Clair; Jahoda, Marie; Deutsch, Morton; and **Cook, Stuart W.** *Research Methods in Social Relations.* New York: Holt, Rinehart & Winston, 1967. Covers the basic social-science research methods.

Smith, Rea W. "25 Years of Shoring Up The Profession," *Public Relations Journal,* May 1981, pp. 38–40.

Strenski, James B. "New Concerns for Measurement," *Public Relations Journal,* May 1981, pp. 16–17.

Strenski, James B. "Techniques For Measuring Public Relations Effectiveness," *Public Relations Quarterly,* Spring 1982, pp. 21–24.

The Wall Street Journal Index. (Available from Dow Jones Books, P. O. Box 60, Princeton, N.J. 08540). Handy reference volume for researching business topics.

Williams, Frederick. *Reasoning with Statistics: Simplified in Communications Research.* New York: Holt, Rinehart & Winston, 1968.

PRACTICAL APPLICATIONS

PART TWO

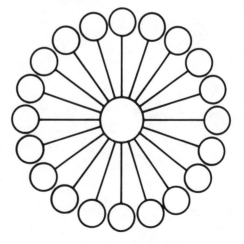

7
Public Relations Writing Fundamentals

WRITE MAKES MIGHT

The ability to write easily, coherently, and quickly distinguishes the public relations professional from others in an organization.

Not that the skills of counseling and judgment aren't just as important; some experts argue that these skills are far more important than knowing how to write. Maybe. But if one doesn't know how to write—how to express ideas on paper—one may have less opportunity to ascend the public relations success ladder.

Simply put, few managers are good writers. They usually come from finance, legal, engineering, or sales backgrounds, where writing is not stressed. But when they reach the top, they are expected to write articles, speeches, memos, and testimony. Here they need advisors, who are often their trusted public relations professionals.

What does it take to be a public relations writer?

For one thing, it takes a good knowledge of "the basics." Although practitioners probably write for a wider range of purposes and use a greater number of communications methods than do other writers, the principles remain the same, whether writing an annual report or a case history, an employee newsletter or a public speech.

The next three chapters will explore the fundamentals of writing—*first* discussing public relations writing generally and news releases in particular, *second* reviewing writing for reading, and *third* discussing writing for listening.

WRITING FOR THE EYE AND EAR

Writing for a reader differs dramatically from writing for a listener.

A reader has certain luxuries a listener does not have. For example, a reader can scan material, study printed words, dart ahead, and then review certain passages for better understanding. A reader can check up on a writer; if the facts are wrong, for instance, a reader can find out pretty easily. To be effective, writing for the eye must hold together under the most rigorous scrutiny.

On the other hand, a listener gets one opportunity to hear and comprehend a message. If he misses the message the first time around, there's usually no second chance. This situation poses a special challenge for the writer—to grab the listener quickly. If the listener tunes out early in a speech or a broadcast, it's difficult to draw him back to the listening fold.

WRITING FUNDAMENTALS

Few people are "born writers." Like any other discipline, writing takes patience and hard work. The more you write, the better you should get, provided you have mastered the basics. Writing fundamentals do not change significantly from one form to another.

What are the basics?

According to counselor F. John Pessolano, a New Yorker who teaches other practitioners how to write, the basics are part theory, part practice, and part common sense. Here's Pessolano's three-part formula for writers, from the novice to the novelist:

The idea must precede the expression.   Think before writing. Few people can observe an event immediately, grasp its meaning, and sit down to compose several pages of sharp, incisive prose. Writing requires ideas, and ideas require thought.

Ideas must satisfy several criteria:

○   They must relate to the reader.
○   They must engage the reader's attention.
○   They must concern the reader.
○   They must be in the reader's own self-interest.

Sometimes, ideas come quickly. Other times, they don't come at all. But each new writing situation does not require a new idea. The trick in coming up with clever ideas lies more in borrowing old ones than in creating new ones. An old idea, refined to meet a specific communications objective, can be most effective. Stated another way, never underestimate the importance to a writer of maintaining *good files.*

Don't be afraid of the draft.   After deciding on an idea and establishing the purpose of a communication, a rough draft should come next. It is a necessary and foolproof method for avoiding a mediocre and half-baked product.

Writing, no matter how good, can usually be improved with a second look. The draft helps one organize ideas and plot their development before committing them to a written test. It often enhances writing clarity if you know where you will *stop,* before you start.

Organization should be logical; it should lead a reader in a systematic way through the body of the text. Sometimes, especially on longer pieces, an outline should precede the draft.

Simplify, clarify, aim.   In writing, the simpler the better. The more people who understand what you're trying to say, the better your chances for stimulating action. Shop talk, jargon, and "in" words should be avoided. Clear, normal English is all that's required to get an idea across. In practically every case what makes sense is the simple over the complex, the familiar over the unconventional, and the concrete over the abstract.

Clarity is another essential for writing. The key to clarity is "tightness"; that is, each word, each passage, each paragraph must belong. If a word is unnecessary, a passage redundant, a paragraph vague—get rid of it. Writing requires judicious editing; copy must always be reviewed with an eye toward cutting.

Finally, writing must be aimed at a particular audience. Few communications can be all things to all people, so a writer must have the target group in mind and tailor the message to reach them. To win the minds and deeds of a *specific* audience, one must be willing to sacrifice the understanding of certain others. Writers, like good companies, can't expect to be "all things to all people."

FLESCH READABILITY FORMULA

Through a variety of writings, Dr. Rudolf Flesch has staged a one-man battle against pomposity and murkiness in writing.*

According to Flesch, anyone can become a writer. His formula, in fact, suggests that if people would only write like they talk, they would all be able to write better. In other words, if people were less inclined to obfuscate their writing with 25-cent words and more inclined to substitute simple words, then not only would communicators communicate better, but receivers would receive more clearly.

There are countless examples of how Flesch's simple dictum works. For instance:

○ Few would have remembered William Shakespeare had he written sentences like, "Should I act upon the urgings that I feel or remain passive and thus cease to exist?" Instead, Shakespeare's writing has stood the test of centuries because of sentences like, "To be or not to be?"

○ A scientist, prone to scientific jargon, might be tempted to write, "The biota exhibited a 100 percent mortality response." But oh how much easier and infinitely more understandable to simply write, "All the fish died."

○ One of President Franklin D. Roosevelt's speech writers once wrote, "We are endeavoring to construct a more inclusive society." F.D.R. changed it to, "We're going to make a country in which no one is left out."

○ Even the most famous book of all, The Bible, opens with a simple sentence that could have been written by a twelve-year-old: "In the beginning, God created the heaven and the earth."

---

* Among the more significant of Flesch's books are *Say What You Mean*, *The Art of Plain Talk*, *The Art of Readable Writing*, and *How to Be Brief: An Index to Simple Writing*.

Wes Pedersen is director of communications and public relations for the prestigious Washington-based Public Affairs Council, the professional organization of the nation's corporate public affairs executives. He holds numerous awards for both public relations and journalistic writing, as well as editing and publishing. He also has received several "Communicator of the Year" honors. A former newspaper editor and foreign correspondent, Mr. Pedersen was for ten years the author of "The World Today," a column published in 112 countries. Among the books he has written is the international best-seller, *Legacy of a President*. Mr. Pedersen also is editor of the scholarly *Public Affairs Review* and of a monthly column in the *Public Relations Journal*, magazine of the Public Relations Society of America.

How important is writing in public relations?

Good writing is vital to any effective, sustained practice.

Are writers born or made?

Most veteran writers, I suspect, would answer "born." The typical writer does seem to have an instinct for the right word and the right phrase in the right order. But that's usually a developed trait, one that can be traced back to early reading and learning habits. The youngster who *likes* to read gains an almost automatic grasp of the niceties of grammar and composition, to the point where parents and teachers alike soon label the pupil a "born" writer. But writing talent can be developed later in life, too. The important thing is that at some point—in grade school, high school, college, or beyond—you are imbued with the desire to improve your writing skills. I've known beginning reporters who seemed totally lacking in writing ability but who blossomed under the tutelage of skilled, patient editors. Teachers, of course, see the same thing, even in graduate school. Almost anyone can become a writer if the desire and determination are there.

How do you approach each writing assignment?

I begin by asking questions, and I ask them in a story conference, not in a casual conversation. I insist on that. I want full agreement from the start on *what* it is that I am expected to write, the purpose it's expected to achieve, the audience it's expected to reach, the media to be targeted, and the time the first draft is due—and the last draft. I'll need to know the answers to all those questions if I am to do the job properly and if I'm to avoid misunderstandings. If I get a "Gee, I don't know" response to any of my questions, I'll make suggestions as to style, media, and so forth. I'll try to do all of this as diplomatically as possible, of course. I don't want to waste my time guessing about any aspect of an assignment, but I don't want to ruffle the feathers of a client either.

What do you do next?

Once I have the answers to the basic questions, I begin my research. I'll want all the information I can get on the subject on which I'll be writing—everything I can assemble in the time allotted me. Even if the client has a great deal of the necessary background information waiting for me, and has experts on hand to brief me, I'll still want to see what else is available. I'll check the computer data banks, reference books, newspaper files, library, and any other resources that seem promising. I'll be looking particularly hard for *current* facts and figures and for any significant information that hasn't been publicized before.

Do you prepare an outline before writing?

Yes. I know that some writers claim they don't need outlines, but I find them helpful for all but the most basic articles or speeches. Not only do they remind me of the key points I want to make, and in what order, but they speed up my writing. I don't have to stop every so often to ask myself "Now what do I do?"

It's at this point that I do the actual writing. Once I've finished the draft, I'll go over it at least twice to see where I can improve it. Then I'll check it out with the client and make whatever changes he or she might want. I'm prepared to do three or four rewrites if that's what it takes to complete the job to everyone's satisfaction. Public relations

is no place for a writer who's so sensitive or arrogant that he balks at rewriting his own copy.

How would you assess the state of writing among public relations practitioners today?

It's erratic, extremely erratic. Some public relations writing *is* absolutely first rate, as good as any of the offerings of the country's top analysts and reporters. But some of it is so embarrassingly amateurish that it puts the entire public relations profession to shame. The rest of it falls somewhere in between, usually at the passing-grade mark or above.

What are the differences between public relations writing and journalistic writing?

If it's simply a matter of imparting information, there should be no difference whatever. But that situation rarely applies. In journalistic writing, emphasis is on the presentation of facts. In public relations writing, it is more likely to be on the promotion of an organization, an activity, a product, a policy, a personality, or a point of view. In journalism, the goal is to reveal. In public relations, it may be to obscure. In journalism, balance is sought in reporting pros and cons. In public relations, the balance may be tilted—the positive accentuated, the negative minimized if not ignored. In journalism, brevity is prized by all editors, except those serving publications of record. In public relations, detail is often insisted upon by the client or employer. In journalism, editorial comment in news stories is frowned upon. In public relations, it is often inserted in an effort to explain, clarify, or "add punch." In journalism, facts flow together naturally in a news or feature story or broadcast. In public relations, they're pieced together in what is hoped will appear to be a natural order but is actually calculated to serve a specific objective. In journalism, writers benefit from the skills and advice of editors with long years in the business. In public relations the "editors" are

(Interview continued)

likely to be the client and the account executive, or the company "brass," who know what *they* want, not necessarily what media people demand.

Is the news release dead?

No, it's like Dracula—virtually impossible to kill. Editors keep impaling it on spikes and entombing it in wastebaskets, but it survives. It probably always will. It's too well established with too many people in public relations or on the fringes of public relations. They regard it as *the* way to get out the word.

The concept of the news release remains sound. The problem lies in its abuse. *Everyone* puts out news releases, but few of the releases deal with genuinely newsworthy topics, and fewer still are professionally written. Personal contacts with editors and reporters remain the most effective means of insuring usage of materials. If a practitioner is recognized as a good news source, attention *will* be paid to telephone calls, letters, memos, fact sheets, and releases alike.

What's the best test of effective writing?

Continuity is the real test of effective writing. Does the text *flow?* Do the most important facts appear at the outset? Do the less important items appear in descending order, including the background information and the explanations? Can the text be cut after three paragraphs, or ten paragraphs, or twenty? And will the reader still have the feeling that, whatever the length, he has read a complete story?

How do you overcome writer's block?

I try to minimize the chances for blocks by doing a detailed outline before I begin writing. It's rare for a block to occur if I know what points I'm going to make and in what order. When I *am* stumped for the right transitional phrase or if a paragraph doesn't seem to jell, I'll put down whatever comes to mind, put a check mark beside that particular passage, and go on writing. When I've finished the manuscript, I'll go back and look at that page. Chances are the wording will flow much better than I'd thought at the time I wrote it, or a solution will raise its lovely head with just a little bit of thought. For me, the important thing is to avoid stopping in mid-page or mid-text to do battle with myself.

Is there anything else you'd like readers of this book to know?

Yes, if they take their writing seriously, and do it well, they'll find that *they* are taken seriously by editors and reporters whose respect and friendship can be absolutely invaluable. Media people give long shrift to practitioners they regard as fellow professionals.

Flesch had seven suggestions for making writing more readable:

1 Use contractions, like it's or doesn't.
2 Leave out the word *that* whenever possible.
3 Use pronouns like *I, we, they,* and *you.*
4 When referring back to a noun, repeat the noun or use a pronoun. Don't create "eloquent substitutions."
5 Use brief, clear sentences.
6 Cover only one item per paragraph.
7 Use language the reader understands.

To Flesch, the key to all good writing is *get to the point*.

THE SECRET OF THE INVERTED PYRAMID

Newspaper writing is the Flesch formula in action. Reporters learn that words are precious and not to be wasted. In their stories, every word counts. If readers lose interest early, they're not likely to be around at the story's end.

That's where the inverted pyramid comes in.

Newspaper story form, from which public relations writing derives, is the opposite of that for a novel or short story. While the climax of a novel comes at the end, the climax of a newspaper story comes at the beginning. While a novel's important facts are rolled out as the plot thickens, the critical facts in a newspaper story appear at the start. In this way, if a reader decides to leave a news article early, she has already learned the basic ideas.

Generally, the first tier, or *lead*, of the inverted pyramid is the first one or two paragraphs, which include the most important facts. From there, paragraphs are written in descending order of importance, with progressively less important facts as the article continues; thus the term *inverted pyramid*. (See Figure 7-1 for an exception to the pyramid style, p. 152.)

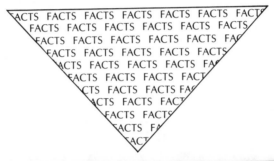

FEATURE
Readability in the insurance industry: telling it like it is[1]

Among the industries opting for more simplified language in customer policies is the insurance industry. The Insurance Services Office (ISO) is one organization committed to the public's clearer understanding of policies.

ISO reported that readability levels increased dramatically with the adoption of a new simplified agreement:

The Old Language (totals 235 words)

In consideration of the provisions and stipulations herein or added hereto and of the premium, this Company, for the term of years from inception date At Noon (Standard Time) to expiration date At Noon (Standard Time) at location of property involved, to an amount not exceeding the amount(s) specified in the Declarations, does insure the insured name in Declarations. . . .

The New Language (totals 23 words)

We will provide the insurance described in this policy in return for the premium and compliance with all applicable provisions of this policy.

Pullman Kellogg NEWS

A Member of the Wheelabrator-Frye Group
Three Greenway Plaza East, Houston, Texas 77046
Arthur L. Dowling, Vice President Advertising and Public Relations

Contact: Ray Waters, Manager of Public Relations   (713) 960-2160

For Release: UPON RECEIPT

CONTINUED COOPERATION IS KELLOGG'S CHRISTMAS PLEDGE

1980 comes to an end, and a new year is about to begin. It is a time to pause; to reflect on the past; to look to the future.

Pullman Kellogg began the year as a division of Pullman Incorporated. In November, Pullman Incorporated was merged into Wheelabrator-Frye, Inc. In 1981, it is planned that the M.W. Kellogg name -- a name synonymous with excellence throughout our industry, throughout the world -- be re-adopted.

In extending wishes for a joyous holiday season and a rewarding new year, Ray Waters, Kellogg's manager of public relations, reaffirmed his department's commitment to strive to reflect that excellence, saying the department will continue to attempt to provide media with information on Kellogg's worldwide activities honestly and speedily -- not only relating to material emanating originally from the department, but in responding to queries received.

"No public relations group can perform its job effectively without earning and retaining the confidence of the press corps," he said. "We will continue to work diligently to deserve that confidence.

"Peace, love and season's greetings to all."

- 30 -

#86 - 12/22/80

United Kingdom Pullman Kellogg Limited, The Pullman Kellogg Building,
Wembley (London), Middlesex HA9 0EE. Telephone (01) 903-8484
The Netherlands Kellogg Continental B.V., De Boelelaan 873, Amsterdam. Telephone 020-42 99 55

The M.W. Kellogg Company NEWS

a subsidiary of Wheelabrator-Frye Inc.

Three Greenway Plaza East, Houston, Texas 77046
Arthur L. Dowling, Vice President Advertising and Public Relations

Contact: Ray Waters Manager of Public Relations   (713) 960 2160

For Release: UPON RECEIPT

Houston, 23 December...Christmas sees an international company with its good name back again, operating under a new president from within a new parent organization, and looking forward to its first full year with the restored name of The M.W. Kellogg Company, under the direction of Robert W. Page, president and chief executive officer. Page had been president of Rust Engineering Inc. of Birmingham, another member company within the Wheelabrator-Frye organization. Wheelabrator-Frye Inc. acquired Pullman Incorporated late in 1980. With that acquisition, Kellogg became a member of the Wheelabrator group.

Ray Waters, public relations manager for the worldwide Kellogg group of companies, said today that 1981, a year of change, has served as a prologue to a decade of commitment to the enhancement of man's condition by the careful exploitation and utilization of his energy resources.

With that corporate commitment came the restatement of what Waters calls Kellogg's public relations credo -- to work with the diverse publics in the best manner possible; to cooperate to the best of his ability to serve their needs and the needs of Kellogg, its sister-companies and its parent organization; and to be as honest and open with those organizations as is humanly possible. He reiterated to the media his often stated belief: "No public relations department can be effective without earning the respect of its publics and without exhibiting, in return, respect for their needs for information and assistance.

"This effort will continue," he said, in extending the best wishes of the season to them.

- 30 -

#55-23 DECEMBER 1981

FIGURE 7-1. *M. W. Kellogg Company news release.* For several years, the Pullman Kellogg company bent the rules of inverted pyramid style each Christmas season. The release above was typical of Public Relations Manager Ray Waters' substitute Christmas card. In 1981, when Pullman changed its name to M. W. Kellogg, the company seized the occasion (right) to combine some new, pertinent corporate information with its Christmas time tradition.
SOURCE: Courtesy of M. W. Kellogg Company.

The lead is the most critical element, usually answering who, what, why, when, where, and occasionally, how. For example, the following lead effectively answers most of the initial questions a reader might have about the subject matter of the news story:

Francisco Franco, Spain's ruler for decades, died this morning in Madrid after suffering a lengthy illness.

FEATURE
The Flesch "sixty-word blacklist"[2]

In his book *Say What You Mean,* Rudolf Flesch expressed particular loathing for the following words, which, he contended, could easily be replaced by substituting the words in parentheses.

1   advise (write)
2   affirmative (yes)
3   anticipate (expect)
4   appear (seem)
5   ascertain (find out)
6   assist (help)
7   complete (fill out)
8   comply (follow)
9   constitute (be)
10 cooperate (help)
11 deceased (dead)
12 deem (think)
13 desire (want)
14 determine (figure, find)
15 disclose (show)
16 effect (make)
17 elect (choose, pick)
18 endeavor (try)
19 ensue (follow)
20 execute (sign)
21 experience (have)
22 facilitate (make easy)
23 failed to (didn't)
24 forward (send)
25 furnish (send)
26 inasmuch as (since)
27 inconvenience (trouble)
28 indicate (say, show)
29 initial (first)
30 in lieu of (instead of)
31 insufficient (not enough)
32 in the event that (if)
33 locate (find)
34 negative (no)
35 obtain (get)
36 personnel (people)
37 pertaining to (of, about)
38 presently (now)
39 prior to (before)
40 prohibit (forbid)
41 pursuant to (under)
42 provide (give, say)
43 represent (be)
44 request (ask for)
45 require (need)
46 residence (home, address)
47 reveal (show)
48 review (check)
49 spouse (wife, husband)
50 state (say)
51 submit (give, send)
52 subsequent (later)
53 substantial (big, large, great)
54 sufficient (enough)
55 supply (send)
56 sustain (suffer)
57 terminate (end, stop)
58 thus (so, that way)
59 transpire (happen)
60 vehicle (car, truck)

That sentence tells it all; it answers the critical questions and highlights the pertinent facts. It gets to the point quickly without a lot of extra words. In sixteen words, it captures and communicates the essence of what the reader needs to know.

This same style of easy and straightforward writing forms the basis for the most fundamental and ubiquitous of all public relations tools—the news release.

THE NEWS RELEASE

The news release is a valuable but much maligned device. Most public relations professionals swear by it. Some newspaper editors swear about it. And everybody uses it to promote activities, communicate policies, and let the public know what their organizations are up to.

A news release may be written as the document of record to state the organization's official position, for example, in a court case or in announcing a price or rate increase. More frequently, however, releases have one overriding purpose: to influence a publication *to write favorably about the material discussed.* Each day, in fact, professionals send releases to editors in the hopes of stimulating favorable stories about their organizations.

Most of the time, news releases are not used verbatim. Rather, they may tip off editors to potential stories or serve as editorial reminders about coming stories. In both instances, the news release forms the point of departure for an original newspaper or magazine story. Too often, as one hardened newspaper editor put it, "Few (releases) are worth the paper they are printed on . . . particularly in this day of escalating paper costs.[3]

Much of the editorial criticism of news releases revolves around the apparent shoddiness with which releases are planned and executed. For example, in one survey of newspaper editors, six factors, in particular, goaded editors most about news releases. They were, in order of onerousness:

1 Information isn't *localized.*
2 Information isn't *newsworthy.*
3 Release contains too much advertising *puffery.*
4 Release is too *long* and *cumbersome.*
5 Release arrived too *late* to be useful.
6 Release was *poorly written.*[4]

Faced with paper shortages, spiraling production costs, shrinking news holes, and intense deadline pressures, editors simply don't have time to wade through masses of poorly written, self-serving pap. They're looking for news.

And according to most editors, most releases just don't contain much news. As one city editor, who claimed to receive hundreds of releases daily, scornfully put it:

Most press releases are written for clients and not for reporters. The people who write them must know this, so I don't imagine they will be persuaded to change their practices, which they must feel serve a useful purpose. The fact that it is not a news purpose or even a public relations purpose is probably irrelevant to them. It keeps the fees or the paychecks coming.[5]

Understandably, editors are proud people who don't readily admit to borrowing other people's (particularly public relations people's) ideas. Nevertheless, public

FEATURE
Ten commandments of news releases

Once upon a time, a public relations sage offered the following ten commandments that, alas, get broken from time-to-time.

One

Thou shalt be selective with the releases you send. Don't waste your ammunition on stories that bore you. They'll bore others, too.

Two

Thou shalt not send multiple copies of the same release. It causes confusion and wastes time, but occasionally, *The New York Times,* for one example, has been known to run a release tossed out by one editor but salvaged by another.

Three

Thou shalt have contact names and phone numbers on all releases. Reporters must be able to get in touch with someone to clarify and answer questions. Don't send out announcements if you don't intend to be there when reporters call.

Four

Thou shalt know deadlines. It's a good idea to let reporters know what's coming. That way, if it's especially newsworthy, they can save space and won't be surprised when it arrives close to deadline.

Five

Thou shalt follow up with a telephone call. Don't assume a reporter received an important release. Releases get overlooked. Messages get lost. Newsrooms don't have secretaries. Sometimes reporters miss significant releases. So it's all right to check up from time-to-time. But don't call needlessly.

Six

Thou shalt take no for an answer. If, after having given it your best shot, the answer is "no," forget it. Don't be offended. Don't take it personally. But don't overstay your welcome either.

Seven

Thou shalt find out about standard criteria. All periodicals have guidelines for things like executive changes and company news briefs. You should know these. Requirements may change. And no newspaper editor likes to know his paper isn't being read, especially by those with whom he deals.

Eight

Thou shalt know and respect the meaning of "exclusive." Exclusive means just that—giving a release to one publication at the expense of its competition. It does not mean giving it to two publications at the same time. Also, it does not mean giving the release to one television station and one newspaper. If reporters get burned, they tend to remember.

Nine

Thou shalt not send releases to people who left the publication years ago. Few things disturb an editor more than receiving mail addressed to a deceased predecessor.

Ten

Thou shalt get to know reporters before needing one. Even if a reporter doesn't use all your releases, it helps to get to know her. Public relations people occasionally forget that reporters are people too. (At least most are.)

relations ideas and releases are used regularly in most publications and serve as an integral part of newspaper content. If a release pierces the "print barrier" in a newspaper or magazine, verbatim, the sponsor's message takes on the heightened stature associated with objective news reporting (see Figure 7–2).

FORMAT

Format of a news release is important. Since the release is designed to be used in print, it must be structured for easy use by an editor (see Figure 7–3, p. 158). Certain mechanical rules-of-thumb should be followed:

Spacing.   News releases should always be typed and double spaced on 8 ½" by 11" paper. Only one side of the page should be used. No editor wants to go rummaging through a handwritten release or a single-spaced, oversized piece of paper with typing on both sides.

Paper.   Inexpensive paper stock should be used. Reporters win Pulitzer Prizes with stories written on plain copy paper. Nothing irritates an editor more than seeing an expensively embossed news release while watching newspapers die from soaring newsprint costs.

Identification.   The name, address, and telephone number of the release writer should appear in the upper part of the release in case an editor wants further information. It's a good idea to list two names, with office and home telephone numbers.

Release date.   Releases should always be dated, either for "immediate" use or to be "held" until a certain embargoed date. Frequently, a *dateline* is used on releases. It refers to the first line of the release, which tells the place where the story originated.

Margins.   Margins should be wide enough for editors to write on, usually about an inch to an inch and a half.

Length.   A news release is not a book. It should be edited tightly so that it is no more than two pages long. Keep words and sentences short.

Paragraphs.   Paragraphs should also be short, no more than six lines at most. A single sentence can suffice as a paragraph. Because composers may type exactly what they see in *front of them,* syllables should not be split from one line to the next. Likewise, paragraphs should be completed before beginning a new page, to ensure that a lost page in the news or composing rooms will not disrupt completion of a particular thought in the release.

Slug lines.   Certain journalistic slug lines should appear on a release to note such things as "more" at the bottom of a page when the release continues to another page and "30" or "###" to denote the end of the release. Also, page numbers and one-word descriptions of the topic of the release should appear on each page for quick editorial recognition.

David Rockefeller Optimista Sobre Aumento Economía P.R.

David Rockefeller, presidente del Chase Manhattan Bank, citó como un ingrediente principal en la continuada recuperación económica de Puerto Rico, su habilidad para mantener la clase de clima comercial que continuará señalando la isla como un sitio que invita a la inversión exterior.

En un discurso ante la Cámara de Comercio de Puerto Rico en los Estados Unidos, el banquero neoyorquino señaló que eliminando cualquier error serio en la estrategia económica, la economía de Puerto Rico deberá generalmente crecer paralelamente con la economía de los Estados Unidos.

Específicamente Rockefeller declaró que es razonable esperar que Puerto Rico aumente su economía alrededor de un 4%, durante los próximos cuatro años asumiendo que la de los Estados Unidos aumentará también de 4 a 4½ por ciento.

Rockefeller añadió que se sentía entusiasmado por los recientes desarrollos económicos positivos registrados en Puerto Rico, entre los que señaló que el empleo está emergiendo de los bajos niveles de la recesión.

A tales efectos señaló que el total de empleados en la isla está aumentado en una tasa anual de alrededor del 4½ por ciento.

Dijo también que el gobierno puertorriqueño desarrolla un programa para consolidar la deuda pública en un corto término y además reducir sus planes de préstamos, así como los de pertenecientes a las corporaciones públicas.

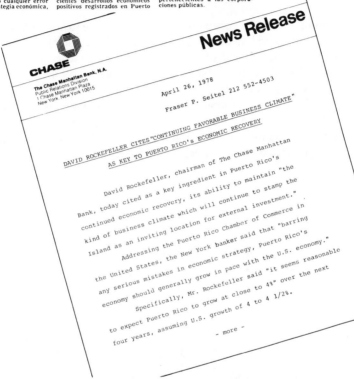

4% growth in island's economy foreseen by David Rockefeller

NEW YORK (UPI) — David Rockefeller, chairman of the Chase Manhattan Bank, Thursday cited as a key ingredient in Puerto Rico's continued economic recovery the island's ability to maintain "the kind of business climate which will continue to stamp it as an inviting location for external investment."

Addressing the Puerto Rico Chamber of Commerce in the United States, the New York banker said that "barring any serious mistakes in economic strategy, Puerto Rico's economy should generally grow in pace with the U.S. economy."

Specifically, Rockefeller said "it seems reasonable to expect Puerto Rico to grow at close to 4 percent" over the next four years, assuming U.S. growth of 4 to 4½ percent.

Rockefeller said he was "encouraged" by a number of positive recent economic developments in Puerto Rico, including:

—Continued emphasis of the Government Development Bank on sound and conservative practices of debt management. "The government has now embarked on a program to consolidate short-term debt and reduce its own borrowing plans and those of its public corporations," Rockefeller said.

—Employment seems to be re-emerging from the dismal levels of the recession. Rockefeller said the total number of people employed on the island is increasing at an annual rate of about 4½ percent.

Further, he said, while unemployment in March was still high at 17 percent, "when you compare this with the level of 19 percent in February and 20 percent in December, it suggests real improvement."

—Another area of encouragement is agriculture, where the government has begun to promote the development of import substitution crops such as rice and vegetables and the production of beef and poultry.

Rockefeller added that recent economic statistics in Puerto Rico's construction industry, which was hard hit by the recession, are also encouraging. However, he said, "the private sector is advancing at a much slower pace" than renewed construction activity in the public sector.

Business Climate 'Aids' Puerto Rico

David Rockefeller, chairman of the Chase Manhattan Bank, Thursday cited as a key ingredient in Puerto Rico's continued economic recovery, its ability to maintain "the kind of business climate which will continue to stamp the island as an inviting location for external investment."

Addressing the Puerto Rico Chamber of Commerce in the United States, the New York banker said that "barring any serious mistakes in economic strategy, Puerto Rico's economy should generally grow in pace with the U.S. economy."

Specifically, Mr. Rockefeller said "it seems reasonable to expect Puerto Rico to grow at close to 4 percent" over the next four years, assuming U.S. growth of 4 to 4½ percent.

Mr. Rockefeller said he was "encouraged" by a number of positive recent economic developments in Puerto Rico, including:

Continued emphasis of the Government-Development Bank on sound and conservative practices of debt management.

"The government has now embarked on a program to consolidate short-term debt and reduce its own borrowing plans and those of its public corporations," Mr. Rockefeller said.

Employment seems to be re-emerging from the dismal levels of the recession.

Mr. Rockefeller said the total number of people employed on the island is increasing at an annual rate of about 4½ percent. Further, while unemployment in March was still high at 17 percent, "when you compare this with the level of 19 percent in February and 20 percent in December, it suggests real improvement."

FIGURE 7–2. *A news release that hit.* Although editors don't like to admit it, sometimes news releases score with point-blank accuracy. In this case, a news release was picked up verbatim by a wire service, translated into Spanish, and given wide circulation in the sponsor's target markets.

SOURCE: Courtesy of The Chase Manhattan Bank.

Headlines.   Headlines are optional. Often, headlines are avoided and releases are begun one-third down the page to allow editors to devise original headlines. Some practitioners prefer headlines to "pre-sell" an editor on the gist of the news release that follows.

Proofreading.   Grammar, spelling, and typing must be perfect. Misspellings, grammatical errors, or typos are the quickest route to the editorial wastebasket.

Timing.   News release writers must be sensitive to editorial deadlines. Newspapers, magazines, and broadcast stations work under constant deadline pressure. A general interest release should arrive at an editor's desk a week to ten days in advance of the paper's deadline. Since "stale news is no news," a release arriving even just a little late might just as well have never been mailed.

To ensure that releases reach editors on time, many institutions either hand-deliver them or have them delivered by a messenger service. These practices are particularly common in metropolitan areas. Prompt delivery also can be ensured through the use of a commercial wire service, such as PR Newswire or Business Wire.

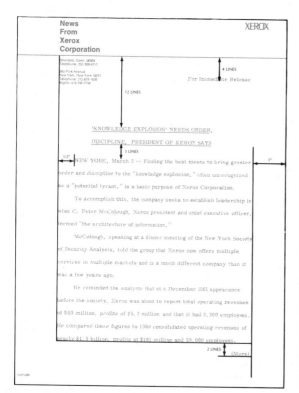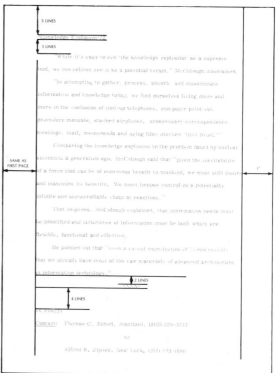

FIGURE 7–3.   *Xerox news release.* The appearance of a news release, like its content, must be professional. This sample from Xerox Corporation contains all the pertinent structural elements of a properly executed news release, including contact names and numbers, slug lines, and spacing.

SOURCE: Courtesy of Xerox Corporation.

STYLE

The style of a news release is almost as critical as its content. Sloppy style can break the back of any release and ruin its chances for publication. Style must also be flexible and evolve as language changes.

For those who think that worrying about capital letters, commas, and proper spelling are relatively insignificant concerns, note the price many companies pay for poor style, according to a leading designer of corporate annual reports:

> We have found that 25 to 50 percent of a company's last-minute changes—and charges—are due to tinkering with capitalization, punctuation, and other choices of style. We have also found that style varies from company to company and from year to year with no apparent reason, resulting in an unprofessional tone in too many annual reports.[6]

Most public relations operations follow the style practiced by major newspapers and magazines, rather than by book publishers. This news style is detailed in the various guides published by such authorities as the *Associated Press, United Press International,* and *The New York Times.*

The press must constantly update its style to conform to changing societal concepts. While release style is subjective and ever-changing, a particular firm's style must be consistent from one release to the next. The following are examples of typical style rules:

Capitalization. Most leading publications use capital letters sparingly; so should you. Editors call this a *down style,* because only the most important words begin with capital letters.

Abbreviations. Abbreviations present a many-faceted problem. For example, months, when used with dates, should be abbreviated, such as Sept. 2, 1975. When the day of the month is not used, the month should be spelled out, such as September 1975. Days of the week, on the other hand, should never be abbreviated. First mention of organizations and agencies should be spelled out, with the abbreviation put in parentheses after the name, such as Securities and Exchange Commission (SEC).

Numbers. There are many guidelines for the spelling out of numbers, but a general rule is to spell out numbers up through nine and use figures for ten and up. Figures, on the other hand, are perfectly acceptable for such things as election returns, speeds and distances, percentages, temperatures, heights, ages, ratios, and sports scores.

Punctuation. The primary purpose of punctuation is to clarify the writer's thoughts, ensure exact interpretation, and make reading and understanding quicker and easier. Less punctuation rather than more should be the goal.

Colon. The colon introduces listings, tabulations, and statements and takes the place of an implied *for instance.*

Comma. The comma is used in a variety of circumstances, including setting off connecting words, separating two words or figures that might otherwise be misunderstood, and setting off nonrestrictive clauses.

Exclamation point. In general, exclamation points should be resisted in releases. They tend to be overkill!!

Hyphen. The hyphen often is abused and should be used carefully. A single hyphen could change the meaning of a sentence completely. For example, "The six-foot man eating tuna was killed" (meaning the man was eating tuna) probably should be punctuated "The six-foot, man-eating tuna was killed."

Quotation Marks. Quoted matter is enclosed in double or single quotation marks. The double marks enclose the original quotation while the single marks enclose a quote within a quote.

Spelling. Many words, from *adviser* to *zucchini,* are commonly misspelled. The best way to avoid misspellings is to always have a dictionary within reach. When two spellings are given in a dictionary, the first spelling given is always the preferred one.

These are but a few of the stylistic stumbling blocks that writers must consider. In the news release, style should never be taken lightly. The style, as much as any other part of the release, lets an editor know what kind of company issued the release and how competent a professional wrote it.

CONTENT

The cardinal rule in release content is that the end product be *newsworthy.* The release must be of interest to an editor and readers. Issuing a release that has little chance of being used by a publication serves only to crush the credibility of the writer.

When a release is newsworthy and of potential interest to an editor, it must be written clearly and concisely, in proper newspaper style. It must get to the facts early and answer the six key questions. From there, it must follow inverted pyramid structure to its conclusion. For example, the following is not a proper lead for a release:

CLEVELAND, OHIO, MARCH 7, 1982—Chief Justice Warren Burger will speak tomorrow in Cleveland. He will speak at 8 P.M. He will address the convention of the American Bar Association. His address will be a major one and concern the topic of capital punishment.

Why would an editor discard this lead? In the first place, it does not get to the heart of the issue—the speech's topic—until the very end. Secondly, it's wordy. If the editor decided to use it at all, he'd have to rewrite it. Here's what should have been submitted:

Chief Justice Warren Burger will deliver a major address on capital punishment at 8 P.M. tomorrow in Cleveland before the American Bar Association convention.

While the second sample cut the verbiage in half, the pertinent questions still got answered: *who* (Chief Justice Warren Burger), *what* (will deliver a major address on capital punishment), *where* (Cleveland), *when* (tomorrow at 8 P.M.), and *why* (American Bar Association is holding a convention, at which he is speaking). Note that *how* in this case is less important. But whether the reader chooses to proceed further into the release or not, the story's gist has been successfully communicated in the lead.

News releases can be written about almost anything, but three frequent subjects are product and institutional announcements, management changes, and management speeches.

FEATURE
The style of equality

Dealing with gender isn't easy for today's writer. No matter how hard a writer tries to be even-handed in treating men and women in print, he—or she—is bound to offend someone.

In the early 1980s, the Congress acted to revise the Interstate Commerce Act by introducing a "gender-neutral terminology" section to the Bus Deregulation Bill. Among other refinements, the section called for "news boy" to be replaced by "newspaper carrier" and "lineman" to be replaced by "line maintainer."

In the mid-1970s, the Washington Press Club also published guidelines for the elimination of such bias in the media. The club's subcommittee on professional equality adopted the following four general rules:

1 Terms referring to a specific gender should be avoided when an alternative term will do. For example, use *business executive* instead of *businessman,* and *city council member* for *councilman.*

2 If no alternative gender-free term has yet achieved widespread acceptance, then use the term that accurately identifies the gender of the person. For example: *Robert Strauss, chairman of the Democratic National Committee; Mary Louise Smith, chairwoman of the Republican National Committee.*

3 Where neither a gender-free term nor any term accurately designating gender is yet in common use, continue to employ the old terminology, even where not literally accurate. For example: *yeoman first class Betty Jones; Mary Smith, a telephone company lineman.*

4 No occupational designation should include a qualification as to the person's gender, unless the sex of the individual is pertinent to the story. Qualifiers imply the occupations are inappropriate for the individuals holding them. For example, *woman lawyer* or *male nurse* would not be acceptable.

In addition, the subcommittee recommended avoiding the following terms: *man-made* (use instead: synthetic, manufactured, artificial); *man-on-the-street* (use instead: the ordinary citizen, the average worker); *man-power* (use instead: personnel, worker, work force); *man and wife* (use instead: husband and wife or man and woman); *co-ed* (use instead: student).

Despite attempts by many to eliminate sex-bias in writing style, satisfying everyone is a near-impossible task for any writer. He or she generally can't win.

THE "ANNOUNCEMENT"

Frequently, practitioners wish to announce a new product or institutional development, such as construction plans, earnings, mergers, and acquisitions, or company celebrations.

The announcement release should have a catchy yet significant lead to stimulate an editor to capitalize on someone else's (the practitioner's) creative idea. For example:

"Tennis whites," the traditional male court uniform, will yield to bright colors and fashion styling this spring as Jockey spearheads a new wave in tennis fashion with the introduction of a full line of tennis wear for men.

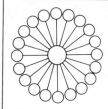

MINICASE
Bungling the Bromo news release

BROMO CORPORATION

CONTACT: Lance Ravenoo

Release Date: Hold for Sept. 20, 1983

Bromo Company Announces Revolutionary Digital Clock ~watch

LINCOLN, SEPT. 21, 1983—Bromo Corporation today announced they would begin marketing immediately a revolutionary digital wristwatch, capable of withstanding more pressure than any other digital watch on the market.

The new watch, described by scientists as "an amazing piece of modern machinery," was produced in Bromo's Lincoln, Texas plant. The watch was market-tested in the Lincoln, Nebraska area and was universally applauded by test participants.

"I've never seen a watch absorb so much punishment," was the response of one participant.

According to Lance Ravenoo, Bromo's director of marketing, "We believe this watch will outpace any other timepiece on the market. It's capacity to withstand abuse is simply unbelievable."

The Bromo watch, which is also waterproof, comes in two styles: a "nautical" that retails for $37.50 and the "free spirit" which retails for $380.00.

QUESTIONS

1 If you were an editor, would you use the Bromo news release?
2 How many errors can you spot?

The creation of the first manufacturing joint-venture company in Romania involving a Romanian company and an American firm was announced today by the Romanian Ministry of Machine Tools and Electro Techniques and Control Data Corporation.

Typically in an announcement release, after the lead identifies the significant aspects of the product or development, a spokesperson is quoted for additional product information. Editors appreciate the quotes because then they do not have to interview a company official. For example:

The new, lightweight plastic bottle for Coca-Cola began its national rollout today in Spartanburg, S.C. This two-liter package is the nation's first metric plastic bottle for soft drinks.

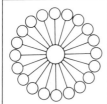

MINICASE
Promoting a president at Oswego U.

As public information director of Oswego University, you are advised that the university's Board of Trustees has selected the fifteenth president in the school's history.

He is Wilson W. Waters, a 1952 graduate of Oswego, who has most recently served as the school's Dean of Students.

In researching Waters' background, you uncover a few other interesting facts:

○ He is fifty years old, married to the former Renee Siggerson of Yankton, South Dakota.

○ He was born in Oswego and spent the first twenty-one years of his life there.

○ He has a master's degree from Brown University and a Ph.D. from Harvard.

○ He is 6'9", Jamaican, and played fifteen years in the National Basketball Association.

○ He had been Dean of Students at Oswego for ten years.

Your assignment, according to the board, is to publicize the Waters announcement as extensively as possible in local and national media.

QUESTIONS

1   Are these facts sufficient to write a news release about the new Oswego president? What additional information would help?

2   From the data given, what angle would you pursue for local Oswego editorial consumption?

3   What would your lead be for national media consumption?

4   Are there any facts given that you wouldn't use in the release?

"We are very excited about this new package," said John H. Ogden, president, Coca-Cola U.S.A. "Our two-liter plastic bottle represents an important advancement. Its light weight, toughness, and environmental advantages offer a new standard of consumer benefits in soft drink packaging."

The subtle product "plug" included in this release is typical of such announcements. Clearly, the organization gains if the product's benefits are described in a news story. But editors are sensitive to "product puffery" and the line between legitimate information and puffery is thin. One must always be sensitive to the needs and concerns of editors. A professional avoids letting the "thin line" of product information become a "short plank" of puffery.

THE "MANAGEMENT CHANGE"

Newspapers are often interested in management changes, but editors frequently reject releases that have no "local angle." For example, the editor of the Valdosta, Georgia *Citizen* has little reason to use this announcement:

NEW YORK, N.Y., SEPT. 5, 1983—Jeffrey O. Schultz has been named manager of the hosiery department at Bloomingdale's Paramus, N.J. store.

On the other hand, the same release, amended for local appeal, would almost certainly be used by the Valdosta *Citizen:*

NEW YORK, N.Y., SEPT. 5, 1983—Jeffrey O. Schultz, son of Mr. and Mrs. Siegfried Schultz of 221 Starling Lane, Valdosta, has been named manager of the hosiery department at Bloomingdale's Paramus, N.J. store.

Sometimes one must dig for the local angle. For example, suppose Mr. Schultz was born in Valdosta, but went to school in Americus, Georgia. With this knowledge, the writer might prepare the following release, which would have appeal in the newspapers of both Georgia cities:

NEW YORK, N.Y., SEPT. 5, 1983—Jeffrey O. Schultz, son of Mr. and Mrs. Siegfried Schultz of 221 Starling Lane, Valdosta and a 1972 graduate of Americus High School, was named manager of the hosiery department of Bloomingdale's Paramus, N.J. store.

While penetrating local publications with the management change release is relatively easy once the local angle has been identified, achieving publication in a national newspaper or magazine is much harder. *The Wall Street Journal,* for example, will not use a management change announcement unless the individual has attained a certain level of responsibility, usually corporate vice-president or higher. In other words, if a release involves someone who has not attained senior executive status at a major company, forget it, at least as far as *The Wall Street Journal* is concerned.

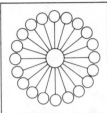

MINICASE
Selecting the right lead

The president's speech on corporate social responsibility is one for which he seeks wide press coverage. He believes that somewhere in the following excerpt lies the key for maximum media exposure:

> By and large, I believe the typical American business is keenly aware of its social responsibilities. But while most companies have recognized the need for social responsibility, many have had difficulty in applying the concept to daily operations.
>
> To some, *social responsibility* has meant stepping up financial contributions to urban projects. To others, the term has become synonymous with programs to minimize pollution, train the hard-core unemployed, or counsel the disadvantaged.
>
> But that is not enough.
>
> Specifically, I believe the time has come for companies to move beyond narrow notions of corporate social responsibility and to adopt instead a more deep-rooted and pervasive framework of ethical policies and procedures. What we need now is social responsibility that underlies every decision the corporation makes.
>
> The challenge now, as I see it, is to institutionalize ethics by shaping specific corporate codes of conduct and by integrating ethical practices more firmly into corporate policy.

QUESTION
Based on this speech excerpt, what would your lead be?

For national consumption, it is the importance or uniqueness of the individual or company that should be emphasized. For example, an editor might not realize that the following management change is unique:

WASHINGTON, D.C., JUNE 6, 1983—Yolanda King of Sacramento, Cal. today was promoted to the rank of admiral in the United States Navy.

However, the same release stands out clearly for its news value when the unique angle is played up:

WASHINGTON, D.C., JUNE 6, 1983—Yolanda King of Sacramento, Cal. today was named the first woman admiral in the history of the United States Navy.

While one can never go wrong being straightforward in a news release, a local or unique angle to help sell the story to an editor should always be investigated.

FEATURE
A good editor is gutsy

Good editors must be willing to take bold strokes. They must chop, slice, and cut through unnecessary words. Bad grammar, misspellings, incorrect punctuation, poorly constructed sentences, misused words, mixed metaphors, non sequiturs, cliches, redundancies, circumlocutions, jargon—all are their mortal enemies.

Regrettably, many public relations writers, like many newspaper reporters, are not as careful in writing as they should be. Here, for your editing pleasure, is a typical cross section of the worst that professional writers have to offer:
What's wrong here?

○ The present incumbent is running for re-election.

○ The smell of war returns to the capital, and I am listening seriously.

○ She was strangled to death in her bed.

○ He was held on charges of negligible homicide.

○ She is the widow of the late Nelson Apfelbaum.

○ The coffee service is supported by replicas of chicken legs, which belonged to Mrs. Abraham Lincoln.

○ Yesterday, a car battery exploded in his face while helping a stranded motorist.

○ If elected, he promised to evoke stiff penalties for drunken drivers.

○ Although Jessie Owens is dead, his feats live on.

○ It was the general consensus of opinion that Nelson was innocent.

○ Not only was her enthusiastic exuberance catching, but it was also contagious.

THE "MANAGEMENT SPEECH"

Management speeches are another recurring source of news releases. The key to a speech news release is selecting the most significant portion of the talk for the lead.

A good speech will generally have a clear thesis, from which a lead will naturally flow. Once the thesis is identified, the remainder of the release simply embellishes it. For example:

BOONEVILLE, MO., OCT. 18, 1983—Booneville Mining Company is "on the verge of having several very profitable years," Booneville Mining President Marsha Mulford said today.

Addressing the Booneville Chamber of Commerce, the Missouri mining company executive cited two reasons for the positive projections: the company's orders are at an all-time high, and its overseas facilities have "turned the corner" on profitability in the current year.

Normally, if the speech giver is not a famous person, the release should not begin with the speaker's name but rather with the substance of the remarks. If the speaker is a well-known individual, leading with a name is perfectly legitimate. For example:

> Secretary of Commerce Malcolm Baldridge called today for a "new attitude toward business investment and capital formation."

The body copy of a speech release should follow directly from the lead. Often, the major points of the speech must be paraphrased and consolidated to conform to a two-page release. In any event, it is often a significant challenge to convert the essence of a management speech to news release form.

THE IMPORTANCE OF EDITING

Editing is the all-important final touch for the public relations writer. In a news release, a careful self-edit can save the deadliest prose.

An editor must be judicious. Each word, phrase, sentence, and paragraph should be weighed carefully. Good editing will "punch up" dull passages and make them sparkle. For instance, "The satellite flies across the sky" is dead. But, "The satellite roars across the sky" is alive.

In the same context, good editing will get rid of passive verbs. Invariably, this will produce shorter sentences. For example, "The cherry tree *was* chopped down by George Washington." Shorter and better is "George Washington *chopped* down the cherry tree."

Editing should also concentrate on organizing copy. One release paragraph should flow naturally into the next. Sometimes it just takes a single word to unite the two adjoining paragraphs. Such is the case in the use of the word *size* in the following example:

> The machine works on a controlled mechanism, directed by a series of pulleys. It is much smaller than the normal motor, requiring less than half of a normal motor's components.
> Not only does the device differ in size from other motors, it also differs in capacity.

Writing, like fine wine, should flow smoothly and stand up under the toughest scrutiny. Careful editing, therefore, is a must.

168   PRACTICAL APPLICATIONS

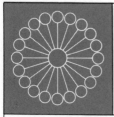

CASE STUDY
The Raina, Inc. news release

BACKGROUND: The Raina, Inc. Carborundum plant in Blackrock, Iowa has been under pressure in recent months to remedy its pollution problem. Raina's plant is the largest in Blackrock. While the company has spent $1.3 million on improving its pollution control equipment, black smoke still spews from the plant's smokestacks, and waste products are still allowed to filter into neighboring streams.

The pressure on Raina, Inc. has been intense of late. To wit:

○ On Sept. 7, Andrew Laskow, a private citizen, called to complain of the "noxious smoke" which was befouling the environment.

○ On September 8, Mrs. Lizzy Ledger of the Blackrock Garden Club called to protest the "smoke problem" which was wreaking havoc with the zinnias and other flowers in the area.

○ On September 9, Clarence "Smoky" Salmon, president of the Blackrock Rod and Gun Club, called to report that 700 people had signed a petition against the Raina plant's pollution of Zeus Creek.

○ On September 10, WERS-Radio editorialized that "the time had come to force area plants to act on solving pollution problems."

○ On September 11, the Blackrock City Council announced plans to enact an air and water pollution ordinance for the city. The Council invited as its first witness before the public hearing, Leslie Sludge, manager of the Raina Carborundum Blackrock Plant.

NEWS RELEASE DATA:

1   Leslie Sludge, manager of Raina Carborundum's Blackrock Plant, appeared at the Blackrock City Council hearing on September 13.

2   Sludge said Raina Carborundum already has spent $1.3 million on a program to "clean up" pollution at its Blackrock plant.

3   Raina had received 500 "complaints calls" in the past three months protesting its pollution conditions.

4   Sludge said Raina was "concerned about environmental problems but profits are still what keeps our company running."

5   Sludge announced the company had decided to commit another $2 million for pollution abatement facilities over the next three months.

6   Raina Carborundum is the oldest plant in Blackrock and was built in 1900.

7   Raina's Blackrock plant employs 10,000 people, the largest single employer in Blackrock.

8 Raina, Inc. originally scheduled its "pollution abatement" program for 1984, but speeded it up because of public pressure in recent months.

9 Sludge said that the new "pollution abatement" program would begin in October, and that the company projected "real progress in terms of clean water and clean air" as early as June 1983.

10 In 1975, Raina, Inc. received a "Presidential Award" from the Environmental Protection Administration for its "concern for pollution abatement."

11 An internal Raina, Inc. study indicated that Blackrock was the "most pollutant-laden" of all Raina's plants nationwide.

12 Sludge formerly served as manager of Raina's Fetid Reservoir plant in Fetid Reservoir, New Hampshire. In two years as manager of Fetid Reservoir, Sludge was able to convert it from one of the most "pollutant-laden" plants in the system to the "cleanest," as judged by the Environmental Protection Administration.

13 Sludge has been manager of Blackrock for two months.

14 Raina, Inc.'s new program will cost the company $2 million in all.

15 Raina will hire 100 extra workers especially for the "pollution abatement" program.

16 Sludge, 35, is married to the former Polly Usion of Wheeling, West Virginia.

17 Sludge is author of the book, *Fly Fishing Made Easy.*

18 The bulk of the expense for the new "pollution abatement" program will be spent on two globe refractors, which purify waste destined to be deposited in surrounding waterways, and four hyperventilation systems, which remove noxious particles dispersed into the air from smokestacks.

19 Sludge said, "Raina, Inc. has decided to move ahead with this program at this time because of its long-standing responsibility for keeping the Blackrock environment clean and in response to growing community concern over achieving the objective."

20 Former Blackrock plant manager Fowler Aire was fired by the company in July for his "flagrant disregard for the environment."

21 Aire also was found to be diverting Raina, Inc. funds from company projects to his own pockets. In all, Aire took close to $10,000 for which the company was not reimbursed. At least part of the money was to be used for pollution control.

22 Aire, whose whereabouts are presently not known, is the brother of J. Derry Aire, Raina's vice president for finance.

23 Raina, Inc.'s Blackrock plant has also recently installed ramps and other special apparatus to assist handicapped employees. Presently, Blackrock has 100 handicapped workers in the Raina, Inc. plant.

24 Raina, Inc.'s Blackrock plant started as a converted garage, manufacturing plate glass. Only thirteen people worked in the plant at that time.

25 Today, the Blackrock plant employs 10,000, covers fourteen acres of land, and is the largest single supplier of plate glass and commercial panes in the country.

26   The Blackrock plant was slated to be the subject of a critical report from the Private Environmental Stabilization Task-force (PEST), a private environmental group. PEST's report, "The Foulers," was to discuss "the 10 largest manufacturing polluters in the nation."

27   Raina, Inc. management has been aware of the PEST report for several months.

QUESTIONS

1   If you were assigned to draft a news release to accompany Sludge to the Blackrock City Council meeting on September 11, which items would you use in your lead, i.e. who, what, why, where, when, how?

2   Which items would you avoid using in the news release?

3   If a reporter from the *Blackrock Bugle* called and wanted to know, "What happened to former Blackrock manager Fowler Aire?," what would you tell him?

NOTES

1   "From 235 Words to 23: Insurance Industry Makes Strides in Language Simplification," *PR Reporter* 21, no. 14 (3 April 1978):2.

2   "The 60-Word Blacklist" (p. 72) from *Say What You Mean* by Rudolph Flesch. Copyright © 1972 by Rudolph Flesch. Reprinted by permission of Harper & Row Publishers, Inc.

3   Charles Honaker, "News Releases Revisited," *Public Relations Journal,* April 1981, p. 25.

4   Bill L. Baxter, "The News Release, An Idea Whose Time Has Gone," *Public Relations Review,* Spring 1981, p. 30.

5   Charles Honaker, *op. cit.*

6   Corporate Annual Reports, Inc., "Guide to Business Writing Style" (New York: Author, 1975), p. 1. Available from 112 E. 31 St., New York, N.Y.

SUGGESTED READING

Ayer Press. *Ayer Public Relations and Publicity Stylebook.* Philadelphia, Pa.: Author, 1975. A guide to copy preparation for the publicist.

Baxter, Bill L. "The News Release: An Idea Whose Time Has Gone?" *Public Relations Review,* Spring 1981, pp. 27–31. Professor Baxter recommends concrete steps public relations practitioners can take to bring releases up to a new standard.

Blewett, Steve. "On Being A Pro: A House Organ Editor Speaks," *Public Relations Quarterly,* Summer 1981, pp. 9–10.

Erb, Lyle L. "Experts Misuse of Language: Part One," *Public Relations Quarterly,* Spring 1982, p. 32.

Erb, Lyle L. "Writer's Notebook," *Public Relations Quarterly,* Spring 1981, p. 32.

Erb, Lyle L. "Writer's Notebook," *Public Relations Quarterly,* Winter 1981–82, p. 32.

Flesch, Rudolf. *The Art of Plain Talk.* Paperback ed. New York: Macmillan, 1962.

————. *Say What You Mean.* New York: Harper & Row, 1972.

Fowler, H. W. *A Dictionary of Modern English Usage.* Oxford, England: Oxford University Press, 1926.

Greaser, Constance U. "Writers, Editors and Computers," *Public Relations Journal,* March 1982, pp. 26–28. "Hacking Through The Paper Jungle," *Public Relations Journal,* August 1981, p. 26.

Hayakawa, Samuel I. *Writing Language in Thought and Action.* 4th ed. New York: Harcourt Brace Jovanovich, 1978.

————. *The Use and Misuse of Language.* New York: Fawcett, 1973.

Honaker, Charles. "News Releases Revisited," *Public Relations Journal,* April 1981, pp. 25–27. Honaker explains why editors are repulsed by the steady and overwhelming flow of releases that are poorly written, fatuous, and without news value.

Jordon, Lewis, ed. *The New York Times Manual of Style and Usage.* New York: McGraw-Hill, 1977.

Rivers, William L. *Writing: Craft & Arts.* Englewood Cliffs, N.J.: Prentice-Hall, 1975.

Shaw, Harry. *Twenty Steps to Better Writing.* Totowa, N.Y.: Littlefield, Adams, 1975.

Strunk, W., and **White, E.B.** *Elements of Style.* New York, N.Y.: Macmillan, 1972.

TRADITIONAL STRENGTH

Writing for reading has traditionally been among the strongest areas for most public relations professionals. Most practitioners entered public relations through the field of print journalism. Accordingly, most practitioners were schooled in the techniques of writing for the eye. Today, of course, a background in the print media is not particularly necessary to practice public relations work. Indeed, as noted, public relations professionals today gravitate into the field from a variety of backgrounds —from law, television, general management, political science, and education.

Nonetheless, demonstrating a facility for writing for reading continues to be a basic requirement for public relations work.

While the news release is the most frequently used communications vehicle designed to be read, there are additional writing weapons in the practitioner's arsenal. Each has its own purpose and style. This chapter will review several writing vehicles: the biography, the backgrounder, the feature story, the case history, the byliner, the memorandum, and the pitch letter.

8
Writing For the Eye

Each of these may stand alone as individual communications. Often, several are combined as limited elements in a press kit (to be discussed later), which may provide editors with story ideas. The practitioner must know when each particular vehicle is appropriate.

THE BIOGRAPHY

Next to the press release, the most popular tool is the biography, often called the *biographical summary* or just plain *bio*. The bio recounts pertinent facts about a particular individual. Most organizations keep a file of bios for all top officers. Major newspapers and wire services prepare stand-by bios on well-known people for immediate use on breaking news, such as sudden deaths.

STRAIGHT BIOS

The *straight bio* lists information, factually and straightforwardly, about an individual in descending order of importance, with company-oriented facts preceding more personal details. For example:

David Rockefeller became chairman of the board of directors and chief executive officer of The Chase Manhattan Bank, N.A. in New York on March 1, 1969 and of The Chase Manhattan Corporation upon its formation on June 4, 1969.

During his career with Chase Manhattan, Mr. Rockefeller gained a worldwide reputation as a leading banker and spokesman for the business community. He spearheaded the bank's expansion both internationally and throughout the metropolitan New York area and helped the bank play a significant role as a corporate citizen.

Mr. Rockefeller joined The Chase National Bank as an assistant manager in the foreign department in 1946. He was appointed an assistant cashier in 1947, second vice-president in 1948, and vice-president in 1949.

From 1950 to 1952, he was responsible for the supervision of Chase's business in Latin America, where, under his direction, new branches were opened in Cuba, Panama, and Puerto Rico, plus a representative office in Buenos Aires.

NARRATIVE BIOS

The *narrative bio*, on the other hand, is written in a breezier, more informal way. This style gives spark and vitality to the biography to make the individual come alive. For example:

David Rockefeller, who has been described as a man possessed of "a peculiar blend of enterprise, prudence, knowledge, and dedication," was born in Manhattan on June 12, 1915. His mother was the former Abby Aldrich, daughter of Senator Nelson Aldrich of Rhode Island. She had met John D. Rockefeller, Jr., the shy son of multimillionaire John D. Rockefeller, when he was an undergraduate at Brown University in Providence.

John D. Rockefeller, Jr. was anxious that his children not be spoiled by the fortune his father had created and therefore put them on strict allowances. The household atmosphere was deeply religious, with one of the children reading the scriptures each morning before breakfast. Mrs. Rockefeller was an exceptional woman, with a strong interest in the arts. She and David were very close.

Throughout David's academic career, he attended schools in which the Rockefeller family had an interest—either philanthropic, sentimental, or both. Abby and John D.,

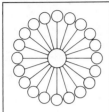

MINICASE
Grepso the clown bio

As the public relations director for WAAH-TV, you are assigned to write both a straight and narrative bio on the station's ever-popular Grepso the Clown. Here are eight key facts:

1 Grepso's real name is Howie Barmad. He is 45 and a former light-heavyweight boxing contender.

2 Grepso was born in Jersey City, New Jersey.

3 He joined WAAH ten years ago as a newscaster, later worked as a weatherman, and five years ago became Grepso the Clown.

4 Grepso was educated at Harvard University, where he received a B.A. degree in philosophy and graduated Magna Cum Laude.

5 He has been voted "clown of the year" for three years in a row as northeastern chairman of the United Cerebral Palsy Telethon.

6 Grepso lives in Basking Ridge, New Jersey. His hobbies include collecting tropical fish, snorkeling, and fingerpainting.

QUESTION
From the data given, how would you write a straight bio on Grepso? A narrative bio?

III had attended traditional private schools, but David and his three other brothers were sent to Lincoln School, an experimental venture conducted by the Teachers College of Columbia to try out the progressive techniques of John Dewey.

Because of its personal tone, a good narrative bio is more difficult to write than the standard bio, which allows little room for embellishment.

THE BACKGROUNDER

Background pieces, or *backgrounders*, generally provide additional information about the institution making an announcement. Backgrounders are usually longer and more general in content than the news release. For example, a two-page release announcing the merger of two organizations may not permit much description of the companies involved. A four- or five-page backgrounder provides editors with more depth on the makeup, activities, and history of the merging firms. Backgrounders are usually not used in their entirety by the media but rather are excerpted.

Subject matter dictates backgrounder style. Some backgrounders, like Example One, are written like a news release, in a snappy and factual manner. Others, like Example Two, take a more descriptive and narrative form.

Lyle L. Erb is a columnist for *Public Relations Quarterly*. Mr. Erb was in the newspaper business for 36 years. He edited *Seminar, a Quarterly Review For Journalists*, for nine years and published *In Black and White*, the eclectic newsletter for those who write and edit for publication, for three years. Now retired, Mr. Erb is a consultant in Pacific Beach, California.

How would you assess the state of public relations writing today?

Deplorable. That is a generality, but in general, accurately descriptive of most of the press releases, scripts, pitch letters, etc., that come to me for review.

What are the fundamentals you consider sacrosanct in writing?

Be brief. Use short words. Write short sentences, short paragraphs. Eschew obfuscation. Avoid cliches, slang, fad words. Shun

**EXAMPLE ONE:
BACKGROUNDER—THE MAGNAVOX COMPANY**

The Magnavox Company, founded in 1912, is a leading manufacturer of quality products in the areas of consumer electronics, home furnishings, music, mobile home and recreational vehicles, government, and industry.

The company has over 20,000 employees working in three operating groups: the consumer electronics group, the home furnishing and music group, and the government and industrial group.

Government and industrial group. This division has historically been oriented to engineering and manufacturing products for the Department of Defense. In recent years, an extensive effort has been made to develop a significant posture in the industrial electronics field. Specific products are communications systems, position location and navigation systems, and specialized information gathering and processing systems for both government and industry.

hyperbole and circumlocution. Be direct—active, not passive. Have respect for the tools of our trade, the words we work with. Don't use words like "sacrosanct."

Do you think anyone can master public relations writing skills?

No. (I assume you mean "everyone.") Many college graduates today can't write a simple sentence. They are ignorant of basic rules of grammar. They can't spell. Yet some of them are successful public relations practitioners.

As a columnist, what kinds of pitch letters do you especially appreciate?

Those that DO NOT begin with "danglers": "As a writer, I want you to know . . ." "As an investor, there is an opportunity . . ." For example: In this question, what does the phrase "as a columnist" modify?

What advice would you give a colleague who had to write a public relations feature and couldn't get started?

Do your research thoroughly. Decide what you want to say. Tell them you're going to say it. Say it. Tell them what you said.

What constitutes a good press kit?

A good one presents the facts—"Just the facts, ma'am"—about the product, service, or person. A bad one exaggerates, overemphasizes, intensifies, and is replete with italics, capital letters, and astounders!

How does one become a "good" writer?

By writing. Writing, revising, and rewriting. A good copy editor can improve almost anyone's writing. *Good* writing is not necessarily *fine* writing. As one sage put it, "When you think you have written an especially fine line, blot it out. It will do wonders for your style." Remember that facility is not felicity. "You write with ease to show your breeding, but easy writing's curst hard reading." (Thomas Moore's *Life of Sheridan*.) The writing may be easy. It's the revising and rewriting that's hard work.

Is there anything else you'd like readers of this book to know?

There is no such thing as "good public relations writing," just as there is no such thing as "good journalistic writing" or say, "good legal writing." Good writing is good writing. Bad writing is what gave rise to such opprobrious terms as *journalese* and *legalese*. Good writing communicates. And that's what public relations is all about. (We are not speaking here of fiction or belles lettres.)

EXAMPLE TWO:
BACKGROUNDER—SICKLE CELL DISEASE

The man was a West Indian Black, a 20-year-old student in a professional school in Illinois. One day in 1904, he came to James B. Herrick, an eminent Chicago cardiologist, with symptoms Herrick had never seen before and could not find in the literature. The patient had shortness of breath, a disinclination for exercise, palpitation, jaundice, cough, dizziness, headache, leg ulcers, scars from old leg ulcers, many palpable lymph nodes, pale mucous membranes, muscular rheumatism, severe upper abdominal pain, dark urine, and anemia. Blood smears showed many odd-shaped cells, but what arrested the eye was the presence of numerous sickle-shaped cells.

Herrick kept the patient under observation for many years. He did not suspect that he was looking at a disease that afflicted millions of people, including thousands of Blacks in America.

In devising a backgrounder, a writer enjoys unlimited latitude. As long as the piece catches the interest of the reader/editor, any style is permissable.

NEWS NEWS NEWS
from *ROYAL-GLOBE*

110 WILLIAM STREET NEW YORK N.Y 10038
212 732 3456

CONTACT   Frank J. Morris/ Guy Staffa
Date   February 27, 1978
No.   15

RELEASE   IMMEDIATE

ROYAL-GLOBE SPONSORS
INSURANCE LUNCH-O-REE
FOR NEW YORK SCOUTS

NEW YORK -- Royal-Globe Insurance Companies, which sponsored the first Greater New York Councils, Boy Scouts of America Insurance Lunch-O-Ree a decade ago, will again sponsor the annual event on April 13, 1978, at the Waldorf-Astoria Hotel.

"In underwriting costs of this Lunch-O-Ree, Royal-Globe assures the entire proceeds of the event will go to support the Greater New York Councils, BSA, which serves more than 80,000 youths and adult leaders," noted Royal-Globe President J. Roy Nicholas, chairman of the Lunch-O-Ree. "The Greater New York Councils is the largest scouting organization in the country, and 82 per cent of its budget is used to support program services to youths," Mr. Nicholas added.

A highlight of the Lunch-O-Ree will be the presentation of "Good Scout" awards to Harold A. Eckmann, chairman of the Atlantic Companies, and John M. Regan Jr., chairman, Marsh & McLennan Companies, Inc., both in New York City. Each year, the awards are presented to industry leaders who best exemplify the ideals of the Boy Scouts of America.

Tables of ten are $750 and individual tickets are $75 each. For tickets, contact Linwood C. Wiley Jr., finance director, Greater New York Councils, 345 Hudson Street, New York, N.Y. 10014, (212) 242-1100. The sales goal is 1,000 tickets.

We Think You Should Know . . .

Royal-Globe Insurance Companies are part of Royal Insurance, an international insurance group that offers coverage in more than 80 countries, writes policies in 17 languages and collects premiums and pays losses in 121 currencies.

In the United States, the history of the Companies reaches back to the founding of the Newark Insurance Company in 1811. Today, Royal-Globe does business in all 50 states and writes premiums of over $800 million through a network of more than 125 offices and 6,000 skilled employes countrywide.

During its many decades of service in the United States, Royal-Globe has withstood many catastrophies: the Chicago fire and the San Francisco earthquake and conflagrations; hurricanes, depressions and the dislocation of wars. While some others have faltered, we have grown and continue to provide markets for the protection of people and business.

Royal-Globe is noted for meeting the needs of a changing society. The Companies were first to provide fire insurance for the Pacific Coast in 1853 and insured the first self-sustaining nuclear chain reaction in 1942 at the University of Chicago.

Ever-growing financial resources, a countrywide network of service offices, thousands of skilled employees committed to maintaining the corporation's tradition of superior service to policyholders and producers, and well over a century of experience in this country evidence Royal-Globe's reputation as a leader in the insurance field.

FIGURE 8-1 This backgrounder supplements information on the release's corporate sponsor.

THE FEATURE

Closely related to the backgrounder is the feature story. Features in magazines or newspapers are the opposite of news items. They're often light and humorous, although some are serious.

One of the foremost sources of feature writing is *The Wall Street Journal*. Each business day, the *Journal's* front page is dominated by three "leader" articles, most written in a time-tested feature writing style. Basically, the *Journal* system separates each story into three distinct parts, sometimes labeled as the *D-E-E System*.[1]

DESCRIPTION

The typical *Journal* story begins by *describing* an existing situation, often with a light touch, in a way that readers relate directly to their own environment. For example:

> Seated at student desks in a small room, prospective Delta Airline pilots pore over a battery of psychological tests.
>
> "This is ridiculous," mutters one of the four applicants. "What do these tests have to do with whether I'll make a good pilot? What the hell does it matter whether I like to sing in the shower?"
>
> It may matter a great deal.[2]

EXPLANATION

The second part of the *Journal* feature *explains* how a situation, trend, or event came to be. It is often historical in nature, stating dates, places, and people from the past. It often relates how other factors (economic, sociopolitical, or environmental) may have come to bear on the topic. For example:

> Delta is among hundreds of U.S. concerns that are turning more to psychologists for guidance in deciding who gets what job.
>
> Through testing and interviews, psychologists help screen prospective employees and select promotion candidates—occasionally all the way up the corporate ladder.
>
> The trend isn't new.[3]

EVALUATION

The final section of the *Journal* feature *evaluates* the meaning of what is contained in the first two parts. It often focuses on the future, frequently quoting sociologists, psychologists, or other experts on the meaning of the phenomenon discussed. For example:

> "We're not interested in exposing or destroying a man," says Melvin Reid, president of a management consulting firm that does psychological testing. "We're interested in coming to general conclusions that both employee and employer will find useful in selection and placement."[4]

THE CASE HISTORY

For public relations purposes, the D-E-E approach is a natural in feature assignments. The case history, for example, is frequently used to tell about a customer's favorable use of a company's product or service. Generally, the case history writer works for the company whose product or service is involved. Magazines, particularly trade journals, often welcome case histories, contending that one person's experience may be instructive to another.

Case history articles generally follow a five-part formula:

1   They present a problem experienced by one company but applicable to many other firms.
2   They indicate how the dimensions of the problem were defined by the company using the product.
3   They indicate the solution adopted.

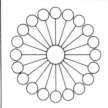

MINICASE
The lethargic lubar works

You've been assigned to write a case history article for *Modern Metal Markets* magazine by your client, Belch Weather, the nation's fourth largest producer of lubar equipment. Here are the facts:

1   A year and a half ago, Zazu Industries could not produce enough dorts in its Bythorn factory, despite running three shifts. As a result, Zazu was not keeping pace with demand and risked losing important orders.
2   Zazu's vice-president of production examined the production records of the Bythorn factory and visited the plant. She spent several days inspecting the production line and talking to supervisors and workers. She concluded that the lubar equipment, purchased ten years ago, was not as fast or efficient as it should be.
3   Zazu detailed the specifications for the equipment, informed suppliers, and took competitive bids. Eventually, the lubar equipment of Belch Weather was purchased.
4   Although Belch Weather's was not the least expensive equipment, it turned out to be the most cost-effective. It could, with minor adaptations, turn out three sizes of dorts: large, medium, and small. Competitive equipment could only turn out two sizes. Belch Weather's equipment also produced 400 units an hour, compared with 275 units on the old equipment and 410 units on the equipment of Belch Weather's nearest competitor. However, the competitor's price was much higher than Belch Weather's.
5   Zazu has been using Belch Weather equipment since that time. In that period, only three of twenty-six machines have been out of working order. Production has improved, and Zazu is now able to go to a two-shift operation at an annual savings of $1 million. This amount each year over a five-year period will offset the cost of buying Belch Weather's lubar equipment.

QUESTIONS

1   If you worked for Belch Weather, how would you apply the D-E-E method to this case history?
2   How would your approach differ if you worked for Zazu Industries?

4 They explain the advantages of the adopted solution.

5 They detail the user company's experience after adopting the solution.

Incorporating the D-E-E approach into the case history writing process may interest an editor in a particular product or service. Done skillfully, such a case history is "soft sell" at its best—beneficial to the company and interesting and informative to the editor and readers.

THE BYLINER

The by-lined article, or *byliner*, is a story signed and ostensibly authored by an officer of a particular firm. Often, the byliner is ghost-written by a public relations professional. In addition to carrying considerable prestige in certain publications, byliners also allow corporate spokespeople to express their views without being subject to major reinterpretation by the publication.

Perhaps the major advantage of a byliner is that it positions executives as experts. The fact that an organization's officer authors an informed article on a subject means that not only are the officer and the organization credible sources but also, by inference, that they are perhaps *more* highly regarded on the issues at hand than their competitors. Indeed, the ultimate audience exposed to a byliner may greatly exceed the circulation of the periodical in which the article appears. Organizations regularly use byliner reprints as direct mail pieces to further their image with key constituent groups. Such use of reprints will be further discussed in Chapter 10.

It is often a good idea for a writer to outline the byliner, noting at the outset the major points the author wishes to get across. Although most byliners are more formal than case histories and generally contain many facts and figures, they still can lend themselves to the D-E-E writing approach.

THE MEMORANDUM

Humorist Art Buchwald tells of the child who visited his father's office. When asked what his dad did, the son replied, "He sends pieces of paper to other people, and other people send pieces of paper to him."

Most people who work know a great deal about memoranda. Inside many organizations, the memo is the most popular form of communication. Memos are written for a multitude of purposes and adopt numerous forms. While most everyone gets into the memo-writing act, writing memos correctly takes practice and hard work.

The key to writing good memos is clear thinking. Many memos reflect unclear thinking and are plagued by verbosity and fuzzy language. Inverted pyramid style is often a good way to compose a memo. More often, *rewriting* turns out to be the key. As professor Marvin Switt has put it:

> Rewriting demands a real openmindedness and objectivity. It demands a willingness to cull verbiage so that ideas stand out clearly. And it demands a willingness to meet logical contradictions head-on and trace them to the premises that have created them. In short, it forces a writer to get up his courage and expose his thinking process to his

own intelligence . . . It demands that you put yourself through the wringer, intellectually and emotionally, to squeeze out the best you can offer.[5]

Practitioners, in particular, must write good memos. Frequently they must prepare long, internal *white papers, position papers,* or *standby statements* that should clearly outline the firm's position. Such documents are used to respond to inquiries on sensitive subjects and can't afford to be vague or subject to misinterpretation.

In general, the more textually taut a memo is, the less chance it will fall prey to others in the organization who are prone to pounce on it. One rule of thumb for memo writing is to pretend to send the memo to yourself as a straight telegram at your own expense. Chances are, the less your telegram costs, the more effective the memo will be.

THE PITCH LETTER

The pitch letter is a sales letter, pure and simple. Its purpose is to interest an editor or reporter in a possible story, interview, or event. (Figure 8–2 gives examples of pitch letters.) Although letter styles run the gamut, the best are direct and to the point, while at the same time, catchy and evocative. The pitch letter's lead, unlike a typical

---

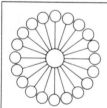

MINICASE
The misleading memo

To: Public Relations Department
From: Rita Rey, Public Relations Director

It has recently been brought to my attention that many of the press comments our organization has been receiving in the negative may stem from our policy of refusing all press interviews, regardless of the publication making the request.

Obviously, such negative stories do our company no good with its many publics and often present an unfair and misleading presentation as to our philosophy and approach. I wish therefore to inform all concerned—those who have refused interviews in the past and all others as well—that we will immediately change our policy to entertain all requests from the press and judge each on its merits.

If there are any questions about company policy on this matter, please contact me.

QUESTIONS
1 What's wrong with this memo?
2 How would you improve it?

IF you EVER WANT TO SEE tHE little N⊙TiONAL LAmpOON aLive AgaiN iN YOUR CRUmmy MailBOX, you KNOw whAt you HAVE to Do!!!

you've BeEN WaRNed.

DON'T PLAY CUTE.

National Lampoon

This Is Your Last Chance . . .

Say good-bye, sweetheart. This is it! You can kiss the $7.95 one-year subscription to the *National Lampoon* good-bye just as you've said *au revoir* and *harry verderchi* to the fifty-cent gallon of gas, the ten-cent cigar, and the twenty-cent bus ride.

The price is going up and we're giving you fair warning. We're not saying exactly how much we're going to charge for the new one-year subscription but — it's less than the gross national product of Yugoslavia and more than a rubdown in a midget massage parlor.

The reasons for the increase in price are numerous in addition to greed:

1. The cost of paper has skyrocketed. All right, let's examine that. What does it mean to a magazine operation? Well, our editors drink a lot of coffee and this means an increase in the price of coffee cups. They throw paper airplanes around the room while trying to think of funny things to say. Up your cost of paper airplanes by 50 percent.

2. The cost of typewriters has increased. This doesn't affect us since no one on our staff knows how to type.

3. The cost of manufacturing has increased. This means that our editor in chief will be paying more for his Mercedes-Benz this year, and that means more for you to kick in. Would you ask the editor in chief of the world's most widely read adult humor magazine to drive around in last year's Mercedes-Benz?

4. The price of grain is spiraling. (We don't know what that means, but it is an exact quote from the *Wall Street Journal* so it must be important.)

O.K., put this all together and it means — raise the subscription prices. No more $7.95. So, this is it. This is your last chance. From here on in, it's clipsville. You pay more.

If you really want to save, take out a two- or three-year subscription. The savings are so big that we actually lose money every time you or anyone else subscribes for two or three years. We do it only because our subscription manager is insecure and he wants to know that he'll have at least a handful of people around for a long time.

No more message. If you want the latest in yocks, mirth, and lovable satire, subscribe today and subscribe at these pre-inflation prices.

Sincerely,

Herbert Hoover

Herbert Hoover
Subscription Manager

FIGURE 8–2. Pitch letters should be enticing, catchy, and evocative. And while these examples from the subscription department of the *National Lampoon* magazine may not exactly qualify as bona fide pitch letters, they certainly are enticing, catchy, and evocative. SOURCE: Courtesy of The National Lampoon.

gossipy and rambling personal letter, should hit the reader between the eyes with a punchy, direct-mail marketing approach. Good pitch letters usually contain several key elements:

First, they open with a *grabber*, an interesting statement that impels the reader to read on. Next, they explain why the editor and/or publication should be interested in the "pitch" or invitation. Finally, they are personally written to specific people, rather than being addressed to "editor" (which is the journalistic equivalent of "occupant").

A variant of the pitch letter is the *query letter*, in which the practitioner asks an editor to consider an article on the company's or client's product. Normally, the query letter will describe the product in some detail and invite the editor to respond if interested in pursuing the suggested story.

Pitch letter mechanics are similar to those of the release. Writing should be sharp and pointed. Whenever possible, length should be held to one page. Spelling of names, especially the editor's, should be perfect. Facts and statements in the letter should be carefully checked.

Importantly, practitioners should remember that editors regularly receive many pitch letters. If an editor isn't interested in a pitch, don't badger her. The trick is to capture in the letter the essence of a story that she can't afford to pass up.

OTHER TOOLS

Other public relations tools may be helpful in certain infrequent situations. For example:

THE ROUND-UP ARTICLE

While many publications discourage publicity about a single company, they encourage articles that summarize, or *round up*, the experiences of several companies within an industry. These *survey* articles may be initiated by the publications themselves or frequently through the suggestions of public relations people. Weaker or smaller companies, in particular, can benefit from being included in a round-up story with stronger, larger adversaries. Thoroughly researching and drafting round-up articles is a good way to secure articles that mention the practitioner's firm in favorable association with top competitors. Wire services, in particular, are regular users of round-ups.

THE FACT SHEET

Fact sheets are short documents that compactly profile an organization. They generally support the information in news releases and back-grounders. Editors find fact sheets helpful in quickly supplying resource material for articles. Figure 8–3 shows an example of the fact sheet.

THE Q & A

The question and answer form, or *Q&A*, often substitutes for or complements a fact sheet in conveying easy-to-follow information. In the Q&A, the writer lists frequently asked questions about the subject and then provides appropriate answers. Often, a skillfully written Q&A can substitute for a personal interview between an editor and a company official.

FIGURE 8–3. Fact sheet samples. The Coca-Cola Company uses a variety of fact sheets to embellish its releases and backgrounders.
SOURCE: Courtesy of Coca-Cola Company.

THE PRESS KIT

Press kits often are distributed to the media in conjunction with an announcement. Press kits incorporate several methods of communication, including graphics, for possible use by newspapers and magazines.

A "bare-bones" press kit consists of a news release, backgrounder, and perhaps a photo. This kit may be all the media require to understand and portray an announcement. Other announcements might require a fact sheet or a Q&A. It is important to weigh carefully each item in the press kit. While an editor will require a certain amount of information to understand a story, he won't appreciate being overwhelmed by too much copy and too many photos. When making up a press kit, the ability to judge how much is enough becomes critical. Figure 8–4 shows the press kit used to unveil a statue marking the twenty-fifth anniversary of David Rockefeller on Wall Street.

In preparing a press kit, public relations practitioners must keep the following points in mind:

○ Make sure information is accurate, thorough, and answers the most fundamental questions a journalist may have.
○ Provide sufficient background information to allow the editor to select his own story angle from the materials prepared.
○ Don't be too commercial. Offer balanced, objective information.
○ Confine opinions and value judgments to quotes from credible sources.
○ Never lie. It's tantamount to editorial suicide.
○ Visually arresting graphics may mean the difference between using the item in the next day's paper and throwing it in the same day's waste basket.

FEATURE
Don't—repeat *don't*—use "do not"

In writing for the eye, public relations practitioners should keep in mind that publications sometimes mistakenly drop out words in print.

Invariably, the most important words are the ones dropped.

For example, the public relations officer of the labor union who issues a statement that "We do not intend to strike," may have his quote appear in the next day's paper as "We *do* intend to strike"—the "not" having been inadvertently dropped by the paper.

A slight yet significant change.

The remedy: use contractions.

It's pretty hard to drop out a significant word or distort the intended meaning when the statement is "We *don't* intend to strike."

A small but not entirely insignificant point to remember.

THE CHASE MANHATTAN BANK. N.A.

Public Relations Division 1 Chase Manhattan Plaza New York, N.Y. 10015

release: Immediately

MONUMENTAL SCULPTURE BY JEAN D
ON CHASE MANHATTAN

A monumental, 42-foot high scul
by the renowned French artist Jean Du
1 Chase Manhattan Plaza where it has
months.

The sculptur
cial community k
Bank, to mark h
largest outdoor
attend the unv

The 25

daily as it '
trunks with
glass and a
polyuretha
built to '
in the op

I'
large pu
Merrill

FACTS ABOUT DUBUFFET SCULPTURE

Size   Stands 42 ft. high - weighs 25 tons.

Structure   Fiberglass resin skin - like the hull of a molded
            boat sandwiched over a core of cellular aluminum
            and mounted on a steel framework anchored to the
            plaza structure.

Completion Fabrication of the
            vision

            der M. Dubuffet's super-
            l-a-half. This was done
            Perigny-Sur-Yerres near
            : May. The sculpture
            .9 and is being provided
            enjoyment of the down-
            l of his 25th anniversary

            luding the effect of
            n the plaza.

            d Merrill, Inc.
            in charge);
            rge of design).

            bbed anodized aluminum
            956 and completed
            t high, and the
            derground levels.

            to public use. The
            culpture stands
            usual sculpture
            The floor of the

A WORLD OF FANTASY: Pedestrians on the Chase Manhattan Plaza take
on a Lilliputian-like quality in contrast to the massive sculpture.

FIGURE 8–4. *Dubuffet sculpture press kit inclusions.* Although a press kit can have an unlimited number of materials, often a complete story can be told with just a few strategic documents. In this case, a news release, fact sheet/backgrounder, and photograph tell the whole story.

SOURCE: Courtesy of The Chase Manhattan Bank.

THE STANDBY STATEMENT

Organizations sometimes take actions or make announcements that they know will lead to media inquiries or even public protests. In such cases, firms prepare concise statements to clarify their positions, should they be called to explain. Such standby statements generally are defensive in nature. They should be brief and unambiguous so as not to raise more questions than they answer. Such events as executive firings, layoffs, price increases, or extraordinary losses are all subject to subsequent scrutiny by the media and therefore are proper candidates for standby statements.

TO WRITE OR NOT TO WRITE

Written methods of communication are often overused. Everyone from editors to corporate presidents complain they get "too much paper." So before the professional even thinks of putting thoughts on paper, she assesses her plan, asking herself these questions:

1 **Will writing serve a practical purpose?** Have a use in mind for the communication before you write it. If you can't come up with a purpose, don't write.

2 **Is writing the most effective way to communicate?** Face-to-face or telephone communication may be better and more direct than writing. Writing occasionally is used as an excuse for not calling or seeing someone in person. In most cases, it's better to resolve a situation quickly; there is no quicker method than going directly to the source.

   Sometimes, too, the written word is "lifeless." An audiovisual presentation to a training group, for example, may be more interesting and effective than a training manual. Again, the objective of the message dictates the form.

3 **What is the risk?** Writing is always risky. Just ask a lawyer. Retracting a printed comment is a lot harder than taking back an oral one. Before committing words to paper, carefully weigh the risks. In the early 1970s, a "confidential" internal memo from an ITT lobbyist made its way into the hands of syndicated columnist Jack Anderson. Anderson printed the memo verbatim. The memo concerned sensitive negotiations between ITT and the U.S. Justice Department. Once the secret document was published, ITT's reputation took a severe tumble. Should the memo have been written? No. Could ITT have avoided the scandal? Absolutely.

4 **Are the timing and the person doing the writing right?** Timing is extremely important in writing. A message, like a joke, can fall flat if the timing is off. Timing, of course, depends on the particular subject and the circumstances surrounding it. The question "Would it be better to wait?" should always be asked before writing.

   Also important is consideration of the person doing the writing. A writer should always ask if she is the most *appropriate* person to write. Perhaps the message is right, but someone at a different level or in a different position in the organization may be able to write it better.

   The pen—or the typewriter—is a potent weapon. But, like any weapon, writing must be used prudently and properly to achieve the desired objective.*

---

* For an interesting analysis of when to write and when not to write, see Dan J. Forrestal, "It's the Little Things that Count," *Public Relations Quarterly*, Summer 1974, pp. 17–18.

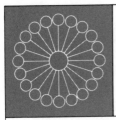

CASE STUDY
The leather pitch letter

In January 1981, Dr. Jane Mellenkamph of the University of Idaho completed experimentation on a novel process through which genuine leather could be made water repellent.

With this process, for the first time ever, leather could be washed with ordinary laundry soap and water. Dr. Mellenkamph immediately patented her leather-treating process and spread the word throughout the leather-tanning industry.

In June, Samuel S. Sobelham, president of Associated Leather Tanners of Atlanta, purchased all rights to Dr. Mellenkamph's patent. Sobelham, a veteran in the industry, considered the Mellenkamph formula the most revolutionary breakthrough in history. Sobelham was convinced that glove manufacturers would "fall all over each other" to purchase his specially-treated, water-resistant leather.

But Sobelham misjudged his market.

For the next year, he tried unsuccessfully to create an interest in the new product. "We've heard all these washable leather stories before," echoed most of the glove manufacturers. "There's no such thing as a washable leather; don't bother us," was the reply he heard most often.

By June 1982, Sobelham concluded it was useless to deal directly with manufacturers. He would have to go around them to the only group who could force glove manufacturers to act—the general public.

He turned to public relations counselor Ed Andrews to come up with a plan to inform the public about the new product. He explained to Andrews that this product was developed at the critical stage of the tanning process and exceeded any federal washability standards. Sobelham said there was no other product like it on the market. He said that the only reason glove manufacturers weren't yet interested in the product was they frankly couldn't and didn't believe it.

Andrews returned to his small shop and considered his strategy to put the product "on the map" and convince glove manufacturers that public interest in and potential demand for the product was keen.

Three days later, Andrews was back to Sobelham with the following plan.

He thought that they could hold a press conference in the Grand Ballroom at New York City's Plaza Hotel at 12 noon on July 1.

Rather than billing it as a traditional press conference, it would be a "fashion show" at which professional models would exhibit all kinds of expensive and nonexpensive gloves made of washable leather. The gloves themselves would run the gamut of textures, styles, and colors.

In addition to the gloves and models, the highlight of the conference would be a long table on which crystal bowls filled with various materials—

axle grease, chicken fat, chocolate ice cream, coffee, grape juice, etc.—would be placed. After exhibiting the gloves to the crowd, each model would dip the gloves in a different bowl. After dipping gloves, the models would then deposit them into two washing machines at the front of the room. The gloves would then be washed and the results dramatically revealed to the crowd.

This unique fashion show, Andrews reasoned, could provoke important headlines from the nation's influential fashion editors attending. With favorable stories from the fashion press, glove manufacturers around the country would be bidding for Associated Leather Tanners patented process.

Sobelham reacted with one word to Andrews' idea, "Boffo!"

When Andrews returned to his office, he realized that the fashion editors would have to be drawn to the fashion show through a pitch letter. He knew that each day, most major fashion editors received ten to twenty such letters inviting them to various functions. Sometimes the pitch letter meant the difference between an important attendee and a no-show. Therefore, Andrews figured, his pitch letter had to be tight, catchy, and enticing. In other words, perfect.

If it wasn't and the editors failed to show, the Ed Andrews public relations firm would be minus one client.

QUESTIONS

1 What are the essential facts that Andrews must get into his pitch letter?

2 If you were Andrews, would you send every editor the same pitch letter or would particular editors get different versions?

3 If you were Andrews, what would you say in your pitch letter?

NOTES

1 Timothy Hubbard, "Anatomy of Excellence," *Columbia Journalism Review*, Fall 1968, pp. 31–33.

2 John Koten, "Psychologists Play Bigger Corporate Role in Placing of Personnel," *The Wall Street Journal*, 11 July 1978, p. 1. Used by permission of Dow Jones & Co., Inc.

3 Ibid.

4 Ibid., p. 20.

5 Marvin H. Switt, "Clear Writing Means Clear Thinking Means...........," *Harvard Business Review*, January-February 1973, p. 62.

SUGGESTED READING

Allen E. Sturges. *Allen's Synonyms and Antonyms*. New York: Harper and Row, 1949.

Berrey, Lester V. *Roget's International Thesaurus*. 3rd ed. New York: Thomas Y. Crowell, 1962.

Brown, Leland. *Effective Business Reporting*. Englewood Cliffs, N.J.: Prentice-Hall, 1973.

Darrow, R. *House Journal Editing*. Danville, Ill.: Interstate, 1975.

Dyer, Janet. " 'Predictable': The Watchword For 1980 Reports" *Public Relations Journal*, August 1981, p. 9. Annual report layouts for the 1980s from many different companies seem to follow the same format time after time.

Fernald, James C. *Funk & Wagnalls Standard Handbook of Synonyms, Antonyms and Prepositions*. New York: Funk & Wagnalls, 1947.

Grabow, Bert G. "10 Laws of Report Production," *Public Relations Journal*, August 1981, pp. 18–19. Grabow discusses the 10 uncodified laws of annual report production.

Grey, David L. *The Writing Process: A Behavioral Approach to Communicating Information and Ideas*. Belmont, Calif.: Wadsworth, 1972. Gives good pointers for developing objectivity toward one's own work.

Hemphill, Phyllis D. *Business Communications and Writing Improvement Exercises*. Englewood Cliffs, N.J.: Prentice-Hall, 1974.

Honaker, Charles. "News Releases Revisited," *Public Relations Journal*, April 1981, pp. 25–27.

Lesikar, Raymond V. *How to Write a Report Your Boss Will Read and Remember*. Homewood, Ill.: Dow Jones-Irwin, 1974.

Lustig, Theodore. "The Trade Show as Report Theme," *Public Relations Journal*, August 1981, pp. 14–17.

McKechnie, Jean L. *Webster's New Twentieth-Century Dictionary*. New York: World, 1975.

Miller, Martin and **Pagani, Frank.** "Upgrading Small Company Reports," *Public Relations Journal*, August 1981, pp. 12–13.

G&C Merriam Co. *The Merriam-Webster Book of Word Histories*. Springfield, Mass.: Author, 1976. Rejects the "port out, starboard home" theory for the meaning of *posh*. But under the *G*'s alone you can learn the origin of *genius, gin, goon, gorgeous, gossip, gridiron*, and other words of interest.

————. *The Merriam-Webster Pocket Dictionary of Synonyms*. Springfield, Mass.: Author, 1972. Useful for careful attention to shades of meaning and for short examples of good usage by established writers.

————. *The Merriam-Webster Thesaurus*. Springfield, Mass.: Author, 1978. Contains more than 100,000 synonyms, antonyms, idiomatic equivalents, related words, and contrasted terms.

Oxford University Press. *The Compact Edition of the Oxford English Dictionary*. Oxford, England: Author, 1971.

Riblet, Carl, Jr. *The Solid Gold Copy Editor*. Tuscon, Ariz.: Flacon, 1972.

Rivers, William L. *Writing for Mass Media*. Englewood Cliffs, N.J.: Prentice-Hall, 1974. Contains information and helpful tips about writing for all media.

————. *Free-lancers and Staff Writer: Writing Magazine Articles*. Belmont, Calif.: Wadsworth, 1972.

Wales, L. *Practical Guide to Newsletter Editing/Design*. Ames, Iowa: Iowa University Press, 1976.

THE SPOKEN WORD

Writing for listening involves the spoken word. When a person hears a speech, radio broadcast, or television announcement, he generally gets one crack at the message. If he misses it the first time around, he rarely gets a second chance.

The key to writing for listening is to write as if speaking. Use simple, short sentences, active verbs, contractions, and one- and two-syllable words. Let phrases stand alone.

In brief, be brief.

This chapter will touch on the most widely used methods of communicating to be heard, including speeches, broadcast releases, public service announcements, and film scripts.

As people read less and watch and listen more, writing for the ear becomes increasingly important for the public relations professional. Accordingly, where once the province of public relations was dominated by print-oriented professionals, today, more and more practitioners enter the field with strong radio and television orientations.

9
Writing for the Ear

THE SPEECH

Speech writing has become one of the most coveted public relations skills. Increasingly, speech writers have used their access to management to move up the organizational ladder. The prominence they enjoy is largely due to the importance top executives place on making speeches.* Today's executives are called upon by government and special interest groups to defend their policies, justify their prices, and explain their practices to a much greater degree than ever before. In this environment, a good speech writer becomes a valuable asset.

Most executives rely on public relations professionals to write their speeches and, in many cases, to contribute to the speech's ideas. The work is demanding; according to Pittsburgh speech writer James G. Busse, a writer must possess certain basic qualifications: "the ability to unite words and ideas skillfully and reasonably fast; a talent for getting along with top executives; an understanding of the realities of economics and business; a working knowledge of the world and its people; an inherent curiosity; a healthy respect for deadlines; the ability to write for oral presentation; good judgment in deciding what corporate managements should and shouldn't be saying; and the discretion to keep his mouth shut about his work."[1]

To Chrysler Corporation speech writer Chuck Connolly, the speech writer becomes a "surrogate chairman." As Connolly put it, "When I have to write the top man's speech, I'm literally forced to figure out policy, compress it, and make it cogent from the point-of-view of the chairman. Therefore, when I sit in on meetings to dig for my information, I'm not just a recorder. I'm a strategist."[2]

THE SPEECH WRITING PROCESS

The speech writing process breaks down into four components: a) preparing, b) interviewing, c) researching, and d) organizing and writing.

PREPARING

One easy way to prepare for a speech is to follow a "4W" checklist. In other words, answer the questions *who, what, where,* and *when.*

Who.   The *who* represents two critical elements, the speaker and the audience.

A writer should know all about the speaker: how he speaks, how he uses humor, how he reacts to an audience, what his background is, and what his personality is like. It's almost impossible to write a speech for someone you don't know.

The writer also should know something about the audience. What does this audience feel about this subject? What are its predispositions toward the subject and the speaker? What are the major points with which it might agree? The more familiar the writer is with the *who* of a speech, the easier the writing will be.

What.   The *what* is the topic. The assigned subject must be clearly known and well defined by the writer before beginning formal research. If the writer fails to delineate the subject in advance, much of her research will be pointless.

---

* A poll commissioned by *PR Reporter* (Vol. 20, no. 50, 19 December 1977, p. 2) found speech making to be the major public relations activity in which chief executives participated.

FEATURE
Speech writing pays

Not every practitioner wants to be a speech writer. Some can't take the deadlines. Others shy away from the responsibility of creating ten to fifteen pages of prose out of a few ideas. But for many who do accept the challenge, speech writing pays, not only in prestige, but also in remuneration.

In government, experienced writers typically earn in the $35-$45,000 or GS-15 pay range.

In the corporate ranks, the "scarcity of top corporation executive speech writers has pushed typical salaries into the $40-$80,000 range."[3] Indeed, large companies will frequently hire top freelance speech writers, who charge between $1,500-$4,000 per speech.

One drawback of the executive speech writer is the frequent feeling of insecurity, brought about by management change. As one writer put it, "As an extension of the executive's mind and often being neither fish nor fowl with an organization, the position tends to have all the security of a point leader in an infantry platoon."[4]

Nevertheless, speech writing has become a fine art, practiced by an increasing number of practitioners intent on winning greater management respect and earning more money.

Where. The *where* is the setting. A large hall requires a more formal talk than a roundtable forum. Often, the location of the speech—the city, state, or even particular hall—bears historic or symbolic significance that can enhance a message.

When. The *when* is the time of the speech. People are more awake in the morning and get sleepier as the day progresses, so a dinner speech should be kept short. The *when* also refers to the time of year. A speech can always be linked to an upcoming holiday or special celebration.

INTERVIEWING

Interviewing speakers in advance is essential. Without the chance to interview the speaker, the results can be dismal. A good interview with a speaker often means the difference between a strong speech and a poor one. Stated another way, the speechwriter is only as good as his access to the speaker.

In the interview, the speech writer gets some time—from as little as fifteen minutes to over an hour—to observe the speaker firsthand and probe for the keys to the speech. The interview must accomplish at least three specific goals for the speech writer:

Determine the "object" of the talk. The "object" is different from the subject. Whereas the subject is the topic, the object is the purpose of the speech—that is, what exactly the speaker wants the audience to do after she is finished speaking.

Robert L. Fegley recently retired after forty-one years in public relations and advertising positions with the General Electric Company. At the time of his retirement, he was Staff Executive-Chief Executive Officer Communications at GE's headquarters in Fairfield, Connecticut. In that capacity, he counseled GE Chairman Reg Jones in the planning and performance of his public affairs activities. In 1979, *Business Week* cited Mr. Fegley as one of the nation's "Top 10 Executives in Corporate Public Relations."

The subscribers of *PR News* also voted him "PR Professional of the Year." In 1981, he received the "PR Man of the Year Award" of the University of Texas.

How hard is it to write an executive speech?

All good writing is hard work, but speech writers face special difficulties. They're writing words that will be presented as the thoughts and feelings of another person. Many clients unconsciously resent this and tend to fight it. A supple and adaptive mind, a chameleon style, a ready store of knowledge on many subjects, a collaborative attitude, and much patience—these all help.

How does one become a speech writer?

The best way to start is to write a few speeches as special assignments. If you like it and the client likes you, you've got a lucrative career underway. If not, you can always fall back on your original job.

How does one approach the speech writing assignment?

Quickly fill yourself in on the audience and the occasion. What topics, what messages, would be worth the time of both the speaker and the audience? Then talk it over with the speaker and decide what specific points to make. A written outline helps build the story line and get client agreement. Next, do thorough research to be sure that the talk

Does she want them to storm City Hall? To love big business? To write their congressmen? The interviewer's essential question must be, "What do you wish to leave the audience with at the conclusion of your speech?" Once the speaker answers this question, the rest of the speech should fall into place.

will be authoritative and persuasive. Then write, review with the speaker and other individuals whose responsibilities are affected, and revise until the speaker is happy.

Is there a general format to most speeches?

The good ones all contain surprises, so no single format suffices. But the great speeches are those that change minds and incite action. For these, the talk should start with a dramatic statement of the problem, including eye-opening anecdotes or statistics that make it an urgent matter. Then state your proposed solutions in clear one–two–three terms. End with an appeal to the heart and an expression of confidence that things can be changed.

How liberally should a speech writer use humor?

It depends entirely on the speaker. If he or she is a witty person or a good story-teller, by all means give full rein to this aspect of the speaker's personality. Otherwise, lay off.

How cognizant of the "spoken word" should a speech writer be?

Write for the ear, not for the eye. There's a difference. Writing for the ear is usually more colloquial, more concise, more direct, more pungent. Two good practices for speech writers: read every draft aloud and give speeches of your own. Then you will learn to hear the meanderings and superfluities that lose an audience.

Should a speech writer experiment with rhetorical flourishes?

Today's audiences respond to direct and candid speech and are quick to spot the pretentious speaker as a phony. But there are time-tested rhetorical techniques—challenging questions, self-deprecating wit, original and quoted aphorisms, rhythmic changes—that work as well today as they ever did.

How important is it to know the speaker?

The writer must insist on dealing directly with the speaker. He can't do a decent job through intermediaries. It's an intensely personal relationship, and he always faces the diplomatic assignment of reassuring those who are worried about his access to "the chief." The best speaker-writer relationships are those that build over time into mutual trust and collaboration.

What are the characteristics that distinguish a good speech writer from a mediocre one?

The really good ones are something more than wordsmiths. They become personal advisors on how to exert leadership. Alexander Hamilton to George Washington; Ted Sorenson to John Kennedy. They bring their own intellectual contribution to the development of policy and see each speech in the context of a larger strategy.

Is there anything else you'd like readers of this book to know?

Speech writing is usually a loner's job, not ordinarily the best path to a top management position. But the speech writer for the chief executive officer can earn good money and enjoy the prestige of a person in a unique position to influence policy. That is, until the CEO retires. Then, unless the writer has been a bit foresighted, it is customary to bury the slave with the caliph.

Determine the speaker's main points. Normally, an audience can grasp only a few points during a speech. These points, which should flow directly from the object, become touchstones around which the rest of the speech is woven. Again, the writer must determine the three or four main points during the interview.

Capture the speaker's characteristics.   Most of all during the interview, the writer must observe the speaker. How comfortable is she with humor? How informal or deliberate is she with words? What are her pet phrases and expressions? The writer must file these observations away, recall them during the writing process, and factor them into the speech.

RESEARCHING

Like any writer, speech writers sometimes develop "writer's block," the inability to come up with anything on paper. One way around writer's block is to adopt a formalized research procedure.

First, dig into all literature, books, pamphlets, articles, speeches, and other writings on the speech subject. Prior speeches by the speaker are also important documents to research. A stocked file cabinet often is the speech writer's best friend.

Second, think about the subject. Bring personal thoughts to bear on the topic. Presumably, the speaker has already discussed the topic with the writer, so the writer can amplify the speaker's thoughts with his own.

Third, seek out the opinions of others on the topic. Perhaps the speaker isn't the most knowledgeable source within an organization about this specific subject. Economists, lawyers, accountants, doctors, and other technical experts may shed additional light on the topic. Outside sources, particularly politicians and business leaders, are often willing to share their ideas when requested.

ORGANIZING AND WRITING

Once preparation, interviewing, and research have been completed, the fun part begins. Writing a speech becomes easier if, again, the speech is organized into its essential elements: introduction, thesis, body, and conclusion.

Introduction.   A speech introduction is a lot like handling a bar of soap in the shower: the first thing to do is get control. An introduction must grab the audience and hold its interest. An audience is alert at the beginning of a talk and is "with" the speaker. The writer's job is to make sure they stay with him.

The speech writer must take full advantage of the early good nature of the audience by making the introduction snappy. Audience members need time to settle in their seats, and the speaker needs time to get his bearings on the podium. Often, the best way to win early trust and rapport with the audience is to ease into the speech with humor.

For example:

> I understand full well that a conference speaker should have one overriding priority: to make it short. Perhaps I'll steal a page from my neighbor's eight-year-old son who was told to write a brief biography of Benjamin Franklin. He wrote, "Benjamin Franklin was born in Boston. At an early age he moved to Philadelphia. As he walked down the street a lady saw him and started laughing. He married the lady and discovered electricity!"

Thesis.   The thesis is the *object* of the speech, its purpose or central idea. A good thesis statement lets an audience know in a simple sentence where a speech is going and how it will get there. For example, its purpose can be to persuade:

> The federal government must allow home football games to be televised.

Another thesis statement might be to reinforce or crystallize a belief:

Sunday football viewing is among the most cherished of winter family home entertainments.

The purpose of yet another thesis statement might be merely to entertain:

Football viewing in the living room can be a harrowing experience. Let me explain.

In each case, the thesis statement lets the audience know early what the point of the speech will be and leads them to the desired conclusion. Many writers prefer to skip the thesis and hit the audience throughout the speech with the central idea in a three-part organization, commonly described as:

Tell 'em what you're gonna tell 'em.
Tell 'em.
Tell 'em what you told 'em.

Body.   The speech body is just that—the general body of evidence that supports the three or four main points.

While facts, statistics, and figures are important elements, writers should always attempt to use comparisons or contrasts for easier audience understanding. For example, note the comparisons in the following two passages.

It took eighty years for the telephone to be installed in 34 million American homes. It took sixty-two years for electrical wiring, forty-nine years for the automobile, and forty-seven years for the electric washing machine to arrive in that same number of homes. Television reached that saturation point in a mere ten years.

In a single week, 272 million customers passed through the checkout counter of American supermarkets. That's equal to the combined populations of Spain, Mexico, Argentina, France, West Germany, Italy, Sweden, Switzerland, and Belguim.

Conclusion.   The best advice on wrapping up a speech is to do it quickly. As the old Texas bromide goes, "If you haven't struck oil in the first twenty minutes, stop boring." Put another way, the conclusion must be blunt, short, and to the point. It may be a good idea to orally review the major points and thesis one last time and then stop. For example, the following is an excellent conclusion—short but sweet:

In closing, it was Malcolm Muggeridge who said, "There is no such thing as darkness; only the failure to see." We in the business community are playing not to lose instead of playing to win. Let's play to win.

THE SPOKEN WORD

Since speeches are meant to be heard, the writer should take advantage of tools that emphasize the special qualities of the spoken word. Such devices can add vitality to a speech, transcending the content of the words themselves. Used skillfully, these devices can elevate a mediocre speech into a memorable one. Here are a few:

1 **Alliteration,** the repetition of initial sounds in words, was used in this description of the press in a speech given by former Vice-President Spiro T. Agnew:

Nattering nabobs of negativism.

2 **Antithesis** incorporates sharply opposed or contrasting ideas in the same passage. President Kennedy was famous for his savvy use:

> Let us never negotiate out of fear, but let us never fear to negotiate. . . . Ask not what your country can do for you, ask what you can do for your country.

3 **Metonomy** substitutes one term for another closely associated one; it gives a passage more figurative life. For example, the following passage, without metonomy, is flat:

> Ladies and gentlemen, people of Rome, and all of you from the surrounding area, I'd like your attention for the next few moments.

But note the difference when metonomy is used:

> Friends, Romans, countrymen, lend me your ears.

4 **Metaphor and simile** figuratively connect concepts having little literal connection, such as the use of the torch symbol in the following President Kennedy passage:

> Let the word go forth from this time and place to friend and foe alike, that the torch has been passed to a new generation of Americans born to this century and unwilling to witness or permit the slow undoing of those human rights to which we are committed today at home and around the world.

5 **Personification** gives life to inanimate objects, animals, or ideas, such as in the following passage from William Hazlett:

> Prejudice is the child of ignorance.

6 **Repetition** is the use of the same words or phrases over and over again. For example, Churchill's use of the phrase *we shall* in the following:

> *We shall* fight on the beaches, *we shall* fight on the landing-grounds, *we shall* fight in the fields and in the streets, *we shall* fight in the hills. *We shall* never surrender . . .

Such ear-oriented devices cannot be used for every speech. But a professional will not be reluctant to experiment with them, because they form the very essence of writing for listening.

USING HUMOR

Speech humor can either be a godsend or a curse. It's a tricky business. Humor in a speech should never be too ambitious, because the typical executive is not Johnny Carson. High comedy, rapid-fire jokes, and satire should be avoided at all costs. In general speech humor must follow three rules:

It must be relevant.   A speaker won't win support by rattling off unrelated jokes. Rather, humor must be an integral part of the talk, used to either underscore a point or introduce one. For example, the following illustration is a good way to introduce a speech about competitiveness and getting ahead:

> When Woodrow Wilson was governor of New Jersey, a very ambitious young civil servant called him at his home at 3:30 one morning and said urgently, "Mr. Governor, I'm sorry to wake you, but your state auditor has just died and I'd like to know if I can take his place."

Mr. Wilson thought that over for a moment and then replied, "Well, I guess it's all right with me, if it's all right with the undertaker."

It must be in good taste.   Topics such as sex, weight, age, race, and religion should ordinarily be avoided in a speech. People are just too touchy. If there is even the slightest chance that a joke might offend the audience, don't use it. One safe target is the speaker himself. A speaker willing to poke fun at himself can generally win the admiration of the audience. For example, after the Kennedy-Nixon television encounters that contributed to Nixon's presidential election defeat in 1960, Nixon quipped: "I am a dropout from the Electoral College. I flunked debate."

It must be fresh.   Stale humor can sour an audience. A joke that goes over well for millions of people on network television would not be a good candidate for a subsequent speech because too many people have heard it. Speech writers must carefully select humor for its crispness. Some organizations subscribe to topical humor services to keep speakers current. Other institutions hire freelance joke writers for executive speeches. In each case, speech writers try to avoid the fate of Samuel Johnson's English student, whose paper provoked the professor to respond:

I found this report to be good and original. However, the part that was good was not original. And the part that was original was not good.

Humor is worth experimenting with. It can spark a dull speech. It can give credibility to an unsure speaker. But it's explosive, so handle it with care.

TIGHTENING THE TALK

Editing is the final responsibility of the speech writer. Like any other form of writing, the speech must be tight. After completing the draft, the writer should carefully review each sentence and word. One way to tell if a speech makes sense and moves smoothly is to recite it aloud and have someone listen to it. By obtaining "advance audience reaction," a writer can present his final product with more assurance.

How long it takes to write a speech depends on the subject's complexity. Normally, a double-spaced page of speech type takes two to two and a half minutes to read. A twenty-minute, major address may be ten to twelve pages in length and take several days to write, exclusive of research and preparation time.

As a general rule, no speech should ever exceed twenty minutes. Most people will just not sit still these days for long addresses. So no audience will be upset at a speaker who gives a twenty minute speech when scheduled to speak for forty minutes. Indeed, it's much better to leave the audience "hungry" for more than it is to leave them "fed up" after too much.

Some of the most famous "speeches" in history were the shortest:

○ General Douglas MacArthur, upon leaving Corregidor, promised, "I shall return."
○ Martin Luther King, leading a Civil Rights march in the South, proclaimed, "We shall overcome."
○ And the shortest speech of all, General Dennis McAullife, upon being ordered to surrender by the Nazis, defiantly replied, "Nuts!"

Now those are short—but memorable—speeches.

EMBELLISHING THE SPEECH

After a speech is written and approved, the skillful public relations practitioner will embellish it to help stimulate readership or republication.

Having endured the arduous process of preparing a speech, the public relations professional has a responsibility to interest others in the talk. Ordinarily, the widest dissemination of an executive speech is through the public media. With many such speeches vying for editorial space, interesting an editor in using a speech is a difficult challenge. One device is to give the speech a provocative title. The title is the first thing an editor sees. If it's snappy, she may choose to read on. Occasionally, in fact, a good title may influence an editor's decision to use excerpts of the speech in print.

Another device to help disseminate executive speeches to a wider audience is through the creation of a *speaker's bureau.* A speaker's bureau, generally established and managed by a firm's public relations group, is an office through which company speakers are recruited, assigned, and equipped with verbal ammunition. In other words, after willing speakers are located in the organization, the public relations department selects appropriate community forums, schedules the speakers, and prepares them with speeches. Often, a speech written for a top executive can be "recycled" through the speaker's bureau and used by many different speakers in various settings. Thus, the speaker's bureau can be an excellent community relations tool and speech dissemination device. However, setting up and maintaining a speaker's bureau entails a great deal of work and must be worth the investment in time.

The key to speech writing, just like any other kind of writing, is experience. With speech writing becoming a more competitive and sought-after pursuit among practitioners, it is unfortunately difficult for an interested novice to break in. However, most political candidates or nonprofit community organizations are more than willing to allow beginners to try their hand, generally for no compensation, at drafting speeches. For the budding writer, such voluntarism is a good way to learn the ropes of speech writing. For few other activities in public relations offer as much fulfillment—both spiritually and monetarily—as does speech writing.

RADIO, TELEVISION WRITING

As many as two-thirds of the American public get their news from radio and television. Almost every American home has at least one TV set and several radios. Indeed, there are more U.S. homes with television sets than with indoor plumbing. As a nation we have about 1,000 TV stations, 8,000 radio stations, four national TV networks, cable TV networks, and scores of national and regional radio networks. Radio is with us constantly, and TV, while not yet quite as mobile, seems almost as pervasive.

Unfortunately, TV and radio are the animals public relations people generally understand the least. For one thing, as noted, many practitioners were trained in the print medium and feel more comfortable dealing with newspapers and magazines than they do dealing with their electronic counterparts. Additionally, many feel that radio and TV provide limited publicity opportunities compared to the larger news holes of the average daily newspaper.

Like it or not, TV and radio are extraordinarily powerful forces in our society. Practitioners can no longer opt to ignore them. The following discussion briefly introduces fundamentals for dealing effectively with radio and TV broadcasters.

FEATURE
Every picture tells a story

As executive speech making has become more important, a plethora of counseling firms have sprung up to advise executive speakers on how to create and deliver winning speeches.

Among the most novel concepts was developed by Communispond, Inc. Because most executives are neither comfortable at a podium nor confident in their ability "to perform" before a large audience, Communispond came up with the concept of *drawing pictures* to replace formal written speeches.

Essentially, after gathering all available evidence and support material and outlining in words what they wanted to cover, Communispond-trained executives were encouraged to draw pictures, called *ideographs,* to properly reflect the subject at hand. For example, if a corporate speaker wished to express the notion that "the ship of American capitalism" was being fired upon by "Socialist salvos" around the world, he might sketch an ideograph similar to the one at the right.

In this way, Communispond-trained speakers were taught to use their "nervousness" to

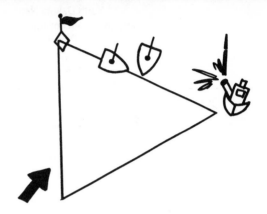

convey natural, human conviction. In other words, not constrained by lifeless written copy, an executive was free, as Communispond put it, "to speak as well as you think."

While not right for everyone, Communispond's unique approach, when mastered, allowed for a much more extemporaneous and lively discourse than the average prepared text. Fortunately however (at least as far as corporate speech writers are concerned), most executives still insist on the security blanket of a full-blown, written text.

THE BROADCAST NEWS RELEASE

The principle document in reaching broadcast editors is the basic news release. Most public relations departments don't take the time to prepare special releases for broadcast use. But well they might, because broadcast style differs materially from written style.

For example, while the following release might be fine for print use, it would have trouble in a broadcast context:

GRAND FORKS, N.D.—The North Dakota National Bank today announced it was lowering its home mortgage lending rate to 12 percent from 12½ percent, effective immediately.

Marcus D. Pickard, III, president and chief executive officer of North Dakota National Bank, said, "We are lowering the home mortgage rate because of increasing competitive pressures in the mortgage market and the trend of declining interest rates generally."

Mr. Pickard added that this was the first reduction in the home mortgage rate in North Dakota in five years.

Fine for print, perhaps. But this translation would be a much better lead for broadcast:

GRAND FORKS, N.D.—The home mortgage rate is coming down.

North Dakota National Bank today announced it was lowering its home mortgage rate to 12 percent from 12½ percent, effective immediately.

Bank President Marcus Pickard said the move was taken because of "competitive pressures and the trend of declining interest rates."

This marks the first reduction in North Dakota's mortgage rate in five years.

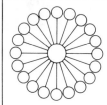

MINICASE
The bank broadcast release

Chase Manhattan Bank is one of the world's premier authorities on the energy industry. It employs a department of energy economists and is a leader in energy lending around the world. The bank is concerned with maintaining and enhancing its relationships with energy companies and regularly distributes information about the energy industry to the media.

The following is a typical Chase print release about the energy industry:

NEW YORK, N.Y.—The Chase Manhattan Bank reported today that some of the abnormal factors influencing the net earnings of a group of representative petroleum companies "continued to play a major role in the first quarter of this year," resulting in gains of 43 percent in the United States and 167 percent in the rest of the world. However, the gains are likely to be short-lived, the bank said.

The bank's monthly publication, *The Petroleum Situation*, found that worldwide, the companies earned 111 percent more than the year-earlier period; however, "Well over half of the worldwide increase in profits can be traced to accounting procedures involving inventories.

Chase energy economists explained that many importing nations require the companies to treat inventories on a first-in first-out basis as well as carry very large inventories as a safety measure. "The petroleum companies are required to apply the cost of inventories acquired months earlier to their current revenue. Under this system, radical changes in the cost of inventories, either up or down, will have a major impact on profits," the bank said.

According to *The Petroleum Situation*, "That is exactly what happened in the first quarter of this year."

QUESTIONS

1 In writing for broadcast, what are the most important messages that Chase wishes to convey?

2 What elements in this print release are inappropriate for broadcast use?

3 How would you translate this print release into appropriate broadcast form?

This release would be an ideal news item on a local radio or TV newscast. Normally, such an item lasts ten, twenty, or thirty seconds, no more. Infrequently, an important item may take a minute to cover. Generally in writing for broadcast, the shorter the better. Material must catch the listener early. The story should be told in the first two or three sentences, allowing the listener to "tune out" early. In other words, in most broadcast writing, the inverted pyramid must be much more "pointed" to capture a listener's attention.

The following checklist may be helpful in writing for radio and TV:

1 **Use simple, declarative sentences.**
Awkward, overly dramatic, and unnatural:

> Turning the first spade of sod on the site of the new $3 million University Center today, Mayor Grumble hailed the Dexter University building program as a "great step forward for the state's finest university."

Better:

> Construction began today on the three million dollar Dexter University Center. Mayor Grumble, on hand for the dedication, called the school's building program "A great step forward for the state's finest university."

2 **Numbers and statistics should be rounded off.**
No one will remember:

> The Ajax Company today announced year-end earnings of $999,765.

But they may remember:

> The Ajax Company today announced year-end earnings of slightly under one million dollars.

3 **Attribution should usually precede the quote.** For example:

> Hospital administrator Christie Gardner says, "Winston Hospital will not bow to pressure."

4 **Try to avoid direct quotes.** Direct quotes often lead to long, clumsy sentence structure. Paraphrase instead.

5 **Personalize whenever possible.** The following is a good print but a poor broadcast lead:

> The Bureau of Labor Statistics announced today that the cost of living has gone down another 2 percent in the last quarter.

Personalize it for broadcast:

> If you hadn't noticed, your grocery bill is coming down. That was the good news today from the Bureau of Labor Statistics, which announced that the cost of living has declined 2 percent for the quarter.

6 **Avoid extended description.** Middle initials, for example, or full corporate titles are unnecessary in the time-constrained environment of broadcast news. For instance, in print, say:

> Marie M. Daniel, president and chief executive officer of Avorn Products, Inc.

In broadcast say:

> Avorn Products President Marie Daniel.

7 Avoid hackneyed expressions and cliches. Trite phrases should be avoided in all writing. But in broadcast, such phrases are particularly annoying. Hackneyed jargon changes yearly, but these are typical shopworn expressions:

> in the wake of
> passed away
> riot-torn
> scandal-ridden
> flatly denied
> sharply rebuked

Public relations people should aim for radio and TV more often. More releases should be written with the needs of broadcasters in mind. The skillfully written and placed broadcast release can often carry a more powerful potential for achieving results than an equivalent print release.

PUBLIC SERVICE ANNOUNCEMENTS

The public service announcement, or *PSA,* is a radio or TV commercial, usually from ten to sixty seconds long, which is broadcast at no cost to the sponsor. Nonprofit organizations, such as the Red Cross and Community Chest, are active users of PSAs. Commercial organizations, too, may take advantage of PSAs for their own nonprofit activities, such as blood bank collections, voter registration drives, health testing, and the like. The spread of local cable television stations has expanded the opportunity for placing PSAs on the air. Nevertheless, radio PSAs still are far more widely used.

Unlike news releases, radio PSAs are generally written in advertising-copy style—punchy and pointed. The essential challenge in writing PSAs is to select the

---

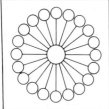

MINICASE
The Shreveport Shriners PSA

The Shreveport Blood Bank is approaching dangerously low levels and urgently needs to replenish its supply. The Shriners, in their traditional spirit of community service, have volunteered to organize a city-wide blood drive.

The Shriners will tour the city in five roving bloodmobiles. The drive will begin Monday, August 21 and end Sunday, August 27.

Each of Shreveport's three major radio stations has agreed to run PSAs on the blood drive. As the Shriners' public relations director, you have been asked to compose three different PSAs: ten-second, thirty-second, and sixty-second spots.

QUESTION
What would you say in the three PSAs for the blood drive?

small amount of information to be used, discard extraneous information, and persuade the listener to take the desired action. For example, this is a typical 30-second PSA:

> The challenge of inflation has never been more serious than it is today . . .
> The need for strong national leadership has never been more pressing than it is today . . .
> Americans must tell their elected leaders to stop spending and regulating and start listening to the people.
> But they won't until *you* demand it.
> Until you demand they stop over-spending,
> stop crippling our economy with needless regulation,
> stop suffocating America with outrageous taxes.
> *You* can make a difference.
> This message brought to you by Hooter Valley National Bank.

While PSAs may combine voices and sound effects for radio, and film for television, the most frequently used type of PSA is the spot announcement designed to be read by station personnel or recorded by the sponsoring organization. The following ten-second PSA is an example:

> I'm Mario Andretti, and I've had some close shaves in my racing career. The National Safety Council tells us that 500 people will be killed on the highways this Memorial weekend. Be one of the safe ones: Drive carefully and live.

In timing PSAs, it is best to read statements aloud to more accurately predict the length of time they will take on the air.

According to survey research, broadcasters use three primary criteria in determining which PSAs make the air: a) sponsorship, b) relevance of the message to the community, and c) message design. In terms of sponsorship, the reputation of the sponsor for honesty and integrity is critical. As to the relevance of the message, urgent social problems, such as health and safety issues and education and training concerns all rank high with broadcasters. In message design, the more imaginative, original, and exciting the message, the better the chance of it getting free play on the air.[5]

FILM SCRIPTS

Film is another important medium for public relations people, especially for those working for national associations and large consumer products companies. Hundreds of firms sponsor films for schools and community groups. Most are professionally written and produced. For example, Modern Talking Picture Service, Inc., the nation's largest sponsored film distributor, handles films and collateral services for more than 700 clients.

Writing a film script demands linking audio messages with video ones. The writer must not over-explain the video, but rather add just enough dialogue to enhance the visual message.

One common film script format is for video directions to be listed on the left side of a page and audio directions and dialogue on the right.

Although practitioners rarely get involved in writing film scripts, some do supervise commercial film companies commissioned to create a sponsored film. In this context, familiarity with the medium helps greatly.

"MORTGAGE MONEY AVAILABLE" TV SCRIPT

Video	*Audio*
Establishing shots of houses, Then CU's of individual homes on the block.	ANNCR: Most Americans agree that saving enough money today to make a downpayment on a new home is a big problem.
	At least that's the way it used to be.
Cut to Max Karl in front of home of couple we will use in sync sequence. Then go to CU of Karl on camera.	According to Mr. Max Karl, chairman and founder of Mortgage Guaranty Insurance Corporation, the country's oldest and largest private insurer of mortgages, most people are not aware of how easy it is to obtain home financing if they qualify for mortgage insurance.
	KARL: A lot of young married couples these days have pretty good incomes, and they can easily carry monthly mortgage payments on a home of their own. But with the high cost of living, not many young families have been able to save enough money for a downpayment, which could be as much as $10,000 or $12,000 on a $50,000 house.
	By asking home lenders if they qualify for private mortgage insurance, called a *magic loan*, a family can now be eligible to buy their dream house for as little as five percent down!
Cut to couple on camera, either in front of house, or in backyard barbecuing.	ANNCR: One couple that agrees with Mr. Karl is George and Catherine Schron of New York.
Pull back from couple and house.	HUSBAND: We've always wanted a house of our own, but with the huge downpayment requirements we began to lose hope of ever moving from our apartment.
	WIFE: We liked what we saw here and were about to leave because we figured the downpayment would be the same as most other places. But the realtor told us about a magic loan and our lending officer said our downpayment would only be $2,600!
	We couldn't have bought this house if it wasn't for magic money!
	ANNCR: From New York, this is Richard DePalma reporting.

FIGURE 9–1 *A sixty-second TV newsclip entitled "Mortgage Money Available."* This TV clip, produced by Ries and Geltzer Public Relations Agency of New York City for Mortgage Guaranty Insurance Corporation, is a typical one distributed to TV stations for use in local newscasts. Note only one direct "plug" for the sponsoring organization. SOURCE: Courtesy of Ries, Cappiello, and Colwell.

FEATURE
Film shorthand

Writing for film also has its own shorthand. For example:

CU: *close up*;
MS: *medium shot*;
SIL: *silent film*;

SOF: *sound-on-film*;
cut: *switch from one scene to another*;
dissolve: *switch gradually from one picture to another.*

"THE SILENT PARTNER"[6]
(CHAMPION SPARK PLUG COMPANY)

Video	Audio
CU of spark plug	The spark plug is a curious critter. It can deliver better gas mileage, quicker engine starting, lower emissions, faster acceleration and greater engine power.
Fade to car on highway	While most of us depend on spark plugs to get around, few of us have any idea what they are and how they work. Spark plugs serve as "silent partners" in our day-to-day transportation.
CU of title card MS of animated power king	There was a time when power was king and high performance was the name of the game.
Dissolve to coughing cars	But that was before petroleum and clean air became known as precious resources.
Dissolve to puzzled engineers	Automotive engineers worked for years to find the key to performance while ensuring energy savings and environmental soundness.
Dissolve to engine	They investigated every part of the car engine to find the key to progress.
CU of muscular spark plug	After years of searching, it was concluded that the spark plug was the strongest, most powerful element in the engine.
Dissolve to engine block	New engine developments made spark plugs even more crucial for the average driver.

TV NEWSCLIPS

One of the more controversial public relations broadcast tools is the TV newsclip or film news release, in which a practitioner packages a film clip describing a news event involving an organization.

TV newsclips are generally produced by outside production services. They run from thirty to ninety seconds and are designed to be incorporated into TV newscasts. Most such newsclips are used on local newscasts. Sports films, in particular, get wide use.

A rule of thumb in producing a TV newsclip is to allow the sponsor one audio and one video "plug" within the clip, as illustrated in Figure 9-1. For example, tobacco firms have had success placing TV newsclips on auto races—their identification neatly embedded in the passing race cars.

In other cases, the sponsoring agency may be a more integral part of the clip itself. For example, Toy Manufacturers of America produced a TV newsclip on how to choose a Christmas toy. The clip played before 103 million people throughout the nation. Brunswick Corporation created a clip demonstrating new equipment at a major bowling tournament. This clip also received wide play. Western Electric produced a clip that took a behind-the-scenes look at the company's massive communication complex for a national political convention.

The key in each of these cases and the key in every saleable TV newsclip is the newsworthiness of the clip itself. Also, in dealing with television, newsclips must be professionally produced, scripted, and edited. Such a clip may cost a sponsor between $3,000 and $6,000 including production and national distribution, depending on the number of stations covered. A successful TV clip should return a sponsor at least $5 of commercial air time for each $1 invested.[7]

While many large stations will not use privately packaged clips as a matter of principle, organizations have nevertheless found the distribution of such clips to be worthwhile. While the deck may be stacked against the use of such film releases, the possibility of reaching an audience of millions of viewers with the impact of sight and sound is indeed an enticing one.

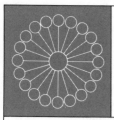

CASE STUDY
The chairman's speech

C hairman Byron Klapper of the Middletown United Way Drive is to address the employees of Middletown Power and Light on the importance of the United Way. Russell Gaye, the newly appointed public relations director of United Way, is to draft Chairman Klapper's speech. Gaye is summoned to the chairman's office to conduct a thirty-minute interview on the speech.

The interview commences.

"Mr. Klapper, it's a pleasure to meet you."

"It's nice to meet you too, Russell. I understand you're newly arrived in Middletown."

"Yes, sir. I'm originally from Seattle, lived there my whole life and only have been in Middletown for a month."

The two discuss Seattle and mutual friends for about seven minutes, when Russ shifts the conversation to the speech.

"Mr. Klapper, I know this is the kick-off speech for United Way, and I assume you'd like to make it something special."

"Yes, I think that's right. I believe in this talk. I'd really like to get to the heart of the United Way campaign and talk about what it means to each individual participant."

"You know, in Seattle, I often heard the United Way criticized for its high administrative budget, insufficient support for community-oriented charities, and things like that. Does that kind of criticism bother you?"

"Yes it does. Particularly because it isn't at all the case. Certainly not in Middletown. Our administrative budget is low, and the charities we support are all community-oriented. I mean how can you say that the Middletown Children's Shelter is not a significant community charity?"

"Absolutely, I couldn't agree more. I have a friend who works at the Shelter and the work they do there is marvelous."

They proceed to speak about the Shelter for another five or six minutes, when Russ again turns back to the speech.

"Mr. Klapper, on the speech, do you want to say anything about the goals of the United Way drive this year?"

"Absolutely. I think we should enumerate that our goal for the city of Middletown is $10 million this year. Middletown Power and Light, of course, will play a significant role in reaching that goal. In fact, they just set their individual goal this morning. I think that's very important to get into the speech, and I also think we should speak a little bit about each individual's responsibility in supporting United Way."

"Do you want at all to allude to Middletown Power and Light's contribution last year?"

"Well, what do you think? Last year, you know, the Middletown Power and Light contribution was way off—about $50,000 less than the previous year. Of course, that was in a period of economic downturn."

"I'm not sure we're out of the downturn yet. Seattle certainly hasn't recovered. Do you think we are?"

"I think we're beginning to see signs of substantial recovery. As you know, national GNP is up and unemployment seems to be declining. In general, I'm relatively optimistic that the economy will continue to improve."

"I know we only have a couple minutes left. How would you like to end the speech?"

"Well, I think, Russ, I'd like to stress the importance of individual responsibility in the United Way drive. This really is a matter of individuals taking leadership on their own for a very, very worthwhile cause."

"Thanks very much Mr. Klapper. I'll have the speech draft up to you tomorrow."

QUESTIONS

1 As a speech writer, how would you rate Russ's interview?

2 Do you think the interview gave him the information he needs to produce a speech?

3 Did he successfully ascertain the subject of the speech? The object? The main points?

4 What do you think he learned about Mr. Klapper's personality, use of humor, approach to the subject, etc.?

5 From what was learned at the interview, and using the United Way material below as a guide, write an eight-minute, four-page speech for Mr. Klapper.

WHAT IS THE UNITED WAY?

The United Way is a locally based voluntary effort, developed over the years since 1887 in over 2200 towns and cities in the United States, to raise funds efficiently, to allocate those funds effectively, and to plan and coordinate human service programs competently.

Last year United Way raised more than $1.78 billion from 37 million contributors to finance 37,000 local, state and national health, welfare and recreation services which serve almost 32 million families. United Way planning organizations seek continually to coordinate and balance the programs and services of all human service agencies regardless of how they are financed or the auspices under which they operate. Both governmental and voluntary organizations are involved. Each United Way organization is autonomous and locally controlled. The funds raised are allocated on the basis of community need to various service agencies by local committees composed of men and women volunteers from all walks of life.

Millions of men and women of all ages are United Way volunteers. They serve in agency programs and on boards and committees to

WHAT DOES UNITED WAY DO?

guide the work and set policies for agencies and United Way organizations. A recent study indicates that volunteers throughout the nation contribute about 8.4 billion hours of service a year. Many of these hours are devoted to serving United Way and its affiliated agencies.

The United Way is the local community's means of dealing with human problems relying on volunteer initiative, commitment, responsibility and participation. It is a system by which people help their neighbors voluntarily. It develops new ways to solve old and new problems. It involves citizens in strengthening and integrating the health and social service programs of both governmental and voluntary organizations.

Services supported by the United Way include family counseling, foster care, adoptions, day care for children, meals on wheels for the homebound, homes for the aging, rehabilitation for the handicapped, Salvation Army, Boy and Girl Scouting, camping, neighborhood houses, community centers, boys and girls clubs, visiting nurses, well-baby clinics, childrens hospitals, Red Cross, Urban League, health research, USO, special inner city programs for the poor and minority groups, YM and YWCA's, scholarships and job training.

WHAT IS UNITED WAY OF AMERICA?

United Way of America is the national association of local United Way organizations. It was created and is supported by them. It exists to help them do a better job of serving their communities. United Way of America serves its members:

1. through the recruitment and training of personnel for professional service in local United Ways;

2. by facilitating the exchange of ideas and experience among the members;

3. through consultation in the local community or via telephone or letters;

4. through the production of manuals and handbooks to guide local operations;

5. by collecting and analyzing pertinent statistical data and publishing the results for local use;

6. by interpreting the United Way movement to other national organizations, to government, corporations, organized labor and others;

7. by providing a coordinated national communications program to familiarize the American people with and to enlist their support for the objectives and activities of the United Way movement and the organizations associated with it;

8. by keeping abreast of national developments of significance to the United Way and interpreting and explaining them to local leaders.

NOTES

1 James G. Busse, "The Ghost in the Executive Suite," *TWA Ambassador Magazine*, June 1978, p. 43.

2 Wesley Poriotis, "Is There Life After Manuscript?" *Public Relations Journal*, July 1981, p. 22.

3 Jerry Tarver, "Washington Newspaper Reports on the Role of the Speech Writer," *The Effective Speech Writer's Newsletter*, 4, no. 1 (June-July 1978): 2.

4 Ibid.

5 R. Irwin Goodman, "Selecting Public Service Announcements for Television," *Public Relations Review*, Fall 1981, pp. 26–28.

6 Used by permission of Champion Spark Plug Company.

7 Hilliard A. Schendorf, "ABCs of TV News Film," *Public Relations Journal*, June 1977, p. 19.

SUGGESTED READING

Ashley, Paul P. *Say It Safely: Legal Limits in Publishing, Radio & Television.* Seattle: University of Washington Press, 1969.

Associated Press. *Broadcast News Stylebook.* (Available from the author, 50 Rockefeller Plaza, New York, N.Y. 10020.) More generalized style than the UPI book; suggests methods and treatment for the preparation of news copy, with information pertinent to AP broadcast wire operations.

Bremer, Roslyn. "Pointer for a Successful Q&A." *Public Relations Journal*, April 1975, p. 48. Required reading on how to handle a question and answer session.

Broadcasting Publications. *Broadcasting.* (Available from the author, 1735 DeSales St. N.W., Washington, D.C. 20036; published weekly on Monday.) The basic news magazine for radio, television, and cable television industries, reporting all activities involved in the entire broadcasting field.

Daily Variety. (Available from 1400 N. Cahuenga Blvd., Hollywood, Calif. 90028). Trade paper for the entertainment industries, centered mainly in Los Angeles, with complete coverage of West Coast production activities; reports from all world entertainment centers.

Glade, Otto W. "Getting Additional Mileage Out of that Speech," *Journal of Organizational Communication* 4, no. 4 (1975): pp. 20–22. What to do with speeches once they've been written and polished.

Goodman, R. Irwin. "Selecting Public Service Announcements for Television," *Public Relations Review*, Fall 1981, pp. 25–34. Insights into what information a station's public service director is looking for in deciding what PSA to air.

Martel, Myles. "Combating Speech Anxiety," *Public Relations Journal*, July 1981, pp. 20–21. The tension-laden self-consciousness that hits most speakers can be alleviated by a proper attitude toward the five elements discussed in this article.

Monroe, Alan H., and **Ehninger, Douglas.** *Principles of Speech Communication.* Glenview, Ill.: Scott, Foresman, 1974.

Novelli, William D. "You Can Produce Effective PSAs," *Public Relations Journal*, May 1982, pp. 30–32.

Poriotis, Wesley. "Is There Life After Manuscript?" *Public Relations Journal*, July 1981, pp. 22–23.

Smith, Richard N. "How To Get Publicity Mileage From Your Speech," *Public Relations Journal*, July 1981, pp. 21, 28.

Tarver, Jerry. "How to Put 'Good' Humor in Your Next Speech." *Public Relations Journal*, February 1975, pp. 15–17.

United Press International. *Broadcast Stylebook.* (Available from the author, 220 E. 42nd Street, New York, N.Y. 10017.) Designed to help people write the kind of copy used by an announcer. It's not a rule book, but it suggests methods and treatment for the proper preparation of news copy, with examples of wire copy and brief comments on correct and incorrect methods of newswire copy preparation.

Variety. (Available from 154 W. 46th St., New York, N.Y., weekly, published on Wednesday.) Paper publishes news, features, and commentary each week on every aspect of show business, with extensive reviews of productions around the world.

Vinci, Vincent. "How to Be a Better Speaker." *Nation's Business*, November 1973, pp. 70–72. Tips for getting your message across to an audience.

Welsh, James J. *The Speech Writing Guide.* New York: John Wiley and Sons, 1968.

10
Public Relations Marketing

In the late 1970s and early 1980s, companies began to realize that public relations could play an expanded role in marketing products.

Until then, most marketers treated public relations as an ancillary part of the promotional element in the marketing mix. They were concerned primarily with making sure their products met the needs and desires of customers, were priced competitively, distributed widely, and promoted heavily through advertising and merchandising. Gradually, however, these traditional notions among marketers began to change for several reasons.

○ Consumer protests about product value and safety and government scrutiny about product demands began to shake historical views of marketing.

○ Product recalls—from automobiles to tuna fish—generated recurring headlines.

○ Ingredient scares began to occur regularly.

○ Advertisers were asked to justify their messages in terms of social needs and civic responsibilities.

○ Rumors about particular companies—from fast-food firms to "pop rock" manufacturers—spread in brushfire manner.

○ General image problems of certain companies and industries—from oil to banking—were fanned by a continuous blaze of criticism in the media.

The net impact of all this was that, while a company's products were still important, customers also began to consider a firm's policies and practices on everything from air and water pollution to minority hiring.

Beyond these social concerns, the effectiveness of advertising itself began to be questioned. The increased number of advertisements in newspapers and on the airwaves caused "clutter" and posed a significant burden on advertisers to make the public aware of their products. In the 1970s, the trend towards shorter TV advertising "spots" helped result in three times as many products being advertised on TV as there were in the 1960s. In the 1980s, the spread of cable added yet another multi-channeled outlet for product advertising. Against this backdrop, the potential of public relations as an added ingredient in the marketing mix became increasingly more credible.[1]

THE MARKETING PLAN

For public relations to be effective as a tool in marketing, it must be introduced early in the marketing plan, rather than as an afterthought.

The plan should carefully lay out the organization's objectives, strategies, and tactics for promoting and selling a product. Public relations may be used in the marketing plan to realize a number of objectives:

1 Helping a company and product name become better known.
2 Helping introduce new or improved products.
3 Helping increase a product's "life cycle," i.e., complementing advertising and sales promotion with additional product information.
4 Seeking out new markets and broadening existing ones at reduced costs.
5 Establishing an overall favorable image for the product and company.

Basically, public relations can play a critical role in "positioning" a product appropriately in the market. A product's *position* is the image the product conveys in the public mind. For example, if the public truly believes that "Coke Is It," then the product positioning strategy of Coca Cola has worked. When the public really believes that the folks at Allstate are "The Good Hands People" or that the group from Avis really does "Try Harder"—that's effective product positioning. Companies spend millions trying to position their products in the public mind.

Public relations offers a practical and inexpensive device for conveying product messages and helping position a firm's products. About eight of ten new products fail to catch on. The cost of these annual failures has been estimated in the billions of dollars. Public relations, then, should be involved early and integrated fully into the marketing plan. Whether in helping market a new product or in enhancing the staying power of an old one, public relations can make a telling difference in product success.

PRODUCT PUBLICITY

In light of the difficulty today in raising advertising awareness above the "noise" of so many competitive messages, marketers are turning increasingly to product publicity as an important adjunct to advertising.

Although the public is generally unaware of it, a great deal of what it knows and believes about a wide variety of products comes through press coverage. Articles in the newspaper's "living" section that describe the attributes of a brand of Burgundy or the advantages of down coats or enriched dog foods often arise from product publicity information distributed by the manufacturer.[2]

Traditional product publicity—whether it introduces a new product or promotes a long-standing one—focuses on some feature of the product that appeals to the public. More recently, companies have begun to link products or brands to events or issues that help publicize the product while positioning it in the public mind. Such an approach has been dubbed by public relations counselor Art Stevens as *brandstanding*.

Such tie-ins can range from the sponsorship of conferences and special-interest brochures to the presentation of contests and sporting events (See Figure 10-1.

To Stevens, effective brandstanding must have the following characteristics:

1 The event or issue linked to a product must invite publicity, i.e. it must be newsworthy.

2 The people attracted must be users or potential users of the product.

3 There must be a meaningful or necessary link between the product and the event. In other words, tying the product with the event must make sense.

4 The link should be evident but not intrusive. The product must be subservient to the event or issue.

5 A concurrent program of promotion must support the effort. The event shouldn't just lie there without proper promotional back-up.

6 Follow-up evaluation of results is important to see if the event should be subject to continuing sponsorship.[3]

In an increasing number of cases, companies have found that by associating with a certain type of sponsorship—quality tennis, golf, or track and field events, for example—the firm's image not only is promoted but also enhanced.

THIRD-PARTY ENDORSEMENT

Perhaps more than anything else, the lure of "third-party endorsement" is the primary reason smart organizations value product publicity as much as they do advertising. *Third-party endorsement* refers to the tacit support given a product by a newspaper, magazine, or broadcaster who mentions the product as "news."

Advertising often is perceived as self-serving. People know that the advertiser not only created the message, but also paid for it. Publicity, on the other hand, which appears in news columns, carries no such stigma. When a message is "sanctified" by third-party editors, it is more persuasive than advertising messages, where the self-serving sponsor of the message is identified.[4]

Editors have become sensitive to mentioning product names in print. Some, in fact, have a policy of deleting brands or company identifications in news columns. Public relations counselors argue that such a policy does a disservice to readers, many of whom are influenced by what they read and may desire the particular products discussed. Counselors further argue that journalists who accept and print public relations material for its "intrinsic value" and then remove the source of the information, give the reader or viewer the false impression that the *journalist* generated the facts, ideas, or photography.[5]

Howard Geltzer is president and co-founder of Geltzer & Company, Inc., a New York City public relations agency. Mr. Geltzer serves as strategist and management supervisor on the agency's accounts. He has written numerous articles and booklets on the concept of positioning in public relations, including *Positioning in PR, Positioning for Hospitals,* and *A Marketing Strategy For Colleges in the 1980s.* Prior to starting Geltzer & Company, Mr. Geltzer spent six years in advertising and public relations positions at General Electric, McGraw-Hill Publications, and *Family Health* magazine.

How important is public relations in the marketing mix?

Public relations or product publicity should function as part of a troika of tactics consisting of 1) advertising, 2) sales, and 3) publicity. The most effective way to launch a concerted, strategic program is to use in harmony these three tactics. The best approach is to implement publicity first, followed by promotion and advertising. Publicity, preceding advertising and sales promotion, maximizes its most important attribute: providing newsworthy material to editors.

How do you promote a client's product?

First, we determine what the marketing intelligence is from the client's viewpoint. We also attempt to find out the divergent opinions within the client organization. Usually,

Equally reprehensible are the public relations practitioners who try to place "sponsored" features without disclosing promotional origins. In other words, some companies will distribute cartoons or stories—either directly or through mail order services—without identifying the sponsor of the material. Obviously, such a practice raises ethical questions. Understandably, editors do not soon forgive firms who sponsor such "anonymous" articles.

Most good marketers will use product publicity as an effective complement to advertising. They know that positive publicity adds credibility to advertisements. In rare cases, marketers may forsake advertising entirely and plow all their funds, on a much more limited scale, into public relations.

there is no unanimity. The divergence may come from product vs. technical people, staff vs. field, or one geographic area vs. another. We next talk to editors to find out what information they know about the product, area, or industry.

Usually, people in the trenches have a pretty good idea about what is going on so we speak to salespeople. The end result is to have a public relations plan that supports the advertising and promotion program and includes product and marketing intelligence from all sources.

Can public relations be more effective than advertising?

I hesitate to use the term *more effective* because, except for unique cases like Sony Walkman, it is difficult to isolate the impact of advertising vs. promotion. Public relations reaches the mind of the prospect by third party endorsement. If the reader sees the news of the product or service in a publication that he respects, he'll tend to believe it, and it will have more of an impact than an ad or trade promotion. But, rather than say that one approach is more effective than another, I would prefer to say that the three tactics working in harmony are much more effective than any single discipline working by itself.

How difficult is it to secure publicity for a client's product?

In a general sense, it's not difficult at all. It is simply a matter of developing the appropri-

ate position, marketing strategy, and specific newsworthy niche for the client's product or service, making sure it is in harmony with the client's advertising and promotion programs, and approaching the editors with determination, energy, and a hard-hitting attack. Editors are looking for interesting and innovative story ideas. The role of the publicity person is to make sure that the information is presented in a way that the editors will find interesting and useful.

What should the proper relationship be between a client and a public relations agency?

The client provides the market, industry, and product intelligence. He details the specific problems and competitive needs. The agency responds with energy, creativity, coordinated marketing, and strategic impact.

What are the advantages of using a public relations agency?

An outside agency provides perspective and overview. Depending on the task, the outside agency is often more efficient and cost-effective. I have found that internal PR people spend enormous amounts of time in meetings and serving the requests of internal management rather than focusing on what editors need and what will create an impact in a publication or on the air. The role of an outside agency, in my opinion, is a separate dimension from that of in-house people. The full force of the effort must focus on the needs of editors, rather than the specific desires of the client.   (Interview continues)

RESPONDING TO NEGATIVE PUBLICITY

While third-party endorsements can help a product, the public specter of "shoddy merchandise" can cause irreparable product damage. When Ralph Nader publicly denounced General Motors' Corvair as being "unsafe at any speed," the media publicized the charges; several years later, the Corvair was no more. Bon Vivant, a New Jersey soup maker, had its vichyssoise recalled by the Food and Drug Administration when a couple was stricken with botulism after sampling a can. The incident was duly reported in the media, and the company never recovered.

How should a product be rolled out in a promotional sense?

We feel that PR ought to be first. The best impact that you can achieve with an editor is to provide news. That is, provide the information to an editor or broadcaster before it has appeared in advertising or dealer or trade programs. Sometimes it is necessary to compress the rollout time frame to a short period. Sometimes it can be timed over the course of a year. But, in all cases, the editors should know about the product, service, or new concept before ads or trade information break.

How do you measure success?

The ground rules for accountability ought to be set in advance. The agency is responsible for informing the client what should happen and what the parameters are, before the program is launched. It is unfortunate that many clients' expectations are way beyond what PR can accomplish. Thus, there is disappointment and, in some cases, bad relationships. But if PR is going to be a marketing tool, there should be marketing impact. If there is going to be impact, it ought to be measurable.

In the case of Sony Walkman, we had a specific number of units that we hoped would be sold in a specific period. In the case of other product programs, we wanted to achieve sufficient dealer impact to stock the product on a regular basis and have salespeople promote the use and application. Very often we will suggest that the client take an awareness research study in advance, so that another one can be administered at the end to specifically find out the impact of the product publicity program.

How would you promote the products of a small company with many competitors?

Once again, every product requires a *position* in the minds of editors as well as the prospective market. Sometimes this position is not easy to develop. There are many products that are the same. In these cases, sometimes it's necessary to reposition the product of the competitor.

I have never seen a product or service to which a positioning strategy could not be applied. The way to develop a PR program begins with the positioning strategy for the product or service. Once that is accomplished, the next step is to follow through with editors and broadcasters in a viable, marketing-oriented strategic publicity plan.

Occasionally, products are faulty and deserve to be publicly pilloried. Other times, criticism may be less justified. In any event, nine rules should be followed when a firm's products are attacked publicly:

1 **Don't ignore the criticism.**   Unless an organization is very lucky, attacks on it or its products won't go away. A response will have to be made eventually. But always consider the source. Not every critic deserves to be taken seriously. Evaluate the credibility of the source before acting.

2 **Don't waste time.**   A response is much better *sooner* than *later*. Get the facts quickly. Don't respond without knowing all the pertinent details. Time the response to secure maximum impact.

3 **Don't use cosmetic surgery.**   Negative criticism can't be turned around with short-term solutions. Move quickly to devise total solutions to alleviate the problem. Piecemeal solutions will only cause the product and the organization to "twist slowly, slowly in the media."

4 **Don't overlook the consumer's viewpoint.**   Sometimes a company that believes in its own integrity and the integrity of its products can be so sure that it is doing right that it overlooks the most essential viewpoint—that of the consumer. This mistake can be fatal.

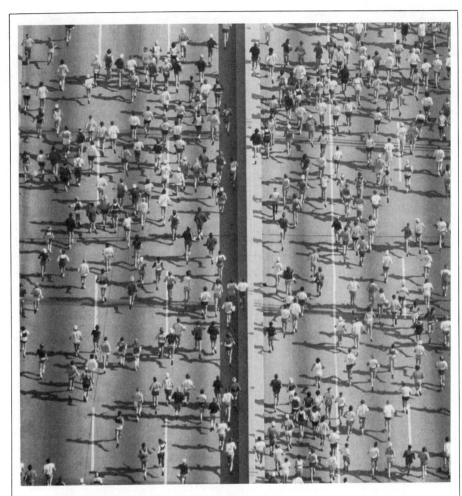

What they did for love. *For the love of running—the triumph that follows the torment—a record 12,530 men and women finished the 1980 New York City Marathon. □ There's nothing like it in the world of distance running. The size of the field. The enthusiasm of the endless onlookers. The exhilarating scenes along the five-borough course. □ Manufacturers Hanover is pleased to be a major sponsor of the annual New York City Marathon, just one in a series of running events we sponsor around the world. Because we admire the pluck and perseverance that runners embody.* **MANUFACTURERS HANOVER**

FIGURE 10–1 Manufacturers Hanover New York City Marathon. Manufacturers Hanover Trust of New York City is one bank that has clearly associated itself with sporting events. In addition to the New York City Marathon, which has become an institution in the international world of track and field, Manny Hanny regularly sponsors professional baseball, hockey, golf, and a variety of other athletic events. Why? Perhaps, as this ad suggests, the bank wishes to emulate the kind of "pluck and perseverance" that athletes embody.

SOURCE: This ad reprinted with the express permission of Manufacturers Hanover Trust.

FEATURE
E.T.'s favorite candy

One of the most spectacular "third party endorsements" of all time occurred in 1982, when Universal Pictures approached Hershey Foods Corp. for a promotional tie-in between Hershey's candy and the hero of a new Universal science fiction picture.

Hershey, as it turned out, was Universal's second choice. Reportedly, the company's first choice, M&M/Mars, turned down the original offer to tie-in its M&M candy.

Hershey, however, accepted in behalf of its Reese's Pieces candy and, in a practice unheard of in Hollywood promotion deals, paid no money for the movie plug—so grateful were the film makers to land the candy company's endorsement.

The rest, of course, is history.

The movie was "E.T. The Extra-Terrestrial," the biggest box office draw in the history of moviedom. Early in the movie, the lovable but famished E.T. follows a trail of brown, yellow, and orange Reese's Pieces to the little boy who would become his friend and savior.

After the film's first two weeks, Reese's Pieces sales tripled. After its first month, sales of Reese's Pieces were up 70 percent. Hershey, in fact, put up $1 million of promotional money, the largest public relations offensive for a single brand in Hershey history, to extol the virtues of "E.T.'s favorite candy."

Although the Hershey people were ecstatic over their adopted hero, they were unsure at first about the affiliation. As one put it, "Our major concern was what kind of creature was this going to be? Is this going to be an X-rated space creature?"

Fortunately, for Hershey, its vice president for new business development saw still pho-

5 **Shoot for key publics.** Know who's most influential. Consumer reporters, consumer advocates, politicians—all may be able to set the record straight if they are reached quickly and effectively. Direct approaches to these pivotal individuals can convert potential disasters into minor brush fires.

6 **Don't overlook the positives.** While some contrition may be necessary, don't go overboard. The product may have many redeeming virtues and one specific flaw. If that can be corrected quickly and inexpensively enough, the product may rebound sharply. Don't spoil its chances by over-confessing.

7 **Involve top management.** Public relations spokespersons may not be enough to convince skeptical publics that a company intends to correct its product problem. A committed and concerned top manager speaking openly and honestly in the media about the company's corrective plans is a most persuasive method.

8 **Don't quote too many people.** In any product publicity crisis, the less spokespersons, the better. It's easier to stay organized and consistent in responses if only a few designated spokespersons express the company's official position.

tos from the unreleased film and concluded, "He was a strange-looking creature. But I told all our executives, 'You're gonna *love* him.' "[6] They did.

SOURCE: Courtesy of Hershey Foods Corp.

9 Think long-term. Always consider the lasting impacts that a prolonged product publicity crisis will have on a company.

PUBLIC RELATIONS MARKETING ACTIVITIES

In addition to product publicity, a number of other public relations activities are regularly used to help market products. These activities include article reprints, trade show participation, the use of spokespersons, special events, and consumer-oriented appeals.

ARTICLE REPRINTS

Once an organization has received product publicity in a newspaper or magazine, it should "market" the publicity further to achieve maximum sales punch. Marketing can be done through article reprints aimed at that part of a target audience— wholesalers, retailers, or consumers—who might not have seen the original article. Reprints also help reinforce the reactions of those who read the original article.

As in any other public relations activity, reprints should be approached systematically, with the following ground rules in mind:

1 **Plan ahead,** especially if an article has major significance to the organization. Ideally, reprints should be ordered before the periodical goes to press so that customers can receive them shortly after the article hits the newsstands.

2 **Select target publics** and address the recipients by name and title. This strategy will ensure that the reprint reaches the most important audience.

3 **Pinpoint the reprint's significance** either through underlining pertinent information in the article, making marginal notes, or attaching a cover letter. This way, the target audience will readily understand the significance of the reprint.

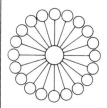

MINICASE
The Walkman public relations/advertising campaign

In 1980, when Sony Corporation introduced the world's smallest stereo cassette player, the "Walkman," it decided to launch a worldwide marketing campaign without the benefit of consumer advertising. Instead, Sony employed the public relations firm of Geltzer & Company, Inc., pioneers in the concept of product positioning, to help launch the Walkman.

Geltzer defined *product positioning* as "finding a hole no one else is using and showing how your product best fills this need." In the case of the Walkman, the product was positioned as a powerful, portable, high-quality sound-producing, personal entertainment vehicle. Complicating the public relations product launch however was the fact that the Walkman didn't meet any current demand and also was expensive—about $200.

To combat these drawbacks, Geltzer & Company organized a multi-faceted public relations program:

○ Nationwide publicity in "upscale" magazines and newspapers talked about the new "stereo-to-go" as a Christmas gift.

○ Models in advertisements for exclusive products from Christian Dior sheets to Gloria Vanderbilt fashions began appearing adorned with Sony Walkmans.

○ Silent disco contests were held in prominent clubs for "movers and shakers," listening to their Walkmans and gyrating to their own, personal beat.

○ In the midst of New York City's crippling subway strike in 1980, office workers on bridges, bikes, and city streets were regularly photographed wearing their Walkmans (generously furnished by Geltzer & Company employees).

○ Predictably, it wasn't long before Johnny Carson began satirizing the Walkman in free, late-night network television jabs.

4 **Integrate the reprint** with other similar articles and information on the same or related subjects. Often, several reprints can be combined into a single mailing piece. Also, reprints can be integrated into press kits and displays.

TRADE SHOWS

Trade show participation enables an organization to display its products before important target audiences. The decision to participate should be looked at with the following factors in mind:

1 **Analyze the show carefully.** Make sure the audience is one that can't be reached effectively through other promotional materials, such as article reprints or

---

By the end of 1980, 500,000 Walkmans had been sold—one of Sony's most successful innovations ever. A major portion of the credit went to Sony's unique marketing approach of attaining considerable positive publicity without the benefit of advertising assistance.

COURTESY: Sony Corporation of America.

QUESTIONS

1 Do you think the Walkman's unique marketing approach would lead to as much, more, or less recognition as other similar, nationally-advertised cassette players?

2 What would be your impression of the Walkman upon seeing it in the newspaper photographs and advertisements?

3 What else could Geltzer & Company have done to incorporate public relations techniques into the marketing campaign of the Sony Walkman?

local publicity. Also be sure the audience is essential to the sale of the product. For example, how responsible are the attendees for the actual purchase?

2 **Select a common theme.** Integrate public relations, publicity, advertising, and sales promotion. Unify all elements for the trade show and avoid, at all costs, any hint of interdepartmental rivalries.

3 **Make sure the products displayed are the right ones.** Decide well in advance exactly which products are the ones to be shown.

4 **Consider the trade books.** Often trade magazines run special features in conjunction with trade shows. Editors need photos and publicity material early enough to make these special editions. Always know what special editions are coming up as well as their deadline schedules.

5 **Emphasize what's new.** Talk about the new model that's being displayed. Discuss the additional features, new uses, or recent performance data of the products displayed. Trade show exhibitions should reveal innovation, break-through and "newness."

6 **Consider local promotional efforts.** While in town during a trade show, an organization can enhance both the recognition of its product and the traffic at its booth by doing local promotions. This strategy means visiting trade magazine editors and local media people to stir up publicity for the product during the show.

SPOKESPERSONS

In recent years, the use of spokespersons to promote products has increased. Spokespersons shouldn't disguise the fact that they are advocates for a particular product. Their purpose is to air their sponsor's viewpoint, which often means going to bat for a controversial product.

An example is the tobacco industry. In the early 1970s, with smoking ads banned on television and radio, the Tobacco Institute, funded by the major tobacco companies, launched a far-reaching speakers campaign to get its story to the public. During the first three years of the campaign, tobacco speakers appeared in 350 cities in forty-eight states and received coverage on 1,300 television and radio shows and in almost 300 newspapers. William Kloepfer, Jr., public relations director for the Tobacco Institute, described the approach:

> We do not try to sell cigarettes or promote smoking. Our public relations objective is to bring a seemingly closed subject back to the level of controversy in the public's mind. We are not attempting to win the argument or make the public view smoking as harmless. We want the public to understand that there is a scientific controversy which has to be resolved by research—not propaganda.[7]

Spokespersons must be articulate, fast on their feet, and thoroughly knowledgeable about the subject. When these criteria are met, the use of spokespersons as a marketing tool can be most effective.

In the 1980s, the spokesperson approach was refined to encompass corporate chief executive officers (CEOs) as lead company spokespeople. For example, Frank Perdue, the CEO of a local New York chicken supplier, literally singlehandedly put his company on the map through advertising and publicity personal appearances. Soon, rent-a-car chairpeople, clothing designers, airline CEOs, and numerous others began appearing regularly to speak for their company's products or services. Then too, in the 1980s, the concept of using celebrities to endorse products also spread. Trusted show business stars (Bob Hope, Robert Young), athletes (Julius Erving, Pete Rose), and overnight celebs (Philippe Petit, the World Trade Center skywalker), all cashed in on the endorsement craze. However, as the feature on p. 233 explains, sometimes dealing with celebrity endorsements introduces unforeseen problems.

SPECIAL EVENTS

Special public relations events also help to market products. They are designed to capture media attention by linking a firm's product with the event created. For example, when Senator William Proxmire wanted to find out if city workers were worth what the taxpayers paid them, he climbed aboard a New York City garbage truck and became a sanitation worker for a day—all in the spotlight of media cameras. When Parker Brothers sought continued recognition for its traditional Monopoly game, it borrowed a bank branch for a day and staged a real life monopoly game—with real money. When Columbia Pictures introduced the movie *Close Encounters of the Third Kind*, it flew more than 300 reporters to Los Angeles and New York for special press screenings, at which the journalists were given leatherette bags and tape recorders labeled CE3K. The movie became a box-office sensation.

There are no particular rules for special events. (Figure 10–2 illustrates a ski tournament sponsored by Fleischmann's.) They range from lavish media extravaganzas to simple ground breaking and open house ceremonies. Sometimes they are

FIGURE 10–2 *Fleishmann Margarine Ski Tournament.* In 1979 Fleischmann's Margarine sponsored a special national cross-country ski competition. Fleischmann's name was prominently displayed on all of the competitors at the more than forty ski touring centers and recreational facilities that hosted the competition.

SOURCE: Courtesy of Padilla & Speer, Inc.

risky, especially when the party is held and no one from the media attends. Nonetheless, done sparingly and conceived thoughtfully, special events can prove a significant enhancement in the marketing of a product.

CONSUMER-ORIENTED PUBLIC RELATIONS

Public relations also helps market products through appeals to consumerist demands. Sponsoring nutritional recipes, publishing consumer information advice, and lobbying for consumer-oriented legislation all help market a company's products. If consumers believe a company sincerely is concerned about their welfare, their trust may translate into purchase decisions. Moreover, a company that voluntarily acts in the public interest, without being prodded by the government, generally can expect to receive a good deal more favorable publicity than a competitor forced to comply with regulation or legislation. Figure 10–3 shows consumerist information provided by a large grocery store chain, General Foods Corporation.

MARKETING FOR THE ENTREPRENEUR

For the small entrepreneur starting out in her own business, public relations sophistication can be a real boon. A small operation can effectively use public relations techniques to enhance marketing of its products and itself.

The key in using public relations techniques to market a small company is the same as promoting a large company: before any public relations program can be considered, solid results must be achieved. In other words, performance must always precede publicity.

Before thinking of a public relations program, an entrepreneur should consider the following six questions:

1 **What are our long-range goals and objectives?** A clear statement of mission will help the organization target its potential audiences. How many clients does it serve now? Does it want to grow? How fast? Is the mission complementary to the human services, educational, cultural, or arts activities in the community? What problems does the company hope to solve?

2 **What are our short-term goals?** Each short-term objective must be evaluated against the longer-range mission so that an appearance of hurtling from one short-term goal to another can be avoided.

3 **Who needs to know about us?** By clearly identifying the individuals or groups that need to know each particular objective, the entrepreneur can lock on the appropriate channel of communication to reach that individual or group.

4 **What are we doing now?** The entrepreneur should first carefully audit her communication efforts, from updating mailing lists to analyzing how she normally reaches key publics.

5 **What else can we do?** The entrepreneur should look inward to see if there are programs on which she can capitalize by publicly telling the firm's story.

Sane talk about fats, cholesterol and your heart

Should you cut back on all fats, saturated and unsaturated? Is there new thinking on cholesterol? Below is a new U.S. Dietary Guideline, with comment from General Foods.

Most Americans eat far too much fat, period.

The fat we should cut down on includes *all* fat...animal and vegetable, saturated and unsaturated. Some fats tend to increase our blood cholesterol, and too much fat of any kind can make us overweight.

Science is divided about the connection between the fats and cholesterol we eat, the cholesterol and triglycerides in our blood, and heart disease. The simple cause-and-effect relationships aren't as certain as we once thought.

U.S. health officials simply do not think you should gamble with too high an intake of fat and cholesterol while the debate over proof rages on.

As you study the Guideline below, remember there are no easy answers. And these underlying principles become even more important:

1. Select from a wide **variety** of foods in each basic food group to help avoid adding too much fat or cholesterol to your diet.

2. Use **moderation** when you eat foods known to be high in fat, or cholesterol.

3. As you change your eating habits, be sure to maintain a proper **balance** of nutrients. If you decide to cut down on fatty meats, for example, turn to other sources of protein, such as lean meats, fish, poultry, and dried beans.

Next: Sane talk about starch and fiber. To date, General Foods has reprinted three of the seven U.S. Dietary Guidelines and plans to reprint the remaining ones soon in this newspaper. The seven Guideline titles are:
1. Eat a variety of foods.
2. Maintain ideal weight.
3. Avoid too much fat, saturated fat and cholesterol.
4. Eat foods with adequate starch and fiber.
5. Avoid too much sugar.
6. Avoid too much sodium.
7. If you drink alcohol, do so in moderation.

1 How much fat should you avoid?
There is no single answer, but most of us could afford to eat about one third less fat. It's high in calories, and being overweight increases risk of heart attack.

2 Should we cut down on all fat?
Yes!! Fat has 250 calories per ounce, twice the calories of carbohydrates or protein. The fats in nuts and olives are equal in calories to the fats in whole milk or ice cream. Margarine has just as many calories as butter. When you reduce fats, don't just avoid one type. Cut down across the board.

3 Are there special problems with saturated fats?
Foods high in animal fat are usually high in cholesterol. Many studies show that eating too much saturated fat can increase blood cholesterol and triglyceride levels for many people.

4 What is cholesterol and where does it come from?
Cholesterol is a fat-like substance that is a normal part of blood and all body tissue. It is essential for the synthesis of certain important hormones. There are several different forms of blood cholesterol. When too much is present in your bloodstream, it can contribute to the clogging of your arteries and increase your risk of heart attack. Some cholesterol is supplied by the food you eat, but your own liver produces it even if you have *no* cholesterol in your diet.

5 Can you eat a high-fat, high-cholesterol diet and still have normal blood cholesterol levels?
For some people the answer is yes, but it's not a license to steal. Have a doctor check the cholesterol and triglyceride levels in your blood annually.

6 Can you go on a low-fat, low-cholesterol diet and still have high blood cholesterol?
Yes. For some people, the body chemistry does not respond to these dietary changes. And there is evidence that, for some, the protein and carbohydrates in the diet can affect cholesterol and triglycerides in the blood. Nonetheless, a low-fat, low-cholesterol diet *will* help many people.

7 Why is there controversy over these recommendations?
There is genuine uncertainty about the relationship between diet and heart disease. Not all people react the same way. There is tremendous variation in the response of individuals to dietary fat and cholesterol. Another part of the controversy has an optimistic note: The rate of heart attacks has declined significantly in the last ten years.

8 How do you tell saturated from unsaturated fats?
Most saturated fat comes from animal sources and is hard like butter or cheese, or fat on meat. Most unsaturated fat is of vegetable origin and liquid, like corn oil. *But there are exceptions!* Many animal fats, such as pork and butter fat, also contain substantial amounts of unsaturated fats. And some vegetable oils like coconut or palm are actually saturated. When vegetable oil is hydrogenated, as in solid shortening or "regular" margarine, it becomes partially saturated.

9 What other common risk factors can affect your heart?
In addition to smoking and high blood pressure, there's stress. Heredity. Drinking too much. Not exercising. Overexertion. Being overweight. Or being a diabetic, to name a few.

10 Does the basic principle, "Eat a variety of foods," still stand when it comes to fats and cholesterol?
More than ever. Your body needs *some* fat. All saturated fats and cholesterol need not be eliminated, particularly if they come in a food rich in other nutrients, like milk or eggs.

11 Should you give up eggs, shrimp, liver?
No. Unless your doctor advises you that your blood cholesterol levels are too high, don't feel that you must totally avoid high-cholesterol foods like shellfish, organ meats and eggs. They can be plentiful sources of the protein and important vitamins and minerals you need. *Moderate.* Don't eliminate.

12 Do you need fat at all?
Most people would reject a diet without fat as unpalatable. And remember some fat is essential for a healthy body. It is better to cut down your use of fats, than to try to eliminate them totally.

13 Should you switch to polyunsaturates?
Scientists are reexamining the evidence. They're now less convinced that increased use of polyunsaturates is the most effective and safe way of lowering blood cholesterol. So moderate your intake of *all* fats.

General Foods urges you to study the U.S. Dietary Guidelines

Inset reproduction of U.S. Dietary Guidelines pamphlet:

U.S. Dietary Guidelines

3 Avoid Too Much Fat, Saturated Fat, and Cholesterol

If you have a high blood cholesterol level you have a greater chance of having a heart attack. Other factors can also increase your risk of heart attack—high blood pressure and cigarette smoking, for example—but high blood cholesterol is clearly a major dietary risk indicator.

Populations like ours with diets high in saturated fats and cholesterol tend to have high blood cholesterol levels. Individuals within these populations usually have greater risks of having heart attacks than people eating low-fat, low-cholesterol diets.

Eating extra saturated fat and cholesterol will increase blood cholesterol levels in most people. However, there are wide variations among people—related to heredity and the way each person's body uses cholesterol.

Some people can consume diets high in saturated fats and cholesterol and still keep normal blood cholesterol levels. Other people, unfortunately, have high blood cholesterol levels even if they eat low-fat, low-cholesterol diets.

There is controversy about what recommendations are appropriate for healthy

Americans. But for the U.S. population as a whole, reduction in our current intake of total fat, saturated fat, and cholesterol is sensible. This suggestion is especially appropriate for people who have high blood pressure or who smoke.

The recommendations are not meant to prohibit the use of any specific food item or to prevent you from eating a variety of foods. For example, eggs and organ meats (such as liver) contain cholesterol, but they also contain many essential vitamins and minerals, as well as protein.

Such items can be eaten in moderation, as long as your overall cholesterol intake is not excessive. If you prefer whole milk to skim milk, you can reduce your intake of fats from foods other than milk.

To avoid too much fat, saturated fat, and cholesterol

• Choose lean meat, fish, poultry, dry beans and peas as your protein sources
• Moderate your use of eggs and organ meats (such as liver)
• Limit your intake of butter, cream, hydrogenated margarines, shortenings and coconut oil, and foods made from such products
• Trim excess fat off meats
• Broil, bake, or boil rather than fry
• Read labels carefully to determine both amount and types of fat contained in foods

Note: Underlinings and numbers for editorial comment by General Foods.
© General Foods Corporation, 1980

FIGURE 10–3 *General Foods Consumerist Information.* General Foods complements its advertising with marketing promotion in the form of consumer-oriented product publicity and public relations programs.

SOURCE: Courtesy of General Foods Corporation.

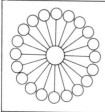

MINICASE
Marketing the Jordache look

In the 1980s, few companies could boast as successful a link between public relations and marketing as Jordache, the maker of what used to be called dungarees and are today called blue jeans.

Jordache was the creation of Joe Nakash, who began in New York City in the late 1970s with $25 in his pocket, sleeping in the bus terminal by night and sweeping floors by day.

After beginning several jeans stores in Brooklyn with his brothers, Ralph and Avi, Joe Nakash borrowed $300,000 to begin his own jeans manufacturing company. Using the first names of himself and his brothers and adding a "che" because it "sounded French," Joe Nakash invented Jordache and with it "the Jordache look." Then the fun started.

The Nakash brothers decided to blow their entire new business loan on promotion.

○ They bought time on "60 Minutes" and ran an ad featuring a topless Lady Godiva and a young man wearing Jordache jeans. CBS objected strongly to the commercial, and Jordache achieved significant publicity over its rejection. Meanwhile, orders for Jordache jeans began to pour in.

○ The brothers attracted additional publicity when they refused to make jeans larger than size 36 so that only the lean could wear them. Predictably, the Jordache ads provoked cries of "sexism" and "exploitation of women." Equally predictably, the company returned the volley, insisting loudly that

6 **Do we have the money to do what we want?** Many entrepreneurs have limited budgets. Advertising costs money. So does postage. So do telephones. Therefore, a pivotal part of the entrepreneur's public relations role is to determine what the proposed program will cost and either scale it back appropriately or work to obtain the funds to do it.

If the entrepreneur decides that publc relations support will be helpful and can be afforded, the following rules may help secure added recognition for a small firm:

Work to achieve visibility.   A entrepreneur in a small company can try to publicize the company through free publicity in the media. Local media are generally receptive to the announcement of a new firm, new officers, new products, and new locations of local business operations. An entrepreneur who takes the time to become familiar with local journalists may find a few willing to use the company's announcements.

their product connoted "vivaciousness and healthy attractiveness." The debate was great media copy.

○ When The New York Times banned a Jordache topless couple ad because "the couple was smiling," the company reshot the ad with the models *not* smiling. Jordache then publicly censured the Times for practicing its own brand of morality. More coverage resulted.

○ When rival firms began to counterfeit Jordache jeans, the Nakash brothers hired a legal and detective team to track them down and invited reporters to come along for the kill. This too, got extensive coverage.

○ When a Jordache blimp crashed at take-off, leaving the invited reporters with a nonevent, Jordache models were delivered by ambulance to the press conference site and turned a fiasco into a party.

While such product publicity techniques may have smacked of the days of P.T. Barnum, the Nakash brothers didn't seem to mind. They seemed content with an image that had, in four years, parlayed brother Joe's original $25 into a $350 million, 8,000 employee business.

QUESTIONS

1 Why wouldn't the Jordache public relations/marketing strategy work for other companies?

2 Do you think the word-of-mouth publicity that the Jordache stunts provoked was helpful for the company's image?

3 Was the decision not to market jeans beyond size 36 a good one?

4 How would you rate the Jordache public relations thrust in terms of clearly positioning the company?

Compose a facilities brochure. No matter how small the firm, a brochure describing itself (its products, prices, and philosophy) is a good idea. A facilities brochure can serve as a "calling card" to potential customers. Done in a quality manner, such a brochure may suggest prestige and credibility, both vital attributes for any business.

Use direct-mail marketing. Once a facilities brochure is created, it should be mailed to customers and prospects. In this context, it is often wise to use an outside, professional mailing service and mailing list supplier. The facilities brochure should have a return response coupon or a postage-paid response care to facilitate customer inquiries.

Work at becoming known in the community. Small businessmen should be joiners. They should join the local Chamber of Commerce, Better Business Bureau, civic clubs such as Rotary and Kiwanis, Junior Achievement, or Big Brother/Big Sister. Achieving recognition in a community isn't difficult if one is willing to put in the work and the hours. For a businessman in a small company, such active participation in community affairs can mean valuable business contacts.

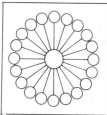

MINICASE
The dubious "Wonder" bread

In the 1970s, the Federal Trade Commission (FTC) claimed that an ITT Continental Bakers product, "Wonder Bread," was not, as its advertising intimated, "unique." Wonder Bread, according to the FTC, was just the same as any other bread. The "revelation" of the less-than-unique bread was carried prominently in national media.

Rather than slinking off to nurse its wounds, ITT came out slugging.

The company launched an immediate advertising campaign stressing Wonder Bread's enriching value. It sent public relations and management personnel on visits to newspaper editors to discuss the dangers of the FTC action, the truth of its own advertising, and the enriching value of the bread. It created and distributed a Wonder Bread press kit, in which the dangers of a federal agency interfering unduly with consumer preference were discussed. It implemented a "recipe campaign," in which recipes using Wonder Bread were distributed to newspapers and magazines throughout the country. It hired well-known nutritionists to tour major markets and educate consumers on the enrichment aspects of bread.

The ITT campaign seemed to neutralize the negative impact of the FTC announcement, and its sales were not materially hurt.

QUESTIONS

1 How successful do you think ITT would have been had the company waited until one month after the FTC announcement to launch its public relations program?

2 Do you think advertising was a necessary component in ITT's program? Why or why not?

3 Might ITT have adopted a "softer sell" campaign to repudiate the FTC's charges? Would this have been more or less effective than the actual campaign?

4 What other public relations activities might ITT have incorporated in its Wonder Bread campaign?

The shoes of the thunder man

Getting celebrities to endorse products is an increasingly popular form of product promotion.

Like everything else, getting Burt Reynolds to drink your beer or convincing Bo Derek to endorse your cosmetics costs money. Sometimes, big money—as much as $100,000 a year for top stars.

Occasionally, celebrities get confused over exactly what they are endorsing. Take the case of Darryl Dawkins, the immense professional basketball center affectionately dubbed "Chocolate Thunder."

In the spring of 1982, Dawkins signed a $50,000-a-year endorsement contract with Nike sneakers.

In return for wearing Nike shoes when in uniform, Dawkins was promised a share in a royalty pool to which Nike contributed 10 to 20 cents for each pair of shoes sold. Dawkins also was promised a Nike bonus of $10,000 if voted the most valuable player in the National Basketball Association or if he finished first in league scoring or rebounding.

Nike also supported the Dawkins sponsorship by printing 20,000 "Chocolate Thunder" posters.

In light of all this, it was understandable that Nike executives were just a bit dismayed when Dawkins showed up on the basketball court wearing shoes made by Pony Sports & Leisure.

Nike promptly sued its errant charge for compensatory damages for the useless posters and punitive damages for fraud.

Actually, Nike was lucky. According to the company's general counsel, another athlete once wore shoes with one company's stripe on one side and another company's mark on the other and tried to collect from both!

"When we caught him, he said that if he'd had any more room, he would have tried three."[8]

Consider advertising.   Advertising for a small business can, of course, be tremendously helpful. However, it is not a necessity. Advertising, as noted, is expensive and can prove wasteful if it is not used strategically. Advertising in the telephone classified directory is probably a good idea; so, too, is sticking to the local media. Print advertising for a small business should have some built-in mechanism, such as a coupon, to indicate reader response.

Most small entrepreneurs have limited means. Therefore, to increase "reach" and recognition in the marketplace, a wise entrepreneur will take advantage of public relations techniques to enhance marketing initiatives.

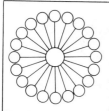

MINICASE
The consumerist can

I n mid-1972, talk in the food industry centered around the anticipated action of the Food and Drug Administration to release nutrition labeling standards for food producers. It was expected that the FDA would take a year to introduce its voluntary standards.

Rather than waiting for the FDA mandate, Del Monte, the world's largest canner of fruits and vegetables, announced a program to begin labeling the nutritional content of its major products.

This massive relabeling campaign created shock waves in its industry. For the first time, a major canner intended to list the levels of carbohydrates, minerals, and vitamins on its cans. The move triggered a number of complimentary articles in the business press and an equal number of "sour grapes" comments from Del Monte's competitors. Some argued, in fact, that General Foods, Campbell Soup, Pillsbury, and several other food processors had been offering nutritional information before Del Monte announced its massive program. But unlike the others, Del Monte had launched a major advertising and public relations campaign to promote its labeling project.

As one industry observer summed up the Del Monte program, "We are entering the era of the marketing of nutrition."[9]

QUESTIONS

1 What do you suspect were the objectives and strategies of the Del Monte labeling program?

2 What were the benefits of the timing of Del Monte's announcement?

3 How did Del Monte believe it would be able to differentiate its nutrition labeling program from those of its competitiors?

THE AGE OF "PUBLIC RELATIONS MARKETING"

Marketing professor Philip Kotler has said that the days of traditional product marketing may be giving way to a more subtle, "social" or "public relations" marketing. According to Kotler, companies must deal with dwindling resources, inflation continuing to limit buying power, consumers becoming more sophisticated, environmental and quality-of-life considerations, and government control. With these worries, companies may be just as concerned about staying in business as they are with maximizing sales.[10]

In light of these changing societal characteristics, a new kind of *radical marketing* may develop:

1 **Quality-of-life**   Rather than being the "seller science," the purpose of marketing in the future may be to assist sellers in selling better, buyers in buying better, and governments in regulating better. *Quality* rather than *quantity* may become the most important variable in marketing goods and services.

2 **Interest orientation**   Rather than being "needs-oriented," marketers in the future may be more "interest-oriented." That is, they may serve the educational or social interest of consumers more than anything else.

3 **External decision-making**   Rather than sellers freely setting prices and controlling marketing factors, external parties may be represented in the marketing decision-making process.

4 **Nonsegmentation**   Rather than varying their product offerings as they choose, marketers may be limited to offering less differentiation in styles, colors, and models.

5 **Less may be better**   Rather than catering to all the wants of consumers, future marketers may have to concentrate on conserving resources and counteracting increased and unnecessary costs to customers.

While radical marketing is not yet upon us and perhaps may never be, Kotler's thesis underscores the importance of marketers thinking beyond traditional notions of product, price, distribution, and promotion as the key elements in selling a product.

More and more, managements of consumer product companies are inviting public relations input in marketing program development. Brand and product promotion managers increasingly are recognizing that public relations programs can address specific marketing objectives with the same precision as advertising and with equal or better cost efficiency. Indeed, some predict that we are on the threshold of a major readjustment in marketing promotion.[12]

By the end of the 1980s, in fact, cable TV and media proliferation may provide a communications base that not only will increase the importance of public relations in the marketing mix but also might well permit product public relations to become an equal partner to product brand advertising.

CASE STUDY
Rely tampons

Procter & Gamble (P&G), one of the nation's most successful marketers, entered the $1 billion-a-year menstrual products industry in early 1980, when its Rely tampons went into national distribution. Rely, which the company had test-marketed since 1974, had drawn rave reviews. Indeed, said one industry analyst, "The consumer preference was one of the greatest they ever had for a new product."

Rely was an immediate success. The product won almost 20 percent of the U.S. market in less than six months. The key to P&G's success was superior product performance. Rely had improved absorbency, an important plus for the 50 million women who used tampons. Other tampon manufacturers soon added "thirsty fibers" to their products to compete with the P&G market blockbuster.

Little noticed by P&G and other manufacturers was a case reported in Colorado in 1978 of a sometimes-fatal disorder called toxic shock syndrome (TSS). Upon being identified, the U.S. Center for Disease Control in Atlanta began to study this disease, which caused vomiting, diarrhea, plummeting blood pressure, rashes, fever, and occasionally death.

In May 1980, the Center reported an increase in the incidence of the disease, the primary victims being menstruating women. In June, the Center linked toxic shock with tampon use, although it said, "no particular brand of tampon is associated with unusually high risk."

Then, on September 18, 1980, the bottom fell out for P&G.

On that day, Rely tampon was singled out as "an increased risk," even though "cases of TSS have occurred with tampons produced by all five of the major U.S. tampon manufacturers," according to the Center.

Immediately, P&G executives met with officials of the Food and Drug Administration, which regulates tampons. On September 19, consumer groups publicly called for the recall of P&G's Rely brand.

Faced with a media disaster and fearing a product recall, P&G didn't hesitate. On September 23, it voluntarily took Rely off the market and agreed to launch a print and broadcast campaign urging women to return tampons already purchased for a refund. Other super-absorbent tampons, however, remained on the market.

To hasten scientific progress into TSS, P&G devoted a staff of in-house researchers to investigate the problem and then committed another $2 million to research TSS at fourteen private institutions.

Despite its prompt handling of the Rely matter, P&G was served with 400 lawsuits from surviving victims and next-of-kin of those who died from TSS after using Rely tampons.

Additionally, the company took a $75 million write-off on its Rely business and was stuck with almost 900,000 cartons of Rely packages (which were ultimately used as an "alternate heat source" for the company's plants).

On the public relations side, however, the company was universally praised for voluntarily taking Rely off the market before being forced to by the government. Investors hailed the company for not allowing the Rely crisis to overwhelm it—for controlling the situation rather than having the TSS controversy control the company. Moreover, P&G was commended for not allowing the incident to interfere with the marketing of its many other successful products, such as Tide detergent, Crest toothpaste, Folgers coffee, and other well-known brands. All functioned as usual during the crisis.

P&G's Chairman Edward Harness promised his stockholders that the Rely debacle did not mean the end of P&G in the tampon business. Harness pointed out that Rely's introduction was the culmination of more than 20 years of P&G research. Also, importantly, he told the shareholders that the company absolutely believed, "There is no medical or scientific evidence of which we are aware that Rely is in any way defective or that any of its ingredients are harmful or contribute to the development of toxic shock syndrome."

But, Harness concluded, the fact that the company's scientists believed Rely to be harmless was less important than P&G's long-held view "that the company and the company alone is responsible for the safety of our products. To sacrifice this principle could over the years ahead be a far greater cost than the monetary losses we face on the Rely brand."

QUESTIONS

1 What might have happened if Procter & Gamble had publicly disputed the 1980 finding of the Center for Disease Control?

2 What other options did P&G have besides removing Rely from the market?

3 How badly do you think P&G's public image was tarnished by the Rely controversy and subsequent lawsuits?

4 Could there have been a potential "spillover impact" on other P&G products from negative public opinion?

5 Had you been public relations director of one of the other four U.S. tampon manufacturers, what public relations response would you have recommended to your management in the wake of the P&G decision?

Helpful hint in answering questions:
Reflecting on what advice he would give to companies who someday might find one of their products similarly caught up in a safety controversy, retired P&G Chairman Harness, advised: "Keep the ball in your own court if you can. Do it right before somebody else does it wrong for you."

For further information on the Rely tampon case, see: Steve Byers, "Two Cases of How to Handle a Public Problem," *The Milwaukee Journal*, October 2, 1980, p. 17; Nan Robertson, "Toxic Shock," *The New York Times Magazine*, September 19, 1982, p. 32; Dean Rotbart and John A. Prestbo, "Killing a Product: Taking Rely Tampons Off Market Put Procter & Gamble Through a Week of Agonizing," *The Wall Street Journal*, November 3, 1980; Pamela Sherrid, "Tampons After the Shock Wave," *Fortune*, August 10, 1981, pp. 114–129.

NOTES

1 Richard M. Detwiler, "Yes, Virginia, It's All True—What They Say about Third Party Endorsements," *Public Relations Journal,* May 1974.

2 Art Stevens, "Brandstanding: Long-Lived Product Promotion," *Harvard Business Review,* May-June 1981, p. 54.

3 Ibid.

4 Detwiler, op. cit.

5 Milton Williams, "Deleting Product Identification," *Editor & Publisher,* 26 June 1976, p. 33.

6 Stephanie Mansfield, "Sweet Success: Reese's Cashes on E.T.'s Candy Cravings," *The Washington Post,* 14 July 1982, p. B1.

7 Cited in Nancie Gee, "Tobacco Speakers Roam U.S.," *Publicist,* July/August 1977, p. 1.

8 Tamar Lewin, "Conflict Over Endorsements," *The New York Times,* 2 August 1982, p. D-1, 3.

9 "Del Monte—Living with New Labeling Rules," *Business Week,* 3 February 1973, pp. 42–45.

10 Philip Kotler, "Marketing Management in an Era of Shortage," speech before the New York-New Jersey Chapter of the American Marketing Association, Rutgers University, Newark, N.J., November 10, 1974.

SUGGESTED READING

Fornell, Cloes. "Efficiency in Marketing Communication." *Marquette Business Review.* Summer 1975, pp. 80–89.

Green, Paul E., and **Wind, Yoram.** "New Way to Measure Consumers' Judgements." *Harvard Business Review 53,* no. 4, July/August 1975, pp. 107–117.

Greyser, Stephen A. "Changing Roles for Public Relations," *Public Relations Journal,* January 1981, pp. 18–25.

Jefkins, F. W. *Marketing and PR Media Planning.* New York: Pergamon, 1974.

Levitt, Theodore, "Marketing Myopia." *Harvard Business Review 53,* no. 5, September/October 1975, pp. 26–48. Management's failure to analyze its markets and customers' needs could account for some degee of corporate decline.

Mayall, Robert L. "Does Anybody Here Know How To Play This Game?" *Public Relations Journal,* June 1981, p. 33.

Musgrave, Philip J. "Make Your Marketing Communications System Sell." *SAM Advanced Management Journal 40,* no. 3, Summer 1975, pp. 23–30.

Siles, Madonna. "Using Paid-for Research and Creativity from Ads As PR Program Base Is a Communications Dollar-Stretcher." *Industrial Marketing,* March 1975, pp. 52–53.

Stevens, Art. "What's New In Product Publicity?" *Public Relations Journal,* December 1981, pp. 16–17. Brandstanding is one way product publicity can address specific marketing objectives with the same precision as advertising and with equal or even better cost-efficiency.

Webster, Frederick E. *Social Aspects of Marketing.* Englewood Cliffs, N.J.: Prentice-Hall, 1974.

Zufall, Dorothy L., "How To Adapt Marketing Strategies In Health-Care Public Relations," *Public Relations Journal,* October 1981, p. 14.

T raditionally, organizations have used advertising to sell products. Only occasionally—for example, the railroads and utilities in the 1920s—did firms use advertisements for purposes other than product promotion.

In 1936, Warner & Swasey initiated an ad campaign that stressed the power of America as a nation and the importance of American business in the nation's future. After World War II, Warner & Swasey continued ads promoting the free enterprise system and opposing government regulation of business.

This unique type of advertising—the marketing of an image rather than a product—became known variously as *institutional advertising, image advertising, public service advertising,* and *public relations advertising.*

Where promotional advertising was hard sell, public relations advertising was softer. Where promotional advertising talked about the particular virtues of using specific products, public relations advertising focused on the general image the company wished to convey and the public issues it wished to confront. While promotional advertising sought purchasing action for its products, public relations advertising sought support for its positions.

11
Public Relations Advertising

Such ads typically were used to announce name changes, management changes, merger plans, or other information that promoted the company in general rather than its products in particular. This kind of specialized advertising remained very much the exception rather than the rule until the 1970s.

ADVERTISING PRESSURES OF THE 1970s

In 1970, U.S. corporations spent a little over $150 million to advertise images and issues. By 1974, the amount spent on such advertising increased to $220 million.[1] One reason for this tremendous growth can be summarized in a single word: *pressure.*

By the early 1970s, pressure began to build for a reshaping of traditional advertising approaches. For a variety of reasons, companies had no choice but to strengthen their role in institutional advertising.

APPROACHING ERA OF SHORTAGES

The sudden jolt brought about by the Arab oil embargo of the early 1970s changed the rules for a number of advertisers. Oil companies, in particular, no longer had to worry about selling their products, but rather about staying in business.

PUBLIC SKEPTICISM

The more sophisticated, college-educated public of the 1970s intuitively distrusted advertising. One study found that even among business people, 42 percent felt "the public's faith in advertising is at an all-time low." Moreover, many thought that business—and especially big business—had shifted its role in the public psyche from hero to villain.[2]

CONSUMERIST AND REGULATORY CHALLENGES

Advertising's most ferocious critics were in the consumerist and regulatory areas. Consumer advocates and regulators began to zero in on large corporations and the advertisements they ran. Soon, large companies became once again "everyone's favorite candidate for slaughter."[3]

COUNTER ADVERTISING

With attacks reminiscent of the earlier muckrakers, consumer advocates of the 1970s went after big business advertising with a vengeance. The weapon they used to attack corporate advertisers was the same tool corporate advertisers used—advertising.

Public interest groups sprang up on both coasts to create their own ads in answer to the claims of large corporate advertisers (see Figure 11-1). One such concern, Public Media Center (PMC) of San Francisco adopted as its creed:

> To represent the unrepresented—in the task of providing media access to those who have important, often vital information or concerns to share with the public but who have been denied access to the communications media in this country because of a lack of funds, a lack of professional skills or because their message was deemed 'too controversial.'[4]

Not only did groups like PMC have the funds (private donations) and skills necessary to create professional advertising, they targeted most efforts at questioning the claims of established advertisers. For example, a typical consumerist-sponsored ad from PMC was a radio spot protesting nuclear power plants. In the ad, an announcer for nuclear plants explained that nuclear technology, like all technology, was a great advancement. The ad finished by the tape speeding up and going out of control.

While radio and television stations and newspapers were not obligated to accept such public service advertising, a few publications and stations, particularly those on public broadcasting channels, accepted the ads. When such counter advertising was accepted, it ran free of charge, falling (on the broadcast side) within the Federal Communications Commission Fairness Doctrine that allows equal time for opposing viewpoints on controversial issues.

CORRECTIVE ADVERTISING

Increased federal pressure was another major reason for the spread of institutional advertising in the 1970s. The Federal Trade Commission (FTC), for years one of the meeker government agencies, suddenly "sprouted teeth" in 1970 when it waged a vigorous campaign to deter advertisers from making claims they could not back up with material facts.[5]

The cutting edge of the FTC offensive was a corrective advertising campaign, where advertisers had to correct any advertising claims found to be false and misleading.

An example was Ocean Spray Cranberry Juice Company, which claimed that its product contained "more food energy" than other drinks. *Food energy,* according to the FTC, meant nothing more than calories. The commission ordered Ocean Spray to run ads stating clearly that previous claims of having more food energy simply meant that the product contained more calories.

While the FTC succeeded in the Ocean Spray case, it was less successful in an attempt to force ITT Continental Baking to run corrective treatment for its Wonder Bread ads. The commission claimed Wonder Bread wasn't any different than other breads even though it boasted it "could build strong bodies 12 ways." The commission claimed that by "implying Wonder Bread is unique," the company's advertising was misleading. ITT appealed the FTC ruling, and a judge ruled, "the record fails, by a wide margin, to show that asserted false aspects of this advertising are presently contributing to Wonder Bread sales or that such aspects have ever had any impact on sales."[6]

In addition to attempts at corrective advertising, government regulators also tried to "counter" certain advertisements to which they objected. In 1967, for example, the government ordered TV and radio stations to make free time available for messages that said cigarette smoking was dangerous to health. Eventually, cigarette manufacturers removed their ads from the airways. Interestingly, in the first year cigarette advertisements disappeared from TV and radio, cigarette sales rose to record levels.

Another government maneuver to regulate advertising claims was the FTC's Substantiation Program, which attempted to make advertisers document claims they made on price, safety, performance, and effectiveness. While most advertisers strongly objected to harsh FTC scrutiny, by the mid-1970s, most had toned down their claims about products they couldn't fully defend. In sum, the rules and the substance of advertising changed dramatically in just a few years.

INTERVIEW
Steve Rivkin

S teve Rivkin is executive vice president of Trout & Ries Advertising, Inc. He also is a member of the agency's board of directors. Prior to joining the agency in 1974 as an account supervisor, Mr. Rivkin was assistant to the vice president of corporate affairs at IU International Corp., a Philadelphia-based conglomerate. He previously served as associate editor of *Iron Age Magazine.* Mr. Rivkin is a frequent speaker on advertising and marketing before business, association, and college audiences.

What's the difference among issue, image, and institutional advertising?

Image and institutional advertising are essentially the same. A company attempts to portray itself in one streamlined manner to its employees, prospects, the financial community, whomever. The trick is boiling down a $7 billion corporation with 60,000 employees scattered across five continents into a description tight enough to write down on the back of your business card.

Issue advertising is something else. Here, a company takes a stand on a matter of (usually) public policy and communicates that stand to government officials, customers, prospects, employees—in short, to anyone who can influence its fate.

What do you mean by "positioning" a company?

Positioning a company means getting into the mind of your prospect with a single, memorable concept or set of ideas about that company. The basic approach of positioning is not to create something new and different, but rather to manipulate what's already there, to retie the connections that already exist.

How do you go about positioning an individual company or product?

Positioning a company is actually thinking in reverse. Instead of starting with you or your company, you start with the prospect.

Step one is to research how your company is perceived in the minds of whatever marketplace is important to you. (Perception is more important than reality.) Don't rely on what management says the company's perceived image is. Your audience's answer may be 180 degrees away.

Step two is to get some internal consensus on what position you ideally want to occupy. (If everybody wants to face a different direction, it's going to be a very difficult march.)

Wishing alone won't make it so. So *step three* is to find out who's in the way of obtaining your desired position. (Maybe you'd like to be known as the world's largest maker of digital widgets. Unfortunately, your competitor is the Digital Widget Company and has five times your revenues and three times your awareness in the widget-buying community.)

Step four is money. Do you have enough money to make it happen? Communications is incredibly expensive today. It takes money to establish a position; it takes money to hold a position once you've established it.

Positioning is also a process that's cumulative. *Step five* is a willingness to hang in there with the same basic idea, year after year. Most successful companies rarely change a winning formula. (How many years have you seen those Marlboro men riding into the sunset? Crest has been fighting cavities for so long, they're into their second generation of kids.)

Finally, you should be sure that your carefully-honed positioning strategy doesn't vanish in a cloud of confusion. *Step six* demands that everything you communicate matches your position. (There's nothing more counterproductive than a speech before a securities analysts group that contradicts the message in the same day's *Wall Street Journal* advertisement.)

As long as an organization's products are good, why should it worry about its corporate image?

It shouldn't have to! (But whoever said life was fair?)

In a multinational, multiproduct, multimedia world, getting noticed is getting tougher. Companies are buying and selling companies at a dizzying rate. Does the reputation of a product or brand automatically transfer along with stock ownership? For most companies, a corporate audience is different than a product audience. (Your banker may not buy your motor oil, but your garage owner isn't going to lend you $10 million either.)

So despite all the good things your product may do and may say about you, your corporate image may ultimately have to stand on its own two feet.

What are the most frequent mistakes organizations make in positioning themselves?

Reaching too far. From some companies' communications, you'd conclude they're just miserable with their current positions. But what's wrong with second place? Pepsi, Avis, Ford, Newsweek, J.C. Penney, Firestone, Zenith, and Chase Manhattan are all considered strong alternatives to the leader.

Trying to be all things to all people. The result is terminal blandness of message.

Choosing the wrong name. The United Shoe Machinery Company disappears into the absolute anonymity of USM Corporation. International Silver Company tarnishes itself into Insilco.

Trying for a free ride. The makers of Alka-Seltzer develop a new product to compete with two cold remedies, Dristan and Contac. They dub it "Alka-Seltzer Plus." But instead of eating into the Dristan and Contac market, the new product wheels around and eats into the Alka-Seltzer market. (One position per product name is the rule.)

This oil executive will go to bed hungry tonight.

Diana Church

HIS COMPANY earned almost two billion dollars in profits* last year, but that's not enough for him. Because he knows the world is running out of fossil fuels, and unless he can move in and monopolize a new power source, in the same way he's monopolized oil, he's going to be out of a job before very long.

That's why he says his company's astronomical profits aren't excessive—because he needs those profits to maintain his power. That's why he's asking for huge new handouts and tax incentives from the taxpayers—because he wants the government to pay the bills, and his company to reap the benefits.

If he doesn't get what he wants, he may not be able to go on collecting his $300,000 a year salary. He may not be able to go on manipulating the world energy market to the benefit of his stockholders and to the detriment of everyone else. He may be forced to give way to a system where the public controls the public resources for the public good.

If you think America's energy supply is too important to be left to a few huge multinational conglomerates, write your elected representatives and tell them that. The oil industry is making its voice heard in Washington. Isn't it time the shivering majority was heard from?

*
After-tax oil profits—1973
(millions of dollars)

	First nine months of 1973	Increase over 1972
Exxon	1,656	59.4%
Mobil	571	38.3%
Texaco	839	34.9%
Gulf	570	60.1%
Standard Calif.	560	39.7%
Standard Indiana	390	32.2%
Shell	253	40.6%
Continental	153	23.4%
Atlantic-Richfield	178	36.9%
Total all nine	5,170	**45.2%**
All oil companies	52,500	**30.3%**

Prepared by Public Interest Communications

ENERGY SHOULD BE EVERYBODY'S BUSINESS

FIGURE 11–1. *Counter advertising.* These two ads, both critical of the nation's oil companies, were prepared by Public Interest Communications in the early 1970s and ran free-of-charge in several newspapers.

The oil companies have us over a barrel

THE NATION'S OIL COMPANIES control the nation's energy supply. And when they want something, they get it. All they have to do is claim that it's not profitable enough for them to produce the energy we need, and the government rushes to make all the concessions the industry wants. The government doesn't even have its own figures on the nation's oil supply—they get all their figures directly from the industry, and make no attempt to have them independently verified.

So if the oil industry wants higher prices, relaxed environmental requirements, the Alaska pipeline, offshore drilling, more tax handouts, and less competition from independent dealers, they simply allow a shortage to occur, and hold our energy supply for ransom.

We think it's time energy policy was based on public need, not corporate greed.

Don't be left out in the cold—write your congressman and insist on public control of the public's resources.

After-tax oil profits—1973
(millions of dollars)

	First nine months of 1973	Increase over 1972
Exxon	1,656	59.4%
Mobil	571	38.3%
Texaco	839	34.9%
Gulf	570	60.1%
Standard Calif.	560	39.7%
Standard Indiana	390	32.2%
Shell	253	40.6%
Continental	153	23.4%
Atlantic-Richfield	178	36.9%
Total all nine	5,170	**45.2%**
All oil companies	52,500	**30.3%**

ENERGY SHOULD BE EVERYBODY'S BUSINESS

EMERGENCE OF IMAGE ADVERTISING

In the face of such hostile pressure from its critics, advertising in the 1970s took a new turn. Advertisers sought to broaden the use of nonproduct ads to create more responsible images for their firms. Instead of products, they advertised programs, many of which were in the public interest. They talked about social responsibility, equal employment hiring, and minority assistance. Figure 11-2 is a good example of image advertising by Gulf in early 1972.

This shift from institutional advertising to image advertising was a subtle one. As one ad agency executive put it, "It was a shift from what the company is doing to

---

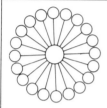

MINICASE
ITT ad campaigns strike back

ITT's response to the Wonder Bread challenge was typical of the company's use of advertising to strike back publicly when threatened.

Today, ITT is one of a very few companies that budgets well over $10 million on public relations advertising for the performance of a variety of purposes from making the company more memorable to raising employee morale to attracting investors and customers. Indeed, ITT has a long record of fighting back with public relations advertising.

In the 1960s, ITT's problem was anonymity. The company's surveys showed that two-thirds of the public knew it vaguely or not at all. Even its own executives, hard-pressed to keep up with the rapidly-diversifying conglomerate, jokingly referred to ITT as "International This & That."[7]

To help position it more clearly in the public's mind, ITT began an extensive advertising program using as its theme, "Serving people and nations everywhere."

In the early 1970s, ITT's involvement in U.S. and international politics made it a lightning rod for growing anti-big business sentiment. In 1972, a published memo allegedly written by an ITT lobbyist linked settlement of Justice Department antitrust charges against the company with a purported ITT pledge of $400,000 to finance the Republican convention. A year later came revelations that ITT had offered advice and money to the Nixon Administration and the Central Intelligence Agency to help unseat Chilean President Salvador Allende.

Although the company vigorously denied any wrongdoing, its reputation was tarnished and its damaged name appeared frequently in front-page headlines.

In response, ITT increased its advertising budget to $7 million in 1974 from $1.3 million the previous year and changed its advertising message to portray the company as a technologically sophisticated one that "cares about

why it is doing these good things for the public.[8] Advertising headlines of the period underscored the social responsibility theme:

At U.S. Steel, Community Life is Our Life-style

At Chase, We Helped the Black Magazine That's Helping Black Businessmen

At Texaco, We Don't Talk about Opportunities, We Create Them

For awhile, image advertising ruled the day. But almost as quickly as they had appeared, the image ads began to run into problems.

---

people and uses its profits to help improve the quality of life." ITT's new slogan: "The best ideas are the ideas that help people."

The first commercial in this new series featured a woman staring at viewers as she soberly announced, "I'm going blind." Explaining that she suffered from night blindness, she told how a binocular-like device made by "the people at ITT" enabled her to see.

Later, market research confirmed that awareness of ITT had grown materially as had the number of people who identified ITT as a company that was "very profitable," "makes quality products," and "cares about the general public."

In 1981, another survey revealed that people were confused between ITT and AT&T. ITT executives became worried, particularly because AT&T's controversial agreement with antitrust regulators to break up its company promised to keep the phone company in the spotlight for several months.

With 60 percent of the public confusing the two firms, ITT's response was a commercial in which an ITT telephone operator answered a caller with, "No, dear, you want AT&T, not ITT. We are two totally different companies." She then went on to explain in clear, crisp, and human detail what ITT really does.

Most people viewed ITT's public relations advertising as highly effective. Said one Indiana University marketing professor, "They're saying something, not just blowing their horn." A 1982 survey by Roper Organization Inc. revealed that among sixteen large companies, ITT ranked in the top half in terms of people viewing it favorably. Summarized ITT's vice president for corporate relations and advertising, "You can never sit back, rest on your oars, and say the job is done. It is absolutely never done."

QUESTIONS

1 How effective do you think ITT's theme line of the 1960s was in combating the company's anonymity with the public?

2 Do you think such a slogan would have been believable in the 1970s?

3 What was the objective of the ad featuring the woman going blind?

4 If you were ITT's public relations director, what other activities might you institute to complement the company's ads?

The trouble with being a big, successful oil company is that nobody believes a word you say.

If you've made up your mind that the guys who run oil companies are bad guys, this isn't your ad.

But if you like to keep an open mind, keep reading. And when you're through, we'd like you to believe one thing: that Gulf is every bit as concerned about preserving and restoring the environment as you are.

One way we can get you to believe this is to tell you what we're doing. So here's what we're doing:

First, we've spent a lot of money fighting pollution for many years—$45 million in 1971 alone, and a projected $196 million during the next five years. And it's bought us some very useful equipment and processes.

It's bought us (and our neighbors) smokeless flare tips at plants and refineries—to insure 100% combustion of hydrocarbons when gases are vented for safety measures.

Closed circuit TV monitoring of flares for combustion

FIGURE 11–2. *Gulf advertisement.* This oil company ad, which appeared in Black Enterprise Magazine in 1972, is a typical "image ad."

SOURCE: Courtesy of Gulf Oil.

control. Roofs that float on liquid storage tanks to prevent vapor formation and escape. Gulfining—a process that removes sulfur from home heating oil. And hydrodesulfurization—to produce fuel that reduces sulfur dioxide emissions at industrial and power generating plants.

We're also making progress in abating automotive exhaust emissions. With low-lead gasoline. And a smoke-suppressant additive that helps to minimize emissions from diesel-powered vehicles.

Before you can correct pollution, you have to trace it. So we built three mobile detector vans to use at Gulf plants: one pinpoints emissions into the air; another pinpoints emissions into the water; and the third determines on the spot the best way to treat effluents.

We transport vast amounts of petroleum by transoceanic tankers. So we use special loading devices that keep accidental spills on board or in dock—and out of the water. And we have a major research program on clean-up technology.

We're concerned with wildlife, too. That's one reason we donated the land for the Tinicum Wildlife Preserve in Pennsylvania. It's a major stopping place for migratory birds that travel the Atlantic Flyway. And we've assisted several environmentalists in getting an interstate highway reconstructed so that the natural state of the land can be preserved.

One of the problems with preserving natural resources is that we're simultaneously fighting a national energy shortage. So we're looking for new, ecologically sound fuel sources from coal, tar sands and shale. And we've entered the nuclear energy field. Our choice of nuclear power systems is a High Temperature Gas-cooled Reactor (HTGR) that uses less uranium and discharges only about ⅔ as much waste heat as other nuclear systems now in commercial operation.

We may some day face a water shortage. So we've developed a way to purify brackish water and are working on ways to desalt sea water economically.

This is some of the work Gulf is doing. We know we have a lot more to do. But we're determined to do it. And we'd like you to believe that.

An Equal Opportunity Employer
Gulf Oil Corporation

PROBLEMS

By the mid-1970s, people began to distrust image advertising. As one student of the field put it, "Enchantment with image ads lessened because of their attempts to try to 'con' audiences, and because too many ignored the rules of sound communication by trying to impose the advertisers' message on the public."[9]

Then too, issues involved in image advertising were more complex than those involved with selling products. Images by nature are amorphous, while products are tangible. While people believed the merits of a particular toothpaste or a bar of soap because they could taste or feel them, they were less likely to take on faith the corporate meaning of *brotherhood, teamliness,* or *social responsibility* simply by being told that the advertiser practiced it.

Finally, image advertising was suspect even within many of the corporations sponsoring it. In many cases, top management, perhaps because of its lack of understanding about the objectives behind image advertising, apparently didn't trust its own ads.[10]

Moreover, feedback measurements on image ads were difficult to conceive and implement. Management, which may have grudgingly accepted image advertising on faith, seemed to grow tired of the idea quickly.

ISSUE ADVERTISING EMERGES IN THE 1980s

The logical extension of image advertising was the birth of issue, or advocacy, advertising in the mid-1970s and its further blossoming in the 1980s.

Issue advertising, unlike its predecessor, didn't aim to be all things to all people. Its objective was to convey the sponsor's viewpoint on matters of some controversy. Ads were informational, factual, and persuasive. Many tried to be hard-hitting and let the public know exactly where the firm stood on certain issues.

The growth of issue advertising in the 1980s was attributable to several factors:

○ Many business executives believed that journalists were, in the words of business professor S. Prakash Sethi, "economic illiterates," who limited the extent to which business would be given a fair hearing in the media.

○ Corporate leaders became more aggressive in responding to their critics, recognizing that past silence generally had been counterproductive.

○ A Supreme Court decision in 1978 (the Bellotti Case discussed in Chapter 22) held that corporate speech was entitled to First Amendment protection, thereby eliminating many earlier restrictions against such speech. As Chase Manhattan Bank Chairman Bill Butcher put it, "A company not only has rights and privileges like an individual person, but also responsibilities and duties. Any person who claims his rights but shuns his responsibilities fails to contribute to the betterment of mankind and, therefore, has no claim on the respect of mankind. I believe the same holds true for corporations."[11]

○ The news media, stunned by a proliferation of corporate advertisements criticizing its treatment of business (Figure 11-3) began to acquiesce to corporate requests for "equal time."

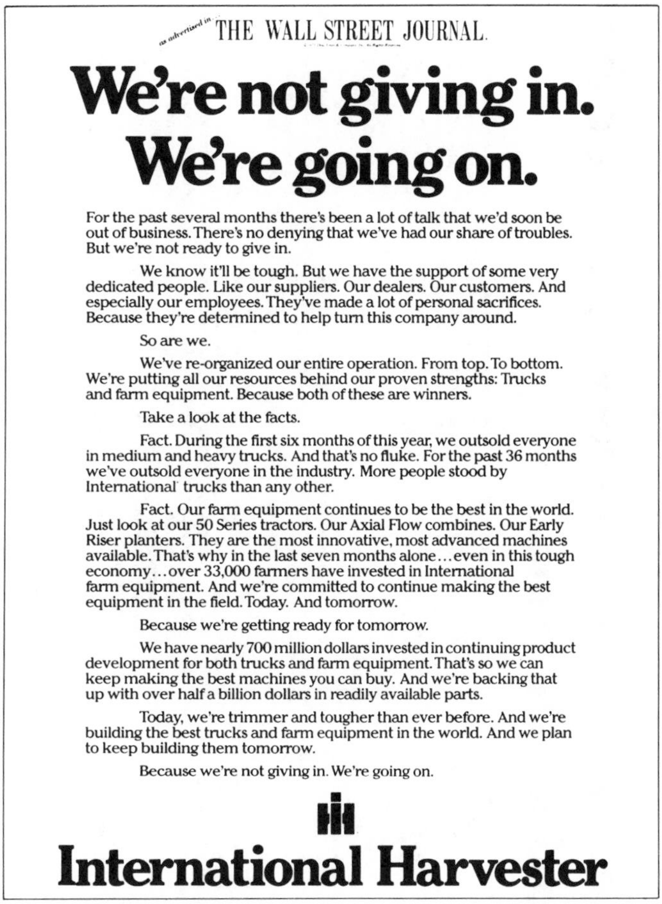

FIGURE 11-3. *International Harvester advertising.* In the summer of 1982, the huge International Harvester Company was widely rumored in the media to be on the verge of bankruptcy. To counter such damaging talk, the company hammered back with this full-page ad in The Wall Street Journal.

Courtesy of International Harvester.

as advertised in THE WALL STREET JOURNAL.

We're not giving in. We're going on.

For the past several months there's been a lot of talk that we'd soon be out of business. There's no denying that we've had our share of troubles. But we're not ready to give in.

We know it'll be tough. But we have the support of some very dedicated people. Like our suppliers. Our dealers. Our customers. And especially our employees. They've made a lot of personal sacrifices. Because they're determined to help turn this company around.

So are we.

We've re-organized our entire operation. From top. To bottom. We're putting all our resources behind our proven strengths: Trucks and farm equipment. Because both of these are winners.

Take a look at the facts.

Fact. During the first six months of this year, we outsold everyone in medium and heavy trucks. And that's no fluke. For the past 36 months we've outsold everyone in the industry. More people stood by International trucks than any other.

Fact. Our farm equipment continues to be the best in the world. Just look at our 50 Series tractors. Our Axial Flow combines. Our Early Riser planters. They are the most innovative, most advanced machines available. That's why in the last seven months alone...even in this tough economy...over 33,000 farmers have invested in International farm equipment. And we're committed to continue making the best equipment in the field. Today. And tomorrow.

Because we're getting ready for tomorrow.

We have nearly 700 million dollars invested in continuing product development for both trucks and farm equipment. That's so we can keep making the best machines you can buy. And we're backing that up with over half a billion dollars in readily available parts.

Today, we're trimmer and tougher than ever before. And we're building the best trucks and farm equipment in the world. And we plan to keep building them tomorrow.

Because we're not giving in. We're going on.

International Harvester

Networks began allowing corporate institutional commercials to include a great deal more advocacy or controversial content than had previously been the case. ABC-TV for one allowed Kaiser Aluminum & Chemical Corporation to present an unedited rebuttal to an earlier ABC report on unsafe aluminum housing wire. ABC also began to accept issue commercials on its late-night programming. Not to be outdone, CBS devoted an entire 1981 edition of "60 Minutes" to a critical look at itself, providing opportunity to various observers, including corporate media critics, to comment on the program's practices in covering news stories.

By 1980, almost 90 percent of America's independent television stations were accepting advocacy or opinion commercials, compared to about 50 percent in 1975. Moreover, a survey by the Association of National Advertisers Inc. revealed that 200 U.S. corporations collectively spent close to $675 million annually for what could be classified as public relations advertising during the period 1977-1981.[12]

While companies previously had occasionally discussed "issues" in their advertising, the issue ads of the 1980s were much more pointed than at any previous time. Figure 11-4, for example, shows an ad from DuPont designed to inform critics of the relative safety of aerosol spray cans.

FIGURE 11-4. *DuPont advertising.* DuPont's "issue advertising" campaign in the mid-1970s was aimed at responding to criticisms of the family of chemicals known as chlorofluorocarbons. Courtesy of DuPont.

ISSUE ADVERTISING IN THE OIL INDUSTRY

By far the leading proponent of issue advertising was the oil industry, barraged by critics who claimed it profited from the nation's energy miseries. The realization of worldwide energy shortages, as one advertising executive put it, made it nonsensical "to promote traffic into Arco stations when there wouldn't be enough gas to go around."[13]

Initially, the oil companies reacted to the energy crisis by sponsoring factual ads explaining the origins of the problem and exhorting the public to conserve energy. But these ads failed miserably. As Texaco's advertising general manager put it:

> We had not done as good a job as we should have in bringing our story to the people and their representatives. We sincerely believe the facts are on our side, but we failed to bring those facts home to the public. We cannot afford to fail again.[14]

The direction the industry chose to "prevent failure" was that of hard-line issue advertising. For example, in late 1974, when legislators challenged oil firms on the truth of their supply shortage, Texaco responded with full-page ads claiming: "We're Not Holding Back Anything."

Of all the large companies, none was more demonstrative and vocal in issue advertising than Mobil Oil. Mobil bought space opposite newspaper editorial pages across the country each Thursday to holler, plead, and proselytize. Mobil didn't mince words. "Don't read these ads if you've made up your mind about oil profits," began a typical ad. Another urged readers to "fight the two-times-two-equals-five logicians who think the same outfit that brings you the U.S. Mail can find oil three miles under the ocean bottom" Strong words. Tough talk. Admonition bound to evoke criticism. To wit:

> While the big guns of Mobil's ads on the Op-Ed page thundered their message to the groggy readers of *The New York Times*, a team of fast-talking Mobil flacks were busying themselves with the public interest consumer groups and environmental groups.[15]

These Mobil ads (further illustrated in Figures 11–5 through 11–7) that created such controversy were largely the idea of Mobil's public affairs director, Herbert Schmertz, a former labor lawyer and assistant to Robert Kennedy. The ads were conceived and written by Mobil's public relations staff and executed by an advertising agency. Schmertz attempted to place Mobil's issue ads on television networks, but they initially rebuffed him, saying that such advertising would precipitate "demands for equal time."[16] Schmertz then turned the rejection by the networks into a public relations victory by offering to buy equal time for his adversaries. The networks refused the offer.

As previously noted, the impact of Mobil's advocacy advertising campaign was difficult to measure. A 1976 Louis Harris survey revealed that Mobil was regarded somewhat more favorably than some other oil companies. Of the people who were familiar with Mobil, 69 percent regarded it as a "progressive, forward-thinking company" compared with an average of 66 percent for all the oil companies in the survey. On the question of "helping to improve the quality of life," 60 percent thought well of Mobil, compared with an average of only 53 percent for all the companies. No company came out well on the question of "keeping profits at reasonable levels"; only 34 percent agreed that Mobil did so.[17]

If we tell you oil companies don't make enough profit, you'll have a fit. Oil companies don't make enough profit. Sorry.

It has been more than five years since we first ran an advertisement under this headline. Back, even, before our profits were called "obscene."

Today, the oil industry is being charged with things like "ripoffs" and "profiteering." And the reason for these accusations hasn't changed much since 1972: continued misunderstanding about just how profitable the industry *really* is.

In the years since the oil embargo brought on that "obscene profits" nonsense, for example, Mobil's annual *revenue* has increased steadily. But our revenue, like your salary, is shared with federal, state, and local governments. It also pays the bills, buys crude oil, and pays royalties.

What's left after all the bills and taxes are paid is net income, or *profit,* which last year amounted to just 3.8 cents for every dollar Mobil Oil took in. Out of this profit, dividends are paid to shareholders. What's left provides some of the money to look for new supplies of oil and gas. In fact, looking for oil and gas is so expensive, we have to borrow money to help finance the search.

Mobil Oil's profit per dollar of revenue of 3.8 cents is substantially lower than the 4.6-cent average return on revenue for all U.S. industry. Measured by the same yardstick, the oil industry as a whole last year was just a little better than average, with a 5.0 percent return on revenue. But this still can't hold a candle to the 8.5 percent return for the pharmaceutical industry, 6.4 percent for broadcasting and motion pictures, or 6.1 percent for soaps and cosmetics, to name just three other industries.

Another measure of corporate profitability is return on shareholders' equity—net income expressed as a percentage of the company's net worth. Last year, that number for Mobil Oil was 13.2 percent, the oil industry was at 13.0 percent, and all U.S. industries were at 13.3 percent.

These results put oil about halfway down a list headed by the broadcasting and motion picture industry, whose return on shareholders' equity for 1976 was a whopping 21.0 percent. Others near the top were soaps and cosmetics, 16.3 percent; and publishing and printing, 14.7 percent. Motor vehicles were slightly better than oil at 13.8 percent. Food was below oil at 12.8 percent and office equipment was at 11.5 percent. So, many industries did better than we did and others did worse.

And last year wasn't an unusual one, either for us or other industries. With few exceptions, oil industry profits have traditionally been near the median for U.S. industry as a whole.

In the final analysis, these comparisons provide ample proof that the myth of oil company "greed" is just that—a myth. If more is needed, however, it can be found in a recent financial analysis of 30 petroleum companies. It showed that, in the years since the embargo, the companies' profits increased by $6.7 billion, while their investments increased $14.6 billion. In other words, they *spent* more money than they *earned* in profits, borrowing against the expectation of future earnings.

This fact probably prompted a recent draft study made for the Federal Energy Administration to say: **"Return on oil company stockholder equity is not excessive compared with other manufacturing industries.... Oil companies have consistently been making capital expenditures in excess of available internally generated funds.... It appears that a choice may have to be made between allowing higher profits or probably seeing lower capital expenditures for privately financed energy development efforts."**

And that's why we say we don't make enough profit.

Mobil

©1977 Mobil Corporation

FIGURE 11–5. *Mobil ad—profits.* In 1977, when Senator Henry Jackson labeled oil company profits "obscene" at a congressional hearing, Mobil immediately challenged the assertion.

SOURCE: © 1977 Mobil Oil Corporation.

Indeed, Mobil's management made no claim that the company had moved public opinion on specific issues. However, few argued that the program was not without value. Indeed, Mobil has continued its advertising activism into the 1980s. As one public relations agency executive put it, "The days of sweetness and light in image advertising are over. Mobil's ads are vigorous and show that the company has conviction."[18]

Why do we buy this space?

For more than 11 years now, we've been addressing Americans with weekly messages in principal print media. We've argued, cajoled, thundered, pleaded, reasoned and poked fun. In return, we've been reviled, revered, held up as a model and put down as a sorry example.

Why does Mobil choose to expose itself to these weekly judgments in the court of public opinion? Why do we keep it up now that the energy crisis and the urgent need to address energy issues has eased, at least for the present? When our problems are with cost-cutting and increasing productivity, not with voters, politicians and customers?

Our answer is that business needs voices in the media, the same way labor unions, consumers, and other groups in our society do. Our nation functions best when economic and other concerns of the people are subjected to rigorous debate. When our messages add to the spectrum of facts and opinion available to the public, even if the decisions are contrary to our preferences, then the effort and cost are worthwhile.

Think back to some of the issues in which we have contributed to the debate.

● Excessive government regulation—it's now widely recognized that Washington meddling, however well intentioned, carries a price tag that the consumer pays.

● The folly of price controls—so clear now that prices of gasoline and other fuels are coming down, now that the marketplace has been relieved of most of its artificial restraints.

● The need for balance between maintaining jobs and production and maintaining a pristine environment—a non-issue, we argued, if there's common sense and com-promise on both sides, a view that's now increasingly recognized in Washington.

Over the years, we've won some and lost some, and battled to a draw on other issues we've championed, such as building more nuclear power plants and improving public transportation. We've supported presidents we thought were right in their policies and questioned Democrats and Republicans alike when we thought their policies were counterproductive.

In the process we've had excitement, been congratulated and castigated, made mistakes, and won and lost some battles. But we've enjoyed it. While a large company may seem terribly impersonal to the average person, it's made up of people with feelings, people who care like everybody else. So even when we plug a quality TV program we sponsor on public television, we feel right about spending the company's money to build audience for the show, just as we feel good as citizens to throw the support of our messages to causes we believe in, like the Mobil Grand Prix, in which young athletes prepare for the 1984 Olympics. Or recognition for the positive role retired people continue to play in our society.

We still continue to speak on a wide array of topics, even though there's no immediate energy crisis to kick around anymore. Because we don't want to be like the mother-in-law who comes to visit only when she has problems and matters to complain about. We think a continuous presence in this space makes sense for us. And we hope, on your part, you find us informative occasionally, or entertaining, or at least infuriating. But never boring. After all, you did read this far, didn't you?

Mobil

FIGURE 11–6. *Mobil ad—Why This Space?* Eleven years after it began its op ed advertising series, Mobil was still going strong in 1982. While some criticized the company for "preaching to the choir," Mobil pushed on. Why? Well, as Mobil itself put it, "When our messages add to the spectrum of facts and opinion available to the public, even if the decisions are contrary to our preferences, then the effort and cost are worthwhile.

SOURCE: © 1981 Mobil Oil Corporation.

PURPOSES OF PUBLIC RELATIONS ADVERTISING

Traditional public relations or nonproduct advertising—as opposed to image or issue positioning—is still very much in practice for specific purposes. Advertising can be appropriate for a number of mutually supportive activities:

1 **Mergers and diversifications**   When a company merges with another, the public needs to be told about the new business lines and divisions. Advertising provides a quick and effective way to convey this message.

2 **Personnel changes**   A firm's greatest asset is usually its managers, its salespeople, its employees. Presenting staff members in advertising not only impresses a reader with the firm's pride in its workers, it also helps build confidence among employees themselves.

FIGURE 11-7.   *Mobil's turkey.* Occasionally, in the midst of "talking turkey" on public issues, Mobil took a deep breath and relaxed its offensive.

3 **Organization resources** A firm's investment in research and development implies that the organization is concerned about meeting the future intelligently, an asset that should be advertised. The scope of a company's services also says something positive about the organization.

4 **Manufacturing and service capabilities** The ability to deliver quality goods on time is something customers cherish. A firm that can deliver should advertise this capability. Likewise, a firm with a qualified and attentive servicing capability should let clients and potential clients know about it.

5 **Growth history** A growing firm, one that has developed steadily over time, and that has taken advantage of its environment, is the kind of company with which people want to deal. It is also the kind of firm for which people will want to work. Growth history, therefore, is a worthwhile subject for nonproduct advertising.

6 **Financial strength and stability** A picture of economic strength and stability is one that all companies like to project. Advertisements that highlight the company's financial position earn confidence, customers, and corporate stockholders.

7 **Company customers** Customers can serve as a marketing tool, too. Well-known personalities who use a certain product may be enough to win additional customers. This strategy may be especially viable in advertising for higher-priced products like expensive automobiles or sports equipment.

8 **Organization name change** Occasionally, firms change their names (Jersey Standard to Exxon, American Metal Climax to AMAX, Inc., First National City Corporation to Citicorp). To stick in people's minds, a name change must be well promoted and well advertised. Only through constant repetition will people become familiar with the new identity.

9 **Trademark protection** Companies such as Xerox and Coca Cola, whose products are household names, are legitimately concerned about the improper generic use of their trademarks in the public domain. Such companies run periodic ads to remind people of the proper status of their marks. In one such ad, a perplexed secretary reminds the boss, "If you had ordered forty photocopies instead of forty Xeroxes, we wouldn't have been stuck with all these machines."

10 **Corporate emergencies** Occasionally, an emergency situation erupts—a labor strike, plant disaster, a service interruption. One quick way to explain the firm's position and procedures without fear of distortion or misinterpretation by editors or reporters is to buy advertising space. This tactic permits a full explanation of the reasons behind the problem and the steps the company plans to take to resolve the dilemma.

THE FUTURE

The pressures on companies, particularly large firms, will not soon abate. Regulatory pressures, consumerist demands and class action suits will probably continue to plague big business. As firms continue to seek a voice in public issues, it is likely that nonproduct advertising, especially issue advertising, will continue, limited only by a firm's willingness to spend money.

FEATURE

Issue advertising to the rescue

While many companies in the 1980s began using issue advertising to go on the offensive against critics, issue ads were useful as a quick defense too.

Consider the following chain of events involving Citibank, among the world's most powerful institutions.

On December 21, 1981, after Soviet-style authoritarianism had snuffed out a Democratic movement in Poland, The Wall Street Journal quoted a high ranking Citibank executive as saying, "Who knows which political system works? The only test we care about is: *Can they pay their bills?"*

On December 22, the Journal and other newspapers around the nation began receiving steaming letters to the editor denouncing the Citibank quote.

On December 23, the President of the United States, in a nationally televised address, urged Americans to place a candle in their windows in solidarity with the Polish people.

Three days later, on December 26, there appeared a full page ad in The New York Times, headlined "Peace and Freedom on Earth," picturing a lighted candle and quoting the President's call for all Americans to show support for their brave Polish brethren (see p. 259).

The ad's sponsor?

Yup.

Additionally, as more companies become concerned about the free enterprise system, capital formation, the trade-offs between environmental considerations and economic growth, and a host of other subjects, they are likely to take their case directly and immediately to the public via advertising.

Indeed, in the summer of 1979 when First National City Travelers' Checks objected to the television commercials of rival American Express, it took the issue directly to the public with full-page newspaper advertisements that screamed: "Yes, those TV commercials for American Express Travelers' Checks are false and misleading."[19]

Again, in the winter of 1982, the nation's three largest hamburger makers, McDonald's, Burger King, and Wendy's squared off in television ads accusing each other of offering less substantial products. In both the travelers' check and the hamburger case, the two genres of issue and product advertising successfully had been combined.

The effectiveness of issue advertising, particularly with legislators and nonbusiness opinion leaders, remains an open question. Critics charge that many image and issue ads are examples of big companies "talking to themselves." Indeed, most issue advertisers consider managers at other companies important targets for such advertising.

The likelihood of continued nonproduct advertising presents important new challenges for public relations professionals who are used to dealing with adversary

Courtesy of Citibank.

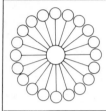

MINICASE

The Junior Achievement ad

T he Omaha, Nebraska Junior Achievement Society wants to run an advertisement extolling the free enterprise system. Public relations director
Allan Louis is asked to compose the ad from the following excerpts of a
speech by Junior Achievement's chairperson:

> The free enterprise system carries the lifeblood of this nation. But it is in
> serious trouble.
>
> The initiative, the innovation, the hope, and the freedom that have given this
> country's people more of the fruits of life and liberty than mankind has ever enjoyed,
> are in a state of unease.
>
> It's about time we admitted that the free enterprise system in this country can't
> survive . . . unless those of us who should be defending the system, who should be
> working to improve it, fight to save it.
>
> That is the issue.
>
> The essence of the American proposition has always been that free people
> can be trusted to know what's best for them. Edmund Burke, a thinker whose ideas I
> very much like, once observed, "The true danger is when liberty is nibbled away—for
> expediency—and by parts."
>
> We are in that danger now. Government regulation and a feeling that 'bigness
> is badness' is cutting into our free enterprise system.
>
> This system has made us the richest nation on earth. Our standard of living is
> higher, our consumers have more choices, and our people have jobs.
>
> Clearly, wealth is better than poverty. Free enterprise is better than any alter-
> native. At Junior Achievement we are working to maintain and expand that system.
>
> This should be everyone's goal.

QUESTIONS

1   Louis plans to write one page of copy for this ad. What would you suggest
    he write?
2   Presuming your copy is approved, how might you illustrate it?

publics. They are also used to working with top management and reflecting management's position to the public. As advertising moves further into the realm of issues
and positions, public relations professionals will be called upon to play a greater role.

Already, advertising departments in many companies have moved within the
public relations/communications sphere. Then too, as noted, the nation's largest
independent public relations counseling firms have been taken over by some of the
major advertising agencies, the assumption being that advertising and public relations are complementary tools in the solution of modern communications problems.

To be sure, as organizations are called upon to explain themselves more on such issues as credit, guarantees, social responsibility, minority hiring, and advertising and product claims, public relations practitioners will be asked to pick up an increasing share of the decision-making and creative burden.

In so doing, practitioners must be sensitive to using the relatively new channel of advocacy advertising in a responsible manner. As Professor S. Prakash Sethi puts it,

> Increased access to the marketplace carries with it the obligation to use such access in a responsible manner. Business has most to lose from public misinformation and, therefore, should take every possible step to improve the quality of public information and debate. This would lead to better public understanding of complex issues affecting business and society and would improve the process of public policy formulation.[20]

Clearly, the real advertising giants in the 1980s and beyond may not be those companies who triumph in the marketplace of products, but rather those who are effective in the marketplace of ideas.

CASE STUDY
The bank that cried "wolf"

In the fall of 1975, The Chase Manhattan Bank told the world, through a series of advertisements in major national media, that it was "very worried." The object of Chase's concern was an impending "shortage of capital," which the bank thought threatened the nation. Chase said in its ads that the United States was "underinvesting $4 million each day," and that if this trend continued, there would be a "shortfall of $1.5 trillion" in ten years. Translated into common terms, this shortfall would mean a decline in growth and prosperity in the United States. To underscore its concern, Chase announced it had decided to cry "Wolf!" and said it would debate the capital formation argument "anywhere, at any time."

One person who wanted to take the bank up on its offer was a twenty-eight-year-old data processing executive in Helena, Arkansas, Robert Sitarzewski. Seeing the Chase ads in a national magazine in September, Mr. Sitarzewski wrote Chase's Chairman David Rockefeller, saying, "You don't know what you're talking about." Sitarzewski then challenged the New York banker to a public debate.

After several weeks, Mr. Sitarzewski received a response from Chase's corporate communications director advising him that although Mr. Rockefeller would not be able to debate, the bank's chief domestic economist would accept the challenge.

And so the "Great Debate" was planned.

"Wolf!"

The Chase is crying "Wolf!" Again. And we mean it. Again.

America is faced with a shortage of capital. Capital vital to the healthy growth this nation must have if it is to maintain and improve the living standards of all Americans.

In 1952, we published a study warning against government disincentives to the continuing search for natural gas. We raised more caution flags in 1956, 1957, and 1961 about industry's ability to continue "to deliver low-cost petroleum energy."

We were accused of crying "Wolf!" at that time. And indeed we were. But it was no pretense.

Our warnings were based on hard facts which became even harder with every disappearing drop of cheap imported oil.

Today we face an equally hard set of facts regarding the level of capital formation and mounting capital needs:

Fact 1: The next ten years will require twice as much capital as the past ten.

Fact 2: It will take a tremendous effort of husbanding sources and resources — far more than it took to win World War II or to put a man on the moon.

Fact 3: We will be lucky if there is as much as $2.6 trillion for building and rebuilding our industrial capacity.

Fact 4: Set against the needs of $4.1 trillion, there'll be a shortfall of $1.5 trillion.

Which means we will be under-investing $400 million a day every day for the next ten years.

The highest priority of our economy right now should lie in the nurture and stimulation of capital formation. Because everything the American people need and want grows out of that.

How do we deal with the problem?

Chase proposes a six-part action program:

• Provide sufficient inducements for an ever-growing base of personal savings.

• Establish more realistic guidelines for depreciation allowances.

• Give preferential tax treatment for retained corporate earnings used for investment purposes.

• Ameliorate our relatively harsh treatment of capital gains compared with that of most other countries.

• Stabilize our monetary and fiscal policies to prevent violent swings in the economy.

• Eliminate unnecessary controls. And do away with outmoded government regulations and agencies that restrict our free market economy.

Capital formation must be government's business, businesses' business, labor's business, banking's business — everybody's business.

Your business.

CHASE

Courtesy of The Chase Manhattan Bank.

In the spring of 1976, Chase sent Richard Everett, vice-president and head of Chase's domestic economic policy unit, to Helena, via the bank's private jet. Mr. Everett was accompanied by an entourage of several bank employees.

The event attracted print and electronic media representatives from across the country. Network television covered. Wire services were represented. The *Washington Post* sent its reporter. So did *The New York Times.*

As the wife of Helena's mayor put it, "This is the first time since the Civil War we've had this many Yankees in town."

During the debate in a local community college auditorium, Mr. Sitarzewski told the audience of about 600 that the free functioning of the market would allocate the nation's resources adequately. He said the bank's proposals to stimulate capital investment would "destroy the American capitalistic system."

Mr. Everett parried that the federal government would have to provide more tax incentives for industry, encourage personal savings, and attract foreign investments "or the economy would suffer major setbacks."

And who won the "Great Debate"?

Most of the hundreds of follow-up media accounts called the contest "a draw." The Associated Press, however, quoted one member of the audience as saying, "Sitarzewski clearly won because he made the bank come to Helena, Arkansas."

QUESTIONS

1 Do you think the bank handled the challenge correctly?

2 How would you have modified Chase's response?

3 Do you agree with the audience member that Sitarzewski won the debate?

4 What do you think Chase got out of the debate?

5 From a public relations standpoint, was Chase justified in participating?

NOTES

1 Mead & Bender/Communications, "Advertising in the National Interest" (Boston, Mass.: Author, January 1979).

2 Steven A. Greyser and Bonnie B. Reece, "Businessmen Look Hard at Advertising," *Harvard Business Review,* May-June 1971.

3 "Problems of the Credibility of Big Business, *National Observer,* 26 January 1975, p. 14.

4 Public Media Center Annual Report, 1974/1975. (Available from the Public Media Center, 2751 Hyde St., San Francisco, Calif. 94109.)

5 Staff report to the Federal Trade Commission on the Ad Substantiation Program, prepared by Hon. Frank E. Moss, 31 July 1972. (Available from the U.S. Government Printing Office, Washington, D.C., order no. 80-9410, 1972.)

6 "ITT Continental Baking Unit Is Backed by Examiner on Wonder Bread Ads," *Wall Street Journal*, 29 December 1972, p. 4.

7 Bill Abrams, "How ITT Shells Out $10 Million or So a Year to Polish Reputation," *The Wall Street Journal*, 2 April 1982, p. 116.

8 Audrey Allen, "Corporate Advertising: Its New Look," *Public Relations Journal*, November 1971, p. 6.

9 Philip Lesly, "Business Faces a Change of Voice," *Public Relations Journal*, November 1971, p. 15.

10 W. H. Depperman, "PR Advertising Is a Misunderstood Tool," *Advertising & Sales Promotion*, April 1966.

11 Willard C. Butcher, "Total Corporate Responsibility in the 80s," Address at the University of North Carolina, Charlotte, North Carolina, 16 October 1981.

12 Peg Dardenne, "The Cost of Corporate Advertising," *Public Relations Journal*, November 1981, p. 30.

13 Audrey Allen, op. *cit.*

14 "Oil's New Sell," *Time*, 11 November 1974, p. 30.

15 Alexander Cockburn and James Ridgeway, "How Big Oil Pushes Its Message," *The Village Voice*, 6 October 1975, p. 17.

16 Michael Gerrard, "This Man Was Made Possible by a Grant from Mobil Oil," *Esquire*, January 1977, p. 142.

17 Irwin Ross, "Public Relations Isn't Kid Glove Stuff at Mobil," *Fortune*, September 1976, p. 202.

18 "Hammond Backs 'Message' Advertising," *Jack O'Dwyer's Newsletter*, 29 October 1975, p. 3.

19 Advertisement in *The Washington Post*, 21 August 1979, p. A7.

20 S. Prakash Sethi, "Battling Antibusiness Bias: Is There a Chance of Overkill?" *Public Relations Journal*, November 1981, p. 64.

SUGGESTED READING

Burton, Philip Ward. *Advertising Copywriting*. 3rd ed. Columbus, Ohio: Grid, 1974.

Dardenne, Peg. "The Cost Of Corporate Advertising, *Public Relations Journal*, November 1981, pp. 30–35, 38–42.

"Garbett, Thomas F. "Corporate Advertising: The What, The Why, and The How," New York: McGraw-Hill, 1981.

Herpel, George L., and **Collins, Richard A.** *Specialty Advertising in Marketing*. Homewood, Ill.: Dow Jones-Irwin, 1972. Good discussions about a much-neglected part of public relations.

Mandez, Maurice I. *Advertising*. Englewood Cliffs, N.J.: Prentice-Hall, 1974.

Quera, Leon. *Advertising Campaigns: Formulation and Tactics*. Columbus, Ohio: Grid, 1973.

Sachs, William S. "Corporate Advertising: Ends, Means, Problems," *Public Relations Journal*, November 1981, pp. 14–17.

Sethi, S. Prakash, "Battling Antibusiness Bias: Is There A Chance of Overkill," *Public Relations Journal,* November 1981, pp. 22–24, 64.

Welty, Ward. "Is Issue Advertising Working?" *Public Relations Journal,* November 1981, p. 29.

"When You Are Considering Corporate Advertising," *Public Relations Journal,* November 1981, p. 21. Guidelines on approaching the task of running an advertising program.

Wright, John S.; Warner, Daniel S.; and **Winter, Willis L., Jr.** *Advertising.* New York, N.Y.: McGraw-Hill, 1971.

More and more, public relations people are turning to outside suppliers for assistance in specialty areas. From photography and graphic arts, to the orchestration of seminars and other special events, to space-age communications techniques such as teleconferencing and satellite news dissemination, public relations support services have increased in use and value to practitioners. While it is helpful to know something about photography and how to use it for annual reports, brochures, and special projects, a professional photographer may be needed. While a familiarity with design and layout techniques is useful, for important reports a professional designer may be required. Likewise, while a practitioner should feel comfortable with film, when it's time to tell the company's story on celluloid, an experienced film maker may be solicited.

The same holds true for a score of other support activities, including translations, mailing services, distribution wire services, directories, messengers, and press clipping and broadcast transcription services.

12
Support Services

WRITING AND RESEARCH SUPPORTS

Probably the two most significant supports a practitioner needs in writing are a good, unabridged dictionary and a thesaurus. To these might be added *Bartlett's Familiar Quotations* and a *World Almanac* or encyclopedia.

Freelance writers are available, but most public relations people do their own writing. Research support, however, is frequently needed. Many organizations, especially larger ones, have their own libraries, many of which are affiliated with local libraries for expanded research capability. Trade associations, including the Public Relations Society of America, also maintain information centers for the use of members.

Additionally, there are a number of directories that identify research sources in a myriad of fields. One way to tap such directories is to consult an overall guide book, such as *Guide to American Directories,* published by Klein & Company. Major newspapers, such as *The New York Times* and *The Wall Street Journal*, provide computerized index services to articles and subjects covered in the publications.

Another type of writing support is the use of national feature services to prepare and disseminate client publicity essentially to smaller, local newspapers around the country. Such services furnish copy in two forms: printed matrices (called *mats)* and camera-ready copy (copy that is ready to be photographed for offset newspaper use). Mats are made of heat-resistant, coated paper, from which copper and brass newspaper plates are made for the traditional letterpress newspapers. The letterpress process, however, is much less common today than the photo-offset process, and most feature services specialize in furnishing camera-ready copy (see Figure 12–1).

A derivative of the general interest mat service is the special-interest service, such as a minority media service that covers the nation's 1,500 minority media outlets. A release to 1,000 minority daily newspapers and 2,800 weekly newspapers, mostly in the suburbs, may bring up to 100 to 400 clippings at a cost of just under $2,000 to a sponsor. Add potential television and radio outlets, and the cost may escalate to just under $3,000 for comprehensive coverage of the nation's minority media.

The success ratio for such feature services is high, and clients regularly receive extensive newspaper mentions for their publicity material.

Broadcast services, which likewise package and distribute recorded and taped messages, support public relations efforts in radio and television placement. Such services produce features ranging from chief executive interviews to consumer tips, all laced subtly with the sponsoring agency's name.

PHOTOGRAPHIC SUPPORTS

Photos, if used properly, can enhance brochures, annual reports, or even news releases. Any practitioner involved with printed material should know the basics of photography.

Photography has a language all its own. For example:

○ **Air brushing** is used by artists and retouchers to blank, gray down, or obscure details in a photograph. Clouds, smoke, steam, and the like, may be "air brushed" in.

FIGURE 12–1. *Mat service publicity.* These newspaper articles are distributed by one of the nation's major feature services, North American Precis Syndicate. Precis produces them from organizational publicity and distributes finished copy to close to 4,000 suburban newspapers.

SOURCE: Courtesy of North American Precis Syndicate, Inc.

How should an organization go about selecting a public relations agency?

Public relations activities are an essential part of the operations of all types of organizations, ranging from nonprofit agencies with staffs of less than twenty people to multinational corporations with personnel in the many thousands. Dealing with legislators, employees, shareholders, financial contributors, vendors, dealers, customers, and other publics is the responsibility of public relations people. A vital question for any organization is whether to provide its own public relations people on full or part-time staff and/or retain a public relations agency. The decision is similar to that of retaining an outside counselor with regard to law, accounting, and other services.

What kind of an organization requires outside public relations help?

Smaller organizations sometimes find it is more economical and efficient *not* to have advertising, accounting, legal, and public relations people on staff, but rather to utilize outside agencies. Larger organizations generally have internal people for all of these functions, and then supplement their staff with one or more outside agencies. Therefore, the first decision to be made is what are the public relations needs, objectives, and goals and then to decide whether these

Richard Weiner is chief executive of Richard Weiner, Inc., a major public relations agency in New York City specializing in publicity for products and services. A prolific writer, Mr. Weiner is the author of seven widely-used books in the communications field, including *Professional's Guide to Publicity, Professional's Guide to Public Relations Services,* and *News Bureaus in the U.S.*

○ **Bleeding** is reproducing a photo on a printed page without one or more of the traditional white margins. A bleed picture extends to the very trim-edge of the page to heighten the drama of the photo.

○ **Cropping** is marking off or cutting off a portion of a photo to change the proportions or composition. Often, a skillful cropping job can heighten the drama of a photo.

functions can be handled more economically and efficiently internally and/or externally.

What can an outside agency offer that an in-house public relations capability cannot?

The outside agency is more likely to be proficient in media relations, and thus, more capable of attempting to achieve significant publicity in major media. The public relations agency also can provide objectivity that is necessary with regard to counseling, especially as it may relate to sensitive problems. Furthermore, the outside agency may have a particular body of experience and expertise in dealing with the special problems and needs of an industry or specific organization. Top management of an organization is more likely to respect, and act on, the advice of an outside counselor as compared to staff people.

How does a publicist choose appropriate media for a specific story?

In setting up a publicity program, the publicity agency—or any publicist—first determines the desired goals and audiences. From this comes a list of media which are capable of reaching and influencing these audiences.

Are there specific steps you follow in seeking publicity for a client's product?

The outside agency often starts with an objective analysis of the attitudes of relevant publics to the organization, particularly if there is a crisis or other problem, such as sales decreases or hostility from government, consumer, labor, environmental, or other groups.

How do you organize a press conference?

The most important decision in organizing a press conference is whether or not to hold it. Generally when in doubt, the answer should be "no"! There are few things more embarrassing than a press conference to which no one comes, and such events have been known to take place. Next, decisions must be made with regard to content, time, place, participants, materials, agenda, and other details. Perhaps the most important element is the invitation to be sent a week or more prior to the event.

This invitation, which can range from a tip sheet (which lists the who, what, where, when, and why) to a letter or printed announcement, should be sent to appropriate media people and then followed-up by telephone. If an event is important enough to warrant a press conference, then it also warrants a rehearsal. Particularly for spokespeople who are relatively inexperienced, it sometimes is extremely helpful to hold a simulated press conference shortly before the actual conference. The publicist should have an extensive checklist, including a variety of details, such as sign-in receptionist, microphones, if necessary, seating arrangements, availability of telephones, and other communications aides.

How can an organization monitor the press coverage it receives?

In addition to providing a photographer and audio or video service to make a transcript of the press conference (for purposes of the record, as well as subsequent publicity uses), the publicist may want to retain a clipping

(Interview *continues*)

○ **Glossy print** is a photographic print suitable for reproduction, having a smooth, polished surface.
○ **Reducing** makes a photo smaller than the original reproduction. Its opposite, *enlarging,* makes the reproduction larger than the original.
○ **Retouching** corrects blemishes to improve an original print or negative.
○ **Scaling** measures the size and proportion of a photograph for reproduction.

bureau or broadcast-monitoring service. Clipping bureaus provide vital information, and almost every publicist subscribes to one or more bureaus on a continuing or occasional basis. The quickest way to obtain a broadcast transcript is to work directly with the program producer or staff. Local stations will often provide radio tapes or television films at little or no cost. Of course, nothing replaces personal monitoring of major media.

How does one keep abreast of changes in communications?

New books and media directories are reviewed and new services described in such journals as *Advertising Age, Public Relations Journal, Media News Keys, Jack O'Dwyer's Newsletter,* and other publications. *PR Reporter,* the weekly newsletter published in Exeter, New Hampshire, frequently includes a supplementary "Tips and Tactics" sheet with practical tips on specific public relations problems. *Public Relations News,* the weekly newsletter published by Denny Griswold in New York, devotes half of each issue to a case study which often includes procedural details.

Is there anything else you'd like readers of this book to know?

As public relations becomes more extensive and complex, most practitioners tend to become "generalists," and therefore must turn for assistance to specialists, outside vendors, and intermediaries. Each person must decide how to use the multitude of specialized services that exist. The objectives, concepts, and other major decisions remain the responsibility of the individual public relations practitioner.

While a detailed discussion of photographic terms and techniques falls beyond the scope of this book, public relations practitioners should be relatively conversant in photographic terminology and be able to recognize the attributes that characterize good photos:

1 They should be "live," in real environments with believable people instead of stilted and obvious model shots in studios (see Figure 12–2).
2 They should focus clearly on the issue, product, image, or person that the organization wishes to emphasize, without irrelevant, visually distracting clutter in the foreground or background.
3 They should be eye-catching, creatively using angles—overhead, below, to the side—to suggest movement on the part of the photographer.
4 They must express a viewpoint—an underlying message.

These kinds of shots are often difficult, especially for the novice photographer. It often makes sense, therefore, to hire a professional. Some organizations are fortunate to have photographers on staff. Others must hire freelancers who may charge upwards of $1-2,500 per day for annual report work.

Almost as important as the photograph itself is the coordination of photographic assignments. Practitioners should work closely with the photographer and the intended subject, notifying both well in advance of specific needs and dates. Too often, a photographer must wait—and charge for—a day or two just for a setup to be

FIGURE 12–2. *Two publicity photos.* "Big Blue Marble," ITT Corporation's award-winning public service children's TV series, used a variety of photos to stimulate publicity interest. The photo at right shows singer Melba Moore, Big Blue Marble spokesperson, and friends on a playground. The photo at left portrays two Big Blue Marble volunteers at the show's Pen Pal Computer Center. If you were a newspaper editor, which photo would you use?

SOURCE: Courtesy of International Telephone and Telegraph Corporation.

ready. (Worse, photos taken in hasty setups may show safety hazards or outdated equipment, necessitating costly retouching or even reshooting.) Finally, photographers may not understand the nuances behind a public relations photo without the counsel of the person who scheduled the shot. Consequently, planning for and following through on photographic assignments becomes a critical responsibility for practitioners.

Just as photos say something about the nature of an organization, interesting graphic design suggests innovation and leadership. Annual report design, for example, is big business. Many firms, large and small, refuse to cut corners in the design of printed material. Charts, typography, photo captions, headlines—even paper stock—are important elements in conveying a corporate image.

Today, expressing an institutional personality is such a critical and delicate challenge that outside assistance generally is considered a wise and necessary investment.

AUDIOVISUAL SUPPORTS

Before using audiovisual materials, public relations professionals first must consider two things: a) the objectives of their presentation and b) the audience they intend to reach.

As with any other type of media, audiovisual materials are channels through which a presentation's content is delivered to an audience. The purpose of that

TABLE 12-1   Pros and cons of five audiovisual vehicles

Material	Advantages	Limitations
I. SLIDE SERIES A form of projected audiovisual materials easy to prepare with any 35MM camera.	**1** Prepared with any 35mm camera for most uses. **2** Requires only filming, with processing and mounting by film laboratory. **3** Colorful, realistic reproductions of original subjects. **4** Easily revised, updated, handled, stored, and rearranged. **5** Can be combined with taped narration for greater effectiveness. **6** May be played through remote control presentation.	**1** Requires some skill in photography. **2** Requires special equipment for closeup photography and copying. **3** Prone to get out of sequence and be projected incorrectly.
II. FILM STRIPS Closely related to slides, but instead of being mounted as separate pictures, the film, after processing, remains uncut as a continuous strip.	**1** Compact, easily handled, and always in proper sequence. **2** Can be supplemented with captions or recordings. **3** Inexpensive when quantity reproduction is required. **4** Projected with simple, lightweight equipment. **5** Projection rate controlled by presenter.	**1** Relatively difficult to prepare locally. **2** Requires film laboratory service to convert slides to film strip form. **3** In permanent sequence and therefore cannot be rearranged or revised.
III. OVERHEAD TRANSPARENCIES A popular form of locally-prepared materials, requiring overhead projector for presentation.	**1** Can present information in systematic, developmental sequences. **2** Simple-to-operate projector with presentation rate controlled by presenter. **3** Requires limited planning. **4** Can be prepared by a variety of simple, inexpensive methods.	**1** Requires special equipment, facilities, and skills for more advanced preparation methods. **2** Projection technique may be cumbersome and lack finesse of more remote processes.

presentation—to motivate, to inform, to educate, to guide thinking, to instruct, etc.—must be established first before the specific audiovisual medium is selected.

A practitioner has available a variety of audiovisual channels, each of which, as Table 12–1 indicates, presents its own advantages and limitations. Again, in preparing for especially important presentations, it may be wise to seek professional audiovisual help in devising a compelling presentation.

TABLE 12-1 *continued.*

Material	Advantages	Limitations
IV. MOTION PICTURES Films involving motion and increased degree of complexity.	1 Particularly useful in describing motion, in showing relationships, or giving impact to subject. 2 Ensures consistency in material presentation. 3 Heightens "drama" in material presentation. 4 Allows special techniques in presenting content.	1 May be expensive to prepare in terms of time, equipment, materials, and services, e.g. $1–5,000 per minute for finished product. 2 Requires careful planning and production skill.
V. MULTI-IMAGE/MULTIMEDIA Combination of visual materials used together for specific purposes, either concurrently or in succession.	1 Can create strong emotional impact on viewers, can rivet attention. 2 Use of photographs, slides, filmstrips, and motion pictures in combination. 3 Provides for more effective communications in certain situations than when only single medium is used.	1 Requires additional equipment, complex set-ups, and careful coordination during planning, preparation, and use.

GRAPHICS SUPPORTS

Closely related to photographic and audiovisual supports is the use of graphic arts. Artwork too must be planned with sufficient consideration for objectives and audiences.

A well-conceived visual design and layout of an organization's graphics presentation is essential in conveying a particular impression. While a comprehensive discussion of graphics is not appropriate, key design principles include such things as simplicity, unity, emphasis, and balance.

○ **Simplicity** of design merely means limiting design elements to present one idea at a time. Elements should be easy to read and easily understood.

○ **Unity** is the relationship among the elements of a visual display. These, too, must be clear and easily understandable.

○ **Emphasis** in a visual refers to highlighting the center of interest and attention, through the use of size relationships, perspective, color, space, and the like, so that an audience understands the purpose of the communication.

○ **Balance**, either formal or informal, can add to the visually arresting nature of an illustration or design.

While public relations practitioners are not expected to be experts in graphic art, they are expected to understand the critical role that graphics can play in conveying a particular image for an organization. (See Figure 12-3.)

DISSEMINATION SUPPORTS

Prompt and targeted dissemination of communications materials is vital. A variety of outside services are available to assist in this process.

MESSENGER SERVICES

To many large companies, an external messenger delivery service is invaluable in disseminating press material, particularly in urban areas. Important news releases *must* make it to the media in time for editing and placement. A story that arrives late in the afternoon for the 6 o'clock news doesn't stand much chance. Most large cities have messengers to move news, messages, and parcels around town in a hurry. In major cities, certain messenger services specialize in public relations accounts. These firms are well aware of the immediate nature of public relations work.

COMMERCIAL WIRE SERVICES

News wire is even faster than messenger delivery. Commercial services, such as PR News Wire and Business Wire, have offices around the country ready to distribute client news releases on their own private wire. Unlike copy offered to Dow Jones, Reuters, the Associated Press, or United Press International (which may reject or use only portions of a release), commercial wires charge clients to run their complete releases. Many newspapers subscribe to such services, usually ensuring a firm that its release will at least make it into the newspaper's wire room.

MAILING SERVICES

Most large cities are served by direct-mail firms that can provide clients addresses by zip code. Such firms as Associated Release Service, Inc., Media Distribution Services, Inc., and PR Aids are experts in disseminating news material accurately, quickly, and to the right publication. These companies maintain and guard their own computerized media mailing lists, which are periodically updated to acknowledge the frequent staff changes at publications and broadcast outlets. Each mailing house tailors its distribution list to fit the needs of its clients. For example, a company with a message directed to farmers may want its release distributed solely to farming journals and editorial writers who specialize in farm affairs. Mailing services also have the capacity to *localize* releases, to modify master news releases to emphasize a local ingredient for particular markets. For example, an announcement by a firm's president may be localized so that a regional vice-president becomes the source of the information.

RADIO-TV SERVICES

In recent years, a number of services have sprung up to assist public relations professionals in placing their publicity messages on radio and television.

One of the most exotic such services is NEWSLINK, which uses satellite communications links to transmit publicity to hundreds of television stations

The Corporate Signature

Our signature is an arrangement of our mark and logotype. It is considered as one design element in any layout or application situation. A complete corporate signature must be used whenever identification is necessary. Each authorized arrangement has an established relationship between the mark and logotype. This relationship is not to be altered or changed in any way.

DAVID'S
Lemonade

Preferred form
for vertical format

O DAVID'S

Preferred form
for horizontal format

DAVID'S O
Lemonade

Alternate form
for horizontal format

FIGURE 12–3. *David's Lemonade.* Simplicity, unity, emphasis, and balance must all be clearly defined for powerful corporate design. These excerpts from the corporate identity manual of David's Lemonade, the creation of Fulton + Partners Inc., is an example of design that works.

SOURCE: Courtesy of Sanders Printing Corporation.

equipped with satellite reception. The NEWSLINK teletype advisory system alerts news directors to every transmission and attempts to "sell" them on its contents in advance. Customer-produced newsclips of broadcast quality are then fed to receptive television stations in a matter of seconds. The NEWSLINK feed is delivered twice a day, and the normal transmission charge for a one-minute clip is $1,000. This compares to a video cassette mailing charge which, depending on the number of copies involved, may cost three or four times as much as the NEWSLINK satellite system.

In a related context, the phenomenon of teleconferencing as a means of disseminating organizational news also is growing. Teleconferencing combines television with phone hook-ups so that participants can be seen and questions asked even from remote locations.

In one successful teleconference in 1981, General Mills announced the results of a survey of working families through an elaborate 18-city, satellite TV hookup. With General Mills executives presiding at a press conference in New York, reporters from around the country called in to pose questions about the survey. This two-way electronic press conference helped generate first-hand publicity in each of the cities involved. A similar hookup, organized by the Burson-Marsteller public relations agency, reintroduced Extra Strength Tylenol in late 1982 after the product was removed from the market (See Case Study, p. 492). The Tylenol teleconference received front page publicity across the nation.

Beyond the space-age devices of satellite communications and teleconferencing, radio production houses, sponsored film creators and distributors, news clip services, and a vast variety of other supports exist to assist practitioners in reaching the electronic media.

MEDIA DIRECTORIES

Another support is the media directory, which describes in detail the various media. For example:

1 *Ayer Directory of Publications* lists about 20,000 publications, including daily and weekly newspapers as well as general circulation, trade, and special interest magazines. *Ayer* also includes the names, addresses, and phone numbers of publication editors.

2 *Bacon's Publicity Checker* provides data on almost 5,000 U.S. and Canadian trade and business publications, organized in some 100 categories—from accountants and advertising, to woolens and yachting. *Bacon's* includes editors, addresses, and phone numbers.

3 *Broadcasting Yearbook* contains information on radio and TV stations in the United States, Canada, and Latin America. It also lists key personnel, addresses, and telephones.

4 *Editor & Publisher Yearbook* lists newspapers (daily, weekly, national, black, college and university, foreign language) and their personnel across the United States.

5 *Working Press of the Nation* is a five-volume effort. It lists locations and editorial staff for the following media: newspapers, magazines, radio, television, feature writers, syndicates, and house magazines.

6 Specialized directories from *Hudson's Washington News Media Directory* and *Congressional Staff Guide* to the *Anglo-Jewish Media List* and various state media directories, published by state press or broadcasters' associations, are also excellent resources.

MEASUREMENT ASSISTANCE

After an organization has distributed its press materials, it needs an effective way to measure the results. A variety of outside services can help.

PRESS CLIPPING BUREAUS

Some agencies will monitor company mentions in the press. These press clipping bureaus can supply newspaper and magazine clippings on any subject and about any company. The two largest, Burrelle's and Luce, each receive hundreds of newspapers and magazines daily. Both services dispatch close to 50,000 clippings to their clients each day. Burrelle's, for example, employs about 800 people and subscribes to about 1,800 daily newspapers, 9,000 weeklies, 6,000 consumer and trade magazines, and various other publications.

These bureaus may also be hired in certain regions to monitor local news or for certain projects that require special scrutiny. Most charge monthly fees plus about seventy cents per clipping. For a practitioner who must keep management informed of press reports on the firm, the expense is generally worthwhile.

BROADCAST TRANSCRIPTION SERVICES

Press clipping bureaus generally are not equipped to monitor radio and television stations for client mentions. Consequently, specialized transcription services have arisen to monitor broadcast stories. A handful of such broadcast transcription services exist in the country, the largest being Radio-TV Reports, Inc., with offices in several cities. This firm monitors all major radio and TV stations around the clock, checking for messages concerning client companies. After a client orders a particular segment of a broadcast program, Radio-TV Reports either prepares a typed transcript or secures an audiotape. Costs for transcripts are relatively high, with a one-page

Broadcast transcription entered the company a firm called Mediascan supplied clients with daily verbatim transcripts of network news programming, transmitted by computer to word processors.

CONTENT ANALYSIS SERVICES

A more sophisticated analysis of results in the media is supplied by firms that evaluate the *content* of media mentions concerning clients. Firms like PR Data, Inc. of Rowayton, Connecticut, use computer analysis to discern positive and negative mentions about organizations. Although this measurement technique is rough and somewhat subjective, it nevertheless enables an organization to get a clearer idea about how it is being portrayed in the media. However, such "press clipping computer analysis" stops short of being a true test of audience attitudes.

TREND WATCH SERVICES

Another relatively recent wrinkle in public relations services is the rash of so-called trend watch companies that have sprung up. These firms specialize in assessing and analyzing trends that loom on the horizon.

Perhaps the most prominent such firm is the Naisbitt Group of Washington, D.C., which culls about 125,000 items each year for clients from Sears to Westinghouse who yearly pay $15,000 for the service. John Naisbitt, author of the best-selling *Megatrends,* and other trend watchers predict broad social, economic, and political developments with which companies wish to keep abreast so they're not surprised later on. For example, Naisbitt successfully predicted both the end of mandatory retirement a year before it was legislated by Congress as well as the decline of nuclear power long before the Three Mile Island accident in 1979.

While the vast majority of trend watch data is, in the words of one subscriber, "good cocktail party chatter" of little practical use, many companies think it wise to hire such a service. Understandably, the competition is fierce.[1] Competitors include Cambridge Reports, Inc., which gets almost $6,000 for a service consisting of quarterly packets of eight one-page reports, and Yankelovich Corporate Priorities, which publishes a report costing $32,000. One reason companies may think it necessary to subscribe was summed up by the vice president for government and industry affairs at Alexander & Alexander Inc., an insurance broker and trend watch client. "It's no longer enough to make as good a product as you can," he said. "There are other things that can blow you out of the water."[2]

OTHER SERVICES

Other services exist that can provide the public relations professional with everything from motion pictures to social secretaries, from food consultants to sky writers, from party-arranging to pyrotechnic experts for fireworks displays.

Translation services are available in most major cities to translate press materials into Spanish, French, German, Italian, Japanese, and even Chinese, Russian, and Arabic (Figure 12–4).

FIGURE 12–4. *Chinese typewriter.* In 1979, in conjunction with the normalization of relations between the United States and China, the Media Factory, Inc., a New York translation service, began marketing this Chinese typewriter, primarily for firms doing business with the Chinese. The cost of this item was $1,750.

SOURCE: Courtesy of the Media Factory.

PRACTICAL APPLICATIONS

Corporate identification firms (a hot item in recent years) examine and recommend changes in a firm's name and corporate image, and then in its stationery, signage (signs on offices, equipment, etc.), and collateral materials (business cards, etc.). Yearly retainer fees for such firms often can extend into the six-figure latitude.

Film services also are useful for stimulating audience comprehension and interest in an organization. Today's ten- or twelve-minute public relations films are of high quality, complete with skillful scripting, production, and direction, featuring professional actors in leading roles. It is not unusual for such films to cost companies six-figure sums, although more reasonably priced films (i.e., below $25,000) are certainly possible.

SPECIAL EVENTS

Finally, a variety of support services exist to assist public relations professionals in organizing special events. These are the off-beat occurrences such as meetings, conventions, cocktail parties, lunches, open houses, tours, award ceremonies, and the like, with which practitioners invariably are confronted some time in their careers.

Often, the public relations professional is called on to organize such events. As a first step in this role, the practitioner should compose a checklist of do's and don'ts in planning the event. In general, every special event organizer should prepare for the following:

○ **Invitations**   How simple or elaborate should the announcement of the meeting be? What should it say? Who should be invited?

○ **Speakers**   Who should speak? Who should introduce the speakers? What arrangements must be made for the speakers?

○ **Facilities**   What about lighting, seating, audiovisual supports, temperature of the room, and many, many other considerations?

○ **Food**   What's the hotel menu look like? What's the reputation of the hotel's food? How many waiters and bartenders will be in attendance?

FEATURE
THE CARDINAL RULE OF SPECIAL EVENTS

The cardinal rule of special events planning is that as soon as you've concluded that you have successfully anticipated every potential emergency—think again.

Consider the case of the special events planner responsible for the 6 P.M. St. Louis Election Day cocktail reception, who, upon arriving at the hall, was told that Missouri law prohibits alcohol being served before the closing of the polls at 7 P.M.

There are few worse plights for a meeting planner than to have to stand around for an hour with 200 snarling executives—all sipping club soda.

○ **Hotel procedures** Which hotel manager has been assigned to the event? Have arrangements been personally checked and a dress rehearsal held? Have arrangements been made for special procedures for checkout, billing, or transportation?

FIGURE 12–5. *A special event.* Occasionally, a specially conceived event can attract extensive publicity. In 1959, when The Chase Manhattan Bank was in the midst of constructing its downtown One Chase Manhattan Plaza headquarters, photographer Robert Mottar asked the hundreds of workers to freeze for a moment so that this picture could be recorded for posterity. It also was reported in many of New York City's daily newspapers, which acknowledged both the bank and its new location.

SOURCE: Courtesy of The Chase Manhattan Bank.

○ **Miscellaneous** What kind of decorations have been arranged? What kind of press accommodations have been made? Have telephones been designated for event use? What kind of back-up facilities are available? Etc., etc., etc.

In planning major events, public relations professionals generally are well advised to seek outside help. In general, practitioners can find just about any type of assistance by consulting local directories and industry source books, which periodically are updated to include the ever-changing variety of external services that support public relations work. Often, outside help doesn't come cheap. But the savings in aggravation and worry when an outside expert is hired usually turns out to be well worth the price.

CASE STUDY
Chino Chemicals

The Chino Chemical Company of Albuquerque, New Mexico, was concerned about pending state and federal chemical legislation. Essentially, the legislation would have prohibited the manufacture of certain chemicals produced at Chino plants, because of the suspicion that such chemicals were harmful to plant workers and neighbors. Chino officials argued that even if the chemicals were harmful, the likelihood of the kind of proportions necessary to cause any damage were unlikely to be reached at any of Chino's plants. Still, the company worried about the pending bills.

In order to "get the jump" on any legislation, Chino decided to launch a publicity campaign giving its side of the pending controversy. Chino's hope was that its workers, many of whom were Mexican Americans, and Congressional constituents around the country would see the logic of the Chino arguments and voice their opinions to their legislators.

Chino was convinced that only a nationwide publicity barrage could effectively mobilize public opinion in its favor. Its public relations staff, however, was limited to two professionals and one secretary. Clearly, outside support was needed. The question was, what kind of outside support?

"It seems to me," said Chino public relations director Denise Zeeman, "that what we really need is a professional writer who can capture our arguments lucidly and then translate them onto the printed page. We could then pick it up from there."

Zeeman reasoned that once the press materials were written, she and her staff could then do a thorough enough job of disseminating the arguments to the media.

"After all," Zeeman reasoned, "we have excellent contacts with all the dailies in Albuquerque and I, personally, know two of the television station managers. It seems to me the dissemination part of this is easy, once we get the writing done."

QUESTIONS

1 Do you agree with her reasoning on the need for outside support?

2 What support would you have requested?

3 What target audience should Chino try to reach? What kinds of media would best appeal to that target audience?

4 If Zeeman is successful in reaching the media outlets she mentioned, would you call the Chino public relations program a success? Why not?

5 Do you agree that outside public relations support is necessary for Chino?

NOTES

1 Bill Abrams, "John Naisbitt Makes A Handsome Living Reading Newspapers for Big Corporations," *The Wall Street Journal, 30 September 1982, p. 55.*

2 Ibid.

SUGGESTED READING

Congressional Quarterly. *Washington Information Directory.* Washington, D.C.: Author, 1982. This handy reference guide lists more than 5,000 information sources in Congress, the executive branch, and private associations. It eliminates the time-consuming task of finding out who does what and where.

Foegen, J.H. "Inflation Deserves At Least A 'Day'!" *Public Relations Quarterly.* Summer 1981, pp. 12–14.

Fox, James F. "The Prevention of Cruelty to Speakers," *Public Relations Journal.* July 1981, pp. 12–14.

Fox, James F. "Program Chairman: Moderator or Menace?" *Public Relations Journal.* July 1981, pp. 12–14. The job of program chairman requires etiquette, amenity, and attention to detail, but these qualities often are overlooked.

Gebbie Press. *All-in-One Directory.* 1982 ed. (Box 1000, New Paltz, N.Y. 12561.) A basic reference, providing brief address and chief editorial executive listings. Radio section lists over 6,500 stations, both commercial and educational, with addresses and network affiliations. The television section lists over 900 commercial and educational stations. Also has complete listings of black media, including black-oriented radio stations.

The Hollywood Reporter. (Available from 6715 Sunset Blvd., Hollywood, Calif. 90028). Daily Monday through Friday trade paper for entertainment industries, emphasizing movies and television, but also covering Las Vegas and Broadway.

Kappes, Jorja L. "Localizing Awards Programs For Greater Effectiveness," *Public Relations Quarterly,* Spring 1981, pp. 27–28.

Kemp, Jerrold E. *Planning & Producing Audiovisual Materials,* 4th Edition New York: Harper & Row Publishers, 1980, Chapter 7.

Media News Keys. (Available from 150 Fifth Avenue, New York, N.Y. 10011.) Published on Monday, this service paper with a monthly cumulative index reports on network and local television in over thirty-five top market metropolitan areas of the country. Also reports programming trends and changes in major market areas.

National Research Bureau. *Working Press of the Nation.* (Available from author, 242 N. 3rd Street, Burlington, Iowa, 52601). Five volumes, each covering a different medium —newspapers, magazine, radio-TV, feature writers, syndicates and house organs.

O'Dwyer, Jack, ed. *O'Dwyer's Directory of Corporate Communications.* New York: J.R. O'Dwyer, 1982. Mr. O'Dwyer's guide provides a full listing of the public relations departments of nearly 3,000 companies and shows how the largest companies have defined public relations and have staffed and budgeted for it.

———. *O'Dwyer's Directory of PR Firms—1982.* New York: J.R. O'Dwyer, 1982. This directory has listings on 1,200 public relations firms. In addition to information on executives, accounts, type of agency, and branch office locations, the guide offers a geographical index to firms and cross-index to more than 8,000 clients.

Peter Glenn Publications. *National Radio Publicity Directory.* 1976 ed. (Available from author, 17 E. 48th St., New York, N.Y. 10017.) Carries listings on programs on over 1,800 stations throughout the United States, covering local talk shows, with a separate category for network and syndicated radio shows. Listed by state.

PR Aids' Party Line. (Available from 221 Park Ave. South, New York, N.Y. 10003.) An information service weekly, published on Monday, listing editorial placement opportunities in all media, including network and local radio and TV.

Public Relations Aids, Inc. (221 Park Ave. South, New York, N.Y. 10003.) Computerized media system that lets a client select local broadcast media by market, type of programming, power of radio stations, network for TV, department (news, program, women's interest, public service, etc.).

Public Relations Plus. *New York Publicity Outlets—1979.* (Available from author, Washington Depot, Conn. 06794.) A basic guide to newspapers, magazines, radio, TV within a fifty-mile radius of New York City.

———. *TV Publicity Outlets—Nationwide.* (Available from author, Washington Depot, Conn. 06794.) This publication is the only quarterly TV directory offering information on over 2,300 contacts for television programs across the country.

Selame, Elinor, "Keeper Of The Mark," *Public Relations Journal,* November 1981, pp. 44–46. A graphics department can help improve a corporation's outdated identity system.

Weiner, Richard, ed. *News Bureaus in the U.S.* New York: Richard Weiner, 1981. This media guidebook lists information on 500 bureaus maintained by newspapers, magazines, business publications, and wire services in twenty-three major cities.

———. *Professional Guide to Public Relations Services.* 2nd ed. Englewood Cliff, N.J.: Prentice-Hall, 1980. Describes and evaluates more than 1,000 services including clipping bureaus, mailing house media guides, translators, prop houses, film and record producers and distributors, and mat suppliers.

———. *Syndicated Columnists.* New York: Richard Weiner, 1979. This book gives information on how to locate major columnists in twenty-four subject categories as well as offering a description of the major syndicates and columnists.

THE PUBLICS

PART THREE

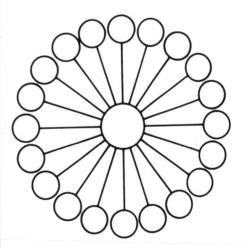

13
Employees

A HOT TICKET

The first step in promoting positive external public relations is achieving good internal public relations.

If management speaks out of one side of its mouth to its external constituencies and out of the other to its internal ones, it will lose credibility. Employees must be solidly on management's side. Without their support, a company is unlikely to communicate convincingly with the outside world. At base, every employee is a public relations spokesperson for the organization. And no organization today can afford to talk out of both sides of its mouth. Indeed, more and more, practitioners are finding that "sound public relations begins at home."[1] (See Figure 13-1.)

Internal communications has become a hot ticket in public relations. Management traditionally tended to view employees as a mass, rather than as individuals, each with individual interests, needs, and wants.[2] Now good management realizes that a satisfied and enthusiastic employee is an extremely effective and credible public relations advertisement.

The "employee public" is composed of several subpublics: hourly workers, salaried workers, supervisory staff, union members, official staff, craftsmen, and white-collar workers. Given such a diverse mix of subpublics, mass communications, aimed at no group in particular, may not succeed.

Internal communications, like external messages, must be targeted to reach specific subgroups. Communications must be *continuous* to consistently reinforce management's interest in its employees.

In recent years, several trends have emerged affecting employee communications.[3]

 **Allied Corporation**
P.O. Box 2245R
Morristown, New Jersey 07960

Chairman of the Board

September 30, 1982

Dear fellow employees:

Our proposed acquisition of Bendix Corporation and our purchase of 39 percent of Martin Marietta Corporation present us with great opportunities.

I'd like to share with you the reasons for our action and the benefits we see for all concerned — you, our customers and our shareholders who will be asked to approve the transaction later this year.

Both Bendix and Martin Marietta are fine companies. They are important participants in the American economy and have grown substantially in sales and earnings over the past five years. We expect that trend to continue as the two companies contribute significantly to Allied's profitability.

We will be delighted to welcome Bendix into Allied. Bendix has many fine businesses. They are generally leaders in the automotive and industrial markets they serve.

We are particularly enthusiastic about the role Bendix will play in the expansion of our new electrical/electronic core business area, begun with the acquisitions of Eltra and Bunker Ramo and enhanced by our accelerated R&D program. Bendix has a fine reputation in the high-technology aerospace electronics field and therefore when Bendix approached us, we saw an excellent opportunity to extend our own business interests at an affordable cost.

In addition, the Bendix acquisition helps to fulfill two of our corporate goals:

● It improves the balance between income from manufacturing operations and income from oil and gas and from commodity products which are so vulnerable to every swing of the economic pendulum and

● It lowers our 65% corporate tax rate by increasing domestic source income

The price tag, of course, is a big one and I've been asked how this $1.9 billion transaction can be justified at a time when economic conditions have forced us to cut back production and lay off personnel.

My answer is that Allied, like American industry in general, must build for the future if we are to turn this nation around and get back on the path to prosperity. This is why we have diversified our company, why we have pressed on with capital spending despite the recession and why we have quadrupled our investment in research and development in four years. These actions help ensure our future and the creation of many more opportunities and jobs.

Moreover, our cost-cutting programs, as painful as they've been, have been necessary to reduce the impact of the recession and to make us even stronger competitors when times improve. It is the low-cost producer of high-quality products who has a competitive edge hard to beat.

This acquisition, as exciting and beneficial as it is, has substantially increased our long-term indebtedness and to reduce it to a more comfortable level will require some action. This is a manageable problem. I plan to appoint a task force of Allied/Bendix personnel to analyze our options and make recommendations, stressing to them that in these unsettled economic times, there is a need not only to preserve jobs but to create them.

Aside from the opportunities which this acquisition offers Allied, I think another useful purpose has been served: It brought to a halt a dispute which was potentially very damaging to both Bendix and Martin Marietta, their employees, their shareholders and their customers.

I believe that both Allied and Bendix will grow faster together than either could have grown alone and that our combined commitment to research and development of new technology — more than $400 million in 1982 — will make us more competitive in the international arena, an important factor at a time when U.S. industry has been losing ground to overseas producers.

Both Allied and Bendix have strong management and quality technology, manufacturing capabilities and products. And with our combined workforce of more than 110,000 people, we will grow together in service to our customers and profitability for our shareholders.

Edward L. Hennessy Jr.

Edward L. Hennessy, Jr.

FIGURE 13–1 *Allied employee ad.* So important has employee communications become that when Allied Corporation proposed to acquire Bendix Corporation in 1982, Allied took the unprecedented step of running a full-page ad in leading newspapers to explain the deal to employees.

COURTESY: Allied Corporation.

○ **Externalization of Communications**   With a greater emphasis on relations with the media, government officials, opinion leaders, and external constituencies of all stripes, the need has intensified for employee communication not only to be in sync with the external program but also to play a larger role in the overall corporate communications function.

○ **Targeting of the Organization**   As progovernment interest groups swipe at corporations, in particular, employees become much more important to their firms as voters, advocates, and concerned citizens through the political process.

○ **Characterization of the Internal Audience**   Employees no longer accept organizational pronouncements at face value. The staff today is generally younger, better educated, increasingly female, ambitious, and career-oriented at all levels. Today's more "hard-nosed" employee demands candor in communication.

○ **Businesslike Approach to Employee Communications**   Larger budgets and staffs in internal communications functions have allowed a greater emphasis on research-oriented services such as climate studies, effectiveness audits, economic education programs, and the like.

○ **Nonprint Emphasis**   Face-to-face communication has been emphasized while more impersonal, print-oriented communication has diminished in relative importance. More emphasis has been placed on small group meetings, visibility of top executives, and use of audiovisual, particularly video, communications.

The goal of any employee communications must be credibility. The task for management is to convince employees that it not only wants to communicate with them but that it wishes to do so in a truthful, frank, and direct manner.

CREDIBILITY: THE KEY

The employee public is a savvy one. Employees can't be conned because they live with the organization every day. They generally know what's going on, whether management is honest with them or not. That's why management must be truthful.

One employee communications manager summarized the problem succinctly;

About the only authority you hold today as a manager is the authority of your passion for the truth and your integrity. The sticks are pretty much gone. The carrots are not what they used to be. Loyalty to the organization per se is pretty much gone. Your best hope is your credibility with your people.[4]

Surveys show that employees desperately want to know top management's views on a host of internal matters. For example, employees want to find out in what direction an organization is headed, why it has chosen to go that way, and what their personal role in the new direction will be. While employees understand that policy decisions rest with management, they nevertheless appreciate and desire the opportunity to contribute to policy formulation.[5]

In dealing with organized labor, in particular, communications candor is extremely important for management. The role of the union in the organization must clearly be understood by public relations professionals, whose job is to enhance communications between management and union members. In times of economic

INTERVIEW
Roger D'Aprix

Roger D'Aprix is a New York-based consultant with the international consulting firm of Towers, Perrin, Forster & Crosby. He is the author of *Communicating for Productivity*, published in 1982 by Harper & Row. Mr. D'Aprix is a frequent lecturer and speaker on employee communication and is the recipient of the Fellow Award, highest award of the International Association of Business Communicators. Formerly, he was manager of employee communications for Xerox Corporation.

What are the fundamental public relations principles in dealing with employees?

I think that there is only one. Employees are *the* primary public relations audience for any organization. They have the greatest interest, concern, and attachment to the organization for the obvious reason that their personal fate is so closely intertwined with the fate of that organization. The great irony is that they usually are the most neglected, most lied-to constituency in American business. Accordingly, they often undo otherwise effective communication with the public-at-large.

Should certain information, e.g. corporate layoffs, lost discrimination suits, etc., be kept from employees?

It is naive in the extreme to withhold such information. For one thing, employees have multiple sources of information, including their own powerful grapevine. For management to pretend that not talking about the issue is somehow to "withhold" it from them is nonsense. They know already, and they long for someone to level with them on what the event means. The tactic of trying to withhold bad news only serves to increase the resentment people feel over the event. That's especially true with layoffs.

What are the most effective ways to communicate to employees?

The single most effective way is face-to-face. And the best person to do it is the boss. Unfortunately, we have tended to neglect this powerful technique and to rely on depersonalized media to do the job. After face-to-face communication comes all of the traditional media—house publications, news-letters, A-V media, and the like. But they are much inferior to face-to-face communication.

Is the employee house organ an outmoded concept?

No, it's not outmoded. It just needs to be used more intelligently. Its primary content should be the major issues of the business related in terms that mean something to employees. Everything else should be merely frosting on the cake.

What are the characteristics that distinguish good employee communicators from medi-ocre ones?

The chief characteristics are honesty, a will-ingness to communicate on a timely basis, and concern for the dignity and welfare of the workforce. Those are all of the attributes that senior management should manifest in doing this vital job, which is their responsibil-ity and not the responsibility of the profes-sional communicator. If we're talking about the professionals here, I would say the best ones see communication as a process rather than as a product or collection of media, and that's the way they approach their work. They're also persistent and imaginative. The bad ones are all craft-oriented and try to function like internal journalists.

If an organization has a major news event to announce, is it better as a rule that employ-ees receive the announcement first?

Absolutely. Otherwise, they read about the event in the media, and it infuriates them that as members of the organization they have to get their information second hand.

Why are some organizations such poor em-ployee communicators?

They don't really see the employees as the people who make the organization go. Therefore, they communicate as an after-thought to their people rather than in any planned, orderly fashion. Also, they don't provide sufficient staff and dollars to do the job. Finally, they think that tangible programs like house publications really do mean that they are communicating even when the real need is to manage the process of commu-nication.

How can an organization determine its spe-cific employee communications needs?

The best technique is good employee re-search. Hire a good consultant to come in and measure as objectively as possible where the workforce really is in their views of the organization. Determine what the neces-sary techniques are to give people the infor-mation and insights they need to do their jobs better and to feel a greater sense of commitment. In short, measure and then plan and strategize to do the job properly.

Is there anything else you'd like the readers of this book to know?

Yes. Of all of the areas of public relations, this one is probably the ripest for growth and change. There will be more and more need to do this job better. Let's begin to recognize the employee audience for what it is, and let's stop merely giving this area lip service. If done well, it can affect every part of the organization's effectiveness. It can be the lubricant in helping the organization achieve its objectives, but it must reflect and rein-force those objectives. If done badly, it can help bring on alienation, distrust, and disas-ter for the organization. It's a great oppor-tunity which we simply can't afford to ignore any longer.

agony, such as those that have afflicted the nation from time-to-time in the 1970s and 1980s, it is imperative that a sense of teamwork be established between union members—indeed all employees—and management. For example, in the early 1980s when U.S. auto manufacturers suffered dislocations because of declining sales, increased foreign competition, and retooling for more fuel-efficient cars, management and labor in the major auto companies had to work more closely together. Chrysler advertised the benefits of American labor. General Motors announced that hourly workers as well as top executives and members of the board of directors would take pay cuts until the company reemerged. In both cases, the *esprit de corps* was briefly interrupted by subsequent developments. Nonetheless, the spirit of the times demanded that management and labor work together to solve the common problems of their organizations.

It is essential for any organization that employees feel they are appreciated. They want to be treated as important parts of an organization and not be taken for granted. The most important ingredient, then, of any internal communications program must be its credibility.

OBJECTIVES

The first step is to set objectives. Here are several from Rockwell International, a far-reaching conglomerate with offices throughout the United States and around the world:

1 To keep all communications understandable and to avoid ambiguity or lack of clarity.

2 To communicate regularly and not just in crisis situations.

3 To provide completely reliable information and to present all the facts needed to arrive at a reasonable judgment.

4 To disseminate information, particularly about changes—in advance of, not after, the fact when possible.

5 To communicate on the basis of what employees want to know about their company and their jobs; and to provide information helpful to employees in understanding and performing their job responsibilities.

6 To recognize the accomplishments and contributions of employees.

7 To clarify the reasons for policies and procedures; and to build an understanding of the economic "facts of business life" required for a successful operation.

8 To stimulate awareness on the part of employees that the company has a sincere interest in their security and well-being.

9 To help develop a sense of employee pride in association with a progressive company.

10 To encourage employee aid in the company's support of worthwhile community projects and civic affairs.

11 To encourage employees to express attitudes and opinions; and to provide the interest for a free flow of information both upward and downward.

12 To present a continuing overview of company products and operations so employees are knowledgeable about their company.

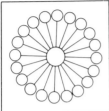

MINICASE
Sparking internal credibility at Arco

The development of Atlantic Richfield Company's *ARCO Spark* publication is a good example of setting out to win internal communications credibility.

ARCO Spark, distributed weekly to more than 40,000 employees and retirees around the world, was Atlantic Richfield's first attempt at company-wide communications on a regular basis. To win credibility for the publication, Atlantic Richfield employee communicators took several bold measures, including a "Letters to the Editor" column that printed some letters that were critical of the company, its management, and even *ARCO Spark* itself. Another segment of the paper was an "Employee Opinion Section," which featured anonymous staff questions and answers. For example: "I would like to know why the chairman rates an annual salary of $625,000 and the president rates $440,600?"

ARCO Spark reported both sides of controversial issues, such as the Arab Oil Embargo of 1973 and the explosion of a ship near a company refinery.

Editors "loosened up" communications language, referring to then Atlantic Richfield President Thornton Bradshaw as *Brad* in headlines and Board Chairman Robert O. Anderson as *Bob*. They also eliminated titles like *Mr.* and *Mrs.* and replaced the company's name with pronouns like *we, us,* and *our.*

They reported on legal actions taken by or against the company, on current lifestyle trends such as transcendental meditation and mid-life crisis, and on the pros and cons of various company programs.

As syndicated columnist Milton Moskowitz observed, "Many publications report only the good news, letting employees get the bad news elsewhere. But when Atlantic Richfield settled out of court on claims arising from a gas leak that killed nine persons in Denver City, Texas in 1975, the *Spark* reported the news on the front page."

As a result of *ARCO Spark's* candor, Atlantic Richfield subsequently produced additional publications for various levels of management with the same brand of credibility.[6]

QUESTIONS

1 How do you think employees reacted to the candor of *ARCO Spark?*
2 If you were editor of *ARCO Spark*, would you have published *all* letters the publication received?
3 If Atlantic Richfield's out-of-court settlement had not received publicity a week after it occurred, would you, as *ARCO Spark* editor, have suggested using the story in your publication?
4 What other kind of features could *ARCO Spark* run to enhance credibility with employees?

Growing out of these general objectives must be a predetermined list of tactical objectives for employee communication. While management concerns vary with changing situations, the following tactical objectives are common in employee communications efforts:

1 Achievement of production quotas to meet delivery promises on schedule.
2 Achievement of quality standards and reduction of defects to meet customer demands.
3 Achievement of cost-reduction goals.
4 Achievement of productivity improvements from new equipment and procedures, changes in facilities, machines, and methods.
5 Introduction of new practices, changes in work standards, restructuring of jobs, changes in classifications and pay rates.
6 Resolution of employee dissatisfaction, strike threats, and strikes through sound understanding of the issues.

EMPLOYEE COMMUNICATIONS METHODS

Once objectives are set, a variety of techniques may be adopted to reach the staff.

The initial tool is research. Before any communications program can be implemented, communicators must have a good sense of staff attitudes.

Perhaps the most beneficial form of research to lay the groundwork for effective employee communications is the internal communications audit. This consists essentially of old-fashioned personal, in-depth interviews to determine staff attitudes about the job, the organization, and its management coupled with an analysis of existing communications techniques. The findings of such audits are often startling, always informative, and never easily ignored.[7]

Once internal communications research is complete, the public relations practitioner has a clearer idea of the kinds of communications vehicles that make sense for the organization.

In the next sections, several of the more popular vehicles of employee communications will be discussed:

1 employee publications
2 management publications
3 annual reports to the staff
4 bulletin boards
5 internal television
6 telephone hotlines
7 face-to-face meetings

EMPLOYEE PUBLICATIONS

Many years ago, the company-sponsored newspaper was considered a good way to prevent barriers between management and employees. While the format and content of the employee newspaper (or increasingly, news magazine) has changed over time, the broad concept of informing the staff through one major corporate publication has stood the test of time. Before creating such a newspaper, an organization must answer several basic questions:

1 Whom will this paper attempt to reach?
2 What kinds of articles will be featured?
3 How should each issue be budgeted?
4 What format will the paper take?
5 What should it accomplish with respect to the target readers?
6 How frequently should it be published?
7 Who in the organization should produce the publication—the public relations or personnel department?

The answers to these questions depend on what organization is doing the asking. Internal communications needs differ from one organization to the next. Figure 13-2 shows various formats chosen by different organizations. In general, papers should clearly interpret management's policies to the staff and, whenever possible, serve as a two-way communications vehicle, expressing staff concerns as well.

Traditionally, employee publications purposely overlooked news about controversial company-related issues. Instead, they included a plethora of items about management's benevolence and employees at work and play. In recent years, a hint of controversy has slowly crept into some employee publications. Also, there is little disagreement that today, the singlemost important subject to employees is job information that affects the organization and therefore themselves and their jobs.

FIGURE 13-2. *Employee publications.* Employee publications take all sizes, shapes, and formats.

Employee newspapers should appear regularly, on time, with a consistent format. Employees should expect them and look forward to them. While there is no pat formula for the types of features that interest employees, according to one employee communications specialist, the following "mix" of employee-related and organization-oriented features usually works well:[8]

Staff photographs.   People love to see themselves in the papers.

On-the-job stories.   People appreciate reading about their neighbor's job.

"How-to-do-it" case studies.   Co-workers' success stories are always interesting, especially if the reader can benefit from the experience. Case studies also aid morale.

Candid camera.   It's fun to see other people caught in the act of being themselves.

Policy-philosophy articles.   People literally crave the background of company policies and philosophies.

Educational quizzes.   People like to learn about the organization, especially if the learning process is in an interesting format, such as a quiz.

Retiree articles.   Retirees are among the most devoted publics of employee papers. Writing about them helps bolster this relationship.

Departmental features.   Written in a lively fashion, features about the activities and successes of different departments can be beneficial for organizational under-standing.

The "you" approach.   The key to writing *for* people is writing *about* people. A good internal newspaper brings the reader directly into the story. This approach enhances knowledge and appreciation of an organization, while instilling pride in the individual.

Employee publications historically have served as principal organizational entry points for public relations beginners. The total U.S. circulation of employee publications has been estimated at more than 200 million—well in excess of the total U.S. daily newspaper circulation. Therefore, job availabilities are more plentiful in the employee publications area than in most other public relations positions.

Indeed, one organization primarily devoted to internal communications, the International Association of Business Communicators (IABC), has, in a relatively short time, come to rival the much older Public Relations Society of America. With about 120 chapters throughout the U.S., Canada, and the United Kingdom, and affiliates in thirty-seven countries, the IABC sets journalistic standards for internal communicators. IABC dues are $80 annually, and the organization's various publications, seminars, and conferences keep members aware of changing concepts not only in internal communications but also in the general area of journalistic writing.[9]

MANAGEMENT PUBLICATIONS

Managerial employees must know what's going on in the organization. The company needs their support. Continual, reliable communication is a way to ensure it.

Many firms publish frequent bulletins for management as updates on personnel changes, office relocations, new telephone numbers, and revised company policies.

Occasionally, special bulletins concerning new product developments, breaking company news, or other matters of urgent interest are circulated.

More formal publications, such as management magazines, often are more technical than related employee newspapers. Additionally, these magazines often are more confidential. For example, a firm may release its corporate mission to all employees through the employee newspaper but may reveal its business profitability objectives only in the management magazine.

This element of confidentiality always is a sensitive one. Employees occasionally object that internal publications don't reveal enough pertinent details about corporate decisions and policy. One common complaint is that outside newspaper reporters "know more than we do about our own firm's activities." While such a limitation may be necessary for certain issues, those who run the organization must try to be as candid as possible with their fellow managers in particular.

Because of the very personal, vested interest of a manager in an organization, management publications are generally among the best read of any internal communication. Don't underestimate them as a way to build confidence in and credibility for top management and promote a "team spirit."

STAFF ANNUAL REPORTS

It often makes sense to print a separate annual report just for employees. Frequently, the lure of this report—published in addition to the regular corporate shareholder annual report—is that it is written for, about, and by the employees.

Most employees do care about their organization, how it functions, and what its management is thinking. The annual report to the staff is a good place to discuss these issues informally yet candidly. While the report can be both factual, explaining the performance of the organization during the year, and informational, reviewing organizational changes and significant milestones during the year, it also can be motivational in its implicit appeal to team spirit and pride.

Staff reports observe few hard-and-fast rules about concept and format. In the report shown in Figure 13-3, the main focus is what it all means to the employee. Staff annuals can be as complex as duplicating the shareholder annual report itself, or as simple as briefly outlining the highlights of the year for the company. Typical features in the staff annual report include the following:

1 **Chief Executive's Letter** A special report to the staff reviewing the performance and highlights of the year and thanking employees for their help.
2 **Uses of Funds Statement** Often a graphic chart describing how the organization used each dollar it took in.
3 **Financial Condition** Frequently a chart describing the assets, liabilities, and stockholders' equity of the corporation.
4 **Description of the Company** Simple, graphic explanation of what the organization is and where its facilities are located.
5 **Social Responsibility Highlights** Discussion of the organization's role in aiding society through monetary assistance and employee participation during the year.
6 **Staff Financial Highlights** General description, usually in chart form, of salaries, benefits, and other staff-related expense items.

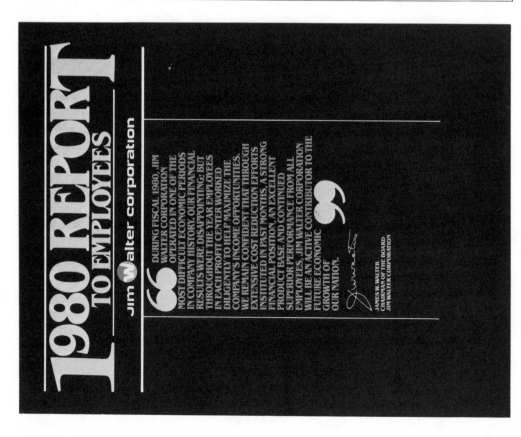

FIGURE 13–3. *Jim Walter employee annual report.* The Jim Walter Corporation is one company that regularly distributes a special annual report to employees—in good and bad times. Even when the company has a sub-par year, management commends employees for their contribution, recognizing an important tenet of employee communication, that winning the approval of the staff is the first step to winning the approval of external publics.

SOURCE: Courtesy of Jim Walter Corporation.

7 **Organizational Policy**   Discussion of current issues (perhaps related to the American enterprise system and capitalism), about which management feels strongly and for which it seeks employee support.

8 **Emphasis on People**   One general theme throughout the report should be the importance of the people who make up the organization. This theme may take the form of in-depth profiles of people on the job, comments from people about their job, and/or pictorial essays on people at work.

Employees appreciate recognition. The special annual report is a measure of recognition that does not go unnoticed—or unread—by a firm's workers.

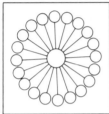

MINICASE
The Quackenbush Beacon

Quackenbush Manufacturing has fifteen plants in ten states. It is a diversified manufacturer, with 30,000 employees and one internal newspaper, *The Beacon*, to reach them.

Editor Sammy Shram prides himself on distributing *The Beacon* without fail every other Wednesday. Since *The Beacon* is the only communications vehicle that unites the entire Quackenbush staff, Shram is responsible for informing employees about company developments and management policy.

At 1:30 on the Monday afternoon before publication, Shram and his public relations colleagues are advised that the Eau Claire plant has blown up. Early reports indicate that five to ten Quackenbush employees may have been killed. Many others are injured. The fire and subsequent explosion were caused, according to rumors, by a disgruntled ex-Quackenbush employee. Only the quick thinking of plant manager Carlos Sledge, who sounded the alarm early, averted a more serious disaster.

Because *The Beacon* will be published in two days, Shram must decide quickly how to treat the Eau Claire disaster. His absolute deadline for copy is in one hour.

QUESTIONS

1 Should Shram run the story in his next edition? Why or why not?

2 If he does, how should he treat it? If he doesn't, should he report it in the edition after next?

3 If you were a reporter for the Eau Claire Daily Blat and had only the information recorded in this case study, how might your report differ from the Quackenbush Beacon's?

BULLETIN BOARDS

Bulletin boards are making a comeback—in corporations, hospitals, and other organizations. For years they were considered second-string information channels, generally relegated to the display of federally required information and policy data for such activities as fire drills and emergency procedures. Most employees rarely consulted them.

But the bulletin board has experienced a renaissance and is now being used to improve productivity, cut waste, and reduce accidents on the job. Best of all, employees are taking notice.

How come?

For one thing, yesterday's bulletin board has become today's "news center." It has been repackaged into a more lively, visual, and graphically-arresting medium. Using enlarged news pictures and texts, motivational messages (Figure 13-4), and other company announcements—all illustrated with a flair—the bulletin board has become a primary source of employee communications. Hospitals in particular have found that a strategically-situated bulletin board outside a cafeteria is a good way to "promote employee understanding and cooperation."

One key to stimulating readership is to keep boards current. One person in the public relations unit should be assigned to this weekly task.

INTERNAL TELEVISION

Recently television has emerged as a medium to reach the staff. Organizations have begun to introduce "video newspapers" to complement their publications. Television also is used extensively for employee training. Many young employees, literally reared on television, may be more inclined than other workers to accept audiovisual communications.

Internal television can be demonstrably effective. A 10-minute videotape of an executive announcing a new corporate policy imparts hundreds of times more information than an audiotape of that same message, which, in turn, contains hundreds of times more information than a printed text of the same message.[10] Organizations that use television effectively have found that the rest of their internal communications program becomes that much more effective when complemented by an integrated video system.

But internal television is not without serious dangers.

For one thing, unless in-house television is of comparable broadcast quality to commercial TV, employees may be "turned off." Because television is a very *visible* medium, the following problems typical of in-house television may scuttle any attempt to reach employees:

1 **Too Much Talk** In-house TV attempts are notorious for "talking heads"— narrators spending interminable minutes narrating without any action on the screen.

2 **Poor Scripts** Script-writing ability is a special skill, difficult to find in the typical organization.

3 **Limited Equipment and Staff** Good quality television demands keeping abreast of technological breakthroughs. Even the wealthiest organizations may

find it difficult and too expensive to try to keep up with the pace of television technology.

4   **Lack of Creativity**   Creativity in television encompasses a number of aspects, including writing, photography, editing, and production. All require special technical expertise typical firms are unlikely to have.

FIGURE 13–4.   Jim Walter bulletin board message. Sometimes the most effective and well-read bulletin board announcements carry simple messages like this.
SOURCE: Courtesy of Jim Walter Corporation.

5 **Failure to Communicate**   If extensive time and effort is put into the technical production of a TV show, the content may be overlooked. Consequently, the people in the target audience may never get the desired message.

6 **Poor Acting**   Public relations professionals, despite what their critics say, generally are not actors. Exclusively in-house casting may not suffice.

7 **Poor Voices**   In television, the voice should fit the subject, script, and audience. This task isn't easy when drawing from existing corporate talent.

8 **Poor Music**   Proper music selection requires skill as well as access to good music libraries.

9 **Poor Direction**   A good director is second in importance only to a good script.

10 **Poor Production Quality**   The sophisticated viewer (the typical employee) is aware of camera moves, lighting, picture framing, editing, sound quality, sound mixing, color, graphics, and art. If they are inferior, the viewer won't be convinced.

11 **Program Length**   Most corporate video directors tend to make programs too long. Any program over twelve minutes may not sustain audience attention.[11]

In addition to insufficient competence and resources, in-house video can also be plagued by poor public relations planning. The key to effective in-house TV is first to examine internal needs, then to plan thoughtfully *before* using the medium, and finally to reach target publics through the most sophisticated and high-quality programming available. If the organization cannot afford high-quality video, it simply should not get involved.

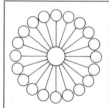

MINICASE
The Bilgewater breakthrough

For twenty years, the *Bilgewater Bugle* has served the faculty of Bilgewater College. The *Bugle* reports regular employee newspaper fare, including research grants, personnel changes, and employee features.

While Bilgewater's public information office has not surveyed faculty opinions about the *Bugle* for some time, director Chico Chesterton feels it's time for a change.

"Television," according to Chesterton, "is the name of the game these days. What we really need is a video house organ to complement the *Bugle*, for faculty and students."

In setting out to convince the college president, Chesterton posits the following:

1 Since students spend more time watching television than they do reading, TV is an excellent way to inform them about the school's policies and programs.

TELEPHONE HOTLINES

The telephone also is receiving wider recognition as a way to reach employees with information.

At The Chase Manhattan Bank, employees are encouraged to call a "telephone hotline" recording that updates the staff each day on news of interest. The Chase hotline provides commuter information, breaking news about earnings announcements, interest rate moves, and management changes.

Another bank, Suburban Trust Company of Hyattsville, Maryland, has introduced a *two-way* telephone hotline. This system, called *Inter-Com,* allows employees to pose job-related questions to public relations representatives. All calls are kept confidential. If an issue requires the knowledge of the caller's supervisor, the employee must first give permission before the supervisor can be contacted.

Understandably, Inter-Com was not an overnight sensation. Initially, employees were wary. Gradually though, as the program lived up to its promise of confidentiality and concern for employee problems, Inter-Com's reputation grew. A key to the program's success was the senior management support it received. As the program's manager put it, "Many of the employee concerns that Inter-Com handles are situations that management would prefer not to deal with. Inter-Com forces decisions. There are occasions when decisions go against the employee, but it is recognized that management should become involved. That involvement may be just as important as the final decision.[12]

The real appeal of two-way hotlines is that they provide immediate feedback. Many companies, Bank of America and IBM among them, have initiated "open line" programs similar to Inter-Com.

---

2 TV monitors can be situated throughout student and faculty lounges, so in-house television may be continuously broadcast during the lunch hour. This way, normal class time need not be disturbed.

3 Students and faculty might be quite willing to watch the lunchtime TV shows as they relax before or after they have eaten or following their normal shopping and browsing time at the numerous stores in the area.

4 People will like seeing their fellow students and teachers in the roles of television personalities.

5 Students will appreciate having a choice between the daily feature films shown in the student union and the in-house TV shows shown in the lounge.

6 The constant broadcast of in-house television may help motivate those who normally sleep in the lounge during their lunch period.

7 By seeing faculty and administration in interviews on the screen at lunchtime, students and teachers will feel closer to and more a part of the college team.

QUESTION
Where does Chico's reasoning fall down?

FACE-TO-FACE MEETINGS

For good staff-management relations, many organizations have concluded that there is no substitute for face-to-face meetings.

Some firms formalize the meeting process by mixing management and staff in a variety of formats, from gripe sessions to marketing/planning meetings. In many organizations, the concept of "two-down" and "three-down" skip level meetings is a popular and productive form of communication. In these, top-level managers meet periodically with employees at levels several notches below them in the organizational hierarchy. Such sessions introduce people who rarely get the opportunity to communicate with each other and often result in productive new ideas and associations that ultimately benefit the firm.

Just as with any other form of communication, the value of meetings lies in their regularity and substance. Meetings held only occasionally will not be as productive as meetings scheduled periodically to realize target communication objectives.

One such successful program is the quarterly, two-way, two-hour Management Open Forum of Cedars-Sinai Medical Center in Los Angeles, a 1,000 bed, 5,000 employee urban facility. This program is designed as a top-of-the-head question and answer session for middle managers. In each get-together, about 15 percent of the hospital's more than 500 managers—department heads are excluded—are encouraged to ask questions of top hospital staff members. Questions are rarely mild and answers generally tell managers why the hospital chooses to take certain actions. The meetings, according to the internal communications manager who runs them, are not only effective but inexpensive to boot.[13]

OTHER METHODS

Several other employee communications methods are available, including the following:

Open houses. An open house gives relatives, friends, and neighbors an opportunity to see the workplace firsthand. Often, industrial firms hold "family nights" at plant locations. These events must be carefully planned and thoroughly organized; committees should be assigned to coordinate such areas as invitations, souvenirs, exhibits, and refreshments.

Management media summaries. In order for management to keep aware of what the media are saying about the organization, regular media summaries can be compiled and distributed. For example, the 3M Company delivers its "News Scanner" service to top management by 10 A.M. daily. The United Technologies Company, in addition to distributing a "Morning News Summary," also posts "Noon News Briefs" in its executive dining room. At Mobil, an elaborate system of newswires, videotape recorders, and press clipping monitors keeps corporate management aware of virtually any item concerning the energy industry or the company.

Employee activities. Many organizations sponsor special after-hours employee activities (subsidized sports, picnics, cultural affairs) to promote employee morale. Workers appreciate these activities; however, organizations should be sensitive about appearing paternalistic in these kinds of sponsorships.

Management-employee task forces.   An off-shoot of face-to-face meetings is the formation of task forces composed of managers and subordinates from throughout the organization. These task forces, charged with such responsibilities as keeping the premises clean, organizing emergency plans, and keeping the company ethical also have an ancillary objective—to enhance employee communications (see Figure 13-5).

BATTLING THE GRAPEVINE

One nemesis of good employee communications is the grapevine. In most organizations, the rumor mill can be devastating. As one employee publication described the grapevine:

> It's faster than a public address announcement and more powerful than a general instruction. It's able to leap from L.A. to San Francisco in a single bound. And its credibility is almost beyond Walter Cronkite.

Rumors, once they pick up steam, are difficult to stop. An organization must work to correct rumors as soon as possible, because employees tend to distort future events to conform to the rumor.

Here's how you can speak up.

Of all the people who will become involved in the Chemical Facts of Life program, none are more important than the 62,000 Monsanto employes and their families.

Starting with our Chairman and President, Monsanto executives already are speaking to nationally prominent groups about the Chemical Facts of Life.

This "Speak Out" portion of the program will be expanded until we have a huge cadre of Monsanto employes giving speeches at every level ranging from civic clubs in the smallest plant community, to major conventions and meetings of national groups.

The task of informing local, state and national lawmakers and regulators will receive special emphasis through intensified activities in our Washington office and a companywide "Grass Roots" program designed to reach legislators on a one-to-one basis.

But most important of all is your role. The role of the employe. We want you to participate in the program. We suggest you take the following steps.

1. Learn the chemical facts.

Over the next several months, we'll provide you with a continuing flow of information through plant newspapers, Chemical Fact Bulletins and in other ways.

(The Chemical Facts of Life booklet itself contains a wealth of material to support intelligent conversation about chemicals and their usage.)

2. Speak out when the opportunity arises.

Several times a day, each of us has an opportunity to speak out on behalf of our industry, our company and our products. To neighbors, relatives, friends, business associates, customers, suppliers.

And even to store clerks, bank tellers, taxi drivers. To anyone we may come in contact with.

3. Send us your comments.

This is not a one-way program. We want your comments, suggestions and advice.

Do you have any thoughts about other ways to tell our message to the country and the world?

Would you like extra materials to distribute among your non-Monsanto associates?

Would you like to participate in a speaker's bureau? Does your civic club or church group need a speaker?

The "Chemical Facts of Life" committee would like to hear from you.

> If you would like to get involved in any way, or if you have any comments, please drop a note to Chemical Facts of Life, Dept. A3NB, Monsanto, 800 N. Lindbergh Blvd., St. Louis, Missouri 63166.

© Monsanto Company 1977

FIGURE 13-5. *Monsanto's Speak Out Program.* This excerpt from a Monsanto Company employee booklet shows the importance of internal communication to achieve an external purpose. Monsanto sought to enlist the aid of its 62,000 employees around the world to "speak out" about the benefits of chemicals in society.

SOURCE: Courtesy of Monsanto.

Identifying the source of a rumor often is difficult if not impossible. Also, it's usually not worth the time. However, dispelling the rumor quickly and frankly is another story. Often a "bad news" rumor—about layoffs, closings, etc.—can be most effectively dealt with through forthright communication. Generally an organization makes a decision after a thorough review of many alternatives. The final decision is often a compromise, reflecting the needs of the firm and its various publics, including, importantly, the work force. Yet, in presenting a final decision to employees, management often overlooks the value of explaining *how* it reached its decision. By comparing alternative solutions so that employees can more clearly understand the rationale of management decisions, an organization may make the bad news more palatable.[14]

Again, the best defense against damaging rumors is a strong and candid communications system. Historically, the function of internal communications has bounced like a billiard ball between the provinces of public relations and personnel. Where the function resides is much less important than the role internal communications plays. If employee communicators are competent and if management stands wholeheartedly in support of their efforts, the culture of an organization will likely be a positive and productive ingredient in the firm's performance.

FEATURE

Plucking ripe fruit from the corporate grapevine

One of the most unique responses to the corporate rumor mill is that of Sun Co. in Radnor, Pennsylvania. *Sun News*, you see, has a columnist whose subject matter is the corporate grapevine.

Columnist Robert Finucane, in fact, will tackle just about any sacred cow in print—from corporate nepotism to the company's system for determining employee salaries.

In one column, Finucane wrote about certain Sun middle managers "who would rather die than say yes or no or anything."

In another column around Halloween, Finucane advised readers to "go trick-or-treating dressed as a five-year plan. All you need is a costume thrown together at the last minute with a lot of holes in it." The Sun planning department wasn't pleased by that one.

Evidently, the grapevine columnist generally gets good reviews from his superiors. Says Sun's chief executive, "Bob doesn't get nasty, doesn't get mean, and I never get the indication that he's using [his] freedom to take a whack at anyone." Adds another senior manager about Finucane, he "obviously has to walk at times at the edge of disrespect and disloyalty—and he manages to do it."

As to the possible effect on the company itself from the meanderings of its internal gadfly, summarized Harold Burson, chairman of New York's Burson-Marsteller public relations firm, "If it is done with taste, with a light enough touch, it could serve to humanize the company to its employees."[15]

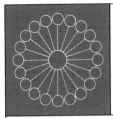

CASE STUDY
Much ado about Mary

nternal gossip and rumors can be devastating to any organization. But rarely in the history of corporate America have internal rumors proved as destructive as the ones that led to the resignation of a promising, young, woman executive from the Bendix Corp. in the fall of 1980.

The saga went like this.

Mary Cunningham, her degree from the Harvard Business School freshly in hand, joined Bendix in June 1979 as executive assistant to the company's chairman, William M. Agee. Prior to entering Harvard, Cunningham had served as a junior officer of The Chase Manhattan Bank for three years.

Agee, himself, was known as something of a corporate maverick. Only in his early 40s—young for a major company CEO—Agee rose swiftly to the top by shaking things up at Bendix through acquisitions, personnel changes, and assorted bold business strokes.

A year after she joined Bendix, Mary Cunningham was promoted to vice president for corporate and public affairs. Although she had no experience in the communications field and the move was roundly criticized by public relations professionals, Agee stuck by the decision.

Inside the company, gossip about the "special relationship" between Cunningham and Agee began to circulate after her promotion. Insiders pointed to a number of public signs that the relationship might be more than strictly a business one. For example:

○ A television camera focused on former President Gerald Ford at the 1980 Republican National Convention in Detroit happened to find Agee and Cunningham sitting next to him.

○ Some Bendix people suggested that Agee was less accessible than he had once been, and Cunningham's growing influence with him did not help to allay suspicions.

○ In August 1980, Agee and his wife of 23 years got a divorce so quickly that it surprised even top officials at Bendix.

In light of the fact that Cunningham, a single woman, and Agee, a newly-divorced man, were so close, it wasn't long before the Agee-Cunningham relationship became the major topic of conversation in the corridors of Bendix.

In September 1980, Agee suddenly fired his chief operating officer and in the wake of that firing, the executive vice president for strategic planning also resigned. Almost immediately, Agee appointed Cunningham as new Bendix vice president for strategic planning—just fifteen months after she graduated from Harvard Business School.

Said Chairman Agee about his new strategic planning director, "She has been my right and left arm ever since she came into the company. She is the most vital and important person within the company and has played an important part in conceptualizing the strategy."

Agee also appeared before the executive committee of the Bendix board to personally refute the rumors about a romantic involvement between himself and Cunningham. Cunningham also appeared at the meeting and offered to resign. But she argued that doing so would appear to corroborate the rumors and set the terrible precedent that, as Fortune Magazine put it, "Rumors can dictate policy." The board did not push for her resignation.

Fortunately for all concerned, the media generally had not yet noticed the rumored Agee-Cunningham relationship.

But then, the Bendix chairman went a tad too far.

At a meeting in late September before more than 600 Bendix employees, Agee acknowledged the rumors about himself and Cunningham. He staunchly defended his strategic planning director on the basis of her qualifications. And he vigorously denied that her advancement had anything to do with "a personal relationship that we have."

Agee apparently believed that a public discussion of the matter would once and for all clear the air. He was wrong.

His comments to the employees set off an avalanche of press coverage, and Mary Cunningham literally became a household word across America. As Fortune put it, "Top corporate executives in the U.S. have been accused of almost everything imaginable except having romances with one another." Predictably, in late October 1980, Mary Cunningham resigned from Bendix.

As for Agee, he said he had learned some valuable lessons from the Cunningham flap, the most salient of which was the old Henry Ford II bromide, "Never complain, never explain." Agee added that he did not believe there would be any long-term, lingering negative impact on Bendix.

Nonetheless, two years later when Bendix attempted to acquire the huge Martin Marietta Corp., the Bendix chairman was again publicly criticized for taking along with him to Bendix-Martin merger discussions his wife of just a few weeks, the former Mary Cunningham.

Summarized one Bendix operating executive as the company got battered in the swirl of rumors surrounding Agee and Cunningham, "It's not like dealing with spark plugs."[16]

QUESTIONS

1 Was it wise for Agee to confront the Bendix executive committee of the board on the Cunningham rumors?

2 Was it wise for him to discuss the Cunningham relationship at the meeting of employees?

3 If Agee had said nothing about the Cunningham situation at the employee's meeting, what might have been the result?

4 Based on this case, do you think "going public" to nip a budding rumor is always the best policy?

5 Had you been Agee's public relations counselor in the midst of the Cunningham controversy, what public stance would you have recommended the company adopt?

NOTES

1 Charles S. Steinberg, "Where Good PR Begins," *Public Relations Journal*, September 1976.

2 Richard W. Darrow, "Employee Communications—Neglected Need," *The New York Times*, 28 December 1975.

3 Roy G. Foltz, "Learning to Speak With One Voice," *Public Relations Journal*, July 1982, pp. 30–31.

4 Roger M. D'Aprix, "The Human Corporation," speech delivered to the Southeast District Conference of the Public Relations Society of America, 8–10 February 1978.

5 Roy G. Foltz, "Credibility: Its Erosion," *The Personnel Administrator*, September 1976, p. 16.

6 "Credibility—The Most Important Ingredient in Communications," *Editor's Newsletter*, January 1978.

7 Ronald Goodman and Richard S. Ruch, "The Role of Research in Internal Communication," *Public Relations Journal*, July 1982, p. 19.

8 Interview with Robert S. Cole, East Coast Public Relations Manager, Bank of America, 5 September 1978.

9 For further information about the International Association of Business Communicators, write IABC, 807 Market Street, Suite 940, San Francisco, Cal. 94102.

10 Douglas P. Brush, "Internal Communications and the New Technology," *Public Relations Journal*, February 1981, pp. 10–11.

11 Jack Moss, "20 Things Wrong with In-Plant AV," *Photo Methods for Industry*, October 1973.

12 "Two-Way Communications Identifies and Solves Problems," *Editor's Newsletter*, June 1978, p. 2.

13 Andrea Platt Hecht, "How to Bring Middle Management Into the Communication Process," *Public Relations Journal*, October 1981, p. 16.

14 "Communicating Bad News," *Kwashe Lipton Newsletter*, Vol. 15, No. 3, July 1982.

15 Erik Larson, "Corporate Grapevine Produces Ripe Fruit for Robert Finucane," *The Wall Street Journal*, 18 March 1981, pp. 1–20.

16 This case was excerpted largely from Peter W. Bernstein, "Upheaval at Bendix," *Fortune*, 3 November 1980, pp. 48–56.

SUGGESTED READING

Allen, Fred T. "Ways to Improve Employee Communications," *Nation's Business*, September 1975, pp. 54–56.

Anderson, Howard J. *Primer of Labor Relations*. Washington, D.C.: Bureau of National Affairs, 1975.

Anderson, Walter, *Handbook of Business Communications*. (Available from Box 243, Lenox Hill Station, New York, N.Y. 10021).

Blewett, Steve. "On Being A Pro: A House Organ Editor Speaks," *Public Relations Quarterly*, Summer 1981, pp. 9–10.

Blicq, R. *On the Move: Communication for Employees*. Englewood Cliffs, N.J.: Prentice-Hall, 1975.

Bormann, Ernest G., and **Howell, William S.** *Interpersonal Communication in the Modern Organization.* Englewood Cliffs, N.J.: Prentice-Hall, 1969.

Brennan, John F. Jr., *The Conscious Communicator: Making Communications Work in the Work Place.* Reading, Mass.: Addison-Wesley, 1975.

Erb, Lyle L. "There's A Moral Here Somewhere," *Public Relations Quarterly.* Winter 1981–82, pp. 23–24.

Foltz, Roy G. *Management by Communication.* New York: Chilton, 1973.

Foulkes, Fred K. "The Expanding Role of the Personnel Function." *Harvard Business Review,* 53, no. 2 (March-April 1975):71–84.

Gitter, A. George. "Public Relations Roles: Press Agent or Counselor?" *Public Relations Review,* Fall 1981, pp. 35–41.

Hogan, Patricia. "A Woman Is Not a Girl and Other Lessons in Corporate Speech." *Business & Society Review,* no. 14 (Summer 1975), pp. 34–38.

McGregor, Douglas. *The Human Side of Enterprise.* New York: McGraw-Hill, 1960.

Preston Publishing. *How to Communicate within the Organization.* New York: Author, 1969.

Seiler, Roger and **Enzer, Michael J.** "How to Select and Use Motivational Films," *Public Relations Journal,* July 1981, p. 26.

Walters, Kenneth D. "Your Employees' Right to Blow the Whistle," *Harvard Business Review,* 52, no. 4 (July-August 1975):25–35.

DEALING WITH THE MEDIA

14
Media

The media *are* (not is!) the public most associated with public relations work. Most people, in fact, believe that the term public relations is synonomous with *publicity*. It isn't. But few people are able to distinguish between securing favorable publicity for an organization and winning positive public relations.

Without question, publicity is a critical activity for most public relations professionals. Indeed, Chapter 15 will be devoted to a comprehensive discussion of publicity in all its aspects. The focus of this chapter will be the broader area of media relations.

A good working relationship with the media is imperative for any successful communications program. Dealing with the media has traditionally been a primary responsibility for public relations practitioners. Media relations, in fact, has developed into a career specialty for many in the field.

Ours is a mass-media society, where learning and knowledge come from newspapers, television, radio, magazines, books, and films. To the traditional means of transmitting information (the classroom, pulpit, lecture hall, and face-to-face) have been added such devices as satellite communication networks, computerized printing technology, and even two-way cable television.

In our society, the media play a major role in shaping opinions, values, and knowledge. Indeed, if an item isn't in the news, it may as well have never happened. If it makes page one, it not only happened but also is important. If it makes page forty, it may have happened, but isn't terribly important. Or so we think.

The mass media also greatly influence today's issues. When they zero in on a particular individual or institution, the results can be devastating. Recent U.S. history is studded with examples of people and agencies whose power and influence have been cut short as a result of their attracting extensive, critical media attention.

Presidential appointments in recent years have been particularly vulnerable:

○ In 1980, President Reagan's choice of Ernest Lefever to become the State Department's human rights executive was publicly chastised, when the media learned that Lefever's Ethics and Public Policy Center had received funding from the Nestle Company in connection with its controversial role in promoting infant formula in lesser developed countries. The media hue and cry against Lefever was so furious that the nominee sadly removed himself from consideration for the State Department job.

Later in the Reagan Administration, the President's trusted aide, Joseph Canzeri, also had to resign after the media dug up several old loans Canzeri had received at favorable rates from his former employer, Laurence Rockefeller.

○ Nor was President Carter's Administration immune from media attack. After newspaper reports revealed questionable personal financial dealings by Bert Lance prior to his being selected by President Carter as the nation's director of the Office of Management and the Budget, the Georgia banker went before the Congress and a national television audience to deny the various allegations. Shortly after his testimony, he resigned from the Administration and ultimately faced criminal charges.

○ President Carter's chief drug advisor, Dr. Peter Bourne, also resigned after newspaper stories revealed first that Bourne had written a false prescription for an employee and later that he had occasionally smoked marijuana.

○ During President Ford's Administration, Secretary of Agriculture Earl Butz resigned when a magazine revealed a tasteless racial joke that Butz had recounted "in confidence" to a reporter aboard an airplane.

The vigilance of the media in exposing fraud, deception, and questionable practices in society is traditional. During the late 1940s, in one of the most celebrated and tragic examples, columnists Drew Pearson and Walter Winchell attacked the nation's first Secretary of Defense, James Forrestal. These attacks contributed to Forrestal's eventual physical and mental breakdown and ultimate resignation. He was hospitalized after leaving office, and in 1949, he jumped to his death from the sixteenth floor of Bethesda Naval Hospital.[1]

The media's crowning achievement in recent years was its exposure of the Watergate break-in, which eventually led to the resignation of President Nixon. The success of the *Washington Post* in getting to the bottom of Watergate triggered an immediate reaction, throughout journalism, to focus on abuses of power in all areas of society. Regrettably, this focus on abuse itself led to abuses by some journalists. Even Carl Bernstein, one-half of the *Post* Woodward-Bernstein Watergate reporting team, concluded that, "Post-Watergate has been marked by the elevation of gossip and celebrity journalism."[2]

Ships that didn't pass in the night

Remember a few years back when the big news turned out to be no news? We saw stories about mysterious ships alleged to be lurking offshore awaiting an increase in oil prices—phantom tankers that no one, not even the Coast Guard, could ever find.

Maybe the media's enlightenment over these specious articles did some good—because nowadays we encounter far fewer energy stories based on phantom facts. Energy reporting has been gaining stature—more depth, more expertise, more sophistication—and one result is a public that's much better informed on energy issues. And we're a lot less upset by what we read about our business.

We've tried to keep up our own record of being forthright and forthcoming when a story involved Mobil—or, for that matter, any energy subject on which our information and insights are sought. We try to tell it like it is. Factually.

And let the ships fall where they may.

Mobil®

FIGURE 14–1. *Mobil Media Ad.* The oil companies have had their share of problems with investigative reporting. However, as this Mobil ad demonstrates, when the oil giants believe the media have learned from past mistakes, they occasionally duly acknowledge.

SOURCE: Courtesy of Mobil Corporation.

Edwin L. Dale, Jr. is Assistant Director for Public Affairs of the United States Office of Management and Budget. For twenty-one years, Mr. Dale was a reporter for *The New York Times,* serving both as an economic correspondent and news reporter in the Washington Bureau and as European economic correspondent in Paris. From 1951 to 1955, Mr. Dale was an economic news reporter in the Washington Bureau of *The New York Herald Tribune.* From 1977 to 1981, Mr. Dale served on the professional staff of the House of Representatives, Subcommittee on Economic Stabilization of the Committee on Banking, Finance and Urban Affairs. He is author of *Conservatives in Power,* published in 1960 by Doubleday, and has written numerous magazine articles in such publications as *Harper's, New York Times Magazine, The New Republic,* and *London Economist.*

What's the consensus attitude of journalists toward public relations people?

Well, I don't think there is any such thing as a consensus. The range of opinion I am sure is quite wide. My view would be that first and often forgotten, public relations people, whether in industry or in the government, are essential—they have to be there—for two reasons. One, as the issuer of formal announcements. And second, as the channel or conduit to higher officials. If that post did not exist, there would be a much more chaotic situation. Therefore, I think that if the public relations position did not exist, whether in a government agency or in business and finance, it would have to be invented.

What do journalists like least about public relations people?

It varies entirely with the quality of the individual. I think the qualities that would most

Nowhere has investigative reporting taken off so dramatically as on "the tube." By the early 1980s, investigative reporting gained a solid foothold in television news. This, too, was not without significant problems. Said Dan Rather about the investigative program that helped land him the top anchor position at CBS News, "On '60 Minutes,' we make mistakes so often, violating the basics of accuracy, clarity or fairness, that sometimes it shatters me. If with our budget and our staff and time, we

turn journalists off, in order, would be, first, untrustworthiness. If public relations people are ever caught lying or half-lying to make their organization look better, they simply are not trusted from then on. Number two, I think, would be lack of knowledge, lack of sophistication about the field that they are supposed to be covering. That would of course vary widely among public relations people; that is, their qualities would vary widely. And, number three, I suppose would be laziness, unwillingness to return calls, and failure to follow through on things that they have pledged to do.

Has your attitude about public relations changed since you switched sides?

No.

Do you think a reporter can ever attain "objectivity"?

Perfect objectivity, no. I think those who set out with their own objective, their own goal to attain as close to objectivity as possible, can come pretty close. The problem arises with journalists who don't really want to be objective, but want to sell a point of view. Those, and they are the majority, who try to attain objectivity I think come quite close. I believe the problem with the press is less the minority who genuinely slant the news to reflect their own point of view than it is the competitive pressures that lead reporters to over-hype and exaggerate stories.

What's the proper role of a spokesperson?

It is to convey as quickly and efficiently as possible the attitude and official pronouncements of his agency or his business and, within boundaries set by his own superiors,

to elaborate on and explain the announcement.

What are the primary responsibilities of the public information director of a government agency?

I think they vary. In the case of some agencies and some public affairs directors, the job is seen as one of selling, promoting a point of view, which is an entirely valid exercise.

This means doing everything from drawing up film slide shows, preparing promotional types of press releases, and the like. The other and completely different version, and I think it's the most important function, is to react to queries, legitimate queries from the press in its broadest sense, including radio and television, and to get the information out accurately, rather than trying to promote a point of view.

Have you observed an improvement in the journalist-public relations person relationship?

I would say the relationship as I have known it, which is now about thirty years worth, has been pretty constant. I don't personally detect any change.

How does a public relations person convince a journalist to treat her organization "fairly"?

I don't know. The best thing I can think of is to tell the truth, to tell all that you are permitted to tell and hope for the best. I don't know any way of convincing, particularly with a journalist who starts with the presumption that a government or a business is evil, or bad. If they start with that presumption then there is very little you can do to change it.

make so many mistakes in exposé material, what's it like under less luxurious circumstances?"[3]

Whether a positive or negative development—or, as is more likely the case, a combination of the two—the emergence of investigative reporting has placed added pressure on public relations practitioners, who, as the primary voice of management, seek honest, fair, and accurate treatment of their organizations in the media.

"OBJECTIVITY" IN THE MEDIA

Total objectivity in reporting is unattainable because it would require complete neutrality and almost total detachment in reporting a story. Most people start with biases and preconceived notions about almost any subject. Reporting, then, is very subjective. Nevertheless, scholars of journalism believe that reporters and editors should strive for maximum objectivity.

After the turn of the century, when muckrakers exposed the questionable practices of the "public-be-damned" capitalistic entrepreneurs, American journalism was dominated by reporters seeking to learn the answers to six key questions: who, what, where, when, why, and how.

After World War I, reporters became more interpretive. Led by the examples of the *New York Herald Tribune* newspaper and *The New Yorker* magazine, reporters embellished stories by going beyond the official viewpoint, interviewing participants in a news event as well as spectators.

After World War II, another reporting refinement began to develop: *advocacy journalism.* Advocacy journalists tended to take sides and support causes in reporting.

By the 1960s, journalists—both reporters and columnists—enlarged the advocacy concept to become more investigative. They sought more depth and meaning in their reporting. Occasionally, they didn't investigate thoroughly enough.

For example, reports that Vice-Presidential candidate Senator Tom Eagleton had been arrested for drunken driving helped remove him from the 1972 ticket. After the candidate had been discredited, columnist Jack Anderson admitted that the story he had initiated was based on questionable information.

In another example, in the early 1970s, when an uprising at New York State's Attica Prison took the lives of several people, journalists didn't question the claim of corrections officials that prisoners had slashed the throats of the hostages. Autopsies revealed that no throats had been slashed and that official versions of what happened were false and misleading.

By the 1970s, yet another form of journalism had begun to develop, so-called *new journalism.* In approaching a story, new journalists secured all the facts that conventional reporters got, but kept going, saturating the story with dialogue, facial expressions, setting details, gestures, habits, manners, and behavioral patterns, hoping to paint scenic pictures for readers. Additionally, this style frequently took liberties in order to juxtapose time sequences and protect actual identities. It was slow to catch on and seemed restricted to pace-setting publications *(New York Magazine, Rolling Stone, Esquire)* as well as campus newspapers. Although it had less application to general newspaper reporting,[4] some of the leading practitioners of new journalism—Jimmy Breslin, Gay Talese, and Pete Hamill, for example—all started by using the form in newspaper writing.

In the early 1980s, new journalism was clobbered by two particularly embarrassing incidents. In one, *New York Daily News* columnist Michael Daly was found to have fabricated a column purporting to be an interview with a woman whose son had been murdered in Ireland. Daly was promptly fired. The other incident was an even more celebrated and more embarrassing case. *Washington Post* reporter Janet Cooke was awarded journalism's highest honor, the Pulitzer Prize, for a front-page story about an eight-year-old heroin addict. As was later revealed, Cooke's searing story lacked only one ingredient—truth. It was, in fact, all a lie created by the fertile imagination of the reporter and slipped by red-faced *Washington Post* editors. Cooke was summarily stripped of her Pulitzer and fired from the *Post.* But the damage was done. By the mid-80s then, while journalists still frequently interpreted what they observed—so-called "trust me" journalism—they also exhibited a renewed sense of the importance of reporting the "true facts."

In general, the who, what, why, where, and when approach to reporting still dominates American journalism. Reporters are interested in learning the "truth" about an issue. Often, finding out requires a high degree of subjective judgment. Thus, if an organization expects fair treatment in print or on the air, the statements of its practitioner must always hold up when subject by the media to a "test of truth." Figure 14-2 describes a journalists' creed.

FEATURE
Turning the cameras on "open Mike"

No investigative journalist has gained as feared a reputation for catching subjects off guard as television reporter Mike Wallace of CBS-TV's "60 Minutes." Indeed public relations professionals live in dread of the day that "Mike Wallace appears at your door."

That's why in January of 1982, many public relations practitioners may have felt a bit more chipper than usual when they read that Mike Wallace had been caught at his own game.

The story started when Wallace took his "60 Minutes" crew to San Diego's Federal Savings and Loan Company to interview a vice president on the plight of low-income Californians—most either Black or Latin with minimal reading skills—who faced foreclosures after signing contracts for expensive air conditioners without realizing their houses served as collateral. As a precondition of the interview, San Diego Federal insisted on filming the proceedings for its own use.

During a break in the filming, with the CBS camera off but the San Diego Federal

camera still rolling, Wallace commented on the complex lien-sale bank contracts.

"You bet your *****they are hard to read," he said, "if you're reading them over the watermelon or over the tacos!" Whereupon, according to observers, Mike began to laugh uproariously. But not for long.

A few weeks later, Wallace learned that the San Diego Federal crew had videotaped his off-hand remark, and he and CBS tried desperately to retrieve the offensive tape from the bank.

They failed, and the story received nationwide coverage. Later, Wallace called the retrieval idea a "lame one" and he and CBS apologized for the racially disparaging remark.

Ironically, during a prior "60 Minutes" show about the behind-the-scenes workings of the broadcast, Wallace was asked how he would feel if a hidden camera one day captured some embarrassing material about him. "I wouldn't like it," he replied.

He was right.

THE JOURNALIST'S Creed

I believe IN THE PROFESSION OF

JOURNALISM.

I BELIEVE THAT THE PUBLIC JOURNAL IS A PUBLIC TRUST; THAT ALL CONNECTED WITH IT ARE, TO THE FULL MEASURE OF THEIR RESPONSIBILITY, TRUSTEES FOR THE PUBLIC; THAT ACCEPTANCE OF A LESSER SERVICE THAN THE PUBLIC SERVICE IS BETRAYAL OF THIS TRUST.

I BELIEVE THAT CLEAR THINKING AND CLEAR STATEMENT, AC-CURACY, AND FAIRNESS ARE FUNDAMENTAL TO GOOD JOUR-NALISM.

I BELIEVE THAT A JOURNALIST SHOULD WRITE ONLY WHAT HE HOLDS IN HIS HEART TO BE TRUE.

I BELIEVE THAT SUPPRESSION OF THE NEWS, FOR ANY CONSIDER-ATION OTHER THAN THE WELFARE OF SOCIETY, IS INDEFENSIBLE.

I BELIEVE THAT NO ONE SHOULD WRITE AS A JOURNALIST WHAT HE WOULD NOT SAY AS A GENTLEMAN; THAT BRIBERY BY ONE'S OWN POCKETBOOK IS AS MUCH TO BE AVOIDED AS BRIBERY BY THE POCKETBOOK OF ANOTHER; THAT INDIVIDUAL RESPONSIBIL-ITY MAY NOT BE ESCAPED BY PLEADING ANOTHER'S INSTRUC-TIONS OR ANOTHER'S DIVIDENDS.

I BELIEVE THAT ADVERTISING, NEWS AND EDITORIAL COLUMNS SHOULD ALIKE SERVE THE BEST INTERESTS OF READERS; THAT A SINGLE STANDARD OF HELPFUL TRUTH AND CLEANNESS SHOULD PREVAIL FOR ALL; THAT THE SUPREME TEST OF GOOD JOURNAL-ISM IS THE MEASURE OF ITS PUBLIC SERVICE.

I BELIEVE THAT THE JOURNALISM WHICH SUCCEEDS BEST—AND BEST DESERVES SUCCESS—FEARS GOD AND HONORS MAN; IS STOUTLY INDEPENDENT, UNMOVED BY PRIDE OF OPINION OR GREED OF POWER, CONSTRUCTIVE, TOLERANT BUT NEVER CARE-LESS, SELF-CONTROLLED, PATIENT, ALWAYS RESPECTFUL OF ITS READERS BUT ALWAYS UNAFRAID, IS QUICKLY INDIGNANT AT IN-JUSTICE; IS UNSWAYED BY THE APPEAL OF PRIVILEGE OR THE CLAMOR OF THE MOB; SEEKS TO GIVE EVERY MAN A CHANCE, AND, AS FAR AS LAW AND HONEST WAGE AND RECOGNITION OF HUMAN BROTHERHOOD CAN MAKE IT SO, AN EQUAL CHANCE; IS PROFOUNDLY PATRIOTIC WHILE SINCERELY PROMOTING IN-TERNATIONAL GOOD WILL AND CEMENTING WORLD-COMRADE-SHIP; IS A JOURNALISM OF HUMANITY, OF AND FOR TODAY'S WORLD.

Walter Williams

DEAN SCHOOL OF JOURNALISM, UNIVERSITY OF MISSOURI, 1908-1935

FIGURE 14–2. *The Journalist's Creed.* This creed was coined after World War I by Dr. Walter Williams, dean of the School of Journalism at the University of Missouri.

SOURCE: Courtesy of University of Missouri School of Journalism.

MEDIA'S VIEW OF OFFICIALDOM

By definition, the media view officials, particularly business and government spokespeople, with a degree of skepticism. Reporters shouldn't be expected to accept on faith "the party line." By the same token, once a business or government official effectively substantiates the official view and demonstrates its merit, the media should be willing to report this accurately without editorial distortion.

Stated another way, the media-business/government relationship should be one of healthy adversaries rather than bitter enemies. Alas, this occasionally is not the case. Journalist Edith Efron has said, referring to the relationship between business and the media, "The antagonism to capitalism on the nation's airwaves, the deeply entrenched prejudice in favor of state control over the productive machinery of a nation, is not subjective assessment. It is a hard cultural fact."[5]

Indeed, some journalists tend to look at government, business, and all forms of authority as "the enemy." Fortunately, such journalists are in the minority. Most want to get the facts from all sides. They acknowledge and respect the practitioner's role in the process. If they are dealt with fairly, they will reciprocate in kind.

Some executives fail to understand that there is an essential difference between the media and their own organizations. This variance, as described by former journalist and presidential press secretary Ron Nessen, is that "The reporter wants to get all the information he can and interpret it as he sees fit while the people in organizations he covers want things to be presented in the best light."[6] Because of this difference, some managements consider journalists to be adversaries, and they fear and distrust the media.

Thoughtful journalists, of course, abhor the "enemy" tag. They implore officials in business and government to continue to talk to the media, to explain complex issues so that the public might better understand them. According to Lewis H. Young, editor-in-chief of *Business Week* magazine, "The chief executive officer has to learn to be comfortable with the press. And the only way to be comfortable with the press is to get to meet media people, to talk to them, to go out for lunch with them, go out to dinner with them, and to get used to the kinds of things that they're going to ask about, what they're interested in."[7]

Based on the deep-seated distrust that some business and government people reserve for the media, Young's wish is no easy task.

OFFICIALDOM'S VIEW OF THE MEDIA

In the early 1980s, the pervasive fear and distrust of the news media among executives, particularly among those in business, diminished just a bit.

In one 1981 study, some 71 percent of executives polled considered themselves "usually accessible to the media." However, some 73 percent of those polled believed that "fewer than half the reporters understand the subject they are writing about."[8]

In another study of top communications officers of 1,300 large corporations, the broad majority said that senior executives were actively participating in news interviews and that, in general, corporate spokesmen were treated "fairly" in most interviews.[9]

However, problems still remained. In yet another 1982 study of 600 high level executives, 73 percent believed that business and financial coverage on television news in particular "is prejudiced against business." On the question of accuracy and willingness to present both sides of an issue, the majority voted against the media.[10]

In general, studies have indicated that as the relative power of the media has increased, most people have begun to trust the media less. In one 1981 survey of Americans, only 16 percent said they had a great deal of confidence in the press, with the figure for television news at 24 percent. This was in sharp contrast to the 41

FEATURE
Media watchdogs

It was bound to happen. So frustrated with the media were business executives in the 1980s that it was only a matter of time before media watchdog organizations began to spring up, most of them financed by large companies.

Perhaps the three most prominent were the Washington-based Accuracy In Media, Inc. (AIM) and The Media Institute and Los Angeles-based Foundation for American Communications (FACS).

AIM regularly berated established media giants, primarily the three television networks and the Washington and New York newspapers, for what it described as distorted left-leaning tendencies. Not surprisingly, AIM officials were considered perpetual burrs in the buttocks of network and newspaper executives. Nonetheless, AIM occasionally got its way through media corrections or, in some cases, reassignment of certain (and invariably, seething) reporters.

The Media Institute singled out the treatment by the media of particular issues—from the handling of the so-called oil crisis in the mid-70s to the portrayal of business executives as "con men, crooks, and clowns" on prime time television programs. (Indeed, many Americans think the typical businessperson is more likely to be portrayed on the TV show, "Dallas" than in the pages of *Fortune* magazine.) While not as rebellious as AIM, The Media Institute also proved effective in occasionally changing errant media ways.

The mission of FACS was to increase the dialogue between media and business. FACS-sponsored conferences on media-business relationships and specific issues of the day regularly sat business executives down with media critics in an open yet civilized setting. FACS seminars seemed to prove that when both sides could see their adversaries face-to-face, they not only didn't fight, but occasionally even liked each other.

percent scored by television news and the 30 percent total for the press in 1973. Summarized one newspaper publisher, "The truth is, a lot of the American public don't much like us or trust us. They think we're too big for our britches."[11]

With the media and the public—particularly government and business officials—still polls apart, the challenge for public relations professionals to foster a closer working relationship between their organizations and the media continues to be a major one.

ROLE OF PUBLIC RELATIONS

How can public relations practitioners correct what may well be a distrusting, fearful relationship between the organization and the media?

First, they can pinpoint the reasons for past grievances. Perhaps the firm has traditionally refused to talk to reporters, played favorites among media people, or gone over a reporter's head to complain to an editor. The first job of a public relations person, then, is to reverse any of these "red flag" practices that may exist.

Second, the organization can also establish a formal media relations policy. (See Figure 14-3.)

Such a policy can include:

1 Appointing one person as the official spokesperson for the organization; ordinarily the public relations director.

2 Implementing an open news policy; informing news outlets of *bad news* as well as *good news.* While many organizations find the reporting of bad news a bit hard to stomach, in the long run it's better for an organization to volunteer and control the announcement of bad news, rather than to let an investigative journalist discover the story and exaggerate its significance.

3 Establishing a news-gathering apparatus within the organization to better keep journalists informed of current developments.

Finally, they can rebuild contacts with the media. Frequently, getting to know journalists can help attain this objective. While some may disagree with the practice of "taking a journalist to lunch," according to Dow Jones News Service Editor Robert L. Rettig, "It is a good idea for practitioners to take press members to lunch to get to know them and their points of view.[12] Such sessions should be low-key, friendly visits, perhaps to introduce story ideas, perhaps not. Such personal contact may pay off in the future.

A good public relations person can be a great help to a journalist. Generally, practitioners are the first people reporters call inside an organization. Frequently, the reporter's questions can be handled directly or channeled to a more knowledgeable source within the organization. Often, the intermediation of a practitioner can help journalists reach company sources.

Organization and Policy Guide

It is frequently in Chase's best interest to take advantage of interest from the media to further the reputation and services of the bank. In dealing with the media, Chase officers must be careful to protect the best interests of the bank, particularly with regard to the area of customer confidence.

The following policies will serve as a guideline for media relationships. Specific questions regarding the media should be addressed to the Public Relations Division.

Inquiries from the Media

Most journalists call the Public Relations Division when they need information about the bank or wish to arrange an interview with a bank officer. Many times, public relations officers are able to handle inquiries directly. Occasionally, however, more complex questions require input from appropriate bank officers. In these cases, inasmuch as journalists are often under deadline pressures, it is important that bank officers cooperate as fully and respond as promptly as possible. Such cooperation enhances Chase's reputation for integrity with the news media.

Less frequently, reporter inquiries will go directly to line officers. In this case, either one of two responses may be appropriate:

1. If a journalist seeks simple, factual information such as Chase's current rate on a particular savings instrument or the factual details of a new bank service, officers may provide it directly.

2. If a reporter seeks Chase policy or official opinion on such subjects as trends in interest rates, legislation, etc., responses should be reviewed with the Public Relations Division. If an officer is unfamiliar with a particular policy or requires clarification of it, he or she should always check first with the Public Relations Division before committing the bank in print.

In talking with a reporter, it is normally assumed that whatever a bank officer says may be quoted and attributed directly to him or her by name as a spokesperson for the bank. An officer not wishing to be quoted must specify that desire to the journalist.

FIGURE 14–3. *Chase Manhattan Bank press relations policy.* This policy is typical of many large organizations. Relationships with the media are generally encouraged, with the public relations division taking overall responsibility for all of the bank's relationships with journalists.

SOURCE: Courtesy of The Chase Manhattan Bank.

Most reporters with whom the bank deals will respect an officer's wishes to maintain anonymity. Most journalists recognize that it is as important for them to honor the wishes of their sources at the bank as it is for the bank to disseminate its comments and information to the public through the news media. Chase's policy toward the media should be one of mutual trust, understanding and benefit.

Interviews With the Media

In order to monitor the bank's relationships with journalists, all requests for interviews with bank officers by journalists must be routed through the Public Relations Division.

As a rule, public relations officers check the credentials of the journalist and determine the specific areas of inquiry to be examined. The public relations officer will then decide whether the interview is appropriate for the bank. When the decision is affirmative, the public relations officer will discuss subject matter with the recommended interviewee and together they will decide on a course of action and Chase objectives for the interview.

A member of the public relations staff is normally present during any face-to-face interview with an officer of the bank. The purpose of the public relations staffer's attendance is to provide assistance in handling the interview situation as well as to aid the reporter with follow-up material.

When a reporter calls an officer directly to request an interview, the officer should check with the Public Relations Division before making a commitment.

Authorized Spokespersons

Vice presidents and above are normally authorized to speak for the bank on matters in their own area of responsibility.

Normally, officers below the level of vice president are not authorized to speak for attribution on behalf of the bank except where they are specialists in a particular field, such as technical directors, economists, etc.

Exceptions may be made in special situations and in concert with the Public Relations Division.

Written Material for the Media

Chase articles bylined by officers may either be written by the officer approached or by a member of the public relations staff. If an officer decided to author his or her own article, the public relations division must be consulted for editing, photographic support and policy proofing.

Occasionally, customers or suppliers may wish to include Chase in an article or advertisement they are preparing. This material too must be routed through the Public Relations Division for review.

FIGURE 14-3 *continued.*

In addition to responding to reporters' telephone inquiries (either as the firm's official spokesperson or as the conduit to more knowledgeable sources), public relations professionals arrange interviews between journalists and executives. Frequently, practitioners sit in on these interviews to assist interviewees and reporters. The role of the practitioner in such situations should not be to obstruct the interview but rather to facilitate it.

At the heart of the journalist-practitioner relationship is credibility and trust. True, the two professions travel to the beat of different drummers, yet they should respect each other's views and responsibilities. Only through mutual respect can adversary relationships between journalists and practitioners be avoided. Journalistic respect can neither be bribed nor bullied. It can only be earned through the consistent practice of fair, open, and honest dealing, and through the highest degree of professionalism.

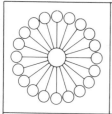

MINICASE
The Kennecott profile

Kennecott Copper Company, the nation's largest copper producer, for many years thought that "no news was good news." Kennecott management generally avoided the media. For a long while, it didn't matter. At least not until 1978, when Curtiss-Wright Corp. announced it planned to make a tender offer to take over Kennecott.

The takeover attempt infuriated Kennecott stockholders, who were unhappy with management's apparent indifference. At Kennecott's annual meeting that year, one elderly shareholder complained that the company had ordered her and her neighbors to "leave their homes to make way for a new mining facility." Another shareholder praised Curtiss-Wright for "awakening our country-club management from its sleep."

Kennecott survived the takeover attempt only through a massive advertising campaign and some last-minute fence-mending, including giving Curtiss-Wright four seats on the Kennecott board of directors. Even before the ballots were officially tallied, Kennecott announced it had asked Hill and Knowlton to be its future public relations counsel. The Kennecott chairman sadly summed up the company's image in the past, "The problem is that we've done a lousy job of public relations."[13]

QUESTION

If you were the Hill and Knowlton executive assigned to the Kennecott account, what would your plan be to resurrect the company's sagging image?

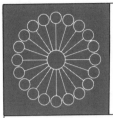

CASE STUDY
The media relations ruckus at Goliath Industries

Compared to most organizations, the media relations policy at Detroit's huge Goliath Industries was exemplary. The company, the nation's largest manufacturer, was generally forthright in its public statements and frequently led industry on such issues as corporate disclosure and South African business policy.

Goliath was such a business leader, in fact, that most observers were puzzled when on May 18, C.A. Wheat, Goliath's vice-chairman and likely successor to the firm's president, unexpectedly resigned.

In response to Wheat's departure, Goliath Industries issued a terse news release indicating that Wheat was leaving "to pursue personal business opportunities." Goliath refused to amplify the brief announcement, despite constant prodding by the media. The company cited as its primary reason for secrecy the concept of privacy with respect to personnel records.

The announcement that Wheat was leaving the $325,000-a-year job started rumor mills humming, not only in Detroit but throughout the nation.

The media, predictably, refused to drop the story. Eventually, one enterprising reporter turned up the fact that Wheat had been asked to leave by Goliath's president as a result of an internal audit that reportedly revealed conflicts in Wheat's handling of a customer with whom Wheat shared business interests.

After this revelation, the Goliath story became fair game for business journalists everywhere. The firm quickly acknowledged the existence of the internal audit but refused to discuss its content, claiming such a "confidential matter" was exempt from its internal disclosure code. Details of the report were subsequently made public by the *Detroit Free Press.* Indeed, even Wheat acknowledged the accuracy of the transactions described, maintaining there was nothing improper about them.

In the months that followed *l'Affaire Wheat,* as the Detroit newspapers called it, it was revealed that the Federal Bureau of Investigation had launched a probe of the matter, and a federal grand jury also had been impaneled to investigate. Eventually, Wheat was cleared of all possible violations of law.

Nevertheless, the positive public image of Goliath Industries had suffered a tremendous blow. *Forbes* magazine labeled it "the industry's biggest public relations blunder in years."

One source close to Goliath's board of directors summed it up by saying, "It could not have been handled any worse."

QUESTIONS

1 Had you been Goliath's public relations director, what strategy would you have recommended on May 18?

2 What would you have suggested the firm do after the revelation of the internal audit?

3 How would you suggest Goliath management handle the Wheat affair at the company's next annual meeting? Should they bring it up at all? What should they say?

NOTES

1 Walter Mills, *The Forrestal Diaries* (New York: Viking Press, 1951) and Jack Anderson with James Boyd, *Confessions of a Muckraker* (New York: Random House, 1979).

2 Cited in "Reporter Attacks Press," *Editor & Publisher,* 4 November 1978, p. 38.

3 "Investigative Reporting: Handle With Care," *RTNDA Communicator,* Radio Television News Directors Association, Washington, D.C., March 1982, p. 5.

4 Tom Wolfe, *The New Journalism* (New York: Harper & Row, 1973).

5 Chester Burger, "How to Meet the Press," *Harvard Business Review,* July–August 1975, p. 62.

6 "Sound Advice about Media Relations," *Public Relations News* 33, no. 47 (21 November 1977): 1.

7 Lewis H. Young, "The Media's View of Corporate Communications in the 80s," *Public Relations Quarterly,* Fall 1981, p. 10.

8 Roger Ricklefs, "Business Relations With the Press: Three Versions of the Way It Is," *The Wall Street Journal,* 6 July 1981, p. 15.

9 "Antagonism: Myth or Reality?" *Public Relations Journal,* November 1981, p. 62.

10 "Business Thinks TV Distorts Its Image," *Business Week,* 18 October 1982, p. 26.

11 "The Press: In Deeper Trouble With the Public," *U.S. News & World Report,* 20 September 1982, pp. 68–69.

12 "Must P. R. and the Press be Adversaries?" *The Corporate Shareholder,* 24 January 1979, p. 3.

13 Robert J. Cole, "Way is Cleared for Curtiss-Wright to Attempt Takeover of Kennecott," *The New York Times,* 3 May 1978 and "Kennecott's Milliken Gets the Message," *Business Week,* 15 May 1978.

SUGGESTED READING

Arlen, Michael J. *The View from Highway 1.* New York: Farrar, Straus and Giroux, 1976.

Blake, R. H., and **Haroldson, E.** *A Taxonomy of Concepts in Communication.* New York: Hastings House, 1975.

Carlson, R. O. *Communications and Public Opinion.* New York: Praeger, 1975.

Chaffee, Steven H., and **Petrick, Michale J.** *Using the Mass Media: Communication Problems in American Society.* New York: McGraw-Hill, 1975.

Charnley, Mitchell V. *Reporting.* 3rd ed. New York: Holt, Rinehart & Winston, 1975. Basic reporting text, with pointers on how news should be written.

Daley, Robert. "We Deal with Emotional Facts." *The New York Times Magazine,* 15 December 1974, pp. 18–19. Contains sharp criticism of network news programs.

DeLozier, M. *Marketing Communications Process.* New York: McGraw-Hill, 1976.

Editor & Publisher Yearbook. (Available from 850 Third Avenue, New York, N.Y. 10022.)

Diamond, Edwin. *The Tin Kazoo: Television, Politics and the News.* Cambridge, Mass.: M.I.T. Press, 1975.

Roper, Burns. *The Growing Importance of Television News and the Medium's Emerging Role in Corporate Public Relations.* New York: Television Information Office, 1965.

Schramm, Wilbur. *Men, Messages, and Media: A Look at Human Communication.* New York: Harper and Row, 1973. An analysis of the communications process and its effects of mass communication in society; contains an insightful look at the "War of the Worlds" broadcast and the Kennedy-Nixon debates.

Shapiro, Andren. *Media Access.* Boston: Little Brown & Co., 1976. A legal guide.

Tebbel, John. *The Media in America.* New York: Thomas Y. Crowell, 1975.

THE ART OF PUBLICITY

No matter if you work for the largest manufacturing company, the poorest politician, or the tiniest nonprofit organization, chances are if you are engaged in public relations work, attracting positive publicity will be among your primary responsibilities.

Securing publicity is perhaps the most well-known aspect of public relations work. Clearly, it is the function most associated with public relations. In most people's minds, as we have noted, publicity *is* public relations.

Publicity, through news releases and other methods, is designed to broaden knowledge and positive recognition about an organization, its personnel, and its activities. Publicity is most often gained by dealing directly with the media, either in reacting to inquiries or in initiating the communication.

Importantly, publicity differs dramatically from advertising, despite the fact most people confuse the two.

15
Publicity Techniques

Advertising possesses the following characteristics:

1 You *pay* for it.
2 You control *what* is said.
3 You control *how* it is said.
4 You control to *whom* it is said.
5 To a degree, you control *where* it's put in a publication or on the air.
6 You control the *frequency* of its use.

Publicity, on the other hand, offers no such controls. Typically, publicity is subject to review by news editors, who may decide either to use all of a story, some of it, or discard it completely. When it will run, who will see it, how often it will be used —all are subject, to a large degree, to the whims of a news editor.

But while publicity is by no means a "sure thing," it does offer two overriding benefits that enhance its appeal, even beyond those offered by advertising:

1 First, while not free, it costs only the time and effort expended by public relations personnel and management in attempting to place it in the media (see Figure 15–1). Therefore, relatively speaking, its cost is minimal, especially compared with advertising and assessed against potential returns.

2 Second and most important, publicity, which appears in *news* rather than in advertising columns, carries the "implicit endorsement" of the publication in which it appears. In other words, publicity is perceived as objective "news" rather than self-serving promotion. This translates into the most sought-after of commodities for an organization—*credibility.* And this is the true value of publicity over advertising.

SECURING PUBLICITY

Gaining access to the media is a common problem among organizations wishing to attract positive publicity. People often complain that "the media are more interested in bad news than in running anything positive." To a degree, this complaint is valid.

While no two reporters or editors can agree on what constitutes news, more often than not news is the sensational, the unusual, or the unexpected. And oftentimes for an organization, this equals "bad news." Indeed, in recent years, large multinationals like Mobil Oil and Kaiser Aluminum have taken the unprecedented step of purchasing media air time to tell their side of a story.

Obviously, most organizations lack the resources to do this. But clearly, every organization yearns to earn positive mentions in the media. This objective is indeed attainable.

Overall, what's required is a basic, common sense knowledge of the media people with whom you're dealing and a sense of courtesy, responsiveness, and respect in dealing with them. It bears repeating: Journalists—or at least most of them—are people too. Treat them that way, and the goal of penetrating the print or broadcast barriers lies within reach. The next several pages offer specific suggestions for developing a positive relationship with the media.

FIGURE 15-1 *Media relations advertising.* Media relations has become so important for many large companies that they now advertise names and locations of their press relations staffs so that journalists know where to obtain information about the firm.

SOURCE: Courtesy of Con Edison, Exxon Corporation, Texaco, and The Tobacco Institute.

A ndrew S. Edson is vice president and general manager of the New York office of Padilla and Speer, a leading Minneapolis-based public relations agency. Mr. Edson's extensive background in public relations includes periods as an account executive for Harshe-Rotman & Druck, Inc. and Ruder & Finn. He also was assistant director of corporate public relations for The Anaconda Company and public affairs manager for Citicorp. Mr. Edson also has taught public relations at Pratt Institute and Syracuse University and lectures frequently on public relations subjects.

How does one deal effectively with the media?

You must know the media you plan to deal with. Read the pertinent publications, listen to or watch the actual program. In short, do your homework beforehand. This will show when you write that first pitch letter or make the introductory call. Honesty also counts. Don't hide under a hundred platitudes once you've established a contact. If you cannot effectively answer a question or aid a journalist, be truthful and let that person know. It'll pay off in the long run.

How important are contacts in media relations?

Very. If you develop a good working relationship with members of the fourth estate, you, too, can engage in a game of "give and go." It's not imprudent to ask a favor or question a journalist. Basically, it's a two-way street. The newsperson wants your help when he or she needs it. Conversely, there will come a day when you will need a favor in return. Good media contacts are invaluable in practicing public relations.

What is the proper relationship between a journalist and a public relations practitioner?

Some say at "arms distance," while others make it a habit of getting to know a journalist on an almost personal and social basis. There really isn't any concrete formula for setting the tone of a practitioner/journalist relationship. Common sense and an adherence to a professional code of ethics, such as that of the Public Relations Society of America, more than anything else, constitute what is proper and improper.

Does it bother you when a journalist calls you a "flack"?

Yes and no. Name calling has been around for a good long time—certainly that of a pejorative nature. What good is it to engage in a war of hurling epithets at a journalist? Who wins? You won't. A true professional can easily sense when he or she is dealing with another professional and the only name worth using is the person's given one or surname.

How do you go about securing a magazine story for a client?

The formula, if you will, pretty much holds true whether you're working for a public relations agency, corporation, nonprofit association, or government. Simply, know your target publication and whether or not your story pitch will fit in its format, whether the subject has been treated in-depth or at all by a book, and what its criteria are for considering an idea. Unless you know the journalist or editor personally, it's best to compose your thoughts on paper. Spell out the rationale in writing, why you believe it will make a good article. Be aware of the magazine's deadline, its readership (is it right for your client?), its reputation, reprint policy, and above all, whether or not your client will cooperate. Finally, especially with the national business and financial books, be aware that they like to be dealt with on almost an exclusive basis. Therefore, it's dirty pool to pitch the identical story to a *Fortune* and a *Forbes,* especially since they compete with

each other. You can, however, offer your pitch to a number of books and see who takes the bait first and then proceed accordingly.

What steps do you follow in publicizing a client?

I first try to put together a publicity plan that will help the client achieve his objectives through proven strategies and action programs. Sure, everyone would love to be in *The New York Times* or *Wall Street Journal,* or on ABC's "Good Morning America" program, but it doesn't always happen. While your client may push for his or her appearance in a national book, the company and its products may be more appropriate for a series of bylined articles in trade publications (not at all unlike hitting a few singles in baseball) before pitching a major book or program. Those singles will help you get a home run, and build a better case for pitching your client before other target media. Keep in mind the reprint potential of trade articles as calling tools for your sales force, for direct mail to shareholders, as information vehicles to financial analysts, and for simplifying a technical subject to a business journalist. Your success or failure, however, shouldn't be measured on the sheer volume of clippings or articles. Always remember what management's objectives were from the outset and go from there.

Is it wise to phone a busy journalist to assess his or her interest in a story?

That depends on how well you know the person, whether he or she is on a breaking deadline, and how comfortable you feel in "cold pitching" a story. If you're aware that the afternoon is the worst possible time to

(Interview *continues.*)

call someone at the *Wall Street Journal,* for example, unless you've a fast-breaking news story, engage in conversation in the A.M. It's certainly faster to discern interest in an idea by telephone than it is by mail.

Are clients understanding when they don't attract publicity?

Some are. Some aren't. If you make the client aware from the outset of the success/failure ratio and don't make any unnecessary promises, then you won't get harmed. All too often, public relations practitioners get overzealous and almost guarantee that certain things will happen when they may not. Unlike advertising, we don't control what gets into print, or heard on the airwaves, or seen on the tube. If you don't succeed, consider doing a post mortem. Ask the media why they didn't use your story. Perhaps it can be repitched or recycled. Learn from your mistakes.

What special tips can you offer in dealing with the media?

Be honest, forthright, and cooperate with the media person in a professional manner. Don't forget to send a proper thank you note when the occasion calls for it. Think of your relationship as continuing, not a one-shot deal. Stay in touch, even if you have nothing in particular to "sell."

VARIETY OF FORMS

Occasionally, events trigger an immediate need to disseminate company news. A sudden change in management, a fire or explosion at a plant, a labor strike or settlement—all engender the need for news publicity. In a more controlled sense, news publicity is used to announce plant openings, executive speeches, groundbreakings, charitable donations, major appointments, and product changes.

Feature. Less news-oriented material provides the media with features: personality profiles on management and company personnel, helpful hints from company experts, case studies of ongoing and successful company programs, innovative ways of opening up production bottlenecks, or unusual applications of new products. Practitioners also often help freelance writers in this task.

Financial. Generally, this material concerns earnings releases, dividend announcements, and other financial affairs. The Securities and Exchange Commission requires that all publicly held companies announce important financial information promptly through the media and news wires.

Product. Publicizing new or improved products has enormous potential to aid bottom-line profits. However, such publicity should be used judiciously so that the media do not feel the organization is going overboard in attempting to boost sales.

Picture. The old maxim "a good photo is worth a thousand words" is particularly true in public relations. Photos frequently can tell a story about a new product or company announcement without the necessity of a lengthy news release.

If the accompanying photo caption of three or four lines is pointed and provocative, the photo has an even greater chance of being used. (See Figure 15–2 for examples of publicity pictures.)

lease directed to a specific person or editor has a greater chance of being read than one addressed simply to "editor."

In smaller papers, for example, one person may handle all financial news. At larger papers, the financial news section may have different editors for banking, chemicals, oil, electronics, and many other specialities. Public relations people should know who covers their "beat" and target releases accordingly.

Public relations professionals also should know the differences in the functions of newspaper personnel. For example, the *publisher* is the person responsible for overall newspaper policy. The *editorial editor* generally is responsible for editorial page content, including the opinion-editorial (op-ed) section. The *managing editor* is responsible for overall news content. These three should rarely, if ever, be called in attempting to secure publicity. That leaves the various *section editors* and *reporters* as key contacts for public relations practitioners.

4   Make personal contact. Knowing a reporter may not result in an immediate story, but it can pay residual dividends. Those who know the local weekly editor

FEATURE
Myopic Meg and the great flack flap

Nobody ever said newspaper editors were the most rational of beings.

Take Meg Greenfield, the respected editorial page editor of the *Washington Post.* Because Ms. Greenfield's domain is widely read by the movers and shakers of America, it is a frequent target of public relations-authored, op-ed articles. So frequent, in fact, that midway through 1982, editorial page editor Greenfield blew her journalistic cork.

In a blistering memo to her fellow editors, Greenfield lashed out at public relations counselors as "wolves," "slaves," and "that damned crowd."

"I, myself, have told some slave or other from (public relations firm) H and K that we don't traffic with press agents, that if her client, a college president, had business to transact with us, then the college president should call," Ms. Greenfield huffed in her "confidential" memo.

Obviously unaware or perhaps unconcerned that politicians and business executives also regularly have their "bylined edi-

torials" ghost-written by public relations people, Ms. Greenfield said she would still entertain these articles as long as public relations agencies weren't involved.

It wasn't long, of course, before the memo leaked and the counter attack began. *Advertising Age* made Greenfield's memo a cause celebré. Soon the editorial page section of the *Post* was flooded both with critical letters and, ironically for Greenfield who wanted to be rid of such things, invitations to lunch from public relations people to explain their views.

One public relations counselor caustically pointed out that Ms. Greenfield didn't write her memo until the *Post's* major competitor, the *Washington Star,* had gone out of business.

In any event, the "great flack flap," as one magazine labled it, seemed to end in a stand-off, with most *Post* editors continuing to accept material from public relations consultants as usual and Ms. Greenfield, as she put it, not getting "this stuff anymore."[1]

or the daily city editor have an advantage over colleagues who don't. Also, when a reporter uses your story idea, follow up with a note of commendation— particularly on the story's accuracy.

5 **Don't badger.** Newspapers are generally fiercely independent about the copy they use. Even a major advertiser will usually fail in getting a piece of puffery published.

    Badgering an editor about a certain story is bad form. So is complaining excessively about the treatment given a certain story. Worst of all, it achieves little to act outraged when a newspaper chooses not to run a story. Editors are human beings, too. For every release they use, dozens get discarded. If a public relations person protests too much, editors will remember.

6 **Use "exclusives" sparingly.** Sometimes public relations people promise "exclusive" stories to particular newspapers. The exclusive promises one newspaper a "scoop" over its competitors. For example, practitioners will frequently arrrange to have a visiting executive interviewed by only one local newspaper. While the chances of securing a story are heightened by the promise of an exclusive, there is a risk of alienating the other papers. Thus, the exclusive should be used sparingly.

7 **When you call, do your own calling.** Reporters and editors generally don't have assistants. Most do not like to be kept waiting by a secretary calling for the boss. Public relations professionals should make their own initial and follow-up calls. Letting a secretary "handle" a journalist can alienate a good news contact. Above all, be courteous.

MAGAZINES

Magazine publishing has experienced a renaissance in the 1980s.

    While some of the nation's most prominent magazines have closed down— *Look* and *Colliers,* for example—many others, particularly specialized publications, have sprung up in their place: from gossip-oriented magazines like *People* and *Us* to publications farther afield such as *Wet,* "the magazine of gourmet bathing," *The Chocolate News,* a bi-monthly featuring every imaginable form of chocolate, and the *Razor's Edge,* which caters to women sporting shaved heads.

    Today, approximately 10,900 magazines are published in the United States. They generally can be classified into the following categories:

General interest. Aimed at the entire population; designed to appeal to all groups. The two largest are *Reader's Digest* and *TV Guide.* While differing in format and treatment, they both appeal to millions of readers.

News. Weeklies that summarize news events, provide background, and add depth to evolving stories. *Time, Newsweek,* and *U.S. News and World Report* dominate this group. *Time,* the first news magazine, which made its debut in 1923, now has a circulation in excess of four million.

Quality. Targeted to a more selective readership. *Smithsonian, National Geographic, Harper's, Saturday Review,* and *The New Yorker* are examples. Often, these

FEATURE
He made the roof but not the cover

The pinnacle of publicity placement is to successfully land a positive photo on the cover of a major magazine.

That's why when *Fortune* magazine asked K mart Chairman Bernard M. Fauber to be photographed for a possible cover photo in September 1982, K mart jumped at the chance.

Given only two days' notice to get the photo to *Fortune's* New York headquarters, the K mart public relations staff cleared Mr. Fauber's schedule, located a cherry-picker truck to lift him to the roof of a K mart store to pose for the picture, and then whisked the film from the company's Michigan headquarters to New York by special courier.

When the long-awaited issue was published, lo-and-behold Ronald Reagan and not Bernard Fauber graced *Fortune's* cover.

Explained the magazine's managing editor, the K mart cover was just one of three alternatives prepared for the issue. Ultimately, President Reagan won, and Mr. Fauber lost.

Mr. Fauber was philosophical in defeat. "If I had to lose out," he said, "I can't think of anyone I'd rather lose out to."[2]

The moral for all public relations publicists: "Never build expectations up too high about imminent positive publicity. Chances are, you—and your client—may be bitterly disappointed."

magazines offer more scholarly writing than news magazines. Others, such as *The Nation* and *The New Republic,* have more limited circulations but command national respect as journals of political insight.

Business-oriented. *Forbes, Business Week, Dun's, Fortune,* and *Barron's* are among the fastest-growing of all periodicals. All influence the attitudes of the nation's business leadership and are the objects of considerable public relations activity.

One area of rapid growth is that of regional business journals. Indeed, the Association of Area Business Publications, organized in late 1978 with fourteen members, soon had fifty publishers with a combined circulation in sixty tabloids and magazines of more than 900,000. And there were perhaps another thirty to forty similar publications across the nation ready to join the group. As the group's executive director explained the boom, "It's very simple. There's a tremendous hunger for local and regional business news. The national business publications can't possibly begin to touch it. And the local dailies, for the most part, do a very poor job."[3]

Trade. Magazines such as *Advertising Age, Supermarket Age, Iron Age, Convenience Store News, Metalworking News,* and many others are trade-oriented and important publicity targets for practitioners serving in specific fields. Most of these are avidly read in the industry.

Men's/women's interest.   These cater specifically to either the men's or women's market. For example, *Playboy* and *Penthouse* are clearly designed for men, while *Cosmopolitan, Vogue, Glamour,* and *Playgirl* are aimed at women.

One recent trend in such magazines has been toward the area of toning up one's flesh. A clutch of new titles—*Shape, Fit, Pretty Body,* and *Slimmer* have taken their place next to the more traditional *Better Homes and Gardens, Lady's Home Journal, Ms.,* and *Mademoiselle.* All, once again, are excellent outlets for potential public relations placements.

Special interest.   Periodicals for virtually every special interest group: black lifestyle—*Ebony* and *Jet;* science—*Popular Mechanics* and *Scientific American;* farming—*Farm Journal;* journalism—*The Quill* and *Editor and Publisher;* sports—*Sports Illustrated, Sport,* and *Runner;* aviation—*Flying, Air Cargo,* and *Aviation Week,* etc., etc., etc.

This is not to mention magazines for airline passengers, homosexuals, classic car owners, apartment dwellers, and marijuana smokers. Indeed, even *Wet* has 45,000 regular readers.

Successful placement.   How does one take advantage of the magazine boom?

Magazine placement differs from newspaper placement in a number of ways. For one thing, magazines have longer "lead times" than newspapers: stories take longer to get printed so articles must be less time-oriented than daily press material and must be written in more of a feature style. They also must be scheduled further in advance. Here are five general suggestions for attempting to place publicity in magazines:

1   **Choose target publications carefully.** Know what the magazine uses. Read and study back issues for at least six months to determine if your subject fits.

2   **Innovate.** Magazines like creative ideas and shun run-of-the-mill material. Suggest new approaches and break new ground. Retreaded news releases seldom have a chance.

3   **Take care with the cover letter.** A short cover letter can help sell a story idea. The letter should state simply why it's in the magazine's best interest to publish the suggested story. The letter should be just thorough enough to interest the editor and make the "sale" without supplying the finished article.

4   **Use exclusives.** With public relations material, many magazines insist on exclusives. For example, *Time* may not accept a feature idea or a bylined guest column from an executive if *Newsweek* has already run such an article from the same executive. As a matter of courtesy and prudence, practitioners should seek only one placement per story idea in a particular magazine category. If the idea is rejected by the first choice, the practitioner should then approach the next choice.

5   **Use freelancers.** Magazines frequently buy articles from freelance writers. Some freelancers know magazine editors well enough to have a feel for what the editors like. A practitioner should stay in contact with freelancers, who are willing recipients of story ideas, which then can be marketed by the writer to magazine editors.

RADIO AND TELEVISION

For more than two decades, radio was the nation's dominant electronic news source. Then came television, and radio slipped into a subordinate position. While the "golden years" of radio may have passed, the medium is still important as a news source. Here are the facts:

1 During the average week, the radio is heard by adults in close to 99 percent of homes with $20,000 or more in annual household income.
2 The number of radios in cars rose from under 50 million in 1962 to 123 million by the end of the 1970s.
3 On a typical day, the average college and high school student spends about three hours with a radio.

As TV has taken on the entertainment characteristics of radio, radio has moved more strongly into news dissemination. At least one all-news radio station is available in major cities, broadcasting a constant stream of news around the clock.

Several radio networks, including ABC, NBC, CBS, and Mutual, compete to service the more than 8,000 stations in the United States. Radio journalists are often receptive to the story ideas of public relations people.

Television also offers a variety of opportunities, particularly on the local level, for groups to tell their stories through film, videotape, and on-the-air interviews. There are about 725 television stations in the United States.

Each week night, about 44 million Americans get their news from one of the three major television network shows. In the 1980s, TV news has experienced a resurgence, with networks launching late night and early morning news shows. Additionally, the networks, local stations, and public broadcasting all feature interview programs to complement nightly news shows. Also, with cable television introducing a host of business and economics-oriented programs, the networks, too, have begun to increase their quantity of business and economic news. Unfortunately, many Americans think that by watching TV, they are getting *all* the news. TV news personnel are the first to admit that their coverage is, by necessity, "capsulized and condensed." The typical thirty-minute show provides less than twenty minutes of news coverage. In terms of words, a TV news show would fill only about one-half of one page of the average daily newspaper. When Edward R. Murrow was reminded of this fact by a listener, he changed his opening from "This is the news" to "This is *some* of the news." People who rely solely on television for their news are missing much of what's happening in the world, the nation, and their own community.

Film and videotape are the special appeals of television and are used liberally to heighten the impact of stories. Practitioners should be aware that occasionally an important story that lacks film may be limited in its air time, while a less important one with film might receive greater play. This, of course, helps influence people's judgments about the relative importance of specific news events. Indeed, broadcasters are often faulted by their critics for using faulty judgment in "visually biasing" viewers with only one side of a story.

Nevertheless, TV's growth is indisputable. In the 1980s, cable television also has grown dramatically. By 1983, almost 30 million households subscribed to cable TV. One result was that the three networks' share of prime-time ratings declined by about 11 percent from 1979 to the early 1980s. Perhaps the most stunning attempt at news on cable was entrepreneur Ted Turner's Cable News Network (CNN), a 24 hour-a-day video news service that has tried admirably to match the networks in world news coverage. Beyond CNN, about 24 million people subscribed to cable in the U.S. by the end of 1982. In addition, companies like Warner-Amex promised further use of two-way systems to link viewers with the programs they watched. The pioneer of such systems, the QUBE Limited two-way system in Columbus, Ohio, proved successful. And Warner-Amex, for one, planned to spend $150 million over three years to expand its two-way capacity. By 1990, projections indicate that half the television sets in America will be hooked up to cable, which will become a $200 billion-a-year industry. Again, the possibility for publicity placement on cable television is enormous.

FEATURE
The private business TV network

"The first business satellite-television system in the world—a system that can reach every community in this country to promote and strengthen our enterprise system."

Thus did President Reagan describe the American Business Network, the nation's first private business television network, launched by the U.S. Chamber of Commerce in late 1982.

Called BIZNET, it transmits programs from the Chamber's Washington, D.C. headquarters via communications satellite to subscribers around the country. Its programs include news reports, political projections, international trade information, small business reports, appearances by government officials, and a rundown of legislative activity.

An additional BIZNET feature is the opportunity for interaction between audience members and speakers through audio hookups. Subscribers generally are state and local chambers of commerce, trade associations, and corporations that purchase their own receiving facilities and pay a $5,000 annual subscription fee.

One reason the Chamber said it started BIZNET was, "The coverage of business issues is not extensive enough and is sometimes quite superficial. Business people need an opportunity to interact frequently with government officials whose decisions are vital to the health of business enterprises. That's what BIZNET is all about."

Predicted Presidential counselor Edwin Meese III about BIZNET, it will "revolutionize the way the business community makes itself heard."

Indeed, the launching of BIZNET may have stimulated other organizations to pilot their own television programming. Also in 1982, American Express launched, via satellite, its own business news program, "How's Business?" to 536 cable systems serving five million households. Another company, Public Affairs Satellite System, also began distributing short news and feature programs produced by businesses to radio and television stations via satellite.

Thus began the era of "narrow casting," especially by business groups, to seize "equal time" with target audiences.[4]

Successful placement. Radio and television may be approached similarly by the public relations professional in pitching publicity material for electronic media placement, using these guidelines:

1 **Generally call, don't write.** Radio and television are more telephone-oriented than newspapers. To begin each day, radio news directors and television assignment editors plot their staff assignments. A phone call to these people—and generally not to reporters or correspondents themselves—during their early scheduling periods may evoke some interest. However, most news directors appreciate advance warning, so an early letter about an upcoming event may be a good idea.

2 **Keep the story simple.** Radio and TV don't have the editorial space that newspapers and magazines offer. Rarely does a radio story last one minute—the equivalent of perhaps a page and a half of triple-spaced copy. Television stories may be a bit longer, but not much. Therefore, the more succinct a story, the better.

3 **Know deadlines.** Deadlines in radio and TV may even be stricter than for newspaper work. Unless a TV story can be filmed or taped in time to return for the six o'clock news (ideally, mid-morning), it will be useless. Radio offers greater flexibility since interviews can be taped on-the-scene or on the telephone and aired immediately. Frequently, short interview snatches or "actualities" from longer interviews will be aired. In any event, it's a good idea to schedule radio and TV publicity early enough in the day to avoid running up against competition from unexpected breaking news.

4 **For TV, be visual.** TV assignment editors are rarely interested in nonvisual stories. "Talking heads" (shots of people moving their mouths and nothing else) are anathema to TV producers. On the other hand, stories that offer dramatic, interesting visuals may have a good chance of being used.

5 **Get to know the talent coordinator/producer.** In placing clients on radio and television talk shows, it helps to know the people who "book the talent." Talk shows are excellent vehicles through which to discuss products, books, or ideas. Earning the trust of the talent coordinator or producer will help ensure that invitations will continue to appear.

WIRE SERVICES

Two news-gathering organizations form the backbone of the nation's news system, supplying up-to-the-minute dispatches from around the world to both the print and electronic media. The Associated Press (AP) and United Press International (UPI) wire services compete to deliver the most accurate news first. Both services write in a simple, understandable style. The AP serves close to 10,000 clients—newspapers, magazines, TV, and radio stations—with UPI serving nearly 7,250. Each has bureaus in more than 100 countries, and both believe it is their role to be there when the news happens.

Staging as intense a rivalry on the financial side are two business wires—Dow Jones and Reuters. These wires specialize in business-oriented news. (Reuters also provides a general news service outside the United States.) When a company releases news that may influence the decision of an investor to hold, sell, or buy its stock, it is required to release the information promptly to the broadest group of investors. In such an instance, Dow Jones, Reuters, and the local press are notified simultaneously. Dow Jones and Reuters news wires, like those of AP and UPI, are found in newspaper offices, brokerage firms, banks, investment houses, and many corporate offices throughout the country.

Additionally, commercial wire services, such as PR News Wire and Business Wire, distribute public relations material to news outlets nationwide. Unlike AP and UPI, these commercial wires charge organizations a fee for running news release stories verbatim on their wires. Such commercial wires serve as an effective backup, ensuring that announcements at least reach news outlets.

Feature syndicates, such as North American Newspaper Alliance and King Features, are another source of editorial material for newspapers and magazines. They provide subscribing newspapers with a broad spectrum of material ranging from business commentaries to comic strips to gossip columns. Some of their writers, such as Art Buchwald, Jack Anderson, and Jane Bryant Quinn, have built national reputations as columnists. Many such columnists depend heavily on source material provided by public relations personnel.

HANDLING INTERVIEWS

Public relations people coordinate interviews for both print and broadcast media. Most executives are neither familiar with nor comfortable in such interview situations. For one thing, reporters ask a lot of searching questions, some of which may seem impertinent. Executives aren't used to being put on the spot. Instinctively, they may resent it. So counseling executives for interviews has become an important and strategic task for the in-house practitioner as well as a lucrative profession for media consultants.

PRINT INTERVIEWS

The following ten do's and don'ts are important in newspaper, magazine, or other print interviews:

1 **Do your homework in advance.** An interviewee must be thoroughly briefed—either verbally or in writing—before the interview. Know what the interviewer writes, for whom he writes, and what his opinions are. Also determine what the audience wants to know.

2 **Relax.** Remember that the interviewer is a person too, just trying to do a good job. Building rapport will help the interview.

3 **Speak in personal terms.** People distrust large organizations. References to *the company* and *we believe* sound ominous. Use *I* instead; speak as an individual, as a member of the public, rather than as a mouthpiece for an impersonal bureaucracy.

4 **Welcome the "naive" question.** If the question sounds simple, it should be answered anyway. It may be helpful to those who don't possess much knowledge of the organization or industry.

5 **Answer questions briefly and directly.** Avoid rambling. Be brief, concise, and to-the-point. An interviewee shouldn't get into subject areas about which he knows nothing. This situation can be dangerous and counterproductive when words are transcribed in print.

6 **Don't bluff.** If a reporter asks a question that you can't answer, you should admit it. If there are others in the organization more knowledgeable about a particular issue, the interviewee or the practitioner should point that out and get the answer.

7 **State facts, back up generalities.** Facts and examples always bolster an interview. An interviewee should come armed with specific data that support general statements. Again, the practitioner should furnish all the specifics.

8 **If the reporter is promised further information, get it to him quickly.** Remember, reporters work under time pressures and need information quickly to meet deadlines. Anything promised in an interview should be granted soon. Conveniently "forgetting" to answer a request may return to haunt the organization when the interview is printed.

9 **There is no such thing as "off the record."** If a person doesn't want to see something in print, he shouldn't say it. It's that simple. Reporters may get confused as to what was "off the record" during the interview. While most journalists will honor an "off the record" statement, some may not. Usually, it's not worth taking the risk. Occasionally, reporters will agree not to attribute a statement to the interviewee but to use it as background. Mostly though, interviewees should be willing to have whatever they say in the interview appear in print.

10 **Tell the truth.** Telling the truth is the cardinal rule. Journalists are generally perceptive; they can detect a fraud. So don't be evasive, don't cover up, and most of all, don't lie. Be positive, but be truthful. Occasionally, an interviewee must decline to answer specific questions. In this case, he should candidly explain why a question can't be answered. This approach always wins in the long run.*

    After the interview, the practitioner might call the reporter to determine his assessment of the interview. Generally, reporters will say frankly how the interview (and the interviewee) turned out. Try to improve the interviewee in future interview situations.

BROADCAST INTERVIEWS

As the broadcast media, particularly television, have become more potent channels of news to the public, executives are being called upon to appear on news and interview shows to air their viewpoints. For the uninitiated and the unprepared, a TV interview can be a harrowing experience.

    To be effective on TV takes practice. Executives and public relations people must accept guidance on acting appropriately before the camera. In recent years, elaborate programs have been constructed by counseling firms to teach executives how to act on TV. The following eleven *do's* and *don'ts* may help in being effective in a TV interview:

1 **Do prepare.** Preparation is the key to successful broadcast appearances. Executives should know the main points they wish to make *before* the interview begins. They should know the audience. They should know who the reporter is

---

* For additional practical pointers, see William J. Ardrey III, "The Editorial Interview: How to Get the Most Out of It," *Public Relations Journal*, 23 January 1973, pp. 19–22; Chester Burger, *op. cit.*, pp. 62–70; and Richard W. Soell, "When Management Meets the Press," *Public Relations Journal*, January 1971, pp. 21–22.

and something about her beliefs. Finally, they should rehearse answering tough hypothetical questions before entering the studio.

2 **Do be yourself.** Appear relaxed. Smiles are appropriate. Nonverbal signs of tension (clenched fists, gripping the arms of a chair, or tightly holding one hand with the other) should be avoided. Gesturing with palms open, on the other hand, suggests relaxation and eagerness to discuss issues. Avoid giggling, smoking, or chewing gum during the interview. Proper posture is also important.

3 **Do be open and honest.** Television magnifies everything, especially phoniness. If facts are twisted, it will show. On TV, a half-truth becomes a half-lie. Establish credibility early.

4 **Do be brief.** TV and radio have no time for beating around the bush. Main points must be summarized at the beginning of sentences. English must be understandable, because neither the reporter nor the public can be expected to be familiar with technical jargon.

5 **Do play it straight. Be careful with humor.** An interviewee can't be giddy, vacuous, or irreverent. Attempts to be a comic may be interpreted as being foolish. However, the natural and relaxed use of appropriate humor may be a big plus for getting a point across. If humor does not come naturally, interviewees should play it straight. That way, they won't look stupid.

6 **Do dress for the occasion.** Bold patterns, checks, or pinstripes should be avoided; so should jewelry that shines or glitters. Skirts should fall easily below a woman's knees. Men's socks should be high enough to prevent a gap between socks and pants. Colors on shirts, socks, suits, and accessories should generally be muted.

7 **Don't assume the interviewer is out to get you.** Arguments or hostilities come through clearly on TV. In a discussion on a controversial subject with a professional interviewer, the guest usually comes out looking like the bad guy. All questions, even naive ones, should be treated with respect and deference. If an interviewee becomes defensive, it will show.

8 **Don't think everything you say will be aired.** TV is a quick and imperfect medium. When Equitable Life Assurance fired several hundred managers, a reporter spent hours chatting with top Equitable executives. That evening, thirty seconds worth of interviews were aired. In other words, to make a point on TV, be brief and direct in responses.

9 **Don't let the interviewer dominate.** Interviewees can control the interview by varying the length and content of their responses. If a queston requires a complicated answer, the interviewee should clarify before getting trapped into an incomplete and misleading response. If interviewees make mistakes, they should correct them and go on. If they don't understand a question, they should ask for clarification.

10 **Don't say "no comment."** *No comment* sounds evasive. If interviewees can't answer certain questions, they should clearly explain why. Begging off for competitive or proprietary reasons is perfectly allowable as long as some explanation is offered.

11 **Do stop.** One regularly practiced broadcast technique is to leave cameras running and mikes on even after an interviewee has responded to a question. Often the most revealing, misleading, and damaging statements are made by

FIGURE 15.3 *Coor's "no comment" ad.* Typical of an enlightened media relations attitude is this ad by Adolph Coors Co., a firm which once had been criticized in the media as espousing a particularly silent attitude.

SOURCE: Courtesy of Adolph Coors Company.

interviewees embarrassed by the silence. Don't fall for the bait; silence always can be edited out later. The interviewer knows that, and the interviewee should, too, before getting trapped.

These are just a few hints in dealing with what often turns out to be a difficult situation for the uninitiated. In general, the best advice for an interviewee is to be natural, straight, and prepared.*

PRESS CONFERENCES

Press conferences, the convening of the media for a specific purpose, are generally frowned upon. Unless an organization has real news to communicate, press conferences can flop. Reporters don't have the time for meetings offering little news. Before attempting a conference, ask this question: Can this information be disseminated just as easily in a news release? If the answer is yes, the conference should be scratched.

Eventually, though, every organization must face the media in a conference, either in connection with an annual meeting, a major announcement, or a presentation to securities analysts. The same rules and guidelines hold true for dealing with the press in conference as in a one-on-one interview. Be honest, candid, forthright, and fair.

Follow these guidelines in a press conference:

1 **Don't play favorites; invite representatives from all major news outlets.** Normally, it makes sense to alert wire services, which in turn, may have facilities to advise their print and broadcast subscribers. For example, both the AP and UPI carry daily listings of news events in major cities.

---

* For additional practical pointers, see Eliot Frankel, "Learning to Conquer 'Mike' Fright," *Washington Journalism Review,* July/August 1982, pp. 29–33; Paul Lockwood, "Speak into the Mike, Please!" *Enterprise,* November 1977; and Dick Martin, *The Executive's Guide to Handling a Press Interview* (New York: Pilot Books, 1977), pp. 12–13.

2 **Notify the media by mail well in advance of the conference and follow up by phone.** Ordinarily, the memo announcing the event should be straightforward and to the point, listing the subject, date, time, and place as well as the speaker and the public relations contact's name, title, and phone number. If possible, it should reach the editor's desk at least seven to ten days before the event. Also, the day before the event, a follow-up phone call reminder is wise.

3 **Schedule the conference early in the day.** Again, the earlier in the business day, the better, particularly for TV consumption.

4 **Hold the conference in a meeting room, not someone's office.** Office auditoriums and hotel meeting rooms are good places for news conferences. Chairs should be provided for all reporters, and space should be allowed for TV crews to set up cameras. The speaker at the conference should preside either from a table or a lectern, so that microphones and tape recorders can be placed nearby.

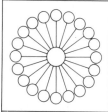

MINICASE

The irate interviewee

Cable Electronics was one of the hottest high-technology firms in the country. So hot, in fact, that *Forbes* magazine asked to interview Chairman Charles Spungen about the company's remarkable growth.

An engineer by background, Spungen had little experience with the press. Nevertheless, he passed up the opportunity for a preinterview briefing from his public relations director, choosing to get a haircut instead. Immediately after the haircut, he greeted *Forbes* reporter James White at the door of his office, and the interview commenced:

White: *Your growth has been phenomenal. To what do you attribute the rapid rise in your profits?*

Spungen: We've been on the ball, Jimmy. And damn good at what we do. Our products are better. Our people work harder. And we produce. Simple as that.

White: *What do you think your competitors have been doing wrong?*

Spungen: In the case of Telcom, they've been playing catch-up ball for four years. They just can't seem to get on track. Suncom is another story. Their management is weak.

White: *What about Apex?*

Spungen: Apex couldn't come in third in a three-man race! But gloriosky! Don't quote me on that one.

White: *What, briefly and specifically, are some of the new products you're working on?*

5 **The time allotted for the conference should be stated in advance.** Reporters should be told at the beginning of the conference how much time they will have. This way, no one can complain later.

6 **Keep the speaker away from the reporters before the conference.** Mingling prior to the conference will only give someone an edge. Keep all reporters on equal footing in their contact with the speaker.

7 **Prepare materials to complement the speaker's presentation.** The news conference is an apt place for a press kit, which should include all the pertinent information about the speaker, the subjects, and the organization.

8 **Let the reporters know the end has come.** Just before the stated time has elapsed, the practitioner should announce to the reporters that the next question will be the last one. After the final question, the speaker should thank the reporters for coming and not take any more questions. After the conference,

---

Spungen: We're looking at a new micro-processing line. I can't say much about it now, but we think it will be revolutionary.

White: *Didn't I read something about that in the trade press several months ago?*

Spungen: I wasn't aware of the story if you did.

White: *I learned that yesterday you were served with a suit from a group of minority and women employees. Can you tell me a bit more about this suit and what it might mean for your company's future profit outlook?*

Spungen: Well, we were notified about that in a confidential correspondence from the court. I absolutely cannot talk about that issue, either to confirm or deny the existence of any such suit.

White: *But wouldn't such a suit be potentially damaging to the company?*

Spungen: Look, we get sued all the time by various people. To highlight a suit by a few disgruntled employees would be playing into their hands. I certainly wouldn't want to get involved in publicizing these people. So let's drop the subject, okay?

QUESTIONS

1 If you were Spungen's public relations director, what would you have included in your briefing (had you had it) prior to the interview?

2 Do you think Spungen's answers were responsive?

3 How would you rate his response to the question about competition?

4 What do you think White might do with the "off the record" information Spungen gave him?

5 Do you think Spungen was right in standing his ground when White raised the minority suit issue? How might he have better handled the question?

FEATURE
The problem of publicity timing

Most everyone appreciates positive publicity. Politicians, in particular, would do just about anything to receive favorable recognition in the media. But occasionally, their timing is just a wee bit off.

Take the case of Illinois Senator Charles Percy, who eagerly called radio networks with his reaction to President Reagan's May 1981 speech to the Congress, Reagan's first after being wounded by an attempted assassin's bullet.

"I thought the President looked good, sounded good, and spoke with vigor," Senator Percy eagerly told the networks.

The only problem, as was later reported by a number of gloating newspapers, was that Senator Percy called in his reaction to the President's speech a full two and a half hours *before* the President delivered it.

An embarrassed Percy aide later explained that the Senator had gotten the full report on the President's condition earlier in the day from a colleague. What the aide didn't need to explain was that Senator Percy and his people had learned that, in dealing with publicity, timing, while not everything, is nonetheless excruciatingly important.

some reporters (particularly broadcast journalists) may want to ask follow-up questions on an individual basis. Do so only if all reporters have an opportunity to share in the one-on-one format.

Remember, the purpose of a news conference (and the reason reporters attend) is that reporters can ask questions. Questions should be handled as they would be with a single reporter. Every reporter should have a chance to speak up. One reporter shouldn't be allowed to dominate.

Often, it is up to the practitioner to make sure that the conference goes according to schedule and format.*

PRESS JUNKETS

A junket usually is billed as an "information visit" by journalists to a particular site, paid for by a sponsoring organization. The purpose of the trip—for example, film critics to Hollywood to screen a new film or travel writers to a far-away island to sample its hospitality—is to secure positive publicity.

Some news organizations flat-out reject junkets. *Harper's Magazine,* for instance, has a policy "not to solicit or accept contributions or subsidies from interested parties on matters on which the magazine plans to write." Others are less doctrinaire. Indeed, less prosperous publications find junkets a good way to report on out-of-the-way places and events that they couldn't afford to cover otherwise. As the *New Republic's* editor put it, "If you have honest people going, they will not be persuaded by the purchase of an airplane ticket for them."

* For additional practical information, see Sam Justice, "Dealing with the Financial Press," monograph, *Corporate Shareholder Press,* September 1978, and Dick Martin, *op. cit.*

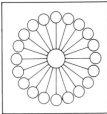

MINICASE
The agitated administrator

Chee Chee Gomez of the Eye Witness News team is at Elmsford Psychiatric Center to film an interview with hospital administrator Neal Shapiro. Earlier in the day an Elmsford patient had escaped and molested a woman in a city park before being captured.

Shapiro—his tie undone and his lip curled—agrees to take a few minutes for the "interrogation."

Gomez: *Mr. Shapiro, how could a patient with such a long history of mental illness be allowed to roam free on the grounds of the hospital and then escape undetected?*

Shapiro: In the first place, our patients are generally supervised as they perform their regular chores during the day. We have about forty very able guards. Each one has either been a regular police officer or a corrections officer and is also trained in working with mental patients. We have had a few, isolated incidents in the past several years, but nothing that I would call major. Our guards, as I said, go through a thorough training period before being assigned here. Generally, they supervise very well, and we haven't had much trouble. This case was a fluke. The man simply slipped away. I mean, what would you have us do? Chain him to his bed? This guy had a real history of severe problems. He should never have gotten away. Somebody just blew it.

But let me add that there was no way we could envision that he would ever do such a thing. For one thing, over the past several months he has been an excellent patient. He has taken his treatment, reacted well to supervision, and generally caused no problems. In this particular case, he probably just slipped away for a second and something snapped.

There is no way, it seems to me, that you can fault the institution on such an isolated incident. I simply do not feel that undue criticism of the institution or our supervisory staff in this case is warranted. Now, that's all I care to say.

QUESTIONS

1 What do you think of Shapiro's response?

2 If you wanted to portray Shapiro and his institution as the villain in this case, how would you edit his answer on film?

3 If you wanted to portray Shapiro and his institution as blameless, how would you edit the film?

4 Were you Shapiro's public relations advisor, how would you have suggested he answer questions?

Nonetheless, journalistic junkets should be arranged with extreme care. Occasionally, in fact, a sponsoring organization has been "sandbagged" by a cynical journalist who accepts the firm's generosity only to write sarcastically of the excesses he and his colleagues received.

The bottom line on junkets then is for public relations professionals to approach them with extreme caution.

PROFESSIONALISM: THE KEY

As is true with any other specialty in public relations work, the key to media relations is professionalism. Because management relies on the practitioners for expertise in effectively handling the media, they must not only know their own organization and management but also must be conversant in and respectful of the role and practice of journalists.

The best public relations/media relationship—indeed, the only successful one—must be one based on mutual understanding, trust, and respect.

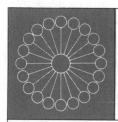

CASE STUDY
Illinois Power's reply

In the 1980s, no network news program had rivalled the incredible impact of CBS-TV's "60 Minutes." Watched each Sunday night by close to 40 million Americans, "60 Minutes" regularly ranks as one of the most popular programs in the nation and is the show most feared by public relations practitioners. When "60 Minutes" comes calling, scandal or at least significant problems can't be far away.

Such was the thinking at Illinois Power Company (IP) in Decatur, Ill., in the fall of 1979 when "60 Minutes" sent reporter Harry Reasoner to find out why the company's Clinton nuclear reactor project was behind schedule and over budget.

What followed—the exchange between "60 Minutes" and Illinois Power —ranks as a classic confrontation in the annals of public relations.

Because Illinois Power suspected that "60 Minutes" aimed to do a "hatchet job," the company agreed to the interviews only if it, too, videotaped the "60 Minutes" filming on its premises.

In other words, IP would videotape the videotapers; it would report on the reporters. Reasoner and his producer reluctantly agreed to the arrangement.

On November 25, 1979, "60 Minutes" broadcast a 16-minute segment on the Clinton plant, charging IP, as the company feared, with mismanagement, missed deadlines, and costly overruns that would be passed on to consumers.

Viewers saw three former IP employees accuse the utility of making no effort to control costs, of slipshod internal reporting, and of fabricating estimates of construction completion timetables. One of the accusers was shown in silhouette with a distorted voice because, as reporter Reasoner intoned, "he fears retribution."

The day after the CBS story, IP's stock fell a full point on the New York Stock Exchange in the busiest trading day in the company's history.

Rather than responding as most companies do with bruised feelings, a scorched reputation, and feeble cries of "foul" to its stockholders, IP lashed back with barrels blazing.

Within days of the broadcast, IP produced "60 Minutes/Our Reply," a 44-minute film incorporating the entire "60 Minutes" segment, punctuated by insertions and narrative presenting the company's rebuttal.

The rebuttal included videotape of CBS film footage not included in the program, much of which raised serious questions about the integrity of the material CBS used. The rebuttal also documented the backgrounds and possible motives of the three former employees CBS quoted, all of whom had been fired for questionable performance. One of the former employees, in fact, was the leader of the local antinuclear group opposing IP.

Initially, the reply tape was aired to a relatively small audience: the company's employees, customers, shareholders, and investors. But word traveled quickly that Illinois Power had produced a riveting, broadcast-quality production, so true to the "60 Minutes" format—ticking stopwatch and all—that it could easily be mistaken for the original itself.

Within a year, close to 2,500 copies of the devastating rebuttal had been distributed to legislators, corporate executives, journalists, and others. Excerpts were broadcast on television stations throughout the nation, and the IP production became legendary. As *The Wall Street Journal* put it, "the program focuses new attention on news accuracy . . . Although even a telling, polished, counter-program like Illinois Power's can't reach the masses of a national broadcast, the reply tape has proven effective in reaching a significant 'thinking' audience."[5]

Even CBS was impressed. The producer of the original "60 Minutes" segment called the rebuttal highly "sophisticated," especially for a company that had first seemed to him to be a "down-home cracker barrel" outfit.

The Illinois Power tape soon spawned imitators. Companies like Chevron, Union Carbide, Commonwealth Edison, and many others began experimenting with defensive videotaping in dealing with television journalists.

And while "60 Minutes" admitted to some sloppiness in its reporting and to two minor factual inaccuracies, it essentially stood by its account. Complained CBS executive producer Don Hewitt, "We went in as a disinterested party and did a news report. They made a propaganda film for their side, using our reporting for their own purposes."

Perhaps.

But one irrefutable result of the dramatic confrontation between the huge national network and the tiny local utility was that Illinois Power Company had earned its place in public relations history as the company that brought mighty "60 Minutes" to its knees.

(Ironically, three years after the Illinois Power confrontation, a *TV Guide* poll discovered that America's "most trusted television journalist" was Harry Reasoner. Evidently, nobody asked Illinois Power.)*

QUESTIONS

1 Do you agree with Illinois Power's original decision to let "60 Minutes" in despite the suspicion that the program would be a "hatchet job"? What might have happened if IP turned down the "60 Minutes" request?

2 If "60 Minutes" had turned down Illinois Power's request to videotape the Reasoner interviews, would you have still allowed the filming?

3 Presume Illinois Power didn't tape the "60 Minutes" filming on its premises. What other communications options might the company have pursued to rebut the "60 Minutes" accusations?

4 Do you think IP did "better" by allowing "60 Minutes" in to film or would they have been better off keeping CBS out?

* For further information on the Illinois Power Case, see *Punch, Counterpunch: 60 Minutes vs. Illinois Power Company*, The Media Institute, Washington, D.C., 1981; and "Turning the Tables on 60 Minutes," *Columbia Journalism Review*, May/June 1980.

NOTES

1 Carl Cannon, "The Great Flack Flap," *Washington Journalism Review*, September 1982, p. 35.

2 Charles W. Stevens, "Cherry Picker Got Him to the Roof, But Not Onto Fortune's New Cover," *The Wall Street Journal*, 15 September 1981.

3 Bill Hogan, "The Boom in Regional Business Journals," *Washington Journalism Review*, July/August 1982, p. 35.

4 Merrill Brown, "News Feature Offered by American Express," *The Washington Post*, 6 August 1982, p. C7; "The Last Word In Business Communication," *Nation's Business*, October 1982, pp. 34–36.

5 *The Wall Street Journal*, 21 April 1980, p. 32.

SUGGESTED READING

Bennett, Michael J. "The 'Imperial' Press Corps," *Public Relations Journal*, June 1982, pp. 10–13.

Caruba, Alan. "Satellite TV: New Way To Educate Physicians," *Public Relations Journal*, October 1981, p. 20.

Fang, Irving E. *Television News*, 2nd ed. New York: Hastings House, 1972. Helpful hints for the user of TV as a publicity outlet.

Golden, Harry, and **Hanson, Kitty.** *Techniques of Working with the Working Press*. New York: Oceana Publicatons, 1962.

Hynds, Ernest D. *American Newspapers in the 1970s*. New York: Hastings House, 1975.

Johnson, Daniel. "Try This Approach For Breaking News," *Public Relations Journal*, September 1981, pp. 28–29.

Kennedy, Bruce M. *Community Journalism.* Ames, Iowa: Iowa State University Press, 1973.

Klein, Ted, and **Danzig, Fred.** *How to Be Heard: Making the Media Work for You.* New York: MacMillan, 1974.

Kowal, John Paul. "Understanding the Media: If a Newspaper Hums, Hum Back," *Public Relations Quarterly,* Summer 1981, p. 11.

Lindt, David, ed. *The Publicity Process.* Ames, Iowa: Iowa State University Press, 1975.

Martin, Dick. *Executive's Guide to Handling a Press Interview.* New York: Pilot Books, 1977.

McCombs, Maxwell E. *Mass Media in the Marketplace.* Journalism Monographs, no. 24. Minneapolis: Association for Education in Journalism, 1974.

River, William L. *Mass Media.* 2nd ed. New York: Harper and Row, 1975, A good reference guide for preparing information to be used by different media.

Roalman, Arthur R. "Ten Sometimes Fatal Mistakes Top Executives Make in Press Interviews," *Management Review,* July 1975, pp. 4–10.

Spitzer, Carlton E. "Fear Of The Media," *Public Relations Journal,* November 1981, pp. 58–63. Business fears the media and usually acts accordingly. It is time for both adversaries to clean up their houses and develop a more productive relationship.

Turow, Joseph and **Park, Ceritta.** "TV Publicity Outlets: Preliminary Investigation," *Public Relations Review,* Fall 1981, pp. 15–24.

Weiner, Richard. *Professional's Guide to Publicity.* New York: Richard Weiner, 1976.

Wolseley, Roland E. *The Changing Magazine: Trends in Readership and Management.* New York: Hastings House, 1973.

Young, Lewis H. "The Media's View of Corporate Communications in the 80's" *Public Relations Quarterly,* Spring 1982, pp. 9–11.

EXPLOSIVE GROWTH

The growth of public relations work, both in dealing with government and in the government itself, has been explosive over the past decade.

The burgeoning of the federal government is a relatively recent phenomenon. Since 1970, some twenty new federal regulatory agencies have sprung up, from the Environmental Protection Agency to the Consumer Product Safety Commission to the Department of Energy to the Occupational Safety and Health Administration. Moreover, according to the General Accounting Office, some 116 government agencies and programs now regulate business. And while in the 1950s and 60s, the business community was primarily interested in keeping government at arm's length, today, as one corporate official put it, "The chief executive is seeing increasingly that more and more of the day-to-day decisions are made, not in his boardroom, but in Washington."[1]

To deal with the larger and more potent government bureaucracy, organizations have upgraded and bolstered their government relations functions.

As for the government itself, its public relations function also has been expanded and enhanced. While President Nixon preferred advertising professionals as his closest advisors, in the Reagan Administration, numerous public relations professionals held key slots.

Ironically, the public relations function traditionally has been something of a stepchild in the government. In 1913, the Congress enacted the Gillett amendment, which almost barred the practice of public relations in government. The amendment stemmed from efforts by President Theodore Roosevelt to win public support for his programs

16
Government

through the use of a network of "publicity experts." Congress, worried about the potential of this unlimited presidential persuasive power, passed the amendment, which stated: "Appropriated funds may not be used to pay a publicity expert unless specifically appropriated for that purpose."

Several years later, still leery of the president's power to influence legislation through communication, Congress passed the "gag law," which prohibited "using any part of an appropriation for services, messages, or publications designed to influence any member of Congress in his attitude toward legislation or appropriations."

Even today, no government worker may be employed in the practice of "public relations." However, the government is flooded with "public affairs" experts, "information" officers, "press" secretaries, and "communications" specialists. The Civil Service Commission estimates that more than 21,300 people are employed in federal public affairs jobs.[2]

In both the government and in the organizations that deal with the government, the practice of public relations has become more important. Through the 1970s, most organizations emphasized *federal* government relations. Today, with the shift in public policy toward more decisions at the state and local levels, government relations closer to home have become more important.

PUBLIC RELATIONS IN GOVERNMENT

Unfortunately, when people think about public relations in government, they tend to envision either a blonde bombshell bursting in air over the Capitol dome, a piggish congressman stuffing cash in his pockets as a secret videotape camera records the scene, or some senator or another checking into a hospital to treat some kind of antisocial behavior. Such predilections are indeed unfortunate and unfair.

Most practitioners in government communicate the activities of the various agencies, commissions, and bureaus to the public. As consumer activist Ralph Nader has said, "In this nation, where the ultimate power is said to rest with the people, it is clear that a free and prompt flow of information from government to the people is essential."

Just as the size and scope of industry public relations activities vary, so too do those in government. Offices range from one employee operations in cities and state capitals to the U.S. Department of Agriculture's $10 million information system radiating from Washington to 146 public affairs officers.

The volume of information initiated in Washington is so great that it is almost impossible for newspapers to cover the Capitol without the assistance of public relations professionals. In the words of columnist James J. Kilpatrick, "Those of us who try to cover Washington, however feebly, are utterly dependent upon the information officers. . . . What counts is the integrity of the information men."

UNITED STATES INFORMATION AGENCY

Most far-reaching of the federal government's public relations apparatus is the United States Information Agency (USIA), which for a brief time was called the International Communications Agency. USIA employs 8,000 people and is America's public relations arm in more than 100 countries around the world. Its budget today is slightly under half a billion dollars. While that might seem rather hefty as public relations budgets go, USIA officials claim that the U.S.S.R. has 77,000 people and a budget of about $3 billion performing this same function.

USIA's primary mission is "to support the national interest by conveying an understanding abroad of what the United States stands for as a nation and as a people; to explain the nation's policies and to present a true picture of the society, institutions and culture in which those policies evolve."[3]

Under the direction of such well-known media personalities as Edward R. Murrow, Carl Rowan, and Frank Shakespeare, the agency has employed a multimedia approach to communications through:

1 **Radio**   Voice of America has 106 transmitters, broadcasts in forty languages and, in an average week, reaches more than 75 million people with a staff of 2,000.

   In addition to Voice of America, the USIA in 1981 adopted plans for Radio Marti, in honor of José Marti, father of Cuban independence. Radio Marti's purpose was to broadcast to Cuba in Spanish and "tell the truth to the Cuban people."

2 **Film and television**   USIA produces and acquires over 200 films annually for distribution in 125 countries and also films news clips for overseas television use.

3 **Media**   About 20,000 words a day are radio-teletyped to 200 overseas posts for placement in media.

4 **Publications**   Overseas regional service centers publish fifteen magazines in thirty-one languages and distribute pamphlets, leaflets, and posters to over 100 countries.

5 **Exhibitions**   USIA designs and manages about fifty major exhibits each year throughout the world, including eastern European countries and the Soviet Union.

6 **Libraries and books**   USIA maintains or supports libraries in over 200 information centers and binational centers in more than ninety countries and assists publishers in distributing books overseas.

7 **Education**   USIA also is active overseas in sponsoring educational programs through 111 binational centers where English is taught and in 11 language centers. Classes draw about 350,000 students annually.

GOVERNMENT BUREAUS

Nowhere has government public relations activity become more aggressive than in federal departments and regulatory agencies. Many agencies, in fact, have found that the quickest way to gain recognition is to increase public relations aggressiveness.

The Federal Trade Commission (FTC), which columnist Jack Anderson once called a "sepulcher of official secrets," opened up in the late 1970s to become one of the most active of government communicators. As a former FTC director of public information described the agency's attitude, "The basic premise underlying the Commission's public information program is the public's inherent right to know what the FTC is doing."[4]

When the FTC found a company's products wanting in standards of safety or quality, it often announced its complaint through a press conference. While corporate critics branded this process "trial by press release," it helped transform the agency from a meek, mild-mannered bureau to an office with real teeth.

R obert Keith Gray is the founder and chairman of Gray and Company, a major national public affairs/public relations firm based in Washington, D.C. Mr. Gray is former vice chairman and head of Washington operations for Hill and Knowlton, Inc. Prior to joining Hill and Knowlton in 1961, he served the Eisenhower Administration in various capacities, including Secretary of the Cabinet and Appointments Secretary. He is author of *Eighteen Acres Under Glass,* an account of his years at the White House. Mr. Gray was co-chairman of the 1981 Presidential Inauguration Committee and director of communications during the 1980 Reagan-Bush campaign.

What makes a good lobbyist?

There is no magic concoction from which a lobbyist is brewed. Likewise, there is no one trait or skill that separates the effective lobbyist from the ineffective one.

A knowledge of the legislative process certainly is essential. The rules under which the House and Senate operate govern the lobbyist's course of action. Plainly and simply, know Capitol Hill, its faces, which are many and always changing, its pace, which can be hectic, and its rules.

A member of Congress survives by keeping one eye on a given issue and the other on the clock, so you have to know the limitations of a Member's time. Prepare your client's case carefully, target your Member; then, when you have been granted an audience, state your case intelligently and crisply. A tip: If it takes less than the time allotted, you will improve your chances for a quick appointment the next time you ask for one.

In lobbying, are "contacts" everything?

No! A good case is far more important than a good contact. A friend in the right place, a press aide who was particularly cordial at a dinner party, your high school sweetheart who vowed to marry a Member of Congress and did—contacts like these can and often do serve the lobbyist well.

But they do not make the lobbyist; it is the other way around. A good lobbyist develops contacts and learns to keep them. The secret is maintaining a productive relationship with a given contact year in and year out. Public relations, lobbying, politics—all are give-and-take professions. The best lobbyists operate under the "What can I do to help you?" maxim.

Lobbying has grown more complicated in the last fifteen years. Back in the days of the single-issue lobbyists, it may have been possible for lobbyists to get automatic votes from pet congressmen, but those days are gone. Today, Members speak and vote their minds. Legislators, however, are open and responsive to a good argument, and the construction and delivery of one—and its applicability to district or state interests or national goals. These are the high cards the lobbyist holds.

What is the most common mistake lobbyists make?

Operating with less than full facts. Know your issue, know it well! There is nothing more basic to the lobbyist than preparation.

On the other hand, the Member should be informed and intrigued by your proposal, not overwhelmed by it. Inexperienced lobbyists sometimes press too hard. They oversell their cases, insist on presenting more information than anyone has time to read or wants to hear.

In your government relations work, are there some clients who you will not accept?

Obviously, we will not accept any client whose request conflicts with national security. We also feel strongly about protecting the interests of clients we already represent. So if a prospective client proposes a project which in turn poses an unresolvable conflict between Gray and Company and an existing client, we would decline the proposal.

What are the fundamental principles of good government relations work?

Lobbying and good government relations work share many of the same tactics. One-on-one confrontations are common in both fields. The more you know about the constituency of the person you are lobbying, the more successful you will be. If you are dealing with a Member of the House or Senate, then know that person's political record.

How will your proposal bear on the Member's district? Will local jobs be affected? How many people stand to benefit from the proposal? What is its effect on taxes, balance of payments, foreign trade? Argue your point on a district as well as national level.

Maintain your credibility. Never leave a Member with facts you cannot verify. If you find you have erred, rush back to square the record. Leave every visit with the welcome mat out for a return.

Finally, work with the staff! A Member's support of your cause may depend on the support of his staff. Staff will do the follow-up work on your case as soon as you walk out the door.

How important are lobbyists in influencing legislation?

Today's legislator, given the preponderance of issues and the limits of time, is overworked and often under-informed. The complexities of our society spread the Member and his or her staff so thin that they can only hope to know the general line on a plethora of issues.

In this arena, the lobbyist offers the legislator refined information about how a certain issue will affect employment, products, prices, etc. The lobbyist thus provides practical application to legislative theory.

The modern legislator understandably is very responsive to those who bring clear understanding to issues. The lobbyist fills an information void with solid facts and persuasive arguments.

(Interview *continues.*)

Other government departments also have stepped up public relations efforts. The Department of Defense had a public affairs budget of $31 million and a staff of over 1,000 people. The Department of Health and Human Services had a public affairs staff of 550 people and a budget of $45 million. The departments of Agriculture and Treasury also have substantial communications staffs. Even the Central Intelligence Agency has a 20-person group of public affairs experts.

THE PRESIDENT

Despite early congressional efforts to limit the persuasive power of the nation's chief executive, the president today wields unprecedented public relations clout.

Almost anything the president does or says makes news. The broadcast networks, daily newspapers, and national magazines follow his every move. His press secretary provides the White House press corps (a group of national reporters assigned to cover the president) with a constant flow of announcements supplemented by daily press briefings. Unlike many organizational press releases that seldom make it into print, many White House releases achieve national exposure.

While most journalists resent administration attempts at news management (some call it news manipulation), most succomb to it. As one publication put it, "The ways a president can influence the news are endless. For example, announcements of favorable developments are made from the White House, while gloomy tidings are usually reported by individual agencies."[5]

Typical of such news management was President Jimmy Carter's Administration in the late 1970s. When his image as a forceful leader began to wane in late 1978, he brought in media specialist Gerald Rafshoon to help improve it. Thereafter, the president began announcing federal grants in local communities, holding town meetings around the country, and even taking adventurous vacations, such as a raft trip down the Idaho rapids. Some believed that even the historic Camp David summit, which brought together the traditional enemies of Israel and Egypt, was (at least below the surface) a "Rafshoon production."

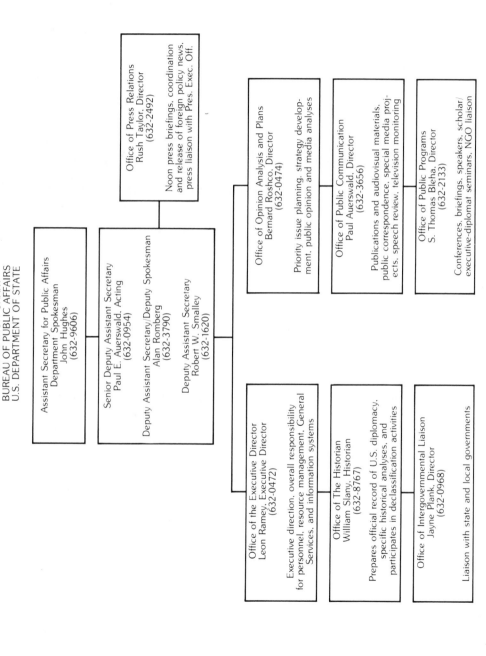

FIGURE 16-1. *State Department public affairs organization chart.* The Bureau of Public Affairs in the U.S. Department of State is typical of the public information mechanism in a federal department. The Assistant Secretary for Public Affairs in the State Department and in most other federal agencies reports directly to the Secretary.

SOURCE: Courtesy of United States Department of State.

Ronald Reagan, as noted, has been perhaps the most masterful presidential communicator in recent history. Reagan was weaned in the movies and on television, and even his most ardent critics agreed the president possessed a compelling stage presence. So formidable have been the persuasive powers of "the great communicator" that when CBS broadcast a critical 1982 documentary against Reagan's budget cuts, White House reporters objected strenuously to the president and his aides singling the broadcast out for criticism. "How can you say that it (White House criticism) is not going to have a chilling effect on our profession?" moaned a Washington correspondent.[6] In the face of such media angst, the White House dropped its offensive.

Later in the spring of 1983, when Reagan's Interior Secretary James Watt forbade the popular music group, the Beach Boys, from performing on the Capitol

FEATURE
The "imperial" press corps

The Washington press corps, the group of reporters assigned to follow the president and report on Washington, has for years warned of the dangers of an "imperial presidency" in which the president becomes omnipotent in his ability to control public opinion.

In recent years however, an "imperial press corps" also has developed among the people who cover the president.

The Washington press corps has expanded enormously within the past twenty years. During President Kennedy's term, fewer than 300 reporters were accredited to cover the White House. Today, the number is around 3,000.

In the old days, when only *The New York Times,* the late *New York Herald-Tribune,* and the *Chicago Tribune* had bureaus with ten or more members, Washington coverage spanned as well as possible the entire government apparatus. Today, by contrast, every paper with any pretention to national significance—the *Boston Globe, Newsday, Atlanta Constitution,* and many others—has at least ten Washington bureau members. The focus of their coverage has shifted inexorably to one person—the president of the United States.

Moreover, the position of White House reporter has become a status symbol in the journalistic profession. Salaries of $40–50,000, relatively rare in most newspaper offices, are commonplace in Washington bureaus. Indeed, with the salaries of congressional and cabinet-level positions limited by law, Washington reporters often make more money—perhaps considerably more—than the newsmakers they cover. For example, network correspondents command six-figure incomes, with each major network assigning two or three such correspondents to cover the White House simultaneously.

Sometime after he had retired, Lyndon Johnson, the first chief executive to be labeled an "imperial president" by the Washington press corps, was asked by a TV reporter what force or influence he thought had done the most to shape the nature of Washington policy.

"You bastards," Johnson snapped in history's first reference to the "imperial press corps."[7]

Mall on July 4th, the President's communication savvy again saved the day. He immediately presented Watt with a plaster foot to symbolize where he "shot himself." The Reagan gesture once again reversed an embarassing situation and resulted in even more goodwill for the "great communicator." Indeed, despite the regular ups and downs of any presidency, it was largely agreed that among President Reagan's most potent skills was his ability to persuade the people.

THE PRESIDENT'S PRESS SECRETARY

Some have called the job of presidential press secretary the second most difficult position in any administration. The press secretary is the chief public relations spokesperson for the administration. Like practitioners in private industry, the press secretary must communicate the policies and practices of the management (the president) to the public.

Often it is an impossible job.

In 1974, Gerald terHorst, President Ford's press secretary, quit after disagreeing with the pardon of former President Richard Nixon. Said terHorst, "A spokesman should feel in his heart and mind that the chief's decision is the right one so that he can speak with a persuasiveness that stems from conviction."[8]

A contrasting view of the press secretary's role was expressed by terHorst's replacement in the job, former NBC reporter Ron Nessen. Said Nessen, "A press secretary does not always have to agree with the president. His first loyalty is to the public, and he should not knowingly lie or mislead the press."[9]

Still a third view of the proper role of the press secretary was offered by a former public relations professional and Nixon speech writer who became a *New York Times* political columnist, William Safire. Said Safire:

> A good press secretary speaks up for the press to the president and speaks out for the president to the press. He makes his home in the pitted no-man's-land of an adversary relationship and is primarily an advocate, interpreter and amplifier. He must be more the president's man than the press's. But he can be his own man as well.[10]

In recent years, the position of press secretary to the president has taken on increased responsibility and attained a higher public profile. Jimmy Carter's press secretary, Jody Powell, for example, was among Carter's closest confidants and frequently advised the President on policy matters. Powell's successor as press secretary, James Brady, was seriously wounded in 1981 by a bullet aimed at President Reagan as they both departed a Washington hotel. Although Brady was permanently paralyzed, he retained his title as presidential press secretary and returned for limited work at the White House.

DEALING WITH GOVERNMENT

The business community, foundations, philanthropic, and quasi-public organizations have a common problem: how to deal with government, particularly the mammoth federal bureaucracy.

Because government has become so pervasive in organizational and individual life, the number of corporations and trade associations with government relations units has grown steadily in recent years.

Government relations people primarily are concerned with weighing impending legislation for its impact on the company, industry group, or client organization. Generally, a head office government relations staff complements staff members who represent the organization in Washington and state capitols.

These representatives have several objectives:

1 To improve communications with government personnel and agencies.
2 To monitor legislators and regulatory agencies in areas affecting constituent operations.
3 To encourage constituent participation at all levels of government.
4 To influence legislation affecting the economy of the constituent's area as well as its operations.
5 To advance awareness and understanding among lawmakers of the activities and operations of constituent organizations.

To carry out these objectives, it is essential to learn one's way around the federal government and to acquire connections. A full-time Washington representative is often employed for these tasks.

To the uninitiated, Washington (or almost any state capitol) can seem an incomprehensible maze. Consequently, organizations with an interest in government relations usually employ a professional representative, who may or may not be a registered *lobbyist,* whose responsibility, among other things, is to influence legislation.

Lobbyists are required to comply with the federal Lobbying Act of 1947, which imposes certain reporting requirements on individuals or organizations that spend a significant portion of time or money attempting to influence members of Congress on legislation. Some have described this act as "vague, essentially unenforceable, and in need of revision."[11]

Indeed, the Supreme Court rewrote the law in 1953 and greatly narrowed the act's application in order to find it constitutional. In point of fact, one need not register as a lobbyist in order to speak to a senator, congressional representative, or staff member about legislation. But a good lobbyist can earn the respect and trust of a legislator.

Because of the need to analyze legislative proposals and deal with members of Congress, many lobbyists are lawyers with a heavy Washington background. Lobbying ranks are filled with former administration officials and Congress members, who often turn immediately to lobbying when they move out of office.

While lobbyists, at times, have been labeled as everything from *influence peddlers* to *fixers,* such epithets are generally inaccurate and unfair. Today's lobbyist is more likely to be "a technician, competent and well-informed in his field . . . performing a vital function in furnishing Congress with facts and information."[12] Indeed, the lobbyist's function is rooted in the first amendment right of all citizens to petition government.

WHAT DO LOBBYISTS DO?

Lobbyists inform and persuade. Their contacts are important, but they must also have the right information available for the right legislator. The time to plant ideas with legislators is well *before* a bill is drawn up, and skillful lobbyists recognize that timing is critical in influencing legislation.

The specific activities performed by individual lobbyists vary with the nature of the industry or group represented. Most take part in these activities:

1 **Fact-finding** The government is an incredible storehouse of facts, statistics, economic data, opinions, and decisions, which generally are available for the asking.

2 **Interpretation of government actions** A key function of the lobbyist is to interpret for management the significance of government events and the potential implications of pending legislation. Often, a lobbyist predicts what can be expected to happen legislatively and recommends actions to deal with the expected outcome.

3 **Interpretation of company actions** Through almost daily contact with Congress members and staff assistants, a lobbyist conveys how her group feels about legislation. The lobbyist must be completely versed in the business of her client and the attitude of the organization toward governmental actions.

4 **Advocacy of a position** Beyond the presentation of facts, a lobbyist also advocates positions on behalf of clients, both pro and con. Often, hitting a congressional representative early with a stand on pending legislation can mean getting a fair hearing for the client's position. Indeed, few congressional representatives have the time to study—or even read—every piece of legislation on which they are asked to vote. Therefore, they depend on lobbyists for information, especially for information on how proposed legislation might affect constituents.

5 **Publicity springboard** More news comes out of Washington than any other city in the world. It's the base for close to 2,000 press, TV, radio, and magazine correspondents. This multiplicity of media makes it the ideal springboard for launching organizational publicity. The same holds true to a lesser degree in state capitals.

6 **Support to company sales** The government is one of the nation's largest purchasers of products. Lobbyists often serve as conduits through which sales are made. A lobbyist who is friendly with government personnel can serve as a valuable link for leads to company business.

"GRASSROOTS" LOBBYING

Particularly effective recently has been the use of indirect or "grassroots" lobbying (as opposed to conventional lobbying by paid agents). The main thrust of such lobbying is to mobilize local constituents of Congress members, together with the general public, to write, telephone, telegraph, or buttonhole members of Congress on legislation.

Grassroots lobbying is a tactic that has been used most effectively by everyone from so-called consumer advocates, such as the Ralph Nader Organization and Common Cause, to President Ronald Reagan. In the early 1980s, a resurgence of citizens' activism, not seen since the 1960s, began to appear. Coalitions formed on issues from arms to economics on both national and local levels. Locally, tenants organizations, neighborhood associations, and various other local groups won significant concessions from government and corporate bodies. Nationally, the Nuclear Freeze Campaign, for one, made its way onto many November 1982 state election ballots and received widespread support.

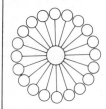

MINICASE
The dubious shrimp

At the Chamber of Commerce's annual holiday cocktail party for legislators and press, Al Henderson, Consolidated Brands lobbyist, ran into Rep. Charley Franklin, a member of the House of Representatives subcommittee on tariff legislation. While savoring shrimp over a bountifully-laden table of hors d'oeuvres, Henderson had the following conversation with Rep. Franklin:

"Charley, it's good to see that your heavy duties on the subcommittee permit you to come down from the hill to relax from time-to-time."

Rep. Franklin smiled as he speared a fat shrimp with a toothpick. "Well, Al, I look on these occasions as an extension of my congressional work, an opportunity to feel the public pulse on key legislative issues."

"Speaking of legislation, Charley, do you see a possibility of the committee acting this session on HR 6821, which would impose duties on imports of seafood?"

Rep. Franklin stopped munching. "It will be difficult to complete action this session, Al. As you know, the administration is dead against it. They see it reversing our long-time, free-trade stance. Besides, we don't want to risk alienating any potential allies."

"Like Russia?" Al demanded. "Those commies are catching seafood right off our shores and then selling it back to us at costs below our processing costs." Al paused and stared at the shrimp he was ready to consume. "Do you think the Chamber would serve imported shrimp?" He whispered, dropping the shrimp back into the dish.

"Since they're here, I'd hate to see them go to waste," Rep. Franklin said, spearing the shrimp Al had put back.

Al grew serious. "Charley, these foreign fishermen not only are hurting the U.S. fishing fleet, but also a lot of processors and canners of seafood. I wish you'd support the measure to bolster America's sagging trade balance."

"O.K. Al, I will keep it in mind when—and if—we get to hearings on HR 6821," Rep. Franklin said, popping in one more shrimp for the road.

QUESTIONS

1 What do you think of Henderson's conversation with Rep. Franklin?
2 Would you have handled it differently if you were Henderson?
3 Is there any statement that Henderson made with which you would disagree?
4 What about Rep. Franklin? How would you assess his reaction to Al's comments?
5 Do you think Al's approach is an example of the most professional kind of lobbying?

The success of such grassroots campaigns was not lost on big business. Business learned that grassroots lobbying—applying pressure from the fifty states and the 435 Congressional constituencies, from corporate headquarters to plant communities—was at the heart of moving the powers in Washington. In one of the most successful grassroots campaigns in history, the upstart money market fund industry in 1981 soundly trounced the more entrenched banking establishment by organizing a massive grassroots letter-writing campaign. Constituents from all over the country wrote their congressional representatives and state legislators "to keep hands off the money funds." One outgrowth was that threatened legislation to limit the funds never was instituted.

Such indirect lobbying may seek to a) persuade community leaders to meet directly with their congressional representative, b) mobilize telephone calls and individualized letters to Congress members, c) instigate mass mailings of postcards or coupons from advertisements, or d) exhort shareholders, members, employees, and customers to pressure Congress.[13]

Whatever the objectives, grassroots lobbying and lobbying in general are very much in vogue. Rare is the group not represented in Washington. The popcorn industry has its Popcorn Institute. The automatic telephone dialing service industry has a lobbyist. Pro-hunters have Safari Club International, and anti-hunters have the Fund for Animals. There's even a billboard lobby, the Outdoor Advertising Association of America. All believe their efforts are worthwhile.

Lobbyists are a gritty breed. Even the underdog is positive that somewhere in the vast network of official Washington there is a friendly ear, no matter how much of a pariah his cause might currently be. His task: to find it, cherish it, nurture it, and finally to ask it a favor.[14]

POLITICAL ACTION COMMITTEES

A relatively new, fast-growing, and perfectly legal mechanism for unified support of political candidates by members of incorporated bodies is the political action committee (PAC).

Between 1974 and 1980, the number of federally registered PACs nearly quadrupled, with the largest increase coming from corporations. Today, one-half of the 2,300 PACs in the United States are sponsored by corporations. The Federal Election Commission, which gathers and reports figures from all PACs, recorded PAC receipts from January 1979 to August 1980 as $113 million, the majority of which went to support political candidates.

For many years, the law prohibited corporations from making direct political contributions. In recent years however, the Federal Election Campaign Act of 1971 with subsequent amendments generally allowed incorporated bodies to "solicit funds, maintain them in a segregated fund, pay all expenses of the fund, and disperse the funds at the discretion of the organization's management.[15]

While some politicians publicly voice concern about the clout of PACs in influencing elections, the facts thus far indicate that such fears are either unfounded or at least premature. The average corporate PAC in 1980 took in $24,000 in contributions, the average trade association PAC, $50,000, and the average labor union PAC, $73,000. These sums were hardly enough to play a dominant role in influencing elections. Also, within organizations themselves, PACs must observe strict rules in carrying out their mandates. All donations must be entirely voluntary with any coercion to contribute strictly prohibited. (See Figure 16–2).

While PACs, to date, have hardly wielded enormous clout in elections, their development will be observed closely as they become more of a factor in the years ahead.

DEALING WITH THE CONGRESS

The name of the game in Washington is influencing legislation. And the key to wielding such influence revolves around having *good* information. Legislators work on information. Hence, it is the timely presentation of accurate information that counts. A key vote may be effected by other considerations from time-to-time, but usually Members of Congress are most sensitive to what will affect the voting in their area.

■ What is ChasePAC?
ChasePAC is a registered Political Action Committee—that is, an organization empowered to solicit donations from Chase personnel and to contribute these funds to political candidates on the federal, state and local levels. ChasePAC's affairs are conducted in accordance with federal and New York State laws. ChasePAC is registered with the Federal Election Commission in Washington and with the State Board of Elections in Albany.

■ What statutory authorization is there for establishment of corporate PACs?
Establishment of corporate PACs has been authorized by the Federal Election Campaign Act and by the New York State Election Law. In fact, operation of a PAC is the only legally sanctioned way in which a bank or corporation may involve itself in fund-raising in connection with any campaign for federal public office. As you know, Chase is prohibited by law from contributing corporate funds to candidates or political committees in connection with any election for federal public office.

■ How many similar Political Action Committees are in existence?
Since enactment of the Federal Election Campaign Act, the corporate PAC movement has mushroomed. Today there are more than 1,000 such committees in existence, including over 100 PACs in the banking industry nationwide and in about a half dozen major banks headquartered in New York City.

■ What is the purpose of ChasePAC?
The purpose of ChasePAC is to provide a convenient way for Chase personnel to pool their personal funds in order to extend tangible support on both the federal and state levels to political candidates whose views on important issues are consistent with Chase positions.

■ How much would any candidate receive from the fund?
It is anticipated that a typical contribution would range between $200 and $400. This level of giving appears to be consistent with the pattern of other corporate Political Action Committees.

CHASE believes that sound government can only be achieved through the full participation of its citizens. As a result, The Chase Manhattan Corporation has established a Political Action Committee (ChasePAC) to give its staff members a means to contribute as a group to responsible men and women who seek public office.

To find out more about ChasePAC and how you can participate in its activities, we invite you to read this Fact Book which has been prepared to explain how ChasePAC works and to answer questions you may have about the organization.

You will also find an enrollment card printed in this booklet. Please use this card at the time you decide to join your fellow Chase staff members in contributing to this political action fund.

If after reading this brochure you have any further questions, you may contact Herbert W. Abrams, Treasurer of ChasePAC, 552-3733.

FIGURE 16–2. Chase PAC Q&A. This question and answer sheet, mailed to each potential member of the Chase Manhattan Bank Political Action Committee, offers the kind of simple explanations that are typical of most corporate PACs.
SOURCE: Courtesy of The Chase Manhattan Bank.

FEATURE
Just keep talking . . .

One of the most disconcerting elements of congressional testimony to the person testifying is the common practice for legislative committee members to conduct private conversations or other business while a witness testifies.

Understandably, such cross-talk and apparent rudeness gets annoying. Inexperienced witnesses will stop, pause, and sometimes even call attention to the non-attention of committee members.

The best advice for any witnesses, however difficult it might be, is to continue their remarks or answers as if they are getting the full attention of the committee.

For one thing, legislators are busy people with many conflicting, simultaneous pressures. For another, legislators are relatively powerful and should not be alienated.

Besides, a stenographer records all comments as a witness testifies and answers questions. And even though committee members may not be listening, their staff aides may well be. Often, staff aides know more than the legislators and wield enormous influence in the legislators' thinking and voting. Therefore, if the Congress Member converses while you testify—just keep talking.

TESTIFY

One way to reach Congress, of course, is through giving testimony, either in connection with legislation, a special investigation, or a nonlegislative study designed to examine a particular issue.

Congressional witnesses must do their homework. They must write out their testimony and know it well enough to explain it confidently and articulately. They should also prepare for sharp interrogation by Members of Congress. Even if testifying on legislation with general backing, there are always at least two points of view that invariably emerge in every hearing—Republicans versus Democrats, conservatives versus liberals, business versus labor, one-worlders versus protectionists—the gamut of ideological, philosphical, ethnic, and religious viewpoints.

WRITE

Another effective means of getting through to a busy legislator is by writing. Since Members of Congress receive scores of letters, the following helpful hints, offered by Washington public affairs counselor John J. Daly, may aid in getting through:

1 Keep letters brief and to the point.
2 Write on business or personal letterhead; always sign your name.
3 Identify the subject clearly. State the name of the legislation about which you are writing. Give the House/Senate bill number or, at least, a short abbreviation or nickname of the bill.

4 State the reason for writing. Personal experience is the best supporting evidence. Explain how the issue affects you, your family, business, or profession, or what effect it could have on your state or community.

5 Don't cry "wolf." Not every governmental action is going to put a person out of business and members of Congress are sensitive to unnecessarily extreme claims.

6 Don't be argumentative. A letter is not a debate. Its purpose is to convince, not intimidate.

7 Don't name-call. Identifying the "enemy" adds nothing to the dialogue.

8 Ask for the legislator's position on the issue when he replies. As a constituent, you're entitled to know.

9 Consider timing. The best time to write is when a bill is in committee. Legislators are more responsive when a bill is still being discussed in the committee forum.

10 Congratulate them on the good things, don't write just to complain. Praise is more likely to be remembered.

11 Don't send the local newspapers the text of your letter. That's blackmail. Neither members of Congress nor anyone else appreciates such a tactic.

12 Avoid form letters. Often, lobbying groups direct thousands of letters to Congress members, all saying the same thing. The typical Congressional response is to toss out these form appeals. It's much better to tailor each letter you write.

VISITING THE CAPITOL

Perhaps the most effective way of reaching legislators is to visit them.

First, arrange to meet your representative or senator early in a Congressional session, not to press for consideration of particular legislation but rather to introduce yourself.

If there is particular legislation in which you are interested, go see your legislator early in the process. This means you must track the subcommittee calendars closely. Decisions in subcommittees are critical and their impact grossly underestimated.

When you get through the door of your representative's office, realize that his time is short. Usually, you've got fifteen minutes to make your case. What the representative wants to know is this:

1 What's the problem?

2 What does it mean to my state or district in terms of the economy, jobs, or the general welfare?

3 How can I help?

Tell your representative of your concern as simply and succinctly as possible.

After the visit, follow up with a short letter to the legislator or his legislative aide and keep track of legislative developments. An occasional reminder nudge may be helpful. But too much pressure will be counterproductive.

Most of all, just as in dealing with the media, the best relationships between you and your legislator or his all-important aides are developed over time and based on mutual trust.[16]

DEALING WITH LOCAL GOVERNMENT

In 1980, Ronald Reagan rode to power on a platform of "New Federalism," calling for the shift of political debate and public policy decisions to state and local levels. Thus it became more important for public relations people to deal with local, state, and regional governments.

Dealing with such local entities, of course, differs considerably from dealing with the federal government. For example, opinion leaders in communities (those constituents with whom an organization might want to affiliate to influence public policy decisions) might include such sectors as local labor unions, teachers, civil service workers, and the like. Building consensus among such diverse constituents is pure grassroots public relations.

Larger organizations, in particular, will be challenged in the years ahead by proposals to raise state and local taxes, especially new users fees and variable rate schedules. The new stringency in funding government social programs also will create increased demands for greater business participation in community affairs. As schools, museums, libraries, hospitals, and other not-for-profit institutions feel the federal pinch, local businesses will be asked to take up the slack.[17]

The very nature of state and local issues makes it impossible to give one, all-encompassing blueprint for successful government relations strategies. Public relations advertising may be appropriate in some cases. Area philanthropic contributions may be called for. And certainly, closer contact with local legislators to impress them with the investment, facilities, and jobs created by the organization will become

FEATURE

"Glassroots" government relations

When Cencom of Wisconsin sought public support for a telephone rate increase in 1982, it went straight to the opinion leaders it knew would make a critical difference—local *bartenders.*

Specifically, Cencom's public relations strategy was to sell the rate increase, in advance, to such influential citizens as bartenders, barbers, and hairdressers through local dinner meetings. At the dinners, company spokespersons reeled off facts about interest rates, cost inflation, and discount competition and responded to the questions of guests.

Cencom reasoned that these people, plus a smattering of restaurateurs, gas station owners, and grocers, were eminently more influential than such people as ministers, politicians, and newspaper editors. Consequently, the latter were ignored and the former invited to dinner.

And did this "glassroots" government relations foray at bartenders work? Well, a few weeks after the dinners, Cencom's rate hearing was held. Nobody bothered to come. And the Wisconsin Public Service Commission awarded the phone company $586,000 of the $638,000 it sought in higher rates.[18]

increasingly important. On the other side of the coin, local governments themselves face a growing public relations challenge from increasingly cantankerous public sector unions.

Clearly, through the remainder of this decade, increased government relations attention will be directed at effectively reaching the relatively new audiences of state, local, and regional lawmakers.

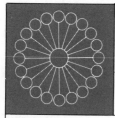

CASE STUDY
The cocktail party

Acquiring important contacts is essential among Washington-based corporate representatives. Because Washington is largely an "after hours" city, effective lobbyists will usually make themselves available for social gatherings with officials and aides to secure contacts.

Olga Twill, a top Washington lobbyist for the Bernard Hamilton Company (BHC), attended a Georgetown cocktail party for the visiting ambassador of Pago Pago. Also in attendance at the cocktail party was one Gilda Gumshoe, a secretary in the office of Senator Waldo (Fitz) Fitzman, junior Democratic senator from Utah. Sen. Fitzman was chairman of a special subcommittee on pension reform, with special interest in the area of "inside information."

Twill was vitally aware of the closed Fitzman hearings, especially in light of the fact that the BHC pension fund was one of those suspected of being handled with "inside information." This suspicion stemmed from the belief that BHC reaped a large profit through the sale of more than one million shares of Morris Mortgage Trust (once the nation's largest mortgage trust) just a month before the trust declared bankruptcy. Bernard Hamilton, chairman of BHC, was a member of the board of directors of the Third City Bank (Morris Trust's leading creditor), and some suspected him of having "inside information" about the trust's imminent demise.

While BHC and its chairman had not been publicly charged with dubious practices, Twill and her associates believed the Fitzman hearing would soon get around to BHC. Nevertheless, Twill had no idea when the "Fitzman shoe" would drop.

As the party progressed and the guests became more talkative through increased libation, Twill sauntered over to the visiting ambassador and recognized he was talking to a familiar figure, whom she vaguely placed as one of Sen. Fitzman's assistants. She stopped short and nonchalantly gazed about the room, focusing on the conversation between the woman and the ambassador.

"Tell me more, Miss Gumshoe, about your boss. He seems to be one of the most mysterious men these days," the ambassador was saying.

"Senator Fitzman has kept a relatively low profile as this city goes," the woman said, "but he's got a bombshell coming up next Tuesday that should make every paper in the country."

"Oh?" said the ambassador.

"That's right. Our pension fund hearings have really landed a big catch. I can't tell you who is involved, but he's one of the biggest men in the corporate world, and his company probably even has offices in Pago Pago."

"What do you mean you've *landed* this fellow?" the ambassador asked.

"What I mean is we've caught him using information to help his own company at the expense of the American people; in other words, using information that wasn't released to the public."

"That sounds quite exciting," the ambassador rejoined. "And when do I learn the identity and affiliation of this culprit?"

"Next Tuesday morning, Mr. Ambassador, at ten o'clock. And if you'd like, you could be my guest at a real, live Washington press conference when we announce it to the world. Just stop by the Madison Hotel Ballroom next Tuesday. I'll look for you then."

"Fine," said the ambassador.

As the conversation concluded, Twill was already halfway out the door. The overheard conversation, she thought, plainly pointed to her boss, Bernard Hamilton, as the subject of next Tuesday's press conference. Twill returned to her office and called Milt Stokes, BHC's public relations director, at his home. She told Stokes about the conversation she had overheard and suggested that BHC had seven days to plan strategy in anticipation of the press conference.

After his conversation with Twill, Stokes called Bernard Hamilton and suggested they get together first thing in the morning.

At the meeting with Stokes the next day in his office, Hamilton made the following points about his knowledge of the Morris Trust case:

1 Yes, he was a member of the board of directors of Third City Bank. Generally, the board did not discuss specific loans made by the bank. However, he did recall that the Morris Trust situation was discussed at least peripherally at one or two board meetings. However, no recommendations to foreclose on the loans had been made by the board, nor was it in the board's province to recommend action on individual loans.

2 Yes, BHC's pension fund manager did supervise the divestiture of Morris Trust shares over a two-month period, although Hamilton was not exactly sure of the dates and amounts of each sale of Morris Trust stock. He denied having spoken at length to the pension fund manager, a fellow named Spiro Rivkoon, about Morris Trust. He did have several conversations with Rivkoon about the pension fund portfolio, and perhaps Morris Trust had been discussed parenthetically, but he couldn't recall discussing it in depth.

3 He was well aware of his confidential obligations to Third City Bank not to discuss inside information about a particular stock. Moreover, he denied vehemently the allegation that he would ever act on inside information about any company.

4 While he was not aware of just when Rivkoon "got BHC out" of Morris Trust stock, he thought that some of it was done after the stock nosedived, thus encumbering some loss to the BHC portfolio. In any case, he was relatively certain that Rivkoon got his information to "get out" through the normal, public channels of information.

5 He knew full well, as did many other people, that Morris Trust was on the verge of collapse for several months. He also knew that bankers were

frantically pleading with the government to try to establish some subsidy to help the trust through its difficulties. However, he was certain that this information was not widely circulated because of the panic it might cause in the market. He denied trading in Morris Trust stock as a result of this information.

6   He personally owned no Morris Trust shares.

7   He was also cognizant of the BHC internal regulation barring any member of the company to "provide investment knowledge to internal fund managers about companies about which the BHC employee has privileged knowledge." Hamilton himself had drafted this recommendation for the BHC Policy Guide five years before.

After reviewing his thinking about the Morris Trust case, Hamilton told Stokes that BHC "must be ready if Fitzman's committee is going to come down hard on us."

"It's in your lap, Milt," Hamilton intoned. "Let me know what you recommend."

QUESTIONS

1   What public relations strategy would you recommend that BHC adopt in this case? What specific procedural steps would you recommend that Hamilton follow to fulfill these strategic objectives?

2   How should BHC respond? Through what medium? When should BHC respond; that is, what kind of "timing" implications are involved? Who should do the responding for the company? Where should the response come from?

3   Is there anything BHC should not reveal about the Morris Trust situation? Why?

NOTES

1   Vasil Pappas, "More Firms Upgraded Government-Related Jobs Because of Sharp Growth in Federal Regulations," *The Wall Street Journal*, 11 January 1980, p. 1.

2   Dom Bonafede, "Uncle Sam: The Flim Flam Man," *Washington Journalism Review*, April/May 1978, p. 66.

3   *45th Report to the Congress*. Washington, D.C.: United States Information Agency, June 30, 1977.

4   David H. Buswell, "Trial by Press Release?" *NAM Reports*, 17 January 1972, pp. 9–11.

5   "Managing the News, White House Style," *U.S. News & World Report*, 4 September 1978, p. 17.

6   "White House Fights Back," *Washington Journalism Review*, June 1982, p. 38.

7   Michael J. Bennett, "The 'Imperial' Press Corps," *Public Relations Journal*, June 1982, pp. 10–13.

8   Robert U. Brown, "Role of Press Secretary," *Editor & Publisher*, 19 October 1974, p. 40.

9   I. William Hill, "Nessen Lists Ways He Has Improved Press Relations," *Editor & Publisher*, 10 April 1975, p. 40.

10   William Safire, "One of Our Own," *The New York Times*, 19 September 1974, p. 43.

11 Frederick J. Krebs, assistant general counsel, Chamber of Commerce of the United States, in testimony before the Senate Government Affairs Committee, 14 February 1978.

12 Jules Witcover, "The Lobbyist's Act," *The Washington Post*, 16 March 1975, p. 26.

13 Charles Mohr, "Business Using Grass-Roots Lobby," *The New York Times*, 17 April 1978.

14 Gordon Chaplin, "Lobbying the Underdog," *Washington Post Magazine*, 28 May 1978, p. 18.

15 William L. Dupuy, "The Political Action Committee and the Public Relations Practitioner," *Public Relations Quarterly*, Spring 1981, p. 14.

16 E. Bruce Peters, "You Can Be Wise in the Ways of Washington," *Enterprise*, December 1981/January 1982, pp. 8–9.

17 Jan Rogozinski, "The New Federalism and Public Relations," *Public Relations Journal*, March 1982, p. 16.

18 Inesm Salazar, "To Lobby for Higher Phone Rates, Cencom Took Bartenders to Dinner," *The Wall Street Journal*, 6 October 1982, p. 29.

SUGGESTED READING

Bernays, Edward L. "The PR Proficiency of the Reagan Administration," *Public Relations Quarterly*, Spring 1981, p. 20.

Brown, David H. "Government Public Affairs—Its Own Worst Enemy," *Public Relations Quarterly*, Spring 1981, pp. 4–5.

————. "Information Officers and Reporters: Friends or Foes?" *Public Relations Review*, Summer 1976, pp. 29–38.

Chaplin, Gordon. "Lobbying the Underdog." *The Washington Post Magazine*, 28 May 1978, pp. 18–22.

Chittick, William O. *State Department, Press, and Pressure Groups*. New York: John Wiley and Sons, 1970. Examines the role of a public information officer with regard to the press, lobbyists, and administrators.

Commission on Freedom of the Press. *Government and Mass Communications: A Report from the Commission on Freedom of the Press*. 2 vols. 1947. Reprint (2 vols. in 1). Hamden, Conn.: Shoe String Press, 1965.

"Courting Industry's New Board Member: Government," *Industry Week*, 18 October 1976, pp. 82–86.

Crouse, Timothy. *The Boys on the Bus: Riding with the Campaign Press Corps*. New York: Random House, 1973.

Deakin, James. *Lobbyists*. Washington, D.C.: The Public Affairs Press, 1966. Examines how lobbyists are organized in Washington.

Dexter, Louis A., and **White, David.** *People, Society, and Mass Communications*. New York: Free Press, 1964.

Dunn, Delmar D. *Public Officials and the Press*. Reading, Mass.: Addison-Wesley, 1969.

Dupuy, William L. "The Political Action Committee and the Public Relations Practitioner," *Public Relations Quarterly*, Spring 1981, pp. 14–16.

Gilbert, William H. *Public Relations in Local Government*. Washington, D.C.: International City Management Association, 1140 Connecticut Ave. NW, 1975.

Goldstein, Stephanie. "Hi, I'm From Government, and I Want to Help You," *Public Relations Journal*, October 1981, pp. 22–24.

Goulding, Phil G. *Confirm or Deny: Informing the Public on National Security.* New York: Harper and Row, 1970.

Herbers, John. "Citizen Activism Gaining in Nation," *The New York Times,* May 16, 1982.

Hesse, Michael B. "Strategies of the Political Communication Process," *Public Relations Review,* Spring 1981, pp. 32–47.

Hiebert, Ray E., and **Spitzer, Carlton E.,** eds. *The Voice of Government.* New York: John Wiley and Sons, 1968.

Hudson, Howard Penn. "Working with Federal Government," *Public Relations Quarterly,* Spring 1981, pp. 6–13. Relations with the federal government are less hostile today than in previous years. There is more acceptance that one can work within the framework of the government.

Hudson, Howard Penn, and **Hudson, Mary Elizabeth,** eds. *Hudson's Washington News Media Contact Directory.* (Available from 2626 Pennsylvania Ave. N.W., Washington, D.C. 20037.) A directory listing the Washington correspondents for major newspapers (listed by state or origin), news bureaus, foreign newspapers and news services, radio and TV networks (both domestic and foreign), magazines, specialized newsletters and periodicals, freelance writers, and photographic services.

Kelley, Stanley, Jr. *Professional Public Relations and Political Powers,* Baltimore, M.D.: Johns Hopkins University Press, 1956.

Miller, William H. "Business Gets Its Lobbying Act Together." *Industry Week,* 5 December 1977, pp. 66–76.

Pimlott, J. A. *Public Relations and American Democracy.* Rev. ed. Princeton, N.J.: Princeton University Press, 1971

Reaburn, Gordon C. "How to Get Congress' Attention," *Public Relations Journal,* May 1981, p. 42.

Relyea, Harold C. "The Freedom of Information Act: Its Evolution and Operational Status." *Journalism Quarterly,* 54, Autumn 1977, pp. 538–544.

Rivers, William L. *The Adversaries: Politics and the Press.* Boston, Mass.: Beacon Press, 1970.

————. *The Opinionmakers.* Boston: Beacon Press, 1965.

Robinson, Gilbert A. "The New Look At CIA," *Public Relations Journal,* December 1981, pp. 12–15.

Rogozinski, Jan. "The New Federalism and Public Relations," *Public Relations Journal,* March 1982, pp. 12–14, 16. The shift of public policy decisions to the state and local levels will give new importance to local attitudes and create new challenges for public relations.

Rosenbaum, Morris Victor. "Effective Public Relations with Washington, D.C." *Public Relations Quarterly,* Summer 1967, pp. 7–23.

Ruder, William, and **Nathan, R.** *A Businessman's Guide to Washington.* New York: Macmillan, 1975.

Sigal, Leon V. *Reporters and Officials: The Organization and the Politics of Newsmaking.* Lexington, Mass.: D.C. Health and Company, 1973. Reporters and government officals define news differently.

————. "Lobbying, Ethics and Common Sense," *Public Relations Journal,* February 1982, pp. 34–36.

Spitzer, Carlton E. "Should Government Audit Corporate Social Responsibility," *Public Relations Review,* Summer 1981, pp. 13–28.

Wise, David. *The Politics of Lying: Government Deception, Secrecy, and Power.* New York: Random House, 1973.

RESPONSIBILITY TO THE COMMUNITY

President Calvin Coolidge once said, "The business of America is business." Today, some argue, "The business of business is America."

In the early 1960s, any business executive worth his salt would have stated immediately that a company's job is to make money for its owners—period. Indeed, Nobel Prize-wining economist Milton Friedman argued just that; that the corporation's responsibility is to produce profits and that the cost of corporate social goals amounts to a hidden tax on workers, customers, and shareholders.

Professor Friedman is in the minority. More and more, companies and other organizations acknowledge their responsibilities to the community: helping clean the air and water, providing jobs for minorities, contributing money and talent to solve urban problems, and, in general, helping enhance the quality of life for everyone.

Today's "enlightened" self-interest among executives has taken time to develop. The social and political upheavals of the 1960s forced organizations to confront the real or perceived injustices inflicted upon certain social groups. The 1970s brought a partial resolution of these problems as government and the courts together moved to compensate for past inequities, outlaw current ones, and prevent future ones.

The 1970s also saw a more conciliatory response from business toward societal concerns. Indeed, business bore a major share of carrying out social programs because it was the principal repository of the nation's economic resources.[1]

17
The Community

In the 1980s, the conflict between organizations and society has become one of setting priorities—of deciding *which* community group, for example, deserves to be the beneficiary of corporate involvement. Most corporations today accept their role as an agent for social change. As Federated Department Stores President Howard Goldfeder put it:

> We continue to be mindful of the fact that we are citizens of the communities we serve, that we're neighbors, voters, taxpayers, that our children attend the same schools, drink the same water, drive the same streets and highways as our customers.[2]

Basically, every organization wants to foster positive reactions in the community and avoid negative ones. To achieve community acceptance and approval, most organizations, regardless of size, find the role of community relations a critical one. What positive community relations boils down to is convincing neighbors that the organization is a good citizen, cares about its community, and offers a good product or service at a fair price.

THE COMMUNITY

The community of an organization can vary widely, depending on the size and the nature of the business. The "mom and pop" grocery store may have a community of only a few city blocks, the community of a Buick assembly plant may be the city where the plant is located, the community of a multinational corporation may embrace much of the world.

Who are the principal members of a firm's "community"? At the local level, there are several discrete types of community members.

Community leaders. These are the shapers of opinion in the community: public officals, major employers, "old guard" families, vocal advocates, and occasionally, "informal" thought leaders. They can generally be reached through regular contact at influential local groups, face-to-face meetings, and special mailings.

Local press. It is important to get to know the local news media for effective community relations. Attempting to coerce the media by purchasing or canceling advertising should not be contemplated. Much more practical is getting to know local journalists in an informal, low-pressure way.

Civic groups. There are many ways to reach local civic groups: regularly donating to local charities, using radio programs, forming a speakers' bureau to meet local organizations, filling emergency needs, or providing free movies for use by nonprofit groups.

Students, faculty, school officials. Educating young people and informing their mentors about the benefits of the firm is time well spent. Eventually, students will become customers and employees.

Municipal employees and local officials. It makes sense for organizations to encourage employees to take active roles in city council, the police or fire commission, civil defense, and other municipal agencies. Concerned citizenship on the individual level translates directly into corporate community concern.

Local merchants, industrialists. A brief congratulatory letter to a business person recently honored or promoted is always welcomed. So too, are visits to new merchants, industry officials, and new residents to acquaint them with the local company.

Again, key constituencies vary from community to community. Each organization must learn which members of its community are capable of influencing others. For example, knowing which civic group is more influential with the alderman and which alderman is more influential with the mayor may be of crucial importance to the management of a local organization. Identifying and being able to tap such "influence networks" is a valuable property of the community relations specialist.

WHAT THE COMMUNITY EXPECTS FROM THE ORGANIZATION

Communities expect from resident organizations such tangible commodities as wages, employment, and taxes. But communities also expect certain intangible contributions, too, such as:

Appearance. The community hopes that the firm will contribute positively to life in the area. It expects facilities to be attractive with care spent on the grounds and plant (see Figure 17-1). Increasingly, community neighbors object to plants that belch smoke and pollute water and air. Occasionally, neighbors will organize to oppose the entrance of factories, coal mines, oil wells, drug treatment centers, and other facilities suspected of being harmful to the community environment. Government, too, is acting more vigorously to punish offenders and to make sure that organizations comply with zoning, environmental, and safety regulations.

Participation. As a "citizen" of its community, an organization is expected to participate responsibly in community affairs, such as civic functions, park and recreational activities, education, welfare, and support of religious institutions. Organizations generally cannot shirk such participation by blaming "headquarters policy."

Stability. A business that fluctuates sharply in volume of business, number of employees, and taxes paid can adversely affect the community through its impact on municipal services, school loads, public facilities, and tax revenues. Communities prefer stable organizations that will grow with the area. Conversely, they want to keep out short-term operations that could create temporary boom conditions and leave ghost towns in their wake.

Pride. Any organization that can help "put the community on the map" simply by being there is usually a valuable addition. Communities want firms that are proud to be residents. For instance, to most Americans *Battle Creek, Michigan* means cereal, *Hershey, Pennsylvania* means chocolate, and *Armonk, New York* means IBM. Organizations that help "make the town" usually become symbols of pride.

INTERVIEW
Carlton E. Spitzer

Carlton E. Spitzer is senior vice president in the Washington division of Manning, Selvage & Lee, a leading national public relations agency. Previously, Mr. Spitzer was corporate vice president for public affairs at Borden, Inc. and director of public information for the U.S. Department of Health, Education & Welfare. Mr. Spitzer is co-editor of the *Voice of Government,* published by John Wiley & Sons. He has written numerous magazine articles on corporate public affairs. His latest book is *Raising the Bottom Line: Business Leadership in a Changing Society,* published in 1982 by Longman, Inc.

What should the proper relationship be between an organization and the community?

The riots of the 1960s, erupting as they did from long-neglected human needs, made clear, I think, that business enterprises must engage fully in community life. Business is not expected to forsake its own goals but simply to identify its goals within the context of broad community needs and objectives. Simply, its function cannot be, or appear to be, contrary to or indifferent to community life.

What constitutes an organization's "social responsibilities"?

A business cannot succeed in a vacuum. Profits cannot be maximized in a declining market. A business cannot find strength by exploiting or seeming to exploit the needs of its customers. If a business is to sell its products or services, it must protect its markets. That is both social responsibility and good business sense. Today, every type of community and national organization is turning to business for financial, managerial, and technical help. The challenge, I think, is for business to respond intelligently but avoid unreasonable public expectations for its performance. Business can't afford to dominate the community process, and it can't close the gap created by reduced federal spending. Business must communicate with the public much better than it has in the past. Social responsibility—or *corporate public involvement,* the new phrase coined by John Filer and Stanley Karson to reflect a business-like approach, more pragmatism, and less do-gooding—means that business must be proactive, get out front and lead.

How socially responsible are most organizations today?

Being socially responsible in the past meant supporting the Urban Coalition, the National Alliance of Businessmen, and perhaps giving money to black colleges. Those were the classic responses to domestic upheaval in the late 1960s. When the smoke cleared and the yelling stopped, most business executives were anxious to return to "business as usual." They were surprised to find they could not. Ralph Nader, the Rev. Jesse Jackson, and other voices for affirmative action, consumer rights, and environmental clean-up forced business into a new mode. Jackson signed contracts with big companies guaranteeing the hiring and promoting of minorities, buying from minority-owned suppliers, and other actions the companies might have done on their own but did not. Companies complain bitterly about being regulated, yet the record is clear that without the force of regulation few companies would have done much in addressing equal rights or cleaning up foul air or filthy water. The role of government regulation in those area was necessary. The trouble is that business tends to resist all regulation. It has for years. Too many executives still cling to the tired notion that it is sufficient for a company to provide jobs, purchasing power, and tax payments. The more successful entrepreneurs today are those who understand the interdependence between company and community and who involve themselves in community life. Still, the majority of business executives are a long way from accepting the reality that social and economic planning must be permanently fused if our private enterprise system is to survive in the long-term.

What's the difference between public relations and public affairs?

I used to think I knew. In the late 1960s, I foolishly accepted an invitation from the National Association of Manufacturers to write a piece for their publication explaining the difference between public relations and public affairs. I wrote that public affairs was concerned with public issues, governmental affairs, and the complex of communication processes, internal and external, that challenge every kind of bureaucratic structure. I also wrote, to the displeasure of some of my associates, that public affairs people were becoming a part of top management in most companies whereas, historically, public relations executives had skillfully carried out the decisions of top management. I said that by and large, public affairs types were different because they were dealing with broader issues and at higher levels. Well, some of my friends disagreed. They were understandably upset for they had indeed been counseling their managements for years on broad issues under the banner of public relations. What is clear to me in the 1980s is that whether one is titled counselor, communications director, public affairs vice president, or public relation manager, one is deeply and importantly involved in helping the enterprise or institution relate to its constituencies and is listened to attentively by top management. Titles have multiplied and diversified. I no longer pay much attention to them. I do pay close attention to job descriptions, reporting lines, and, of course, performance.

How would you answer someone like Milton Friedman who says that an organization's only "social responsibility" is to pay as high a return as possible to its shareholders?

I don't think Milton Friedman agrees with Milton Friedman that corporate officers have no responsibility other than to make money for their stockholders. A company executive is surely acting responsibly when he spends corporate profits to clean up the environment and thereby minimizes government regulation, which is both expensive and unwanted. A company executive is surely acting responsibly when he or she considers the social consequences of business decisions and thereby minimizes consumer unrest, labor problems, and other potential trouble areas that can injure reputation and diminish sales.

(Interview continues.)

Just where would Dr. Friedman draw the bottom line for business if society crumbles around it? How can any business succeed if society falters? As for stockholders, people today invest across the board, in many companies and commodities. The stockholders' interest is best served by corporate policies which contribute to the kind of society in which business can grow and prosper. Donald MacNaughton, chairman of The Hospital Corporation of America and a former chairman of Prudential Insurance, has said that maximizing profit at the expense of social and human values is a losing game. The concern should be, he says, for balancing profits with social and human values. Professor Friedman is much too smart to believe in one-dimensional management. I think he put himself out on a limb a long time ago. He ought to smile and climb back. I personally don't know of any top executive who shares such a limited view of management responsibility in the 1980s.

How enlightened is American business management today?

Management is much more organized and sophisticated in its dealing with government at all levels and pressure groups of all kinds. But perhaps only 10 percent of top management actually embrace the concept that business enterprises are social as well as economic institutions and therefore have a clear and profound obligation to society, including the obligation to tell the public what they are doing and why. Fortunately the 10 percent represent industry leadership, who have spoken out strongly for long-term planning, building for the future, and less pressure on managers for favorable quarterly earnings reports. The short-sighted way we measure and reward managers is terribly damaging to our nation. When business is open, caring, and involved, there is less need for government rules and regulations and less cause for pressure groups to make demands, and more time and incentive to think ahead.

Therefore, I hope and believe that business generally is becoming more enlightened.

How can a group organize for community relations?

Analyze community needs by talking directly with the mayor, Chamber of Commerce, United Way, community and minority groups, especially emerging cutting edge groups; with teachers, elected officials, police authorities, agencies for the elderly and handicapped. Take time. Mobilize company resources and talents to address select community needs most natural to one's own enterprise. Coordinate activity with other local companies to make sure that *all* pressing community needs are being addressed collectively. Speak out, if others do not, against racism and for cooperative community action. Be as serious about community relations as you are about making a profit.

Is there anything else you'd like readers of this book to know?

There is much that organizations can do voluntarily, cooperatively, effectively, and more imaginatively to improve society than any government bureau could ever conceive or carry out. If business takes leadership, and I pray it does, the private enterprise system will endure, and the nation will be strengthened. If business declines the opportunity it has, it may not get a second opportunity. Government will then move back into the marketplace, taking over more firmly than before. I would hope that industry, in the future, would concentrate on the business of peace, the products of peace, the profits that can be realized from producing services and products to keep the world whole and sane and together. Industry has the information, technology, and power to join with government in leading the nation and the world out of its pressing social and economic stress, given time. The question remains, does industry have the wisdom?

IF EVERYBODY LOVES NEW YORK SO MUCH, WHY IS IT SO DIRTY?

With all the hoopla about "I Love New York," everybody seems to have overlooked something—the garbage problem.

Maybe love is blind. Because New York does have a major litter problem. On Broadway. In front of our movie theaters. Our best restaurants. Your neighborhood. And unless we all do something about it fast, it'll reach awesome proportions.

So let's not put up with it anymore. When you see a piece of litter, it won't hurt to pick it up. If there's a pile of loose garbage in front of a restaurant, don't eat there. If your neighborhood store has a mess out front, tell them. It'll do you some good and it'll do the store some good. Who knows—New York may wind up not only a great place to visit, but an even greater place to live. For more information on how to clean up your city, call We Care About New York, Inc. at 619-3100.

THE CHASE IS ON

NEW YORK LET'S CLEAN UP NEW YORK.

We Care About New York, Inc. and the City of New York

FIGURE 17–1. *Corporate clean up.* Every community wants its corporate citizens to care about its appearance. In this case, The Chase Manhattan Bank let its customers know that it, too, cared about cleaning up its headquarters city.

COURTESY: The Chase Manhattan Bank.

WHAT THE ORGANIZATION EXPECTS FROM THE COMMUNITY

Organizations expect to be provided with adequate municipal services, fair taxation, good living conditions for employees, a good labor supply, and a reasonable degree of support for the business and its products. When some of these requirements are missing, organizations may pick up and move to communities where such benefits are more readily available.

New York City, for example, experienced a substantial exodus of corporations during the 1970s when firms fled to neighboring Connecticut and New Jersey as well as to the Sun Belt states of the Southeast and Southwest. These became commercial centers through policies of tax moratoriums, lower labor costs, and business incentives. New York state and city legislators responded to the challenge by working more closely with business residents in such areas as corporate taxation. By the early 1980s, the corporate flight to the Sun Belt not only had been arrested, but some firms decided they agreed with the "I Love New York" ad campaign and returned to the state.

The issue for most urban areas, faced with steadily-eroding tax bases, is to find a formula that meets the concerns of business corporations while accommodating the needs of other members of the community.

COMMUNITY RELATIONS OBJECTIVES

A written community relations policy can help an organization achieve rapport with its neighbors. Employees, in particular, must understand and exemplify their firm's community relations policy; to many in the community, the workers *are* the company. A community relations policy, then, must clearly define the philosophy of management as it views its obligation to the community.

Equally important, a clear set of community relations objectives must be enumerated so that employees have a clear idea of the organization's goals in promoting favorable public opinion within the community. Typical objectives might include the following:

1   To tell the community about the operations of the firm: its products, number of employees, size of payroll, tax payments, employee benefits, growth, and support of community projects.

2   To correct misunderstanding, reply to criticism, and remove any disaffection that may exist among community neighbors.

3   To gain the favorable opinion of the community, particularly during strikes and periods of labor unrest, by stating the company's position on issues involved.

4   To inform employees and their families about company activities and developments so that they can tell their friends and neighbors about the company and favorably influence opinions of the organization.

5   To inform people in local government about the firm's contributions to community welfare and to obtain support for legislation that will favorably affect the business climate in the community.

6   To find out what residents think about the company, why they like or dislike the organization's policies and practices, and how much they know of company policy, operations, and problems.

7 To establish a personal relationship between management and community leaders by inviting leaders to visit the plant and offices, meet management, and see employees at work.

8 To support health programs through contributions of both funds and services of employees to local campaigns.

9 To contribute to culture by providing funds for art exhibits, concerts, and drama festivals and by promoting attendance at such affairs.

10 To aid youth and adult education by cooperating with education and teachers in providing student vocational guidance, plant tours, speakers, films, and teaching aids, and by giving financial support to higher education.

11 To encourage sports and recreational activities by providing athletic fields, swimming pools, golf courses, and tennis courts for use by community residents, and by sponsoring teams and sports events.

12 To promote better local and county government by encouraging employees to run for public office or volunteer to serve on administrative boards; by lending

Our Guiding Principles

Over our long history we have evolved standards and values guiding the management of the company that comprise an unwritten creed. These beliefs are central to conducting our affairs responsibly in fulfilling our obligations to shareowners, employees, customers and the communities in which we work.

Two contemporary developments suggest that a more formal statement of the company's principles is in order. One, the substantial increase in the size and geographic breadth of the company, and, two, the growing interest of the public in the ethical practices and social commitments of business. To be responsive to these new needs, our Board of Directors two years ago approved a written declaration of the canons that have guided this company's operations for so many years.

Since these are not static rules to be filed, but active principles to be practiced, they have recently been reviewed and again endorsed.

Implicit in the responsible conduct of the affairs of the company is one fundamental consideration — our consistent compliance with all pertinent laws, regulations and ethical standards.

These principles are personal and important to us. Obviously, they are not unique. We share many of them with other responsible and successful members of the business community.

We set forth these guiding principles looking ahead to continued growth for our company, improvement in the quality of life of our people and continued constructive relationships with the communities closest to us.

T. M. Ford
Chairman and President

FIGURE 17–2. *Emhart's obligations.* The principles enumerated here by the chairman and president of the Emhart Corporation represent the obligations the company believes it has to its corporate community.

COURTESY: Emhart Corporation.

company executives to community agencies or to local government to give specialized advice and assistance on municipal problems; and by making company facilities and equipment available to the community in times of emergencies.

13   To assist the economy of the community by purchasing operating supplies and equipment from local merchants and manufacturers, whenever possible.

14   To operate a profitable business in order to provide jobs and to pay competitive wages that increase the community's purchasing power and strengthen its economy.

15   To cooperate with other local businesses in advancing economic and social welfare through joint community relations programs, financed and directed by the participating organizations.

All these community relations objectives not only make sense in terms of social responsibility, but they also make good business sense as well. Many organizations, from hospitals to department stores to corporate multinationals, have learned that an

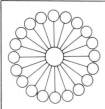

MINICASE
The malodorous emissions[3]

When an organization fails to maintain continuing communication with its neighbors, the results can range from distrust to hostility. Such a situation faced Mystik Tape (MT), a part of Borden Company.

In 1953, MT built a plant in Northfield Village, a sparsely populated suburb of Chicago. By the mid-70s, the community had become affluent, populous, and residential. The MT operation had grown to more than seven acres and over 600 employees, annually producing 100 million square yards of pressure-sensitive tapes.

Although MT tried for years to avoid environmental pollution, the problem of malodorous vapor emissions remained. At the high school across the street from the plant (built on land donated by MT), students complained that their breathing was affected (though the company was convinced the fumes were "nontoxic to anyone and offensive to only some").

Faced with community pressure, MT took the following steps:

1   It ordered a custom-made incinerator to consume virtually all the offending substances and convert them into harmless, odorless products.

2   It hired a public relations agency to help develop a continuing community relations program.

3   It recruited a younger general manager, experienced in listening to and acting on community complaints.

4   It surveyed community residents to see if they were aware of the plant's contribution to the community.

effective community relations program can translate into ample benefits in recruitment, tax treatment, and public support for the organization and its beliefs.

EMERGENCE OF PUBLIC AFFAIRS

In recent years, community relations has evolved into the more all-encompassing activity of public affairs. While a precise definition of *public affairs* is elusive, this Conference Board definition is a good one:

> A significant and substantial concern and involvement by individuals, business, labor, foundations, private institutions, and government with the social, economic, and political forces that singly or through interaction shape the environment within which the free enterprise system exists.

The emergence and expansion of public affairs activities is a response to public demands that organizations act responsibly in employee hiring and promotion, product safety and pricing, advertising, merchandising, and labeling.

---

5 It held a press briefing at which a newly-created post of community relations manager was announced.

6 It mailed a six-page folder, "This is Mystik Tape," to all residents and media in the area.

7 It established a quarterly community bulletin, addressed to "Dear Neighbors," describing MT's contributions and donations to the community.

8 When the huge oxidizer arrived, it was left on view outside the plant for two weeks. Then came a dedication ceremony, attended by civic leaders, followed by a demonstration and a plant tour.

9 New practices were introduced. Community residents received welcoming letters and samples of Mystik tape. MT executives addressed science and business classes and school assemblies. A "Science Student of the Year" award was established.

These efforts produced a turnaround in community attitudes, and the firm received many letters of praise from residents and business leaders. Complaints and expressions of anti-MT sentiment, especially from high school students, virtually disappeared.

QUESTIONS

1 What other steps could MT have taken?

2 What might have resulted if MT had done nothing and just tried to tough it out?

3 Do you think MT went overboard and did too much? If so, what would you have eliminated?

4 Now that it has the community's goodwill, would you advise MT to taper off its programs?

PUBLIC RELATIONS VS. PUBLIC AFFAIRS

Distinctions between public relations and public affairs are often blurry. In some organizations, the functions may overlap.

Certain differences, however, are clear. The public affairs function usually operates through either the political or social service process; practitioners tend to be knowledgeable about liberal arts or political science. In contrast, public relations usually operates through the communications process, with practitioners oriented toward journalism.

As public relations counselor John W. Hill once said, "The difference between the two functions is marked by an exceedingly fine line. Actually, the two activities are brothers under the skin."

While no clear-cut distinction between the two functions has yet been established, the team concept of many large organizations helps guard against duplication of efforts. In smaller operations, these two functions often are combined.

Crisis planning. The most significant test for any public affairs operation comes when the organization is hit by a major accident or disaster. How an organization comports itself in the midst of a calamity may influence how it is perceived for years to come. Poor handling of a disaster may damage an organization's reputation, and the firm itself may be sued. It is essential therefore that the facts of any emergency be handled intelligently and forthrightly with the news media, employees, and the community-at-large.

The key to mitigating a disaster lies in crisis planning. Years ago in the airline industry, "crisis planning" meant that "one of the pr man's first responsibilities when a crash occurred was to paint over the company's name" on the wreckage before news photographers arrived.[4] Fortunately, times have changed.

Today, organizations from airlines to hospitals prepare for potential crisis by brainstorming the possible problems and creating contingency plans to deal with them (see Figure 17–3). One quintessential principle in dealing with a crisis is not to "clam up" when disaster strikes. Invariably, the first tendency of executives is to say, "Let's wait until all the facts are in." The fallacy in this is that in saying nothing, an organization is perceived as already having made a decision. That angers the press and compounds the problem. On the other hand, inexperienced spokespeople, forced to nervously speculate or use sensationalistic language, e.g. "slammed, careened, plowed" are even worse. The solution is neither silence nor sensationalism. Rather, as a senior Dow Chemical communications manager put it:

> The public must be fully informed frequently and accurately through the media from the outset . . . by credible senior spokesmen accustomed to dealing with the media in a responsible, respectful manner, who understand and can explain clearly in lay language complex information.[5]

An example of a company that moved quickly to head off a brewing crisis was Rexnord Inc. in the days following a 1979 Chicago DC-10 crash. The crash, which killed 273, was suspected to have been caused by the loss of a bolt Rexnord feared it had manufactured. The firm issued a statement saying that it was sure that tests would reveal the bolt was not at fault, and it encouraged questions about the part. Rexnord eventually was exonerated from any blame. When the dust settled, its chief executive explained, "We had no legal obligation to go out in front, but we wanted to

```
                    PUBLIC RELATIONS DEPARTMENT

                          DISASTER PLAN

   I.  Notification:

       Medical center public relations will be notified of a "code orange" by the
       page operator.  During hours other than 8:00 a.m. - 5:00 p.m., Monday -
       Friday, the page operator will notify the public relations officer on call,
       who will notify the public relations director of the "code orange."

  II.  Person In Charge:

       The director of public relations is responsible for all print and electronic
       media contact during a "code orange."  Until the public relations director
       can be reached, the on call public relations officer will assume the
       responsibilities of the director.

 III.  Staffing Call Up:

       All available public relations officers will be notified by the director
       or designee of the "code orange" and asked to report to the hospital.

  IV.  Responsibilities/Procedures:

       A.  During a disaster, medical center public relations is responsible for:

           1.  Managing press relations from the command center in 2500 north.

           2.  Establishing and maintaining a press room in Ross Hall 101.

           3.  Manning the telephones in the public relations office.

       B.  The director of public relations will assign the public relations
           personnel available to staff the press room, the public relations
           office and the emergency room.  The director will then report to the
           command center in 2500 north to direct all public relations activities.

       C.  Press room, Ross Hall 101 - public relations officers will:

           1.  Remain in Ross Hall room 101.

           2.  Maintain direct contact with the public relations officer in
               the command center.

           3.  Respond to all press inquiries.  Notify press and communications
               media of the established press room in Ross Hall room 101.

           4.  Act as spokespersons as deemed appropriate by the public relations
               director.  Assist in the selection of a spokesperson.

           5.  Post signs in the following areas directing the press to the press
               room:    Ross Hall lobby; Ross Hall room 101; 23rd Street
               entrance to the hospital.

           6.  Obtain emergency phones from the public relations office
               and install in jacks provided in room 101.

       D.  Public relations office, Ross Hall 712 - public relations officers
           will:

           1.  Remain in the public relations office.

           2.  Man the phones in the public relations office.

           3.  Refer all calls from families of victims to the social
               work supervisor in the main lobby of the hospital at
               extension____.

           4.  Request the television/radio media to announce that persons
               wishing to donate blood may contact or go to their local Red
               Cross collection center.
```

FIGURE 17–3. *Hospital public relations disaster plan.* Most hospitals have crisis preparedness plans as a contingency for avoiding chaos when a plane crash or a fire, for example, swells the emergency room with victims.

do so. . . . I've been talking and writing articles about the public losing faith in business and this was something we needed to do."[6]

Although crisis plans differ from organization to organization, the following principles should be considered:

1   Develop a written crisis communications plan that defines individual roles, and distribute it widely.
2   Identify a single spokesperson, preferably a public relations officer, for the organization in time of crisis.
3   Be certain that information released is accurate and precise. Consider legal ramifications of information released.
4   Let all personnel know the proper procedure for reporting during crisis situations. It's a good idea to designate crisis officers within departments.
5   Share the institution's plans for releasing information in a crisis situation with the news media. Being partners with the media in time of crisis is greatly preferable to being adversaries.
6   Let news people know that information violating an individual's right to privacy or jeopardizing the organization's legal rights may have to be withheld during a crisis.
7   Coordinate communications plans with the community hospital.
8   Develop a means of notifying families and company officials of serious injuries before releasing the information publicly.

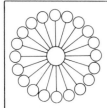

MINICASE

Bulletin: Moko chief executive dies in copter crash . . .

Those were the chilling words that clattered over the Dow Jones wire ticker late one afternoon in the headquarters of Moko Electronics Inc. Moko Chairman and Chief Executive J. Raul Espinosa had been killed in a freak helicopter accident.

Never in her twenty years in public relations had Moko's corporate communications director Molly Tullia been faced with such a tragedy.

Tullia knew that in addition to the great personal tragedy that the company and its people had suffered, the publicly-traded firm also risked a significant loss of confidence among investors if the disaster was not handled correctly.

Tullia and Moko's chief operating officer agreed that in addition to expressing the firm's profound grief, it was also critical to convey that Moko was well positioned to continue to perform profitably, despite the tragedy. This was particularly important because Moko had just completed a turnaround year in

9 Be specific in the guidelines to be followed. Guidelines should be organized in the communications approach, thorough in apportioning responsibilities, and aggressive in carrying out the plan precisely if a crisis should arise.[7]

SOCIAL ACTIVISM HANGS ON

The activist movement, which began on college campuses in the late 1960s during the Vietnam War, has today evolved into a tamer movement, a movement that pressures corporations to deal responsibly with societal issues. Here's a sampling of activist groups that regularly tweak corporate America:

Project on corporate responsibility. Formed in the late 1960s, the project's early efforts were directed primarily at General Motors. The project got credit for "shaking up" the automaker into appointing the first black to its board of directors, naming an air pollution expert as the firm's first vice president of environmental activities, and depositing $5 million in minority-owned banks.

Nader's raiders. The several organizations spearheaded by consumer crusader Ralph Nader publish reports on abuses in a wide range of areas: air pollution, banking, birth control pills, nursing homes, government regulatory agencies, corporate democracy, and so on.

Council on economic priorities. The Council provides information to investors wishing to base investment decisions on the social policy of corporations as well as on their financial performance.

---

profitability after suffering two consecutive years of declining profits. The company could ill afford the perception that the death of its chairman would cause it to return to its losing ways.

To prevent that perception, Tullia made the following statement to the media:

> The Moko company and all its employees are profoundly saddened by this great personal tragedy. J. Raul Espinosa was the guiding light in streamlining Moko's operations over the past several years to return the company to its traditional position as a leader in the electronics industry.
>
> Mr. Espinosa dedicated himself to building a deep, broadly-skilled Moko management team. Largely through his efforts, the company has begun to implement its long-term strategic plan for the 1980s.
>
> It is a testimony to the dedication and ability of J. Raul Espinosa that the company he helped build is today positioned better than at any time in its 100-year history.

QUESTIONS

1 What do you think of the Moko media statement? Does it accomplish the company's objectives?

2 How does the statement make you feel about Espinosa? About the future of the company?

National affiliation of concerned business students.   This group, formed in the mid-1970s, is primarily concerned with social activism among business school students. It has backed such reform proposals as guaranteed annual income for all Americans, negative income tax, consumerism, and the application of private management techniques to the public sector.

National council of churches.   This group, composed of more than thirty Christian denominations, lobbied aggressively in the 70s and 80s against corporate and university support for the apartheid policies of the South African government.

In addition to these larger, more organized groups, corporate shareholders concerned about a wide variety of miscellaneous issues regularly let organizations know how they feel. The emergence of so many social activists has caused the term *social responsibility* to become a permanent part of the corporate lexicon.

RESPONDING THROUGH SOCIAL RESPONSIBILITY

Social responsibility has been defined as a social norm. This norm holds that any social institution, including the smallest family unit and the largest corporation, is responsible for the behavior of its members and may be held accountable for their misdeeds.[8]

In the late 1960s, when the idea was just emerging, initial responses were of the "knee jerk" variety. A firm that was threatened by increasing legal or activist pressures and harassment would ordinarily change its policies in a hurry. Today, however, organizations and their social responsibility programs are much more sophisticated. As one practitioner put it, "Social responsibility today is treated just like any other management discipline—you analyze the issues, evaluate performance, set priorities, allocate resources to those priorities and implement programs that deal with issues within the constraints of your resources."[9]

Many companies have created special committees to set the agenda and target the objectives. The primary concerns of the Corporate Responsibility Committee of The Chase Manhattan Bank are illustrative:

1   To continue Chase's leadership in equal opportunity employment, both at home and abroad.
2   To foster a broader and healthier economic base in New York City and other areas served by the bank.
3   To encourage housing and community development facilities.
4   To improve the physical and cultural environment of the bank's community.
5   To initiate comprehensive international social responsibility programs.

CATEGORIES OF SOCIAL RESPONSIBILITY

Social responsibility touches practically every level of organizational activity, from marketing to hiring, from training to work standards. A partial list of social responsibility categories might include the following:

Product lines. Dangerous products, product performance and standards, packaging, and environmental impact.

Marketing practices. Sales practices, consumer complaint policies, advertising content, and fair pricing.

Employee services. Training, counseling, and placement services, transfer procedures, and educational allowances.

Corporate philanthropy. Contribution performance, encouragement of employees to participate in social projects, and community development activities.

Environmental activities. Pollution control projects, adherence to federal standards, and evaluation procedures of new packages and products.

External relations. Support of minority enterprises, investment practices, and government relations.

Employment of minorities and women. Current hiring policies, advancement policies, specialized career counseling, and opportunities for special minorities such as the physically handicapped.

Employee safety and health. Work environment policies, accident safeguards, food, and medical facilities.

More often than not today, organizations have incorporated social responsibility into the mainstream of organization practice. Most firms recognize that social responsibility, far from being an add-on program, must be a corporate way of life.

For example, Levi Strauss, Xerox, IBM, and others encourage employees to take time off to participate in community projects. Xerox employees have built wheelchair ramps for handicapped persons in Detroit, cleared land and built picnic tables in a park near Houston, and served as juvenile probation officers in St. Louis. Leaves for such projects may range from a month to a year to several years.[10]

Banks, particularly those in urban areas, have designated target neighborhoods for community economic development and special housing financing projects. Chase Manhattan, for example, focused such community redevelopment efforts in the predominately minority areas of Jamaica, Woodside, and Bedford Stuyvesant in different New York City boroughs.

Little wonder why in 1977, business rose up in unified opposition to the suggestion by Commerce Secretary Juanita Kreps that the government establish a "Social Performance Index" to appraise the efforts of individual companies in such areas as environmental controls, affirmative action, minority purchasing, resolving consumer complaints, and product testing. To many executives, "The scheme constituted a public scorecard that would put corporations in competition with each other for public favor, with the Commerce Department acting as referee."[11] To many business people, already sold on the importance of social responsibility, such a government scorecard was just not necessary.

As former Chase Chairman David Rockefeller put it:

The business sector is undertaking increasingly to make genuine headway against major urban problems. More must be done, certainly. More to emphasize coordinated programs than isolated projects; more to strengthen the educational system to overcome the difficulties of upgrading performance; more to promote cooperative efforts among business, government and the minority communities. But the heartening signs of progress to date suggest a willingness on the part of this vital triad to cooperate, fully recognizing that in striving for solutions they are living up not only to the best of American ideal but also to the wisest of American self-interest.[12]

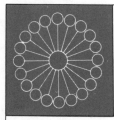

CASE STUDY
Three Mile Island

P rior to March 28, 1979, most of the nation's electric utilities had little use for public relations and preferred a low-key business style, out of the public spotlight and off the front page.

Occasionally, a utility official would come forward to defend the industry, particularly the cause of nuclear power, in the face of adversary criticism. For example, in 1978 when a magazine in Harrisburg, Pennsylvania wrote about a fictional disaster at a nearby nuclear power plant, Chief Executive Officer Walter Creitz of the Metropolitan Edison Company, which operated the plant, publicly complained about the "blatantly distorted" writing. Later, when the York *Daily Record* ran a four-page series calling attention to "grave safety defects" at a plant, Creitz again spoke up, calling the series tantamount "to someone yelling fire in a crowded theater."

How ironic.

For on March 28, 1979, Creitz, Metropolitan Edison, and the Three Mile Island plant plunged into the scariest nuclear nightmare in the nation's history. Overnight, Three Mile Island and nuclear power became the most prominent issues in the country, with newspapers, magazines, and network broadcast media all focused on the events in southeastern Pennsylvania.

What happened was that an accident in the reactor's core caused the danger of a "meltdown," which could ultimately have led to lethally radioactive gases escaping into the atmosphere. Initially, Metropolitan Edison spokespersons explained that a pump had broken down in the reactor, and that this malfunction was regarded by engineers as a normal aberration and no cause for panic. This reassurance sounded suspiciously akin to the script of *The China Syndrome,* a current Jane Fonda movie about a nuclear accident.

On March 28, Metropolitan Edison spokespersons announced that a small amount of radioactive water had leaked onto the floor of the reactor's containment building. They said that they had declared an emergency and had notified proper state and local authorities. State police thereupon blocked off the bridges leading to the 600-acre island.

The company then issued a statement:

> There have been no recordings of any significant levels of radiation and none are expected outside the plant.
>
>   The reactor is being cooled according to the design by the reactor cooling system and should be cooled by the end of the day. There is no danger of a meltdown. There were no injuries either to plant workers or to the public.

Shortly after the company released this statement, Pennsylvania officials helicoptered over the plant and detected a small release of radiation ino the environment.

How much radioactivity had leaked?

When reporters persisted, Creitz said, "I'll be honest about it: I don't know."

By March 30, Harrisburg was inundated with 300 reporters from around the world. In the days to follow, Pennsylvania officials, as well as representatives of the National Nuclear Regulatory Commission, were calling the Three Mile Island plant failure "one of the most serious nuclear accidents to occur in the United States." Nevertheless, Metropolitan Edison spokespersons still contended, "We didn't injure anybody. We didn't overexpose anybody. We didn't kill a single soul. The release of radioactivity off-site was minimal."

In the days and months after the incident, the industry became a national scapegoat. Interestingly, when Senator Edward Kennedy requested Creitz to testify to the health subcommittee a few days after the accident, Creitz declined and sent a subordinate in his place.

The events at Three Mile Island did not reflect well on public relations practitioners. For example, the governor of Pennsylvania said that "the lack of credible information" was of major public concern.[13] Journalists on the scene agreed: "Sources and public-information people were hard to reach. When reached, they gave out conflicting stories. And it turned out they were all guessing."[14]

Largely because of the events at Three Mile Island, the future of nuclear power in America appeared unclear. What was clear, however, was that largely because of the confusion over Three Mile Island, the nuclear power industry had seriously damaged its credibility.

Perhaps the only bright spot in the otherwise dim immediate future of the industry was the boon Three Mile Island provided to public relations. A year after the accident, Metropolitan Edison officials invited reporters on a tour of the renovated Three Mile Island facility in anticipation of hearings on the possible restarting of the unit. In addition, the nuclear power industry itself launched "truth squads" to tour the country, frequently shadowing antinuclear celebrities like Jane Fonda and her husband, Tom Hayden, to debate the virtues of nuclear power on radio and television. Because of Three Mile Island, the industry had, indeed, come out of the closet.

"Just because we're no longer thought of as the community good guys," said one utility communications director, "doesn't mean we're going to roll over and play dead." Said another, "It's either fight or give up the ship."

QUESTIONS

1 What mistakes did Metropolitan Edison make in its public relations approach at Three Mile Island?

2 Should the company have been better prepared for a potential accident at its plant?

3 Had you been Metropolitan Edison's public relations director, what role would you have suggested for Creitz? For yourself?

4 If you were named the new public relations director of Metropolitan Edison two months after Three Mile Island, what would be your first project?

5 How would you suggest the industry set about to "pick up the pieces" in terms of its damaged credibility?

NOTES

1 S. Prakash Sethi, "Business and Social Challenge," *Public Relations Journal,* September 1981, p. 31.

2 *How to Survive Happily in the Community and with the Press and the Government.* Federated Department Stores, Inc., 7 West 7th Street, Cincinnati, Ohio 45202, February 1981.

3 Adapted from *Public Relations News,* 31, no. 44 (3 November 1975): 3–4. Reprint permission from *PR News,* 127 East 80th Street, New York, N.Y. 10021.

4 Thomas Petzinger Jr., "When Disaster Comes, Public-Relations Men Won't Be Far Behind," *The Wall Street Journal,* 23 August 1979, p. 1.

5 Michael Cooper, "Crisis Public Relations," *Public Relations Journal,* November 1981, p. 53.

6 Cited in Michael A. Verespej, "DC 10 Tragedy Tests Rexnord's Krikorian," *Industry Week,* 6 August 1979, p. 36.

7 Excerpted from R. Seymour Smith, "How to Plan for Crisis Communication," *Public Relations Journal,* March 1979, pp. 17–18.

8 Donald K. Wright, "Social Responsibility in Public Relations: A Multi-Step Theory," *Public Relations Review,* Fall 1976, p. 25.

9 Interview with Andrew R. Baer, manager of public relations, The Equitable Life Assurance Society, 21 January 1979.

10 "On the Job," *Money,* November 1974, p. 28.

11 Carlton E. Spitzer, "Should Government Audit Corporate Social Responsibility?" *Public Relations Review,* Summer 1981, p. 14.

12 David Rockefeller, "Corporate Responsibility: A Call for Joint Business Investment in Society," *Black Enterprise,* March 1972, p. 85.

13 Albert B. Crenshaw, "Thornburgh Faults Information Quality after A-Plant Incident," *The Washington Post,* 22 August 1979, p. A9.

14 Peter M. Sandman and Mary Paden, "At Three Mile Island," *Columbia Journalism Review,* July/August 1979, p. 47.

SUGGESTED READING

Backman, Jules, ed. *Social Responsibility and Accountability.* New York: New York University Press, 1975.

Cole, Richard L. *Citizen Participation in the Urban Policy Process.* Lexington, Mass.: D. C. Heath, 1974.

Cooper, Michael. "Crisis Public Relations." *Public Relations Journal,* November 1981, pp. 52–57.

Effrat, Marcia Pelly. *The Community: Approaches and Applications.* New York: Free Press, 1974.

Escobar, Frank. "Public Relations and the Minority Community." *Public Relations Journal,* July 1981, pp. 27–28. Public relations programs have not kept pace with organizations' attempts to resolve their problems with minority communities.

Finn, David. *The Corporate Oligarchy.* New York: Simon and Schuster, 1969.

Harrison, Bruce. "Environmental Activism's Resurgence." *Public Relations Journal,* June 1982, pp. 34–36. Despite a national commitment to environmental health, activists are stepping up their activities, including fund raising and grass-roots campaigns.

Hawley, Willis D. and **Wirt, Frederick M.** *The Search for Community Power.* Englewood Cliffs, N.J.: Prentice-Hall, 1974.

Litschert, R., and **Nicholson, E.** *Corporate Role and Ethical Behavior.* New York: Van Nos Reinhold, 1977.

Londborg, Louis B. *Public Relations in the Local Community.* New York: Harper and Row, 1950.

Nolan, Stephen, and **Shayon, Diana.** *Profiles of Involvement.* Philadelphia: Human Resources Corporation, 1972. Gives examples of social action projects from various corporations.

Peak, Wilbur J. "Community Relations." *Public Relations Handbook.* 2d ed. Edited by Philip Lesly. Englewood Cliffs, N.J.: Prentice-Hall, 1978.

Reich, Charles A. *The Greening of America.* New York: Random House, 1970.

Sethi, S. Prakash. "Business and Social Challenge." *Public Relations Journal,* September 1981, pp. 30–31, 34. Business cannot participate effectively in the political process until it articulates who and what it is socially and what role its products and services play culturally, according to the author.

Sethi, S. Prakash. *Up Against the Corporate Wall.* Englewood Cliffs, N.J.: Prentice-Hall, 1977.

Sutula, Dolores A. "Community Education as a Communications Tool." *Public Relations Journal,* February 1981, pp. 27–28. An example of how one hospital tackled major community relations problems.

Tisch, Preston Robert. "A Way to Rebuild Public Confidence in Business." *Nation's Business,* April 1976, pp. 20–23.

Walton, Clarence, ed. *Ethics of Corporate Conduct.* Englewood Cliffs, N.J.: Prentice-Hall, 1977.

Warren, Roland L. *Perspectives on the American Community.* Chicago: Rand McNally, 1973.

18
Consumers

DEALING WITH CONSUMERISM

American consumers today—more than at any other time in our history—are well aware of their rights. Consumers simply will not tolerate defective merchandise, misleading advertising, packaging and labeling abuses, quality and safety failures, inadequate service and repair, diffident corporate complaint-handlers, incomprehensible or inadequate guarantees and warranties, and slow settlements when products don't live up to advance claims.

In other words, doing business means dealing with consumerism, and the movement is exerting increasing clout in the marketplace.

Conditions that enabled Ralph Nader's "Public Citizens, Inc." to collect over $1 million annually from consumers throughout the nation testify to the public's acceptance and support of the movement. Surveys corroborate that consumers believe in it. A typical research study found that most people supported the following consumerist efforts:[1]

1 Formation of a federal agency for consumer advocacy.

2 Adoption of a periodic convention for government, business, and consumer representatives to construct long-term consumer policies.

3 Establishment of consumer complaint bureaus in local communities.

4 Creation of independent test centers to evaluate the safety of potentially dangerous products, to be run by either government agencies or private consumerist groups.

5 Adoption of *consumer affairs* as a compulsory subject in high schools.

6 Requirement of large companies to employ senior officers responsible for consumer affairs.

7 Encouragement of large corporations to include on their boards of directors several public or consumer representatives.

As the findings of this study suggest, many Americans believe that consumers need assistance in ensuring that products and services meet the highest standards of safety and quality.

GROWTH OF THE CONSUMER MOVEMENT

Although consumerism is considered to be a relatively recent concept, legislation to protect consumers first emerged in the United States in 1872 when Congress enacted the Criminal Fraud Statute to protect consumers against corporate abuses. In 1887, Congress established the Interstate Commerce Commission to curb freewheeling railroad tycoons.

The first real consumer movement came right after the turn of the century when journalistic muckrakers encouraged legislation to protect the consumer. Upton Sinclair's novel *The Jungle* revealed scandalous conditions in the meat-packing industry and helped establish federal meat inspection standards as Congress passed the Food and Drug Act and the Trade Commission Act.

In the second wave of the movement, 1927-1938, consumers were safeguarded from the abuses of manufacturers, advertisers, and retailers of well-known brands of commercial products. During this time, Congress passed the Food, Drug, and Cosmetic Act.

By the early 1960s, the movement had become stronger and more unified. President John F. Kennedy, in fact, proposed that consumers had their own "Bill of Rights," which contained four basic principles:

1 The Right to Safety To be protected against the marketing of goods hazardous to health or life.

2 The Right to be Informed To be protected against fraudulent, deceitful, or grossly misleading information, advertising, labeling, or other practices, and to be given the facts needed to make an informed choice.

3 The Right to Choose To be assured, whenever possible, access to a variety of products and services at competitive prices.

4 The Right to be Heard To be assured that consumer interests will receive full and sympathetic consideration in the formulation of government policy.

In 1962, the first National Consumer Advisory Panel was established to "bring to the president's attention matters relating to the consumer." Two years later, President Lyndon Johnson appointed the first Special Assistant to the President for Consumer Affairs. In 1971, President Richard Nixon expanded the concept still further with the creation of the Office of Consumer Affairs, which was given broad responsibility to analyze and coordinate all federal activities in the field of consumer protection.

FEDERAL CONSUMER AGENCIES

A massive government bureaucracy attempts to protect the consumer against abuse: upwards of 900 different programs, administered by more than 400 federal entities. Key agencies include:

Justice Department. The Justice Department has had a consumer affairs section in the antitrust division since 1970. Its responsibilities include the enforcement of such consumer protection measures as the Truth in Lending Act and the Product Safety Act.

Federal Trade Commission (FTC). The FTC, perhaps more than any other agency, has vigorously enforced consumer protection in recent years. Its national advertising division covers television and radio advertising, with special emphasis on foods, drugs, and cosmetics. Its general litigation division covers areas not included by national advertising, such as magazine subscription agencies, door-to-door sales, and income tax services. Its consumer credit and special programs division deals with such areas as fair credit reporting and truth-in-packaging.

Food and Drug Administration. The FDA is responsible for protecting consumers from hazardous items: foods, drugs, cosmetics, therapeutic and radiological devices, food additives, and serums and vaccines.

Consumer Product Safety Commission. This bureau is responsible for overseeing product safety and standards.

Office of Consumer Affairs. This agency, the central point for consumer activities in the government, publishes literature to inform the public of recent developments in consumer affairs.

From time to time in recent years, federal legislators have attempted to add yet another consumer protection agency to the federal government's arsenal. In 1978, perhaps more indicative of the public's disdain for new spending than of the belief that consumer protection had gone far enough, efforts to create a federal Consumer Protection Agency were soundly defeated.

Indeed, by the early 1980s, the public had become increasingly disenchanted with nonstop government growth. With "the cost of government regulation" estimated at over $100 billion per year,[2] Presidents Carter and Reagan both preached a platform of reducing the size of government bureaucracy. Under Carter, several industries, most notably the airlines, were deregulated. Ironically, with the regulatory "gloves offs," several airlines couldn't compete and went bankrupt. Under President Reagan, the FTC, in particular, toned down its investigative offensive into the affairs of business. While some applauded this removal of government intervention in the market process, others objected that unregulated companies would run roughshod over the American consumer.

By the mid-1980s, the jury was still out in determining whether more or less government protection was beneficial to the consumer.

Jean Way Schoonover is president of Dudley-Anderson-Yutzy Public Relations Incorporated, a major New York City-based public relations agency that specializes in food and consumer-oriented public relations. Ms. Schoonover was named "Advertising Woman of the Year" in 1972 by the American Advertising Federation. In 1976, she was awarded the New York Women in Communications Matrix Award and Amita's Golden Lady Award.

Are consumers today more "enlightened"?

Consumers today are more conscious of their rights and the value of their goodwill. They view companies, products, and services in a more critical manner; whether they are more enlightened is difficult to judge.

Are companies today more "enlightened"?

Companies are also more aware of consumer opinion and of the power of comsumers to make known their opinions through the media. Companies are therefore more conservative than they might otherwise be.

What is the general state of consumer relations in American companies?

PRIVATE CONSUMER ACTIVISTS/PUBLICATIONS

The consumerist movement has attracted a host of activists in recent years.

Private testing organizations, which evaluate products and inform consumers about potential dangers, have proliferated. Perhaps the best known, Consumers' Union, was formed in 1936 to test products over a wide spectrum of industries. It publishes the results in a monthly magazine, *Consumer Reports,* which reaches more than one million readers. Often, an evaluation in *Consumer Reports,* either pro or con, greatly affects how customers view particular products.

Consumers also have begun taking a more active role in their own affairs. The Consumer Federation of America was formed in 1967 to unify lobbying efforts for proconsumer legislation. Today, the federation consists of 200 national, state, and local consumer groups, labor unions, electric cooperatives, and other organizations with consumer interests.

The state of consumer relations in American companies today is generally good, but the function might suffer if business has to continue to retrench because of a faltering economy.

What is the future of the consumer movement?

The consumer movement will continue to exert influence, almost as an institutionalized part of our environment, but its impact will be less than in the past, except in problem areas.

What are the responsibilities of a company to the consumers of its products?

The responsibilities of a company to consumers of its products are to produce good products which provide a good value, and to stand behind those products in terms of quality, performance, and safety. The company should be candid about risks and how to minimize them.

How useful are corporate ombudsmen?

They are useful, provided they have real authority and access to top management. They provide a central point valuable to consumers on the one hand by their responsiveness, and valuable to the company on the other by their ability to communicate to management the problems and opportunities from the consumers' viewpoint.

What should a company do if its products are criticized in the press?

If a company's products are criticized in the press, it should: a) examine the validity of the criticism, b) take remedial steps if necessary, c) if unjustified, rebut the criticism with facts presented in a dispassionate manner, d) take the offensive, if necessary.

What do you recommend as a general strategy in dealing with the various consumer agencies of the government? In dealing with the Ralph Naders of the world?

As a strategy for dealing with consumer agencies in government, we recommend that they build good contacts, set up regular channels of communication, give them advance information on developments, present data to support claims as early as possible. As for dealing with the Ralph Naders of the world, make no personal charges or attacks; respond to criticisms with facts; be aware that they often create ersatz issues that may or may not require response. If the issue has no basis, it is likely to die a natural death. Responding to it merely prolongs the attention to it and/or gives the impression that there is substance to the claim.

BUSINESS GETS THE MESSAGE

Obviously, few organizations can afford to shirk their responsibilities to consumers. Consumer relations divisions have sprung up, either as separate entities or as part of public relations departments. The title *vice-president-consumer relations* is showing up with more frequency on corporate organization charts.

In many companies, consumer relations began strictly as a way to handle complaints, an area to which all unanswerable complaints were sent. Such units frequently provide an "alert" system to management. In recent years, some companies have broadened the consumer relations function to encompass such activities as developing guidelines to evaluate services and products for management, developing consumer programs that meet consumer needs and increase sales, developing field training programs, evaluating service approaches, and evaluating company effectiveness in demonstrating concern for customers.

In adopting a more active consumerist philosophy, many firms have found that consumerism/customer relations need not be a defensive posture. Rather, positive customer relations can be effective as a marketing tool to enhance an organization's reputation as a concerned supplier of products that satisfy consumer desires.

Accordingly, the consumer affairs function has grown in stature. Today, there is a Society of Consumer Affairs Professionals in Business (SOCAP). In a poll of its members, SOCAP found that 80 percent regularly reported consumer trends to management, 70 percent developed consumer education materials on a regular basis, half met occasionally with consumer representatives, and nearly half consulted with government agencies on a periodic basis.

PHILOSOPHY

Most companies begin with the premise that customers, if they are to remain customers, deserve to be treated fairly and honestly. Historically, the companies that initiated their own activist consumer affairs units have been those to escape the wrath of outside activists.

The Grand Union Company, second oldest food chain in the nation, is a good example. Grand Union's consumer affairs department began in 1970 to recommend policies and procedures to the company, monitor performance, and effect changes in the best interests of consumers. Stealing a page from JFK, Grand Union drew up its own "Consumer Bill of Rights," which is illustrative of a forward-thinking, consumer-oriented company:[3]

We believe that the consumer has a right to know.

Grand Union was among the first to introduce unit pricing or listing price-per-measure information on its packages. More than 5,000 Grand Union items were unit-priced, and the company explained how to use the new system by displaying large window posters and placards in its stores.

We believe that the consumer has the right to choose.

Grand Union made it policy to always give customers a choice between nationally-advertised brands and its own brand.

We believe that the consumer has the right to expect to find advertised specials in the store, in adequate quantity and variety.

Grand Union was among the first to offer "rain checks," entitling customers to purchase out-of-stock specials at the same price even after the sale had concluded.

We believe in the consumer's right to protection from unsafe products.

Grand Union was among the first to voluntarily switch to a system of open dating, allowing customers to determine the freshness of perishable and semiperishable products. The company also maintained its own test laboratory and sponsored in-store cleanliness programs.

We believe in the consumer's right to be heard.

In addition to its complaint bureau, Grand Union provided customers with addressed, postage-paid letter forms, pens, and writing desks in its stores. The company promised that each letter received would be acted upon and replied to promptly.

We believe that the consumer has a right to be completely satisfied in any dealings with the company.

Grand Union advertising stressed nutritional education as well as straight product messages. Early in the mid-70s fuel crisis, Grand Union converted its company fleet

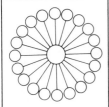

MINICASE
The nontoxic chemicals[4]

In the mid-1970s, the Monsanto Company of St. Louis could read the writing on the wall—and also in newspapers and magazines. As Monsanto's advertising and promotion director explained it:

> We'd been reading the same newspapers and watching the same TV as the public and observed a great deal of negative, one-sided information about chemicals. People were horrified by the hazards of chemicals because they lacked a balanced view. Someone had to speak up and inform the public of what we and other companies are doing to reduce the risk.

So in 1977, Monsanto launched a full-scale program to expose the truth about chemicals.

The company's first effort was aimed at employees. It prepared a booklet, *The Chemical Facts of Life,* which was distributed internally.

It began a Monsanto company Chemical Facts of Life Speakers Bureau and recruited "speak out" trainees among its staff. One of the company's most outspoken spokesman was its chairman and president, John W. Hanley, who delivered numerous speeches on the chemical risk/benefit issue.

Monsanto also created a film on the contribution of chemicals and devised a twenty-eight-unit education exhibit to tour the country.

Finally the company launched a national advertising campaign to inform consumers about the contributions to society that chemicals make. In its television ads, Monsanto used prominent scientists to convey the chemical message.

Although Monsanto's name was never overemphasized in either the advertising or the booklet, nevertheless the company felt its major investment was well worth the price. As Monsanto's advertising director put it, "If the public develops a more balanced perspective on the chemical issue, sooner or later it's going to be felt by the people who regulate and legislate us."

QUESTIONS

1 Do you think Monsanto's campaign was worth the investment?

2 What purpose was served by beginning the campaign with employees?

3 Was the national advertising campaign a wise idea?

4 Should Monsanto have made its consumer relations thrust more company-oriented and less generic?

of almost 200 trucks in the New York metropolitan area from gasoline to diesel power, thus reducing pollution. The company also stopped burning its trash and instead had it carted away or recycled.

All in all, the Grand Union Consumer Bill of Rights demonstrated that an enlightened consumer relations policy makes good business sense.

CONSUMERIST OBJECTIVES

Building sales is the primary consumer relations objective. A satisfied customer may return; an unhappy customer may not. Some typical goals might include the following:

Keeping old customers.   Most sales are made to established customers. Consumer relations efforts should be made to keep these customers happy. Pains should be taken to become responsive to customer complaints and reactions.

Attracting new customers.   Every business must work constantly to develop new customers. In many industries, the prices and quality of competing products are similar. Customers may base decisions among brands on how they have been treated.

Marketing new items or services.   Customer relations techniques can influence the sale of new products. Thousands of such products flood the market each year. And the vast array of information about these products can confuse the consumer. In 1980, General Electric research revealed that while consumers want personalized service and more information on new products, they generally lack the time to investigate a product fully before buying. Consequently, General Electric established the "GE Answer Center," a national, toll-free, 24-hour service that informed consumers about new GE products and services. Building such company and product loyalty lies at the heart of a solid consumer relations effort.

Expediting complaint handling.   Few companies are free of complaints. Customers protest when appliances don't work, errors are made in billing, or deliveries aren't made on time. Many large firms have established response procedures. Often, a company ombudsman can salvage a customer relationship with a speedy and satisfactory answer to a complaint.

Reducing costs.   To most companies, an educated consumer is the best consumer. Uninformed buyers cost a company time and money—when goods are returned, service calls are made, and instructions are misunderstood. Many firms have adopted programs to educate customers about many topics: what to look for in choosing fruits and vegetables, how to shop for durable goods, how to use credit wisely, how to conserve electricity. In Figure 18-1, booklets from Shell Oil provided tips to consumers on a variety of topics. Most companies find no value in taking advantage of the customer. In the long run, if customers use products and services wisely and happily, they will return to buy again.

CONSUMER PROGRAMS

Some of the nation's most marketing-oriented firms are leaders in creating innovative consumer relations programs. Most apparently feel that by investing in consumer relations activities, they are safeguarding and ensuring future sales.

Here are some of the more novel approaches to consumer relations:

1 The major automobile companies all are engaged actively in consumer relations, although each takes a different tack. The Ford Motor Company established a Consumer Affairs Board, which met periodically to mediate unresolved product complaints and render binding judgments on the company and its dealers. Ford's initial board consisted of educators, dealers, and motor vehicle officials. At General Motors, each car division offered specific consumer relations programs for dealers, introducing them to techniques for handling complaints and for getting to the root of customer dissatisfaction. Chrysler Corporation held seminars for its dealers on handling customer complaints and conducted "Women on

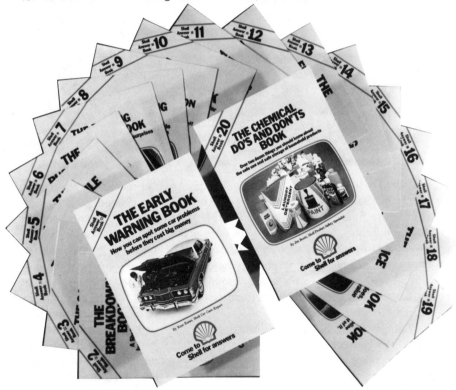

FIGURE 18–1. *Shell answer books.* Typical of the desire of the nation's oil companies to present a proconsumerist image, Shell Oil published a complete set of easy-to-read, illustrated manuals, teaching people how to care for their cars, their homes, and themselves. The free booklets were available in Shell stations around the country.

SOURCE: Courtesy of Shell Oil Company.

Wheels" workshops, dealing with basic car repair and maintenance. Chrysler also introduced free, long-term warranties, intimating its confidence in the reliability of its product.

2   Food and pharmaceutical firms have taken leadership in listing product ingredients and nutritional information on their packages. Del Monte was among the first food processors to list ingredients and nutritional information on its labels and to offer customers further product information on request. Eli Lilly offered a similar product labeling service for its drug items and went one step further by providing information on labels for immediate antidotal analysis in case of emergencies. Lilly's favorable consumerist record helped it weather an attack against its Darvon product in 1979 and another against its Oraflex product in 1982.

3   Other companies, from appliance sellers (Sears, General Electric, and Whirlpool) to banks (Citibank, Chemical Bank), have translated jargon into easily understandable English on their warranties and loan agreements. Gulf went so far as to publish a booklet on "The Art of Complaining," so its customers would know how to voice complaints, to whom to voice them, and what to expect in response.

FEATURE
Reconsidering the recall policy

Under President Carter, the National Highway Traffic Safety Administration (NHTSA), as the Case Study at the conclusion of this chapter indicates, was the most aggressive of government agencies in exposing suspected car and tire safety problems. Frequently, the NHTSA would issue news releases warning consumers of possible defects in their cars and tires.

When President Reagan took office in 1980, the NHTSA became less aggressive, at least in publicizing its activities. As NHTSA Administrator Raymond Peck put it, "The purpose of this agency is not to create publicity . . . and not to excoriate or condemn the manufacturers."[5]

In August 1981, both the *Washington Post* and *The New York Times* revealed that Ford Motor Company and the Chrysler Corporation had stopped issuing public notices of car recalls for repair of safety defects, choosing instead to notify car owners directly. When questioned about this policy, Ford responded that it would no longer issue press releases on recalls routinely unless "significant" safety hazards were involved.

The Ford and Chrysler revelations immediately triggered outraged cries from consumer advocates, including Joan Claybrook, President Carter's NHTSA Administrator, who said that in the past, manufacturers publicized recalls "because they knew that if they didn't, the NHTSA would."

Shortly after the unannounced recall story hit the press, the auto companies reversed field. Said Ford, "To avoid any misunderstandings, the company will henceforth make public announcement of safety recalls of vehicles simultaneously with notifying owners."

415

All of these companies and many more like them have recognized that in consumer relations, as in many other activities in the public relations field, the best defense is a good offense.

OFFICE OF THE OMBUDSMAN

At many companies, the most immediate response to consumerism has been the establishment of "ombudsman" offices. The term *ombudsman* originally described a government official—in Sweden and New Zealand, for example—appointed to investigate complaints against abuses of public officials. In most firms, the Office of the Ombudsman investigates the complaints made against the company and its managers. Such an office generally provides a central location customers can call to seek redress of grievances.

A five-year study of consumer complaint handling commissioned by the U.S. Office of Consumer Affairs suggested two important caveats for suppliers of consumer goods and services.

1 Consumers who do *not* complain when they are dissatisfied are often unhappy enough to switch product brands, companies, or both.
2 Since marketing costs are extremely high, it may be less expensive to resolve the complaints of existing customers than to win new ones.[6]

Some companies (for example, General Motors, American Motors, Chrysler, ITT, and Whirlpool) have installed special telephone lines that allow consumers to call the ombudsman by dialing direct and toll-free. The ombudsman also monitors the difficulties customers are having with products. Often, the ombudsman can anticipate product or performance deficiencies. Skillful complaint-handling personnel—who are cheerful, positive, knowledgeable, and genuinely concerned with solving consumer problems—not only can keep customers happy but can also serve to correct and prevent customer problems in the future.

THE FUTURE OF CONSUMERISM

Despite periodic legislative setbacks and shifting consumerist leadership, the cause of consumerism seems destined to remain strong. Although critics may argue that "nobody uses unit-pricing and nobody wears seat belts," the push for product safety and quality will likely increase in the years ahead.

Congress and federal agencies today subject companies to more scrutiny in their consumer policy. The phrase *"caveat emptor"* (let the buyer beware) has been replaced by *"caveat venditor"* (let the seller beware). For example, in 1960, there were fewer than 50,000 product liability cases, dealing with faulty merchandise, warranties, or performance. By 1970, the number had mushroomed to 500,000 cases. Through the 1980s, the number of such cases may surpass one million annually.

The tidal wave of consumerism can only be met by sophisticated planning from business firms. Indeed, companies now audit their programs to assess corporate policies in terms of how well they protect consumer rights.[7] In essence, the corporate consumerist challenge is to keep one step ahead of legislators and activists by introducing safety, performance, and service standards that show the company's good faith and public interest.

Occasionally, as in the tragic murders from cyanide-laced Tylenol in 1982 (see Case Study at conclusion of Chapter 22), a company cannot avoid the harsh glare of negative publicity about its products. However, in the long run, the firm that lives by a proconsumer philosophy should prosper. Conversely, the firm that ignores the push of consumerism may not only experience difficulty in growing, but also in remaining a viable business enterprise.

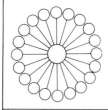

MINICASE
A day in the life of the ombudsman

So you want to handle consumer complaints?

Here is a random selection of complaints received by the consumer affairs division of The Chase Manhattan Bank. How would you have handled them?

1   A businessman, carrying an attaché case, made a deposit at a midtown branch before going to his office. Inadvertently, he left his case on the main banking floor. By the time he discovered his missing attaché, the police bomb squad had smashed the innocent case and cordoned off the area. The owner asked the bank for a replacement. Would you have given it to him?

2   A woman, after making a deposit and leaving the bank, reported that a huge icicle fell from the bank's roof and nearly hit her. She complained bitterly to consumer affairs. How would you appease her?

3   A young installment loan customer claimed his car was removed for reclamation because of delinquent loan payments. He claimed he had paid the loan on time and objected to the illegal seizure. Upon checking, it was determined that several loan payments were, in fact, delinquent. Nevertheless, the car was returned, in a very damaged condition. The young man sought reimbursement for repairs. What would you recommend?

4   A customer complained she received no response to her numerous letters and memos concerning the hostile treatment accorded her at the local branch. After investigation, it was learned that the woman was a nuisance to branch officers, yet kept a very healthy balance in her savings account. Further, all the correspondence to which she referred was written on the backs of checks she submitted in payment for indebtedness to the bank. How would you handle this problem?

5   The executor of an estate complained that he received a card reading, "Best wishes in your new residence," when the executor's client, a customer of the bank, had died. What remedial action would you recommend?

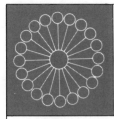

CASE STUDY
The unfortunate Firestone 500s

The Firestone Tire and Rubber Company first began feeling the heat on its 500 steel-belted radial tire in 1976, when the Center for Auto Safety, a Washington-based organization once associated with Ralph Nader, received numerous complaints about tread separations and blowouts.

"During 1977, the Center studied the tire complaints in its files and found that half of them were leveled against Firestone, with the great bulk of these involving the 500 radial."[8] Later that year, the Center's director wrote the president of Firestone and suggested the company shift half its advertising budget into "quality control." In his letter, the Center's director urged the company to "recall the defective tires before more innocent people are killed and injured." The Center thereupon turned its data over to the National Highway Traffic Safety Administration (NHTSA).

The NHTSA, chaired by a former Nader associate, decided to launch its own survey of tire performance. It mailed 87,000 survey cards to people who had bought new cars equipped with radial tires. Respondents were asked to indicate their tire brands and to report whether they had experienced blowouts or other problems. While less than 10 percent of those surveyed responded to the questionnaire, many of the 5,400 who did respond criticized the Firestone radial.

Firestone acted immediately to suppress the study on the grounds it was "statistically unsound because of the small response."[9] The company further claimed that the resultant publicity would damage its business. The U.S. District Court granted a restraining order.

However, the company's litigious actions piqued the curiosity of people who had been unaware of the radial tire crisis. In particular, the episode aroused the suspicions of a U.S. congressman, who decided to hold hearings on the issue.

To make matters worse, the NHTSA study was leaked to the press, and the Firestone name was further tarred in public.

The leak of the NHTSA study enraged Firestone officials. The company responded to NHTSA requests for data on its 500 tires with bitterness, foot-dragging, and appeals for more time to "research" NHTSA questions.

At the hearings on its tires, Firestone sent its chief counsel as sole representative. The Firestone lawyer read a prepared statement and then was subjected to spirited cross examination by hostile legislators. Moreover, the Firestone witness was preceded to the stand by a parade of consumers, all testifying against the 500 radial.

By the fall of 1978, the NHTSA had released its "initial determination" that the Firestone 500 had a safety-related defect, and it recommended that Firestone recall the tires immediately. The company responded by denying that there was anything wrong with the tires, calling the 500 radial "safe and reliable."

On October 23, 1978, a story in the *Wall Street Journal* began:

> Firestone Tire and Rubber Co., bowing to government pressure, said it will soon begin mailing recall notices covering about 10 million of its "500" steel-belted radial tires.
>
> The company expects that about half that number of tires will actually be returned by their owners for replacement and that the recall will cost it about $135 million after taxes.

A month after Firestone's announcement about the recall notices, the *Washington Post* reported that Firestone's ten-page mailgram to tire dealers "led to mass confusion" because "it contained apparent inaccuracies over what tires would or would not be accepted under the terms of the recall."

Incredibly, a full two years after Firestone's recall, the company had to pay an additional $500,000 civil fine and recall another 400,000 radial tires. Explained the NHTSA administrator, "Firestone learned that these tires were likely to fail the standard before our testing revealed it, but the company did not notify us and recall the tires."[10] Consequently, Firestone was faced with paying the largest civil penalty ever assessed under the National Traffic and Motor Vehicle Safety Act.

In a post mortem of the Firestone 500 situation, *Time* magazine assessed the situation thusly: "A classic public relations fiasco."

QUESTIONS

1 How would you assess Firestone's consumer relations response to the radial tire controversy?

2 What should have been Firestone's posture in light of the study of its radials?

3 Should Firestone have sought a restraining order to bar the release of the NHTSA study?

4 How might Firestone's appearance at the hearings have been better handled?

5 Had you been the consumer affairs director, what strategy would you have recommended upon being apprised in 1976 of the controversy?

6 What posture would you advise the company adopt for the rest of the 1980s?

NOTES

1 "The Consumer Confronts the Businessman," *Across the Board*, November 1977, p. 83.

2 Address by Willard C. Butcher, President, The Chase Manhattan Bank, at Commonwealth Club of California, San Francisco, Cal., 15 September 1978.

3 The Grand Union Company, *Corporate Responsibility Report*, pamphlet (Elmwood Park, N.J.: Author, 1973).

4 Adapted from Jeff A. Williamson's "Monsanto Company: A Chemical Company Leader Assumes the Role of Industry Spokesman and Public Educator," *Madison Avenue Magazine,* February 1979, pp. 90–92.

5 Peter Behr, "Recalls of Ford's Escort, Lynx Not Announced to the Public," *The Washington Post,* 12 August 1981, pp. 1–16.

6 Robert M. Cosenza and Jerry W. Wilson, "Managing Consumer Dissatisfaction: The Effective Use of the Corporate Written Response to Complaints," *Public Relations Quarterly,* Spring 1982, p. 17.

7 Larry J. Rosenberg, John A. Czepiel, and Lester C. Cohen, "Consumer Affairs Audits, Evaluation, and Analysis," *California Management Review,* Spring 1977, pp. 12, 13.

8 Arthur M. Louis, "Lessons From the Firestone Fracas," *Fortune,* 28 August 1978, p. 46.

9 Ibid., p. 47.

10 "Firestone to Pay Fine of $500,000 in Recall Dispute With U.S. Unit," *The New York Times,* 13 May 1980.

SUGGESTED READING

Barksdale, Hiram C., and **French, Warren A.** "Response to Consumerism: How Change is Perceived by Both Sides." *Business Topics* 23, no. 2 (Spring 1975): 55–67.

Communications Counselors. *Capital Contacts in Consumerism.* (Available from author, 1701 K Street, NW, Washington, D.C. 20006.)

"Corporate Cocoon? Top Executives Keep Tabs on Consumers or Contend They Do." *Wall Street Journal,* 1 July 1976, p. 1.

Cosenza Ph.D., Robert M. and **Wilson, Jerry W.** "Managing Consumer Dissatisfaction: The Effective Use Of The Corporate Written Response To Complaints." *Public Relations Quarterly,* Spring 1982, pp. 17–19.

Dinsmore, William H. "Please Allow Eight Weeks . . ." *Public Relations Quarterly,* Winter 1981–82, pp. 28–29.

Harrington, Michael. *The Twilight of Capitalism.* New York: Simon and Schuster, 1976.

Henry, Kenneth. *Defenders and Shapers of the Corporate Image.* New Haven, Conn.: College and University Press, 1972.

Kangun, Norman; Cox, Keith K.; Higginbotham, James; and **Burton, John.** "Consumerism and Marketing Management." *Journal of Marketing* 39, no. 2 (April 1975): 3–10.

Morganstern, Stanley. *Legal Protection for the Consumer.* New York: Oceana, 1973.

Ramparts Magazine editors. *In the Marketplace: Consumerism in America.* New York: Harper & Row, 1972

Rowat, Donald C. *The Ombudsman Plan: Essay on the Worldwide Spread of an Idea.* Toronto: McClelland and Stewart, 1973.

Silk, Leonard, and **Vogel, David.** *Ethics and Profits.* New York: Simon & Schuster, 1976.

Stein, Harry J. "The Muckraking Book in America, 1946–1973." *Journalism Quarterly* 52, no. 2 (Summer, 1975): 297–303.

Ways, Max. "Business Needs a Different Political Stance." *Fortune* (September 1975): p. 97.

GROWTH OF FINANCIAL RELATIONS

Financial relations—or, as it is called, investor relations or just IR—has been a growth area in public relations since the 1960s. Financial relations generally blends the skills of finance and writing with knowledge of the media, marketing, and, more recently, government, because of its increased role in the capital markets.

Financial relations was born in the mid-1930s, shortly after the passage of the Securities Act of 1933 and the Securities Exchange Act of 1934, which dealt with protecting the public from abuses in issuance and sale of securities. Financial relations existed in relative obscurity until the 1960s, when investors rushed to the stock market to strike their fortunes. Stock prices escalated, and IR enjoyed a heyday. The euphoria ended in the early 1970s as the investing public grew increasingly disenchanted with stocks. Indeed, the number of individual shareholders in 1975 was less than in 1970. Nevertheless, just about 32 million Americans own shares in publicly owned corporations.

19
Investors

IR emerged from the problems of the early 1970s as a smarter, more focused, sophisticated practice.[1] Its principal objective remained to achieve favorable recognition for a company in the eyes of investors.

In the 1980s, the investor relations job basically breaks into three parts:[2]

Compliance. This results from the increased number of regulations and rule changes promulgated by a wide variety of government agencies, not the least of which is the Securities and Exchange Commission (SEC). IR practitioners must have a comprehensive knowledge of government regulations, most particularly SEC reporting requirements.

Institutional investor needs. IR practitioners must be able to satisfy the needs of the institutional investor community—the banks, insurance companies, and mutual funds that oversee the investment of pension funds and other assets managed by institutions. In 1980, the 300 largest institutions managed more than $1,000 billion of investment funds, attesting to their overwhelming importance as IR targets.

Individual investor needs. The third element of the IR mix involves convincing individuals to invest their savings in common stocks, particularly the common stock the IR professional is marketing.

Little wonder that chief executives pay good money for IR professionals. Recent salary surveys indicate that IR practitioners generally are paid in the high range of all public relations salaries, with the better IR pros earnings upwards of $100,000 a year. Not surprisingly, the financial relations field has become a specialized one in which the inexperienced are at a particular disadvantage.

ESSENCE OF INVESTOR RELATIONS

A public company must communicate promptly and candidly any information, both good and bad, that may have an effect on its securities. Practitioners must see that shareholders receive such information fully, fairly, and quickly so that they can decide whether to buy, hold, or sell the company's securities.

The institutions and individuals who own the common stock of a company are, in effect, the owners of that corporation. The shareholders, in person or by proxy, elect the Board of Directors, who in turn select the officers who run the company. So in theory, at least, shareholders (who own the company) influence the operations of that company. In practice, corporate officers manage companies with relative independence. Nevertheless, shareholders constitute a critical public for any firm.

Shareholders and potential shareholders also serve as an important source of additional corporate funds through equity capital, used for a company's expansion and diversification. If a company is stymied in its efforts to raise equity capital, it may find its growth opportunities limited.

Why do investors buy a company's shares? The first requisite must be performance. A company that fails to perform can't expect good communications to sell its stock. On the other hand, a thoughtfully planned and executed financial communications program may materially enhance the market popularity of a company that performs well.

ORGANIZING THE PROGRAM

The most effective way to reach the investing public—individuals as well as institutions—is through a systematic program of financial relations, ordinarily managed by an investor relations director. Frequently, programs are bolstered by the retention of a financial relations counseling firm.

Since most public companies perpetually compete for equity capital, an organized investor relations program is essential. While communications tools such as the annual and quarterly report are important, practitioners also must communicate directly with investors, potential investors and their intermediaries, securities analysts, brokers, and funds managers.

The IR professional must be outgoing, a good communicator, a good salesperson, knowledgeable in finance and accounting, and conversant in the language of Wall Street. The rapidly changing practice of financial relations also means the IR director must be up-to-date on recent SEC rulings.[3]

FINANCIAL RELATIONS AND THE SEC

The Securities and Exchange Commission, through a series of comments and complaints over the years, has painted a general portrait of disclosure requirements for practitioners (Appendix B).*

The SEC's overriding concern is that all investors have an opportunity to learn about "material" corporate information as promptly as possible. Through its general antifraud statute, Rule 10b-5, the SEC strictly prohibits the dissemination of false or misleading information to investors. It also prohibits "insider trading" on the basis of material information not disclosed to the public.

Such insider information prompted the SEC in 1972 to charge Liggett & Myers and its communications director with giving advance earnings information to certain securities analysts and institutions. The basis of this complaint was that Liggett & Myers conveyed the "material" information to the insiders about two hours before releasing the news to the general public.[4]

Besides cracking down on insider information, the SEC also has challenged public relations firms on the "accuracy" of information they disseminate for clients. In 1971, the SEC charged the public relations counsel of the Pig 'n Whistle Corp. with issuing press releases and other material that "contained false and misleading statements." The SEC's complaint intimated that it was the responsibility of the public relations firm to authenticate the data contained in client news releases.[5]

The responsibility of practitioners to disseminate corporate news fully, fairly, and promptly has expanded in recent years. As a former SEC chairman put it, "There once must have been a time when the role of financial public relations officers was completely enjoyable and not terribly troublesome. Today, everyone who participates in the process of getting information to the public assumes a certain amount of responsibility for its adequacy and accuracy."[6]

In response to such pleas, in 1982 the SEC issued a 95-page release, "Adoption of Integrated Disclosure System," which attempted to bring some order to the chaos of SEC requirements. Essentially, the new SEC document attempted to make more uniform the instructions governing corporate disclosure of information.

---

* Each year, Hill and Knowlton compiles an extensive list of corporate reporting requirements, which it publishes in *Public Relations Journal*. The list included in Appendix B appeared in Robert W. Taft, "Order out of Chaos," *Public Relations Journal*, April 1982, pp. 25–37.

INTERVIEW
James O. Rollans

James O. Rollans is vice president of corporate communications at California's Fluor Corporation, where he is responsible for developing and implementing communications strategies on Fluor's business outlook, company performance, and objectives for the financial community, shareholders, the media, and employees. Mr. Rollans is a leading authority in the field of investor relations, having been responsible for the function at such leading corporations as Dart & Kraft Inc., The Chase Manhattan Bank, and B. F. Goodrich Company. He has also held a variety of financial management positions with the Singer Corporation.

What is the essence of Investor Relations?

Stock prices are determined in the marketplace, *not* in the corporate suite! This statement has been the guiding philosophy of investor relations since its inception as an acknowledged corporate function in the 1950s. The communications objective that has flowed from this philosophy is to transmit sufficient information to investors in a timely manner so that *they* can fairly value the corporation's stock.

Can investor relations impact the stock price?

In a word 'yes', but it's a word that needs explanation. We operate in the real world, and Wall Street and the investment process is even worse than that. The price of a stock gets down to information—the right information, in the right hands, at the right time. Investor relations makes that happen. (Please, under no circumstances do I mean selective or insider information!)

Said another way—poor investor relations can result in a stock being undervalued. This happens when the right information isn't in all the right hands or isn't available at the right time. Good investor relations will assure that the company and its performance and prospects get full exposure and, in the process, full value.

How do you know if your stock is fairly priced?

There are some who would tell you that fair market value can be determined with precision. Don't you believe it. If it were true, as the old saying goes, these people wouldn't be selling statistical modeling programs. They would be sitting on the fantails of their yachts in Newport Beach, California clipping coupons.

However, tracking the price performance of your stock vis-a-vis the overall market indicators and direct investment competitors can and should be done. This comparison will give some measure of investor relations effectiveness as well as some idea of what level of financial performance investors demand.

With what general body of knowledge must an investor relations professional be conversant?

The investor relations professional is a jack-of-all-trades and master of many. Preferably, the person will hold an MBA from a leading university with a major in finance and a minor in communications or journalism and be someone who has had direct business experience in the industrial sector or with a financial institution and who understands the investment process and basic security laws.

What separates the successful investor relations pro from the not so successful?

The best in this field view the company through the eyes of several key players: the chief executive officer, chief operating officer, chief financial officer, largest institutional investor, smallest individual investor, most critical investment analyst or stock broker, most skeptical Securities and Exchange Commission attorney, to name just a few. Keeping the information flowing so that these audiences can clearly understand the issues from their unique perspectives and make the necessary decisions is what the job is all about.

How does a company start an investor relations program?

A company starts an investor relations program by first having a clear set of expectations for the function and properly organizing it within the corporate structure. All key executives must be made aware that the function is being put in place and that their support and help is needed and expected. Next, the position must be filled by someone who fits the management team, understands the job, and can get it done. Finally, a comprehensive investor communications program should be developed including identification of current and potential investors, security analysts, and stock brokers along with check points to ensure that the program is on target.

How important is a company's annual report?

The annual report is the single most important document in the investor communication process. It is the first document that potential investors will request and where they will get their first impression of the company. It also is the key reference document used by investment professionals.

How should the investor relations professional handle "bad news"?

Under the heading of bad news and what to do about it, there is only one rule to remember and two good reasons to remember it. The rule is: when faced with bad news, make sure that the company is the first to announce it. There is no exception to this rule! The two good reasons are 1) it will get out anyway so control it and discuss not only the problem but what management is doing to resolve it and 2) the company will only maintain its credibility if it is willing to discuss bad news as well as good news. If two

(Interview *continues.*)

reasons aren't enough here's a third: stock prices are discounted more for rumored problems than for problems that are identified and candidly discussed by management.

Is there anything else you'd like readers of this book to know?

Perhaps the most difficult aspect of managing an investor relations program is making sure it is well-paced and on track. The reason is, the only person in the process in a position to judge whether the job is being done well is the person actually performing the job. Only the investor relations person can take measure of all the factors that go into the communication decisions. A further complication is that criticism can be constant and from all directions.

Management's view is generally that investors and security analysts should be more familiar with the business, more understanding, more patient. Investors and analysts on the other hand often feel that results could be better and the communication could be more candid.

The investor relations professional must consider this input carefully, separate out the constructive ideas, be extremely critical of the program and of his own personal contribution, and then implement the necessary adjustment. This may sound harsh, but the best test of a "job well done" may well be that no one will notice. The best communications are never obvious.

SOURCES OF INVESTOR INFORMATION

Investors receive corporate information from securities analysts, public media, and corporate communications vehicles such as annual and quarterly reports, news releases, and annual meetings.

SECURITIES ANALYSTS

Securities analysts greatly influence the buying habits of institutional investors and others. In recent years the professional investment community has shrunk, and this has hit securities analysts. Between 1968 and 1975, the number of New York Stock Exchange member firms dropped from 646 to 506, a decline of 22 percent. Employment in the New York securities industry during the same period dropped by 40,000 people.

Today analysts are asked to follow an increasing number of companies, with the average analyst keeping tabs on upwards of forty firms. Frequently analysts aren't able to evaluate a company that does not meet rigid criteria in terms of market value, capitalization, and trading volume. Additionally, many analysts today are young with little experience, further complicating the role of the practitioner. Nevertheless, in financial relations, analysts are a key public and must be reached.

To reach analysts effectively, credible communications must play a major role. As such, a firm's management should be accessible, because no matter how good a company's earnings record is, without accessibility, a corporate message will likely fall on deaf ears.[7] Good practitioners make sure that key analysts are heavily exposed to corporate management.

Analyst meetings, presentations, and field trips are most important. A luncheon appearance before the New York Society of Security Analysts, for example, can be a significant platform for reaching Wall Street. Company-sponsored meetings in secondary cities also can serve to broaden interest in a company. Finally, inviting analysts to tour plants, visit headquarters, and meet corporate management on a firm's own turf is another way to introduce and educate analysts about a company and its leadership.

In the 1980s, surveys have indicated that analysts primarily are interested in information that "looks ahead."[8] They seek to learn every factor that might affect earnings—from management's long-range plans to prospects for the industry as a whole. They want presentations that go beyond shareholder documents. And, again, they want to *see* a management team that is forceful, vibrant, and committed to sound corporate growth.

FINANCIAL PRESS

The stock exchanges insist that material corporate announcements must be released by the fastest available means. Ordinarily, this means that such information as top management changes and dividend or earnings announcements must be disseminated by telephone, telegraph, or hand delivery to media outlets. Basically, companies are expected to release material information through the following channels:

Major wire services. Dow Jones & Company, Reuters Economic Service, Associated Press, or United Press International.

Major New York City newspapers. One or more of the New York City newspapers of general circulation that publish financial news, most specifically *The New York Times* and *The Wall Street Journal.*

Statistical services. Particularly Standard & Poor's Corporation and Moody's Investor Service, which keep complete records on all publicly-held companies.

Private wire services. Services such as PR News Wire and Business Wire guarantee for a fee that corporate news is carried promptly and reaches newspaper newsrooms and brokerage offices.

Achieving broad disclosure for a small company is not easy. While a major corporation automatically attracts the attention of the financial community, the smaller firm, in order to satisfy disclosure requirements, may have to use paid wire services and direct mailings to shareholders. For example, to "make" the Dow Jones wire, a firm's stock must be listed in the national or supplemental list of *The Wall Street Journal.* The burden of proof in conforming to disclosure requirements, however, rests squarely with the issuer, so a company must take appropriate measures to assure that SEC requirements for prompt disclosure are met.

Practitioners can also benefit from positive stories about the company in the media. Investment community professionals read the trade press avidly. Strategically-placed articles in trade media discussing technological innovations or effective strategies may boost a company in the eyes of security analysts, stockbrokers, and institutional portfolio managers.

The latest wrinkle in communicating financial information is television. In addition to the recent phenomenon of videotaped annual meetings and annual reports (which will be discussed shortly), increased interest in financial matters has promulgated an array of investor-related television programs. The nation's top financial show, "Wall Street Week," reaches millions of viewers each week on the Public Broadcasting System (PBS). Its success influenced the development of another PBS

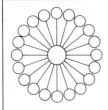

MINICASE
Texas Gulf Sulphur

Probably the most far-reaching and widely-publicized court case involving SEC disclosure law was that of the Texas Gulf Sulpher (TGS) Company in the 1960s.

In late 1963, TGS discovered ore deposits in Canada. Although a potentially spectacular find, the company made no public announcement about the discovery. In subsequent weeks, TGS quietly purchased hundreds of acres of surrounding land, and company officers purchased additional shares of TGS stock on the open market. Eventually, as more ore was found in 1964 and officers continued buying TGS stock, rumors circulated concerning the company and its mineral treasure. On April 12, 1964, the company distributed a press release that termed the rumors "unreliable" and stated that drilling "to date hasn't been conclusive." Despite the negative announcement, TGS officers continued to buy company stock.

Four days later, almost six months after the original discovery, TGS announced it had "made a major strike of zinc, copper, and silver." The price of TGS stock immediately skyrocketed.

After extensive litigation, the U.S. Court of Appeals ruled that TGS officers had violated SEC disclosure laws. The court said that TGS officials traded on inside information and passed on tips to their friends, who also bought the stock on insider knowledge. The court also ruled that TGS, on April 12, "issued a false and misleading press release," in violation of Rule 10B-5.

TGS officers (including the director of public relations) and their friends were punished for trading on the information not fully disclosed to the public. The case proved conclusively that a company's failure to make known material information (information likely to be considered important by reasonable investors in determining whether to buy, sell, or hold securities) may be in violation of the antifraud provision of the Securities and Exchange Acts. The TGS case remains today as a landmark in the history of public relations law.

QUESTIONS

1 If you had been the public relations director of Texas Gulf Sulphur in 1963, what communications steps would you have recommended the company take after it discovered rich ore deposits in Canada?

2 If, as TGS public relations director, you had not been told by management until April 12 of the ore deposits and then were asked to put out the release denying rumors of a rich ore find, what would you have done?

financial program, "The Nightly Business Report," a broad-based, half hour look at the financial news of the day. In 1982, the nation's first television network devoted to financial news, appropriately named the Financial News Network, was born to give cable viewers an around-the-clock look at everything from commodity prices to leading economic indicators to international news events with potential market impact. With narrowcasting—communicating signals to smaller, more targeted, more focused population segments—becoming ever more sophisticated, it is likely that television, particularly cable TV, will play an increasingly important role in financial news dissemination as the decade progresses.

CORPORATE COMMUNICATIONS TOOLS

A company has numerous financial communications methods at its disposal, including the annual report, quarterly reports, annual meeting, and fact books.

THE ANNUAL REPORT

The annual report is a company's key financial communications tool. Many investor relations professionals swear by it. Others argue that the annual report is exaggerated in importance, contending that the ideal annual report might simply read:

> Dear Shareholder,
> We did well in 1980. Earnings and sales were up. Customers were happy and buying. Your dividend was increased. Thanks for purchasing our stock and not selling it.

Clearly, such brevity is not the trend. Each year, annual reports increase from 10–40 percent in size and become more complex in nature.[9] In addition to companies providing more detailed data on their individual lines of business, financial structure, and foreign operations, they also use the reports to promote their views on topics from social responsibility to government regulation. The overriding purpose of the report remains as a basic marketing tool, one that builds image and provides product and financial data for analysts, customers, and investors.

While the individual elements and general tone of annual reports change gradually over the years and between firms, most reports include the following:

Company description. This should include the company name, its headquarters address, a description of its overall business, and a summary of its operations in both narrative and numerical form. Many firms begin their annual reports with a one-page, easily readable summary of financial highlights.

Letter to shareholders. The letter ordinarily incorporates a photo of the firm's chairperson and president. It covers these key areas: accounting of last year's achievements, discussion of the general and industry environment in which the company operated over the past year and will operate in the future, discussion of strategies for growth, general operating philosophy for the future, new product and capital spending plans, and general targets for increased earnings and returns.

Optionally, the letter might cite management's major concerns either for the company or for the environment in which it operates. Most of all, the letter to shareholders must be written in simple, understandable language, be short on rhetorical flourishes, and long on fact. For example, the following excerpt from the 1982 annual report of the Wisconsin Securities Company of Milwaukee, includes perhaps the world's most candid letter to shareholders. Wrote president George M. Chester:

> It is surprising so few stockholders sold their Wisconsin Securities stock. . . In truth it was a difficult year. . . But George Chester still has a job, thanks to his many relatives.[10]

Financial review.   In light of the SEC's increasing demands for corporate disclosure, many companies have expanded financial reviews to encompass the data historically included in other reports, such as the 10-K. Financial reviews generally include five- or ten-year summaries of such items as sales, cost of goods, operating costs, operating margin, expenses, capital expenditures, income taxes, and net earnings, and such salient shareholder information as price/earnings ratios, debt ratios, return on assets, and return on equity.

Management's discussion and analysis.   This complement to the financial review is a general discussion of the factors influencing the numbers in terms of earnings performance, operating income and expenses, asset growth, and the other key financial indicators.

Management/marketing/issues discussion.   The annual report's narrative section may be devoted to a general profile of key managers, an explanation of the company's markets or products, or essays detailing the company's view on emerging public issues. Many annual report watchers contend that such public issues analysis is even more important than the massive financial data that annual reports include. As Richard A. Lewis, president of Corporate Annual Reports, has said, "Corporations are blunting one of the sharpest communications tools by having to cram them so full of financial data, most of which is incomprehensible to the average shareholder."[11]

Graphics.   Photographs and charts are critical to the annual report. Most people have limited time to read, and a dynamic chart or striking photo may be enough to draw readers into the report's body. The high prices of freelance annual report photographers (some upwards of $2,500) are testimony to the importance companies place on good photos.

Companies go to great lengths to simplify financial terminology and technical jargon in annual reports. Security Bank and Trust Company of North Carolina put a crisp dollar bill in each copy of its 1977 annual report to encourage shareholders to read it. International Paper asked financial columnist Jane Bryant Quinn to explain in an ad, "How to read an annual report." The 1983 annual report of Terminal Data Corp., a manufacturer of microfiche equipment, included a microfiche card containing the contents of fourteen earlier annual reports. While most don't go quite that far, the majority of companies treat their annual reports as the primary vehicle to reach and entice existing and potential shareholders. (Figure 19-1 shows examples of annual reports.)

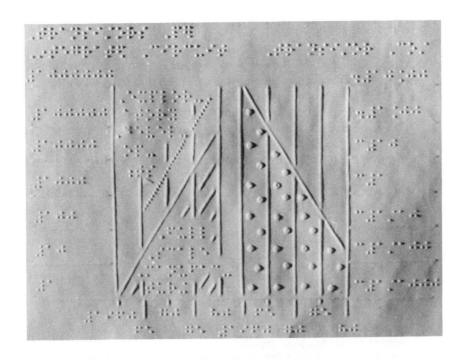

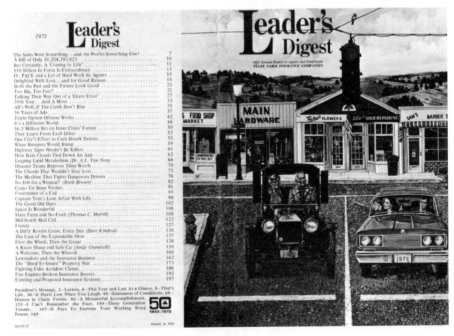

FIGURE 19–1. Annual reports come in all sizes and shapes. AT&T (top) produces a braille version complete with a "talking book" phonograph record, which goes to more than 1,000 blind AT&T investors and requires three months to prepare. To celebrate its 50th anniversary, State Farm Insurance Company produced a replica of the familiar *Reader's Digest* as its annual report for agents and employees.

SOURCE: Courtesy of State Farm Insurance and AT&T.

In the early 1980s, companies like International Paper and Emhart Corporation pioneered the transfer of the annual report from paper to videotape. When surveys indicated that most investors devote an average of just five to fifteen minutes to printed reports, both firms decided that electronic annual reports might be the answer.[12] Both companies tried to remain true to their printed annual report format by featuring the same elements, including the chairman in a starring role, in the video version as well. Both firms advised stockholders in advance that the televised reports would be cablecast at a particular time on a particular channel, and both seemed pleased with the results. Emhart, in fact, lent cassettes of the annual report program to interested stockholders. Summarized Dean William F. May of the New York University Graduate School of Business, "Moving from the hard, cold printed page into the warmth of television serves a tremendous purpose in [educating] the shareholder—current and potential—on the nature of the company. It gives it flesh and blood."[13]

QUARTERLY REPORTS

Quarterly reports, or interim reports, keep shareholders abreast of corporate developments between annual reports.

In general, the SEC recommends that the quarterly report include comparative financial data for the most recent quarter and year-to-date for the current and preceding year. Such items as net sales, costs and expenses, gross and net income, assets, liabilities, net worth, and earnings per share should always be included. So too should a letter to the shareholders, analyzing the important developments during the quarter. In recent years the SEC has been less rigorous in its quarterly report requirements, and some firms have cut back on expenses in producing such reports.

ANNUAL MEETING

Once a year, the management of public companies is required to meet with the shareholders in a forum. Occasionally, annual meetings inspire fear and trepidation among managers unused to the glare of public questioning and skepticism. Indeed, several "annual meeting gadflies" travel from annual meeting to annual meeting probing managements on unpleasant, difficult, and occasionally, embarrassing subjects. The existence of these gadflies has led some managers to view the meeting with a degree of loathing.

In one celebrated instance in 1982, General Motors (GM) Chairman Roger Smith proposed having two annual meetings on the same day. The first meeting, said Smith, would be a short business meeting, attended by all of GM's top managers, at which no shareholder questions would be entertained. The second meeting would be held miles away from the first and would feature a designated GM executive to answer shareholder questions. So great was the opposition to Smith's proposition that GM, several days before its meetings, announced, on second thought, that it would hold only one annual meeting after all.

A well-planned and executed annual meeting enables corporate managers to communicate effectively with investors (see Appendix C for an "Annual Meeting Checklist"). Here are a few hints for organizing a successful meeting:

Management speeches. Beginning with short, punchy speeches from the chairman, president, or both establishes the tone for the meeting. These speeches set an

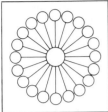

MINICASE
The unheard of merger

Minidata is a computer software company with less than $1 million in annual sales. Its stock is listed on the Over-the-Counter list. Through the years, Minidata has rewarded its approximately 1,000 shareholders with steadily increasing profits.

Minidata intends to sign an agreement to acquire Rosemary Software (RS), another computer software company, doing about $600,000 in annual sales.

Minidata financial relations chief Jennie Barmad would like to publicize the RS acquisition as broadly as possible. However, Barmad is aware that neither company qualifies to be covered by the Dow Jones wire or any other major financial medium. She is concerned that if the company's acquisition receives no coverage, the firm will be in violation of SEC disclosure requirements.

QUESTIONS

1 What should Barmad do to ensure disclosure?
2 What might Barmad do to achieve additional publicity?
3 If the proposed merger receives no publicity, might the firm be accused by the SEC of purposely avoiding disclosure law?

upbeat tempo for the rest of the meeting, emphasizing current developments and perhaps even announcing quarterly earnings or management changes.

Stockholder voting.   Voting includes choosing directors and auditors and deciding on proposals presented by shareholders. Management's viewpoint on these proposals is spelled out in previously mailed proxy statements.

Question-and-answer sessions.   The Q&A portion of the meeting is the reason that many stockholders attend. They like to see management in action, answering pertinent questions from the floor. How managers handle questions is thought to reflect their competence in running the company.

Management must be thoroughly briefed in advance about potential questions. Indeed, managers should plan answers *before* the meeting. Preparing for Q&A sessions may require monitoring other corporate annual meetings, preparing briefing books on potential questions, and even meeting in advance with potential questioners. Some managements, for example, find it worthwhile to lunch with those stockholders known to ask questions at annual meetings—i.e. gadflies— to find out in advance what's on their minds.

Questions should be handled candidly, succinctly, and, whenever possible, in a light, nonthreatening manner. Most stockholders agree that the best meetings are those conducted in a friendly atmosphere. After all, stockholders "own" the business. A manager's "light touch" at an annual meeting may win over even the most skeptical stockholders.

Special embellishments. The best companies spark their annual meetings by introducing special, imaginative touches.

○ W.R. Grace & Co. held one annual meeting in Boston and provided shareholders with a free lunch and plant visit, followed by a tour of the historic bicentennial sites of Lexington and Concord.

○ Wometco Enterprises each year treats shareholders to a first-run showing of a feature film. The company consistently draws a good 10 percent of all shareholders at the annual meeting.

○ Norton Simon, Inc., like a number of other leading consumer product companies, gives each shareholder a package of products, including spaghetti sauce, moisturizing creams, and bottles of wine and soda.

○ Western Union Corporation, like other companies concerned with employee communications, broadcasts its annual meeting to employees at fifty locations in the United States via the company's microwave and satellite transmission facilities.

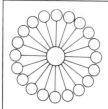

MINICASE
The Adelstein letter

The following is the letter to shareholders in the current annual report of Adelstein, Inc., national manufacturer of ball bearings.

Dear Friends:
All things considered, 1980 wasn't a bad year for your company.

While earnings declined by 10 percent, sales nevertheless reached the $300 million mark last year. We experienced strong demand in most of our domestic markets. However, unexpected environmental difficulties in both our Brazilian and Argentine operations caused a downturn in earnings. Our cut of the dividend in the last quarter was also a direct outgrowth of the problems in Brazil and Argentina.

We had great concern once again this year about the rate of domestic inflation in the United States. In order to continue to ensure that our shareholders will receive growth in earnings and dividends, inflation must be kept to a minimum. This is why we feel strongly that it is Adelstein's responsibility to speak out both on the federal and local levels about the evils of inflation. One way Adelstein acts to circumvent the dangers of inflation is through diversification around the world.

○ Other companies have begun to videotape annual meetings and produce tightly-edited, 30-minute cassettes that capture the sense and atmosphere for shareholders who can't attend in person. Since most of a company's shareholders don't make it to the annual meeting, the introduction of video annual meetings may have real potential for the future.

The best annual meetings are amicable gatherings. The promise of "goodies" to be handed out after the meeting helps convey a positive feeling throughout the proceedings. To prevent a meeting from being dominated by a hostile questioner, specific procedures on speaking from the floor should be clearly announced and enforced.

In sum, the annual meeting, like any other communications tool, should be used actively to promote goodwill and further the positive perception of the corporation among its shareholders.

FACT BOOKS/SHEETS

Corporate fact books and fact sheets are statistical publications distributed primarily to securities analysts and institutional investors as supplements to the annual report. They "unclutter" the annual report and turn it into a broad, interpretive document to which the individual shareholder can easily relate.[14]

Our ball bearing operations in Central America and Canada experienced strong growth last year. Central America operations grew by 6 percent, and Canadian operations, while not growing in percentage terms, nevertheless continued to achieve good operating performance.

Our South American performance, on the other hand, was limited by the problems in Argentina and Brazil. In the year to come, we are confident about the near-term future of Adelstein, Inc. The uncertainty in the economy must be counteracted by strong management controls and rigorous enforcement of expense monitoring. Last year, in an increasingly expansionary inflationary period, Adelstein's expenses increased by 14 percent year-to-year. This year, we plan to do even better.

Clearly, with our plans and strategies firmly in place, we expect Adelstein's operating and financial condition to continue to improve in the coming year.

Todd O. Adelstein
Chairperson of the Board

QUESTIONS

1   If you were an Adelstein stockholder, would you be pleased with this letter?
2   Did the letter leave out any areas?
3   Did it leave any questions unanswered?
4   From what you read in the letter, how would you assess Adelstein's prospects for improvement next year?

In general, fact books and fact sheets not only save money, but often have significantly more impact on a busy security analyst searching for a quick view of a company's position and prospects. A visually-arresting and substantive document, regardless of its size, can serve as an important shareholder relations vehicle (see Figure 19–2).

OTHER SPECIALIZED COMMUNICATIONS

Periodically, companies complement the traditional arsenal of financial communications with specialized vehicles.

Investors' guides. These mini-fact books give a general corporate description and list leading products, office locations, and financial highlights. Such guides introduce a company and frequently contain tear-out cards for acquiring additional corporate information.

Private television packages. In addition to video annual reports and meetings, videocassette packages showing presentations by corporate officers can be shipped directly to portfolio managers and analysts around the country at a comparatively low cost. Video can extend and expand an executive's time and deliver the corporate story to a larger, more targeted financial public, over a wider geographic area.[15]

FIGURE 19–2. Fact books and fact sheets come in a variety of sizes and shapes. All, however, have the same objective: to give as clear and accurate an organizational snapshot in as brief a time as possible.

Dividend stuffers. Frequently practitioners include management messages in dividend mailings. Shareholders tend to take seriously mailings that include checks; thus these mailings help greatly in delivering the firm's ideas.

Paid advertising space. Periodically, a company can reprint its income statement or balance sheet to encourage a broad audience to find out more about its securities.

TAKEOVERS/PROXY CONTESTS/TENDER OFFERS

Infrequently, a company is faced with as trying a situation as occurs in corporate America—an outsider takeover attempt. In most cases, a substantial decline in the company's stock price might precipitate an outsider's attempt to "take over" the firm in one of two ways:

○ A tender offer for shares of stock, in which the raiding party offers shareholders cash, securities, or both; or

○ A proxy contest, in which certain shareholders attempt to oust present management by obtaining sufficient shareholder votes to seize control of the board of directors.

In most cases, such an "unfriendly takeover" is inimical to current management, which intensively fights back to ward off the raider. More often than not, as Figure 19-3 on page 441 graphically illustrates, the public battle gets grimy.

Often, it is the job of the IR professional to establish the preparatory steps to be taken prior to a takeover attempt, including an outline of the moves to resist the actual takeover. Overall strategy must be based upon the maintenance of an excellent relationship with stockholders, particularly with those who hold a large amount of stock.

Specific IR activities might include the following:

○ Appoint a defense committee.

○ Prepare and update a "Large Stockholder's List."

○ Maintain a "watch" to determine whether company shares are being accumulated rapidly.

○ Step up personal contacts with important stockholders in order to secure their loyalty.

○ Increase contacts with top-flight securities analysts and investors to improve chances of obtaining intelligence from them.

○ Prepare envelopes for emergency stockholder mailings.

○ Retain professional proxy solicitors.

○ Prepare basic letters and new release forms to be sent immediately to stockholders within hours of learning about the takeover attempt.

○ Prepare lists of major newspapers in which takeover defense advertisements might appear. Prepare the ads themselves.

○ Organize a public relations campaign to enhance the image of the company both internally and externally.

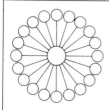

MINICASE
Handling the antinuke shareholders

Associated Nuclear, Inc. (ANI) expects a tough annual meeting because of well-publicized recent problems with nuclear facilities around the country. ANI owns several nuclear plants itself.

E.K. Janeway, the dour ANI chairman, pounds the gavel and the questioning begins.

Questioner: *My name is Scotty Margolin, and I own five shares. Mr. Janeway, how do you justify the corporation's nuclear activities today?*

Janeway: The simple answer is, we don't believe there is a nuclear problem in the country. Such talk is exaggerated, distorted, and generally untrue.

Questioner: *My name is Rosie Kierstein, and I own ten shares. How can you glibly dismiss a question that concerns the possibility of nuclear radiation causing a potential hazard to human life?*

Janeway: Very easily. I don't buy the premise. Next question.

Questioner: *My name is John Gilbert, and I represent 2,000 shares. How many lawsuits does the company face today, and how many are related to the problems that are being currently reported in the press?*

These are but a few of the actions that must be taken in anticipating and dealing with a takeover attempt. Often, the hiring of outsiders, expert in dealing with proxy contests and takeover attempts, is a necessity. With the number of takeover attempts escalating in the 1980s, the key to mounting an effective takover defense remains to continually practice open and honest communications with shareholders.

CREDIBILITY

The real bottom line in financial communications is improving corporate credibility. Investors show support only when they believe in a firm and its management. Obfuscation, fudging, and gobbledygook have no place in communicating with investors, who want to know all the news, the bad as well as the good, quickly and accurately.

Because corporate candor is the only path to credibility and respect, these general guidelines should be followed in communicating with the investment community:

1 **Be aggressive.** Aggressive companies don't necessarily acquire the reputation of being "stock promoters." Companies today must compete vigorously for

Janeway: We are faced with thirty lawsuits today. Since each is being litigated, I can't comment further.

Questioner: *My name is Bret Schultz, 100 shares. How confident are we that the safety procedures we follow at our nuclear plants can avoid the problems that have been recently reported?*

Janeway: Our safety requirements are strictly enforced by government regulators. If there's a problem, the government is just as much to blame as private companies.

Questioner: *Patrick Watson, five shares. Could problems like the ones being reported around the country happen at an ANI plant?*

Janeway: That's a very hypothetical question. Anything could happen anywhere, but I doubt we'll have trouble.

Questioner: *My name is Frank O'Connor, and I own five shares. I want to say that I, frankly, am appalled at you, Mr. Janeway, for dismissing these questions with such a blasé and uncaring attitude.*

Janeway: Since that is not a question, you are out of order. Please sit down.

QUESTIONS

1 How would you rate Janeway's treatment of the stockholders? His control of the annual meeting?
2 How would you have suggested the questions be answered?
3 If you were an ANI shareholder, what would you think of your management?

visibility. Analysts and investors want to keep informed. Therefore, aggressive communications, truthfully delivered, are the best kind.

2 **Promote success.** The record ordinarily does not speak for itself. Companies must communicate to investors an intelligent evaluation of their securities, competitive position, and market outlook.

3 **Meet despite bad news.** Companies should meet with investors in bad and good times; investors need constant communication. If there are problems at a firm, investors want to know what management is doing to solve them. Most of all, investors hate surprises.

4 **Go to investors; don't make them come to you.** Investors expect to be courted. Firms need to broaden investment ownership. Therefore, a company should volunteer information rather than make investors pry it loose.

5 **Enlist investors in the public policy area.** As noted, there are 32 million stockholders in the United States today. The implications of even partially mobilizing this vast constituency are awesome. Historically, corporations have not sought out stockholder support for public policy viewpoints, which seems a

FIGURE 19–3. *Chock Full o'Nuts ad.* In late 1982, the Chock Full o'Nuts Company waged a furious takeover defense against the challenge of a dissident group of shareholders led by New York financier Jerry Finkelstein. This ad was typical of the bitterness of the battle, which was ultimately won by management.

SOURCE: Courtesy of Chock Full o'Nuts.

440

tragic mistake. To accomplish meaningful legislative and regulatory reforms in favor of free enterprise, all concerned parties, shareholders and management alike, must join the fight.

Among the best examples to date of mobilizing investors was the offensive launched by AT&T to stop the Telecommunications Act of 1982, aimed at nullifying parts of the Justice Department proposal requiring AT&T to divest its 22 local operating companies. As Figure 19-4 suggests, AT&T urged shareholders to barrage the Congress in order to, as AT&T Chairman C. L. Brown put it, "stop this bill in its tracks." Although such a "form letter" approach occasionally backfires, in this case, AT&T share owners responded enthusiastically, and the bill was killed.

In general, then, the best financial relations policy is an active and open one. Investors need to be informed and want to learn more about the companies whose stock they hold. To improve corporate credibility, a firm and its investor relations professionals must work at it—*all* the time.

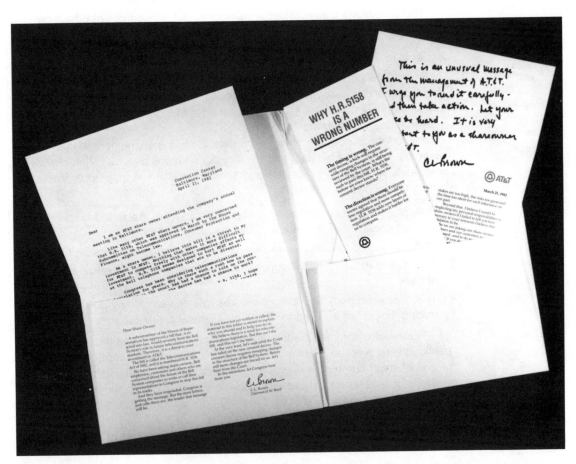

FIGURE 19–4. *AT&T shareholders materials.* In 1982, AT&T successfully enlisted shareholder support to defeat H.R. 5158 before it could be passed into law. The company went so far as to prepare letters for shareholders to sign and then send off to their Congressional representatives.

SOURCE: Courtesy AT&T.

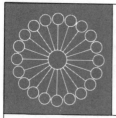

CASE STUDY
The raid on Microdot

One of the most difficult tasks for any financial relations professional is dealing with an unfriendly corporate takeover attempt. Occasionally, when a company's stock is selling well below its book value, it becomes an attractive target for such an attempt. When one company attempts to raid another by tendering for its shares, communications must be used quickly and aggressively to ward off the raider.

Such was the famous case with Microdot, one of the nation's outstanding medium-sized growth companies, which was caught in a classic takeover battle.

Microdot management, like the managements of hundreds of other companies with low stock prices, good earnings records, and an abundance of cash, was well aware that it was ripe for a takeover attempt.

At 4:45 P.M. on Tuesday, December 2, the inevitable happened.

Microdot's president, Rudolph Eberstadt, Jr., received a call that General Cable Corporation, headquartered in Microdot's hometown of Greenwich, Connecticut, planned to make a cash tender offer for Microdot stock at $17 a share, versus that day's closing market price of $11.75.

Microdot did not want to be taken over. Rather, management wished to remain independent. Eberstadt and his investor relations director, Allan Howell, immediately sprang into action to try to stave off a takeover attempt by implementing the following controls:

1 They placed strict surveillance on Microdot's copying machine to reduce the risk that confidential documents might be purloined.
2 They hired around-the-clock guards for Microdot's headquarters facility.
3 They called in "debugging" experts to check the company's office and phones.
4 They interviewed all Microdot employees in a search for any possible information that could be used to attack the General Cable bid.

Howell also suggested adopting a communications thrust based on the "public interest premise" that if General Cable's bid was successful, it spelled the end of small companies everywhere. Indeed, as Eberstadt was to write in hundreds of later letters, "If General Cable is successful, then there will be no future IBM, no Xerox, no Polaroid. They will be choked off, smothered as soon as they start to show their real growth potential."

Among the communications measures Microdot adopted to defend itself were the following:

1 It ran a series of newspaper advertisements under such headlines as "Are you next?" aimed at appealing to the stockholders and managements of other medium-sized companies.

2   It sent letters and Mailgrams to its shareholders on an average of more than twice a week during the two-month tender fight.

3   It asked shareholders to write to General Cable board members, SEC officials, and legislators about the unfairness of the General Cable bid.

4   It took its case to the U.S. Congress and obtained a hearing before the Senate Banking Committee.

5   It sought to embarrass the opposition, even running critical advertisements in the hometown of the General Cable president.

6   It wrote "Are you next?" letters to the chief executive officers of sixty-four medium-sized companies.

7   It produced a brochure titled "How American Business Feels about General Cable's Raid on Microdot" containing responses from the CEOs of the medium-sized companies to whom it had written.

8   It wrote to the top two or three executives of the nation's fifty largest banks, urging them "to take a public stand in favor of credit only for purposes of increasing productive resources of this country by declaring that your bank is opposed to financing surprise takeover raids that add nothing to America's economy."

9   Three days after the announcement of General Cable's proposed offer, it increased its quarterly dividend to twenty-five cents a share from fifteen cents. It then wrote to shareholders a month later stating that the increased rate was in line with a new company policy to pay out between one-third and one-half of its earnings.

10 It issued a press release on December 23 forecasting that next year's earnings would increase 41 percent over estimated current year's per share results. (Actually profits turned out to be only 16 percent higher in the next year.)

11 It kept channels opened to the press, Congress, and regulators, aggressively pursuing its viewpoint in the public arena.

The end result of Microdot's efforts was success in eluding the General Cable bid. General Cable, in fact, wound up suing Microdot, alleging the dissemination of misleading information.

When the dust settled, Microdot had located an alternative merger partner (or "white knight"), more to the liking of Microdot management and willing to offer a higher price than General Cable. Several months after General Cable launched its takeover challenge, Northwest Industries paid $21 a share for Microdot stock and effectively took over the company.

QUESTIONS

1   How important was Microdot's adoption of the "Are you next?" theme in its defense?

2   Do you think Microdot was wise in so tenaciously publicizing its case?

3   If you were a Microdot shareholder, what would have been your response to the Microdot program?

4   If you were General Cable's financial relations manager, what strategy would you have recommended your company follow in response to the Microdot defense?

NOTES

1   Winthrop C. Neilson, "Is There a Future for Investor Relations?" *Public Relations Journal,* April 1978, p. 16.

2   Peter G. Osgood, "Investor Relations in the Eighties," *Public Relations Journal,* April 1981, p. 6.

3   Anne F. Hamby, "Structuring a Financial Relations Program," *Public Relations Journal,* April 1978, p. 21.

4   "SEC Extends Scope to PR," *Jack O'Dwyer's Newsletter 5,* no. 8 (23 February 1972): 1–3.

5   Earl C. Gottschalk, Jr., "Liability of PR Firms for Clients' Releases is Questioned Again," *The Wall Street Journal,* 5 June 1972, p. 14.

6   Ray Garrett, Jr., "The Role of Financial Public Relations," address before the Publicity Club of Chicago, Chicago, Illinois, March 13, 1974.

7   Brian McBain, "What Motivates an Analyst to Follow a Company?" *Public Relations Journal,* April 1977, p. 12.

8   Gabriel Werba, "What Analysts Want to Hear," *Public Relations Journal,* April 1982, p. 19.

9   "The Annual Report 1978: Thick and Innovative," *Business Week,* 16 April 1979, p. 114.

10 "George M. Chester Thanks Relatives," *The Wall Street Journal,* 25 April 1983, p. 81.

11 Cited in Peg Dardenne, "Emerging Trends in Annual Reports," *Public Relations Journal,* September 1977.

12 Jane Wollman, "Annual Reports Go Video," *Savvy,* August 1982, p. 21.

13 John F. Budd, Jr. and Bruce Pennington, "Financial Reporting By Television," *Public Relations Journal,* April 1982, p. 40.

14 "The Hard Facts about Facts Books," *The Corporate Communications Report 5,* no. 3 (October 1973): 1–4.

15 Joseph H. Snyder, "Color Video—An Emerging Investor Relations Tool," address at Opinion Research Corporation's Second National Financial and Investor Relations Executive Briefing, New York, N.Y., December 12, 1977.

SUGGESTED READING

Andrew, Gordon G. "Corporate Factsheets." *Public Relations Journal,* April 1982, pp. 43–45.

Berg, Stephen. "DOs & DON'Ts To Attract Investors." *Public Relations Journal,* April 1982, pp. 22–24.

Budd Jr., John F. "Financial Reporting By Television." *Public Relations Journal,* April 1982, pp. 38–40.

Cannella, Vincent. "Integrated Disclosure: Betwixt and Between." *Public Relations Journal,* August 1981, pp. 8–9.

"Dow Jones Ticker Tape Criteria." *Public Relations Journal,* Public Relations Journal, April 1982, p. 49.

Dunk, William P. and **Kraut, G.A.** "Investor Relations: What It Isn't." *Public Relations Journal,* April 1982, pp. 12–14.

Epstein, Chuck. "Put Your Financial News On The Tube." *Public Relations Journal,* April 1982, pp. 41–42.

Epstein, Marc. "Cleaning up the Annual Report: the Accountant's Responsibility to Society." *Business and Society Review* 13 (Spring, 1975): pp. 83–85.

Fischer, George, L. and **Davenport, C. R.** "Are You Telling the Story They Want to Hear?—What Investors Want to Hear." *Public Relations Journal*, April 1981, pp. 14–18.

Halbrecht, H. "What the Investor Relations Executive Should Do for Your Company." *Management Review* 64, no. 2. (February 1975): pp. 18–25.

"Investor Relations Check List for the 1980s." *Public Relations Journal*, April 1982, p. 14.

Kahn, Herman. *The Future of the Corporation.* New York: Mason and Lipscomb, 1974.

Louviere, Vernon. "Treating Each Stockholder as an Individual." *Nation's Business* 63, no. 12 (December 1975): pp. 49–50.

Marcus, Bruce. *Competing for Capital.* New York: John Wiley and Sons, 1975.

"Meeting the Analysts." *Industry Week* 185, no. 10 (9 June 1975): pp. 38–40.

Neilson, Winthrop C. and **Barnes, Douglass M.** "Five Keys To Better IR." *Public Relations Journal*, April 1982, pp. 16–17. Traditional skills, strategies, and programs must be complemented with new ones to meet today's capital market challenges.

Nolan, Joseph. "Protect Your Public Image." *Harvard Business Review*, March/April 1975, pp. 135–142.

Osgood, Peter G. "Investor Relations in the '80s." *Public Relations Journal*, April 1981, pp. 6–8.

Putman, George. "What the Analysts Want to Know." *Public Relations Journal* 31, no. 4 (April 1975): pp. 15–17.

Roalman, A. R. *Investor Relations Handbook.* New York: Amacon, 1974.

"The SEC, the Stock Exchange, and Your Financial Public Relations." New York: Hill & Knowlton Financial Relations Unit, 1972.

Silk, Leonard, and **Vogel, David.** *Ethics and Profits: The Crisis of Confidence in American Business.* New York: Simon and Schuster, 1976.

Taft, Robert W. "Order Out Of Chaos." *Public Relations Journal*, April 1982, pp. 25–37.

Taft, Robert W. and **Raynolds, Edward O.** "Going Public." *Public Relations Journal*, April 1981, pp. 19–24, 32.

Werba, Gabriel. "What Analysts Want To Hear." *Public Relations Journal*, April 1982, pp. 18–20.

Zausner, M. *Corporate Policy and the Investment Community.* New York: Ronald Press, 1968.

While most people employed in public relations today work for business organizations, the public relations field in associations, hospitals, non-profit organizations, the military, and many other groups is an expanding one.

By the same token, while the activities of most public relations practitioners are aimed at communicating with employees, the media, the government, the community, consumers, or investors, other "special" publics also are important. Reaching such publics as women, ethnic groups, and senior citizens, in fact, has become of vital importance to public relations and marketing practitioners in recent years.

While any chapter on such special publics inevitably risks both sins of omission in leaving someone out or commission in uneven treatment of those discussed, some discussion of the special areas of public relations as well as special interest groups with whom public relations professionals deal is a necessity.

Therefore, this chapter will introduce several unique groups with which all public relations professionals should at least be somewhat familiar.

20
Special Publics

WOMEN

Although women have always been a prime target for advertisers (especially for products related to the roles of homemaker and mother), it was not until the women's liberation movement of the 1960s and 70s that women became a primary group for public relations. By the 1980s, women had indeed come "a long way baby."

Women constitute an important source of discretionary income in the labor force. Some 63 percent of all American women between the ages of eighteen and sixty-four work outside their homes. By 1990, more than 70 percent of such women could be working and may outnumber their stay-at-home counterparts by approximately three to two.[1] Three-quarters of all working women are employed full time (thirty or more hours per week). More than two-thirds of women with school-aged children also work. Households with working wives have median incomes almost 40 percent greater than those with nonworking wives.

That women recently have been more conscious of sexual bias against them has greatly affected the public relations field. In the employee relations area, for example, women have been vocal in demanding proper pay, opportunities for promotion, and rights in the workplace. Practitioners obviously must be sensitive to the special problems in reaching women and must avoid condescending or sexist language in internal messages.

Women also are critical in the areas of consumer relations and product publicity. Women still do about 90 percent of family food shopping and are increasingly responsible for the purchase of expensive items such as automobiles and furniture. Working women have proven less brand loyal and less easily persuaded than their nonworking counterparts. Moreover, they have different "media habits" because they have less leisure time to read or watch television.[2]

ETHNIC GROUPS

Major companies, institutions, and government agencies have spent considerable time, money, and energy during the last decade attempting to resolve problems involving the minority community.

However, although ethnic groups may be categorized into a particular racial subculture, in reality, such groups are themselves composed of a series of market segments based on demographic, economic, psychological, and sociological factors. Therefore, targeting public relations programs to meet the needs of such ethnic groups becomes difficult and generally has not met with great success.[3]

BLACKS

There are over 27 million American blacks, earning a total income in excess of $80 billion. The number of families with incomes of over $15,000 quintupled since 1970.

Certain segments of blacks have scored impressive income gains compared to caucasian counterparts. Median income for black females runs about 92 percent of the income of white women. Black males, by contrast, barely reach 70 percent of their white counterparts' income. Black husband-wife families have incomes that are 59 percent of their white counterparts.

Like women, blacks have steadily integrated the traditionally white male marketplace, but many can still be reached effectively through special media. Black-oriented magazines (*Ebony, Jet, Black Enterprise,* and *Essence*) are natural vehicles. So, too, are the black-oriented dailies of major cities, such as the *Amsterdam News* in New York and the *Daily Defender* in Chicago. Indeed, while blacks make up 12 percent of the U.S. population, 45 percent of the population in fourteen major U.S. cities is composed of black residents. Black-oriented newspapers in major cities are controlled, for the most part, by active owners whose personal viewpoints dominate editorial policy. Black-oriented news media should definitely be included in the normal media relations functions of an organization.

HISPANICS

Hispanics make up a growing portion of the labor and buying markets in such major cities as New York, Los Angeles, San Antonio, Miami, Chicago, and Kansas City. There are at least three separate Hispanic markets in the United States—Cubans in Florida and the Northeast, Mexicans in the Southwest, and Puerto Ricans in the Northern metropolitan areas. Each speaks a slightly different language and displays different cultural values. In these markets, organizations need to publish bilingual literature and employ bilingual customer service representatives. Radio stations and newspapers communicating in Spanish, such as New York's *El Diario* and *La Prensa,* are prominent market voices in reaching Hispanics.

Smart organizations have realized that Spanish is the second language of the Western Hemisphere and seek to assist Hispanics in becoming more fluent in speaking English and more literate in writing English. Increasingly, U.S. television stations carry some Spanish language programming. And at least one public relations agency, Fleishman Hillard, has devoted an entire division to serving Hispanic needs.

AMERICAN INDIANS

In certain areas of the country, Arizona, New Mexico, and Utah, for example, the American Indian public is as important as the Spanish-speaking one in urban centers. In recent years, increased communications efforts have been undertaken to explain the special plight of the American Indian. The Navajo tribe, for instance, numbers 130,000 and is beset by such problems as high unemployment, infant mortality, and an average life expectancy of forty-four years. The tribe has benefited by increased publicity; corporations have enlarged existing operations on Navajo reservations, and increased tourism has aided the Navajo cause.

OTHER MINORITIES

America has always been a second homeland for people from other countries. People from Vietnam, India, the Mideast, and the Slavic nations frequently are important publics for companies and obviously must be reached through special communications.

YOUTH

The youth market is huge business for many manufacturers but a difficult market to reach. To effectively reach young people fourteen to twenty-five requires approaches that identify closely with the interests of various subgroups, such as students,

teaching, and research positions at universities in North Dakota and Wisconsin.

How does university relations work differ from other types of public relations practice?

University relations is part of a broader concept, "institutional advancement," which embraces public relations, alumni affairs, and development (fundraising). These three functions combine to produce a total program designed to foster understanding and support for a college or university.

The university is not a corporation, dedicated to making a profit. It is an association of human beings basically concerned with the spirit of learning, serving a mission of teaching, research, and public service. The most significant goals of a university are not precise targets, but high ideals—the enrichment of the minds and lives of its students, the advancement of knowledge, the increase of understanding among human beings, and the unending search for truth.

The job is to conceptualize, design, and implement programs that facilitate a systematic two-way process of interaction between the university and its internal and external publics. When various segments of the university better understand each other, they can better contribute to decisions and actions.

What are the specific publics with which a university relations professional deals?

University relations personnel commonly speak of "internal publics" and "external publics." Internal includes students, faculty,

Harvey K. Jacobson serves on the faculty of the University of Michigan as associate professor of communication and has been Acting Vice President for University Relations. A recognized authority in the evaluation/planning area of public relations programs for educational institutions, Dr. Jacobson is author/editor of *Evaluating Advancement Programs*, published by Jossey-Bass Publishers in 1978. A frequent contributor to professional literature, he has published more than fifty journal articles, research reports, and book chapters. Before accepting his appointment at Michigan in 1974, Dr. Jacobson was Director of University Relations at the University of North Dakota and was engaged in various administrative,

administration, and nonacademic staff. External includes alumni, legislators, parents and families of students, news media, donors, prospective donors, governing boards, government officals (local, state, and federal), minority groups, labor unions, other colleges and universities, religious organizations, business executives and merchants, the chamber of commerce, corporations, foundations, learned societies, accrediting associations, cultural groups, education officials (superintendents, principals, and counselors), prospective students, women's groups, occupational groups (physicians, dentists, lawyers, engineers, and others) and the general public.

What are the primary activities in university relations work?

The organization of university relations functions may be as distinct as the nation's 3,000 colleges and universities themselves, but many of their operations incorporate common activities. Here is a listing of nine program areas: information services, publications services, special events, internal communication, research and evaluation, administrative services, government relations, alumni relations, and donor relations.

What are your objectives in promoting a university?

"Promoting" is not the proper word; it is misleading, confining, and one-directional. Much more preferable is the transactional model. University relations covers relations of an institution with the publics on which it depends for viability. Responsible university relations officers are change agents who engage in exchange relationships, applying the social sciences to bring about adjustment at the highest level between publics and the organization. The university relations professional seeks to develop relationships that lead to mutual adaptation.

How important is fundraising in your job?

The fund-raising dimension of university relations work is very important and is steadily rising in significance. American colleges and universities, including many in serious financial difficulty, increasingly have turned to their graduates and to corporations and foundations for support and survival.

What kinds of special communications vehicles can be used in dealing with minorities or other special publics?

A college or university can build relationships between the institution and minority/special interest communities by three basic and complementary approaches: helping the institution as a whole improve its awareness and understanding of the interests and concerns of minorities and special interest groups, instilling in university relations staff members the philosophy that coverage of these concerns is important to the institutions and that treatment is fair and representative, and tailoring information and communication programming for minority- and ethnic-oriented media and groups.

Is there anything else you'd like readers of this book to know?

Changes on the political, social, economic, and technological fronts suggest that institutions of higher education face a rapidly-changing environment. It is instructive to identify major trends and examine their implications for university relations practitioners. Here are factors that should be anticipated: rise of the research-based manager, increased emphasis on finance, greater attention to substance, greater dependency upon volunteers, greater need to condense the message, a growth in process-centered news, and repeated tests of professional competence.

teenagers, and even dropouts. Young people listen to radio but don't read much. In the early 1980s, among the most successful cable networks was MTV, a nonstop video-music channel catering to the young. In a related sense, companies like 7-Up began sponsoring rock group tours in the mid-80s, again to reach the affluent youth market.

Many firms (record companies, movie distributors, clothing manufacturers, food suppliers) devote special programs to young people.

Even companies that don't initiate special programs recognize the importance of young people as future employees, customers, and neighbors. Such firms often "piggyback" onto established activities (Boy Scouts, Girl Scouts, 4-H Clubs, Junior Achievement) by sponsoring contests, scholarships, and awards.

SENIOR CITIZENS

While the purchasing power of senior citizens may shrink as they withdraw from the work force, they are an increasingly vocal minority of 25 million. For example, they have effectively lobbied for liberalization of Social Security benefits and legislation prohibiting forced retirement of workers at age sixty-five.

FIGURE 20–1. *Chase Center 60.* The Chase Manhattan Bank introduced a special banking program to respond to senior citizens.

SOURCE: Courtesy of The Chase Manhattan Bank.

Senior citizens can be reached through publications such as *Modern Maturity*, published by the American Association of Retired Persons. Seniors are considered a prime public for life and health insurance, group travel tours, and real estate in warm climates.

As the American population continues to mature, as more people opt for earlier retirement, and as life expectancies continue to increase, senior citizens will likely become an even more important public for many companies (see Figure 20-1). Like women and minority groups, they have even begun to be more militant, as exemplified by the development of the Gray Panthers organization, to realize their objectives.

EDUCATORS

Teachers form a primary link with future employees and consumers. They also are influential in advising government officals; indeed, many legislative proposals emanate from educational journals. As such, educators comprise an important public.

Many companies regularly visit campuses so that executives, students, and teachers can exchange ideas. DuPont, for example, sponsors an annual educators' conference, where professors and top management discuss topics of mutual interest. Public relations firms such as Hill and Knowlton have begun educational divisions to cater to this special market.

Within the university, communication has taken on a stronger role. Offices of university relations have combined with alumni offices at many colleges to mesh communications and fund-raising activities and to encourage alumni community support for school development. University relations offices perfor most of the same public relations functions as industry departments—from media relations to employee communications.

In addition to occasional fund-raising duties, educational or university relations frequently includes other activities, unknown to corporate public relations. Such duties as advising the student yearbook staff, encouraging faculty participation in academic/professional organizations, promoting morale and prestige among faculty families, and advising the student newspaper all generally fall within the purview of educational relations specialists.[4] While salaries for educational relations professionals often are less than their corporate counterparts, duties and responsibilities are similar. Indeed, with schools facing rising tuition costs and diminishing government revenues, the role of the educational relations professional becomes ever more important.

NONPROFIT ORGANIZATIONS

Practitioners employed with nonprofit organizations, such as the Red Cross or Salvation Army, primarily are involved with fund-raising and the recruiting of volunteers. To stimulate favorable public opinion in support of their organizations, practitioners must continually develop public confidence through internal and external channels.

Public relations tasks in a nonprofit group include securing legislative endorsement for organization-sponsored measures, informing members about organization activities, improving internal relations, and keeping interested parties up-to-date on the group's plans and objectives.

Even with scarce financial and human resources, a nonprofit organization can launch successful programs. For example, a minimum public relations plan for a low-budget organization might consist of the following elements:

Newsletter.   Factual, periodic (monthly or bimonthly), intriguing.

Pamphlets.   Up-to-date, comprehensive explanation of the organization—what it is and what it does.

Publicity.   Ongoing news and feature releases written clearly and interestingly.

Exhibits.   Simple, portable; should reveal the essence of the organization and its mission.

Speeches.   Short, to-the-point explanations of the organization's role in society.

In general, all of the public relations products of the organization should be of the highest quality, true to the facts, and designed with key audiences in mind, especially when one considers that in the not-for-profit world, public relations often is the mission of the organization.

ASSOCIATIONS

Public relations programs are conducted by more than 11,000 national industrial associations, some 500 national professional associations, and approximately 10,000 regional, state, and local associations (see Figure 20-2). Typical of these are the National Association of Manufacturers (NAM), the American Trucking Association, the National Rifle Association, the U.S. Chamber of Commerce, and the American Bar Association.

An association is fundamentally a public relations vehicle dealing daily with the challenge of first conveying and then "selling" its viewpoint. Not unsurprisingly, association executives have a keen awareness of the value and impact of organized, professional public relations. Unlike nonprofit organizations, which must constantly work to raise money, associations generally are well-endowed by their members. To a large degree, in fact, associations are in the business of lobbying in behalf of their members.

Whereas years ago, association communications primarily meant media relations or production of educational and editorial materials, the scope of activities of association public relations today is diverse. In addition to lobbying, association public relations includes public opinion research and planning, publicity, advertising, information action, government relations support, conferences, special events, training programs, and on and on. Accordingly, association public relations staffs and budgets also have been increasing.

As Jim Low, former president of the American Society of Association Executives, put it, "The only way to survive in the fast-paced world of associations is to learn to communicate . . . outstanding communications programs are the only way to realize success."[5]

An expanding array of interest groups have begun associations—most headquartered in Washington—to keep an eye on the government and win the favor of the public. Indeed, association public relations is as much a Washington growth industry as any other.

Because industries and companies are so diverse, the business community increasingly has relied on such groups as the NAM, Business Roundtable, and Business Council to speak for business as a whole. The NAM, for instance, with headquarters in Washington, represents about 20,000 manufacturers and is active in all phases of public relations work from press relations and booklet preparation to clergy relations and lobbying.

FIGURE 20–2. *Scrap iron sculpture.* One way for business and professional associations to secure favorable publicity is by making contributions and staging events to highlight their activities. The Institute of Scrap Iron and Steel combined both activities in presenting to the Smithsonian (as a gift to all Americans) a thirty-ton sculpture constructed entirely of iron and steel scrap materials. Called *Isis,* the scupture was the subject of extensive national publicity and resulted in tremendous recognition for its sponsor.

SOURCE: Courtesy of the Institute of Scrap Iron and Steel.

HEALTH AND HOSPITALS

The health and hospital industry is the nation's third largest employer, a $100 billion enterprise consisting of 7,000 institutions that serve hundreds of millions of people annually. Hospitals in recent years have faced escalating pressures from rising costs, active consumerism, and government intervention. Accordingly, the use of public relations techniques, particularly in enhancing a hospital's image and promoting its services to diverse publics, has become more important.

Because more people are using hospitals, costs for hospital services have skyrocketed, and hospitals have become centers of scientific progress. For these reasons the public has become intensely interested in hospital news. Hospitals have recognized the need to keep the public informed.

"Marketing" has become the watchword in hospital public relations. Basically, public relations practitioners must market the health services people need rather than creating an artificial demand.[6] Community needs must mesh with institutional needs to determine the services offered by the hospital, who will be served and how, and what effect this will have on pricing, referral, and access to health care.

Another major marketing objective is to educate hospital publics through such public relations vehicles as "open houses" that demonstrate and explain services, sponsorship of health and medical events and seminars, and distribution of health-related information through newspaper columns, radio spot announcements, and tele-

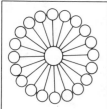

MINICASE

Happy birthday Virginia Mason[7]

In 1980, Virginia Mason Medical Center of Seattle, Washington celebrated its sixtieth anniversary.

A public opinion survey in the fall of 1979, which revealed a general lack of awareness about the Center's programs, was disturbing news to the medical and administrative staff. Clearly, a heightened public relations effort was needed. And the Center set out to achieve it with the sixtieth anniversary.

It targeted the following audiences:

○ **Patients**   The core of Virginia Mason supporters was hospital and clinic patients. They comprised a key target group. Communications efforts included a special overview film, "Medical City," for closed-circuit use in patient rooms. Additionally, a Medical Center booklet was prepared and given to all new patients.

○ **Employees**   Two thousand potential community emissaries worked at the Medical Center. To enhance their role in the anniversary, a week-long birthday celebration for employees, "Happy Birthday, Virginia!" was sponsored, featuring a birthday card contest, a "present" day, and a Center-

phone "hotlines." Indeed, the increase of medical-care costs has enhanced the importance of health education as a primary source of hospital-community interaction.

Community relations is a key aspect of the marketing-communications job. Practitioners must keep neighborhoods informed about such controversial programs as alcohol and drug treatment and involve area residents as much as possible in hospital affairs. In a marketing sense, practitioners must constantly seek out human interest stories for the media to demonstrate the hospital's concern for its community.

Public relations also will play a major role in the continuing development of health maintenance organizations (HMOs), associations of physicians that emphasize early detection of potential health concerns. Some predict HMO enrollment will grow to upwards of 20 million people by 1990. HMOs compete directly with traditional insurance carriers. The public relations challenge of HMOs includes persuading the public that regular health maintenance can detect and help prevent illness and persuading doctors that the HMO approach also makes sense for their participation.

With hospital costs continuing to rise, medical practices being placed under increased scrutiny, and corporate chains taking over an increasing number of hospitals and other health care facilities, the importance of hospital public relations promises to increase in the future. In a related context, public relations has become crucial to health care advertising, because it is the only way a prescription drug manufacturer can go directly to the consumer.

---

wide birthday party. Morale was high, and employees quickly got into the spirit.

○ **Donors/Friends** Center board members and other supporters received a special calendar, marking the anniversary, as well as the Medical Center booklet. An anniversary issue of the hospital's community publication also was prepared. And a community-based program for health-care policy issues was introduced.

○ **General Public** Solid-state exhibits for the hospital, research center, and clinic libraries were sponsored, highlighting the Medical Center's role in the community. Beyond this, the major public anniversary vehicle was a newspaper supplement in a *Seattle Times* Sunday edition, with a circulation of 400,000.

Results of the anniversary program indicated that the marketing communications approach was a powerful one. Perhaps the key indication was that a letter of appeal in the midst of the anniversary celebration generated Virginia Mason more than $1 million in community contributions, surpassing the amounts of the previous years. Everyone associated with the hospital considered the program a smashing success.

QUESTIONS

1 What additional public relations programs could Virginia Mason have adopted for its sixtieth anniversary?

2 What additional methods of measurement could it have used to analyze the results of its public relations program?

MILITARY

Like hospital public relations, public affairs activities in the military also have become more important in recent years. With more than one-quarter of every U.S. taxpayer's dollar going to the military budget, people are legitimately interested in how the military spends their money.

The communications apparatus of the Department of Defense (DOD) and the military services is a complex one, involving over 1,000 people. Military public information officers, like their counterparts in industry, are responsible for internal communications as well as external media and community relations work. Just as corporate public relations practitioners must answer ultimately to their stockholders, military public information people must answer directly to the taxpayers who support them.

The public information principles of the military establishment also are equivalent to those of many organizations. In the case of the Army, for example, the overriding public information objective is to "fully inform the public of the Army's unclassified activities."[8] To meet this objective, the Department of the Army (DA) follows these principles:

1 DA agencies will provide unclassified information about the Army and its activities to the public. DOD and DA policy require prompt and maximum disclosure of information.
2 Requested Army records will be released under AR 340-17.
3 Unfavorable news will be released with the same care and speed as favorable news. Candor is essential in dealing with the public.
4 Promotional, self-serving news is suspect in terms of truth and accuracy and should be avoided. Generating news events designed for media coverage conflicts with the spirit and intent of this regulation.
5 DA officials must not discuss publicly matters that are the responsibility of other governmental agencies, e.g., foreign policy is a responsibility of the Department of State.
6 Information classified in the interest of national security will not be disclosed.
7 Public affairs officers and staffs will not initiate or conduct programs for psychological warfare purposes.[9]

In recent years, especially following the unpopular Vietnam War, the military's public information efforts were designed to build confidence in and support for America's fighting forces. Indeed, improving the image of the military has been essential in recruiting volunteers, in winning support for increased military weaponry, such as the B-1 Bomber, and in generally reestablishing the role of the military as a respected force in our society.

OTHER SPECIAL PUBLICS

Again, it is impossible in one small chapter to list all of the important special publics with which public relations activities are concerned. However, among the more prominent publics with whom practitioners deal are the following:

DISTRIBUTORS/DEALERS

Consumer product manufacturers sell nearly all their output to wholesale distributors and retail dealers. Some oil companies and auto manufacturers have distribution/dealer networks in the tens of thousands. The responsibility for coordinating an effective distributor/dealer communications program often becomes another essential job for the public relations department (see Figure 20-3).

SUPPLIERS

Manufacturers depend on suppliers for raw materials. Suppliers occasionally complain about unfair practices, high prices, and favoritism. To improve relations with suppliers, companies have launched supplier communications programs, supervised by practitioners. For example, at Western Electric each of the firm's 40,000 suppliers is introduced to Western Electric's policies and practices through a booklet called *Glad to See You.*

COMPETITORS

Competitors, too, must be reached through periodic communication. Unfair, monopolistic competition is the archenemy of America's competitive enterprise system. Companies must keep competitors constantly aware of their practices and discourage any feeling among the competition of price-cutting, secret stealing, quality misrepresentation, or theft of employees. Especially today, when many industries have tended toward oligopolistic organization (control by just a few firms), individual companies are increasingly sensitive to the importance of making known their own fair and competitive beliefs and practices.

RELIGIOUS GROUPS

Traditional religious values ebb and flow with the changing trends in society. Groups such as the National Council of Churches, B'nai Brith, and the Fellowship for Christian Athletes have responded against this trend with aggressive public relations campaigns.

Recent years have seen a revival in fundamentalist religious groups. From relatively modest beginnings in the Bible Belt, ministers such as Jerry Falwell and Oral Roberts have come to command huge syndicated television audiences. From such ministries have sprung activist organizations from the Moral Majority to the National Pro-Family Coalition to the Coalition for Better Television, all preaching a conservative, fundamentalist line.

ENVIRONMENTAL GROUPS

Environmentalists, too, recently have reemerged as prominent activists in the halls of Congress and the corridors of industry. President Reagan's choice of James Watt as Secretary of the Interior in 1980 was a lightning rod for a new surge in environmental activism. Traditional environmental groups, such as the Sierra Club, Friends of the Earth, and the National Audubon Society, all experienced monetary and membership growth in the wake of Watt's appointment.

While the environmentalist furor triggered by Watt may subside, it is unlikely that environmental leaders will soon back off from the activist battleground they have

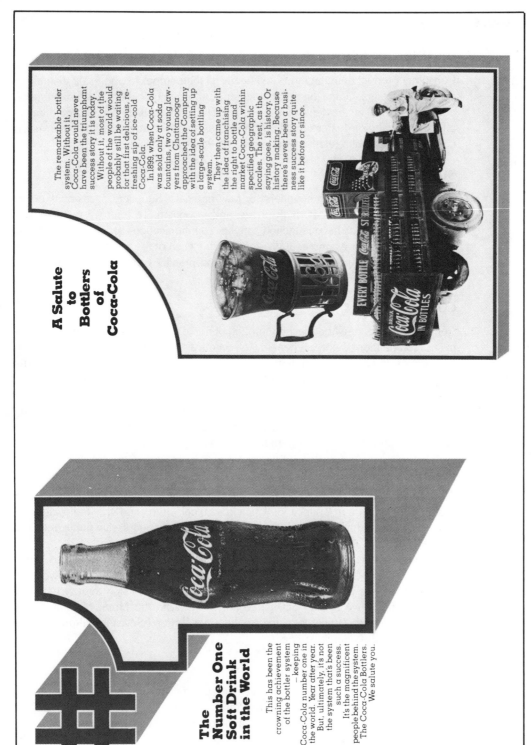

FIGURE 20-3. *Coca-Cola bottlers salute.* To the Coca-Cola Company, few in the organization are any more important than the people who bottle the soft drink. This is an excerpt from a special Coca-Cola publication designed especially to applaud its bottlers.

SOURCE: Courtesy of Coca-Cola Company.

FIGURE 20–4. *Captain America fights to conserve energy.* In 1980, the U.S. Department of Energy, in conjunction with the Campbell Soup Company and the Marvel Entertainment Group, launched a nationwide "Youth Energy Conservation Program" by using comic book hero Captain America to fight the villains of conservation, who carelessly refused to close doors, turn off lights, and conserve energy. The program was launched with a special reception at the White House, where Captain America himself played the starring role and received extensive nationwide publicity.

established in fighting for the cause of environmentalism.[10] The reawakening of environmental activism means that industry and labor must continue in the years ahead to seek a balance in environmental and economic values (see Figure 20–4).

SPORTS FANS

Sports fans have developed into a major and distinct special public. Sports public relations is among the most important aspects of a college athletic recruiting program or a professional team's recognition efforts. Many general managers in professional sports today began as public relations directors. With sports fans growing increasingly discontent with high stadium prices and more petulant millionaire ballplayers, sports public relations in the years ahead will be as important an aspect as any other in professional sports.

Obviously, there is no such thing as the "American public," because America is composed of hundreds of small subgroups. It is the task of public relations professionals to identify special publics, determine their needs, communicate with them about their firm's plans and programs, and ultimately win their support.

CASE STUDY
Procter & Gamble's symbol

I n the early 1980s, the nation's mightiest marketer, Procter & Gamble Company (P&G), was faced with one of the most bizarre public relations problems in modern memory. A whispering campaign, apparently begun by certain fundamentalist religious groups in the South, suddenly erupted nationally, associating the company and its "moon and stars" trademark with Satanism and devil worship.

The rumors first surfaced in 1980 when P&G began getting thousands of phone calls about stories that company officials "had confessed" on the Phil Donahue and Merv Griffin network television shows that P&G supported devil worship. Incredibly, no such appearances by P&G executives ever took place on the shows.

Nonetheless, the company later found that several pastors had passed on the rumors from their pulpits. Leaflets urging parishoners to boycott the company's well-known products—Crest toothpaste, Ivory soap, Folgers coffee, and the like—began to show up in supermarkets. A typical flyer reported P&G's president as saying "as long as the cults and gays have come out of the closet, he was going to do it too. He said he told Satan that if he would help him prosper, he would give his heart and soul when he died. He gives Satan all the credit for his riches."[11]

Despite the absurdity of the rumor, P&G soon began to realize many people apparently took the preposterous stories seriously. Wrote one 75-year-old woman, "In the beginning God made the tree. Where did Satan get Charmin?"[12] By 1982, the company was receiving well over 10,000 questions a month about its "relationship" with the devil.

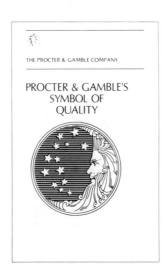

BILLY GRAHAM

July 31, 1982

Unfounded rumors have been spread that the Procter & Gamble Company has some connection to devil worship.

Unfortunately, some of these false accusations have been spread in various churches.

These rumors claim that the Procter & Gamble 100-year-old trademark with its famous moon and 13 stars representing the 13 colonies has something to do with the supporting of satanism and devil worship. I have found this to be absolutely false. I urge Christians everywhere to reject these false rumors and to be reminded that it is a sin to "bear false witness."

Billy Graham

CBS NEWS

A Division of CBS Inc.
524 West 57 Street
New York, New York 10019
212/975 435

Dear Ms. Gilbert:

In response to viewer inquiries regarding Procter & Gamble and the erroneous impression that executives of your company have appeared on 60 MINUTES, we have informed those viewers that at no time has any executive of P&G appeared on our broadcast. Further we don't recall the name Procter & Gamble ever being mentioned by us in any connection.

Sincerely,

Don Hewitt
Executive Producer
60 MINUTES

Ms. Kathy Gilbert
Public Affairs Division
The Procter & Gamble Co.
P.O. Box 599
Cincinnati, Ohio 45201

June 10, 1982

ABC News   7 West 66th Street   New York, New York 10023   Telephone 212 887-4002

Av Westin
Vice President
Executive Producer

July 20, 1982

Mr. John G. Smale
President
Proctor & Gamble Co.
6th and Sycamore St.
Cincinnati, Ohio 45201

Dear Mr. Smale:

The ABC News Magazine 20/20 has received numerous phone calls and letters from the public asking if Proctor and Gamble representatives, including you, have been interviewed on 20/20 concerning your company, its trademark and/or satanism/devil worship. We have advised those viewers that no Proctor and Gamble representatives have ever discussed those subjects on our broadcast.

Sincerely,

Av Westin
Vice President
ABC News

AW:bjh

cc: Mr. Patrick J. Hayes
     Section Manager-Public Affairs
     Proctor & Gamble

& THE OLD-TIME GOSPEL HOUR
LYNCHBURG, VIRGINIA 24514

June 1982

To Whom It May Concern:

It is unfortunate that such false accusations regarding the Procter & Gamble Company are made in the first place, but even more concerning that they can be spread as rumor by people who call themselves Christians.

I have discussed these rumors with the Chairman of the Board of Procter & Gamble, who happens to be from my home town in Virginia, and I am certain neither he nor his company is associated in any way with satanism or devil worship. Christians have a responsibility to know the truth before spreading stories and, in this case, the truth is there is no story to tell. I urge people everywhere to help put an end to these unfortunate rumors.

Sincerely,

Jerry Falwell

JF:dd

The International Radio and Television Outreach of Thomas Road Baptist Church

Clearly, it was time for P&G to blast back. And that's exactly what the company did.

○ It armed its Cincinnati headquarters consumer services division with a full explanation of the symbol that had represented the company since the 1850s. P&G's fifteen consumer services staff members patiently explained to caller after caller that the symbol started as simple markings on crates of Star Candles, an early P&G product, and evolved over the years to a formal design of a man-in-the-moon, a popular figure of the 1800s, and 13 stars representing the original colonies. A brochure, "Procter & Gamble's Symbol of Quality," was dispatched to anyone who wanted it.

○ An elaborate tracking system was established to chart the geographical sweep of the rumors as well as the nature of rumor-oriented calls.

○ The company notified news outlets about its problem and asked for their help. In response, network news and talk show producers wrote public letters to P&G, confirming the falseness of rumors that company executives had appeared on their programs.

○ P&G sent out a mailing to 48,000 southern churches and enlisted the aid of religious leaders like Jerry Falwell and Billy Graham in counter attack. Summarized Rev. Graham in his public letter, "I urge Christians everywhere to reject these false rumors and to be reminded that it is a sin to 'bear false witness.' "

○ Finally, the company announced it would take legal action to stop the spread of the rumors. It filed suits in Georgia and Florida, charging several individuals with "libeling the character" of P&G by circulating "false and malicious" statements about the company and by calling for a boycott of its products. To underscore the seriousness of its case, P&G retained former U.S. Attorney General Griffin Bell to represent it in Atlanta.

Interestingly, all but one of the P&G suit defendants sold products of competing consumer goods companies, although there was no evidence that the companies themselves were pushing the rumor.

In any event, P&G's tough public relations response stimulated a flurry of publicity, including national newspaper, magazine, and network television coverage. While *Advertising Age* suggested in an article that P&G's vocal public relations campaign itself helped spread the rumor about the symbol, most felt the P&G offensive was a good idea. After the rumor-deflating publicity, P&G reported that the number of queries to its consumer services department had fallen by half.

As the company's public relations manager described the strategy during the crisis, "Sure, it's a hard-nosed approach. But the rumor has gotten so big that we had to do something dramatic to stop it. We want people to know we are taking this very seriously."[13]

QUESTIONS

1 Do you think P&G could have averted the spread of rumors by immediately changing its corporate symbol?

2 Do you agree with the P&G strategy to "escalate" the rumor campaign by taking its case to the national media? What alternative public relations strategies might the company have adopted?

3 Do you agree with critics who claimed that the P&G public relations program was an "overreaction" to an insignificant, special public?

4 Do you agree with the company's strategy to emphasize the *corporate* name in its counterattack and downplay individual product names?

5 Had you been P&G's public relations manager, would you have decided on such an aggressive campaign?

NOTES

1 U.S. Department of Labor, Washington, D.C., 1976.

2 NBC Radio Network, *Working Women,* booklet (New York: Author, 1978).

3 Frank Escobar, "Public Relations and the Minority Community," *Public Relations Journal,* July 1981, p. 27.

4 Robert L. Hoskins, "Public Relations Opportunities in Two-Year Colleges," *Public Relations Review,* Fall 1981, p. 20.

5 Edith A. Fraser, "Association Public Relations: The State of the Art," *Public Relations Journal,* October 1981, p. 18.

6 Dorothy L. Zufall, "How to Adapt Marketing Strategies to Health-Care Public Relations," *Public Relations Journal,* October 1981, p. 15.

7 This case was largely adapted from Nancy C. Hicks and David T. McKee, "Integrated Strategies: A Successful Approach to Hospital Public Relations," *Public Relations Journal,* October 1981, pp. 14–16.

8 *Army Public Affairs Public Information,* Army Regulation #360–5, Department of the Army, Washington, D.C., 15 July 1979, pp. 1–2.

9 Ibid.

10 Bruce Harrison, "Environmental Activism's Resurgence," *Public Relations Journal,* June 1982, p. 35.

11 Marilyn Dillon, "P&G Clings to Trademark Despite Rumors," *Cincinnati Enquirer,* 23 July 1982.

12 Sandra Salmans, "P. & G.'s Battles With Rumors," *The New York Times,* 23 July 1982, pp. D1, D4.

13 Terry Bivens, "Bedeviled By a Wild Rumor, They Fight Back," *Philadelphia Inquirer,* 1 August 1982, p. 1-D.

SUGGESTED READING

Bateman, J. Carroll. "Public Relations for the Business and Professional Association." *Public Relations Handbook.* 2d ed. Edited by Philip Lesly. Englewood Cliffs, N.J.: Prentice-Hall, 1978.

Bates, Don. "Non-Profit Health and Social Welfare Public Relations Comes of Age." *Public Relations Journal* 32 (August 1976): 24–25.

Block, Bee F., and **Taylor, M. Elliott.** "Bridging the Public Relations Gap between Hospital Provider and Consumer." *Public Relations Journal* 28 (August 1972): 16–21.

Curtis, Lynn A. "The Power of Neighborhood Self-Help Programs." *Public Relations Review,* Spring 1982, pp. 6–14.

Escobar, Frank. "Public Relations and the Minority Community." *Public Relations Journal,* July 1981, pp. 27–28.

Foegen Ph. D., J. H. "Enough Attention For Older Readers?" *Public Relations Quarterly,* Winter 1981–82, pp. 18–20. A survey of some of the largest daily newspapers to see if older people are getting their share of attention in the nation's papers.

Harrison, Bruce. "Environmental Activism's Resurgence." *Public Relations Journal,* June 1982, pp. 34–36.

Haynes, Jim. "Public Relations In The Academic Institution." *Public Relations Quarterly,* Summer 1981, pp. 21–24.

Hicks, Nancy J. and **McKee, David T.** "Integrated Strategies: A Successful Approach To Hospital Public Relations." *Public Relations Journal,* October 1981, pp. 14–16.

Himes, Joseph S. *Racial and Ethnic Relations.* Dubuque, Iowa: William C. Brown, 1975.

Hoskins, Robert L. "Public Relations Opportunities in Two-Year Colleges." *Public Relations Review,* Fall 1981, pp. 42–52.

Hussain, Kheteeb M. *Development of Information Systems for Education.* Englewood Cliffs, N.J.: Educational Administration Series, 1973.

Kobre, Sidney. *Successful Public Relations for Colleges and Universities.* New York: Hastings House, 1975.

Kurtz, Harold P. *Public Relations for Hospitals: A Practical Handbook.* Springfield, Ill.: Charles Thomas, 1969.

Mayer, Frank. *Public Relations for Public School Personnel.* Midland, Mich.: Pendell, 1974.

Pulley, Jerry L. "Principal and Communication: Some Points of Interference." *NASSP Bulletin* 59, no. 38F (January 1975): 50–14. Discusses several factors that can sabotage an educator's communications efforts.

Rimer, Irving L. "How the Non-Profits Do It." *Public Relations Journal* 31, no. 9 (September 1975): 24–25. The annual reports of nonprofit organizations do the job, although they have certain limitations in budget and focus.

Rowland, Wesley A., ed. *Handbook of Institutional Advancements.* San Francisco: Jossey-Bass, 1977.

Saul, Louise. "School Boards Turning to Public Relations Experts to Keep Parents Informed." *The New York Times,* 1 September 1974.

Schmidt, Frances, and **Weiner, Harold N.,** eds. *Public Relations in Health and Welfare.* New York: Columbia University Press, 1966.

Stephens, Lowndes F. "Professionalism of Army Public Affairs Personnel." *Public Relations Review,* Summer 1981, pp. 43–56. The results from a survey of Army personnel attempts to broaden the knowledge of this specialized public relations field.

Sutula, Dolores A. "Community Education as a Communications Tool." *Public Relations Journal,* February 1981, pp. 27–28.

Unruh, Adolph, and **Willier, Robert A.** *Public Relations for Schools.* Belmont, Calif.: Fearon-Pitman Publications, 1974.

Yetman, Norman R., and **Steele, Hoy C.** *Majority and Minority: The Dynamics of Racial and Ethnic Relations.* Boston: Allyn & Bacon, 1975.

21
The International Community

TRANSCENDING INTERNATIONAL BOUNDARIES

In recent years, the public relations activities of multinational corporations, religious organizations, the tourist industry, universities, and government increasingly have transcended national boundaries. Ours is an interdependent world, and in order for such activities as trade and commerce to prosper, the problems of communicating verbally and symbolically across national and cultural borders must be overcome. This, in essence, is the challenge of international public relations.

Historically, U.S. business firms were not particularly interested in sales abroad. Until recently, in fact, the U.S. market itself provided enough diversity to fully occupy most companies. However, with the incursion into the U.S. market of the Toyotas, Lufthansas, and Perriers of the world, U.S. companies increasingly have looked to expand their reach into overseas markets.

Those companies that have already ventured overseas find that international trade is not at all the same as domestic commerce. It is more complicated, conditions of competition abroad often are unfair, and barriers not found in domestic markets confront the potential overseas trader.[1] Indeed, Americans often are surprised to learn that they must sell, design, and package a product differently in Canton, China compared to the way they do it in Canton, Ohio.

Public relations has been described as the "Achilles Heel" of the multinational corporation. Despite the fact that a global program can offer optimum benefits to clients in planning, controlling, and assessing worldwide programs, only a few counseling firms are capable of executing projects on a worldwide basis. Consequently, most programs of multinational companies have been carried out in an ad hoc manner.[2]

In many countries, such as Japan, India, and France, the public relations function may take on great significance for an organization. If a company should, through lack of knowledge, run afoul of local customs in the host country, its operations in that country could be hindered. Steeped in customs and the "do's and don'ts" of doing business in a different country, a practitioner can help steer management past the shoals and pitfalls of trouble. Indeed, the practitioner may fill an important role in helping formulate management policy vis-à-vis the host nation.

THE INTERNATIONAL PROFESSIONAL

In addition to possessing the more traditional public relations skills, the overseas practitioner must be a combination marketing tactician, diplomat, trouble shooter, and government relations expert. A skillful professional can help prevent a foreign government from legislating against a company or even nationalizing its property or ordering its removal.

To win acceptance in any community abroad for an idea, product, or person, it is essential to be thoroughly familiar with the customs, beliefs, and history of the area, current economic and political realities, newest fashions, and, perhaps most importantly, the language.

At the same time, the effective international representative must have a thorough and current knowledge of what is going on back home. A misinformed representative can communicate the wrong message locally because he hasn't been adequately briefed.

In effect, international public relations representatives are the communications link between the host country and the home office. It is essential therefore that they convey to the local constituency a fair and accurate portrayal of the organization's positions and, to the home office, a candid "climate analysis" of the local area.

ORGANIZING FOR INTERNATIONAL PUBLIC RELATIONS

In the typical multinational company, the international public relations manager usually reports both to the headquarters public relations director and to the international department. This latter relationship is extremely important because the international practitioner must be intimately involved with line activities and decisions.

Practitioners are situated in strategic overseas locations. Some U.S. multinationals, for example, position representatives in the Caribbean to cover Latin America, in Hong Kong or Tokyo to cover Asia and the Far East, and in London or Paris to cover Great Britain and western Europe. In recent years, companies have expanded public relations coverage to the Mideast and Africa.

Counseling firms also have expanded their international capabilities. Large agencies (Hill and Knowlton, Burson Marsteller, Ruder & Finn) represent three kinds of clients on the international level:

1 American firms doing business internationally.
2 Foreign companies competing for business in the United States.
3 Foreign governments seeking to advance the interests of their nations in the United States.

Additionally, several public relations networks have developed over the years, linking U.S. counterparts with counselors in other parts of the world to establish quality international standards and take the guess work out of such relationships.[3] The key attraction in such networks is the lure of commissioning an established and experienced local presence. Services range from small spot jobs in one country to coordinated worldwide campaigns. The network concept permits smaller agencies to compete with multi-office giants for certain types of business. Among the largest of such networks are International Public Relations Group of Companies, Local Media, and the Pioneer Group.[4]

THE STATE OF PUBLIC RELATIONS ABROAD

There is no question that international public relations continues to experience healthy growth. The International Public Relations Association, established in the early 1950s, "to contribute to the growth and professionalism of public relations practice on a worldwide basis," has over 700 members in sixty countries. However, the practice of public relations varies in sophistication from country to country.

Canadian public relations is the rival of American practice in terms of level of acceptance and management respect for the function and maturity of the profession. Most major Canadian firms have optimum-sized staffs, and the Canadian Public Relations Society is extremely active.

Public relations in *Europe*, on the other hand, is not as well developed. The obvious complication is language—360 million people speaking twelve different languages, accompanied by varying traditions, cultures, and economies. *British* public relations is as well developed as any practice within Europe, with professionals liberally sprinkled throughout government and industry. Public relations in *France* has developed more slowly, with internal communications growing in emphasis. In *West Germany*, the practice is mixed, wavering under the threat of becoming a collective noun for all activities encompassing sales, stunts, publicity gimmicks, and show-business tricks.[5]

In *Asia*, public relations also has evolved slowly. *Japan* has the most highly developed practice, with more than 100 full-time firms. In Japan the field runs the gamut from press relations to employee communications to management counseling. Elsewhere in Asia, the practice is less active, although countries such as *India* and *China* have recently experienced progress in the public relations area.

In *Latin America*, the scene is more chaotic. In many countries, *relaciones publicas* is used interchangeably with the functions of marketing and advertising. *Mexican* public relations, which began in the 1930s, is more highly developed than in most other Latin America areas. Mexican schools of higher learning often teach the

INTERVIEW
Donald Lightfoot

Donald Lightfoot is chairman and managing director of International Public Relations (PVT) Limited, Zimbabwe. Mr. Lightfoot has extensive communications experience in Africa, to which he emigrated in 1948. Until 1965, he served in the broadcast area, including a period as director-general of the Northern Rhodesia and Zambia Broadcasting Corporations. After forming his own advertising agency and public relations consultancy in Lusaka, Zambia, Mr. Lightfoot purchased the oldest public relations organization in Zimbabwe in 1978 and developed it into the foremost organization in the country with over 40 clients covering all sectors of the economy and the community.

What are the requisites for a public relations practitioner in a foreign country?

Apart from a thorough knowledge and experience in public relations together with the tools of the profession and opportunities available, the most important qualification is a comprehensive knowledge of the country and area in which the operation is carried out. This extends to the leading personalities in central and local government, commerce, and industry, as well as to those directly involved in every facet of society within the country.

What aspect of public relations is most important in a foreign country?

I can only really relate this to my experience over the past thirty-four years in Central Africa where I have seen the emergence of black governments taking over from the previous colonial regimes. A new and different generation of policy and decision makers have emerged, many of whom, although holding most valuable qualifications, have little practical experience of the duties and responsibilities they are called upon to exercise. Government relations then, both central and local, are of prime importance. Equally important is the relationship with the media, which has undergone dramatic changes from projecting colonialistic attitudes of the past into the hopes and aspirations of the majority of the population now represented by a popularly-elected government. In this latter connection, industrial relations also has gained much greater importance as has human relations in the dealings of top management with the workforce and the population in general.

Another important aspect of public relations falls within the field of education aimed at all ethnic groups at all levels of activity within the country. Its major function must be to provide an opportunity for communication between peoples who previously had no forum for such a vital aspect of the country's life and development. Taking Zimbabwe as a prime example, in the past there was little contact between black and white, between certain sections of the white population, and between blacks of different tribal groupings. Without the bringing together of these various sections of the community, in which public relations has a most important role, misunderstanding, hostility, and adverse reaction to the necessary far-reaching changes taking place will continue to the detriment of the country and the population.

What is the state of public relations practice outside the United States?

The approach in many countries, particularly in parts of Africa, is much less aggressive, less sophisticated than in the United States. It is much more necessary to adopt an attitude of education within the public relations field for, in the main, a large proportion of the target audience is unsophisticated and needs to be enlightened and encouraged to a much greater degree than in the more developed countries. Another essential difference is the facilities available to practitioners. The electronic age has not yet materialized to the same extent as in the United States and other more developed countries. Consequently, there is a much more personalized aspect within the public relations field with more direct contact with community leaders and the media. In many instances, this can provide more positive results than when contact is remote.

Is international public relations a growing field?

Yes. Africa provides a perfect example of the growth of international public relations. There is the desire and necessity from both internal and external individuals and organizations to learn more about what is going on and the potential in the outside world for the development of better understanding between peoples and nations, on the one hand, and, on the other hand, about the comparatively new countries in Africa of which little is known and who on many occasions suffer from this ignorance. Through the development of international public relations, there is the greater realization of the opportunities available for the development of trade between the various regions of the world. There is much more positive appreciation of this, certainly in Africa, as the result of the expansion that is taking place in the profession within the international field.

How important is public relations work outside the United States?

Certainly in Africa, of the most vital importance. It must also be appreciated that apart from a considerable ignorance of the development in the field that is taking place not only in their own countries and on the continent itself but throughout the world, there is the added complication that the majority of the population of Africa is to some large extent illiterate and consequently a different approach is necessary within the communications process. There is also a great search for knowledge in every form, and public relations is the ideal manner in which to provide this.

How would you characterize the development of public relations practice in Africa?

It has been little short of phenomenal over the past twenty years. Prior to this, it was almost non-existent, largely due to the underdevelopment of the continent. Coupled with this was an almost total lack of media. Today this situation has gone through dramatic change. Substantial development has taken place through the establishment of primary and secondary industry. Local manufacture of consumer commodities has expanded most

(Interview *continues*.)

considerably and continues to do so. There is a ready market due to the improved living conditions of the population at all levels. Commercial and services industries have been established to a degree never previously experienced. There has been a spectacular development within the communications systems with all forms of media now available for the dissemination of information in all its various forms.

What is the structure of African public relations?

There are now professional consultants and practitioners in almost every African country and an increasing number of organizations are establishing their own internal public relations units. There now exists an overall African body—The Federation of African Public Relations Associations—to which all local associations and institutions are encouraged to affiliate. This development has not so far been as successful as was originally hoped, but it is, nevertheless, a most positive step in the coordination of public relations expertise and practice within the context of the entire African continent.

Is there a legitimate need for professional public relations work in Africa?

The requirement for professional public relations, the manner in which it has developed and is continuing to expand in all fields, is typified by the situation experienced in Zimbabwe over the past few years. This country was faced with the imposition of sanctions by the United Nations following the illegal unilateral declaration of independence by the previous colonial regime in 1965. This was followed by a bitter liberation war lasting several years until independence was achieved in 1980. During this period, public relations was reduced to the lowest possible level. Almost every organization ceased to disseminate information on its activities. The strictest form of censorship was enforced by the authorities. Rhodesia, as it was then known, became a closed book and was tight-lipped on anything going on within the country. Similarly, external organizations were supposedly not dealing with the country in conformity with the United Nations sanctions resolution and naturally kept any involvement with Rhodesia under secure wraps.

Today the situation is completely different. Every opportunity is taken to project images in the form of corporate development and to make available the fullest possible information across the board whenever and wherever this falls within the usual scope of public relations activity. In these terms, Zimbabwe has now taken its proper place alongside the other nations of Africa and of the world. To some extent, it is a completely new country but at the same time it has progressed tremendously over the past twenty years, providing a unique example of the needs and application of public relations practice and development.

subject, and the government and local companies recognize its importance. As in other continents, the growth of American companies in Latin America, complete with local public relations staffs, has helped translate the function and its worth into the cultures of other nations. One problem in certain countries, such as *Argentina, Chile,* and *Uruguay,* is more repressive control of the media by the government.

In *Africa,* the field is growing. The first All-Africa PR Conference was held at Nairobi, Kenya, in 1975. Traditionally, the practice in Africa has been closer to propaganda than to the more open U.S. approach. Obviously, the totalitarian and authoritarian regimes that dominate Africa influence communications. Likewise, public relations concepts have been slow to filter into the markets of the *Eastern Bloc,* the *Soviet Union,* and the *Arab* nations. Here again, the growth public relations may experience in the rest of the 1980s will likely emanate from the expansion of American practitioners working in host nations.

THE MEDIA OVERSEAS

In many foreign countires, the term *public relations* is a euphemism for *press relations*. Working with the press abroad is not easy; there often is a language barrier, and in many countries, the government controls the media.

In some foreign nations, company developments (sales, earnings, and management changes) are not considered news. In Canada, for example, most management change announcements would have to be paid for to make the newspapers. Here are some other idiosyncracies in dealing with the media in other nations:

○ The time-honored U.S. press lunch to introduce products, management changes, or financial information is much less the case overseas, where frequently the company meets the press after work at the close of the business day.

○ Press conferences in countries like West Germany, Switzerland, the Netherlands, Norway, and Sweden begin promptly on the appointed hour. Elsewhere, it is customary to wait fifteen to thirty minutes.

○ Press conference attendees in some countries must include government officials, local bankers, and other dignitaries. In other nations, local custom dictates that the company's customers and representatives be included.

○ Press kits usually should be composed in both English and the main language of the host country. The press kit should contain (in addition to immediate news and a background on the company) statements on the benefits the company offers the host country.[6]

DEALING WITH FOREIGN CLIENTS ABROAD

There is nothing magical about providing public relations services in overseas markets. As noted, the key element in dealing effectively overseas lies in the development of a good working knowledge of the language, customs, climate, and people of the particular host area. Other suggestions for dealing effectively overseas in a public relations context include the following:

○ Be innovative, flexible, and prepared to take risks. Stated another way, don't believe what works in Canton, Ohio etc.

○ Develop continuing dialogue with consumer, business, and government leaders in the host country.

○ Use the expertise of other local public relations practitioners or agencies.

○ "Network" through contacts with foreign government and trade offices in the United States, foreign service people, commercial attaches of foreign consulates, and visiting representatives.

○ Introduce philanthropic programs locally.

○ Dismiss the myth that overseas media will never report events unless paid for. If activities are newsworthy, chances are local media won't ignore them.[7]

Importantly, public relations practitioners operating abroad shouldn't think they have to "out-native the natives." No one will expect the local practitioner to be a linguistic expert or fully knowledgeable in the country's customs. However, convincing one's host of a willingness to learn about the local country will help immeasurably in ingratiating the public relations practitioner abroad.

FEATURE
Press relations Japanese style

In Japan, press relations is practiced in a most peculiar manner, at least according to American standards.

News dissemination in Japan is controlled by press clubs. Only club members are eligible to receive news releases and attend press conferences. Each club jealously guards its prerogatives. Financial news is covered by the Bank of Japan Press Club, which includes reporters from some fourteen selected media specializing in finance and insurance. Tokyo has about forty such clubs, all attached to government ministries and nonprofit business organizations.

Each club has two or three *Kanji*, or chairmen, who serve on a rotating basis and wield considerable power. They arrange attendance of members at press conferences, distribute press releases to members, and are virtually omnipotent. When a company or public relations firm intends to call a press conference or distribute a news release at a press club, it first must inform the Kanji and ask approval at least one day in advance. The Kanji can singlehandedly boycott press conferences or refuse to distribute releases. They are justified in doing so when the release doesn't contain sufficient information, is misleading, or lacks newsworthiness.

Critics contend that press clubs serve to create "closed shops" so far as news coverage is concerned. Typically, a firm can distribute information about a press conference only after the event is held at the press club.[8]

THE FOREIGN PRESS IN THE UNITED STATES

Many foreign publications house bureaus in New York City and Washington, D.C. The foreign press represents the single most important source of information about America for hundreds of millions of people throughout the world.

There are more than 1,000 active representatives of foreign media in the United States, representing more than 500 news organizations. About 80 percent of the U.S. foreign press corps represents European media; Japan is also broadly represented.

Most foreign correspondents are interested mainly in American politics. Normally, about one-half of a correspondent's time is spent on politics and the other half on such subjects as science, art, business, crime, civil rights, and finance. Foreign bureaus often are one-person operations, and an active international public relations representative can keep foreign journalists constantly serviced with topical and timely information for use in overseas markets.

REPRESENTING FOREIGN CLIENTS IN THE UNITED STATES

One growth area for U.S. public relations firms has been their retention by foreign companies and governments seeking to expand their influence in America. Some firms, in fact, report yearly retainers upwards of $100,000 in behalf of foreign organizations.

Just as U.S. multinational companies need public relations assistance abroad, foreign multinationals need help in doing business in the United States—whether in introducing a product, setting up a subsidiary, opening a new plant, or expanding existing operations. A U.S. consultant can be of tremendous value in counseling on working with state and federal legislatures and agencies as well as with the press.

Foreign countries retain the services of public relations counselors to fill a variety of needs such as:

○ Advancing political objectives.

○ Counseling on the probable U.S. reaction to the government's projected action.

○ Advancing the country's commercial interests, e.g. sales in the U.S., increased U.S. private investment, tourism, etc.

○ Assisting in communications in English.

○ Counseling and help in winning understanding and support on a specific issue that may undermine the client's standing in the U.S. and the world community.

○ Helping modify laws and regulations inhibiting the client's activities in the United States.[9]

A foreign government that seeks to hire an American public relations firm often begins by having its embassy in Washington solicit competitive bids. The winner is expected to provide expertise in disseminating "positive news" to the media and other public opinion channels. Often it may be necessary to explain to foreign clients—some of whom may totally control the flow of news in their own countries— how an independent press works.

Typically, a consultant begins the assignment by identifying potential sources of public opinion and by surveying news coverage about the client country. After researching attitudes about the country, activities may be suggested, such as the following:

1 Selectively contacting influential writers and editors and providing them with background information about the country.

2 Inviting media to visit client countries. These expense-paid trips (*junkets*) are often frowned upon by responsible media.

3 Checking with foreign policy experts, educators, business leaders, and government officials about current American attitudes toward the country. The results of these surveys, as well as more formal research, are turned over to the client.

Representing foreign nations is often a difficult and unpopular task. Sydney S. Baron & Co., for example, encountered severe criticism for representing the pro-apartheid government of South Africa. So, too, did Ruder & Finn, when it employed the wife of Senate Foreign Relations Committee member Jacob Javits to work on the agency's Iran Air account. President Carter's brother, Billy, drew public fire for representing Libya's terrorist leader Mohamar Khadafy. Carl Byoir & Associates, a major U.S. public relations firm, has never been able to shake completely the image inspired by its founder, who was accused of propagandizing for the Nazis while working on the German Railroad Association account in the 1930s.

Counselors who work for foreign governments must register with the Department of Justice and list all their activities on behalf of a foreign principal, including compensation received and expenses incurred.[10]

THE OUTLOOK

Multinationals have been under constant attack abroad from a variety of critics, including supra-national bodies, national governments, international labor, and consumer and religious groups. This clamor will not soon diminish and is likely to intensify.

Since 1980, in fact, at least three major cross-border, activist campaigns against major corporations have surfaced.

○ One was a brief international boycott at Coca-Cola over allegations that its Guatemalan bottler had used the local army to squash labor unions.

○ Another was a campaign against major banks and corporations who maintained trade, investment, and lending relations with South Africa, on the grounds that these operations helped support apartheid. One result of this campaign was the withdrawal of deposits by church and university institutional investors from banks that participated in South African loans. Another result was the announcement by some major banks that they were discontinuing the practice of lending to South Africa.

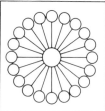

MINICASE
The Nestle infant formula boycott[11]

In 1977, a coalition of some forty groups drawn from church, health, and consumer organizations met at the University of Minnesota at an organizing conference on infant formula. This group, called INFACT, combined its forces with the New York City-based Interfaith Center on Corporate Responsibility, a church coalition of 17 Protestant denominations and about 180 Roman Catholic groups, to attack the Nestle Company and its practices in marketing infant formula to third world nations.

The quarrel between the corporation and the activists had two basic elements. *First,* its critics charged that Nestle marketed infant formula too aggressively, thus discouraging breast-feeding, normally nutritionally best for infants. *Second,* activists pointed to the dangers of improper use of infant formula, such as mixing it with polluted water in third world nations.

By the early 1980s, the infant formula topic had become a major aspect of the North-South dialogue, with formula makers depicted by their adversaries as corporations interested more in profits than in people.

In 1981, the World Health Organization (WHO), a specialized United Nations agency, adopted a Code of Conduct for the international marketing of infant formula. Essentially, the WHO document eliminated all promotional efforts, leaving Nestle and other infant formula companies to serve as passive "order takers" rather than marketers. In light of the WHO code, about 20 countries immediately adopted national codes on infant formula.

○ The third campaign, by far the most heralded, was the worldwide boycott of Nestle, the large Swiss multinational, that dominated the infant formula business in third world countries. Ironically, as the minicase below describes, the Nestle boycott started in the United States, where the Swiss company has never produced or marketed infant formula.

The threat to multinationals lies in the prospect of local regulations involving widely differing controls, sanctions, and curbs in dozens of different countries. The practice of public relations therefore will loom larger in a corporation's response to local pressures. To survive in an increasingly nationalistic overseas atmosphere, multinationals must tie their policies and practices as closely as possible to the aspirations and goals of host countries. They must increase and make known their efforts to upgrade job skills, bring more nationals into local and international management, seek out opportunities to improve their public image, and prove themselves honest and sincere residents rather than undesirable aliens.[12]

To accomplish all this, multinational companies abroad will have to rely increasingly on the sound judgment and competent technical skills of international public relations practitioners.

The gauntlet laid down by the activists posed a major public relations challenge to Nestle. Indeed, when a Nestle subsidiary took over management of Washington's Mayflower Hotel, pickets turned out in great number. Moreover, U.S. retailers were petitioned to stop handling Nestle products.

Although Nestle's credibility originally was badly weakened, it eventually bounced back with an innovative public relations response.

○ In 1981, it opened the Nestle Coordination Center for Nutrition in Washington, D.C. The Center worked to develop a comprehensive, computerized information system on primary health care and infant and maternal nutrition.

○ Nestle's next step in 1982 was to formally support the WHO code by issuing detailed instructions to its marketing executives around the world and to local authorities in countries where no national code had been adopted. Nestle's directives prohibited mass media advertising, direct sampling to mothers, and participation in trade or consumer promotion in the infant formula area.

○ Finally, also in 1982, Nestle established an Infant Formula Audit Commission to review any allegations that the company had violated WHO or national codes. To chair the panel, Nestle named former U.S. Secretary of State Edmund Muskie.

QUESTIONS

1 Had you been Nestle's public relations director, what initial strategy would you have recommended the company follow in light of the worldwide infant formula challenge?

2 In addition to the three public relations programs Nestle began, what other alternative responses might the company pursue?

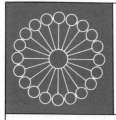

CASE STUDY

The new international image

Mondo Fruit Inc. had traditionally been one of the most powerful agricultural companies operating in the Western Hemisphere. Throughout Latin America, rightists and leftists alike called it the "octopus." The company's tentacles stretched into every country where bananas are grown, embracing hundreds of thousands of acres of farms, towns, cities, and ports. Mondo Fruit owned ships, railroads, and even a communications system. Everywhere it operated, it was a country within a country, funding schools, clinics, hospitals, even collecting the garbage.

It also was accused of running local governments. One writer described Venezuela, for instance, as "a province of Mondo Fruit." The company was charged constantly with helping to overthrow dictators it did not get along with. So pervasive was its influence that Central America became known as "the banana republics" even though the region's main crop was coffee, not bananas.

Such political involvement darkened the company's image in Latin America. Demonstrations against Mondo Fruit were common.

Eventually, the Mondo Fruit relationship with the governments of Central America began to wane. A new breed of proud, self-conscious, nationalistic leader began to emerge. So, too, did an aggressive labor union movement and a professional and business class of residents. In 1980, when Mondo Fruit became part of a larger company, Loco United, its image began to change.

Loco United was considered the model of the modern U.S. multinational corporation that recognized the importance of corporate social responsibility in host nations. Loco United management set out to implement several new programs and upgrade existing ones to enhance the company's reputation in the region. For example:

1 It paid its employees more than other agricultural workers, about twice as much as cattle and coffee workers, and also more than clerical and industrial workers.

2 It provided many fringe benefits, including free housing and free electricity. In Venezuela, if a worker chose to live in a "company house," Loco United built the house and set up a special loan program for workers to purchase their own homes.

3 It provided free medical care and paid vacations.

4 It instituted a Community Action Program, employing native social workers to educate employees on such concerns as nutrition, sanitation, and child care.

5 Wherever possible, it turned over its commissary to Central Americans. In Chile, it turned over its schools to the government, though it continued to pay half of the teachers' salaries. Ironically, while it tried to give the

government its company-owned hospital in Venezuela, the union preferred to have the company maintain it.

6 It also instituted an Associate Growers Program, in which it sold land to former local company workers, supplied them with technology in irrigation, and aided them in disease and pest control.

As Loco United's chief executive put it, "We have a responsibility to our employees, the people of the countries in which we operate, and the countries themselves. We're convinced that it is in our interest to feel this way."

QUESTIONS

1 In 1980, what do you think Loco United decided were its primary short- and long-range public relations objectives?

2 Why did Loco United play down the Mondo Fruit name when it took power?

3 What was the importance of Loco United's Community Action Program? The Associate Growers Program?

4 What special strategy would you suggest for Loco United in dealing with the press in the various countries in which it operates?

5 What other programs might you suggest?

NOTES

1 Robert L. Mayall, "Does Anybody Here Know How to Play This Game?" *Public Relations Journal*, June 1981, p. 33.

2 Ray Josephs, "A Global Approach to Public Relations," *Columbia Journal of World Business*, Fall 1973, p. 93.

3 Ernest Wittenberg, "Getting It Done Overseas," *Public Relations Journal*, June 1982, p. 14.

4 "PR Firm Networks Covering the World," *Publicist*, May/June 1977, pp. 1–4.

5 Jules M. Hartogh, "Public Relations in a Changing Europe." *Public Relations Journal*, March 1974, p. 29.

6 "If You're Planning a Press Conference Abroad," *Practical Public Relations*, 12 August 1974.

7 *Public Relations News*, Vol. XXXVIII, No. 47, 29 November 1982.

8 Adapted from "The Press Clubs of Japan," *Burson-Marsteller Newsletter*, August 1975, pp. 1–4. Adapted with permission.

9 Carl Levin, "Representing Foreign Interests," *Public Relations Journal*, June 1982, p. 22.

10 David M. Sloan, "More Nations Seek a PR Polish on Their U.S. Image," *The New York Times*, 6 August 1978.

11 This case was adapted largely from Richard L. Barovick, "Activism On A Global Scale," *Public Relations Journal*, June 1982, pp. 29–31.

12 William A. Durbin, "PR At the Multinational Level," *Management Review*, April 1974, pp. 14, 18.

22
Managing Public Issues

ISSUES MANAGEMENT IS "IN"

Public issues management has become the hottest buzz phrase in public relations.

According to W. Howard Chase, who helped coin the phrase "issues management," more than 200 American companies have created executive posts for issues managers.[1] Basically, the task of such issues managers is to help their organizations define and deal with emerging political, economic, and social issues that may affect them.

Organizations have had little choice in recent years but to increase their role in the public policy process. The free enterprise system in general and certain industries and companies in particular have been challenged by the widening role of special interest groups in the policy process and the dramatic growth of public concern about the quality of life, consumerism, and the environment.

Large companies, in particular, have become increasingly aware that the many external forces surrounding the business world must be scanned, monitored, tracked, and analyzed. Only in that way can their potential effect on the company's image and profits be gauged, can corporate policy toward them be decided, and can strategy regarding them be planned.[2] Such is the domain of issues management.

ISSUES MANAGEMENT DEFINED

W. Howard Chase defined issues management thusly:

> Issues management is the capacity to understand, mobilize, coordinate, and direct all strategic and policy planning functions, and all public affairs/public relations skills, toward achievement of one objective: meaningful participation in creation of public policy that affects personal and institutional destiny.
>
> Issues management is dynamic and pro-active. It rejects the hypothesis that any institution must be the pawn of the public policy determined solely by others.
>
> The noblest aspect of freedom is that human beings and their institutions have the right to help determine their own destinies. Issues management is the systems process that maximizes self-expression and action programming for most effective participation in public policy formation.
>
> Thus, issues management is the highest form of sound management applied to institutional survival.[3] (See Figure 22–1.)

The Public Affairs Council defines issues management in a slightly less grand manner as "a program which a company uses to increase its knowledge of the public policy process and enhance the sophistication and effectiveness of its involvement in that process."[4]

Like public relations itself, there is no precise definition of issues management. Indeed, many suggest that the term "issues management" is another way of saying that the most important public relations skill is counseling management. Even leaders in the issues management movement agree that public relations pioneers like Ivy Lee, Edward Bernays, Carl Byoir, and John Hill all operated as issues managers when they served as personal advisors to the heads of major organizations.

Nonetheless, issues management, as a specialized discipline within organizations, has developed to the point where the embryonic Issues Management Association, founded in the 1980s, today already has around 400 members.

APPROACH TO ISSUES MANAGEMENT

In approaching issues management, one thing must be clear: no one in our society— not a company, not a chief executive officer, not the president of the United States— can singlehandedly "manage issues." The term "issues management" then is something of a misnomer. However, smart organizations can manage their own *response* to issues and therefore, influence the development of public issues in the following ways:

Anticipate emerging issues.   Normally, the issues management process anticipates issues eighteen months to three years away. Therefore, it is neither crisis planning nor post-crisis planning but rather *pre-crisis planning*. In other words, issues management deals with an issue that will hit the organization a year from now, thus distinguishing the practice from the normal crisis planning aspects of public relations.

Selectively identify issues.   An organization can influence only a few issues at a time. Therefore a good issues management process will select several, specific— perhaps five to ten—priority issues with which to deal. In this way, issues management can focus on the most important issues affecting the organization.

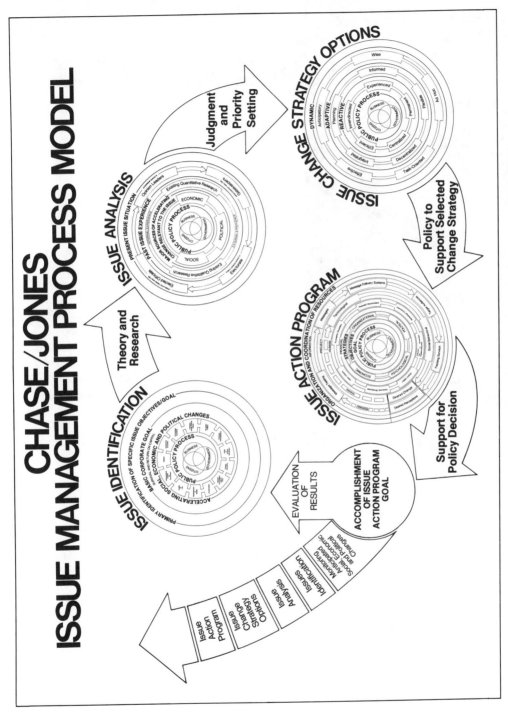

FIGURE 22-1. *Chase/Jones Management Process Model.* A pioneer in the field of issues management, W. Howard Chase, along with Barrie L. Jones, developed this tool for predicting the effect of internal and external environmental changes on the performance of the overall corporate system. The model itself assigns decision-making authority and performance responsibility as well as providing for review and evaluation of issues manager performance.   SOURCE: Courtesy of Howard Chase Enterprises, Inc.

R ay Ewing is Director of Issues Management at Allstate Insurance Companies in Chicago, Ill. Mr. Ewing joined Allstate's public relations staff in 1960, following editing jobs with a business news publisher, radio stations, wire services, and a weekly newspaper. In 1979, he was promoted from Corporate Communications Director to a new position, Issues Management Director. In this position, he also was named secretary of Allstate's Corporate Issues Committee, composed of the company's senior executives with the responsibility to develop corporate policy and action plans for dealing with major current public issues. Mr. Ewing also is president and co-founder of the Issues Management Association.

What is issues management?

Issues management from an organizational standpoint represents an effort at public policy planning; strategic planning is business or profit planning. Issues management relates to outside planning (those forces in the institution's environment that will affect its future existence); strategic planning relates to internal planning (the institution planning its own future structure, businesses, etc.). More specifically, issues management as a process is the identification of emerging issues, prioritization, policy formulation, supporting program development, operational implementation, communication to the appropriate stakeholder groups, and evaluation of results.

How important is issues management for an organization today?

Issues management is the most important management technique developed in the past two decades for the use of senior officers, especially chief executive officers.

Can an organization really "manage" issues?

No. Issues management is not the "management" of issues or the public policy process. It is the management of an institution's efforts to participate in the public policy process.

What kinds of issues does Allstate get involved with?

Because the Issues Management Committee is composed of eleven senior officers (including our chief executive officer and chief operating officer), we concern ourselves with only four or five issues of the highest priority. These are external issues (and internal if they have external implications) which will begin to mature in the next one to three years. They are public policy issues that impact one or more of our stakeholders— public, customers, employees, and shareholders. The issues range from the administration's efforts to transfer some of the social welfare costs from the public to the private sector to the deregulation of the financial services industry.

How does the issues management process work at your company?

Again, issues management is the responsibility of senior management, not a particular department. The Issues Management Committee is a matrix committee, chaired by the Allstate president. Senior officers in charge of practically all major functions sit on the committee. As Issues Management Director, I am secretary to the committee and staff to the chairman.

The Issues Management Committee creates subcommittees to prepare situational analyses, impact analyses, and policy/support plan recommendations for each issue cluster. These subcommittees are interdepartmental, composed of officers and managers considered the most expert in the issue areas. As

Issues Management Director, I have responsibility for coordination between the subcommittees and full committees.

What tangible results have you witnessed as a result of issues management in your organization?

Both line and staff operations have reflected policy decisions made by the senior committee—from products and services to investments and public affairs.

How can a firm begin to organize for issues management?

To get the full benefit of an issues management process, which is a tool for the use of the chief executive officer, it should be created at the top of the company. A matrix committee of senior officers seems the best form. Senior management below the chief executive officer level should be responsible for the work; the chief executive officer for final approval and any adjustments necessary to fit the overall plans of the institution. This approach prevents interdepartmental rivalries, territorial fights, etc. The issues management staff can be officed in public relations, public affairs, government relations, or the planning departments.

Is there anything else you'd like readers of this book to know?

Every public relations practitioner should consider issues management as a potential career path and seek the broader work experiences that will prepare him for it. The psychic income is enormous; the financial income is commensurate.

Deal with both vulnerabilities and opportunities. Most issues, anticipated well in advance, offer both opportunities and vulnerabilities for organizations. For example, in assessing promised budget cuts, an insurance company might anticipate that less money will mean fewer people driving and therefore fewer accident claims. This would mark an opportunity.

On the other hand, promised budget cuts might mean that more people are unable to pay their premiums. This, clearly, is a vulnerability that a sharp company should anticipate well in advance.

Assessing such opportunities and vulnerabilities can play a significant role in determining an organization's philanthropic contributions. For instance, if demographic and economic projections indicate the closing of a particular field office, philanthropic contributions in the community in advance of the closing may help cushion the ultimate blow when the firm departs.

Plan from the outside-in. The external environment—not internal strategies— dictates priority issues selected. This differs from the normal strategic planning approach, which, to a large degree, is driven by internal strengths and objectives. Issues management is very much driven by external factors.

Profit line orientation. While many people tend to look at issues management as anticipating crises, its real purpose should be to defend the organization in the light of external factors as well as to enhance the firm's business by seizing imminent opportunities.

Action timetable. While the issues management process must identify emerging issues and selectively set them in priority order, it also must propose policy, programs, and an implementation timetable to deal with the issues. *Action* is the key to an effective issues management process.

Dealing from the top. Just as a public relations department is powerless without the confidence and respect of top management, so too is it essential that the issues management process operate with the imprimatur of the chief executive. The chief executive's personal sanction is critical to the acceptance and conduct of issues management within a firm.

ROLE OF THE CHIEF EXECUTIVE

No spokesperson has as much public clout as the chief executive officer (CEO). Traditionally, chief executives have been grossly outmatched in influencing public policy. As Howard Chase has put it, "It's no accident that the average American is hard-pressed to name even one important industrial executive. . . . Yet almost everybody recognizes the name of Ralph Nader."[5]

To combat this situation, today's chiefs have stepped up their role in helping form public policy. Many CEOs, especially of larger companies, have become active participants in public affairs, "willing to be interviewed, make speeches, offer public testimony, accept public assignment, and in general show themselves worthy of trust as leaders of important institutions."[6]

These CEOs have realized that to earn trust, they must become more open, forthright, and candid about their organizations, their industries, and themselves.

They have to help people gain a better understanding of what a business corporation is, how it operates, how it perceives its goals and responsibilities, how it views its priorities, how much profit it makes, and where that profit goes.[7]

As chief executives have turned increasingly toward the "management of externalities," so too have public relations departments turned to organizing issues management programs to support the work of their CEOs.

ORGANIZING FOR ISSUES MANAGEMENT

Although in many companies issues management is treated as an informal, ad hoc activity, other corporations have formalized the process to regularly involve specific sectors of the organization (see Figure 22–2). Essentially, issues management breaks down into four basic elements:

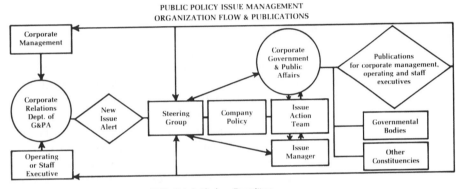

PUBLIC POLICY ISSUE MANAGEMENT
ORGANIZATION FLOW & PUBLICATIONS

KEY: ☐ Individuals or Committees
○ Corporate Government and Public Affairs
◇ Publications

FIGURE 22–2. *Issues management process.* This diagram traces the process at PPG Industries. It pictures the process flow, the principles involved, and the publications used.

SOURCE: Courtesy of the Public Affairs Council.

1 **Identifying Issues and Trends** Issue identification can be accomplished through traditional research techniques as well as more informal methods. Understandably, companies are more concerned with issues that affect them directly. For example, Standard Oil of California organized an extensive campaign to refute criticism of the petroleum industry's use of toxic substances believed to cause cancer. Steel companies, Bethlehem and U.S. Steel, attempted to mobilize public opinion to protest government policies allowing "dumping" of low-priced, foreign steel in the United States.

One way to keep informed of what is being said about a company, industry, or issue is to subscribe to issues-oriented publications of every political persuasion—from *Mother Jones* and *The Village Voice* on the far left to The Liberty Lobby's *Spotlight* on the far right.

2 **Evaluating Issue Impact and Setting Priorities** Evaluation and analysis may be handled by "issues" committees within an organization. Committees can set priorities for issues management action. At the Upjohn Company, for exam-

ple, a senior policy committee (composed of managers in each of the firm's major divisions, as well as public affairs and legal staff members) meets quarterly to set issues priorities.

3 Establishing a Company Position   Establishing a position can be a formal process. After the Upjohn senior policy committee has met and decided on issues, Upjohn's public affairs staff prepares policy statements on each topic. At PPG Industries, individual "issues managers" prepare position papers for executive review on topics of direct concern.

4 Designing Company Action and Response to Achieve Results   The best organized companies for issues management orchestrate integrated responses to achieve results. Typically, companies may coordinate their Washington offices, state lobbying operations, management speeches, advertising messages, and employee communications to forward the firm's point of view.

PUBLIC RELATIONS ROLE

The public relations practitioner can successfully manage the public issues process within a company. Public relations is ideally situated between the public and management; its access both to top management and to outside information makes it the logical focus of such a program.

Public relations also has special advantages in gathering information on issues—internal and external contacts, a sensitivity to external forces, and the ability to articulate ideas. While huge corporations have thus far taken the lead in issues management, one smaller firm, Rexnord, stands out as having formulated a well-developed issues management program. At Rexnord, public relations sits in the "issues management catbird seat." Here's Rexnord's checklist for public relations input in the issues management process:

- Identify and list 100 or more issues.
- Seek out the concerns of other managers about particular issues.
- Categorize those issues.
- Start a central issue file. Let people know where it is.
- Determine issues relevant to the corporation and investigate them in depth.
- Assign priorities to these issues.
- Circulate the issues for management input.
- Learn what other institutions are doing.
- List plans to cause action on the issues.
- Begin a speakers' bureau.
- Determine whether a formal public affairs program is needed to get things rolling.
- Present selected issues at appropriate meetings, e.g., sales meetings, management meetings, and financial meetings.
- Encourage issue-oriented speeches and articles; merchandise them.
- Send letters on the issues to employees, retirees, and shareholders.
- Contact elected officials on the issues.[8]

IDENTIFYING EMERGING ISSUES

No element in the issues management process is more important than identifying salient issues of concern to the organization. In recent years, issues have seemed to affect firms in three separate arenas:

Those aimed at individual companies.   For example, Ford's Pinto gas tanks, Firestone's 500 radials, Allied Chemical's Kepone, Con Ed's problems in New York, and automotive recalls.

Those aimed at whole industries.   The electric utility industry and the mass protest against building nuclear power plants; the effects of TV advertising on children, and how those ads affect the toy, candy, and breakfast food industries; the aerosol industry and the effects of fluorocarbons on the ozone; attacks by women against the insurance and banking industries for their hiring practices.

Those that deal with a larger public interest.   Some industries are caught up in broad arguments about national policy. One only need look at the names of the groups involved in lobbying efforts to determine who's under fire: Friends of the Earth, Action on Smoking and Health, Center for Auto Safety, Citizens for a Better Environment, Environmentalists for Full Employment, Natural Resources Defense Council.[9]

Often, it is groups like these that begin to initiate public policies. Businesses, in particular, must "steal the march" from such groups in influencing policy formation.

In responding to such issues, many firms have taken the approach of Union Carbide Corp, which concentrates its energies and resources on issues that affect its businesses in particular. As its public affairs director explained, "This serves not only to optimize limited resources but to support our credibility. We have no desire to be a corporate gadfly."[10]

Different organizations adopt different approaches to identifying emerging issues. At Alcoa, the first issues explored are those considered dominant by government, academic, and activist organizations. From this examination, about 150 unduplicated issues are chosen, which are then analyzed and separated into general issues categories. From there, key staff members are asked to assess "the top ten issues" with potential impact on Alcoa and its operations. A typical Alcoa priority list would consist of issues in such general categories as economic policy, energy, environment, government policy, health and safety, human resources, tax, trade, productivity and innovation, and a number of other similar generic categories.[11]

ISSUES OF THE DAY

It is unlikely that the debate will diminish soon on such issues as consumerism, energy and environment, health and nutrition, corporate social responsibilities, minority rights, peace and disarmament, and the proper role of the American enterprise system.

We help form public policy.

Corporations are essentially public institutions. The health of the enterprise is largely contingent upon public opinion.

Our role is to serve as counselor, coordinator and catalyst in relations between companies, trade associations and foreign countries and the publics with which they are involved. We clarify the issues. We formulate programs. We communicate the message. And we help form public policy.

In this work we are involved in some of the most important public policy issues of our time.

Our continuing program in the case of landing rights for the supersonic transport Concorde helped to balance questions raised by environmentalists with those who recognize the issues of the speed, efficiency and inevitability of supersonic transport and our traditional close diplomatic ties to England and France. The U.S. Supreme Court decision and the start of service at Kennedy is a gratifying development in this long and difficult campaign.

Our work on behalf of the R.J. Reynolds Tobacco Company is helping assess the potential impact of numerous public issues and concerns.

For the American Seat Belt Council we've helped to position the seat belt and air bag debate in a continuing effort to assure maximum life-saving at minimal cost.

One of the most critical issues of the day is energy conservation. Our efforts in behalf of Dow Chemical Company's Styrofoam brand insulation are helping to educate the public on the need to conserve limited energy resources.

A response to extreme and unfair attacks on sugar and candy with scientific evidence of the nutritional and energy-giving benefits of moderate use of confections is being sought in behalf of the National Confectioners Association.

For client EMI Medical, Inc., we are striving to put into proper perspective the purchase and utilization of the new body and head CAT scanners in the nation's hospitals, weighing the heavy unit costs against the great efficiency, time-saving and pain-saving benefits they provide in comparison to exploratory surgery.

Another continuing public policy problem involves the need for compromise in the area of environmental concerns. We no longer can accept air and water pollution in the name of industrial progress, but at the same time, we cannot sustain a technologically based society if we demand perfection. For Armour-Dial, Division of Greyhound, we interpreted to the community in the area of the company's large soap plant and to media people, government officials and employees the capital equipment program designed to minimize odors and purify discharged waste materials. In the field of nuclear power, for Commonwealth Edison, we interpreted the move toward meeting electricity needs through atomic energy to reduce industrial pollution and at the same time explained the safeguards built into the system.

These examples reflect the scope of our involvement in some of the broad public issues of our times.

EDELMAN

Daniel J. Edelman Inc.

221 N. LaSalle St. Chicago, IL 60601
711 Third Avenue New York, NY 10017
1901 Avenue of the Stars, Los Angeles, CA 90067
703 Market Street San Francisco, CA 94103
1730 Pennsylvania Ave. N.W. Suite 460, Washington, D.C. 20006
Stanhope House, Stanhope Place, London, W22HH, England
Beethovenstrasse 9/6000 Frankfurt, 1 Germany
and DJE International Group affiliates throughout the world.

Brochure available upon request.

FIGURE 22–3. *Public policy issues ad.* Public relations agencies must move quickly to take advantage of emerging communications opportunities. This ad, run by Daniel J. Edelman, Inc., emphasizes its role as one of the nation's leading public relations consultants.

SOURCE: Courtesy of Daniel J. Edelman.

Has America become shortsighted?

America once had a vision of its future.

And that vision led us to become the most productive nation on earth, with our citizens enjoying the highest standard of living of any nation in the world.

Today, inflation erodes our economic growth. Inadequate capital investment limits opportunity and undermines our international competitive position. Our companies are hard pressed to keep up with accelerating technological developments. Productivity has been growing much faster in other major industrial nations than it has in the United States.

Why has American economic performance slipped?

Essentially, we seem to have lost sight of what truly drives our economy and what is required to keep our products and services competitive in world markets. Worse, our vision of the future appears to have narrowed to include only that which is politically fashionable and expedient for the short-term.

It is politically fashionable, for example, to charge that company profits are too high...are a "windfall" ...or are even "obscene." Yet profits constitute the key support for expanding company facilities, financing new research and development, replacing outmoded and inefficient equipment and, ultimately, ensuring greater productivity, higher wages and more jobs.

It's also politically fashionable to demand greater governmental "safeguards," i.e. regulations on the activities of companies. Yet, each year, government regulations cost our society —both companies and individuals—about $100 billion. Much of which could be used instead for new plants, for new products, for new research, for new technology to create new jobs. All of which would make us more competitive in world markets.

It's politically expedient for government—in the interest of "protecting the general welfare"—to spend billions of taxpayer dollars on overregulation without fully weighing costs against benefits. Government overspending, and the resulting federal budget deficit, remains a primary cause of our nation's most serious problem, inflation.

Clearly, we must, as a nation, restore our vision and, with it, our productive capacity.

In the months ahead, we at Chase intend to speak out on the "productive capacity" question: on inflation, on profits, on government regulation, on business investment, on research and development.

Our reason for doing so is quite straightforward. If, as a nation, we are unable to revitalize our productive capacity, Chase's shareholders, customers and employees—together with millions of other Americans —will pay the price. It's a price we need not, and should not, have to pay.

So, we will speak out — as loudly and clearly as we can. We'll do it in our own self interest. And, we believe, in yours.

CHASE

FIGURE 22–4. *Chase eagle.* Companies like The Chase Manhattan Bank are not reluctant to exercise their first amendment rights with a new outspokenness on public issues of national and international concern.

SOURCE: Courtesy of The Chase Manhattan Bank.

In addition to these more general issues, some organizations have seized the "single issues" that seem today to dominate society. For example, while one business firm may launch a public issues program to influence the public's view on such general issues as inflation or recession, another might choose to deal with more specific issues such as gun control or abortion.

Conflicts on these and other issues will continue to be resolved in the public arena. Increasingly, business will seek to be represented, loudly and clearly, in influencing the debate on emerging issues. The debate will require better intellectual resources, better research, and a more sophisticated approach to "issues management" among organizations and their public relations practitioners.

Business firms, in particular, will have to take the offensive in championing more aggressive positions to deal with the arguments of their critics (see Figures 22-3 and 22-4). Reactive responses will not do; companies must be able to "stay in front" of emerging issues. In the years ahead, then, no task will be greater for America's companies and no challenge more significant for professional public relations practitioners than helping "manage" public policy.

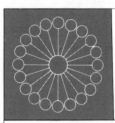

CASE STUDY
The Tylenol murders

For close to 100 years, Johnson & Johnson Company of New Brunswick, N.J. was the epitome of a well-managed, highly profitable, and tight-lipped consumer products manufacturer.

All that changed on the morning of September 30, 1982, when Johnson & Johnson (J&J) faced as devastating a public relations problem as had confronted any company in history. It was on that morning that Johnson & Johnson management learned that its premier product, Extra-Strength Tylenol, had been used as a murder weapon to kill three people.

In the days that followed, another three people died from swallowing Tylenol capsules loaded with cyanide. While all the cyanide deaths occurred in Chicago, reports from other parts of the country also implicated Extra-Strength Tylenol capsules with illnesses of various sorts.

While these latter reports later were proved to be unfounded, Johnson & Johnson and its Tylenol-producing subsidiary McNeil Consumer Products Co., were at the center of a public relations trauma, the likes of which few companies had ever experienced.

Tylenol had been an astoundingly profitable product for Johnson & Johnson. It had been promoted since 1960 as an alternative pain reliever for aspirin. At the time of the Tylenol murders, the product held 35 percent of the $1 billion analgesic market. It contributed an estimated 7 percent to J&J's worldwide sales and almost 20 percent to its profits.

Throughout the years, Johnson & Johnson had not been—and hadn't needed to be—a particularly "high profile" company. Its chairman, James E.

Burke, with the company almost 30 years, had never appeared on television and had rarely participated in print interviews.

Johnson & Johnson management, understandably, was caught totally by surprise when the news hit. Initially, Johnson & Johnson had no facts, and indeed, learned much of its information from the media calls that inundated the firm from the beginning. The company recognized that it needed the media to get out as much information to the public as quickly as possible and in so doing, attempt to prevent a panic. Therefore, almost immediately, Johnson & Johnson made a key decision—to open its doors to the media.

The second day of the crisis, in fact, Johnson & Johnson discovered that an earlier statement that no cyanide was used on its premises was wrong. The company didn't hesitate. Its public relations department quickly announced that the earlier information it had conveyed was false. While the reversal embarrassed the company briefly, Johnson & Johnson's openness was hailed and made up for any damage to its credibility.

Early on in the crisis, the company was largely convinced that the poisonings didn't occur at any of its plants. Nonetheless, Johnson & Johnson recalled an entire lot of 93,000 bottles of Extra-Strength Tylenol associated with the reported murders. In the process, it telegrammed warnings to doctors, hospitals, and distributors at a cost of half a million dollars. McNeil also suspended all Tylenol advertising to reduce attention on the product.

By the second day, the company was convinced that the tampering had taken place during Chicago distribution and not in the manufacturing process. Therefore, a total Tylenol recall did not seem obligatory. Nonetheless, Chairman Burke worried about "the extent to which Johnson & Johnson was becoming deeply involved in the affair. The public was learning that Tylenol was a Johnson & Johnson product and the dilemma was how to protect the name and not incite whomever did this to attack other Johnson & Johnson products."[12]

Burke himself leaned toward immediately recalling all Extra-Strength Tylenol capsules. However, after consulting with the Federal Bureau of Investigation, the J&J chairman decided not to recall all capsules. The FBI was worried that a precipitous recall would encourage "copycat" poisoning attempts. However, five days later, when a copycat strychnine poisoning occurred in California, Johnson & Johnson recalled all Extra-Strength Tylenol capsules—31 million bottles at a cost of over $100 million.

Although it knew it had done nothing wrong, J&J resisted the temptation to disclaim any possible connection between its product and the murders. Rather, even as it moved quickly to trace the lot numbers of the poisoned packages, it also posted a $100,000 reward for the killer.

Nor did the company yield to the temptation to pillory the media, not even when sensation-seekers tried to link a suicide in Philadelphia to the murders in Chicago. Nor did the company rail back at a publicity-seeking Chicago prosecutor, in the midst of an election race, who seized media time to link Tylenol with death and warn the electorate to avoid the product.

Through it all, at the eye of the hurricane, Johnson & Johnson executives remained calm. They communicated the message that "the company was candid, contrite and compassionate, committed to solving the murders and protecting the public."[13]

Through advertisements promising to exchange tablets for capsules, through thousands of letters to the trade, and through statements to the media, the company hoped to put the incident into proper perspective.

At the same time, Johnson & Johnson commissioned a nationwide opinion survey to assess the implications to consumers of the Tylenol poisonings. The good news was that 87 percent of Tylenol users surveyed said they realized the maker of Tylenol was not responsible for the deaths. The bad news was that although a high percentage didn't blame Tylenol, 61 percent still said they were not likely to buy Extra-Strength Tylenol capsules in the future. In other words, while most consumers knew it wasn't Tylenol's fault, they still feared using the product.

But Chairman Burke and Johnson & Johnson weren't about to knuckle under to the deranged saboteurs who poisoned their product. Despite predictions of the imminent demise of Extra-Strength Tylenol, Johnson & Johnson decided to relaunch the product in a new triple, safety-sealed, tamper-resistant package. Many on Wall Street and in the marketing community were stunned by Johnson & Johnson's bold decision.

But so confident was Johnson & Johnson management that it launched an all-out media blitz to make sure people understood its commitment. Chairman Burke appeared on the widely-watched Phil Donahue network television program and skillfully handled sixty minutes of intense public questioning. The investigative news program "60 Minutes"—the scourge of corporate America— was invited by Johnson & Johnson to film its executive strategy sessions to prepare for the new launch. When the program was aired, reporter Mike Wallace concluded that while Wall Street was ready at first to write off the company, it was now "hedging its bets" because of J&J's stunning campaign of facts, money, the media, and truth."[14]

Johnson & Johnson also concentrated on convincing the medical community that its individual users would stay with the product. McNeil aired a special 60-second television commercial of its medical director stressing that the poisonings occurred only in the Chicago area and involved only Tylenol *capsules* not tablets. McNeil also sent about two million pieces of literature to doctors, dentists, nurses, and pharmacists to spread the word that the company's factories weren't the source of the poisonings. The message also asked recipients to help reassure patients and customers that Tylenol in tablet, liquid, or chewable forms wasn't at risk.

Finally, on November 11, slightly more than two months after the murders, Tylenol management held an elaborate video press conference in New York beamed to additional locations around the country to introduce the new Extra-Strength Tylenol package.

Presiding at that news conference, Chairman Burke reviewed what the company had done in the midst of its trauma, introduced plans to resuscitate the product with new packaging, thanked the media for its general understanding and reporting of the facts throughout the crisis, and then called on the press to help Tylenol get a fair chance. At the press conference, Burke referred to the Johnson & Johnson "Credo," conceived by the son of the company's founder, as a key factor in the firm's ultimate decision to stick with Tylenol. (See accompanying figures.)

TRIPLE SAFETY-SEALED, tamper-resistant package for TYLENOL capsules has (1) glued flaps on the outer box, (2) a tight plastic neck seal and (3) a strong inner foil seal over the mouth of the bottle. A bright yellow label on the bottle is imprinted with red letters warning, "Do not use if safety seals are broken."

Our Credo

We believe our first responsibility is to the doctors, nurses and patients,
to mothers and all others who use our products and services.
In meeting their needs everything we do must be of high quality.
We must constantly strive to reduce our costs
in order to maintain reasonable prices.
Customers' orders must be serviced promptly and accurately.
Our suppliers and distributors must have an opportunity
to make a fair profit.

We are responsible to our employees,
the men and women who work with us throughout the world.
Everyone must be considered as an individual.
We must respect their dignity and recognize their merit.
They must have a sense of security in their jobs.
Compensation must be fair and adequate,
and working conditions clean, orderly and safe.
Employees must feel free to make suggestions and complaints.
There must be equal opportunity for employment, development
and advancement for those qualified.
We must provide competent management,
and their actions must be just and ethical.

We are responsible to the communities in which we live and work
and to the world community as well.
We must be good citizens — support good works and charities
and bear our fair share of taxes.
We must encourage civic improvements and better health and education.
We must maintain in good order
the property we are privileged to use,
protecting the environment and natural resources.

Our final responsibility is to our stockholders.
Business must make a sound profit.
We must experiment with new ideas.
Research must be carried on, innovative programs developed
and mistakes paid for.
New equipment must be purchased, new facilities provided
and new products launched.
Reserves must be created to provide for adverse times.
When we operate according to these principles,
the stockholders should realize a fair return.

Johnson & Johnson

Said Tylenol's chairman to the media:

It is our job at Johnson & Johnson to ensure the survival of Tylenol, and we are pledged to do this. While we consider this crime an assault on society, we are nevertheless ready to fulfill our responsibility, which includes paying the price of this heinous crime. But I urge you not to make Tylenol the scapegoat.

I am confident that the news media, working in its own way and according to its own dictates, will help us to dispel these fears about a product that rightfully earned the confidence of the public. We welcome any help we can get from you and others in the vast rebuilding task that lies ahead.[15]

Regardless of the ultimate success of its reintroduction of Extra-Strength Tylenol capsules, Johnson & Johnson had won a major victory on the public relations front. Summarized *The Washington Post*, "Serving the public interest has simultaneously saved the company's reputation. That lesson in public responsibilities—and public relations—will survive at J&J regardless of what happens to Tylenol."[16]

By late December 1982, Johnson & Johnson reported that Tylenol, in a limited test, had recaptured an astounding 95 percent of its prior market share. Morale at the company, according to its chairman, was "higher than in years."[17]

QUESTIONS

1 What might have been the consequences if Johnson & Johnson had decided to "tough out" the initial report of Tylenol-related deaths and not recall the product?

2 Had you been Johnson & Johnson's public relations director, what response would you have suggested to the false rumors disseminated by over-eager journalists and politicians, which popped up immediately after the reported deaths?

3 Johnson & Johnson's public relations strategy was one of "total openness." What alternative public relations strategies did the company have?

4 What specific lessons can be derived from the way in which Johnson & Johnson handled the public relations aspects of this tragedy?

5 Do you think the company made a wise decision by reintroducing Extra-Strength Tylenol?

NOTES

1 "Issues Management, 1976–1982, A Reprise," *Corporate Public Issues*, Vol. VII, No. 12, 15 June 1982, p. 2.

2 Paul Cathey, "Industry Has a New Advance Guard—Issue Managers," *Iron Age*, 23 April 1982, p. 64.

3 "Issue Management Conference—A Special Report," *Corporate Public Issues*, Vol. VII, No. 23, 1 December 1982, pp. 1–2.

4 *Public Affairs Councils, The Fundamentals of Issues Management*, 1220 16th Street, N.W., Washington, D.C.: Author 1978.

5 W. Howard Chase, "Adjusting to a Different Business/Social Climate," *Administrative Management,* January 1979, p. 46

6 Robert L. Fegley, "When Your Chief Executive Goes Public," speech delivered to the Public Relations Society of America, New Orleans, La., November 15, 1978.

7 David H. Simon, "External Pressures on the CEO: Worse Than an Excedrin Headache," *Public Relations Quarterly,* Winter 1981–82, p. 9.

8 David L. Shanks, "Ready for the Issues?" *Enterprise,* February 1979, pp. 13–14.

9 Kalman B. Druck, "Dealing with Exploding Social and Political Forces," speech delivered before Houston Chapter, Public Relations Society of America, Houston, Texas, September 11, 1978. Reprinted in *Vital Speeches of the Day* 45, no. 4 (1 December 1978): 110–114.

10 Paul Cathey, *op. cit.*

11 "Alcoa's Public Issues Survey," *Corporate Public Issues,* Vol. VII, No. 14, 15 July 1982, pp. 1–3.

12 Thomas Moore, "The Fight to Save Tylenol," *Fortune,* 29 November 1982, p. 48.

13 Jerry Knight, "Tylenol's Maker Shows How to Respond to Crisis," *The Washington Post,* 11 October 1982, p. 1 "Washington Business."

14 "60 Minutes," CBS-TV, 19 December 1982.

15 Remarks by James E. Burke, chairman, Johnson & Johnson, at video news conference, New York City, 11 November 1982.

16 Jerry Knight, *The Washington Post,* op. cit.

17 Michael Waldholz, "Tylenol Regains Most of No. 1 Market Share, Amazing Doomsayers," *The Wall Street Journal,* 24 December 1982, pp. 1, 19.

SUGGESTED READING

Chase, W. Howard, ed. *Corporate Public Issues.* Semimonthly newsletter. (Available from Geyer-McAllister Publications, 51 Madison Ave., New York, N.Y. 10010.)

Detwiler, Richard M. "The Myths Of Persuasion," *Public Relations Journal,* April 1982, pp. 52–54.

Drucker, Peter. *Management: Tasks, Responsibilities, Practices.* New York: Harper & Row, 1974.

Federal Register. (Available from Superintendents of Documents, Government Printing Office, Washington, D.C. 20402.) The *Federal Register* provides a method of tracking rules and regulations from government agencies and keeping abreast of changes.

Fegley, Robert L. "How Public Relations Can Help The CEO," *Public Relations Journal,* October 1981, pp. 25–26.

The Fundamentals of Issue Management. Public Affairs Council monograph. (Available from 1220 16th St. N.W., Washington, D.C. 20036.)

Graff, Louis. "The Three Phenomena of Public Relations," *Public Relations Review,* Spring 1981, pp. 17–26.

Griswold, Denny, ed. *PR News.* (Available from *PR News,* 127 E. 80th St., New York, N.Y. 10021.) Weekly newsletter carrying industry news and case studies illustrating public relations problems and solutions.

"Guidelines for Public Relations Professionals," *Public Relations Journal,* January 1981, p. 33.

Lerbinger, Otto. *Designs for Persuasive Communications.* Englewood Cliffs, N.J.: Prentice-Hall, 1972.

Levy, Ronald N. "Public Policy Publicity: How to Do It," *Public Relations Journal,* June 1975, pp. 19–21.

Lukasik, Dr. S. J. "Information For Decision Making," *Public Relations Quarterly,* Fall 1981, pp. 19–22.

O'Dwyer, Jack, ed. *Jack O'Dwyer's Newsletter.* Weekly newsletter. (Available from 271 Madison Ave., New York, N.Y. 10016.)

PR Reporter. Weekly newsletter. (Available from Box 600, Exeter, N.H. 03833.)

Publicist. Bi-monthly. (Available from 221 Park Avenue South, New York, N.Y. 10003.)

Public Relations Review. Quarterly. (Available from the Foundation for Public Relations Research and Education, University of Maryland, College of Journalism, College Park, Md. 20742.)

Simon, David H. "External Pressures on The CEO: Worse Than an Excedrin Headache," *Public Relations Quarterly,* Winter 1981–82, pp. 9–12.

Weaver, Robert A. Jr. "Information Management For The Chief Executive," *Public Relations Quarterly,* Fall 1981, p. 23–25.

GROWTH IN THE 80s

23

The Future

Public relations counselor Philip Lesly, who chaired the Public Relations Society of America's "Task Force on Stature and Role of Public Relations," cited in Chapter One, has suggested that the final part of this century will be "dominated by the human climate—the attitudes of people that determine how all segments of society will function."[1]

Indeed, the "human climate" is now a determining factor in the future of every organization, institution, and nation. Emergence of the human climate as a dominant force in society creates significant opportunities and challenges for public relations.

On the one hand, the field is growing rapidly.

Public relations is a significant growth area in journalism schools; in 1981 there were 8,789 students enrolled and 2,340 graduated. The number of journalism school undergraduates studying public relations—about 10 percent of all journalism undergraduates—nearly doubled in less than five years.[2]

Enrollment in the Public Relations Society of America (PRSA), the field's professional association, is over 11,000. Another 600 new members are added annually. Public Relations Student Society of America today is composed of 123 chapters with 4,000 students. In 1968, there were six chapters and fifty-six students.

The U.S. Department of Labor says public relations jobs will increase faster than the average for all occupations through the 1980s "because of new spots and replacement of individuals who retire or leave the field for other reasons."[3]

The number of continuing education courses in public relations has increased exponentially. In 1971, New York University's continuing education programs in public relations, conducted jointly with PRSA, consisted of two classes and 59 students. By the end of the decade, the program boasted 39 separate courses with more than 1,200 students.[4]

Spending on public relations totals about $2 billion per year. In 1978, the thirty largest public relations agencies had net fee revenues of $140.4 million.[5]

On the other hand, public relations is faced with all the challenges associated with an increasingly popular field. Many want to enter the profession, and competition for most jobs is fierce. Then too, as management becomes more aware of the role of public relations, its performance expectations become greater. So the standards to which public relations professionals are held also have increased. Finally, since in most organizations access to top management is a coveted role and since public relations, by definition, generally is granted ready management access, key public relations positions today are eagerly sought by nonpublic relations managers.

BLOSSOMING OF PUBLIC RELATIONS

That public relations should flourish for the rest of this century can hardly be disputed. Perhaps the primary reason is the "pressure cooker" social and political environment in which institutions must operate today. This new environment, which particularly affects the business corporation, is being shaped by many factors:

○ A growing body of opinion that sees big business as a threat, especially because it has become more active politically.

○ On the trade front, a pronounced swing toward protectionism.

○ Legislative proposals emphasizing job ownership, employee rights, and corporate governance are attracting new adherents.

○ "Product stewardship," an idea that would hold a manufacturer responsible for products in perpetuity, is gaining advocacy.

○ Litigation in a whole variety of areas is reshaping the ground rules of the workplace.[6]

To make matters worse, the public seems to be losing confidence in institutions, particularly business corporations. One 1979 study revealed that only 22 percent of the general population "had confidence in business leadership," down from 55 percent at the beginning of the decade.[7] Clearly, in such a threatening environment, managements require as much thoughtful counsel in dealing with internal and external "political issues" as they do in dealing with more traditional economic influences.

CHALLENGE FOR THE 80s: COUNSELING MANAGEMENT

One reason the remainder of this century promises to mark the most exciting period in public relations history is that chief executive officers will be paying more attention to public relations counsel. Indeed, the CEO can hardly afford to do otherwise.

As Robert L. Fegley, 1979 recipient of the "PR Professional of the Year" award from *Public Relations News,* put it:

Chief executives today need people to help them orchestrate their appearances, develop and articulate their themes, build their media connections, research the issues, develop their positions, and express themselves persuasively. They need counsel on trends and problems among their various constituencies. Public relations people, trained to mediate between the institution and its publics in communications, are peculiarly qualified to help our leaders to lead. And this is true for organizations of all kinds—not only business firms, but government agencies, hospitals, universities, not-for-profit organizations, whatever.[8]

Unlike past decades, when top managers were, by necessity, more concerned with the production, marketing, or financial sides of the business, external pressures today necessitate "a much greater need for businessmen to understand the broad environment in which they operate and to communicate to unfamiliar publics what they can do and are doing to meet public demands."[9] To do this, management must rely more heavily on public relations practitioners to better articulate ideas in the never-ending battle to sway public opinion.

PUBLIC RELATIONS AND THE LAW

In recent years, public relations has been influenced by various court decisions affecting both an organization's right to be heard and its right to be protected against libel.

Because their legal rights to speak out were unclear, business corporations and other institutions traditionally maintained "low profiles" in participating in the public dialogue. Increasingly, the courts have clarified the issue in favor of companies being allowed to publicly express their positions.

In a landmark 1978 case, the Supreme Court struck down a Massachusetts law that permitted a business corporation to speak only on those issues "that materially affect its business, property, or assets." In the case (*First National Bank of Boston et. al. v. Bellotti*), the Court held that companies had the right to spend corporate funds to publicize their opposing views to a referendum to authorize the state legislature to enact a graduated personal income tax.

While the Supreme Court did not attempt to generalize beyond the limits of the *Bellotti* case, the judgment indicated a trend to protect corporations that want to speak out on public issues.

Two other recent Supreme Court decisions further buttress the rights of corporations to speak out. In 1981, the Court struck down a Berkeley, California ordinance limiting to $250 contributions that could be made to individuals and corporations formed to oppose or support local referenda. In 1982, the Court defeated a $1,000 limitation on expenditures by political committees during Presidential elections.

Before joining Monsanto in 1976, Mr. Nolan had been a newspaper editor and correspondent with *The New York Times* and United Press International, a professor of Journalism and Public Affairs at the University of South Carolina, and a senior communications manager at The Chase Manhattan Bank and RCA Corporation. *Business Week* magazine cited him as one of the "Top 10 Executives in Corporate Public Relations." Mr. Nolan has lectured extensively and written articles on public relations and advertising as well as other business subjects in numerous major publications.

What are the most significant challenges that confront the public relations profession?

Gaining management's confidence by providing high-quality advice and being able to measure the results with greater precision than is now being done.

What do you see as the future of public relations education?

More emphasis on the social sciences such as economics, social psychology, and sociology, and less on developing techniques and understanding gadgetry.

What do you see as the prospects for growth in employment in the public relations profession?

Joseph T. Nolan is Vice President, Public Affairs, for Monsanto Company with overall responsibility for public and government relations, advertising, community affairs, and social responsibility. He is a member of Monsanto's Corporate Administrative Committee, the firm's senior policy advisory group, as well as the Environmental Policy and Social Responsibility Committees.

In the area of libel, several recent cases have struck new ground.

○ In 1982, the Philadelphia CBS affiliate was hit with a $5.1 million libel suit by Mayor William Green, when the station aired an erroneous report that Green was the target of a Federal grand-jury investigation of an alleged $50,000 kickback in return for millions of dollars in sludge-removal contracts.

○ CBS-TV itself was hit by a $120 million libel suit filed by Army General William C. Westmoreland, over a 1982 documentary that accused the general of falsifying

I think that employment will expand steadily, but not explosively, over the next decade or two as more and more enterprises understand what public relations can do to help them.

What parts of the field do you see as growth areas in the 80s and beyond?

Both investor and employee relations are likely to increase, but I think that one of the biggest areas of growth will be in dealing with television in all of its aspects. Surveys show that perhaps 80 percent of the public gets its news through television, and yet virtually all public relations departments suffer from a serious "print bias."

What parts of the profession do you see as becoming more limited in available opportunities?

I suspect we've reached the saturation point in the placement area.

What are the greatest threats to the future of public relations?

Inept practitioners—men and women who don't understand thoroughly the enterprise they're trying to represent.

Do you envision that public relations practitioners will be called upon to manage organizations in the future?

The best of the public relations practitioners will move up to top management roles just as marketing specialists, engineers, and lawyers have done in the past.

Will public relations ever attain the same stature as the professions of law or accounting?

If public relations keeps working at its accreditation procedure, improving it as it goes along, and does a better job of policing its ranks, it could very well eventually achieve a place alongside accounting, law, and the other professions. This would be an important development, but its importance should not be exaggerated. The only way to get this kind of stature is to merit it, and that must be done over and over again.

What are the emerging trends you foresee in public relations over the next 20 years?

The most formidable challenge of the rest of the 80s is likely to be managing the new business environment. The decisive issues will be external rather than internal, social and political rather than economic. The pivotal test is making profits for the stockholders and quality products at reasonable prices. The challenge will come primarily from the impact of laws and public opinion.

By the year 2000, what do you predict will be the general state of the practice of public relations?

I predict that major organizations will have a public relations practitioner very near the top, and that they will weigh every major decision in light of its public relations impact just as they do now with respect to its business and financial impact.

enemy troop strengths in Vietnam. After the suit was filed, CBS launched its own internal investigation of the Westmoreland show and found numerous improprieties in the production process.

○ Also in 1982, the *Washington Post* initially lost a $2 million suit after a Federal jury decided that the newspaper libeled William P. Tavoulareas when it alleged that he had used his position as president of Mobil Oil to further his son's career in a shipping business (see Figure 23-1). In May 1983, a federal judge overturned the libel verdict against the Post because the article in question didn't contain "knowing lies or statements made in wreckless regard of the truth." Perhaps as a harbinger of things to come, Mobil in early 1983 took out a highly unusual protection policy against media attacks: defamation insurance. Under the policy, Mobil executives who believe they have been defamed by the media can be reimbursed for most of the legal expenses of bringing the case to court.

"It's a great commentary on our times when a jury finds for an oil company against a newspaper."

Frederick Taylor
Executive Editor, The Wall Street Journal.
quoted in Newsweek. October 25, 1982

To avoid any misquotation, we wrote Mr. Taylor and asked him if the quote were accurate. His entire reply was the following: "I said it. And you can use it."

For several reasons, we think the statement reflects an astonishing degree of irresponsibility—particularly since Mr. Taylor is the Executive Editor of such a prestigious publication. Specifically—

ONE. The statement was made in reference to a unanimous verdict by a jury which found that *The Washington Post* and two reporters had libeled the President of Mobil. This was a personal suit, brought by him as an individual, which he totally paid for himself, to which Mobil was not a party. The jury did not "find for" Mobil. We seriously doubt that Mr. Taylor was unaware of this distinction. After all, his paper provided coverage of the case and clearly reported its private

nature. It was an attempt to substitute a giant oil company as the Goliath attacking the "David-like" *Washington Post.* (Some David!) It was an attempt to erase the fact that the issue in the case involved damage to an individual's reputation. No oil company was involved.

TWO. Even worse, the statement seems to betray a shocking bias. It appears to us that Mr. Taylor thinks oil companies are so venal, so inherently evil that no matter what injustices a newspaper might heap upon them, they should not prevail in a court of law before a jury.

Is Mr. Taylor suggesting that oil companies and their executives be stripped of their civil rights? Or that newspapers should be free to knowingly print false information about them? And, finally, should such behavior be immune from liability?

Mobil

FIGURE 23–1. *Mobil libel suit ad.* The 1982 libel verdict against the *Washington Post* and in favor of the president of Mobil Oil and his son was a chilling one to journalists. In a three column article, in fact, *Wall Street Journal* executive editor Frederick Taylor blamed the verdict on the growing public disenchantment with the press. Mobil, almost immediately, responded to Taylor's charge with this ad.
SOURCE: Courtesy of Mobil Corporation.

All these cases were symptomatic of a growing trend toward organizations becoming more vocal not only in the courts but also in paid advertisements, issue-oriented publications, employee and shareholder information programs, speakers bureaus, and the like. Indeed, with professionals such as lawyers and doctors now given the legal authority to advertise, the challenge to public relations practitioners in organizing such programs will be to carefully avoid appearing to dominate the public marketplace of ideas.

The remainder of this decade will necessitate that public relations professionals become more familiar with certain facets of the law, particularly in the areas of libel, first amendment freedoms, and the laws of federal agencies such as the Securities and Exchange Commission and the Federal Trade Commission.

IMPLICATIONS FOR PROFESSIONALS

The likelihood of greater opportunities in public relations will increase the pressure on practitioners for competence and professionalism in all their activities.

With the role of public relations becoming more important, the domain of public relations counselors is being invaded by nonpractitioners. Some companies, in fact, have turned to lawyers, financial specialists, economists, and operating executives to manage corporate programs. In the 1980s and 90s, practitioners must become immersed in the business of their institutions and their managements, while at the same time commanding a thorough knowledge of the technical aspects of their own field.

Public relations also will have to win the acceptance of management as a true profession and integral part of the management process. To do so, professionals must be willing to handle the most critical public issues confronting their institutions. Only when managements instinctively turn to counsel to solve the more thorny public issues will public relations achieve a universally respected professional status.

This status will help insulate the profession from the severe economic swings to which it has been so sensitive in the past. Frequently, in times of recession, public relations was among the first areas within an organization to feel the axe of budget cuts and staff reductions. In recent years, the profession has made great strides to ensconce itself as a permanent fixture on the organization chart, one equal to production, distribution, and finance. While many CEOs today properly recognize public relations for its long-term contributions, further "missionary work" must be done before practitioners can feel comfortable in times of economic stress.

As a profession that attempts, as part of its mandate, to champion the cause of social responsibility and affirmative action, public relations in the 1980s also must continue to serve as an example of equal employment opportunity. Indeed, a growing number of public relations professionals are women. Fully 36 percent of PRSA's members are women. One executive recruiter predicts, "Over the next twenty years, more than half the labor force in public relations might well be women."[10]

Bearing this out, the fastest growing communications group in recent years has been Women In Communications, Inc. (WICI), founded in 1909 by Theta Sigma Phi, college honorary society for women. WICI has passed the 12,000-member mark and is larger than either the Public Relations Society of America or the International Association of Business Communicators.

FEATURE
Public relations tips for the 80s

The following eleven guidelines for public relations professionals in the 1980s were gleaned from presentations at the National Conference of the Public Relations Society of America in Atlanta in 1981:[11]

1 Be cognizant of the new government public and of the voter demands that brought about the Reagan victory.

2 Go beyond leadership styles to separate the content of the two dynamics that underlie all human value systems: the need for growth through meaningful work and the need to avoid the pain of making a living.

3 Provide comprehensive analysis, guidance and counsel, cooperation with other groups within the organization, and effective internal and external communications.

4 Master computerized information systems and find new ways to use them.

5 Learn the strengths and weaknesses of the new communications technology and how it affects media relations and internal communications.

6 Learn to assess long-term trends, determine policy, shape responses to emerging issues.

7 Inform less and educate more, talk and write less and listen more, do less broadcasting and more narrowcasting.

8 Educate top management to handle media more effectively.

9 Learn to form liaisons with other civilizations and cultures.

10 Use the public relations audit and provide for follow-up studies.

11 View professional development as a continuing investment in human capital.

Critics contend that public relations is an "easy dumping ground" for a firm interested in fulfilling its government equal-employment opportunity quotas. While there may be some truth in this accusation, nevertheless, public relations must continue to offer diverse and challenging opportunities for women and minorities in the future.

LANDING A PUBLIC RELATIONS JOB

The most difficult assignment for any public relations practitioner these days is finding an appropriate job.

As noted, managements pay more for public relations people today and therefore expect more. Competition for public relations positions is fierce. Experience is at a premium. And for each job available, hundreds may apply.

FIGURE 23–2. *Return of King Kong.* In the spring of 1983, the legendary King Kong made a brief but triumphant return to the 88th Floor of the Empire State Building in New York City. The 2,600-pound, 84-foot fabric ape logged over 5,000 newspaper clippings and several hundred television appearances for its sponsor, Robert Keith and Co., Inc. of San Diego. (Which may explain why this is one grinning gorilla.)

COURTESY: Robert Keith and Co., Inc.

Therefore, any public relations job applicant today must have a "strategic approach" to landing a job. Basically, such an approach includes three aspects: the job search, the resume, and the interview. Here are hints in organizing each phase:

JOB SEARCH

Be Focused.

○ Select industries or companies in which you are most interested and with which you may be most familiar.
○ Select speciality areas in which you have experience, e.g. consumer relations, internal communications, speechwriting, graphic arts, etc.; don't be an "unfocused generalist."

Stress Your Strengths.

○ Choose aspects in your background that qualify you for a particular position, such as a facility with language or travel experience.

Know What They're Looking For.

○ Research the specific job before you apply.
○ Find out about the industry, the company, and its management.
○ If you can, find out about the interviewer and anticipate his needs.

RESUME

1 Target it to your potential employer, providing the information he needs to properly evaluate you as a candidate.
2 The "who, what, where, and when" data is essential, but the reasons "why" can be the ice-breaker. Ergo, a brief background of a particular problem and how you helped solve it might be most revealing.
3 Don't be gimmicky. Be straightforward and succinct.
4 Don't mention anything about salary. That comes later.
5 Use a standard form of listing job experience in reverse chronological order and be certain to include all pertinent information such as dates, titles, and most importantly, descriptions of your functions.
6 Point up your strengths and omit your weaknesses. Note areas of in-depth knowledge.
7 Stick to the facts. Leave out the adjectives.
8 Proofread. Proofread. Proofread. If there's a typo, you may be ipso facto out-of-luck.
9 Edit. Limit the resume to one page—a maximum of two—no matter how extensive your background. Some say it should *not* be printed or put on colored stock. The real point is as long as it's neat, clean, and brief, interviewers will read it.
10 While a resume is important, it's only an introduction. Its purpose is to "get you through the door." Period.[12]

INTERVIEW

Pre-interview.

○ Arrive five to ten minutes early so you can relax in the outer office, collect your thoughts, and be refreshed when it's time to go.

○ Look businesslike when you arrive and carry an attache case or briefcase that includes job-getting documents (such as a resumé, a portfolio of writing samples, reference letters, and so on), paper, and pen.

○ Introduce yourself courteously to the secretary and state the purpose of your business.

○ Pronounce the interviewer's name correctly. If you're not sure, ask the secretary.

Interview opening.

○ Greet the interviewer by name and apply a firm handshake.

○ Don't smoke.

○ Allow the interviewer to open the conversation, thus showing your "respect" for her authority.

○ Listen closely to the interviewer and respond accordingly, carefully injecting your own thoughts into the conversation.

Interview development.

○ After a few minutes of opening remarks, begin to develop your sales presentation.

○ Work on scoring points in the limited time available.

○ Be confident not cocky, loose not loud, aggressive not aggravating.

○ Control the interview without being overbearing. After all, it's you—not the interviewer—who wants the job.

Interview closing.

○ Close on a "high note", e.g. summarize a few key credentials in a final statement, express enthusiasm about working for the company, and express appreciation for an interesting chat.

○ If the interviewer offers a brief, take-home project, accept it, unless you don't want the job.

○ Don't leave the office until you know what to expect next.

Post-interview.

○ Recall your reflections of the interview—key comments of the people you met, interesting remarks made by both you and the interviewer—to improve your next interview presentation.

○ Five to seven days after the interview, send a "thank you" letter to the interviewer.

○ In the follow-up letter, reiterate key credentials and provide a brief update on your accomplishments if appropriate.[13]

Again, finding a job in the public relations field today is the toughest task any practitioner will ever pursue. Landing a job requires perseverence, tenaciousness, and total motivation. Public relations executive recruiters and other specialists and individual contact "networks" in the field can be most helpful in seeking a job. But in the final analysis, securing a public relations position depends on one key variable: individual effort.

EMERGING TRENDS

While most professions undergo constant change, few experience more critical or frequent change than public relations. In the 1970s, for example, practitioners were introduced to a tidal wave of primary concerns: consumerism, environmentalism, government relations, and public policy forecasting. Areas of public relations opportunity shifted quickly from marketing publicity, to financial relations, to employee communications, to public issues management. Steadily through the 1970s, the field expanded its horizons and increased its influence.

By the start of the 1980s, the field (both internal departments and external counseling firms) had significantly increased its role as an active rather than reactive force in society. One indication of the field's new maturity was the heightened attempt by advertising agencies to buy public relations units. Indeed, in the early 1980s the largest public relations merger in history was consummated with J. Walter Thompson, one of the nation's largest advertising agencies, acquiring Hill and Knowlton, the nation's largest public relations firm.

For the remainder of the 1980s and beyond, the key challenge confronting the field and the professional is to continue the momentum established in the 1970s. To be sure, the task will not be easy. Numerous pressures on professionals exist both within organizations and outside. The very name *public relations* is being challenged. The trend toward "corporate communications" and "public affairs" is real and threatens to unseat "public relations" in business parlance. Despite the many challenges it faces, the profession appears to be on the threshold of the most significant period in its history. Never before have so many individuals and organizations paid so much for public relations expertise.

As Philip Lesly has put it:

> The future is certain to feel the impact of public relations—by whatever term it is called and by whoever is called on to practice it. The future is there for us in public relations to grow with—if we have the judgment to meet it. It will be up to us to determine whether we sit in on the truly momentous decisions of this generation or merely act as technicians carrying out the initiatives of others.[14]

And that really is the key point.

With its responsibilities expanded, its access to management increased, and its importance to the organization more critical than ever before, public relations is poised to command a leadership role in the management of the organizations of the future.

Whether the field attains this higher stature depends entirely on the calibre and the competence of the men and the women who engage in the practice of public relations for the remainder of this decade and into the 1990s.

FEATURE
All is not won

Despite the strides it has made in recent years and the position of respect it now holds in may quarters, the practice of public relations still has a way to go in several sectors of society.

To wit, the following quotes from recent introductory textbooks in the field of mass communications.[15]

○ "PR is dangerous. Publicists do not often lie, but telling half the truth is an integral part of their business, and stretching the truth is not uncommon."—Peter M. Sandman, David M. Rubin, David B. Sachsman, *Media: An Introductory Analysis of American Mass Communications* (Englewood Cliffs, N.J.: Prentice-Hall, 1976), p. 367.

○ "Many turn to the PR specialists whose prime function is obtaining that space free of charge. (An extreme example of free media coverage happens when fringe political groups kidnap or assassinate well-known people just to focus media attention on their concerns.)"—Edward Jay Whetmore, *MediaAmerica: Form, Content and Consequence of Mass Communication.* (Belmont, Calif.: Wadsworth, 1979), p. 265.

○ "The very term 'public relations counselor' suggests the status-seeking that led undertakers to call themselves morticians, janitors to call themselves maintenance engineers, and garbage collectors to call themselves sanitary haulers."—Charlene Brown, Trevor Brown, William Rivers, *The Media and the People.* (New York, N.Y.: Holt Rinehart and Winston, 1978), p. 384.

Oh well, life would be dull without a continuing challenge.

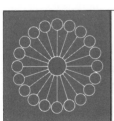

CASE STUDY
The voluntary recall

The practice of public relations can materially influence business decisions, especially as organizations become more aware of and responsible to the many publics upon whom their livelihood depends.

A case in point is the Parker Brothers toy company, which, in 1978, suffered a loss of several million dollars almost solely on the basis of public relations advice. Far from being distraught, Parker Brothers management seemed pleased.

Until April 4, 1978, Parker Brothers had no reason to believe that it had anything but a big winner in its new children's toy, Riviton.

A construction toy for kids six to twelve, Riviton was a great success, with more than 900,000 sets sold in less than two years.

But on April 4, the ninety-six-year-old company was shaken when it learned that an eight-year-old boy in Wisconsin had suffocated with a Riviton rivet in his right lung.

The company further learned that the attorney representing the boy's family had contacted the Consumer Product Safety Commission, which, after an investigation, concluded that the incident was an isolated occurence.

Seven months later, in November 1978, another youngster suffocated on a Riviton rivet in New Jersey.

Although both these deaths were caused by the product's rivets, Riviton nevertheless had met all voluntary and industry-set safety standards. Parker Brothers was under no pressure from any government agency to do anything. However, as Parker's president put it, "We never before in ninety-five years of being in business have heard of a serious accident or fatality resulting from the use or misuse of any of our products."

Parker's management saw four alternatives:

1   It could do nothing. Both accidents resulted from product misuse, and any action the firm took could have been overreacting. Nevertheless, the potential for further misuse clearly existed.
2   The company could issue a statement of warning to the consumer and put the statement on the product package.
3   The product could be modified to eliminate possible hazards. Modification could take months of research and testing.
4   The company could launch a total recall.

Parker Brothers chose option four.

On November 24, Parker's chief counsel notified the Consumer Product Safety Commission of the impending recall. On the same day, Parker Brothers issued the following news release:

BEVERLY, MASS—Parker Brothers today announced the voluntary recall of all Riviton construction toys.

While the Riviton construction toy complies with all safety requirements and does not present a hazard when properly used, Parker Brothers has made the decision to withdraw this product from the market because of two accidental deaths associated with product misuse.

The company reached this decision after the recent death of a nine-year-old child was attributed to choking on a rubber fastening rivet from the Riviton construction toy.

After this announcement, Parker hired extra personnel to answer toll-free telephones and offered full rebates. The company contacted its major customers by telegram and telephone to have them start taking returns immediately. The company also hired extra personnel to dispose of the sets as they arrived, either through incineration or burial.

Seven months after Parker's announcement, the toys were still coming in at the rate of 200 a week. In June 1979, the company reported that 420,000 of the 935,000 outstanding sets had been returned.

The loss to Parker Brothers for the recall was about $10 million. But the company didn't seem to mind.

As Parker's president put it, "By demonstrating our concern for the millions of parents who buy and use our products, we have built a more solid relationship with consumers than ever before."

QUESTIONS

1 Do you agree with the president's assessment that Parker's action would ultimately rebound to the company's benefit?

2 If you were a parent aware of Parker's actions, what would you think of the company? Would you be inclined to purchase Parker Brothers toys for your children?

3 Do you think most companies today, faced with a similar set of circumstances, would have made the same decision as Parker Brothers?

NOTES

1 Philip Lesly, "How the Future Will Shape Public Relations—And Vice Versa," *Public Relations Quarterly*, Winter 1981–82, p. 4.

2 "Items of Concern to Professionals," *PR Reporter*, 29 January 1979, p. 3.

3 *The Occupational Outlook Handbook*. Washington D.C.: U.S. Department of Labor, 1978–1979 edition.

4 "Continuing Education: An Overview," *Public Relations Journal*, June 1978, p. 18.

5 "Image Makers Worry about Their Own Image," *U.S. News & World Report*, 13 August 1979, p. 57.

6 Joseph Nolan, "Business Beware: Early Warning Signs in the Eighties," *Public Opinion*, April/May 1981, p. 14.

7 "The Corporate Image: PR to the Rescue," *Business Week*, 22 January 1979, p. 47.

8 Robert L. Fegley, "How Public Relations Can Help the CEO," *Public Relations Journal*, October 1981, p. 25.

9 "PR: 'The Velvet Ghetto' of Affirmative Action," *Business Week*, 8 May 1978, p. 122.

10 Ibid.

11 "The New Public Relations," *Public Relations Journal*, January 1981, p. 33.

12 Larry Marshall, "Ten Tips For a Job-Getting Resume," Marshall Consultants, Inc., 360 East 65th Street, New York, N.Y. 10021.

13 David Gootnick, "Selling Yourself in Interviews," *MBA*, October/November 1978, p. 37.

14 Philip Lesly, "How The Future," p. 4

15 Carolyn Cline, "The Image of Public Relations in Mass Comm Texts," *Public Relations Review*, Fall 1982, p. 63.

SUGGESTED READING

Careers in Public Relations. (Available from the Public Relations Society of America, 845 Third Avenue, New York, N.Y. 10022.)

Carty, Walter V. "The Message before the Medium," *Public Relations Quarterly* 20 (Spring 1977): 20.

Design for Public Relations Education. (Available from Public Relations Society of America, 845 Third Avenue, New York, N.Y. 10022.)

Fewsmith, Phillips and **Finn, Joan Lockwood.** "When You're On The Wrong Side Of The Desk," *Public Relation Journal,* February 1982, pp. 28–30. A humorous look at what can happen—and often does—when you are interviewed for a job.

Futurist. Bimonthly. (Available from World Future Society, 4916 St. Elmo Avenue, Washington, D.C. 20014.) A journal of forecasts, trends, and ideas about the future on all topics.

Greyser, Stephen A. "Changing Roles for Public Relations," *Public Relations Journal,* January 1981, pp. 18–25.

Hart, Gary. "Emerging Issues for Public Relations," *Public Relations Journal,* January 1980, pp. 11–14, 27, 30–31.

Hershman, Arlene. "Public Relations Goes Public." *Dun's Review,* September 1977, pp. 62–66.

Lesly, Philip. "How the Future Will Shape Public Relations—and Vice Versa," *Public Relations Quarterly,* Winter 1981–82, pp. 4–8.

Lesly, Philip. "Report and Recommendations: Task Force on Stature and Role of Public Relations," *Public Relations Journal,* March 1981, pp. 21–44. Overview analysis of the entire public relations profession and indications of the likely course it might take in the years ahead.

Lesly, Philip. "The Stature and Role of Public Relations," *Public Relations Journal,* January 1981, pp. 14–17.

Lesly, Philip, ed. *Lesly's Public Relations Handbook,* 2nd ed. Englewood Cliffs, N.J.: Prentice-Hall, 1978. See chapter on "Emerging Principles and Trends."

Lindenmann, Walter and **Lapetina, Alison.** "Management's View of the Future of Public Relations," *Public Relations Review,* Fall 1981, pp. 3–14.

Martin, Lee. "A Mixed Bag In The Job Market," *Public Relations Journal,* February 1982, p. 27.

Martinson Ph. D., David L. "How Future Practitioners Define Public Relations, *Public Relations Quarterly,* Spring 1981, pp. 21–22.

Seifert, Walt. "OSU's Graduates Tackle Diverse Fields, Functions," *Public Relations Journal,* February 1982, pp. 14–15.

Skinner, Richard W., and **Shankin, William L.** "The Changing Role of Public Relations in Business Firms." *Public Relations Review,* Summer 1978, pp. 40–45.

"The Corporate Image: PR to the Rescue." *Business Week,* January 22, 1979, pp. 47–50, 54–56.

Traub, Doug. "How To Land That First Public Relations Job," *Public Relations Journal,* February 1982, pp. 16–18. Four senior professionals list writing ability, self-discipline, and leadership among qualities needed to make the grade.

Werle, C. R. "Breaking In: A Different Approach," *Public Relations Journal,* February 1982, p. 18.

Wilcox, Dennis L. "Preparing Today's Students for Tomorrow's PR Careers." *Public Relations Review,* 1, no. 3 (Winter 1975): pp. 47–55.

APPENDICES

Appendix A
Code of Professional Standards

This Code, adopted by the PRSA Assembly, replaces a similar Code of Professional Standards for the Practice of Public Relations in force since 1954 and strengthened by revisions in 1959, 1963 and 1977.

Declaration of Principles

Members of the Public Relations Society of America base their professional principles on the fundamental value and dignity of the individual, holding that the free exercise of human rights, especially freedom of speech, freedom of assembly and freedom of the press, is essential to the practice of public relations.

In serving the interests of clients and employers, we dedicate ourselves to the goals of better communication, understanding and cooperation among the diverse individuals, groups and institutions of society, and of equal opportunity of employment in the public relations profession.

We pledge:

To conduct ourselves professionally, with truth, accuracy, fairness and responsibility to the public;

To improve our individual competence and advance the knowledge and proficiency of the profession through continuing research and education;

And to adhere to the articles of the Code of Professional Standards for the Practice of Public Relations as adopted by the governing Assembly of the Society.

Articles of the Code

These articles have been adopted by the Public Relations Society of America to promote and maintain high standards of public service and ethical conduct among its members.

1   A member shall deal fairly with clients or employers, past and present, with fellow practitioners and the general public.

2   A member shall conduct his or her professional life in accord with the public interest.

3   A member shall adhere to truth and accuracy and to generally accepted standards of good taste.

4   A member shall not represent conflicting or competing interests without the express consent of those involved, given after a full disclosure of the facts; nor place himself or herself in a position where the member's interest is or may be in conflict with a duty to a client, or others, without a full disclosure of such interests to all involved.

5   A member shall safeguard the confidences of both present and former clients or employers and shall not accept retainers or employment which may involve the disclosure or use of these confidences to the disadvantage or prejudice of such clients or employers.

6   A member shall not engage in any practice which tends to corrupt the integrity of channels of communication or the processes of government.

7   A member shall not intentionally communicate false or misleading information and is obliged to use care to avoid communication of false or misleading information.

8   A member shall be prepared to identify publicly the name of the client or employer on whose behalf any public communication is made.

9   A member shall not make use of any individual or organization purporting to serve or represent an announced cause, or purporting to be independent or unbiased, but actually serving an undisclosed special or private interest of a member, client or employer.

10   A member shall not intentionally injure the professional reputation or practice of another practitioner. However, if a member has evidence that another member has been guilty of unethical, illegal or unfair practices, including those in violation of this Code, the member shall present the information promptly to the proper authorities of the Society for action in accordance with the procedure set forth in Article XIII of the Bylaws.

11   A member called as a witness in a proceeding for the enforcement of this Code shall be bound to appear, unless excused for sufficient reason by the Judicial Panel.

12 A member, in performing services for a client or employer, shall not accept fees, commissions or any other valuable consideration from anyone other than the client or employer in connection with those services without the express consent of the client or employer, given after a full disclosure of the facts.

13 A member shall not guarantee the achievement of specified results beyond the member's direct control.

14 A member shall, as soon as possible, sever relations with any organization or individual if such relationship requires conduct contrary to the articles of this Code.

Official Interpretations of the Code

Interpretation of Code Paragraph 2 which reads, "A member shall conduct his or her professional life in accord with the public interest."

> The public interest is here defined primarily as comprising respect for and enforcement of the rights guaranteed by the Constitution of the United States of America.

Interpretation of Code Paragraph 5 which reads, "A member shall safeguard the confidences of both present and former clients or employers and shall not accept retainers or employment which may involve the disclosure or use of these confidences to the disadvantage or prejudice of such clients or employers."

> This article does not prohibit a member who has knowledge of client or employer activities which are illegal from making such disclosures to the proper authorities as he or she believes are legally required.

Interpretation of Code Paragraph 6 which reads, "A member shall not engage in any practice which tends to corrupt the integrity of channels of communication or the processes of government."

1 Practices prohibited by this paragraph are those which tend to place representatives of media or government under an obligation to the member, or the member's employer or client, which is in conflict with their obligations to media or government, such as:
  a the giving of gifts of more than nominal value;
  b any form of payment or compensation to a member of the media in order to obtain preferential or guaranteed news or editorial coverage in the medium;
  c any retainer or fee to a media employee or use of such employee if retained by a client or employer, where the circumstances are not fully disclosed to and accepted by the media employer;
  d providing trips for media representatives which are unrelated to legitimate news interest;
  e the use by a member of an investment or loan or advertising commitment made by the member, or the member's client or employer, to obtain preferential or guaranteed coverage in the medium.

2 This Code paragraph does not prohibit hosting media or government representatives at meals, cocktails, or news functions or special events which are occasions for the exchange of news information or views, or the furtherance of understanding which is part of the public relations function. Nor does it prohibit the bona fide press event or tour when media or government representatives are given an opportunity for on-the-spot viewing of a newsworthy product, process or event in which the media or government representatives have a legitimate interest. What is customary or reasonable hospitality has to be a matter of particular judgement in specific situations. In all of these cases, however, it is or should be understood that no preferential treatment or guarantees are expected or implied and that complete independence always is left to the media or government representative.

3 This paragraph does not prohibit the reasonable giving or lending of sample products or services to media representatives who have a legitimate interest in the products or services.

Interpretation of Code Paragraph 13 which reads, "A member shall not guarantee the achievement of specified results beyond the member's direct control."

> This Code paragraph, in effect, prohibits misleading a client or employer as to what professional public relations can accomplish. It does not prohibit guarantees of quality or service. But it does prohibit guaranteeing specific results which, by their very nature, cannot be guaranteed because they are not subject to the member's control. As an example, a guarantee that a news release will appear specifically in a particular publication would be prohibited. This paragraph should not be interpreted as prohibiting contingent fees.

An Official Interpretation of the Code As It Applies to Political Public Relations

Preamble

In the practice of political public relations, a PRSA member must have professional capabilities to offer an employer or client quite apart from any political relationships of value, and members may serve their employer or client without necessarily having attributed to them the character, reputation or beliefs of those they serve. It is understood that members may choose to serve only those interests with whose political philosophy they are personally comfortable.

Definition

"Political Public Relations" is defined as those areas of public relations which relate to:

a   the counseling of political organizations, committees, candidates or potential candidates for public office; and groups constituted for the purpose of influencing the vote on any ballot issue;

b   the counseling of holders of public office;

c   the management, or direction, of a political campaign for or against a candidate for political office; or for or against a ballot issue to be determined by voter approval or rejection;

d   the practice of public relations on behalf of a client or an employer in connection with that client's or employer's relationships with any candidates or holders of public office with the purpose of influencing legislation or government regulation or treatment of a client or employer, regardless of whether the PRSA member is a recognized lobbyist;

e   the counseling of government bodies, or segments thereof, either domestic or foreign.

Precepts

1   It is the responsibility of PRSA members practicing political public relations, as defined above, to be conversant with the various statutes, local, state, and federal, governing such activities and to adhere. to them strictly. This includes, but is not limited to, the various local, state and federal laws, court decisions and official interpretations governing lobbying, political contributions, disclosure, elections, libel, slander and the like. In carrying out this responsibility, members shall seek appropriate counseling whenever necessary.

2   It is also the responsibility of members to abide by PRSA's Code of Professional Standards.

3   Members shall represent clients or employers in good faith, and while partisan advocacy on behalf of a candidate or public issue may be expected, members shall act in accord with the public interest and adhere to truth and accuracy and to generally accepted standards of good taste.

4   Members shall not issue descriptive material or any advertising or publicity information or participate in the preparation or use thereof which is not signed by responsible persons or is false, misleading or unlabeled as to its source, and are obligated to use care to avoid dissemination of any such material.

5   Members have an obligation to clients to disclose what remuneration beyond their fees they expect to receive as a result of their relationship, such as commissions for media advertising, printing and the like, and should not accept such extra payment without their clients' consent.

6   Members shall not improperly use their positions to encourage additional future employment or compensation. It is understood that successful campaign directors or managers, because of the performance of their duties and the working relationship that develops, may well continue to assist and counsel, for pay, the successful candidate.

7   Members shall voluntarily disclose to employers or clients the identity of other employers or clients with whom they are currently associated and whose interests might be affected favorably or unfavorably by their political representation.

8   Members shall respect the confidentiality of information pertaining to employers or clients even after the relationships cease, avoiding future associations wherein insider information is sought that would give a desired advantage over a member's previous clients.

9   In avoiding practices which might tend to corrupt the processes of government, members shall not make undisclosed gifts of cash or other other valuable considerations which are designed to influence specific decisions of voters, legislators or public officials on public matters. A business lunch or dinner, or other comparable expenditure made in the course of communicating a point of view or public position, would not constitute such a violation. Nor, for example, would a plant visit designed and financed to provide useful background information to an interested legislator or candidate.

10   Nothing herein should be construed as prohibiting members from making legal, properly disclosed contributions to the candidates, party or referenda issues of their choice.

11   Members shall not, through the use of information known to be false or misleading, conveyed directly or through a third party, intentionally injure the public reputation of an opposing interest.

An Official Interpretation of the Code As It Applies to Financial Public Relations

This interpretation of the Society Code as it applies to financial public relations was originally adopted in 1963 and amended in 1972 and 1977 by action of the PRSA Board of Directors. "Financial public relations" is defined as "that area of public relations which relates to the dissemination of information that affects the understanding of stockholders and investors generally concerning the financial position and prospects of a company, and includes among its objectives the improvement of relations between corporations and their stockholders." The interpretation was prepared in 1963 by the Society's Financial Relations Committee working with the Securities and Exchange Commission and with the advice of the Society's Legal Counsel. It is rooted directly in the Code with the full force of the Code behind it and a violation of any of the following paragraphs is subject to the same procedures and penalties as violation of the Code.

1 It is the responsibility of PRSA members who practice financial public relations to be thoroughly familiar with and understand the rules and regulations of the SEC and the laws which it administers, as well as other laws, rules and regulations affecting financial public relations, and to act in accordance with their letter and spirit. In carrying out this responsibility, members shall also seek legal counsel, when appropriate, on matters concerning financial public relations.

2 Members shall adhere to the general policy of making full and timely disclosure of corporate information on behalf of clients or employers. The information disclosed shall be accurate, clear and understandable. The purpose of such disclosure is to provide the investing public with all material information affecting security values or influencing investment decisions. In complying with the duty of full and timely disclosure, members shall present all material facts, including those adverse to the company. They shall exercise care to ascertain the facts and to disseminate only information which they believe to be accurate. They shall not knowingly omit information, the omission of which might make a release false or misleading. Under no circumstances shall members participate in any activity designed to mislead, or manipulate the price of a company's securities.

3 Members shall publicly disclose or release information promptly so as to avoid the possibility of any use of the information by any insider or third party. To that end, members shall make every effort to comply with the spirit and intent of the timely disclosure policies of the stock exchanges, NASD, and the Securities and Exchange Commission. Material information shall be made available to all on an equal basis.

4 Members shall not disclose confidential information the disclosure of which might be adverse to a valid corporate purpose or interest and whose disclosure is not required by the timely disclosure provisions of the law. During any such period of non-disclosure members shall not directly or indirectly (a) communicate the confidential information to any other person or (b) buy or sell or in any other way deal in the company's securities where the confidential information may materially affect the market for the security when disclosed. Material information shall be disclosed publicly as soon as its confidential status has terminated or the requirement of timely disclosure takes effect.

5 During the registration period, members shall not engage in practices designed to precondition the market for such securities. During registration the issuance of forecasts, projections, predictions about sales and earnings, or opinions concerning security values or other aspects of the future performance of the company, shall be in accordance with current SEC regulations and statements of policy. In the case of companies whose securities are publicly held, the normal flow of factual information to shareholders and the investing public shall continue during the registration period.

6 Where members have any reason to doubt that projections have an adequate basis in fact, they shall satisfy themselves as to the adequacy of the projections prior to disseminating them.

7 Acting in concert with clients or employers, members shall act promptly to correct false or misleading information or rumors concerning clients' or employers' securities or business whenever they have reason to believe such information or rumors are materially affecting investor attitudes.

8 Members shall not issue descriptive materials designed or written in such a fashion as to appear to be, contrary to fact, an independent third party endorsement or recommendation of a company or a security. Whenever members issue material for clients or employers, either in their own names or in the name of someone other than clients or employers, they shall disclose in large type and in a prominent position on the face of the material the source of such material and the existence of the issuer's client or employer relationship.

9 Members shall not use inside information for personal gain. However, this is not intended to prohibit members from making bona fide investments in their company's or client's securities insofar as they can make such investments without the benefit of material inside information.

10 Members shall not accept compensation which

would place them in a position of conflict with their duty to a client, employer or the investing public. Members shall not accept stock options from clients or employers nor accept securities as compensation at a price below market price except as part of an overall plan for corporate employees.

11 Members shall act so as to maintain the integrity of channels of public communication. They shall not pay or permit to be paid to any publication or other communications medium any consideration in exchange for publicizing a company, except through clearly recognizable paid advertising.

12 Members shall in general be guided by the PRSA Declaration of Principles and the PRSA Code of Professional Standards for the Practice of Public Relations of which this Code is an official interpretation.

Appendix B
Corporate Reporting Requirements

Including SEC's Integrated Disclosure System, effective May 24, 1982. Prepared by Robert W. Taft, APR, Senior Vice President, Hill and Knowlton, Inc.

Reporting Required For	Securities and Exchange Commission	New York Stock Exchange	American Stock Exchange	Generally Recommended Publicity Practice, All Companies
Accounting: Change in auditors	8-K; if principal auditor (or auditor for a subsidiary) resigns, declines to be re-elected, or is dismissed or if another is engaged. Disclose date of resignation, details of disagreements, comment letters to SEC by auditor on whether it agrees with reasons stated plus other disclosures detailed in 8-K. See also Regulation S-K, Item 304.	Prompt notice to Exchange, 8-K when filed. The NYSE recommends that the independent audit firm be represented at annual meeting to answer questions.	Same as NYSE.	Press release desirable at time of filing 8-K if differences are major. Consider clear statement in annual report or elsewhere on independence of auditors including their reporting relationship to Board's audit committee.
Accounting: Change in method	Independent public accountant must file letter indicating approval/ disapproval of "improved method of measuring business operations."	Prompt notification to Exchange required.	Notify Exchange before change is made and disclose the impact in succeeding interim and annual reports.	Statement of accounting policies is required in annual report. Give some publicity to accounting changes; illustrate how alternative accounting methods affect earnings. Special problems arise in changing LIFO/FIFO methods of accounting for inventory.
Amendment of charter or bylaws	Report if matter subject to stockholders' approval or if change materially modifies rights of holders of any class of registered securities.	Four copies of any material sent to stockholders in respect to proposed changes. Appropriately certified copy of changes when effective.	Ten copies of any material sent to stockholders must be filed with Exchange when effective with certified copy of (a) charter amendments; (b) directors' resolution as to charter or bylaws.	Recommend immediate publicity if change significantly alters rights or interests of shareholders. "Defensive" provision to make takeovers more difficult likely to receive very wide publicity.
Annual (or special) meeting of stockholders	10-Q following meeting including date of meeting, name of each director elected (if contested), summary of other matters voted on.	Four copies of all proxy material sent to shareholders. Prompt notice of calling of meeting; publicity on material actions at meeting. Ten days advance notice of record date or closing transfer books to Exchange.	Ten copies of all material sent to shareholders. Other requirements same as NYSE.	Press release at time of meeting. Competition for news space minimizes public coverage except on actively contested issues. Check NYSE schedules for competing meetings. Recommend wide distribution of post-meeting report to shareholders.

Reporting Required For	Securities and Exchange Commission	New York Stock Exchange	American Stock Exchange	Generally Recommended Publicity Practice, All Companies
Annual report to shareholders: Contents	Required contents listed under Rule 14a-3 of the '34 Act. SEC still encourages "freedom of management expression."	Requirements are more than satisfied by compliance with SEC requirements.	Requirements are more than satisfied by compliance with SEC requirements.	Check printed annual report and appropriate news release to insure they conform to information reported on Form 10-K. News releases necessary if annual report contains previously undisclosed material information. Trend is to consider report a marketing tool.
Annual report to shareholders: Timing and distribution	Annual report to shareholders must precede or accompany delivery of proxy material. (Proxy material should *arrive* at least 30 days prior to annual meeting.) (Form 10-K must be filed within 90 days of close of year.)	Published and submitted to shareholders at least 15 days before annual meeting but no later than three months after close of fiscal year. PROMPTEST POSSIBLE ISSUANCE URGED. Recommend release of audited figures as soon as available.	Published and submitted to shareholders at least 10 days before meeting but no later than four months after close of fiscal year. PROMPTEST POSSIBLE ISSUANCE URGED. Recommend release of audited figures as soon as available.	Financial information should be released as soon as available; second release at time printed report is issued if report contains other material information. NYSE and Amex urge broad distribution of report to include statistical services so company information is available for "ready public reference."
Annual report: Form 10-K	Required by Section 13 or 15 (d) of Securities Exchange Act of 1934 on Form 10-K. To be filed with SEC no later than 90 days after close of fiscal year. (Some schedules may be filed 120 days thereafter.) Extensive incorporation by reference from annual report to shareholders and from proxy statement now make integration of Form 10-K and report to shareholders more practical. (See general instructions G and H of Form 10-K.)	One signed copy must be filed with Exchange.	Three copies must be filed with Exchange. (See Company Guide, p. 253.)	Publicity usually not necessary unless 10-K contains previously unreported material information.
Bankruptcy or receivership	8-K immediately after appointment of receiver. Identify proceeding, court, date of event, name of receiver and date of appointment. Additional 8-K when order confirming a plan of reorganization is entered by court with information on court, date, details of plan, shares outstanding, assets and liabilities at date of order.	Immediate note to Exchange.	Same as NYSE.	Recommend press release at time of 8-K filing. Purpose is to tell creditors how to secure claims, not to notify stockholders of a material development. Further press releases and disclosures handled by receiver under court jurisdiction. Normally very limited.

Reporting Required For	Securities and Exchange Commission	New York Stock Exchange	American Stock Exchange	Generally Recommended Publicity Practice, All Companies
Compensation	See Regulation S-K, Item 402 for exhaustive discussion of how information on management compensation must be presented in filings with SEC, including issuance of stock options and stock appreciation rights.	Not applicable.	Not applicable.	While not generally "material," information on executive compensation is widely reported when proxy statements issued; public relations issues should be discussed in advance of publication.
Control: Change in	Form 8-K. Disclose name of person acquiring control, amount and source of funds, basis of control, date and description of transaction, percent of voting shares held by new controlling person, identity of person from whom control acquired, terms of loans, terms of agreements with old and new management. Statement on Schedule 13D may be required by new controlling persons.	Prompt written notice to Exchange of any change. Immediate release, if material. Recommends directors be identified in annual report.	Prompt written notice to Exchange. Immediate release, if material.	Recommend immediate announcement of any change in control of company. Normally announced by new controlling party.
Default upon senior securities	10-Q if actual material default in principal, interest, sinking fund installment, arrearage in dividends for preferred, registered or ranking securities not cured within 30 days of any stated grace period and if indebtedness exceeds 5 percent of total assets.	Immediate publicity and notice to the Exchange.	Immediate publicity and notice to the Exchange.	Immediate disclosure probably required at time default condition is known; include amount of default and total arrearage, date of default. Consider discussion of method and timing of curing default.
Directors: Change in	8-K if director resigns or refuses to stand because of disagreement and if resigning director writes and requests disclosure of dispute. New directors and officers must personally file Form 3 upon election. Proxy rules require certain disclosures about votes cast for or withheld from individual directors; disclosure of vote on all directors if one or more directors receive 5 percent plus negative vote.	Prompt written notice to Exchange of any change. Immediate release, if material. Recommends Audit Committee for Board. Recommends directors be identified in annual report.	Prompt written notice to Exchange. Immediate release if material. Recommends that company with no outside directors nominate at least two independent directors.	Recommend immediate announcement of any contemplated change in directors. However, no technical requirement for publicity except where control of company changes or key person is added or lost.

Reporting Required For	Securities and Exchange Commission	New York Stock Exchange	American Stock Exchange	Generally Recommended Publicity Practice, All Companies
Dividends	All issuers of publicly traded securities are required to give notice of dividend declarations pursuant to Rule 10B-17. Over-the-counter companies must provide advance notice of record date for subsequent dissemination to investors, extending comparable stock exchange requirements to OTC market. Failure to comply places issuer in violation of Section 10 (b) of the Securities Exchange Act of 1934.	Prompt notice to Exchange and immediate publicity. "Telephone Alert" to Exchange when the action is unusual and during market hours. "Immediate" means even while directors' meeting is still in progress. Ten days' advance notice of record date. NYSE manual implies announcement of management intention prior to formal board action may be required in case of a "leak" or rumor.	Same as NYSE. Notification to Exchange by telephone or telegram with confirmation by letter.	Prepare publicity in advance and release immediately by a designated officer on word of declaration. Publicity especially important when dividend rate changes. Statement of dividend policy now common in annual reports. Statements of "intention" to take dividend action also becoming common.
Earnings	Form 10-Q required within 45 days of close of each of first three fiscal quarters. Include information outlined in 10-Q, Part I, Instruction 4, plus a narrative management analysis in form outlined in Form S-K, Item 303. Summary of quarterly results for two years in "unaudited" annual report footnote. Form 10-K required to report full year's earnings.	Quarterly. Publicity required. Shareholder mailing recommended. NYSE urges breakout of fourth quarter results for AP and UPI P/E ratio computation.	Quarterly. Should be published within 45 days after end of fiscal quarter for all four quarters.	Immediate publicity; do not hold data until printed quarterly report is published and mailed. Release no later than 10-Q filing; annual results as soon as available. Information in news release must be consistent with 10-Q. Breakout of current quarter results together with year-to-date totals desirable in 2nd, 3rd and 4th quarter releases.
Employee stock purchase and saving plans	Form 11-K may be required under 15 (d) of '34 Act. Form S-8 may also be required.	No specific rules.	No specific rules.	Generally no publicity required or recommended. There is increasing trend to mention such programs in annual report.
Environmental matters	Reg. S-K; Item 103; Instruction 5. Disclosure in Forms 10-Q, 10-K and elsewhere under legal proceedings if a) material; b) involves claim for more than 10 percent of current assets; or c) government agency involved and amount likely to exceed $100,000.	No specific provision.	No specific provision.	SEC increasingly believes extensive environmental disclosure is "meaningless and confusing to investors"; has curtailed pressure for extensive timely press release reporting in favor of orderly filings. Handle conservatively.

Reporting Required For	Securities and Exchange Commission	New York Stock Exchange	American Stock Exchange	Generally Recommended Publicity Practice, All Companies
Extraordinary charge or credit; charge to retained earnings	SEC expects discussion of nature of and reason for charge in "Management Discussion and Analysis."	Disclosure recommended for material provisions for future losses, discontinued operations, foreign operations, future costs. Include detail on amounts reserved, subsequently used and remaining available at year-end. Prior notice to Exchange required for any proposed substantial charge to retained earnings by company or by directly controlled subsidiary.	Same as NYSE for charge.	Generally material. Requires immediate disclosure. Press release should precede SEC filings. There is increasing "enterprise" reporting of impact of extraordinary items on earnings per share.
Float: Increase or decrease in	10-Q if an outstanding "class" of securities is changed more than 5 percent by issuance or purchase of securities, or payment of indebtedness. Include this information in 10-K. New rules specify timing and method for company to tender for own shares. See standard SEC treatment in Regulation S-K, Item 202.	Prompt notice when occasioned by actual or proposed deposit under voting trust agreements, etc., and brought to "official attention" of officers or directors. The NYSE requires prompt announcement of a program to purchase the company's own shares.	Prompt announcement upon establishing program to acquire the company's own shares.	Immediate publicity to extent permitted under registration restraints. Report details of statement of purpose required in 10-Q filing. Normally routine but will attract publicity if announcement signals major corporate repurchase program. Ads and releases where company tenders for own shares must conform with SEC filings. Publicity if there is sharp decrease in floating supply which could affect the market in the company's securities.
Foreign currency translation	New FASB No. 52 requires report of foreign currency translation gains or losses as they occur (quarterly).	No requirement.	No requirement.	Recent adoption of FASB No. 52 should reduce or eliminate need for extended discussion of impact of foreign currency translation outside SEC filings except in extreme cases.
Inflation: Impact of	SEC requires adherence to FASB Statement No. 33. Report in two ways in a footnote: the effect of general inflation (constant dollar); the effect of changes in specific prices of materials (current costs). Discussion is still considered "experimental."	No requirement.	No requirement.	Publicity generally not necessary. However expect considerable shareholder and press interest in this section of annual report during periods of rapid inflation.

Reporting Required For	Securities and Exchange Commission	New York Stock Exchange	American Stock Exchange	Generally Recommended Publicity Practice, All Companies
Legal proceedings	10-Q at start, termination of proceedings and in any quarter when material development occurs (generally damage claims in excess of 10 percent of current assets); also any suit against company by an officer, director or major stockholder. See Regulation S-K, Item 103.	No notice to NYSE required unless proceedings bear on ownership, dividends, interest or principal of listed securities, or start of receivership, bankruptcy, reorganization proceedings.	Public disclosure if material. Prompt notice to Exchange.	Public disclosure recommended if outcome of legal proceedings could have material effect on company and news of proceeding has not already become public. Court filings now commonly distributed to key business media with or without press release.
Listing: Initially or on another exchange	Involved and extensive legal work is required.	See listing requirements which are raised or revised frequently (NYSE Company Manual Section B). Dual listing now permitted.	See listing requirements. Dual listing now permitted.	Bulk of routine publicity handled by exchanges. Amex efforts particularly effective in electronic media. Discuss other special opportunities with legal and public relations counsel.
Management discussion and analysis	See Regulation S-K, Item 303 for complete discussion of presentation for both annual and quarterly financial reports.	Not applicable.	Not applicable.	Generally poorly written. SEC seeks greater discussion of liquidity. When well done, offers major opportunity for superior financial communications.
Market Information: Stock prices; Number of shareholders; Dividend payments; Markets where quoted	See Regulation S-K, Item 201, for standard treatment in all SEC filings.	Not applicable.	Not applicable.	Basic information rarely newsworthy in itself but valuable when presented in proper contexts.
Merger: Acquisition or disposition of assets	8-K if company acquires or disposes of a significant (10 percent of total assets or whole subsidiary) amount of assets or business other than in normal course of business. Proxy soliciting material or registration statement may also be required. Check application of Rule 145(b) to any such transaction involving exchange of stock. (See also Tender Offers.)	8-K filed (where assets acquired). Immediate public disclosure. Prompt notice to Exchange where assets disposed of.	8-K filed, for acquisition or disposition of assets. Immediate public disclosure.	NYSE policy requires immediate announcement as soon as confidential disclosures relating to such important matters are made to "outsiders" (*i.e.*, other than "top management" and their individual confidential "advisors"). Immediate publicity, especially when assets consist of an entire product line, division, operating unit or a "substantial" part of the business.

Reporting Required For	Securities and Exchange Commission	New York Stock Exchange	American Stock Exchange	Generally Recommended Publicity Practice, All Companies
Policy statement on handling inside information	No rule.	No rule.	No rule.	Not specifically required by any regulatory authority. Cases involving insider information have turned on whether company had developed and implemented a written policy on disclosure of material, non-public corporate information. SEC requires submission of such statements as part of consent decree.
Prospectus and registration statement	Prospectus must be filed as part of registration statement. Copies distributed to underwriters and dealers in securities offerings, and in turn to investors. Photos of management, products, maps, other visuals permitted. Forecasts may be included in prospectuses and registration statements. See Regulation S-K, Item 500 for extensive discussion of contents.	Seven copies of final prospectus to Exchange. May be used as part of listing application covering the new securities.	Copy of complete registration filing to Exchange. Recent prospectus may be used as part of listing application covering the new securities.	News release, if issued at time of registration, must state from whom prospectus may be obtained. See SEC Rule 134 for permitted content of release at or after initial filing, and SEC Rule 135 for permitted content of release announcing intention to file.
Projection: Forecast or estimate of earnings	See Reg S-K General Policy (b). SEC policy encourages use of projections of future economic performance that have "a reasonable basis" and are presented in an appropriate format. Obligation to correct promptly when facts change. Should not discontinue or resume projections without clear explanation of action.	Immediate public disclosure when news goes beyond insiders and their confidential advisors.	Public disclosure not required initially, but if earnings forecast released, and later appears to be wrong, issuer must correct promptly and publicly.	Projections should be either avoided altogether or widely circulated with all assumptions stated. Projections by others may require correction by company if wrong but widely believed. Once having made projection, issuer has obligation to "update" it promptly if assumptions prove wrong. Press releases and other communications should include all information necessary to an understanding of the projection. Legal counsel should be consulted.

Reporting Required For	Securities and Exchange Commission	New York Stock Exchange	American Stock Exchange	Generally Recommended Publicity Practice, All Companies
Proxy material	Preliminary copies of proxy form and statement filed with SEC at least 10 days prior to shareholder mailing, finals when sent to holders and to each exchange where listed. SEC has broadened disclosure requirements to include additional information on directors, and has changed form of proxy to provide shareholders greater voice in corporate governance. Issuer must disclose in proxy final date for receipt of shareholder proposals.	Immediate newspaper publicity on controversial issues, especially when there is a contest. Four copies of definitive proxy material to Exchange. Ask for advance review in major matters, e.g., to determine Exchange policy; also whether brokers may vote "street name" shares without instructions from customers.	Same as NYSE. Ten copies of all proxy material are required when sent to shareholders.	Normally publicity not needed on routine matters. Press release at time proxy is mailed becoming more common. Press release may constitute "soliciting" material, so caution is advised. Special rules apply in contests; use caution. Corporate responsibility issues: no requirement to identify shareholder proposals by press release prior to meeting. Expanded information on executive compensation is widely used for round-up stories in spring. Review carefully prior to inquiries.
Questionable or illegal payments	Controversial "voluntary" program requires filing under miscellaneous item of Form 8-K. Guidelines for content published by SEC in May '76. Current policy in dispute.	No requirement.	No requirement.	Recommend press release conforming to 8-K at time 8-K is filed. However, no technical requirement for publicity. Recommend adoption of company policy statement on ethical business practices.
Redemption, repurchase, cancellation, retirement of listed securities	File 10-Q if amount of securities decrease is greater than 5 percent of amount outstanding. File 8-K and full general disclosure if the transaction is material. File Schedule 13E-4 on or prior to date of commencement of repurchase offer. File Schedule 13E-3 if going private.	Immediate press publicity. Fifteen-day advance notice to Exchange prior to redemption. Prompt notice to Exchange of any corporate or other action affecting securities in whole or in part.	Fifteen-day advance notice to Exchange prior to redemption. Prompt notice of corporate action that will result in any of these.	Usually advertisement is required. Written notice to security holders. News release.
Rights to subscribe	Registration under the Securities Act of 1933. Prefiling notice covered by SEC Rule 135. Notice to NASD or exchanges 10 days before record date required under Securities Exchange Act antifraud provisions.	Preliminary discussion necessary. Immediate publicity. Important to work out time schedule with Exchange before any action taken. Notice to shareholders in advance of proposed record date.	Preliminary discussion necessary. Immediate publicity. Important to work out time schedule with Exchange before any action taken. Notice to shareholders in advance of proposed record date. Subscription period must extend at least 14 days after mailing date.	Immediate publicity and mailing to stockholders to give all adequate time "to record their interest and to exercise their rights," according to NYSE.

Reporting Required For	Securities and Exchange Commission	New York Stock Exchange	American Stock Exchange	Generally Recommended Publicity Practice, All Companies
Securities: Change in, change in assets securing	10-Q if rights of holders are materially changed directly or through changes in another class of security. Separate item on Form 10-Q for withdrawal or substitution of assets.	Immediate notice to Exchange.	Immediate notice to Exchange. Timely disclosure if materially significant for investors.	Depends on terms. Occurs infrequently.
Segment reporting: (line of business reporting)	See Regulation S-K, Item 101 for standard treatment in all SEC filings.	No requirement. However, "recommended" for inclusion in annual reports.	Same as NYSE.	SEC requirements have created significant opportunities to describe company in clear and detailed fashion. Evaluate filed information for use in all company presentations.
Stockholder proposals	Rule 14a-8 specifies when and under what circumstances company must include shareholder proposal in proxy materials.	No requirement.	No requirement.	SEC interest in "shareholder democracy" is declining. Current liberal rules may change. Publicity normally limited to special "advocacy" publications. General reporting likely at time of annual meeting only.
Stock split, stock dividend or other change in capitalization	10-Q required for increase or decrease if exceeds 5 percent of amount of securities of the class previously outstanding. Notice to NASD or Exchange 10 days before record date under Securities Exchange Act antifraud provisions.	Immediate public disclosure and Exchange notification. Issuance of new shares requires prior listing approval. "Telephone Alert" procedure should be followed.	Same as NYSE.	Immediate publicity as soon as proposal becomes known to "outsiders" whether formally voted or not. Discuss early whether to describe transaction as "split," "dividend" or both and use terminology consistently.

Reporting Required For	Securities and Exchange Commission	New York Stock Exchange	American Stock Exchange	Generally Recommended Publicity Practice, All Companies
Tender offer	Conduct and published remarks of all parties governed by Sections 13(d), 13(e), 14(d), 14(e) of the '34 Act and regulations thereunder. Schedule 14D-1 disclosure required of raider. Target required to file Schedule 14D-9 for any solicitation or recommendation to security holders. (See also Hart, Scott Rodino requirements.)	Consult Exchange Stock List Department in advance. Immediate publicity and notice to Exchange.	Consult Exchange Securities Division in advance. Immediate publicity and notice to .Exchange.	Massive publicity effort required; should not be attempted without thorough familiarity with current rules and constant consultation with counsel. Neither raider nor target should comment publicly until necessary SEC filings have been made. "Stop, look, listen" letter permitted under Rule 14d-9(e).
Treasury stock: Increase or decrease	Check Form 10-Q, items 5 and 6 for possible application. Note: Special rules apply during tender battle.	Notice within 10 days after close of fiscal quarter in which any transaction takes place. Prompt notice of any purchase above prevailing market price.	Same as NYSE. Companies required to notify Exchange on purchase above market price.	Normally no immediate publicity. Reason for action is normally given in annual or quarterly publication before or after event. However, see remarks under "Float," where applicable.

Appendix C
Annual Meeting Checklist

By Frank Widder

The following annual shareholder's meeting checklist can be adapted to serve as a "pre-flight" for almost any major meeting.

I. Meeting Announcement
1 Shareholder's proxy statement and general notice
2 Investment houses, major brokers and institutional investors notice and invitation
3 Financial media invitations
4 Employee notice of meeting
5 Guests

Follow-up (by phone or in person)
1 Investor relations contacts with major shareholders to determine participation, major areas of interest, potential problems
2 Major investment houses involved with company
3 Local financial press
4 Guest relations

II. Management Announcement
1 Notify all key management personnel to make sure they will be there and arrange alternates for those who cannot make it.
2 Notify all members of the board to determine their ability to make the meeting.
3 Arrange flight times and book hotel in advance; guarantee arrival if necessary.

III. Management Coaching
1 Draft basic list of shareholder problems and questions.
2 Arrange meeting with CEO and chairman to prepare answers, with key staff and legal department to run down answers, and practice those answers.
3 Review and practice management speeches.

IV. Presentation Materials
1 Review orders for graphs and slides, compare with financial review speech.

2 Screen any films.
3 Review displays.

V. Agenda
Order of presentations with approximate running times (in minutes).
1 Introduction—Chairman calls meeting to order and introduces board and management (4:00)
2 Opening comments by chairman and review of overall activities of company (6:00)
3 President's message (with visuals) (15:00)
4 Financial report by vice president, finance (with slide highlights) (5:00)
5 Film (20:00)
6 Present proposals in proxy (Limit each shareholder to one statement per issue; hand out ballots to shareholders at beginning.) (20:00)
7 Voting, collect ballots (3:00)
8 General discussion (Limit shareholders to one question each.) (30:00)
9 Announce voting results (3:00)
10 Present company awards of appreciation (2:00)
11 Adjournment (1:00) Total 1 hour, 49 minutes

Agenda allows 20 minutes additional for discussion or for more questions during presentation of proposals. Final agenda will be printed and passed out by ushers at meeting.

VI. Site Preparation
A. Staff
1 Electrician, lighting and sound equipment specialists on hand from 8 A.M. through 5 P.M.
2 Supervisor of custodial, security and equipment staff
3 Walkie-talkie communications network with equipment staff
4 Waiters for lounge
5 Caterers for lounge

533

B. Parking

1 Traffic direction displays at parking lot entrances
2 Parking attendants directing traffic to proper area
3 Signs pointing to meeting entrance in parking lot

C. Entrance/Reception

1 Reception tables with pencils and guest roster
2 Receptionists to staff tables and answer questions about facilities (need to be briefed beforehand)
3 Well-marked rest areas and signs indicating meeting area
4 Unarmed security to control crowd and provide protection
5 Armed security located in discrete areas of meeting room
6 Name tags for all representatives of company

D. Display Area

1 Displays set up along walls, not to impede foot traffic, and checked for operation 24 hours in advance
2 Representatives to staff each booth and be prepared for questions about display
3 Tables to display necessary financial information—annual report, 10-K, proxy statement, quarterlies

E. Lounge Area

1 Adequate seating for participants, guests
2 Breakfast/luncheon tables

F. Meeting Area

1 Sound, lighting, video checks
2 Sound mikes for all stage participants
3 Additional speakers for amplification
4 Alternate hookup in case of failures—sound, lighting and video; alternate film in case of breakage
5 Large screen for slide and film
6 Slide and film projectors for presentation
7 Audio and lighting mixers
8 Portable, remote mikes with long cords for audience questions
9 Tape-recorder hookup to record proceedings

G. Construction

1 Podium constructed high enough for everyone to have direct view of all participants
2 Area blocked off for board and management to view film
3 Area blocked off for lighting and sound equipment

4 Exits properly marked
5 Access to podium and all chairs necessary for seating board and management
6 Logo prominently displayed and lighted above podium

H. Staff

1 Ushers with flashlights at all entrances for seating
2 Security at far corners of room
3 Backstage technicians for sound emergencies
4 Remote mike monitors on both aisles or front and back of room
5 Photographer to shoot proceedings, displays and key presentations

I. Stage Seating Arrangements

1 Podium in middle, chairs to either side
2 Arrange board members in tenure order
3 Management in hierarchy order
4 Chairman sits on board side
5 President on management side
6 Nameplates for all participants on podium
7 Glasses, water, ashtrays

J. Shareholder Seating

1 First-come basis
2 Areas roped off for invited shareholders and guests
3 Areas roped off for film viewing by participants
4 Special area for members not represented on stage—public accountants, special staff, guests

VII. Final Run-Through

1 Day prior complete mock session of annual report, with key principals and timing of presentation—including possible questions and responses.
2 Review slide show and cues four hours before meeting
3 Check screening room communications to begin film. Make sure time is allowed to clear stage.
4 Make sure award is ready for presentation.
5 Handout scripts to key participants and technical people.

VIII. Day of Meeting

1 Review with supervisor that all technical checks are okay.
2 See that all displays are up and working

3 Contact board and management people to check for emergencies in transportation. Arrange backup accommodations if necessary.

4 Sit-down breakfast with key participants to go over agenda and cover any last-minute questions.

5 Go to convention center, check in with supervisor, security head, parking attendant. Insure copies of scripts at podium.

6 Greet participants and guide to lounge.

7 Wait for shareholders and investors, media. Be available for questions and arrange interviews.

8 Sit down and wait.

9 Guide participants, guests to luncheon in lounge. Make sure bar is set up.

10 Have many drinks—and goodnight.

Appendix D

THE SOCIETY OF PROFESSIONAL JOURNALISTS,
SIGMA DELTA CHI

Code of Ethics

THE SOCIETY of Professional Journalists, Sigma Delta Chi believes the duty of journalists is to serve the truth.

WE BELIEVE the agencies of mass communication are carriers of public discussion and information, acting on their Constitutional mandate and freedom to learn and report the facts.

WE BELIEVE in public enlightenment as the forerunner of justice, and in our Constitutional role to seek the truth as part of the public's right to know the truth.

WE BELIEVE those responsibilities carry obligations that require journalists to perform with intelligence, objectivity, accuracy and fairness.

To these ends, we declare acceptance of the standards of practice here set forth:

RESPONSIBILITY:

The public's right to know of events of public importance and interest is the overriding mission of the mass media. The purpose of distributing news and enlightened opinion is to serve the general welfare. Journalists who use their professional status as representatives of the public for selfish or other unworthy motives violate a high trust.

FREEDOM OF THE PRESS:

Freedom of the press is to be guarded as an inalienable right of people in a free society. It carries with it the freedom and the responsibility to discuss, question and challenge actions and utterances of our government and of our public and private institutions. Journalists uphold the right to speak unpopular opinions and the privilege to agree with the majority.

ETHICS:

Journalists must be free of obligation to any interest other than the public's right to know the truth.

1. Gifts, favors, free travel, special treatment or privileges can compromise the integrity of journalists and their employers. Nothing of value should be accepted.

2. Secondary employment, political involvement, holding public office and service in community organizations should be avoided if it compromises the integrity of journalists and their employers. Journalists and their employers should conduct their personal lives in a manner which protects them from conflict of interest, real or apparent. Their responsibilities to the public are paramount. That is the nature of their profession.

3. So-called news communications from private sources should not be published or broadcast without substantiation of their claims to news value.

4. Journalists will seek news that serves the public interest, despite the obstacles. They will make constant efforts to assure that the public's business is conducted in public and that public records are open to public inspection.

5. Journalists acknowledge the newsman's ethic of protecting confidential sources of information.

ACCURACY AND OBJECTIVITY:

Good faith with the public is the foundation of all worthy journalism.

1. Truth is our ultimate goal.

2. Objectivity in reporting the news is another goal, which serves as the mark of an experienced professional. It is a standard of performance toward which we strive. We honor those who achieve it.

3. There is no excuse for inaccuracies or lack of thoroughness.

4. Newspaper headlines should be fully warranted by the contents of the articles they accompany. Photographs and telecasts should give an accurate picture of an event and not highlight a minor incident out of context.

5. Sound practice makes clear distinction between news reports and expressions of opinion. News reports should be free of opinion or bias and represent all sides of an issue.

6. Partisanship in editorial comment which knowingly departs from the truth violates the spirit of American journalism.

7. Journalists recognize their responsibility for offering informed analysis, comment and editorial opinion on public events and issues. They accept the obligation to present such material by individuals whose competence, experience and judgment qualify them for it.

8. Special articles or presentations devoted to advocacy or the writer's own conclusions and interpretations should be labeled as such.

FAIR PLAY:

Journalists at all times will show respect for the dignity, privacy, rights and well-being of people encountered in the course of gathering and presenting the news.

1. The news media should not communicate unofficial charges affecting reputation or moral character without giving the accused a chance to reply.

2. The news media must guard against invading a person's right to privacy.

3. The media should not pander to morbid curiosity about details of vice and crime.

4. It is the duty of news media to make prompt and complete correction of their errors.

5. Journalists should be accountable to the public for their reports and the public should be encouraged to voice its grievances against the media. Open dialogue with our readers, viewers and listeners should be fostered.

PLEDGE:

Journalists should actively censure and try to prevent violations of these standards, and they should encourage their observance by all newspeople. Adherence to this code of ethics is intended to preserve the bond of mutual trust and respect between American journalists and the American people.

Adopted 1926, Revised 1973

Appendix E

OFFICIAL STATEMENT ON PUBLIC RELATIONS

(Formally adopted by PRSA Assembly, November 6, 1982.)

Public relations helps our complex, pluralistic society to reach decisions and function more effectively by contributing to mutual understanding among groups and institutions. It serves to bring private and public policies into harmony.

Public relations serves a wide variety of institutions in society such as businesses, trade unions, government agencies, voluntary associations, foundations, hospitals and educational and religious institutions. To achieve their goals, these institutions must develop effective relationships with many different audiences or publics such as employees, members, customers, local communities, shareholders and other institutions, and with society at large.

The managements of institutions need to understand the attitudes and values of their publics in order to achieve institutional goals. The goals themselves are shaped by the external environment. The public relations practitioner acts as a counselor to management, and as a mediator, helping to translate private aims into reasonable, publicly acceptable policy and action.

As a management function, public relations encompasses the following:

• Anticipating, analyzing and interpreting public opinion, attitudes and issues which might impact, for good or ill, the operations and plans of the organization.

• Counseling management at all levels in the organization with regard to policy decisions, courses of action and communication, taking into account their public ramifications and the organization's social or citizenship responsibilities.

• Researching, conducting and evaluating, on a continuing basis, programs of action and communication to achieve informed public understanding necessary to the success of an organization's aims. These may include marketing, financial, fund raising, employee, community or government relations and other programs.

• Planning and implementing the organization's efforts to influence or change public policy.

• Setting objectives, planning, budgeting, recruiting and training staff, developing facilities—in short, *managing* the resources needed to perform all of the above.

• Examples of the knowledge that may be required in the professional practice of public relations include communication arts, psychology, social psychology, sociology, political science, economics and the principles of management and ethics. Technical knowledge and skills are required for opinion research, public issues analysis, media relations, direct mail, institutional advertising, publications, film/video productions, special events, speeches and presentations.

In helping to define and implement policy, the public relations practitioner utilizes a variety of professional communication skills and plays an integrative role both within the organization and between the organization and the external environment.

INDEX